America

in European Consciousness,

1493–1750

America

in European Consciousness, 1493–1750

EDITED BY KAREN ORDAHL KUPPERMAN

Published for the Institute of Early American History and Culture, *Williamsburg, Virginia, by the* University of North Carolina Press, *Chapel Hill & London*

Manufactured in the
United States of America

The paper in this book meets the guidelines for permanence and durability of the Committee on Production Guidelines for Book Longevity of the Council on Library Resources.

Publication of this book was aided by a grant from the Ahmanson Foundation.

This volume received indirect support from an unrestricted book publication grant awarded to the Institute by the L. J. Skaggs and Mary C. Skaggs Foundation of Oakland, California.

Library of Congress
Cataloging-in-Publication Data
America in European consciousness, 1493–1750 / edited by Karen Ordahl Kupperman.
p. cm.—(Institute of early American history and culture)
Includes bibliographical references and index.
ISBN 0-8078-2166-7 (cloth : alk. paper)
ISBN 0-8078-4510-8 (paper : alk. paper)
1. America—Foreign public opinion, European—History. 2. America—Historiography. 3. Europe—Colonies—America. 4. America—History—To 1810. 5. Public opinion—Europe—History. 6. Collectors and collecting—Europe—History. I. Kupperman, Karen Ordahl, 1939– II. Series.
E18.7.A44 1995
970—dc20 94-5725
CIP

99 98 97 96 95 5 4 3 2 1

The Institute of Early American History and Culture is sponsored jointly by the College of William and Mary and the Colonial Williamsburg Foundation.

TO NANCY LYMAN ROELKER

Contents

Foreword

Newton's laws of motion appear to have application not only to physical objects but also, in some instances, to movements in history. For every action there is a reaction, for every thrust an equal and opposite counterthrust, although we may not always be aware of the latter. When the Europeans, beginning with Columbus, conquered and occupied land in the Americas, they were certainly aware of what they were doing. They were conscious of their own force of change in the New World and were determined, usually ruthlessly, to bring about change. They were much less aware, however, as conquerors tend to be, of what the consequences of their actions were upon themselves and upon the lands from which they came. To this day, far more historical inquiry has been devoted to the consequences for America of the "discovery" of 1492 than to the consequences for Europe.

Yet given the magnitude of this single earth-uniting event, unprecedented in all of human history and destined to occur only once, it is important to ask, What difference did the "discovery" make to European culture and development? In such matters as changes in diet and demography, or growth in trade and maritime prowess, the consequences of the encounter with America were enormous and are fairly apparent, at least from the perspective of the twentieth century. But if one considers what difference the emergence of the New World made to the development of European political theory, literature, theology, law, social philosophy and the "theory of man" (or as we now say, anthropology), economic thought, linguistics, and the fine arts, that is, to the realm of consciousness, the consequences were necessarily more subtle and complex.

The collection of essays that follows is the product of a design that goes back to 1988 and is the result of a convergence of several different factors. The five-hundredth anniversary of Columbus's first voyage obviously had to be reckoned with by the John Carter Brown Library, but beyond that general concern the library had a more immediate reason to focus on European consciousness. Since 1977, with the financial backing of the Readex Microprint Corporation, the National Endowment for the Humanities, and the Andrew W. Mellon Foundation, the library had been engaged in the compilation of a massive guide to early European books with references in them to America. Formally entitled *European Americana: A Chronological Guide to Works Printed in Europe Relating to the*

Americas, 1493–1750 (New York, 1980–94), this work in six volumes, edited initially by John Alden and then by Dennis Channing Landis, more than doubled the known quantity of titles in this subject area. Its only comparable predecessor, Joseph Sabin's *Bibliotheca Americana: A Dictionary of Books Relating to America*, published between 1868 and 1936, recorded approximately 16,000 pre-1750 works, including many "ghosts" and works printed in America, not Europe; *European Americana* records approximately 32,000, and all are truly European imprints and real books. With so many more primary sources made known, we reasoned, the whole subject of the "impact" of the Americas on Europe deserved reexamination.

In 1988, with the aid of a National Endowment for the Humanities planning grant, the library was able to recruit a talented and generous committee to establish the conceptual outlines for a conference on the influence of America on European thought and culture and to make a preliminary list of contributors to it. The members of the planning committee were Fredi Chiappelli of the University of California at Los Angeles; J. H. Elliott of Oxford University; Hans Galinsky of Gutenberg University in Mainz; J. H. McNeill, University of Chicago, emeritus; Anthony Molho of Brown University; Anthony Pagden of Cambridge University; and Sheldon Watts and myself, representing the library.

Several preliminary decisions made by the committee deserve mention here because they clarify what the conference was about, and hence the character of this anthology. First of all, it was decided for several reasons to focus on the period before 1750. That period, before the obvious plethora of reactions to America brought on by the Seven Years' War and the American Revolution, is far more problematical than the period from 1750 to 1800 and after. By the time of the American Revolution, the information flooding into Europe burgeoned to the point that the subject of American influence becomes much less manageable in a single, comprehensive conference. Moreover, 1493 to 1750 is the period encompassed by *European Americana*, the publication of which, it was hoped, would stimulate research in material hitherto little used.

It was also decided at an early stage that we would concentrate on conscious expression, on intellectual life and articulated forms of culture, not on such matters as silent economic and demographic change that were proceeding apace as a direct consequence of the New World encounter but were not overtly integrated into written discussion, debates, and commentary at the time. Although the two may not be entirely separable, we concentrated on intellectual change, not material change. However, from the area of intellectual change and development, we decided to exclude the history of science, under the assumption that the influence of the European discovery of America on the development of science was a vast and relatively unexplored subject that could not be properly addressed in a conference as general as ours was to be.

It should be noted, too, that we did not begin our planning with the intention of demonstrating that America was or was not important to—let alone decisive to—the various manifestations of European culture at the time, the time of Erasmus and of Machiavelli among others, neither of whom, it is said, ever mentioned America. That subtlety was needed in addressing the question specifically of the American influence is immediately made evident by the realization that contemporaneously with information about America pouring into Europe there was also rapidly increasing knowledge of Asia and Africa. Thus if one aims to trace, for example, a rise in cultural relativism and skepticism in European thought, which is often assumed to be the product of better knowledge of the diversity and self-assurance of foreign cultures, was it America or China that provided the most disconcerting new awareness in this respect?

Some twenty-five papers were presented at the America in European Consciousness conference, held on the Brown University campus early in June 1991. They were of uniformly high quality, but for purposes of publication as a book, a selection had to be made. From the many valuable and interesting contributions to the conference, our goal was to come up with ten or twelve essays that represented some degree of excellence, that reflected some of the major themes of the conference, and that would reasonably cohere as part of a total work. It can safely be said that all twelve of the papers in this collection owe a great deal to the intellectual dynamics of the conference as a whole, and with that fact in mind, we have recorded at the back of this volume the complete program of the conference, in recognition of the contributions of all who participated.

The library incurred numerous debts of gratitude in the seven years between the initial planning for the America in European Consciousness conference and the publication of this book. The National Endowment for the Humanities underwrote the planning for the conference and a portion of the cost of the conference itself. The Ahmanson Foundation contributed generously toward meeting the cost of the conference and also assigned a portion of its grant specifically for the purpose of subsidizing the publication of a collection of essays from the conference. The W. Averell and Pamela Harriman Foundation also helped to allay certain costs related to the publication of the essays. The Florence Gould Foundation and the Ambassade de France aux Etats-Unis (through the intervention of Noëlle de Chambrun, cultural and scientific attaché) made possible the participation of a number of French scholars in the conference, including Emmanuel Le Roy Ladurie, administrateur général of the Bibliothèque Nationale, and contributed substantially to meeting the cost of the conference as a whole.

Aside from the benefactions of foundations and other such agencies, the John Carter Brown Library and this volume had the good fortune to be befriended by a distinguished historian of European history who made generosity of mind and spirit her way of life, Nancy Roelker. Through Professor Roelker's support for the library, Karen Kupperman was enabled to have the time free from other obligations to edit this collection.

In this era when the fragmentation of historical research is much lamented, the quincentenary observance may have done some good. We are reminded by it that the central fact of modern history is the expansion of Europe, which began well before Columbus's venture to the west in 1492 but which was incredibly confirmed and reinforced by the discovery of America. The expansion to America in the sixteenth and seventeenth centuries both reflected and underlay the European capacity to attain virtual hegemony of the entire globe within the next two centuries. By focusing on Europe in the early modern period we find the means to understand a great deal more than what happened in Europe alone.

Norman Fiering
Director and Librarian
John Carter Brown Library

Acknowledgments

Many scholars whose names do not appear in the table of contents have contributed to this volume in important ways. A semester's academic leave at the John Carter Brown Library allowed me to tap the resources of that marvelous collection and the knowledgeable and ever-helpful staff to the fullest. The library hosted the conference from which this volume originated and has supported it at every step. I have especially relied on Norman Fiering's support and judgment. Susan Danforth, whose knowledge is unparalleled, helped select and prepare the illustrations. No one has a better eye for a historical image.

Fredrika Teute, editor of publications at the Institute of Early American History and Culture, has helped to shape the collection and the individual essays at every stage. Her editorial hand is a sure guide, and her counsel a source of assurance.

Most of all I want to thank Nancy Roelker, friend and mentor, who died just as the production phase of this project began. She participated in the original conference and was closely involved in the project from its inception. She was always willing to give me the benefit of her advice as problems or questions arose. This is a better, stronger collection because of her, and my own understanding of the issues has repeatedly been enhanced by our conversations.

America

in European Consciousness,

1493–1750

KAREN ORDAHL KUPPERMAN

Introduction

THE CHANGING DEFINITION OF AMERICA

In the years after 1492 the magnitude of the continents upon which Christopher Columbus had stumbled began to penetrate European consciousness. Although Old World venturers had made the crossing before, the consequences were different in the fifteenth and sixteenth centuries. As news of vast, previously unknown lands arrived, Europeans were newly poised to ponder its significance. Renaissance Europe was just approaching the ruptures of the Reformation. Scholarship had flowered with the rediscovery of classical texts and acquisition of the capacity to read them. Because the wisdom of the ancients was presumed to offer the sum of human knowledge, "the veneration of antiquity became more slavish."[1] Yet the ancients, however learned, knew nothing of America.[2] Scholars were forced to deal with an explosion in the number of known species and variety of cultural practices, as religious leaders worked to develop the linguistic skills and knowledge to tackle the vast numbers of unconverted. Uncategorized information and peoples challenged Europeans to "imagine the other."[3]

Some fields of study—geography, for example—blossomed, transforming scholars' view of the world and carving out a place for these disciplines in the universities. But rarely did Europeans accept the novel wholly on its own terms. Often new information was assimilated into inherited ways of thinking so that continuity with ancient knowledge was preserved. Many scholars hung newly acquired lore on inherited structures and thus delayed or blunted its effects. Natural historians and their readers, accustomed to the natural world described by Pliny and the fabulous travel accounts of Sir John Mandeville, could fit new information into the already-established discourse with the exotic East and known people on the margins of Europe.[4] Other disciplines ignored America entirely.

Europeans saw America most immediately as a resource for the Old World. American treasure fed the appetites of European monarchs and merchants, as maize, sweet potatoes, and tobacco fed the masses. Within a very few years, immense and varied efforts were focused on exploiting the newly revealed continents. By the middle of the sixteenth century hundreds of ships crossed the Atlantic annually; these voyages supported colonists, carried treasure, fished the Newfoundland Banks, and carried people back and forth. Although they approached it as consumers, Europeans found their own cultures changing as they undertook to digest America.

Historians looking at the consequences of the Columbian voyages from the vantage point of five hundred years' experience do not agree on how much impact America made on European understanding of the world and its history, nor do they agree on how to characterize the confrontation. Few today write of Columbus "discovering" America. Some employ "encounter," but others find that too placid a word to describe the horrific consequences of the mixing of two previously separate biospheres, especially the impact of diseases to which the Americans lacked acquired immunity, and the resultant havoc wreaked in native cultures. Alfred Crosby, stressing its biological aspect, refers to the expansion of Europe as a "swarming."[5] Others argue that Europe's coming to America is properly seen as an "invasion."[6] The Mexican scholar Edmundo O'Gorman, emphasizing its impact on European thinking, characterizes the process of learning and shaping knowledge as the "invention" of America.[7]

Most recent treatments have dealt with the effects of exploration and colonization on the Americans and their lands and cultures.[8] The authors of the essays in this volume pursue influence in the opposite direction, as they offer a series of case studies that illuminate the process of reception of information about America by Europeans. In doing so they also offer insights into the fundamental problem of how we define and understand shifts in consciousness.

The recent debate over this issue began with the publication of John Elliott's *The Old World and the New, 1492–1650* in 1970. Elliott wrote of the ways in which Europeans tailored news of the lands across the seas to fit inherited models, forcing the strange to become familiar. He reinforced this picture in *First Images of America*, where he wrote of America's "blunted impact" on Europe.[9] Anthony Grafton, continuing this theme, writes that many humanists took up new knowledge from America enthusiastically but found ways to incorporate it into old schemas. "Tradition and innovation, modernity and reverence for the antique seemed compatible."[10]

Other scholars see instead a "vast shaking up of the world . . . as a result of the voyage of 1492."[11] Stephen Greenblatt presents the early explorers as jolted by the "cracking apart of contextual understanding in an elusive and ambiguous experience of wonder."[12] Germán Arciniegas argues in *America in Europe: A History of the New World in Reverse* that "with America, the modern world begins. Scientific progress begins, philosophy thrives. By means of America, Europe acquires a new dimension and emerges from its shadows."[13]

Although they may seem dramatically different, the two positions are not incompatible, because we are studying multilayered consciousness. Reverence for ancient knowledge, for example, may have operated as an obstacle, but it also offered pathways and techniques for understanding the new.[14] What matters is the *way* in which America was assimilated, and it is this that the essays in this collection seek to understand. It is the process of taking in and making sense of the new information that is important and enlightening; resistance or ignorance is just as revealing as openness and receptivity. By 1750 European consciousness accommodated large amounts of new information and regularly established contacts with a wider world. The important question therefore is not so much whether, but *how*, America became part of European consciousness.

Europeans who sought to communicate their impressions of unknown cultures, whether they emphasized their familiarity or their strangeness, were forced to adopt a wide variety of rhetorical strategies. Many of these were old techniques, but employing them to talk about America stretched and strained them.[15] Judgments had to be made in order to write at all, and it is the process of judgment that tells us so much and makes the texts so revealing. Scholars writing today on the aftermath of the joining together of these two worlds are also involved in the stretching and restructuring of categories; many writers seek to tilt our angle of vision so that we can see the encounter in new ways.

Language was basic to the early modern as it is to the modern quest for mastery. Many writers have pointed out that the Europeans' obsession with naming and the establishment of their languages was fundamental.[16] Patricia Seed has written of the various forms of "ritual speech" which were necessary to assert authority, and how each empire's forms symbolized its own sources and objects of authority.[17] J. Brian Harley pointed out that the maps by which the news of discoveries was transmitted to Europeans were also instruments of power; from the beginning of the sixteenth century maps began to show tiny, proliferating veins of European names until soon the coasts were ringed with writing. In these ways the explorers and the colonists in their wake imposed a European order and appropriated the land.[18]

Scholars who seek to focus the modern discourse exhibit the same obsession with naming, as in the debate over whether we should use the word "encounter," "confrontation," "exchange," "invasion," or "invention" to describe what happened in the sixteenth and seventeenth centuries. Some argue that we should refer to the inhabitants of the newly revealed continents as "native peoples" in order to avoid the ethnocentrism involved in the imperialist terms "Americans" or "Indians."[19] Now as in the past each of these words implies an ideological stance. Even more heated has been discussion of the heavy mortality among natives as a result of colonization; some call it "genocide." Clearly, control of naming is as fundamental today as it was then.

Just as the struggle to conceptualize America revealed and wrought change in the intellectual structures of early modern Europe, the contest for control of the

Jean Bellere, "Brevis Exactaque Totius Novi Orbis," from Pedro de Cieza de León, *Parte Primera de la Crónica del Perú* (Antwerp, 1554). John Carter Brown Library.

modern discussion has been enormously productive. Texts of the encounter, some newly available in authoritative forms,[20] now communicate in lively ways that allow us imaginatively to reconstruct the various levels on which exchange occurred. Scholars of literature and art join and compete with historians and anthropologists to draw out the many meanings embedded in texts broadly defined.[21] These texts speak to us of perceptions on all sides and from many ranks and sorts of people. *America in European Consciousness*, first as a conference at the John Carter Brown Library in June 1991, and now as a book, reflects the ferment stirred in the scholarly world by the quincentennial. It brings together the work of scholars from a range of disciplines all committed to understanding the impact of the revelation of formerly unknown continents and peoples to Europeans in a period bridging from the late medieval to the threshold of the modern.[22]

America and Europe came to know each other on many levels over these two and a half centuries. The European-American relationship must be visualized not as steadily, though unevenly, growing knowledge of a constant reality, but rather as a many-stranded spiral of discourse that transformed all participants. Interaction with Europeans changed America radically over these centuries, so America as a subject is elusive. And the opportunities and challenges offered by the newly revealed lands transformed European societies as well. The lands on both sides of the Atlantic were very different in 1750 from what they would have been had the ocean never been crossed. It is the interaction between perceptions and a changing reality that these essays seek to illuminate.

The basic terms of the discussion were set in the very first report. Columbus's first voyage brought back natives and their tools, together with reports of great riches and of many thousands of people ripe for conversion. From the beginning then, even before the magnitude of the news was clear, the two great intertwined themes of colonization appeared fully formed: Christendom had been presented an unprecedented opportunity to preach the gospel, and Europe's reward for this endeavor would be riches beyond imagining. As Columbus advised his sponsors, the Spanish sovereigns: "Your Highnesses ought to resolve to make them Christians: for I believe that if you begin, in a short time you will end up having converted to our Holy Faith a multitude of peoples and acquiring large dominions and great riches and all of their peoples for Spain. Because without doubt there is in these lands a very great quantity of gold; for not without cause do these Indians that I bring with me say that there are in these islands places where they dig gold and wear it on their chests, on their ears, and on their arms, and on their legs; and they are very thick bracelets. And also there are stones, and there are precious pearls and infinite spicery."[23]

Columbus's report, mixing the quest for souls to bring to conversion with the quest for dazzling riches, is the archetype of all European responses to America in being utterly self-referential.[24] America was interesting insofar as it could enhance Europe, either in material goods or in knowledge. Modern scholars have sought and found a very few European writers, such as Bernardino de Sahagún, Roger Williams, or Michel de Montaigne, who seem to have been genuinely interested in the newfound lands and cultures for their own sake. But even these writers undertook their studies to educate readers at home, and to shame Europeans into living up to their own civilized standards.[25] Like their contemporaries, they too saw in the new lands the possibility of enhancing their own societies. America was accommodated through dialogue involving observation, projection, and evolution.

The Essays

One of the most fundamental challenges presented to humanists by knowledge of the hitherto unknown lands across the Atlantic lay in the field of history. The essays in Part I, America and the Historical Imagination, written by and about historians, demonstrate the many possibilities embedded in the texts humanists produced. Peter Burke offers an answer to the problem of how to gauge a shift in consciousness. He imagines a scholar entering a sixteenth-century library and, using the bibliographical aids available at the time, seeking knowledge of America. He then looks at one particular case study, how the writing systems of Mexico and Peru were documented (or not) in contemporary studies of writing. Both modes of approach lead to a minimalist conclusion; America, he argues, was seen as peripheral in the sixteenth and seventeenth centuries.

David Armitage, looking at British historical writing, takes Richard Hakluyt, the great sixteenth-century compiler of exploration accounts, as the progenitor of Britain's special relationship with America. Hakluyt, working at the margins of history where it intersected with geography, itself a newly vivified discipline, was more receptive to the new knowledge and new ways of writing history. The discipline of history was transformed by scholars such as Hakluyt who found the available forms of discourse inadequate. Armitage sees a new theory of history emerging in the seventeenth century. Writers averred that modernity began with the technological advances and the discoveries of the sixteenth century, and the revelation of the Americas was central to this new mentality. But paradoxically, as Europe's thrust toward America helped transform Europe's view of its own history, the American natives continued to be viewed as people outside history, permanently engulfed in an earlier phase. Thus the old relationships between the ancient world, including Europe's own ancestors, and the modern were called in question. Armitage pairs Hakluyt, the chronicler and propagandist who urged the empire's founding, with William Robertson, whose writing of the *History of America* was cut short by the American Revolution and the end of Britain's first empire. Robertson, reflecting on the way in which history had been transformed, argued that only with the discovery of America had it become possible to see the whole scope of human history. Thus Armitage sees profound effects from the reception of American knowledge where Burke argues for little impact.

Both Burke and Armitage agree, however, that Europe's primary response was self-referential. Peter Burke shows European writers congratulating their own culture on the magnificent achievement of the discoveries; America's importance lay in its contribution to the great advances in technology and understanding generated by the Renaissance and Reformation. Newly revealed peoples and lifeways were collected, like the products of far-off lands, in a new spirit of consumerism; they were interesting insofar as they could illuminate European concerns. Could study of them tell scholars something about Europe's own past? Who were the American natives, and what ancient dispersal of peoples accounted for their living so far away? What did revelation of their existence at this time tell Europeans about God's plans for Christendom? Was it a signal of the coming millennium, before which the gospel must be preached to all? Why did God delay this revelation until after the Reformation? What meaning did the disclosure of such vast stores of hitherto hidden knowledge mean for curricula based on study of the ancients who knew nothing of America? All the authors in this collection show early scholars struggling to make sense of America in the only terms meaningful to them: what do these artifacts and the cultures from which they come tell us about ourselves?

The authors in Part II, America Reflected in Europe, writing from a variety of disciplinary approaches, demonstrate how available intellectual forms were harnessed to discussion of American realities. Study of American religions, Sabine MacCormack argues, melded with European scholars' preoccupation with the origins of the religious impulse. Seeing similarities between their own traditions and the newly revealed practices and teachings, they had available to them two models. One was a centrifugal force deep in the past that had dispersed revealed religion. Colonization then involved a reuniting of that split world and restoration to Christianity of peoples who had only a partial and corrupted form. The other was an evolving theory of parallel development according to natural principles of religion. Similarities between religions, in this model, would stem from responses of primitive peoples to the natural world and the attempt to explain it.

Scholars who attempted to solve the puzzle of American religions were deeply interested in the new forms, yet they also represented their observations in shapes that confirmed European norms. It is the selection process, the trimming and tailoring of the information, that makes their enterprise so interesting and important. Through MacCormack's case study, and her intensive analysis of visual as well as written material, we can see the ways in which shifts in consciousness occurred.

Roland Greene's critical analysis of key literary texts shows us the cultural lens through which early explorers and their backers framed the wonders they encountered. He argues that the key and original mode of writing about America was Petrarchan, characterized by the yearning of the author for an ambiguous, tantalizingly indeterminate other, the "reality" of which is the author's own construction. The Petrarchan mode, apparently wholly personal, actually deals with power relations, but in the early colonial setting many of the power claims are fundamentally personal. The first-person anecdote is the classic form of American writing in the early years. The very closeness of his reading allows Greene to open up the subject of the encounter, demonstrating the reverberations generated by the use of color terms to define the lands and their peoples, with all the allure and fear that color evoked.

David Quint's reconsideration of Montaigne's celebrated essay *Des cannibales*, involving close critical analysis in the context of all the *Essays*, enhances our understanding of this key figure and of his writing as a commentary on and exhortation to contemporary France. By placing Montaigne firmly in his own context he demonstrates the futility and anachronism of attempting to pick out "progressive" figures who somehow transcended their own time and place. Montaigne is often treated as exemplary of a tolerant relativism unprecedented in the sixteenth century and is celebrated as one of the creators of the noble savage.

Quint explodes this interpretation by demonstrating that Montaigne wrote to condemn the reported cannibalism among the American Indians as mindless and circular destruction which was ultimately self-immolation. The argument was focused on France; Montaigne's famous praise of the Americans presents them as merely less vicious than his countrymen. The Stoicism of France's decaying warrior aristocracy was Montaigne's principal target; the virtue the nobles celebrated actually was destroying their society. He also wrote to expose the pathetic "blind obstinacy" of those caught up in religious conflict, who gave their lives in refusal to bend over issues that were unworthy of such sacrifice. What was taken for virtue was really self-justifying and perpetual violence.

The three essays in Part II show how familiar texts can be made to yield fresh, and more realistic, readings that illuminate the European-American encounter. In doing so they also serve to demonstrate modes of critical analysis and the way in which certain themes reverberated through early modern discourse.

The essays in Part III, America and European Aspirations, focusing on those who saw new challenges and opportunities in America, take up many of the motifs presented in Parts I and II. For many, especially religious leaders, the revelation of the Americas, coming as it did with the breaking up of Christendom, presented a series of profound challenges. John Headley shows how even basic concepts of space and time were affected. As the world was opened up spatially, religious leaders, Protestant as well as Roman Catholic, argued that the disclosures following Columbus's first venture meant that their times were the last days foretold in Revelation. They had been chosen for a momentous role, nothing less than the culmination of history, before which the gospel must be preached to all nations. World evangelization presented a challenge both exhilarating and daunting.

Headley argues that Tommaso Campanella realized how fundamentally knowledge of America transformed not only Europe's past but also its future as he projected a globalization of Christianity's message and even relocation of sacred sites. Headley's essay helps us to see the complexity of European response to America and of the context in which that response occurred. Where David Quint sees aristocratic Stoicism as a destructive circle holding adherents in its rigid grasp, Headley argues that, in an intellectual such as Campanella, Stoicism linked with Platonism to create the possibility of a new sense of universal community based on natural law among all peoples. Stoicism becomes then a solvent of old rigidities. The early modern response to the encounter, like modern scholarship on it, was always seen through a series of shifting lenses.

Campanella's response to America was, like that of his contemporaries, profoundly Europe-centered. Knowledge about America caused him to change his views of history and of Christianity's task, but the stream of influence was to be all one way. Empire was justified by the need to evangelize, and harsh force could be used on those who resisted. Indians could be used to solve Spain's labor problems. His view of the world was more comprehensive than most, but its center was still in Europe and the goal of history was to make the rest of the world more European. His changed perception did not amount, according to Headley, to "a true transformation of consciousness."[26]

Luca Codignola also treats the challenge and opportunity for evangelization presented to the Holy See by news of huge populations untouched by the Christian message. Codignola's analysis of the church's response elucidates the enormous complexity of that institution. The bureaucratic problem of organizing and directing missions, with momentous consequences for the future of the church flowing from each decision, absorbed leaders until the organization of the Congregation de Propaganda Fide in 1622. That agency, the "least Eurocentric" in the church, then directed mission efforts in the parts of North America colonized by the French and English.

Codignola's discussion of Propaganda raises many of the same issues as Headley's analysis of Campanella. In both we see that the challenge of America provoked an unprecedented widening of perspective, and willingness to rethink the Christian message. But at the same time Propaganda, like Campanella, was also profoundly Eurocentric in assuming that all the world would come under the Christian umbrella. Codignola shows in fascinating detail how, when initial optimism about the susceptibility of coastal natives to conversion was proven false, missionaries responded with reports of more docile and more "civilized" Indians to the west who were anxious for the Christian message. Both Codignola and Headley demonstrate how rejection of Christianity came to be seen as the product of stubborn savagery; natives who were offered and rejected the truth then deserved a far more severe discipline. The harshest rhetoric was the backlash of disappointed naive optimism. But that very optimism, assuming that all Americans would easily give up their own culture and religion for the imported one, is also the most arrogant form of Eurocentrism.

Some of the optimism, and the harshness, stemmed from European thinkers' own confusion over whether the Indians had been known to the ancient world. If, as many thought, they were the descendants of the ten lost tribes of Israel, then they had been exposed to the truths of the Old Testament in the distant past.[27] MacCormack shows that some thinkers even believed the Americans had received the Christian message long ago. Codignola demonstrates the confusion in many minds over whether missionaries were recalling natives to Christianity or introducing it.

This confusion is succinctly summed up in the word used by writers of all religious persuasions to describe the process of conversion: reduction. The Jesuit missions in Paraguay were even referred to as *reducciones.* "To reduce" is a verb with many possible meanings, some obsolete after the seventeenth century. Its original meaning was to restore, especially to a belief, and it carried the implication of bringing back from error. Thus to write of conversion as reduction implied acceptance of the notion that the Indians had fallen away from true religion through a process of attrition.[28] Such belief would certainly account for the easy optimism with which the task was approached.

On the other hand, reduction also carried the modern meaning of bringing to order, obedience, and reason by the use of force or compulsion.[29] The *Oxford English Dictionary* illustrates the meaning "to place under" with American examples. This definition was certainly in the minds of many writers as they mapped a plan of action for dealing with the American natives. From the earliest writings, the Indians were described as "proud"; pride and savagery were seen as inextricably intertwined. Codignola shows that in 1493, as soon as news of the unknown lands was brought, Pope Alexander VI decreed the "barbaric peoples" must be "humbled." Peter Hulme has demonstrated that the association of "truculence" with barbarism lay deep in the medieval past.[30] When writers said of the American Indians that they must be "reduced to civility," the implication of harsh force, wrenching them out of their own structures into some version of European social relationships, seems clear.

The image of reduction, implying the forceful imposition of reason and obedience on peoples who were proud because they were savage, silently covered further confusion in European thinking. Pride was a key attribute, not only of savages but also of aristocratic Europeans. European leaders, particularly those in military roles, participated in a culture of pride that would brook no challenge, however slight. If a single crack appeared, their effectiveness was at an end. David Quint demonstrates the power and pervasiveness of this culture and the lengths to which it carried those who considered themselves most exquisitely civilized. Thus the conclusion is inescapable that Europeans' response to the Indians was influenced by class/status concerns as well as cultural assumptions. As Quint argues, and Headley and Codignola demonstrate, thinking about American experience also resonated with European problems.

Part III also delineates another sort of opportunity and challenge represented by America: transplantation. Slowly over the sixteenth century and increasingly through the seventeenth and eighteenth, humble men and women in some parts of western Europe considered the possibility of emigration. If America offered churchmen the opportunity of great new fields for conversion, it offered ordinary subjects the chance for a security, economic and religious, impossible for many at home. As I try to demonstrate in my essay, the problems generated by the attempt to transplant a version of English society to America forced promoters and colonists to think about the essential elements of their own society. English colonization did not succeed until planners allowed settlers to take control of key elements of the process. Since planters sought control in order to replicate familiar forms abroad, colonizers on both sides of the Atlantic were confronted by the question of what made English society English. Colonization involved self-fashioning on a national level.

Part IV, America and the Scholarly Impulse, presents essays on the actual flow of information and artifacts from America to Europe. Some Europeans actively sought out the new and tried to force those at home to confront it. Many were meticulous reporters, but the process of building a picture was at best imperfect. It is tempting to dwell on the "correct" statements, those we can now see were genuine additions to knowledge. But what bibliographical resources such as *European Americana* allow us to understand is the contemporary context of such works, the sea of pictures, maps, and books in which they floated, and the many ways in which Europeans made sense of the newly revealed lands.[31] In the following discussions of how, and how much, information about America was incorporated into scholarship and which books actually circulated to a large audience, we can see that the reports and analyses we consider most essential may not have seen the light of publication at all in their day. Publication of eyewitness material was sometimes long delayed while other more appealing books dominated. Inaccurate maps were reprinted long after better ones were available. For example, the third edition of Edward Williams's *Virgo Triumphans: or Virginia richly and truly valued*, published in 1650, was illustrated by a map showing the Pacific Ocean just beyond the Appalachian Mountains, an idea first generated by Verrazzano in 1524 and long discredited by the mid-seventeenth century. This map, in which California was decorated with an inset of Sir Francis Drake, was in the portfolio used by William Blathwayt while he was secretary of England's Lords of Trade and Plantations, from 1675 to 1796, and a member of the Board of Trade, from 1696 to 1710.[32]

Images were often reworked and used to represent realities far different from those their creators intended. The map published in Paris as "Nowel Amsterdam en L'Amerique" in the 1670s actually depicts the city of Lisbon. Similarly, engraved versions of John White's late-sixteenth-century paintings of coastal Carolina Algonquian villages appeared as Apache towns in a map by Guillaume de l'Isle in the early eighteenth century.[33]

Modern scholars look for advances in knowledge and understanding, but American information served many purposes for the early modern scholarly world. "Is it true?" may not have been the most crucial test for any particular rendition. It is important to understand the various ways in which information was received and

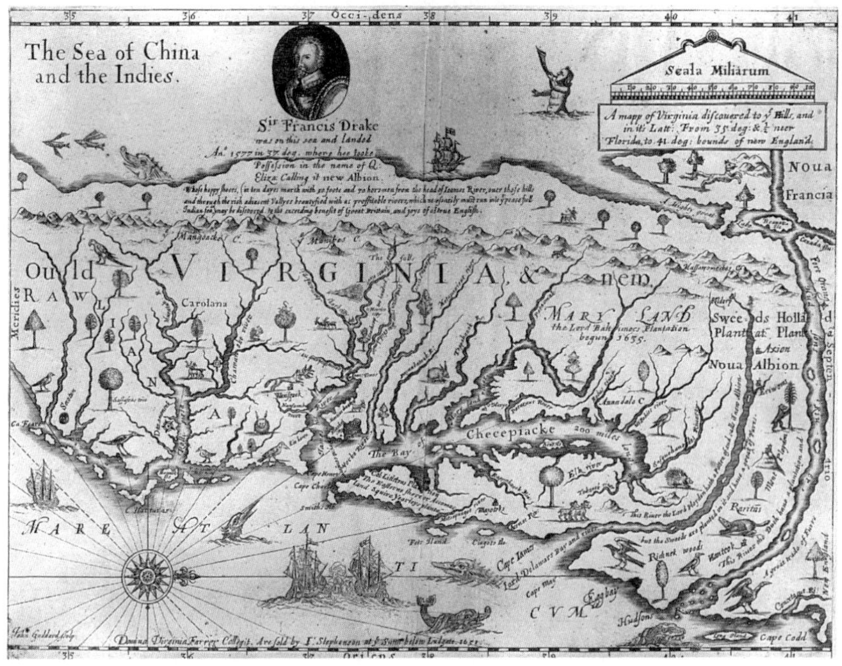

John Farrer, “A Map of Virginia Discovered to Ye Hills” ([London], 1651). John Carter Brown Library.

“naturalized,” and what those differences convey to us about how meaning was assigned and structured. As Christian Feest remarks, Europe both invented and discovered America. The essays in Part IV offer enlightenment on both the progression toward a more accurate and complete understanding of American ethnography and natural history, and on America’s many levels of meanings for European audiences. The authors enable us to see written material progressing to publication and to understand not only the initial selection process but also the way in which maps, prints, and prose continued to change and adapt long after they left their creators’ controlling hands.

A huge amount of new information was taken in, fostering a growing sophistication on the part of Europeans as they assimilated knowledge on a hitherto unimagined scale; Henry Lowood, for example, argues that the number of known species of plants was multiplied fortyfold within 150 years.[34] But all the knowledge and products still served European purposes. As Lowood and Feest demonstrate, they were absorbed in order to solve Old World problems or puzzles, and they were ordered in ways that made sense to Europeans. Scholars naturalized the products of America, decontextualizing them and implicitly denying that their native habitat or setting mattered. Artifacts were validated only as they were seen

[Jollain], "Nowel Amsterdam en Lamerique" ([Paris, ca. 1672]). John Carter Brown Library.

as interesting or valuable in European eyes. From the early years of the sixteenth century, Europeans such as Nicholas Monardes eagerly sought American seeds and slips for planting in their own gardens; as botanical gardens proliferated, scholars came to see such exotic plantings and wrote about their properties. Artifacts from across the ocean were included in exhibits of the exotic, serving European categories so thoroughly that their native origins were obscured. This more "scientific" approach made the newly revealed continents themselves less important. Only with modern ethnographic techniques developed in recent decades is Feest able to present his exhaustive list of American items in European collections, and to reveal the principles on which collectors acted.

Richard Simmons presents another way in which Europeans found America useful; he documents a very large number of books by and about European-Americans in which the new lands and their inhabitants became an imagined, even imaginary, reality for English readers. Books set in America stirred the emotions, and books about new societies, religious and civil, offered instruction. Simmons also documents the huge numbers of books sent home for publication by American religious leaders, demonstrating religious migrants' continued desire to instruct the Old World as they sought refuge for themselves. The outpouring of replies to American authors proves that they were read and their message understood.

Slowly over the long period covered by these essays, some writers moved beyond earlier Europe-centered questions and began to adopt a more sophisticated approach. They ventured to think of America's native peoples as separate societies, quite different from Europe and its past. But many of the essays ask in one way or another whether this growing sophistication always represented an advance over earlier naïveté. Sabine MacCormack, like Christian Feest, sees a tendency in the later years of the period to lump together all native forms under the umbrella of the exotic. This could lead to a new stance, with writers distancing themselves and Europe from the American natives. MacCormack points out that some theorists, notably Isaac La Peyrère and Bernard Fontenelle in the mid-to-late seventeenth century, even ventured to posit, as a radical solution to the perennially discussed problem of the Americans' origin, the idea that they stemmed from a separate creation. Though few scholars on either side of the Atlantic would have gone so far, several of the essays argue for a widespread perception by 1750 that the Americas had little to teach Christendom about its own past.

Consequences

It was not just scholars' perceptions that changed over these two and a half centuries; the peoples and land they described were transformed, and writers' developing perceptions reflected this profoundly different reality. In America the lives of the native populations changed dramatically and tragically over the period from the end of the fifteenth century to the middle of the eighteenth. Populous, thriving nations were reduced by European diseases and declining food supplies to the merest fraction of their former strength.[35] Agricultural peoples became nomadic as they were pushed onto land unsuitable for cultivation; hunting and gathering activities were curtailed by the Europeans' penchant for fencing off land and intensive cultivation. Natives who were caught up in trading and hunting for European consumers became increasingly detribalized; native political and religious structures were often already in disarray because of the leaders' inability to cope with the range of challenges, coupled with high death rates among elders.

All over the two continents Americans were offered the cruel choice of entering the European system, usually in marginal roles, or accepting a far more primitive version of their former cultures. "Savagery" was a self-fulfilling description wherever the newcomers established themselves. Changing descriptions of native life to some extent reflect evolving realities.

The land was also transformed. By the eighteenth century both creoles and natives lived in an environment far different from the America described in the sixteenth century; it had been irrevocably changed by contact and colonization. The "widowed land," bereft of so many millions of its natives through the devastating diseases unwittingly brought across the sea, had been repopulated by Europeans.[36] As colonists took up native lands, they also adopted native crops and exported them to the rest of the world. At the same time, Old World seeds and animals colonized along with the human migrants. Probably no European after the very first explorers ever saw an exclusively American meadow; birds and animals took up seeds carried in the holds of ships and in the guts of animals and spread them far beyond the frontier of contact. Escapees from among the imported horses, cows, pigs, and rats, lacking natural enemies to control them, transformed both American continents long before their human "masters" saw interior lands.

European life was also transformed by its contacts with America. The flooding in of products and information forced creation of structures to organize and establish them. The flow of people out of Europe into the newly revealed lands also changed Old World life. These indirect effects worked in many directions, but they all had one impact in common: unevenly but inexorably they jolted Europe's society and economy in the direction of influence by people farther down the social scale. Cracks in the aristocratic mold would certainly have appeared without America, but the timing and the fault lines were affected by transatlantic enterprises that allowed, even encouraged, assumption of initiative by the excluded. America helped open up Europe.

For example, exposing Europe's consciousness to new information from previously hidden continents forced open the privileged world of scholarship. New voices were heard and new kinds of authority established, the authority of the eyewitness over the classical tradition of Virgil, Pliny, and their interpreters. Anthony Pagden argues that the very nature of authority was stretched and changed in the process.[37] As Henry Lowood demonstrates, the scholars eagerly sought information from travelers. The sources of information about the plants, peoples, and geography of America were ordinary people, the soldiers and mariners who carried out the explorations. John Headley shows how intellectuals such as Tommaso Campanella acknowledged their debt to mariners such as Columbus; ancient wisdom must now be supplemented or even displaced by reports of previously unknown nature. Scholar-venturers such as Gonzalo Fernández de Oviedo y Valdés and José de Acosta affirmed that the wisdom of the ancients must fall before eyewitness experience, the superior source of knowledge.[38]

Explorers such as Hernan Cortés, Samuel de Champlain, and Captain John Smith, whose writings were collected and reprinted by the scholars, described for the waiting audience of intellectuals the realities of American nature. These venturers claimed places alongside the ancients. Bernal Díaz del Castillo, Cortés's companion, compared himself to Julius Caesar: "I was present in many more battles and warlike encounters than those in which the writers say Julius Caesar was engaged, [that is] in fifty three battles, and to record his exploits he had consummate chroniclers, but he was not satisfied with what they wrote about him, so Julius Caesar himself with his own hand made a record in his Commentaries of all the wars he was personally engaged in." Captain John Smith also compared himself to Julius Caesar, who "wrote his owne Commentaries, holding it no lesse honour to write, than fight." He proudly ended his books with the statement "John Smith writ this with his owne hand."[39]

These venturers understood fully the ways in which the printing press had changed the flow of information, and the importance of telling their own stories. Columbus's prologue to the journal of his first voyage told of his resolve "of writing on this whole voyage, very diligently, all that I would do and see and experience." On the return voyage, he faced a terrific storm and his little fleet was down to one ship. He and his mariners first vowed religious pilgrimages if they were delivered. Columbus's second act was to write an account of his voyage and its discoveries, which he wrapped "in a well-tied, waxed cloth and ordered a large wooden barrel brought and he put the parchment in it without anyone learning what it was, except that everyone thought it was some act of devotion; and he ordered it thrown into the sea." The letter beseeched the barrel's finder to take it to the Spanish sovereigns.[40]

Cortés was careful to arrange from across the ocean for the prompt publication of his letters in Europe.[41] And John Smith, whose first long report was published in a disappointingly garbled form before his return from Virginia, thereafter carefully superintended the progress of his books through the press. A flood of books and maps emerged from the travels of Europeans to America and these reports, disseminated through the printed word, claimed an immediacy and legitimacy that few could question.

On the other hand, as Henry Lowood vividly demonstrates, publication of material in its most authentic form was never assured. Some scholars did travel to America, but frequently their writings went unpublished, or were only partially circulated. Thomas Hariot, Ralegh's scientific adviser, is one notable example. Hariot's *Briefe and True Report of the New Found Land of Virginia* (1588) is a classic short description of North America's natural world, but Hariot never published the large natural history he planned.[42] Accident could also intervene; Stephen Parmenius, the Hungarian scholar, died on a voyage to Newfoundland in the late sixteenth century.[43]

English intellectuals experienced a flurry of excitement when one of their number, George Sandys, son of the archbishop of York, went to Jamestown as a colony officer. Sandys was an established author; his book describing his travels through the eastern Mediterranean had already become something of a classic.[44] But, although he wrote letters home to Virginia Company associates and sent one now-lost letter to the naturalist and collector John Tradescant, he spent his scholarly time in Jamestown translating Ovid and wrote nothing about America comparable to his earlier book. His friends expected nothing else; they assumed that American Indians, as primitive peoples, merely recapitulated the characteristics of less interesting Europeans. Michael Drayton's 1622 poem "To Master George Sandys, Treasurer for the English Colony in Virginia," laid out tasks for Sandys:

> Goe on with Ovid, as you have begunne,
> With the first five bookes; let your numbers run
> Glib as the former, so it shall live long,
> And doe much honour to the English tongue:

At the poem's end Drayton asked generally for a "description of the place" and particularly for an account of how the English fared,

> But you may save your labour if you please,
> To write me ought of your savages.
> As savage slaves be in great Britaine here,
> As any one that you can shew me there.[45]

For Drayton and his friends, people without recognizable accomplishments were all alike and all uninteresting.

Such sentiments fueled demands by the men of action that their observations be given credence beyond the writings of those who had only high status to support them. Leaders such as Smith ridiculed the "Tuftaffaty humorists," men of rank who spent all their time in the fort complaining about the rough life. Only those who went into the field and saw firsthand deserved credence.[46] This was more than an intellectual game. Failure to understand the intricacies of native life and to make distinctions between different interest groups could spell the difference between life and death. Subtly the nature of authority and the preeminence of inherited knowledge was transformed, sowing the seeds for even larger transformations to come.

European structures of knowledge were changing in the period of America's revelation, and the flood of new information played a role in that transformation. Even more important, the challenge of thinking about and dealing with America and its peoples forced the pace in fundamental processes of change. David Armitage points out that mapping of European space was just beginning when the geographers were presented with the enormous challenge of organizing information about vast unknown lands.[47]

Basic ideas about communication were also transformed as a result of the American challenge, as Peter Burke demonstrates in his discussion of interest in writing systems. Scholars thought in new ways about the structures of human language and the variety of tongues around the world. The first grammar of a contemporary vernacular language was created in 1492 when Elio Antonio de Nebrija completed his Spanish *Gramática*. Queen Isabella, when presented with it, asked what its purpose was. The answer, given by the bishop of Avila, was "Language is the perfect instrument of empire."[48] The dramatic proliferation of grammars, and, with them, new sophistication about the structure of language, was directly linked to the need to deal with American natives. By 1700 there were twenty-one grammars of American languages and twenty-three of European. Moreover, four American grammars were published before any comparable work on English or Dutch existed. Although few of those who went on to create a philosophical approach to comparative language study may have thought of their enterprise as shaped by the discovery of America, the indirect influence was enormous, as they reduced language to a set of rules by which it could be learned in small steps.[49]

European life was also transformed by the plethora of newly available commodities. Historians have long debated the role of American treasure in the tremendous inflation of the sixteenth and seventeenth centuries. Calorie-rich American foods may have underlain the doubling of population in the same period because while scholarly gardeners cultivated exotic plants, ordinary farmers converted acreage to maize, beans, and sweet potatoes.[50] European foodways were transformed so dramatically that many now-traditional cuisines are based on American foods. As early as the 1670s John Locke was surprised to find maize fields in southern France, where, under the name "bled d'Espagne," it "serves poore people for bred. That which makes them sow it, is not only the great increase, but the convenience also which the blade & green about the stalke yeilds them, it being good nourishment for their cattle."[51]

From its beginnings the drive to explore and colonize all over the world was fueled by a new consumerism, the desire to possess novel luxury goods from abroad. Although this impetus came initially from the wealthy, the influx of goods and their transforming power reached far down the social scale, contributing to the creation of a new consumer culture at all levels. Products such as sugar and tobacco, once only for the super-rich, quickly became items of mass consumption, available to all but the poorest.[52]

Europe's economy was first stimulated by American treasure and products and then boomed in response to America's growing creole population and its demand for manufactured goods. Europe's economic center tilted toward the great Atlantic ports, as producers found vast new markets in American consumers, reversing and reinforcing the earlier flow of products from west to east.[53]

America also became an item of common consumption through the new genre of cheap popular vernacular literature. Stories of drama and adventure centering on European men and women but set in the exotic world across the Atlantic spread consciousness of America across western Europe. Richard Simmons's discussion of eighteenth-century English publishing demonstrates the degree to which America had become a commonplace of popular culture, but often serving as an exotic backdrop for European themes. His research offers an entry into the usually inaccessible consciousness of middling and "poorer sort" men and women and shows their broad, but shallow, knowledge of a transatlantic world. Although few achieved the lasting fame of Daniel Defoe's *Moll Flanders*, many of these books were published again and again across Europe.

Not only was the taste for adventure satisfied, but the new societies' claims to instruct the old found voice in the sermons, psalm books, and treatises sent home for publication and the massive number of books by writers with American experience, for which an apparently insatiable audience existed in England. One exceedingly popular book combined both themes, the instructive voice and American adventure: *The Soveraignty and goodness of God . . . Being a narrative of the captivity and restauration of Mrs. Mary Rowlandson.* This book, the first in the great popular tradition of true stories of Indian captivity (her title page asserts that the book was "written with her own hand"), was written in the form of a sermon. First published in Massachusetts in 1682, it was printed in London the same year and went through many editions. Nancy Armstrong and Leonard Tennenhouse argue that Rowlandson's book, whose popularity grew in the eighteenth century, provided the model for the first modern novel, Samuel Richardson's *Pamela.*[54] Thus, although these publications were all self-referential, interesting insofar as they shed light on European interests, their cumulative indirect effect was dramatic.

Many of the essays in this volume show European intellectuals consuming America and appropriating its cultures, flora, and fauna to elucidate European questions. Intellectuals rarely escaped this framework. But many European men and women did break out, both physically and intellectually, making or accepting a choice to *become* American. Their consciousness of the revealed lands across the Atlantic was far different from the mental world both of the intellectuals and of the popular chapbooks. Although the adventure stories collected by Simmons often centered on the kidnapping of innocent young men and women by rapacious merchants or ship captains or featured the deportation of criminals, huge numbers of people actually chose emigration. Because of this massive transplantation, by the middle of the eighteenth century America became an accepted part of Europe's mental landscape.[55]

For these emigrants America represented the chance to establish ownership of the means of production, land, and to pass the degree of independence that such ownership conferred on to their children. Thus, consciously or unconsciously, emigration meant rejection of Old World relationships, and especially of the

"Hieronymi Benzoni in Indiam Occidentalem I," from Johann Theodor de Bry, *Grands Voyages*, pt. IV (Latin) (Frankfurt, 1594). John Carter Brown Library.

greater dependence to which those who remained at home were condemned. Hundreds of thousands of European men and women emigrated, more or less voluntarily, in the period before 1750. Reconstructing the flow is difficult because Europe's outpouring of population was largely informal. Governments operated behind rather than ahead of the curve of emigration.

Clearly, although literary sources may not provide the evidence to prove it, America represented a powerful reality in the consciousness of ordinary men and women in some parts of Europe. Prospective settlers were not distributed randomly across the landscape; a few regions in each country contributed the great bulk of the emigrants. Andalusia and Extremadura in Spain; England's southern counties, with the later addition of the Scottish highlands and northern Ireland; France's great Atlantic ports and their surroundings; and the Palatinate, Württemberg, and Hesse in Germany all contributed colonists disproportionally. Some regions thus had close ties to America, and their inhabitants knew or knew of someone who had gone there. For these emigrants and their neighbors America took on a personal reality.

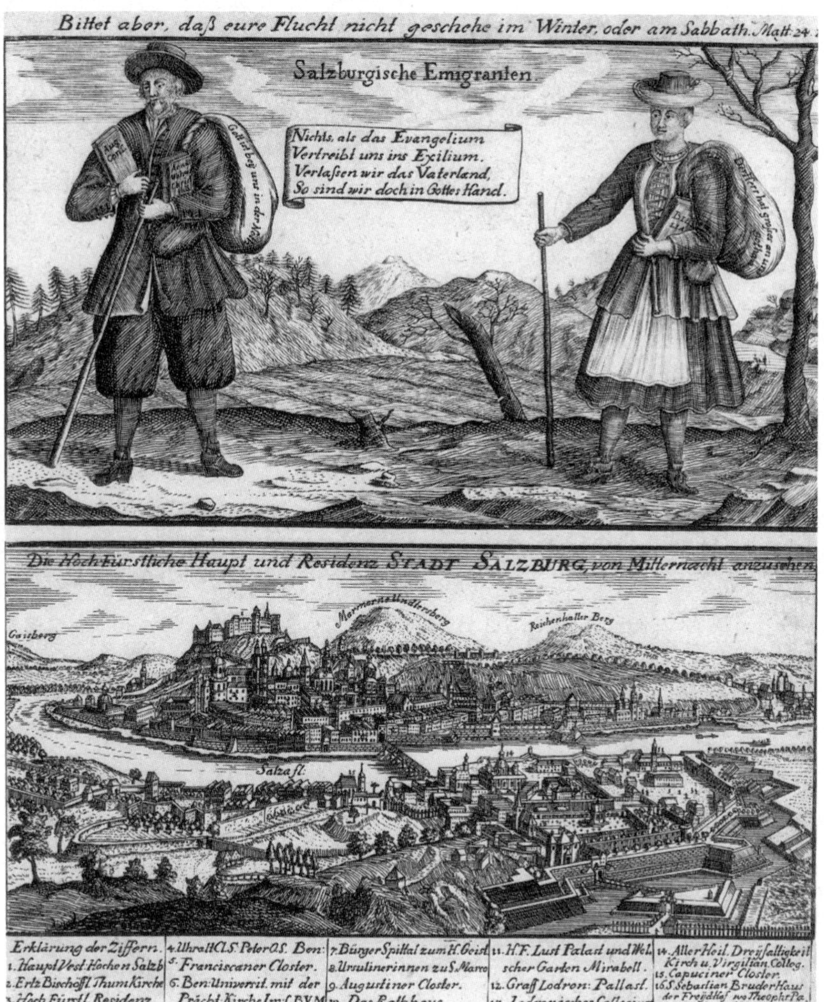

"Salzburgische Emigranten," from *Ausführliche Historie derer Emigranten oder vertriebenen Lutheraner* (Leipzig, 1732). John Carter Brown Library.

Destinations reflected migrants' regional origins, and American locales saw societies reflecting characteristics of the settlers' home regions.[56] Repeated transatlantic voyages were not uncommon. Regions that had contributed heavily to emigration were apt to see transplants returning with stories and goods to feed home dwellers' imaginations. The foundations of many fortunes were laid through early years spent in America, and cities throughout Europe contained men and women who had lived across the Atlantic and knew that world. Richard Simmons refers to the impact of returnees on the life of London. Tokens sent to friends and family at home kept memories alive and made America broadly familiar. Europeans in their turn sought the latest fashions in clothing and books to send to their kin across the Atlantic and thus pictured these items in the American setting.[57]

Colonists were attracted by the prospect of improving their lives. For them America was blank territory in which they could create a new, more perfect Europe without interference from either old or New World complications. For all these migrants, and for those they left behind, America represented the chance to realize European dreams, and their newly constructed societies always constituted a comment on European realities. American arrangements gave colonists unprecedented security, religious and economic, and a new, improved version of Europe. Increasingly, as Luca Codignola demonstrates, these transplanted Europeans/new Americans absorbed the attention of religious leaders in place of the displaced Indians.

The best measure of their success in transplantation is the changing definition of the word "American." In the sixteenth century that name would always connote an Indian, a native of America. Increasingly through the later seventeenth century, and certainly by our closing date of 1750, the appellation "American" was far more ambiguous; most often it referred to a creole, a person of Old World descent born in Europe's New World.

Thus the Atlantic seemed to shrink, its American shore brought closer by the establishment of Euro-American societies. But this new familiarity also hid a greater distance. On every level this paradox reasserts itself: as America became more familiar, a common element in awareness, Europeans also realized the transforming power of that new environment, which reinforced the change in self-perception wrought by the decision to emigrate. The American was more (and less) than a transplanted European. Jasper Danckaerts conveyed the difference vividly as he recounted a conversation with Indians near Cohoes in New York who delightedly distinguished Danckaerts and his companion from the colonists they knew. "Seeing us, they said to each other, 'Look, these are certainly real Dutchmen, actual Hollanders.' Robert Sanders asked them how they knew it. 'We see it,' they said, 'in their faces and in their dress.' "[58]

"Criolian degeneracy" became a theme of transatlantic discourse. In the middle of the eighteenth century the allegation that Old World plants and animals, including human beings, always degenerated in America became a generalized topic of discussion among intellectuals. Charles-Marie de la Condamine, who went to Peru in the 1730s with a French scientific mission, described the Indians as "the enemies of work, indifferent to all motives of glory, honour or knowledge." Antonio de Ulloa, who accompanied Condamine and served long years in America, applied the same charge to Americans of European descent, describing them as intellectually feeble and enervated. French philosophes heatedly discussed whether the discovery of America had been beneficial.[59]

The charge of "criolian degeneracy" allows us to see two key ways in which the effect of America on European consciousness was changing in the first half of the eighteenth century. One is that the charge was answered by Euro-Americans, who now saw themselves as participating in a related but separate culture across the sea. Massive European immigration had caused the most momentous change of all; it had accelerated and routinized contacts and had transformed the reality of America.

Beginning in the seventeenth century and increasingly in the first half of the eighteenth, the new Americans celebrated their difference. As early as 1615 the Franciscan Juan de Torquemada, who spent his entire life from early childhood in Mexico, criticized such predecessors as Herrera, Acosta, and Gómara for their shallowness in describing Indian cultures. As a Euro-American, Torquemada adopted the Incas and Aztecs alongside the Spanish Christians as symbolic ancestors and celebrated them in his *Monarquía Indiana.* To counter charges of cultural backwardness, Juan José de Eguiara y Eguren, rector of the University of Mexico, compiled a massive bibliography with biographical sketches of all Mexican authors and their works, the first volume of which was published in 1755 under the title *Biblioteca Mexicana.* Like Torquemada he emphasized the preconquest accomplishments of the Indians and went on to describe the feats of learning at American universities.[60]

Proudly proclaiming "I am an Indian," Virginian Robert Beverley compared American directness and sincerity to European convolution in his 1705 *History and Present State of Virginia,* where he celebrated "the Plainness of my Dress." His preface set forth the difference: "Truth desires only to be understood, and never affects the Reputation of being finely equipp'd. It depends upon its own intrinsick Value, and, like Beauty, is rather conceal'd, than set off, by Ornament."[61] Later in the century Thomas Jefferson and Benjamin Franklin defended their land and their culture against the philosophes' scorn.

Whereas the defense of their societies as American indicates a break in the experience and expectations of transplanted Europeans and their children from the original assumption that undiluted Old World norms would dominate, the debate over creole culture reveals a powerful continuity in European response. European intellectuals, seeing difference as degeneracy, continued to treat America as a screen on which to project their own fears and fantasies. The projection became more provocative when the actors were men and women like themselves.

The essays in this collection thus cover a deceptively unified topic, America in Europe's consciousness, over a long period that saw enormous change on both sides; this change was in many ways the product of contact and colonization. Many of the essays argue that the third quarter of the eighteenth century saw the real incorporation of America into European consciousness. For many reasons the middle of the eighteenth century marks a turning point and thus a good ending date for this collection. The two and a half centuries since 1493 had seen ingathering and exchange of peoples, goods, and concepts both ways across the Atlantic. After 1750, as the essays below demonstrate, Europeans found themselves looking back at the process of reception. They could ask whether America's revelation had been a good thing; the encounter was over and now was the time to assess its impact. David Hume, for example, wrote in 1754, "It is certain, that, since the discovery of the mines in America, industry has encreased in all the nations of Europe, except in the possessors of those mines."[62] The period was one of consolidation and categorization, synthesis and incorporation.

America as a subject was clearly perceived as different by the middle of the eighteenth century. Euro-Americans defended, and sometimes emphasized, their difference from Old World norms. But they were *Euro*-Americans. The precontact peoples and environment, the subject of so many of the enterprises analyzed in this collection, were now seen as belonging to the past, and the later eighteenth century's reality was the product of European-American exchange.

ACKNOWLEDGMENTS

The author wishes to thank Norman Fiering, James Muldoon, Fermin del Pino-Díaz, Nancy Lyman Roelker, Daniel Slive, Fredrika Teute, Cynthia Van Zandt, and the members of the Brown University History Workshop for their help in shaping this introduction.

NOTES

1. J. H. Elliott, *The Old World and the New, 1492–1650* (Cambridge, 1970), 15–16.

2. On the reconciliation of ancient lore with the revelation of transatlantic lands in the Renaissance, see James S. Romm, *The Edges of the Earth in Ancient Thought: Geography, Exploration, and Fiction* (Princeton, 1992), Epilogue, "After Columbus."

3. James Axtell, "Imagining the Other: First Encounters in North America," in his *Beyond 1492: Encounters in Colonial North America* (Oxford, 1992), 25–74. On the concept of the self versus the other, see Tzvetan Todorov, *The Conquest of America: The Question of the Other*, trans. Richard Howard (New York, 1984), first published as *La Conquête de l'Amérique* (Paris, 1982).

4. Mary B. Campbell argues that the medieval tradition of exotic travel writing was extended to America, and that in Sir Walter Ralegh's *Discoverie of the Large, Rich, and Bewtiful Empyre of Guiana* (London, 1596) the careful reader can see Ralegh breaking through the constraints of the tradition; see *The Witness and the Other World: Exotic European Travel Writing, 400–1600* (Ithaca, 1988), chaps. 5–6. See also Joy Kenseth, ed., *The Age of the Marvelous* (Hanover, N.H., 1991).

5. Alfred W. Crosby, "Ecological Imperialism: The Overseas Migration of Western Europeans as a Biological Phenomenon," *The Texas Quarterly* 21 (1978): 103–17.

6. Francis Jennings, *The Invasion of America: Indians, Colonialism, and the Cant of Conquest* (Chapel Hill, 1975); James Axtell, *The Invasion Within: The Contest of Cultures in Colonial North America* (New York, 1985).

7. Edmundo O'Gorman, *The Invention of America: An Inquiry into the Historical Nature of the New World and the Meaning of Its History* (Bloomington, 1961).

8. On the quincentennial's relative neglect of the impact on Europe, see Helen Nader, "The End of the Old World," *Renaissance Quarterly* 45 (1993): 791–807.

9. J. H. Elliott, *The Old World and the New*, and "Renaissance Europe and America: A Blunted Impact?," in *First Images of America: The Impact of the New World on the Old*, ed. Fredi Chiappelli, 2 vols. (Berkeley, 1976), 1:11–23; also see Elliott's concluding essay in this volume.

10. Anthony Grafton with April Shelford and Nancy Siraisi, *New Worlds, Ancient Texts: The Power of Tradition and the Shock of Discovery* (Cambridge, Mass., 1992), 28–58, 116.

11. Kenneth Maxwell, "¡*Adiós* Columbus!," *New York Review of Books* 40 (1993): 38–45, quote 38.

12. Stephen Greenblatt, *Marvelous Possessions: The Wonder of the New World* (Chicago, 1991), introduction, esp. 19.

13. Germán Arciniegas, *America in Europe: A History of the New World in Reverse*, trans. Gabriela Arciniegas and R. Victoria Arans (San Diego, 1986), quote 2–3. See also the introduction by William H. McNeil entitled "The Legacy of Columbus, or How by Crossing the Oceans He Shaped the Modern World" in Susan Danforth, *Encountering the New World, 1493 to 1800* (Providence, R.I., 1991).

14. Fermin del Pino-Díaz has contributed to my understanding of this point.

15. On scholars' attempts to deal with the problem of categorizing the American natives, see J. H. Elliott, *The Discovery of America and the Discovery of Man* (London, 1972), and Anthony Pagden, *The Fall of Natural Man: The American Indian and the Origins of Comparative Ethnology* (Cambridge, 1982).

16. Particularly interesting treatments are Stephen Greenblatt, "Learning to Curse: Aspects of Linguistic Colonialism in the Sixteenth Century," in Chiappelli, *First Images*, 2:561–80; Peter Hulme, *Colonial Encounters: Europe and the Native Caribbean, 1492–1797* (London, 1986), chap. 2; Anthony Pagden, *European Encounters with the New World: From Renaissance to Romanticism* (New Haven, 1993), 35–36; and Eric Cheyfitz, *The Poetics of Imperialism: Translation and Colonization from The Tempest to Tarzan* (Oxford, 1991). On the way in which naming reflected European hopes, see Roland Greene's essay below.

17. Patricia Seed, "Taking Possession and Reading Texts: Establishing the Authority of Overseas Empires," *William and Mary Quarterly*, 3d ser., 49 (1992): 183–209. The entire April 1992 issue of the *William and Mary Quarterly* is devoted to articles and reviews on the theme "Columbian Encounters."

18. J. B. Harley, *Maps and the Columbian Encounter* (Milwaukee, 1990), sec. 3.

19. Harold Jantz argues that the name America was applied to the southern continent not in honor of the European Amerigo Vespucci, but in an attempt to replicate what was thought to be the native name. He points to names such as Amaracao, Maraca, Marica, Maracaibo, Marahuaca, and El Macareo in the earliest accounts and maps and argues that

the connection of "America" to "Amerigo" was an elaborate Greek language pun. See "Images of America in the German Renaissance," in Chiappelli, *First Images*, 1:97–99.

20. The abstract of Christopher Columbus's *Diario* of the first voyage has been published in a new translation with the original on facing pages and with a concordance of the Spanish; see *The Diario of Christopher Columbus's First Voyage to America, 1492–1493*, ed. Oliver Dunn and James E. Kelley, Jr. (Norman, Okla., 1988). Delno C. West and August Kling have published an *en face* translation and edition of *The Libro de las profecías of Christopher Columbus* (Gainesville, 1991). Margarita Zamora has published a translation of the letter Columbus wrote to the Spanish sovereigns immediately on his landing in Portugal; see "Christopher Columbus's 'Letter to the Sovereigns': Announcing the Discovery," in *New World Encounters*, ed. Stephen Greenblatt (Berkeley, 1993), 1–11. This letter, long thought lost, appears in a sixteenth-century copy of Columbus's *Libro Copiador* (copy book) published by Antonio Rumeu de Armas, *El Libro Copiador de Cristóbal Colón*, 2 vols. (Madrid, 1989).

21. A particularly interesting example is the analysis of the tunics worn by noble Incas as representations of order in R. Tom Zuidema, "Guaman Poma and the Art of Empire: Toward an Iconography of Inca Royal Dress," in *Transatlantic Encounters: Europeans and Andeans in the Sixteenth Century*, ed. Kenneth J. Andrien and Rolena Adorno (Berkeley, 1991), 151–202.

22. On Columbus's medieval mental landscape, see Valerie I. J. Flint, *The Imaginative Landscape of Christopher Columbus* (Princeton, 1992). On the larger context of exploration, see Felipe Fernández-Armesto, *Before Columbus: Exploration and Colonization from the Mediterranean to the Atlantic, 1229–1492* (Philadelphia, 1987).

23. Columbus, *Diario*, 143–45.

24. On Columbus and his enterprise, see William D. Phillips, Jr., and Carla Rahn Phillips, *The Worlds of Christopher Columbus* (Cambridge, 1992), and Felipe Fernández-Armesto, *Columbus* (Oxford, 1991).

25. On this point, see Felipe Fernández-Armesto, " 'Aztec' Auguries and Memories of the Conquest of Mexico," in *The Encounter of Two Worlds in the Renaissance*, *Renaissance Studies* 6 (1992): 288–89, and Wolfgang Reinhard, "Missionaries, Humanists, and Natives in the Sixteenth-Century Spanish Indies—A Failed Encounter of Two Worlds?," in ibid., 360–76.

26. See John Headley's essay below.

27. Karen Ordahl Kupperman, *Settling with the Indians: The Meeting of English and Indian Cultures in America, 1580–1640* (Totowa, N.J., 1980), 107–11.

28. My thinking on this point has benefited from discussion with James Muldoon.

29. See Axtell, *The Invasion Within*, chap. 7. Axtell also reminds readers that colonization reduced the number of Indians dramatically; see *The European and the Indian: Essays in the Ethnohistory of Colonial North America* (New York, 1981), 306–7.

30. Hulme, *Colonial Encounters*, 276, n. 7.

31. John Alden and Dennis C. Landis, eds., *European Americana: A Chronological Guide to Works Printed in Europe Relating to the Americas, 1493–1750*, 6 vols. (New York, 1980–94). This project is based in the John Carter Brown Library.

32. A Map of Virginia discovered to ye Hils, and in its Latt: From 35. deg: & 1/2 neer Florida, to 41. deg: bounds of New England . . . Domina Virginia Farrer Collegit. 1651, no. 22.

33. A version was printed as "Carte de la Nouvelle France," *Atlas Historique*, tom. 6, by Henri Abraham Chatelain (Amsterdam, 1719). For a description, see Helen Wallis, *Raleigh and Roanoke* (London and Raleigh, 1985), 99.

34. See Henry Lowood's essay below.

35. Alfred W. Crosby, *Ecological Imperialism: The Biological Expansion of Europe, 900–1900* (Cambridge, 1986). See John D. Daniels, "The Indian Population of North America in 1492," *William and Mary Quarterly*, 3d ser., 49 (1992): 298–320, on the background and problems of estimating the pre-Columbian population.

36. The phrase "widowed land" is from Jennings, *Invasion of America*, chap. 2.

37. Pagden, *European Encounters*, 54–62. On the claims made for eyewitness authority, and its distancing from the romantic medieval chivalric tradition, see Rolena Adorno's introduction to Irving A. Leonard, *Books of the Brave: Being an Account of Books and of Men in the Spanish Conquest and Settlement of the Sixteenth-Century New World* (Berkeley, 1992), and Campbell, *Witness and the Other World*, chap. 6. See also Christian Feest's essay below.

38. See Lowood's essay below; on Campanella, see Headley's essay below. On Oviedo and Acosta, see David A. Brading, *The First America: The Spanish Monarchy, Creole Patriots, and the Liberal State, 1492–1867* (Cambridge, 1991), chaps. 2, 9, esp. pp. 35, 85. The interaction between scholars and eyewitness texts is the subject of Rolena Adorno, "The Discursive Encounter of Spain and America: The Authority of Eyewitness Testimony in the Writing of History," *William and Mary Quarterly*, 3d ser., 49 (1992): 210–28.

39. Bernal Díaz del Castillo, *The True History of the Conquest of New Spain*, trans. Alfred Percival Maudslay, 5 vols. (London, 1908–16), 5:290–91. On Smith's self-comparison to Julius Caesar, see Philip L. Barbour, ed., *The Complete Works of Captain John Smith*, 3 vols. (Chapel Hill, 1986), 2:41, 3:47; for his proud statement of authorship, see ibid., 2:129, 437, 468; 3:29, 302. For a very interesting discussion of the complexity involved in eyewitness claims, see Beatriz Pastor Bodmer, *The Armature of Conquest: Spanish Accounts of the Discovery of America, 1492–1589*, trans. Lydia Longstreth Hunt (Stanford, 1992).

40. Columbus, *Diario*, 19–21, 361–71.

41. Anthony Pagden, ed., *The Letters of Hernan Cortés* (New Haven, 1986), xliv, lviii. Pagden disputes claims that Cortés was university trained; see xlvi–xlviii.

42. Hariot's *Briefe and True Report* is printed in David Beers Quinn, ed., *The Roanoke Voyages, 1584–90*, 2 vols. (London, 1955), 1:317–87; references to the intended larger work are on 359, 387.

43. David Beers Quinn and Neil M. Cheshire, *The New Found Land of Stephen Parmenius* (Toronto, 1972).

44. George Sandys, *A Relation of a journey begun An: Dom: 1610. Foure bookes, Containing a description of the Turkish Empire, of Ægypt, of the Holy Land, of the remote parts of Italy, and ilands adjoyning* (London, 1615). On Sandys's work, see Richard Beale Davis, *George Sandys, Poet-Adventurer: A Study in Anglo-American Culture in the Seventeenth Century* (London, 1955).

45. Michael Drayton, *Works*, ed. W. J. Hebel, 5 vols. (Oxford, 1961), 3:206–8.

46. Smith, *The Generall Historie of Virginia, New-England, and the Summer Isles*, in Barbour, *Works*, 2:145–46. Smith left Jamestown a decade before Sandys arrived, so the remark was not directed at him.

47. On this process, see Danforth, *Encountering the New World.*

48. Lewis Hanke, *Aristotle and the American Indians: A Study of Race Prejudice in the Modern World* (London, 1959), 8. Nebrija's introduction called language the "companion" of empire; see ibid., 127, n. 31.

49. See John Howland Rowe, "Sixteenth and Seventeenth Century Grammars," in *Studies in the History of Linguistics: Traditions and Paradigms*, ed. Dell Hymes (Bloomington, 1974), 361–79. Rowe points out that all the American language grammars were in Spanish, except for John Eliot's grammar of Massachusett and grammars in Portuguese of two Brazilian languages, Tupí and Cariri. I thank Fermin del Pino-Díaz for pointing out this further meaning of the word "reduction" in colonial discourse.

50. Alfred W. Crosby, Jr., *The Columbian Exchange: Biological and Cultural Consequences of 1492* (Westport, Conn., 1972), chap. 5; Carlo M. Cipolla, *Before the Industrial Revolution: European Society and Economy, 1000–1700* (London, 1976), chaps. 9, 10. For a review of the evidence and arguments on American treasure and the price revolution in Europe, see ibid., 210–17.

51. John Lough, ed., *Locke's Travels in France, 1675–1679* (Cambridge, 1953), 236.

52. On consumption and demand, see Carole Shammas, *The Pre-Industrial Consumer in England and America* (Oxford, 1990), chaps. 1, 4; Jan de Vries, "Peasant Demand Patterns and Economic Development: Friesland, 1550–1750," in *European Peasants and Their Markets: Essays in Agrarian Economic History*, ed. William N. Parker and Eric L. Jones (Princeton, 1975), 205–36; Joan Thirsk, *Economic Policy and Projects: The Development of a Consumer Society in Early Modern England* (Oxford, 1978); Margaret Spufford, *The Great Reclothing of Rural England: Petty Chapmen and Their Wares in the Seventeenth Century* (London, 1984), 21–22; Neil McKendrick, John Brewer, and J. H. Plumb, *The Birth of a Consumer Society: The Commercialization of Eighteenth-Century England* (London, 1982).

53. Cipolla, *Before the Industrial Revolution*, 231–36; T. H. Breen, "An Empire of Goods: The Anglicization of Colonial America, 1690–1776," *Journal of British Studies* 25 (1986): 467–99; Ida Altman and James Horn, eds., *"To Make America": European Emigration in the Early Modern Period* (Berkeley, 1991), 31. See also the essays in Franklin Knight and Peggy Liss, eds., *Atlantic Port Cities: Economy, Culture, and Society in the Atlantic World, 1650–1850* (Knoxville, 1991), for the American side of the equation.

54. Nancy Armstrong and Leonard Tennenhouse, *The Imaginary Puritan: Literature, Intellectual Labor, and the Origins of Personal Life* (Berkeley, 1992), chap. 8.

55. On the choice to emigrate, see David Galenson, *White Servitude in Colonial America: An Economic Analysis* (Cambridge, 1981), esp. chap. 7, and Russell R. Menard, "British Migration to the Chesapeake Colonies in the Seventeenth Century," in *Colonial Chesapeake Society*, ed. Lois Green Carr, Philip D. Morgan, and Jean B. Russo (Chapel Hill, 1988), 99–132, esp. 107–8.

56. On European migration, see Altman and Horn, *"To Make America,"* and Bernard Bailyn, *Voyagers to the West: A Passage in the Peopling of America on the Eve of the Revolution* (New York, 1986), chaps. 1–2.

57. David Cressy, *Coming Over: Migration and Communication between England and New England in the Seventeenth Century* (Cambridge, 1987), chaps. 7, 8, 9, 11. Also see Richard Simmons's essay below.

58. *Journal of Jasper Danckaerts, 1679–1680*, ed. Bartlett Burleigh James and J. Franklin Jameson (New York, 1913), 200.

59. Antonello Gerbi, *The Dispute of the New World: The History of a Polemic, 1750–1900*, rev. and enl. ed., trans. Jeremy Moyle (Pittsburgh, 1973).

60. On the debate over America as an inferior environment, see ibid. On Mexico, see Brading, *The First America*, pt. 2.

61. Robert Beverley, *The History and Present State of Virginia*, ed. Louis B. Wright (Chapel Hill, 1947), 9. I thank Myra Jehlen for this reference.

62. David Hume, "On Money," in *Hume's Essays*, ed. Eugene Miller (Indianapolis, 1985), 286.

Part I

America and the Historical Imagination

PETER BURKE

America and the Rewriting of World History

One of the best-known concepts in intellectual history is that of the "paradigm" or intellectual model, a term put into circulation by the American historian of science Thomas Kuhn. The concept may be illustrated from the history of discovery, noting that Columbus attempted to preserve the traditional model of a world divided into three continents in the face of what Kuhn would call increasing "discrepancies," while Vespucci modified the paradigm and so, in the phrase of Edmundo O'Gorman, "invented" America.[1]

How did historians cope with the change of paradigm? This is the central problem of this essay, located at the crossroads between two lines of inquiry. The first is the study of the "image"—both literal and metaphorical—of the New World. The second is the history of historical writing, conceived in a broad sense to include the historical imagination, the reception of written histories, and other aspects of what has been called the "historical culture" of a given period.[2] My aim is to consider the effect—if not the "impact"—of the European discovery of America on the writing of history in the period 1500–1750.[3] It is obvious that sooner or later the paradigm of world history would have to be revised. The problem is to discover when, where, among whom (readers as well as writers) this revision took place, and the forms which the new paradigm took.

To answer this question, various strategies are possible. The first is to study the monographs on the history of the New World.[4] Their number is impressive, and so is the number of editions of the most popular works. Among the histories of the Americas most frequently republished in the early modern period were the following five: in the first place, the *Historia de la conquista de Mexico* by Antonio de Solís (1691), which went through at least twenty-three editions in five languages (including Danish), between 1684 and 1748; Gómara (eighteen editions in four languages, 1552–1605); Acosta (sixteen editions in six languages, 1590–1624); Benzoni (fourteen editions in five languages, 1565–1612); and Zárate (thirteen editions in five languages, 1555–1742).[5] The modern reader may be surprised by the popularity of Solís. He doubtless owed this popularity to his dramatic style (Solís combined the role of official chronicler of the Indies with that of a successful playwright).[6] In the following century Benito Feyjoó, a leading figure of the Spanish Enlightenment, paid him the compliment of claiming that "infinite" numbers of people were acquainted with the events of the conquest only because of his "beautiful and delicate pen."[7]

Title page of Antonio de Solís, *Historia de la conquista de Mexico* (Madrid, 1684). John Carter Brown Library.

However, before we accept the conclusions of the "maximalists," who enthuse over the effect of the discoveries on European culture, it is necessary to ask how many monographs were written on other parts of the world in this period. To place America in comparative perspective thus involves reading every work of history written at this time. It is therefore necessary to take some kind of short cut. The option I have chosen is to focus on the image of that world in more general works, in so-called universal histories, in bibliographies, chronologies, and encyclopedias.[8]

Following this approach leads to the conclusion that sixteenth-century views of world history were relatively unaffected by the flood of information about the New World which followed the expeditions of Columbus, Cabral, Cortés, and others. An extreme case of this impermeability is the scholar who remarked in 1512 that "whether it is true or fabricated," the discovery of America "matters not at all or very little to the knowledge of Cosmography and History."[9] It is rare for the discovery to be explicitly dismissed in this way, but not so unusual for it to be treated as a second-rate event, or even ignored altogether. The well-known account of the customs of all nations, by Johannes Boemus, for example, first published in 1520 or thereabouts, was organized according to three continents, thus blithely ignoring a discovery made twenty-eight years before. What is more, the book retained this organization in its numerous editions and translations until 1560, when an appendix on America was added to the Italian translation.

It is more common to find historical writers who make only brief and casual references to the new continent. Jean Bodin, for example, mentioned only three titles of books on the history of the Americas in the bibliographical essay in his famous *Method* (1566); Louis Le Roy devoted no more than a chapter to the subject in his reflections on world history, the *Vicissitudes* (1575); Jacques-Auguste de Thou, in his *History of His Own Time* (1604), "allots only one paragraph to the voyages of Columbus and the Portuguese"; and William Camden, in his *Annals* (1615), "gives only four pages to Drake's return with potatoes and tobacco in 1586."[10]

It is true that some sixteenth-century writers did not dismiss America so easily. François Belleforest, for example, devoted a substantial section to the Americas in his *Universal History* (1570).[11] La Popelinière's *The Three Worlds* (1582), a history of ancient and modern discoveries, also devotes considerable space to America.[12] Italian historians in particular emphasized the achievements of Columbus and Vespucci. Thus the continuators of Giovanni Tarchagnota's *History of the World* (1561–63) devoted three pages to Columbus.[13] Francesco Guicciardini interrupted the narrative of his *History of Italy* (1561–64) on more than one occasion to make references to the New World, while the humanist bishop Paolo Giovio (who once interviewed Cortés) discussed the Americas in a number of different works.[14] At the end of the century, Giovanni Botero's multivolume *Universal Relations* (1591–92) provided a substantial amount of information about American history.[15]

Despite such counterexamples, my hypothesis remains the relatively "minimalist" one that America long remained on the margin of world history as viewed by Europeans. To test this hypothesis, let us imagine an early modern scholar visiting a library in order to learn something about the history of the Americas.

He might well have begun by consulting a bibliography—an aid to research which was developing in the sixteenth and seventeenth centuries. The bibliographical chapter in Bodin's *Method* mentioned no more than two authors, Columbus and Vespucci, and stuffed them into a miscellaneous section entitled "Historians of the Ethiopians, Indians, Americans and almost all the Peoples of Africa."[16] The encyclopedic *Theatre of Human Life* compiled by Theodor Zwinger twenty years later mentions seven writers on what he calls the "new world," including Columbus, Vespucci, and Oviedo, combining these (like Belleforest) with writers on Asia.[17] The bibliography of historical works compiled by the Jesuit Antonio Possevino (1597) uses a catch-all category similar to Bodin's, "History of the Ethiopians, Indians, Americans etc," but finds space for fourteen titles, including the Jesuit letters and two poems on Columbus but also the more strictly historical works of Acosta, López de Gómara, Zárate, and others (though not, predictably enough, Las Casas or Benzoni).[18]

The *Universal Alphabetical Index* (1612) compiled by the Italian bishop Federico Giustiniani, an early example of the subject-bibliography, includes an entry on "the New World," citing Peter Martyr, Acosta, and Possevino, and another on "India," in other words, the East and West Indies, adding the names of Columbus, Oviedo, Giglio, Benzoni, Las Casas, and Drake (the bishop seems to have been unusually catholic, rather than Catholic, in his historical tastes). The rival compilation by the Leuven theologian Molanus, the *Library of Materials* (1618) also lumps the historians of the two Indies together but mentions only Peter Martyr, Acosta, Ramusio, and Mariana.[19]

In similar fashion to Bodin and Possevino, the "appendix concerning the historians of particular nations" added by Nicholas Horseman in 1662 to Wheare's lectures on historiography included a single section on India, Africa, and America, citing eleven authors (including Columbus, Cortés, Oviedo, Gómara, Benzoni, and the relatively recent treatises on the origins of the Indians by Grotius, Laet, and Horn).[20] As late as 1713 Lenglet's introduction to historical studies, which included a kind of bibliographical essay, mentioned only six works on America (Grotius and Horn on American origins and Solís, Zárate, Garcilaso, and Las Casas on the conquest).[21] The one exception to the general neglect of America in works of reference in this period is to be found in the elaborate bibliography compiled by Petrus Bolduanus (1620), which devoted five pages to descriptions and histories of America.[22]

Let us turn to the evidence of chronologies. Genebrard's world chronology

(1567) did include the discovery of America but gave it only a brief mention—under the year 1497! (He was clearly a Vespuccian rather than a Columbian.)[23] Similar brevity characterizes most sixteenth-century chronologies. Vignier's chronology (1581) allotted a little more space to Columbus, indeed a whole paragraph.[24] The Jesuit Orazio Tursellini found room for a paragraph on Columbus and another on Cortés in his epitome of world history from the Creation to Pope Clement VIII.[25] In the early seventeenth century, however, J. H. Alsted, a German scholar who taught in Transylvania, showed more enthusiasm. He included Columbus in a "Chronology of Famous Heroes" running from Moses to Maurice of Nassau, while his "Chronology of the Marvels of God" found a place for Vespucci, Cortés, and Pizarro as well.[26]

However, the most widely diffused chronologies, at least in England, were the ones appended to almanacs, summarizing the history of the world from the Creation or the Norman Conquest to the present. In these cases it is the absence of references to the discovery of America which is striking. A sample of twenty-seven almanacs for the year 1699 revealed fifteen with chronologies of world history. All of them mentioned the invention of printing and gunpowder, none the discovery of America. Five contained the stock phrase "The Plantation began in New England," while one also referred to the "Plantation" in Virginia.[27]

In short, I take my stand with the "minimalists" against the "maximalists." The central problem for discussion might therefore be stated as follows. In 1600, or even later, America seems to have had only a minor place in European historical consciousness. By the later eighteenth century, however, its place was a significant one. So when, where, for whom, how, and why did the situation change?

Let us turn to the textbooks on universal history published for university students and others in the seventeenth century. Here we can see America gradually acquiring a more and more important place. For examples of the trend, one might turn to the two rival textbooks published in 1643 in Leiden (where history was relatively prominent in the university curriculum). Johannes de Laet's *Compendium of Universal History* devoted a substantial paragraph to the achievements of Columbus, Vespucci, Cabral, and Magellan, and a sentence to the activities of Cortés in Peru (but nothing to Pizarro). M. Z. Boxhorn's *Universal History* was even more enthusiastic for Columbus and Magellan, though it did not find space for any of the others.[28] A few years later, Georg Horn's *Noah's Ark* (1666), subtitled "a history of empires and kingdoms," appears to be the first textbook of universal history giving anything like a fair share of space to America, about a sixth of the whole. Horn also wrote about the origins of the Americans, a topic which seems to have interested the Dutch in particular.[29]

American history also began to creep into encyclopedias and other works of reference in the course of the seventeenth and eighteenth centuries. The relatively

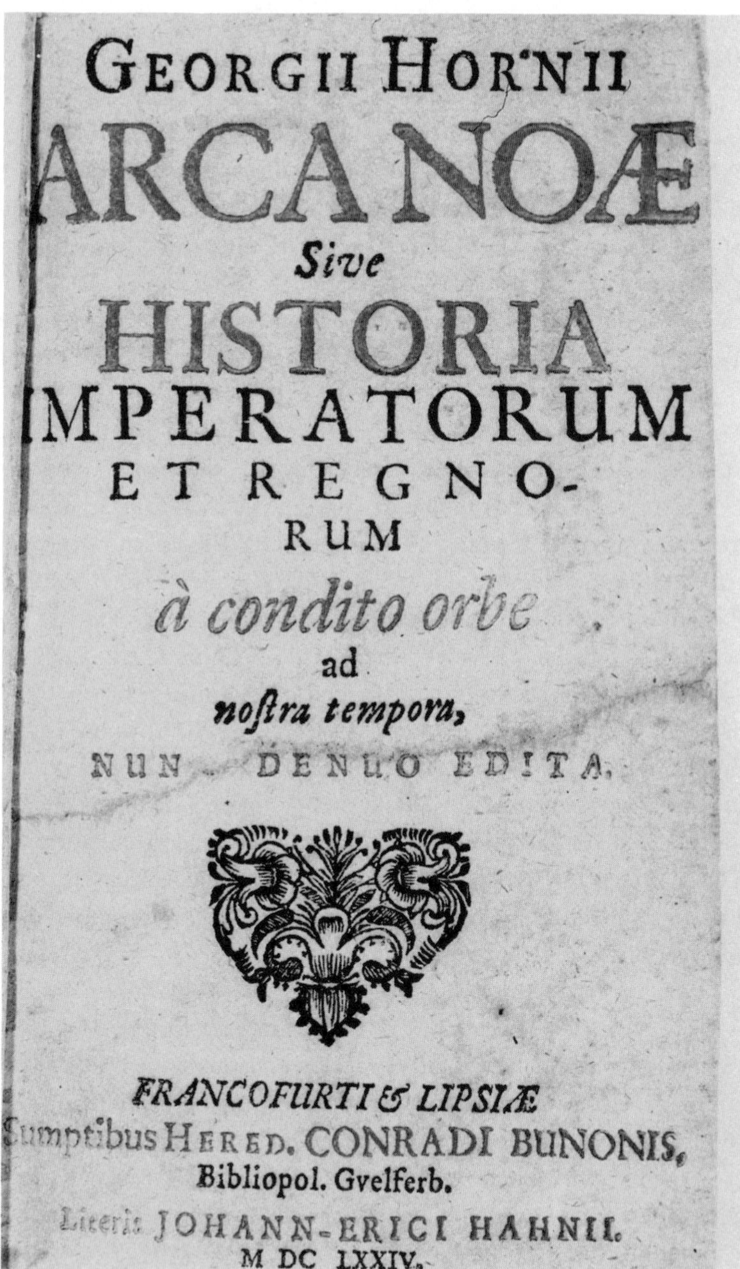
GEORGII HORNII
ARCA NOÆ
Sive
HISTORIA
IMPERATORUM
ET REGNO-
RUM
à condito orbe
ad
noſtra tempora,
NUN DENUO EDITA.

FRANCOFURTI & LIPSIÆ
Sumptibus HERED. CONRADI BUNONIS,
Bibliopol. Gvelferb.
Literis JOHANN-ERICI HAHNII.
M DC LXXIV.

Title page of Georg Horn, *Georgii Hornii Arca Noae* (Frankfurt and Leipzig, 1674). John Carter Brown Library.

concise dictionary of "distinguished people" which the Jesuit G. B. Riccioli included in his *Chronologies Reformed* (1669) included both Columbus and Cortés, and his references included Ramusio.[30] Again, Louis Moreri's *Great Historical Dictionary* has about twenty references to America, including biographical information on Acosta, Anchieta, Cabral, Columbus, Cortés, Las Casas, Pizarro, Sahagún, Vespucci, and Villegaignon (the clerical compiler's interest in missions will be apparent). The main sources quoted are the usual ones, among them Acosta, Herrera, Oviedo, Ramusio.[31]

However, we must be careful not to exaggerate the change. Laurence Beyerlinck's *Theatre of Human Life* (1656), a vast encyclopedia which devoted 740 pages to items beginning with the letter A, gave less than a column to America, "when it was discovered . . . whether it is a fourth continent," and cites only two authors on the subject, Ortelius and Acosta.[32] If America had been absent altogether, one might perhaps have explained the absence in terms of the function of the book, but a brief entry irresistibly suggests lack of interest. Again, Bayle's more famous *Historical and Critical Dictionary*, of 1697, conceived as a kind of anti-Moreri, makes virtually no references to the New World with the significant exception of Brazil—significant because it allows a discussion of the Protestant mission involving Villegaignon and Jean de Léry.[33] Chambers's *Cyclopaedia* (first published in 1728) again makes virtually no reference to the New World. The exception this time is an article under "Inca."[34]

Counting references to the New World in encyclopedias and chronologies has its uses if we want to gauge the relative importance of American history in European consciousness, but it gives us only the outline or the skeleton of the story. The approach clearly needs to be amplified by case studies illustrating the kind of information in circulation and the uses to which it was put. So it may be useful to turn for a moment to the European image of the indigenous cultures of Mexico and Peru. The subject really deserves discussion in detail, with sections on pre-Columbian religions, mythologies, and political systems, not to mention the dramatic decline in the American population following contacts with the West (a subject which already attracted the interest of Ramusio in the sixteenth century and Alsted in the early seventeenth).[35]

It will be necessary to focus on a single theme, and the one chosen is that of the spread of knowledge about indigenous American writing systems. Giovio owned a manuscript of a Mexican history of Mexico, so he was well aware of the system of pictograms. Other Mexican manuscripts were in the possession of Oviedo, Ramusio, and their common friend, the humanist physician Girolamo Fracastoro.[36] Peter Martyr discussed the subject in his fourth decade, but the classic account of the Mexican "hieroglyphics," as he called them, was the one given by Acosta in 1590.[37]

After 1625 European readers could supplement descriptions of this system with images, thanks to the publication by Purchas of what he calls a "Mexican History in Pictures." The manuscript itself (now known as the Codex Mendoza) had an adventurous history. On its way to Charles V, it was captured by the French, passing to Thevet in 1553 and then to Hakluyt, who passed it to Purchas, who was encouraged to print it by Sir Henry Spelman.[38] The Dutch scholar Johannes de Laet used the Purchas edition for the account of Mexican culture given in his *New World* (1633), in which he pointed out discrepancies between its account of pre-Columbian Mexico and the versions of Acosta and Herrera.[39] The Jesuit polymath Athanasius Kircher also used it in the chapter on Mexico in his ambitious comparative study of hieroglyphics, *The Egyptian Oedipus.*[40]

In the case of Peru, Ramusio had already noted the fact that the Indians record important matters by means of strings called "Quippos."[41] A more detailed description of the system, its colors, and knots, stressing its use for keeping accounts, appears in Acosta's history in 1590.[42] Three years after Acosta, the *quipu* feature in Zwinger's encyclopedia, the *Theatre of Human Life*, in the context of reflections on ways of writing history.[43] A fuller account of the system was published by Garcilaso in 1609, and it is on this, together with Acosta, that Johannes de Laet based his summary in 1633.[44]

Curiously enough, when a history of writing came to be written by the Jesuit Herman Hugo, he had nothing to say about these systems (or indeed about Chinese ideograms). He mentioned America only as an example of the amazement of other cultures confronted with the achievements of the West.[45]

America and the Changing Vision of World History

So far I have been concerned with the amount of information accumulated in the early modern period about the history of the New World, and the amount of interest shown in it. It is time to turn to another question. What difference did this interest and information make? Did it give world history a new shape?

It is not difficult to find early modern writers describing the discovery of America as an extraordinary event. The most famous expression of this idea is surely Gómara's much-quoted claim that the discovery was "the greatest thing since the creation of the world, with the exception of the incarnation and death of he who created it."[46] In similar fashion, Oviedo described the circumnavigation of the world by Magellan as "the greatest and most original event since God created the first man and made the world."[47]

Ramusio and Botero were scarcely less hyperbolical. Ramusio called Columbus's enterprise "the most marvellous and the greatest for infinite centuries," while Botero—doubtless with his eyes on the new mission field—declared that "nothing has been greater or more admirable since the Apostles began to preach."[48] In similar fashion, the Franciscan Gerónimo de Mendieta viewed the discovery of America as the fulfillment of Joachimite prophecies about the millennium, while he saw Cortés as a new Moses and also as a compensation for the rise of Luther, as if the New World had been called into existence to redress the spiritual balance of the Old.[49] The Calvinist pastor Pierre Jurieu still believed in 1686 that the discovery showed that the reign of Christ was at hand.[50]

It was not necessary to be a millenarian to view the discoveries as part of a cluster of events revealing the dawn of a new age. A frequently mentioned item in the cluster was the invention of printing. As the Italian humanist Lazzaro Buonamico told the Portuguese humanist Damião Gois in 1539, "Do not think that anything gives fame to our age or its predecessor so much as the method of printing and the discovery of the New World."[51] The French physician Jean Fernel included gunpowder, printing, and the revival (or as we would say, "Renaissance"), of art and literature among the achievements of "this our age," but he pulled out all the stops when he came to describe the discoveries. "Who is ignorant of the fact that . . . the Ocean has been crossed, the Islands discovered, the farthest recesses of India [or the Indies] thrown open, and a large part of the western continent, known therefore as the New World, unknown to the ancients, has, much to our advantage, come to our knowledge?"[52] Jean Bodin echoed this point about those who "open up the farthest recesses of India" in his *Method*.[53] The technological triad of gunpowder, the press, and the compass figured in many discussions of the novelty of the age, most memorably in the work of Francis Bacon.[54]

Protestants added a final event to this cluster, the Reformation. Alsted, for example, declared that "it should not go unobserved that the discovery of the New World, the reform of religion and finally the study of languages and arts began at more or less the same time."[55] Georg Horn, a professor of history at the University of Leiden whose work was mentioned earlier, made the same point a generation later when discussing the discovery of the New World. "Little by little, light began to emerge from all this darkness. The virtual rebirth of literature and the doctrine of the Gospel promised better times. . . . At length what might be called a new world emerged."[56]

One might therefore have expected Christoph Keller (Cellarius), a professor at Halle who produced the first textbook of "modern history" in 1692, to have followed this schema. However, what Keller wrote was essentially a history of Europe in the sixteenth and seventeenth centuries, with references to Asia and North Africa but not to America.[57] Even Condorcet, whose famous sketch for the history of the progress of the human mind adopted a quite new division into periods, passed over the discoveries and began his eighth epoch with the invention of printing. All the same, the discovery of America was one factor in the formation of the idea of a modern or postmedieval age. The convention that modern history begins around 1500, like the idea that the moderns are superior to the ancients—in some respects at least—owes something to Columbus as well as to Gutenberg, Luther, and Charles VIII.[58]

The discovery of America also encouraged new interpretations of the history of the world by bringing information to the notice of European scholars which was not easy to fit into their traditional paradigms. Did the Flood reach America (as Grotius, using Acosta and Herrera, argued), and if not, was it (as Giordano Bruno and Isaac La Peyrère suggested) a purely local phenomenon?[59] Where did the American Indians come from? Were they originally Jews, Carthaginians, Norwegians, or Chinese?[60] What was the relation between Amerindian paganism and the better-known paganism of the ancient Greeks and Romans?[61]

Most important, and the most difficult question of all, did the different human races all descend from a single ancestor or were there, as Giordano Bruno and Isaac La Peyrère suggested (with reference to the Mexicans and Peruvians as well as to the Chinese), "men before Adam"? If the traditional account of the "monogenesis" of humankind was to be replaced by "polygenesis," what would remain of the truth of the biblical account of the Creation? Was the universal history outlined in the Bible no more than the local history of the Jews?[62]

Another way in which the discovery of America affected ideas of world history was by changing the image of the early inhabitants of Europe, or at least by making it more vivid and more precise. The classic example of "the impression that the discovery of the New World made on antiquarian thought of the sixteenth century" is that of the ancient Briton. The impression is easier to illustrate in images than in words. In a manuscript of ca. 1575, now in the British Museum, the Netherlander Lucas de Heere represented ancient Britons like American Indians. His example was followed by John White, by Jacques Le Moyne, by Theodore de Bry (illustrating Hariot's account of Virginia in 1590, and including the famous images of male and female Picts), and by John Speed, on the title page of his *History of Great Britain* (1611).[63]

De Bry made the comparison explicit in a passage declaring that "the Inhabitants of the great Bretannie have bin in times past as savage as those of Virginia." He was followed by Samuel Daniel, in 1612, comparing the "pettie regiments" of ancient Britain with those in the "west world, lately discovered"; by William Camden, in 1615, who compared the ancient Britons with the Eskimos; by Robert Burton, whose *Anatomy of Melancholy* (1621) described the English as "once as uncivil as they in Virginia"; and by Samuel Purchas, with his rhetorical question, "Were not Caesar's Britons as brutish as Virginians?"[64]

Such comparisons were not confined to the ancient Britons. In his *History of New France* (1609), Marc Lescarbot referred to the description of the German

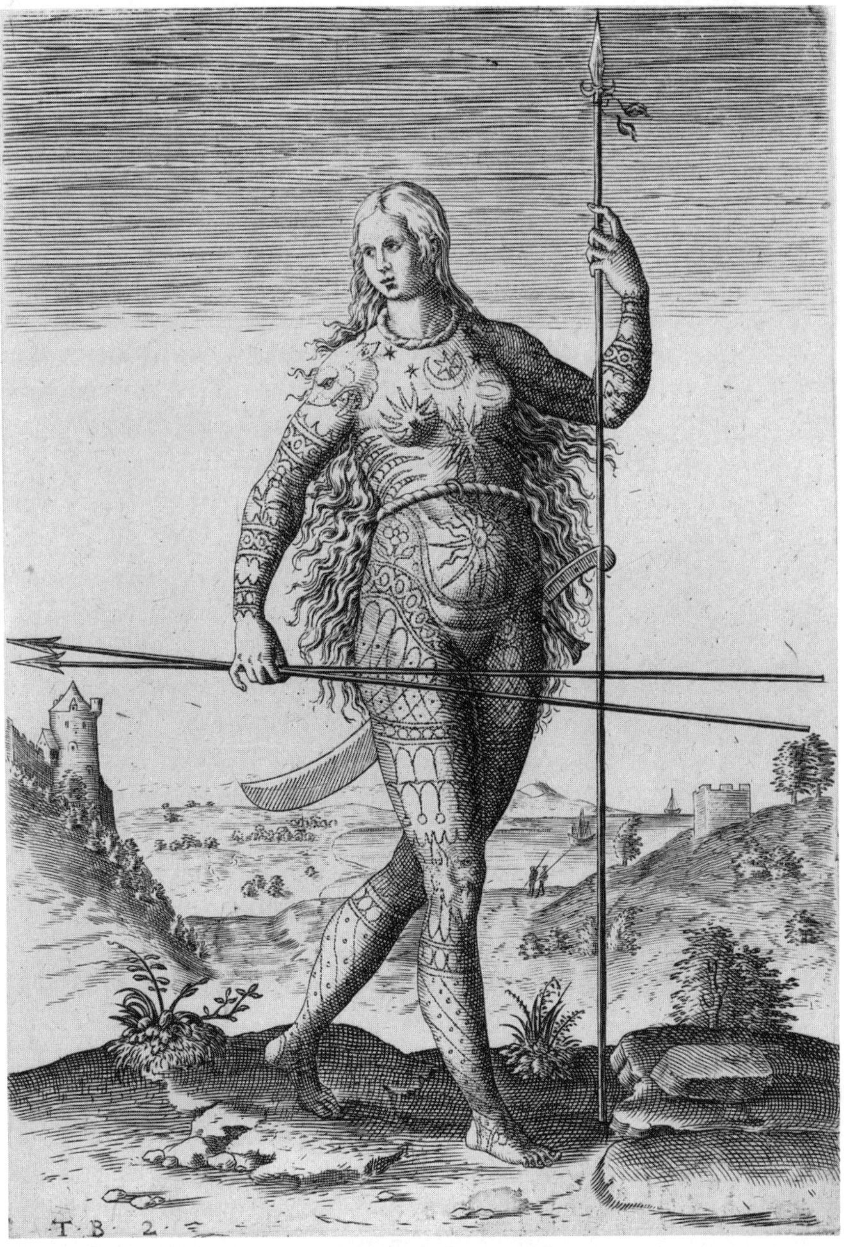

"Femina Pictae icon II," from Johann Theodor de Bry, *Grands Voyages*, pt. I (Latin) (Frankfurt, 1590). John Carter Brown Library.

tribes by Tacitus. A study of *Ancient Germany* (1616) by Philip Cluverius compared the early Germans with the American Indians in several respects, from their nakedness to their religion, and the illustrations to his book, by Nicolaes van Geilenkercken, may owe their "primitive" quality, if not any particular details, to the images of America to be found in De Bry and elsewhere.[65] Burton too included the Germans in his comparison, while Thomas Hobbes used the example of America to reconstruct the "state of nature" in general.[66]

One of the most extended of these comparisons was made by Bernard de Fontenelle in an essay written in the 1690s which noted what the author called the "astonishing similarity between the fables of the Americans and those of the Greeks," taking as an example the parallel between the story of Orpheus and that of "L'Ynca Manco Guyna Capac, fils du Soleil." Fontenelle's conclusion was that the Greeks were once as irrational and primitive as the modern Americans.[67]

The circularity in these arguments from analogy—one of the many productive circularities in intellectual history—is worth a comment. After the American Indians had been perceived in terms of European "barbarians," the tables were turned and the barbarians viewed in terms of the Indians. America thus offered a pristine, indeed a primitive, vision of European antiquity. The rising interest in Homer, at the expense of Virgil, to be detected from the late seventeenth century onward and culminating in the work of Lafitau, Blackwell, and Vico, is linked to this interest in the primitive, whether we explain it by the "impact" of America or explain the concern with America in terms of the new enthusiasm for "savage" places and times.

The difficulty of giving a definite answer to the question of which came first may be illustrated from the case of Vico's *New Science*. Vico's reflections on world history give a central place to a reconstruction of what he called "poetic logic" or "poetic wisdom," a phrase which may be freely translated as "primitive thought," or even *la pensée sauvage*. The third book of his treatise is entirely devoted to the "discovery of the true Homer," arguing that the lack of dignity of the protagonists of the *Iliad* is to be explained by the customs of the barbarous (but heroic) age in which they lived. Vico refers on several occasions to histories and descriptions of America—to Acosta, Hariot, de Laet, Lescarbot, and Oviedo.[68] He is interested in accounts of Mexican hieroglyphics and Peruvian temples and uses information about the Americas to demonstrate the universality of rituals of burial, marriage, and worship. All the same, his reconstruction of poetic wisdom is essentially based on Homer, the *Germania* of Tacitus, and the laws of the Twelve Tables. The most that can be said about the American examples—and even this is conjectural—is that they stimulated Vico to look at his classical sources in a new way.

By encouraging awareness of the difference between the "manners" and customs of different cultures, the discoveries may also have helped, as Amy Gordon has recently suggested, "to bring about the writing of a different kind of history," cultural and social rather than political.[69] The argument is an attractive one, and there is a clear line of development from the digressions on the customs of peoples, presented in a somewhat static manner, to be found in Renaissance historians (following their classical predecessors, notably Herodotus), and the full-fledged histories of manners produced by Voltaire and others in the eighteenth century. However, it is only prudent not to make exaggerated claims in this respect. The shift of interest on the part of historians, which brought the history of manners from the periphery to the center of attention, may well have something to do with the increasing availability of information about customs in America and other places. All the same, the timing suggests that the rise of social history was a response not so much to 1492 as to changes in eighteenth-century Europe itself (from the rise of commerce to the growth of a female reading public).

This sketch has concentrated on developments between 1500 and 1750. In the process, it has revealed a considerable variety of responses to America (or more exactly, to what they called the "new world") on the part of European scholars. Some of them were willing to modify their paradigms to accommodate new data, like La Peyrère, who used the history of America to argue that there were "men before Adam," or Joseph Scaliger, who revised his views on world history in the light of indigenous American chronologies.[70] Others, as we have seen, resisted such modifications to the traditional shape of world history. Some historians, such as Gómara, Oviedo, and Botero, exhibited enthusiasm for the discoveries, while others showed virtually no interest. The next problem on our agenda is surely to examine how this variety was structured. Although it is impossible to examine this question here in the detail it deserves, it may be worth offering a few suggestions for future investigation.

In the first place, there may be national styles of response to America. The Spaniards naturally maintained an interest in their empire, and if they had made more of a contribution to the production of European works of reference such as encyclopedias, it is likely that America would have figured more largely in them. The Italians (Giovio, Guicciardini, Ramusio, and so on), responded warmly to the discoveries at first, in the age when the Americas were associated with Columbus and Vespucci, but they seem to have lost interest in the course of the sixteenth century. The Dutch, despite their relative lack of success in empire-building in the New World, showed considerable interest in that world, as the work of Boxhorn, Grotius, and Laet suggests. They showed a similar interest in Asia and Africa, doubtless because of their deep involvement with long-distance trade.

In the second place, it may be useful to distinguish between the stay-at-homes, who studied America from a distance, and the travelers, who knew it firsthand. In the first group we find Giovio, for example, La Popelinière, and Solís. In the second are Acosta, who spent years as a missionary in Peru, Benzoni, who lived for fourteen years in the New World, and White, who was one of the early settlers in Virginia. The contrast between travelers and stay-at-homes is not one between understanding and prejudice—Montaigne, who never left Europe, is more prepared to understand the "savages" than many people who knew them firsthand—but all the same, it generally led to different styles of account.

In the third place, it may be useful to attempt a sociology of response, distinguishing between the interests of missionaries, merchants, academics, and so on. A concern with America as a mission field is common to such clerical writers as the Italian Jesuit Antonio Possevino, the Spanish Franciscan Gerónimo de Mendieta, and the French secular priest Louis Moreri. Other writers discussed above were involved with trading companies and colonization: Johannes de Laet, for example, with the Dutch West India Company, or Richard Hakluyt with the colonization of Virginia. Gómara was chaplain to Cortés. Benzoni, on the other hand, identified with the colonized, perhaps because he came from Milan, a part of Italy which was under Spanish rule. Academic writers such as Horn and Boxhorn had more reason for presenting a cool, detached account of the history of the New World and generally did so.

Variety has been a major theme of this essay; progress has not. If, however, the period under consideration had been extended a little further, to include the half-century from 1750 to 1800, the temptation to tell a triumphalist story of increasing information and improving understanding of the history of the New World would have been a strong one. Two famous works of synthesis were produced at this time, the abbé de Raynal's *Philosophical History of the Indies* (1770) and William Robertson's *History of America* (1777). Raynal's work had at least twenty-one editions in French before 1800, and nine editions in English. Robertson had at least eleven editions in English (not counting an abridgment) in the same period and was translated into five languages—French, German, Italian, Armenian, and Greek.[71]

That the works of Raynal and Robertson were widely read is suggested not only by the number of editions and translations but also by the survival of the register of borrowers from Bristol Library for the period 1773–84. The register records 111 loans of Robertson and 173 of Raynal (in French or English) in those years.[72] Was Bristol typical, or do these figures reveal the interests of the inhabitants of a port involved in American trade?

That Raynal and Robertson were assimilated into universal history is suggested by the increasing place of America in the cultural histories of the human race written by some German scholars of the time, notably Johann Christoph Adelung, Johann Christoph Gatterer, and Christoph Meiners.[73] The increasing place of America in successive editions of the *Encyclopédie* (which began to appear in 1751) has also been noted.[74] The *Encyclopaedia Britannica* followed the same trend and gave twenty-two pages to the history of Peru in the edition published at the end of the century.[75] A major intellectual issue in the second half of the eighteenth century was the "dispute of the New World," in which the claims of Jean Buffon and Cornelius de Pauw, that the animal and human species to be found in the Americas were inferior to those of other continents, were rejected with vigor by other scholars.[76] This widening of historical horizons fits in well with other aspects of late-eighteenth-century European culture—from a practical awareness of the economic links between continents to the ideal of *Weltbürgertum*, in other words, citizenship of the world, an aspiration shared by intellectuals as diverse as Burke and Herder. The ideal did not endure, however, and horizons narrowed again in the nineteenth century (even if economic links endured and information became more easily available).[77]

In a famous passage of the *Wealth of Nations*, Adam Smith (consciously or unconsciously echoing Gómara), called the discovery of America one of "the two greatest and most important events recorded in the history of mankind," while a few years later the ex-Jesuit Juan Pablo Viscardo called it—with breathtaking simplicity, considering he was a Christian—the "most memorable" event in the annals of the human race.[78] One is reminded of Richard Nixon's reaction to the moon landing of 1969: "The greatest week in the history of the world since the creation." In the eighteenth century, for some intellectuals at least, the discoveries were coming to dwarf the Incarnation. But only in the eighteenth century.

ACKNOWLEDGMENTS

I should like to thank my Emmanuel colleague David Armitage for comments and references, and Karen Kupperman and Fredrika Teute for their constructive criticisms of an earlier draft.

NOTES

1. Thomas Kuhn, *The Structure of Scientific Revolutions* (Chicago, 1962); Edmundo O'Gorman, *The Invention of America: An Inquiry into the Historical Nature of the New World and the Meaning of Its History* (Bloomington, 1961).

2. Hugh Honour, *The New Golden Land: European Images of America* (London, 1975); Fredi Chiappelli, ed., *First Images of America: The Impact of the New World on the Old*, 2 vols. (Berkeley, 1976); on the notion of "historical culture," Bernard Guénée, *Histoire et culture historique dans l'Occident médiéval* (Paris, 1980).

3. J. H. Elliott, *The Old World and the New, 1492–1650* (Cambridge, 1970), chap. 1, "The Uncertain Impact"; Anthony Pagden, "The Impact of the New World on the Old: The History of an Idea," *Renaissance and Modern Studies* 30 (1986): 1–11.

4. On which see Francisco Esteve Barba, *Historiografia indiana* (Madrid, 1964); J. H.

Rodriguez, *História da história do Brasil,* vol. 1 (São Paulo, 1979); and now A. Delgado-Gomez, *Spanish Historical Writing about the New World* (Providence, 1992).

5. Manuel Palau y Dulcet, *Manual de librero hispanoamericano,* 28 vols. (Oxford and Barcelona, 1948–77).

6. Cf. David A. Brading, *The First America: The Spanish Monarchy, Creole Patriots, and the Liberal State, 1492–1867* (Cambridge, 1991), 210–12. This important study had not appeared at the time of the conference on America in European Consciousness.

7. Benito Feyjoó y Montenegro, *Theatro Crítico Universal,* 8 vols. (Madrid, 1781), 4:177.

8. Frank A. Kafker, ed., *Notable Encyclopaedias* (Oxford, 1981); Theodore Besterman, *The Beginnings of Systematic Bibliography* (Oxford, 1935).

9. Johannes Cochlaeus, quoted by David Armitage in his paper, "The New World and English Historical Thought," delivered at the conference on America in European Consciousness.

10. Myron P. Gilmore, "The New World in French and English Historians of the Sixteenth Century," in Chiappelli, *First Images,* 2:519–27; the quotations from 524–25. Cf. André Stegmann, "L'Amérique de Du Bartas et de de Thou," in *La découverte de l'Amérique,* ed. Marcel Bataillon (Paris, 1968), 299–309.

11. François Belleforest, *Histoire universelle* (Paris, 1570), fols. 245–317 (including a few pages on Japan). On him, Benjamin Keen, *The Aztec Image in Western Thought* (New Brunswick, 1971), 148–49.

12. Lancelot Voisin de La Popelinière, *Les trois mondes* (Paris, 1582). On this text, Amy G. Gordon, "Confronting Cultures: The Effect of the Discoveries on Sixteenth-Century French Thought," *Terrae Incognitae* 8 (1976): 45–56.

13. Giovanni Tarchagnota, *Delle historie del mondo,* vol. 2 (Venice, 1563), continued by Mambrino Roseo and Bartolomeo Dionigi, 517ff.

14. Francesco Guicciardini, *Storia d'Italia,* ed. Costantino Panigada, 5 vols. (Bari, 1929), 1:205, 2:130–32; Paolo Giovio, *Historia sui temporis,* vol. 1 (Florence, 1550), bk. 18. On Giovio's scattered references to the New World, Federico Chabod, *Scritti sul Rinascimento,* 2d ed. (Turin, 1967), 266. On Italy generally, Rosario Romeo, *Le scoperte americane nella coscienza italiana del '500* (Milan-Naples, 1954).

15. Giovanni Botero, *Relazioni universali,* 4 vols. (Rome, 1591–95), 1:166–97, 2:243–58. On this work, Chabod, *Scritti,* 326ff.

16. Jean Bodin, *Methodus ad facilem historiae cognitionem* (Paris, 1566), trans. Beatrice R. Reynolds as *Method for the Easy Comprehension of History* (New York, 1945; reprint, 1969), 378–79.

17. Theodor Zwinger, *Theatrum vitae humanae* (Basel, 1586), 1587.

18. Antonio Possevino, *Apparatus ad omnium gentium historiam* (Venice, 1597), bk. 16, chap. 21.

19. Federicus Justinianus, *Index Universalis Alphabeticus* (Rome, 1612); Johannes Molanus, *Bibliotheca Materiarum* (Cologne, 1618).

20. Degory Wheare, *Relectiones hyemales* (Oxford, 1662).

21. Nicolas Lenglet, *Méthode pour étudier l'histoire* (Paris, 1713).

22. Petrus Bolduanus, *Bibliotheca Historica* (Leiden, 1620).

23. Gilbert Genebrard, *Chronographia* (Paris, 1567), "America regio . . . inventa est an. 1497."

24. Nicolas Vignier, *Bibliothèque Historiale*, 3 vols. (Paris, 1581), 3:812.

25. Orazio Tursellini, *Epitome Historiarum*, 4th ed. (Rome, 1625), 370, 382.

26. Johannes H. Alsted, *Thesaurus chronologiae* (Herborn, 1624), 175–76.

27. Cambridge University Library, Hhh.498, a volume of twenty-seven almanacs for 1699. On these chronological tables, Bernard Capp, *Astrology and the Popular Press* (London, 1979), 215–24.

28. Johannes de Laet, *Compendium Historiae universalis* (Leiden, 1643), 506–7, 518; Martin Z. Boxhorn, *Historia universalis sacra et profana* (Leiden, 1643), 1028.

29. Georg Horn, *Arca Noae* (Leiden and Rotterdam, 1666), 455–548.

30. Giovanni B. Riccioli, *Chronologiae reformatae*, 3 vols. (Bologna, 1669), 2:213, 227. Dedicated to one of the Farnese, the book claims Columbus for the Farnese city of Piacenza.

31. Louis Moreri, *Le Grand Dictionnaire Historique*, 3d ed., 2 vols. (Lyon, 1683).

32. Laurence Beyerlinck, *Theatrum vitae humanae*, 8 vols. (Leuven, 1656), s.v. "America."

33. Pierre Bayle, *Dictionnaire Historique et Critique*, 2d ed., 3 vols. (Rotterdam, 1702), s.v. "Barlaeus," "Léry," and "Villegaignon."

34. Ephraim Chambers, *Cyclopaedia* (London, 1728).

35. Brading, *The First America*, 109–10, adds the examples of Motolinia and Mendieta.

36. Giovanni B. Ramusio, *Navigationi e viaggi*, 3 vols. (Venice, 1550–59), 3:preface.

37. José de Acosta, *Historia natural y moral de las Indias* (Seville, 1590), bk. 6, chap. 7, "Del modo de letras y escritura que usaron los mexicanos."

38. Samuel Purchas, *Pilgrimes* (1625; reprint in 20 vols., Glasgow, 1905–7), 15:412ff; Keen, *Aztec Image*, 170–71, 206–7.

39. Johannes de Laet, *Novus Orbis* (Leiden, 1633), 241.

40. Athanasius Kircher, *Oedipus Aegyptiacus*, 3 vols. (Rome, 1652–54), 3:29, 31.

41. ". . . tengono conto delle cose segnalate, con alcune corde fatte di bombagio, che gl'Indiana chiamono Quippos." Ramusio, *Navigationi*, 3:preface. Cf. Marcia and Robert Ascher, *Code of the Quipu* (Ann Arbor, 1981).

42. Acosta, *Historia*, bk. 6, chap. 8, "De los memoriales y cuentas que usaron los indios del Peru." Cf. the description by Pedro de Cieza, written in the sixteenth century but published only in the nineteenth (*Crónica del Perú*, pt. 2, ed. M. Jiménez de la Espada [Madrid, 1880], chap. 12), and that of Poma de Ayala, published only in the twentieth (Guaman Poma de Ayala, *Corónica*, ed. Arthur Posnansky [La Paz, 1944], fols. 358–60).

43. "Peruani chordis versicoloribus, multisque nodis insignitis, et artifico singulari contextis, quorum domus sunt perplenae, multorum seculorum seriem solerter involutam, sine ulla haesitatione exprimunt." Zwinger, *Theatrum*, 1587, with a reference to "Joan Metellus."

44. Garcilaso de la Vega, *Commentarios reales* (Lisbon, 1609), bk. 6, chap. 8; Laet, *Orbis*, 479.

45. Herman Hugo, *De prima scribendi origine* (Antwerp, 1617), preface.

46. Francisco López de Gómara, *Historia General de las Indias* (Saragossa, 1552), dedication: "La mayor cosa después de la creación del mundo, sacando la encarnación y muerte del que lo crió."

47. Brading, *The First America*, 34.

48. Ramusio, *Navigationi*, 3:preface: "la più maravigliosa e la più grande, che già infiniti secoli sia stata fatta"; Botero, *Relazioni*, 4:20: "dalla predicatione degli Apostoli in qua, niuna cosa è stata più grande e più ammirabile."

49. James L. Phelan, *The Millennial Kingdom of the Franciscans in the New World* (Berkeley, 1956), esp. 29–31; Brading, *The First America*, 116.

50. Pierre Jurieu, *Accomplissement des prophéties* (Rotterdam, 1686), vi.

51. Quoted in Elizabeth F. Hirsch, *Damiao Gois* (The Hague, 1967), 103n: "Cave enim putes quicquam nostra superioraque tempora magis posse illustrare quam imprimendi rationem et novi orbis inventionem."

52. Jean Fernel, *De rerum abditis causis* (Paris, 1548), preface: "Quis ignorat . . . classe perlustratum Oceanum? repertas Insulas? intimos Indiae recessus apertos? maximam continentis ad occiduum partem, qua, inde novem orbem appellant, priscis ignotam, nostris magno suo commodo cognitam fuisse?"

53. Bodin, *Methodus*, 360: "iam ut intimos Indiae recessus apertos habeamus" (English translation from *Method*, 301).

54. Elizabeth L. Eisenstein, *The Printing Press as an Agent of Change*, 2 vols. (Cambridge, 1979), 1:21.

55. Alsted, *Thesaurus*, 175: "non est silentio praetereundum, detectionem novi orbis, reformationem religionis, culturam denique linguarum et artium eodem fere tempore coepisse."

56. Georg Horn, *Historia philosophica* (Leiden, 1655), 303, "Novus orbis detectus," and 305–6: "Ex tantis tenebris paullatim clarior lux emergere coepit. Nam et literae quasi renascentes, et ipsa Evangelii doctrina, meliora tempora promittebant . . . Emersit tandem alius quasi orbis."

57. Christophorus Cellarius, *Historia nova, hoc est xvi et xvii saeculorum* (Halle, 1696); on him, Giovanni Falco, *La polemica sul medio evo* (Turin, 1933), 89–93.

58. On the place of America in the *querelle* between ancients and moderns, José A. Maravall, *Antiguos y modernos* (Madrid, 1966).

59. Margaret T. Hodgen, *Early Anthropology in the Sixteenth and Seventeenth Centuries* (Philadelphia, 1964), 207–51; Michel Bligny, "Il mito del diluvio universale," *Rivista Storica Italiana* 85 (1973): 47–63, esp. 53ff.

60. L. E. Huddleston, *Origins of the American Indians* (Austin, 1967); Richard H. Popkin, "The Rise and Fall of the Jewish Indian Theory," in *Menasseh Ben Israel and His World*, ed. Yosef Kaplan (Leiden, 1989), 63–82; Joan-Pau Rubies i Mirabet, "Hugo Grotius' Dissertation on the Origin of the American Peoples and Comparative Methods," *Journal of the History of Ideas* 52 (1991): 221–44.

61. See Sabine MacCormack's contribution to this volume.

62. On these problems, Giuliano Gliozzi, *Adamo e il nuovo mondo* (Florence, 1977), 286–367, 514–621; Paolo Rossi, *The Dark Abyss of Time*, trans. Lydia G. Cochrane (Chicago and London, 1984), 133–36; Richard H. Popkin, *Isaac La Peyrère* (Leiden, 1987), chaps. 3, 4.

63. Thomas D. Kendrick, *British Antiquity* (London, 1950), 121ff, pls. xii–xiv; Stuart Piggott, *Ancient Britons and the Antiquarian Imagination* (London, 1989), 73–86.

64. De Bry quoted by Piggott, *Britons*, 77; Daniel by Kendrick, *Antiquity*, 110; Camden by Hugh R. Trevor-Roper, *Renaissance Essays* (London, 1985), 140; Burton by Piggott, *Britons*, 85; Purchas, *Pilgrimes*, 19, 62.

65. Philippus Cluverius, *De Germania antiqua* (1617; new ed., Leiden, 1631), 108, 156, 168. On him, Hendrik van de Waal, *Drie Eeuwen Vaderlandsche Geschied-Uitbeelding*, 2 vols. (The Hague, 1952), 1:178ff.

66. Thomas Hobbes, *Leviathan* (London, 1651); cf. John L. Myres, *The Influence of Anthropology on the Course of Political Science* (Berkeley, 1916), 22ff.

67. Bernard de Fontenelle, *De l'origine des fables*, ed. J. R. Carré (Paris, 1932), 30–32. It is likely that Fontenelle's source for Peru was the French translation of Garcilaso.

68. Cf. George Kubler, "Vico e l'America precolombiana," *Bollettino Centro Studi Vichiani* 7 (1977): 58–66.

69. Gordon, "Cultures," 53; cf. Eduard Fueter, *Geschichte der neueren Historiographie* (1911; reprint, Leipzig and Berlin, 1925), 291–306, and Hodgen, *Anthropology*.

70. Gliozzi, *Adamo*; Anthony Grafton, *New Worlds, Ancient Texts* (New York, 1992).

71. These minimum figures are based on the catalogs of the British Library and the Bibliothèque Nationale.

72. P. Kaufman, ed., *Borrowings from the Bristol Library, 1773–84* (Charlottesville, 1960), quoted in Peter J. Marshall and Glyndwr Williams, *The Great Map of Mankind* (London, 1982), 57.

73. Michael Harbsmeier, "World Histories before Domestication," *Culture and History* 5 (1989): 93–131.

74. R. Switzer, "America in the Encyclopaedia," *Studies on Voltaire* 58 (1967): 1481–99.

75. *Encyclopaedia Britannica*, vol. 14 (London, 1797), 199–221.

76. Antonio Gerbi, *The Dispute of the New World: The History of a Polemic, 1750–1900*, rev. and enl. ed., trans. Jeremy Moyle (Pittsburgh, 1973).

77. Friedrich Meinecke, *Cosmopolitanism and the National State*, trans. R. B. Kimber (Princeton, 1970).

78. Adam Smith, *Wealth of Nations*, 2 vols. (London, 1776), bk. 4, chap. 7, pt. 3, 235; Juan Pablo Viscardo, *Lettre aux espagnols américains* (Paris, 1799), 1.

DAVID ARMITAGE

The New World and British Historical Thought

FROM RICHARD HAKLUYT TO WILLIAM ROBERTSON

The question of America's place in European consciousness is a classic example of the problem of reception in cultural history. America did not spring fully formed into the imagination of Europe in 1492, nor could its peoples, its flora and fauna, and its sheer geographical existence ever be completely assimilated to European norms. Instead, information about America took its place within a variety of intellectual projects, some of which were more hospitable than others to the fact of its novelty. Those projects in turn shaped a variety of visions of America and its place in time and space. America gradually added to a store of data which often had to be stretched to accommodate the novelty of a New World, but which also predetermined the ways in which that New World would be seen.[1] To speak of the reception of America, rather than its impact or its assimilation, may help us to see more clearly what uses America had within earlier intellectual projects and to what extent America shaped their distinctive features.

In this essay, I shall be examining the intellectual enterprises of Richard Hakluyt and William Robertson in order to show how the historical consciousness of early modern Britain accommodated America. The British experience is notable not least for its belated receptiveness to the New World in the sixteenth century. This was both a practical and an intellectual problem. As Richard Hakluyt told Philip Sidney in 1582, it had been ninety years since "the first discovery of America," but England had yet to get a toehold in those parts of the New World unclaimed by Spain and Portugal. Meanwhile, the philosophical reception of the New World was even more delayed. As William Robertson noted in 1777, it was not until the late seventeenth century that "the manners of the inhabitants [of America] attracted, in any considerable degree, the attention of philosophers."[2] Both Hakluyt's and Robertson's assessments of the reception of America served specific purposes within their own projects. Each stressed the originality and timeliness of their respective historical enterprises, Hakluyt as the humanistic memorialist whose compilations would inspire his countryfolk to action and honor, Robertson as a member of the generation which believed it was able, for the first time, to see human history whole. Information about the New World and its peoples had made such a panoptic survey possible. The Enlightenment project of which Robertson was part depended upon the reception of America into historical consciousness, a process which had barely begun in early modern Britain.

Hakluyt began his historiographical enterprise in the 1580s, when England had no possessions in the New World, while Robertson published his history of America in 1777, just as Britain was fighting to retain its American colonies. Accordingly, Hakluyt's work stood on the cusp of two traditions of history in Elizabethan England: the humanist ideal of history as a Ciceronian *magister vitæ* and the apolitical erudition of the antiquarians who denied any rhetorical or exemplary intent for their researches.[3] Later Robertson, like Gibbon, combined antiquarian erudition with a vision of cosmopolitan and commercial modernity to create the first "philosophical" history of America in English, over a century and a half after Acosta and Herrera had attempted their philosophical histories of Spanish America. The contrast between Hakluyt and Robertson's historical methods and the place of America in their projects marks a shift both in the public status of history in Britain and in the place of America in European consciousness. Yet it shows that, in Britain at least, a comparative history was only possible in the period after 1750, as will be seen from Robertson's intellectual trajectory between 1755 and 1777. The philosophical sophistication of Robertson's *History of America*, and its comparative neglect by later students of historiography, should excuse such straying beyond this volume's chronological boundaries—not least because the vision of modernity implicit in Robertson's *History* can be seen both as the fruit of the reception of America into historical consciousness and as a shaping force in our own historical projects.[4]

The process by which America became a part of British history was as momentous as that by which the New World took its place in British historiography. Indeed, for Hakluyt they were one and the same enterprise. Hakluyt blamed England's tardiness in the race for the New World in part on the intellectual march stolen by the Iberian nations. Not only did they have "those bright lamps of learning (I mean the most ancient and best philosophers, historiographers and geographers) to show them light," but they also had "the lodestar of experience (to wit, those great exploits and voyages laid up in store and recorded) whereby to shape their course."[5] Hakluyt took upon himself the task of supplying England with a documentary account of the New World which would illuminate its maritime history in the Americas and equip its seamen with their own historical "lodestar."

The course of Hakluyt's career shows a specific intellectual project growing and developing with the effort to absorb and order the matter of America. His methods were humanistic, but his ends were ideological. The aim of his enterprise was not simply the English colonization of America but, more precisely, the reorientation of English trade away from short-range commerce in the Mediterranean and

Northern Europe and toward long-distance trade, not least across the Atlantic. In promoting such commercial strategies, Hakluyt was undoubtedly influenced by his commitment to the aims of the Clothworkers' Company, which had paid him a pension in 1578–86, even while he served as a diplomatic chaplain to the English embassy in Paris.[6] Yet such a reading of Hakluyt's intentions is not sufficient to account for the nature of his historical project, nor does it reveal the originality of his works in the context of British historical thought. That can only be shown by an examination of his sources, the development of his enterprise, and the historiographical context within which he worked.[7]

Hakluyt's first published collection, the *Divers Voyages Touching the Discovery of America* (1582), showed both his larger intentions and the awkward foundations on which they rested. His aim was to give continuity to England's endeavors in the New World by linking them back to the history of navigation from the voyages of the Cabots to his present, as if thereby to colonize the very idea of America for England. Yet the contents showed the difficulty under which he was laboring. The only models for his form of history were foreign, and the only accounts he had to hand were those of continental navigators, taken from Ramusio's pioneering *Navigationi et Viaggi* and Jean Ribault's account of the French discovery of Florida, for example. When he came to compile the first version of his *Principall Navigations . . . of the English Nation* (1589), Hakluyt acknowledged only three of "our owne Historians" as sources for his work: the Reformation polemicist John Bale's *Scriptorum Illustrium maioris Brytaniae . . . Catalogus* (1557–59), the martyrologist John Foxe's *Actes and Monuments* (1563–83), and the mid-sixteenth-century translator and anthologist, Richard Eden.[8] Though each of these three supplied matter for Hakluyt's compilation, their status as models is more problematic. Eden was Hakluyt's only English predecessor in the editing and ordering of accounts of the New World. He translated Sebastian Münster's *Cosmographia* in 1553, avowedly to aid Willoughby and Chancellor in their eastward voyages, and two years later he presented a translation of Peter Martyr's *Decades de Orbe Novo* (1511), supplemented with materials from Oviedo, Pigafetta, Paulus Jovius, and others, as a wedding gift for Prince Philip of Spain and Queen Mary.[9] Yet Eden made little attempt to bring any spatial or temporal order to the texts he translated. Foxe's compilation of the lives of ordinary (albeit exemplary, persecuted, and, above all, Protestant) English people in fact seems a much closer inspiration for Hakluyt's collection of individual narratives, and when the East India Company stocked its ships with reading matter in the early seventeenth century, they took both Hakluyt and Foxe on board.[10] Hakluyt may have expanded the social bounds of English historiography, as the voices in his works were largely those of sailors and merchants, but even in this Foxe had preceded him with the butchers and bakers who were the martyr-heroes of his narratives.

DIVERS

voyages touching the discouerie of America, *and the Ilands adiacent* vnto the same, made first of all by our *Englishmen, and afterward by the French-men and Britons:*

And certaine notes of aduertisements for obseruations, necessarie for such as shall heereafter make the like attempt,

With two mappes annexed heereunto for the plainer vnderstanding of the whole matter.

Imprinted at London for Thomas VVoodcocke, *dwelling in paules Church-yard,* at the signe of the blacke beare.

1582.

Title page of Richard Hakluyt, *Divers Voyages* (London, 1582). John Carter Brown Library.

Hakluyt's major achievement in English historiography, and the one which was most rooted in the nature of his materials, was to give a geographical turn to historical writing. The chronicle was still the dominant form of historical writing in England, though it was a senile genre and soon to lapse into obsolescence. Hakluyt's combination of historical and geographical methods spotlighted the inadequacies of a genre which laid history solely along the axis of time, and hence could hardly accommodate the exploration and extension of space. In Holinshed's chronicle, for example, the notice of Martin Frobisher's first voyage in search of the Northwest Passage (1575) was sandwiched between accounts of the hanging, drawing, and quartering of a London goldsmith for clipping coin and of the execution of a husband-poisoner in Tunbridge. Such juxtapositions implied equivalences: once a voyage left English waters it was lost over the historiographical horizon. The chronicle was, however, standing on the threshold of expansion, and the preface to Holinshed's chronicle did acknowledge that "not long before my time, we reckoned Asia, Europa, and Africa, for a full and perfect division of the whole earth," but the discovery of the Americas had the result that "all men, especially the learned, begin to doubt the soundness of that partition."[11] But it was too late for the chronicle to change. New forms of history were arising which would drive it rapidly from the stage, and most were either exemplary and analytical (such as biographies and institutional histories) or, like Hakluyt himself, took the classics and geography as their inspiration (like topographies and chorographies).

Hakluyt's geographical humanism took foreign and classical models for inspiration, just as the Elizabethan antiquarians turned to Strabo, Ptolemy, and Pliny for help in their study of the material traces of the English past.[12] Yet Hakluyt wanted to follow human traces upon the earth, and he strongly disavowed the analytical geography then most in fashion in France: "I am not ignorant of Ptolomies assertion, that *Peregrinationis historia* [the history of Travel], and not those wearie volumes bearing the title of universall Cosmographie . . . is that which must bring us to the certayne and full discoverie of the world."[13] This ambition of a "full discoverie of the world" is reminiscent of his French contemporary Lancelot de la Popelinière's vision of a "perfect" history, though Hakluyt's achievement was much closer to—and was probably influenced by—La Popelinière's hortatory *L'Amiral de France* (published in 1584, while Hakluyt was in Paris) or his geographical-historical *Les Trois Mondes* (1582) than to the general history of humankind announced in *L'Idée de l'histoire accomplie* (1599). Like La Popelinière, Hakluyt had wanted to travel to the New World himself but was prevented from doing so.[14] Hakluyt also referred to *Les Trois Mondes* and *L'Amiral de France* in his own writings and may have been behind the plan to publish a translation of *Les Trois Mondes* in 1583.[15] Yet the limited aims of his own project meant that he did not follow La Popelinière in the direction of his "astonishing project for a kind of general cultural anthropology to be based upon historical and geographical exploration."[16]

The earliest enterprise of Hakluyt's philological humanism was his Latin edition of Peter Martyr's *Decades de Orbe Novo* (1587), in which he subjected his materials to the twin disciplines of time and space. Quoting Abraham Ortelius's famous rule of thumb, "Geography is the eye of history," as La Popelinière had done before him, Hakluyt firmly aligned himself with continental developments in topographical humanism. Besides editing Martyr's complete text, Hakluyt said, he had "added in the margins, after a careful study of the chronology, the dates and other notes necessary to the student," and he had "inserted a geographical map . . . to serve as a plumb-line, mindful of the true saying, that geography is the eye of history." But only with the final edition of his major work, the three-volume *Principal Navigations* (1598–1600), did Hakluyt's geographical-historical method bear its full fruit. As he told Sir Robert Cecil, "Whereas in my two former volumes I was enforced . . . in divers places to use the method of time only (which many worthy authors on the like occasion are enforced unto) being now more plentifully furnished with matter, I always follow the double order of time and space."[17] He laid out the mass of material he had uncovered in over twenty years of research in a sequence stretching from Iceland in 517 to the West Indies in the 1580s, and from King Arthur to the Spaniard Pedro Dias. He grouped the travel accounts in progressive order of time and space and reserved the New World as his triumphant conclusion in the third and separate volume.

Hakluyt's work, through all of its revisions, remained a compilation charting the English diaspora through time and space. Yet it was difficult to place the discovery of America within this historical-geographical scheme, since it was not an event in English history. It was well known and frequently lamented that the discovery of America could have been an event in that history, if only Henry VII had accepted Bartolomé Colon's offer of his brother's enterprise to the Indies. Hakluyt was more concerned than others about this missed opportunity. Sir Walter Ralegh shrugged it off by noting that Bartolomé was "a straunger, in whom there might be doubt of deceipt," especially because few were then willing to believe in any new discoveries. Lawrence Keymis, Ralegh's fellow explorer in Guiana, agreed: who in the 1490s would have believed in "the persuasion and hope of a new found *Utopia*"? The answer, of course, was the Spanish, and in printing two documents recording the offer to King Henry, Hakluyt included the discomfiting news for England that "God had reserved the said offer for Castile."[18]

Columbus's discovery of America for Spain presented a problem of origins for every other European nation. The only solutions were to redefine the nature of the discovery as the sighting of the mainland of North America (in which case Sebastian Cabot could claim the priority on England's behalf) or to push the discovery back even further. The yoking of Welsh public history to that of England by the accession of the Tudor dynasty and the Acts of Union in 1536 and 1543 allowed the

Welsh prince Madoc, who had allegedly fled civil war in 1170 across the ocean to present-day Alabama, to take his place as a native pre-Columbian discoverer. Hakluyt opened the American volume of the *Principal Navigations* with two documents recounting Madoc's exploits, and elsewhere he noted that "it appeareth that the West Indies were discovered and inhabited 322 yeares before Columbus made his first voyage which was in the year 1492."[19] John Dee enforced the claim to North America through Madoc in his "Title Royal . . . to Foreign Regions" of 1580, and many later writers from the 1580s to the 1730s used Madoc to ratify the origins of England's claims in North America and as a stick with which to beat the Spanish.[20] This use of Madoc paralleled Oviedo's identification of the Indies with the Hesperides, which the mythical Spanish King Hespéro had owned in the third millennium B.C.E., or Guillaume Postel's assertions that the New World or Atlantis had been colonized by the descendants of Noah's son Japheth, who had later migrated to Gaul.[21] These were all aetiological fictions, which bucked the process by which historians were attempting to erase such legendary forebears as the Trojan Brutus from national genealogies. No serious claims were ever made through such stories (especially as claims from possession in the New World rapidly overrode those derived from discovery), but they did fulfill an important function as charter myths to validate their respective countries' continuing history in the New World.[22]

For all of his attempts to bring America into the orbit of English history, Hakluyt's work remained resolutely the history of transitory voyages, traffics, and discoveries, not of permanent plantations, colonies, and empire. The Jamestown colony of 1607 did not find a place in any of Hakluyt's compilations (though the Virginia Company did buy a secondhand copy of the triple-decker *Principal Navigations* sometime around 1620).[23] In this, Hakluyt's history was symptomatic of a wider reluctance on the part of English historians to include the plantations in North America within their remit. For example, John Speed's *The Theatre of the Empire of Great Britaine* (1611) made only the most tentative reference to the fact that "at this present in the *new world* of *America* a colonie of Britaines is seated in that part now called Virginea," but the second edition of his work in 1627 gave no further details and made no mention of the extensive migrations to New England of the intervening years.[24] Hakluyt had predicted in his "Discourse of Western Planting" (1584) that the proposed English plantations in North America would provide work for "Cosmographers, hidrographers, Astronomers, [and] historiographers," just as the Spanish crown had employed a principal royal chronicler-cosmographer since 1571 to gather information on its overseas possessions; his hope was never to be fulfilled.[25] The building of an intellectual establishment to aid colonization in Elizabethan England needed mathematicians, physicists, metallurgists, and navigators more than it needed "historiographers."[26] When the crown did appoint a historiographer royal in 1661 the New World was not to be part of his brief—not, at least, until the interests of William Robertson (historiographer royal for Scotland since 1763) turned to America in the 1770s.[27]

The reception of the New World into English historical thought was hampered by method as much as by lack of institutional support. Hakluyt's abjuration of the techniques of continental cosmography, his lack of interest in the kind of universal history proposed by La Popelinière (which Hakluyt, with his copious source materials, was perhaps well placed to contemplate), and his omission of the first plantations meant that his historical achievement would direct English historiography into far different paths from those being followed by contemporary developments in France and Spain.[28] Yet the sheer bulk of his material and the hard-won clarity of his organization meant that the *Principal Navigations* would live on as the founding text of the British Empire (though those words are conspicuously absent from his work) and of the genre of maritime history, which the English were to make peculiarly their own.[29] Hakluyt's achievement is one of the great monuments of English antiquarianism, though its avowed inspirational aim and its aetiological weight helped it to outlive the chorographies and topographies whose development it shadowed.

Hakluyt did not chronicle any English colonies; he was uninterested in the natural history of humanity in the New World; and he accorded 1492 little significance as a turning point in history. British historical thought responded to each of these areas of interest in the century after his death and opened up avenues to be traveled ultimately by philosophical historians who would leave his methods far behind, even as many still drew upon him for empirical information.[30] From Peter Heylyn's *Microcosmus* (eight editions, 1621–39) to John Oldmixon's *The British Empire in America* (1708), America moved from a marginal role in the English cosmographical histories to center stage as England asserted its *imperium* from Virginia and New England through the Caribbean and along the eastern seaboard of America from Newfoundland to the Carolinas. This was accompanied and often informed by the emergence of a creole historiography from the works of John Smith to those of Cotton Mather. The initial reception of a New World was thus followed by the re-creation of many Americas, in the consciousnesses both of metropolitans and of colonials.[31]

The gradual construction of the history of America ultimately overturned conventional accounts of the relationship between antiquity and modernity. Yet, as Robertson pointed out two centuries ago, such a move was neither inevitable nor immediate after the discovery of America. This in turn begs the question of why some thinkers were more receptive than others to the swelling body of information about the New World in the early modern period. The answer lies in the assessment of the nature of the enterprise upon which those thinkers were engaged, and hence the evidential and conceptual needs their projects entailed. The examples of

Thomas Hobbes and John Selden may suffice to illustrate this point. Hobbes was familiar with colonial policy and America through his shareholding in the Virginia and Somers Islands Company and from attending the court of the Virginia Company in his capacity as secretary to William, Lord Cavendish. However, he made strikingly little use of his knowledge in his political works because his whole philosophy was based on axiomatic principles, there being no need for empirical or historical support, least of all for his speculations on the state of nature, which was, in any case, transhistorical and could recur at any moment.[32] Hobbes's friend, Selden, found the matter of America more useful, as when he sought an answer to the puzzle of how foxes came to be in the British Isles. Britain must have been joined to the continent of Europe at some point in its past, he speculated, so that the animals could cross on a land bridge: confirmation of this came from José de Acosta's account of the migration of animals to the New World.[33] Both Selden and Hobbes were engaged, in their different ways, in answering the late-sixteenth-century revival of academic skepticism. The adherents of that revival—most notably Montaigne—found their minimal relativism bolstered by information from the New World. In this context, both Hobbes's comparative indifference to the New World and Selden's instrumental use of its explanatory power without any moral implications may be seen as purposive, and hence characteristic of their attempts to refute the skeptical challenge.[34]

It gradually became clear within more receptive intellectual projects that the native peoples of America challenged historical preconceptions about the nature and dispersal of humanity and that the European encounter with the New World in 1492 had set world history on a new course. Comparative ethnography and a progressive theory of history that was predicated on a vision of commercial society (to which such perceptions gave rise) are usually seen as characteristic of the sociological relativism of Enlightenment historiography. Yet comparative ethnology has its roots in sixteenth-century Spanish views of the New World,[35] and it can also be shown that, for Britain at least, the roots of the Enlightenment's vision of modernity can be found in seventeenth-century English assessments of the consequences of the Columbian encounter. These two movements of ideas had divergent sources, but by the mid-eighteenth century they had begun to run together. The supposed primitivism of the native peoples of North America gave Europe a glimpse of the ancient state of humanity which gradually inspired a new vision of antiquity.[36] Simultaneously, the American Indians' supposed lack of all the distinguishing features of a newly defined modernity made them the objects of evangelization and dispossession on the grounds of their lack of civilization.

A catalog of characteristics was assembled through the course of the seventeenth and into the eighteenth century which gave sharper definition to the image of North American savagery, a supposedly empirical justification for the dispossession of the American Indian, and, reciprocally, confirmation for an increasingly Eurocentric vision of world history. The Indians were not civilized, for they did not live in *civitates* as citizens; they could not be seen as political because they did not inhabit *poleis.* They lacked any sense of private property, in goods or land. They were hunter-gatherers, not settled agriculturalists who could produce surpluses; they had no use of money and hence could not be commercial peoples. They were illiterate and had no sense of history because they had no records of their past. They were in a sense timeless people, whom only external intervention could propel toward civilization and progress. America's reception into European historical consciousness thus had an equal and opposite effect for the native peoples of America. They had unwittingly supplied Europe with a vision of its own history, only to be effectively dispossessed by that European sense of the past.

The view of the American peoples as beings outside history, and hence without rights, was predicated on a particular view of human development which had its roots in the seventeenth-century debates about the significance of America. In this argument, which naturally enforced European rights and superiority over the savage Americans, the late fifteenth century had been the threshold of true modernity for Europe. Along with the recovery of the classics, and the inventions of printing, gunpowder, and the compass, the discovery of America was one of humanity's *Nova Reperta*, which distinguished the moderns from the ancients, and, indeed, Europe from the rest of the surrounding world.[37] In 1757 David Hume, who had just embarked on the third volume of his *History of England*, expressed his regret that he had not begun his work with the reign of Henry VII, for "it is properly at that Period modern History commences. America was discoverd: Commerce extended: The Arts cultivated: Printing invented: Religion reform'd: And all the governments of Europe almost chang'd."[38] By his periodization, and by the factors he chose to emphasize, Hume showed himself heir to a century and a half of historical reflection. In British historical thought, the discovery of America had gradually come to be associated with the accession of the Tudor dynasty, the Henrician Reformation, and the redistribution of wealth and power occasioned by the dissolution of the monasteries. For example, in 1612 Samuel Daniel called the late fifteenth century in England "a time . . . let out into wider notions, and bolder discoveries of what lay hidden before," including the "opening of a new world, which strangely altered the manner of this, inhancing both the rate of all things, by the induction of infinite treasure, and opened a wider way to corruption, whereby Princes got much without their swords." Similarly, in 1655 an official government document justifying war against Spain declared that "the Reformation of Religion, and the Discovery of the West Indies" were "two great Revolutions, happening neer about the same time, [which] did very much alter the State of Affairs in the World." Yet the revolution set in train by Columbus's

Title page of Jan van der Straet [Johannes Stradanus], *Nova Reperta* (Amsterdam, 1600). Folger Shakespeare Library.

voyages came to be seen as above all a commercial transformation. By the 1690s the Scottish projector William Paterson declared that the long-term economic consequences of the discovery of the New World had "so altered the measures of war, shaken the maxims of peace, and otherwise confounded as well as amazed the old, that all thinking men are now become highly sensible how advantageous it is for a people to promote and support their trade, navigation, and industry, and how dangerous to neglect it."[39]

Though it became a commonplace that the late fifteenth century had marked a great shift in the affairs of Europe, not all agreed that the effects of this transformation had been beneficial. Just as Samuel Daniel saw the influx of bullion from the New World as "opening a wider way to corruption," so the mid-seventeenth-century republican James Harrington thought that it had been a blessing in disguise for Henry VII not to have backed Columbus: the riches of America had poisoned the Catholic monarchies of Europe, leaving them "all sick, all corrupted together." (Likewise, Montesquieu thought that the French had done "perhaps imprudently, a very wise thing" in not backing Columbus.) For the truculent Scottish republican, Andrew Fletcher, printing had led to an increase in knowledge, but with the aid of the compass was "a Passage opened by the Sea to the east

Indies and a new World discovered. By this means the luxury of Asia and America was added to that of the Ancients," and Europe thereafter sank "into an Abyss of Pleasures," with a consequent decline in martial valor.[40]

Despite these discernibly negative economic and moral effects of the discovery of the New World, eighteenth-century British historians agreed that crossing the threshold of modernity had brought with it an increase in Europe's self-knowledge. Viscount Bolingbroke, for example, described the late fifteenth century as an "epoch" of "revolution": power had shifted from nobility to crown across Europe; Habsburg-Bourbon rivalry had begun; and "from hence arose the notion of a balance of power in Europe, on the equal poise of which the safety and tranquillity of all must depend." The continuity of such maxims of politics meant that this was the beginning of modern history, and hence that the period held most power to teach the contemporary politician by examples. Hume agreed that true history—history which increased knowledge of government and public affairs—was possible only when printed records became available to the historian. As the classics were dusted off, books rolled off the printing presses, and gunpowder transformed modern warfare, "a general revolution was made in human affairs throughout this part of the world." This assessment of the late fifteenth century as the threshold of modernity and the origin of modern identity persists among both historians and sociologists, though we should now be more critical about the limited meaning of such a history for those parts of the world not encompassed by the Enlightenment's strictly European cosmopolitanism.[41]

The identification of Europe's achievements—classical learning, printing, navigation, commerce, battlefield technology, and political liberty secured through property rights—with modernity implicitly condemned those who lacked these discoveries to irretrievable backwardness and ultimately to colonial subjection. "In the beginning all the World was *America*," wrote John Locke, with the implication that America itself was like the world in its beginnings—uncultivated, unsettled, and unclaimed, and therefore a just prize for any who would productively mingle their labor with the land, assert their property rights, and start off on the road to commerce and civility. As James Tully has recently pointed out, "This Eurocentric convention enframes the eighteenth-century debate and theories of development to this day."[42]

The argument from analogy which linked the American Indian with European barbarism had passed through three stages, propelled by this European ideological self-definition. First, it was believed that the similarity between the New World peoples and the ancestors of Europe implied that the whole of humanity sprang from a single set of parents, whose offspring and heirs had migrated around the globe to populate its surface when "all the World was *America*." Then, the apparent similarities between Algonquians and Picts, for example, could open a window into Europe's past. Finally, such cultural comparisons raised the question of how two peoples so widely separated in time could still appear to be at the same stage of development. The naive comparativism of the seventeenth century was summed up, said William Robertson, by those who had argued " 'that the Germans and the Americans must be the same people.' " But there was a more convincing explanation, derived from the environmental theories of Montesquieu and from the developmental sociology of Adam Smith. Humanity is the same in its essentials the world over, as it has been at all times, and it has followed discernible patterns of development—from nomadic savagery, through the more settled stage of barbarism, to civilization, or, more subtly, from hunter, to shepherd, to farmer, to trader. Any group of human beings, who exist at the same level of development and under similar environmental conditions, will show the same moral and social and political characteristics. Therefore a "philosopher" like Robertson himself would say rather " 'that the human mind, whenever it is placed in the same situation, will, in ages the most distant, and in countries the most remote, assume the same form, and be distinguished by the same manners.' "[43]

Robertson first laid out the principles which were to determine his *History* in an evangelical context in January 1755, when he preached a sermon before the Scottish Society for the Promotion of Christian Knowledge on *The Situation of the World at the Time of Christ's Appearance.* This piece differs from Robertson's later enterprises in its sacred-historical scheme (after all, Robertson, like Hakluyt, was a Protestant cleric), though its broad conclusions about human progress, the origins of society in needs, and the hierarchy of civilizations across the globe are entirely compatible with them. According to Robertson, the successive "empires" of Rome and of Christianity had, for ill and then good, dissolved the barriers which divided the violently independent city-states of antiquity from one another, and commerce had almost completed the unification of the world, which "may now be considered as one vast society, cemented by its natural wants; each part contributing its share towards the subsistence, the pleasure and the improvement of the whole." The evident superiority of Christendom had been extended with "arts and arms" across the globe. All that remained was for that preeminence to be harnessed definitively to the cause of religion in a new age of renovation: "Then might the spirit of Christianity, which languishes so visibly in the places where it hath long been planted, revive with new vigour in unknown lands, and shine with its first splendour, among *the people who now sit in darkness and in the region and shadow of death.*" Proof of the stadial development of society was not far to seek, for those benighted people could be found at home as well as abroad—in fact, the main aim of the sermon was to encourage evangelism in the Highlands and islands of Scotland, where "society still appears in its rudest and most imperfect form."[44] In its concerns with social development, environmental determinism, and the

THE

HISTORY

OF

AMERICA.

By WILLIAM ROBERTSON, D.D.

PRINCIPAL of the Univerſity of EDINBURGH, and HISTORIOGRAPHER to his MAJESTY for SCOTLAND.

VOLUME THE FIRST.

LONDON:

Printed for W. STRAHAN; T. CADELL, in the Strand; and J. BALFOUR, at Edinburgh.

MDCCLXXVII.

Title page of William Robertson, *The History of America* (London, 1777). John Carter Brown Library.

normative superiority of contemporary civilization, Robertson's sermon can be seen as part of a temporal and philosophical sequence in his work which ran from the birth of Christ, through the fall of the Roman Empire, to the discovery of America (in *The Progress of Society in Europe*), and culminated in his crowning achievement, the *History of America.*

Robertson approached his *History of America* crabwise after writing a *History of Scotland during the Reigns of Queen Mary and of King James VI* (1759) and then his *History of the Reign of the Emperor Charles V* (1769). Like Gibbon, he spent much time searching for a historical subject of sufficient scope and significance to display his powers, especially in the aftermath of the success of his *History of Scotland.* Hume urged him to write a study of modern history in the form of Plutarchan biographies (including those of "the great Discoverers and Conquerors of the new World"), while Horace Walpole suggested the history of Sweden, Greece, or the five "good princes" of Roman history, from Nerva to Marcus Aurelius. Robertson chose instead the reign of Charles V, because "the events are great and interesting," among them "the Reformation in Germany; the wars in Italy; the revival of letters; [and] the conquest of the new world."[45] Once Robertson's mind was made up, the research and writing of the history of Charles V's reign took him seven more years, and when it appeared, he had to explain a notable lack in its coverage. "I found that the discovery of the new world; the state of society among its ancient inhabitants; their character, manners, and arts; the genius of the European settlements in its various provinces, together with the influence upon the systems of policy or commerce in Europe, were subjects so splendid and important, that a superficial treatment of them could afford little satisfaction." He therefore proposed a separate history to cover all of these themes at the length, and with the documentation, they deserved.[46] This was to be the *History of America*, planned to cover not only the Spanish, Portuguese, and English settlements from their foundation to Robertson's own time, but also the natural and moral history of the Indians as well. Its ambition and scope were unique in European historical writing, and no comparable synthesis had been attempted, even in Spanish, since the work of Antonio de Herrera a century and a half earlier.[47]

Robertson's *History*, like Gibbon's contemporary enterprise, combined an antiquarian's zeal for sources with a philosopher's analysis of history. To the first end, Robertson accumulated over 280 books and manuscripts on Spanish America alone, which, as a token of his erudition, he listed at the beginning of his *History*, "emboldened by a hint" from Gibbon. He obtained Spanish manuscript sources through the British embassy chaplain in Madrid (though the great archive of Simancas was closed to him). He instituted a search in Vienna for the original of Cortés's first letter to Charles V but turned up instead the *Carta de la Justicia y Regimiento de la Rica Villa de Vera Cruz* and a copy of Cortés's fifth letter. Catherine the Great's doctor interceded on his behalf to obtain accounts of Russian voyages. The Portuguese ambassador in London informed him about the Matogrosso of Brazil. Bougainville supplied accounts of the American Indians, as did two English missionaries to the Iroquois. Most innovatively—yet in belated imitation of the bureaucratic practices of the Spanish principal royal chronicler-cosmographer—Robertson sent out a forty-four-point questionnaire to correspondents throughout the European settlements in the Americas. All of this evidence was necessary because history "produces facts as the foundation of every judgment which it ventures to pronounce," even though the multiplicity of such facts available to the historian in the age of print meant that some boundary had be set to historical curiosity if history itself were to have any relevance and if the historian were not to be overwhelmed by evidence.[48]

Robertson's second aim, to write a philosophical history, set the boundary to historical curiosity in the sixteenth century, because "the political principles and maxims, then established, still continue to operate."[49] It was only with the discovery of America that a philosophical history could be written, for only after that was it possible to view humanity in the full span of its development, from rude hunter-gatherer to polite modern European. The discovery of America "enlarged the sphere of contemplation" "to complete our knowledge of the human species," so that it would at last be possible to "complete the history of the human mind, and attain to a perfect knowledge of its nature and operations." Until the late fifteenth century, the most primitive peoples known to Europe were to be found in the pages of Herodotus, Caesar, and Tacitus. Yet the Scythians and Germans portrayed in their works were agriculturalists, and the historical stage before such a level of social development could only be conjectured. With the discovery of the American Indians, and the increasing knowledge of the peoples of Australasia and the Pacific, conjectural history need be conjectural no more. As Edmund Burke remarked in response to Robertson's gift of a copy of the *History of America*, "The Great Map of Mankind is unrolld at once; and there is no state or Gradation of barbarism, and no mode of refinement which we have not at the same instant under our View."[50] The great Enlightenment project of the history of humanity might at last be fulfilled, though it was only with the Enlightenment's instrumental historicism (as Robertson seems to have realized) that America could take its full place in the historical consciousness of Europe.

Robertson's achievement was to synthesize the widest possible range of written sources, printed and manuscript, on the progress of Spanish conquest and colonization in the Caribbean, Mexico, and Peru; to these he added three discourses which put this synthetic achievement into philosophical perspective. He opened the *History* with a chapter placing the discovery within the general history of navigation and commerce. Though in this Robertson showed himself heir to the British tradition of maritime history (from Hakluyt, through the later collections of voyages, and on to the ideological naval histories of the propagandist London Scot John Campbell, for example),[51] he also aligned himself with the Lockean vision of civilized life, based on property, exchange, and the mutual satisfaction of needs. As Robertson argued, civilization was distinguished by the very idea of property. Property implied the possibility of alienation and exchange to satisfy the differing needs of individuals. "It is to navigation that men are indebted for the power of transporting the superfluous stock of one part of the earth to supply the wants of another." Within this vision of history, the three cardinal events were the crusades ("an event . . . the most extraordinary perhaps in the history of mankind") because they brought shipping and trade in their wake; the invention of the compass ("this event . . . productive of greater effects than any recorded in the annals of the human race"); and the discovery of America itself ("an event no less extraordinary than unexpected").[52] A multiplicity of wants is the true mark of civilization and is the guarantee of the inventiveness, activity, and commerce needed to supply them. Spurred by these urges, Europeans explored their world until they came to the full knowledge of it and its peoples at the beginning of modern history.

Europe's expansion brought it face to face in the Americas with a race of people seemingly indolent, uninventive, and uncommercial, for the most part feebly lolling their way through life, though some, the "more improved" ones, went so far as to burden women with the ignominy of labor. This was the subject of Robertson's other philosophical excursions in books 4 and 7 of the *History*. These unsettled hunting peoples may have been distinguished in their "high sense of equality and independence," but they had no sense of property, so they had little need of law and hence produced only the most minimal forms of government. Here was proof indeed that the key to a people's social development, and hence their place on the ladder of human ascent toward civility, lay in their mode of subsistence. Under such conditions, not even climatic differences would overrule the determining effects of a people's needs, and "a tribe of savages on the banks of the Danube must nearly resemble one upon the plains of the Mississippi. . . . In every part of the earth, the progress of man hath been nearly the same; and we can trace him in his career from the rude simplicity of savage life, until he attains the industry, the arts, and the elegance of polished society." Not even the great empires of Mexico and Peru could be "entitled to rank with those nations which merit the name of civilised," for they neither used metals nor did they domesticate animals. Their pictorial manuscripts represented the first step toward to the attainment of alphabetism, but they had still a long road to travel before they could "be ranked among the polished nations," not least because they had nothing but cacao beans to use as counters of exchange, the discovery of money being "among the steps of greatest consequence in the progress of nations."[53]

Robertson's picture of the native peoples of the Americas, when linked to his vision of human progress from infancy to adulthood, simplicity to civilization, savagery to politeness, held up a mirror to the modernity and maturity of post-Renaissance Europe. European society, now linked together by its common political maxims and the sustaining force of the balance of power, had achieved all that America lacked. It had property, hence law; money, hence trade; printing, hence a sense of history. These were all gradual developments (as Robertson had previously shown in his essay on the *Progress of Society in Europe*), but they had reached the height they now enjoyed during the reign of Charles V. Robertson would have agreed with Hume and Bolingbroke that it was at this point that modern history commences, but this particular vision of modernity would not have been validated without the discovery of America. Robertson had moved far beyond the narrowly English, inspirational, antiquarian vision of Hakluyt, whom he nevertheless praised as the man "to whom England is more indebted for its American possessions than to any man of that age."[54] He had provided the ultimate synthesis, not only of all the available information on the New World and its colonization, but of the twin challenges to antiquity and modernity which America had presented to European consciousness. His philosophical conception of human progress was essentially derived from the challenge of the American Indian to European historical imagination once comparative history across time and space became inferentially possible. The fruits of such comparison had been formed by Locke and his successors into a Eurocentric vision of American backwardness which justified colonization, evangelization, and dispossession. Robertson's achievement was to complete the historical circle by writing a comprehensive history of the New World based on this parallel construction of antiquity and modernity. By carrying off this feat, Robertson is entitled to the accolade for his *History of America* which Arnaldo Momigliano accorded to Edward Gibbon for his history of Rome. We might then take the words from Momigliano's mouth to say that Robertson's "novelty is to be found in the reconciliation of two historical methods rather than in a new interpretation of a historical period." It was Hume himself who awarded perhaps the greatest palm to that achievement, even before the *History of America* was completed, when he wrote in 1770, "I believe this is the historical Age and this the historical nation"; he knew, he said, of eight major histories then on the stocks in Scotland, but "the most sublime of the whole" was Robertson's masterpiece.[55]

Yet history itself overtook Robertson's *History* and condemned it to live as but a fragment of his great design. He had hoped to chronicle not only Spanish America, but the Portuguese and British possessions too. However, the *History* appeared in truncated form only a year after the Declaration of Independence, which, in part, had itself used the very Lockean principles which had once upheld the claims of empire to dissolve the bonds of that empire.[56] Robertson waited patiently to see what the outcome of the conflict might be, in the hopes of resuming his account of the British American colonies, which he had throughout written as the history of colonial rights and metropolitan control; he saw little point, then, in attempting to complete his *History* until it was clear which side of the argument (which he had always seen as confused, and in which he himself had divided sympathies) would win. In the end, he gave up and left the history incomplete, with Virginia dangling in the aftermath of the Glorious Revolution, and New England incongruously rounded off with the Cromwellian conquest of Jamaica; his son published these fragments as books 9 and 10 of the *History* in 1796. Robertson had lost heart and health in the process of waiting for a resolution, and without a philosophical design for his British history which showed the growth of a political entity as a scion of the Old World, not the beginning of a New, political World, he could not complete his project. "As I had written between two and three hundred pages of *excellent* History of the British Colonies in North America," he wrote in 1784, "I long flattered myself that the war might terminate so favourably for G. Britain, that I might go on with my work. But alas America is now lost to the Empire and to me, and what would have been a good introduction to the settlement of British Colonies, will suit very ill the establishment of Independant States."[57]

For all the divergence between their methods and achievements, neither Hakluyt nor Robertson wrote an imperial history which smoothly chronicled the British rise to colonial might. Hakluyt's remained a maritime history and never received within its ambit the first English colonies in North America; Robertson's was a philosophical and cosmopolitan history, cut short by the loss of those colonies. Hakluyt and Robertson stood at either end of the first British Empire as surely as they occupied opposite ends of the spectrum of historical thought in early modern Europe. Hakluyt stood on the threshold of history's emergence from antiquarianism, while Robertson's work was (to Hume's mind, at least) the crowning work of "the historical nation" in "its historical age." If Robertson had remained within the historical scheme Hakluyt had adopted, his enterprise would have been both impossible and superfluous—impossible, because the tools Hakluyt had used would not permit either analysis or comparison; superfluous, because it would have had to end in defeat, secession, and humiliation. Robertson could therefore never have been able to receive America as Hakluyt did, so different were the foundations and aims of his intellectual project. The very contours of that project were determined by a view of human development through time which would have been inconceivable without the preceding two centuries' reception of America into historical thought. Hakluyt had expanded the bounds of history writing in his attempt to receive the New World as an object of antiquarian attention; his successors and those, like Locke, who employed the conclusions of their histories used America as *materiel à penser* to redefine the very idea of civilization and modernity; Robertson, though overtaken by events, attempted to return the historical consciousness of America to the writing of the history of America itself. His achievement should remind us that whenever we speak of early modern history our visions both of history and of modernity are in part the products of the Enlightenment's reception of America into European consciousness.

ACKNOWLEDGMENTS

I am particularly grateful to Peter Burke, Joyce Chaplin, John Elliott, Karen Kupperman, John Pocock, and Joan-Pau Rubiés for their help and comments on earlier drafts of this essay.

NOTES

1. The debate on the reception of the New World can be followed in J. H. Elliott, *The Old World and the New, 1492–1650* (Cambridge, 1970), and "Renaissance Europe and America: A

Blunted Impact?," in *First Images of America: The Impact of the Old World on the New*, ed. Fredi Chiappelli, 2 vols. (Berkeley, 1976), 1:11–23; Michael T. Ryan, "Assimilating New Worlds in the Sixteenth and Seventeenth Centuries," *Comparative Studies in Society and History* 23 (1981): 519–38; Anthony Pagden, " 'The Impact of the New World on the Old': The History of an Idea," *Renaissance and Modern Studies* 30 (1986): 1–11, *The Fall of Natural Man: The American Indian and the Origins of Comparative Ethnology*, 2d ed. rev. (Cambridge, 1986), 4–6, and *European Encounters with the New World: From Renaissance to Romanticism* (New Haven, 1993); Anthony Grafton, *New Worlds, Ancient Texts: The Power of Tradition and the Shock of Discovery* (Cambridge, Mass., 1992).

2. Richard Hakluyt, "To the right worshipfull and most virtuous Gentleman, Master Philip Sydney Esquire," in *The Writings and Correspondence of the Two Richard Hakluyts*, ed. E. G. R. Taylor, 2 vols. (London, 1935), 1:175; William Robertson, *The History of America*, bks. 1–8 (1777), bks. 9–10 (1796), reprint in 3 vols. (London, 1827), 1:273.

3. On these traditions, see D. R. Woolf, "Erudition and the Idea of History in Renaissance England," *Renaissance Quarterly* 40 (1987): 11–48.

4. The only studies which have specifically examined America's place in early modern historiography are Myron P. Gilmore, "The New World in the French and English Historians of the Sixteenth Century," in Chiappelli, *First Images*, 2:519–27; Amy Glassner Gordon, "Confronting Cultures: The Effect of the Discoveries on Sixteenth-Century French Thought," *Terræ Incognitæ* 8 (1976): 45–56; Pagden, " 'The Impact of the New World on the Old' "; and Peter Burke, "America and the Rewriting of World History," in this volume (which suggests the period after 1750 as the moment when the European vision of America was finally consolidated).

5. Richard Hakluyt, *The Principal Navigations, Voyages, Traffiques and Discoveries of the English Nation*, 3 vols. (London, 1599–1600), 1:sig. [*4]^{v}.

6. G. D. Ramsay, "Clothworkers, Merchant Adventurers and Richard Hakluyt," *English Historical Review* 92 (1977): 504–21.

7. As L. E. Pennington remarks of Hakluyt, "Almost no attention has been given to his possible contributions to the discipline of history"; see "Secondary Works on Hakluyt and His Circle," in *The Hakluyt Handbook*, ed. D. B. Quinn, 2 vols. (London, 1974), 2:595. Yet see J. Hamard, "Richard Hakluyt, Historien," *Les Langues Modernes* 42 (1948): 249–59; G. B. Parks, *Richard Hakluyt and the English Voyages*, 2d ed. (New York, 1961), 178–83; and J. H. Parry, "Hakluyt's View of British History," in Quinn, *Hakluyt Handbook*, 1:3–7.

8. Richard Hakluyt, *The Principall Navigations . . . of the English Nation* (London, 1589), sig. *3^{v}.

9. Richard Eden, *A Treatyse of the Newe India* (London, 1553), sig. aaiii^{v}, and *The Decades of the newe worlde or west India* (London, 1555), sig. [Ai]^{v}.

10. Louis B. Wright, *Religion and Empire* (Chapel Hill, 1943), 53, 71.

11. Raphaell Holinshed, William Harrison, and John Vowell, *The First and Second Volume of Chronicles* (London, 1587), 1262, 1.

12. D. R. Woolf, *The Idea of History in Early Stuart England* (Toronto, 1990), 13, 18.

13. Hakluyt, *Principall Navigations* (1589), sig. *3^{v}.

14. For Hakluyt's plan to go to Newfoundland with Sir Humphrey Gilbert in 1583, see

David B. Quinn and Neil M. Cheshire, eds., *The New Found Land of Stephen Parmenius* (Toronto, 1972), 44–45, 174; for La Popelinière's plans, see his letter to J. J. Scaliger, 4 January 1604, reprinted in George Huppert, *The Idea of Perfect History* (Urbana, 1970), 195–97.

15. Hakluyt, *Principall Navigations* (1589), sig. *2v; Taylor, *Writings and Correspondence of the Two Richard Hakluyts*, 2:241, 295n, 398; Edward Arber, ed., *A Transcript of the Registers of the Company of Stationers of London, 1554–1640 A.D.*, vol. 2 (London, 1875), 424.

16. Donald R. Kelley, *Foundations of Modern Historical Scholarship: Language, Law, and History in the French Renaissance* (New York, 1970), 140.

17. Abraham Ortelius, *Theatrum Orbis Terrarum* (Antwerp, 1570), sig. Aiiiir ("Geographia est historiæ oculum"); Lancelot Voisin, Sieur de La Popelinière, *Les Trois Mondes* (Paris, 1583), fol. 35v ("la Geographie est l'œil naturel et la vraye lumiere de l'histoire"); Richard Hakluyt, ed., *De Orbe Novo Peter Martyris* (Paris, 1587), sig. aiiiv–aiiiir; Hakluyt, *Principal Navigations*, vol. 3 (1599–1600), sig. (A2)v.

18. Sir Walter Ralegh, *The Discoverie of the Large, Rich, and Bewtiful Empyre of Guiana* (London, 1596), 99; Lawrence Keymis, *A Relation of the Second Voyage to Guiana* (London, 1596), sig. [A4]v; Hakluyt, *Principal Navigations* (1600), 3:2.

19. Taylor, *Writings and Correspondence of the Two Richard Hakluyts*, 2:290–93.

20. John Dee, "Title Royal . . . to Foreign Regions," British Library MS Cotton Augustus I, 1, iv; Sir George Peckham, *A True Reporte of the Late Discoveries and Possession, Taken in the Right of the Crowne of Englande, of the New-Found Landes* (London, 1583), sig. [Div]r; Humphrey Lhoyd, *The Historie of Cambria*, ed. David Powel (London, 1584), 227–29; Samuel Purchas, *Purchas His Pilgrimage* (London, 1613), 610; John Smith, *The Generall Historie of Virginia, New-England, and the Summer Isles* (London, 1624), 1; *The British Sailor's Discovery* (London, 1739), 12–14, 17, reprinted in *Old England for Ever, Or, Spanish Cruelty Display'd* (London, 1740), 26–29, 35. On the Madoc myth, see Gwyn A. Williams, *Madoc: The Legend of the Welsh Discovery of America* (London, 1979), 31–67, and Richard Deacon, *Madoc and the Discovery of America* (London, 1966).

21. David A. Brading, *The First America: The Spanish Monarchy, Creole Patriots, and the Liberal State, 1492–1867* (Cambridge, 1991), 36; Harold J. Cook, "Ancient Wisdom, the Golden Age, and Atlantis: The New World in Sixteenth-Century Cosmography," *Terræ Incognitæ* 10 (1978): 37.

22. On the justifications for the early claims, see John T. Juricek, "English Territorial Claims in North America under Elizabeth and the Early Stuarts," *Terræ Incognitæ* 7 (1975): 7–22; on "charter" myths, see Keith Thomas, *Perception of the Past in Early Modern England* (London, 1983), 2–3; G. S. Kirk, *The Nature of Greek Myths* (Harmondsworth, 1974), 59–63.

23. D. B. Quinn, "A List of Books Purchased for the Virginia Company," *Virginia Magazine of History and Biography* 77 (1969): 358.

24. John Speed, *The Theatre of the Empire of Great Britaine* (London, 1611), 157.

25. Richard Hakluyt, "Discourse of Western Planting" (1584), in Taylor, *Writings and Correspondence of the Two Richard Hakluyts*, 2:236; David Goodman, *Power and Penury: Government, Technology, and Science in Philip II's Spain* (Cambridge, 1988), 50–87. Even France had a royal cosmographer, and when in Paris Hakluyt met the then incumbent, André Thevet.

26. On colonization and the scientific establishment in Elizabethan England, see especially the essays in John W. Shirley, ed., *Thomas Harriot: Renaissance Scientist* (Oxford, 1974). The English crown had, however, earlier deployed "historiographers" in the Reformation polemic: see G. D. Nicholson, "The Nature and Function of Historical Argument in the Henrician Reformation" (Ph.D. diss., Cambridge University, 1977).

27. Denys Hay, "The Historiographers-Royal in England and Scotland," *Scottish Historical Review* 30 (1951): 15–29.

28. On developments in France and Spain, see, for example, Amy Glassner Gordon, "The Impact of the Discoveries on Sixteenth-Century French Cosmographical and Historical Thought" (Ph.D. diss., University of Chicago, 1974), and Angel Delgado-Gomez, *Spanish Historical Writing about the New World, 1493–1750* (Providence, 1992).

29. G. R. Crone and R. A. Skelton, "English Collections of Voyages and Travels, 1625–1846," in *Richard Hakluyt and His Successors*, ed. Edward Lynam (London, 1946), 65–140.

30. The transition can be traced through John Parker, *Books to Build an Empire* (Amsterdam, 1965); Colin Steele, *English Interpreters of the Iberian New World from Purchas to Stevens: A Bibliographical Study, 1603–1726* (Oxford, 1975); P. J. Marshall and Glyndwr Williams, *The Great Map of Mankind: British Perceptions of the World in the Age of Enlightenment* (London, 1982), chaps. 1–2, 7; and Richard C. Simmons, "Americana in British Books, 1621–1760," in this volume.

31. There is as yet no study comparable to Brading, *The First America*, for British America, but see Richard S. Dunn, "Seventeenth-Century English Historians of America," in *Seventeenth-Century America: Essays in Colonial History*, ed. James Morton Smith (Chapel Hill, 1959), 195–225; Peter Gay, *A Loss of Mastery: Puritan Historians of Colonial America* (Berkeley, 1966); Alden T. Vaughan, "The Evolution of Virginia History: Early Historians of the First Colony," and Harry M. Ward, "The Search for American Identity: Early Historians of New England," in *Perspectives on American History: Essays in Honor of Richard B. Morris*, ed. Alden T. Vaughan and George Athan Billias (New York, 1973), 9–39, 40–62.

32. See Noel Malcolm, "Hobbes, Sandys, and the Virginia Company," *Historical Journal* 24 (1981): 297–321.

33. John Selden, note on Michael Drayton, *Poly-Olbion* (1613), bk. 18, l. 720, in *Works of Michael Drayton*, ed. J. William Hebel, vol. 4 (Oxford, 1933), 385. Selden's source was José de Acosta, *De natura novi orbis* (Salamanca, 1589), bk. 1, chaps. 20–21.

34. See Richard Tuck, *Philosophy and Government, 1572–1651* (Cambridge, 1993), for this reading of Selden's and Hobbes's projects.

35. See Pagden, *Fall of Natural Man.*

36. On this, see Sabine MacCormack, "Limits of Understanding: Perceptions of Greco-Roman and Amerindian Paganism in Early Modern Europe," in this volume.

37. See Jan van der Straet, *Nova Reperta* (Amsterdam, 1600); the quotations from Buonamico, Alsted, Fernius, Horn, et al., in Burke, "America and the Rewriting of World History"; Elizabeth Eisenstein, *The Printing Press as an Agent of Change* (Cambridge, 1979), 20–21.

38. David Hume to Andrew Millar, 20 May 1757, in *The Letters of David Hume*, ed. J. Y. T. Greig, 2 vols. (Oxford, 1932), 1:249; cf. Hume to William Strahan, 25 May 1757, in ibid., 1:251 ("I wish I had from the first begun at that Period. It is really the Commencement of modern History").

39. Samuel Daniel, *The First Part of the Historie of England* (London, 1612), sig. A2^{v}–A3^{r}; *A Declaration of His Highness . . . Setting forth, On the Behalf of this Commonwealth, the Justice of their Cause against Spain* (London, 1655), 517; William Paterson, *Proposals and Reasons for Constituting a Council of Trade* (1701), in *The Writings of William Paterson*, ed. Saxe Bannister, vol. 1 (London, 1859), 27.

40. James Harrington, *The Common-wealth of Oceana* (London, 1656), 272; Charles de Secondat, baron de Montesquieu, *The Spirit of the Laws* (1748), trans. Anne Cohler, Basia Miller, and Harold Stone (Cambridge, 1989), 395; Andrew Fletcher, *A Discourse of Government with Relation to Militia's* (Edinburgh, 1698), 5–6, 9–10, 12. See also Caroline Robbins, "Causes of the Renaissance: The Popular Explanation," *History of Ideas News Letter* 1, no. 2 (1955): 7–10.

41. Viscount Bolingbroke, *Letters on the Study and Use of History* (1735), in *The Works of Lord Bolingbroke*, vol. 2 (Philadelphia, 1841), 239, 243–44, 249–50; David Hume, *The History of England* (1778), ed. William B. Todd, vol. 3 (Indianapolis, 1983), 80–82. For the contemporary identification, see, for example, Zachary Sayre Schiffman, *On the Threshold of Modernity: Relativism in the French Renaissance* (Baltimore, 1991), 5, 6–7; Anthony Giddens, *Modernity and Identity* (Stanford, 1991), 14–21.

42. John Locke, *Two Treatises of Government* (1690), ed. Peter Laslett, rev. ed. (Cambridge, 1988), 301; James Tully, "Placing the 'Two Treatises,'" in *Political Discourse in Early Modern Britain*, ed. Nicholas Phillipson and Quentin Skinner (Cambridge, 1993), 264. For an expansion of Tully's reading of the *Two Treatises* in relation to aboriginal land rights, see "Rediscovering America: The *Two Treatises* and Aboriginal Rights" in James Tully, *An Approach to Political Philosophy: Locke in Contexts* (Cambridge, 1993), 137–76.

43. William Robertson, *The Progress of Society in Europe: A Historical Outline from the Subversion of the Roman Empire to the Beginning of the Sixteenth Century* (1769), ed. Felix Gilbert (Chicago, 1972), 152. On the "four-stages" theory, especially as derived from Smith, see Ronald L. Meek, *Social Science and the Ignoble Savage* (Cambridge, 1976), 99–131, and on Robertson's place in this tradition, ibid., 136–45, and Karen O'Brien, "Between Enlightenment and Conjectural History: William Robertson and the History of Europe," *British Journal for Eighteenth-Century Studies* 16 (1993): 53–63.

44. William Robertson, *The Situation of the World at the Time of Christ's Appearance and its Connexion with the Success of his Religion, considered* (Edinburgh, 1755), 11, 42–44. On the problems of evangelism in the New World, see the "State of the Scottish Society for the Promotion of Christian Knowledge for the Year 1754," appended to Robertson's sermon, ibid., 56.

45. David Hume to William Robertson, [Summer 1759], in Greig, *Letters of David Hume*, 1:314–16; Horace Walpole to Sir John Dalrymple, 22 May 1759; Walpole to Robertson, 4 March 1759; Robertson to Walpole, 20 February 1759, in *The Yale Edition of Horace Walpole's Correspondence*, ed. W. S. Lewis, vol. 15 (London, 1952), 56–57, 50–51, 46.

46. Robertson, *Progress of Society in Europe*, 5.

47. On the *History of America*, see R. A. Humphreys, *William Robertson and His History of America* (London, 1954); E. Adamson Hoebel, "William Robertson: An 18th Century Anthropologist-Historian," *American Anthropologist* 62 (1962): 648–55; Jeffrey R. Smitten,

"Moderatism and History: William Robertson's Unfinished History of British America," in *Scotland and America in the Age of Enlightenment*, ed. Richard B. Sher and Jeffrey R. Smitten (Edinburgh, 1990), 163–79; and Brading, *The First America*, 432–41 (who makes the comparison with Herrera, though to deny Robertson's originality: see 432–33).

48. Robertson, *History of America*, 1:v–x; Humphreys, *Robertson and His History of America*, 16–17; Anthony Pagden, trans. and ed., *Hernán Cortés: Letters from Mexico*, rev. ed. (New Haven, 1986), liii–liv; Robertson, *History of America*, 2:260; Mark Duckworth, "An Eighteenth-Century Questionnaire: William Robertson on the Indians," *Eighteenth-Century Life* 11 (1987): 36–49. For replies to Robertson's questionnaire, see National Library of Scotland MS 3954, fols. 11–93; British Library MS King's 219, fols. 21, 40.

49. Robertson, *Progress of Society in Europe*, 3–4.

50. Robertson, *History of America*, 1:268–69; Edmund Burke to William Robertson, 9 June 1777, in *The Correspondence of Edmund Burke*, ed. George H. Guttridge, vol. 3 (Cambridge, 1961), 350–51.

51. On John Campbell and his naval, Spanish-American, and universal histories, see Guido Abbattista, *Commercio, Colonie e Impero alla Vigilia della Rivoluzione Americana: John Campbell pubblicista e storico nell'Inghilterra del sec. XVIII* (Florence, 1990).

52. Robertson, *History of America*, 1:3, 29, 34, 56.

53. Ibid., 1:300–301, 323–24, 255; 2:254–55, 275–76, 281.

54. Ibid., 3:33.

55. Arnaldo Momigliano, "Gibbon's Contribution to Historical Method," in Momigliano, *Studies in Historiography* (London, 1966), 52; Hume to William Strahan, [August 1770], in Greig, *Letters of David Hume*, 2:230.

56. Tully, "Placing the 'Two Treatises,'" 271–75.

57. Robertson to [Sir Robert Murray Keith?], 8 March 1784, British Library Add. MS 35350, fol. 70^{v} (on which see Humphreys, *Robertson and His History of America*, 14, and Smitten, "Moderatism and History," 175). For Robertson's reaction to the progress of the American war, see "Heads for a Sermon preached by Doctor Robertson, at the Public fast 26 Feby 1778," National Library of Scotland MS 5003, fols. 92^{r}–93^{v}, and Dalphy I. Fagerstrom, "Scottish Opinion and the American Revolution," *William and Mary Quarterly*, 3d ser., 11 (1954): 261.

Part II

America Reflected in Europe

SABINE MACCORMACK

Limits of Understanding

PERCEPTIONS OF GRECO-ROMAN AND AMERINDIAN PAGANISM IN EARLY MODERN EUROPE

The first Europeans to reach America expected to find there things that they already knew. Indeed, this expectation of finding something that is in some respect already known is inherent in discovery of any kind, for without knowledge, there can be no recognition and no understanding. And further, we cannot claim to have discovered something if we do not in some respect understand it. Thus when Columbus arrived in the Caribbean, he described what he saw in the light of long established European ideas about cultural difference and about the nature of human society, and the same is true of the many other Europeans who in due course came to the newly found continent. They all integrated what was new and strange about America into a context of what was familiar and known. When such information was subsequently published and publicized in Europe, further steps were taken in integrating the unknown with the familiar, the result being that, increasingly, the "new things" of America shed the very features that defined them as alien and different. What I would like to do in this essay is to explain some aspects of this process of transformation and its outcomes.

Throughout the sixteenth and seventeenth centuries and beyond, scholars and other learned observers interested themselves in a variety of parallels that might be drawn between the still living civilizations and religions of the Americas and those of the Greco-Roman Mediterranean. This was one of the ways in which American issues came to figure in the—as it were—larger reality of European politics, culture, and religion as perceived by Europeans. It was this larger reality that propelled the study both of the Americas and of the cultures of the ancient Mediterranean, while at the same time stimulating scholars to compare the civilizations of America to those of the ancient world. But these comparisons did not on their own lead to a significantly new perception either of Greco-Roman antiquity or of the Americas.[1] Instead, Europeans spontaneously integrated what they were able to learn about American cultures and religions and about their own past with other concerns of the day, just as we ourselves tend to do now. Over twenty years ago, John Elliott described the impact of America on Europe as an "uncertain" and "blunted" one.[2] The Old World took notice of the New World, but not to the extent of revising established modes of thought in any fundamental way. In addition, many of the major Spanish works on American civilizations written in the sixteenth and seventeenth centuries that we now consider fundamental were not published until modern times, while other specialized works reached only a very small readership.[3] Of the several dozen works published in Spanish that bear on Inca and early colonial Peru, for example, only a small handful, including the histories of Pedro Cieza de León, Francisco López de Gómara, José de Acosta, and Garcilaso de la Vega, were widely consulted and translated into foreign languages.[4] As a result, as Elliott himself suggests, it is often impossible to escape the conclusion that the vast majority of Europeans did not know very much about America, and that much of what they thought they knew was wrong or, at any rate, misleading.[5]

Sixteenth-century depictions of the Inca capital of Cuzco afford a telling glimpse of the process whereby Europeans reformulated the "new things" of America to suit their expectations. Pedro Sancho, secretary to Francisco Pizarro, the conqueror of Peru, wrote an account of the invasion of Peru in which he included a description of that city. He mentioned Cuzco's fine stone buildings and straight but narrow streets traversed by water canals that left just enough room for a man on horseback to pass on either side. Sancho also referred to two rivers crossing Cuzco and described the city's main square, which was overlooked by the palaces of Inca rulers. The fortress above Cuzco, containing stores of arms and quarters for a garrison, was enclosed by a triple wall of huge boulders, each of which, according to Sancho, would have required three Spanish wagons joined together for its transport.

Sancho's verbal sketch, however rudimentary, has sufficient detail for the reader to conjure up a visual image of Cuzco, and this is what Sancho's Italian illustrator in effect did. The image he created, however, bears no realistic resemblance to Cuzco as it then was but instead transforms it into an imaginary Renaissance city of sorts (fig. 1).[6] We recognize the main square framed by what might be described as the palaces that Sancho mentioned. The figure being carried across the square in a litter is the Inca Atahuallpa, whom the Spanish invaders killed in 1533. Two rivers cross the city, just as Sancho had written, and water canals run along the center of some streets. But these streets are wide, and the fortress is a fiction based on European, not Andean, models. For good measure, Cuzco, like most European cities of the period, is fortified by an enclosing wall, although no such wall existed, and none was mentioned by Sancho. Another careful description of Cuzco by an eyewitness, the historian Cieza de León, was transformed into an image of a

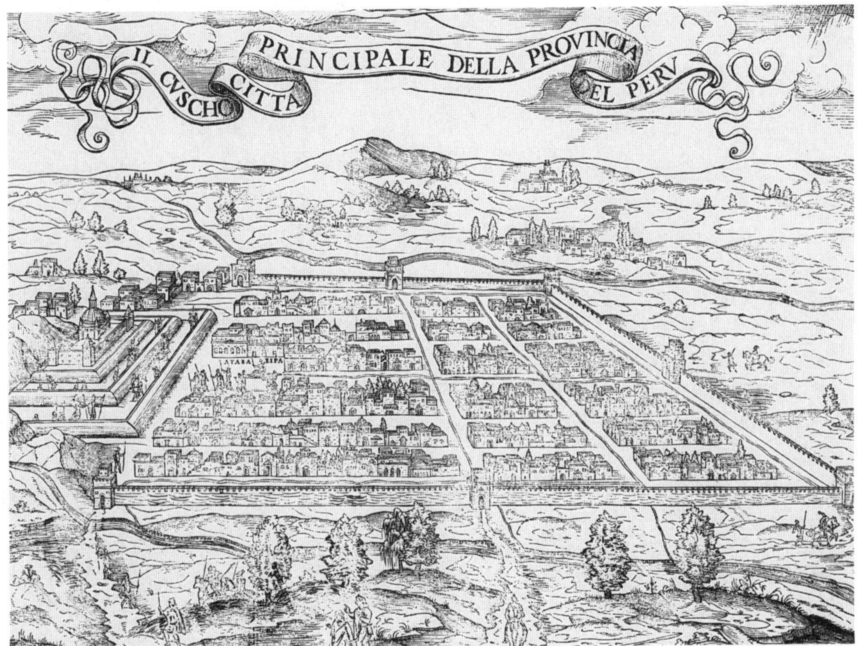

Fig. 1. "Cuzco, capital of the province of Peru," engraving, from Gian Battista Ramusio, *Navigationi e viaggi* (Venice, 1606). Getty Center, Resource Collections.

similar kind (fig. 2). Here we have no plan, but a view of the city at a distance. The figures in the foreground perhaps are Francisco Pizarro with Atahuallpa's successor, Manco Inca, who is dressed in a somewhat fanciful rendering of Inca costume.[7]

Misleading as these depictions appear to be, they are not merely the fancies of illustrators, as becomes clear if we compare them to sixteenth-century representations of ancient Rome during the various phases of its development. Theodore de Bry, who also produced an illustrated folio volume about America, thus engraved a set of plates to accompany an erudite study of Roman topography by Bartolomeo Marliano, which include three sketches designed to make clear the evolution of the city. The first shows Romulus's *Roma quadrata* with city walls pierced by four gates and forming a square that encloses four of the canonical seven hills of Rome, each of which is surmounted by a temple (fig. 3). Next comes the Rome of the sixth king, Servius Tullius, which is octagonal and has eight regions, with the walls enclosing all the seven hills (fig. 4). The Rome of Augustus, finally, is round and has sixteen regions, each with its gate, and a greater number of temples and monuments (fig. 5).[8] All these depictions, with every one of their different components, had a perfectly respectable foundation in antiquarian research, because Marliano mentioned only such buildings and sites as he could document from the

Parte primera de la

y ricos adõde los ſeñores d̃l Cuzco ſalian a tomar ſus plazeres y ſolazes. Aqui fue tambien, donde el gouernador don Franciſco Piçarro mando quemar al capitan general de Atabalipa Chalicuchima. Ay deſte valle á la ciudad del Cuzco cinco leguas: y paſſa por el el gran camino real. Y d̃l agua de vn rio que naſce cerca de eſte valle ſe haze vn grande tremedal hondo, y que con gran dificultad ſe pudiera andar, ſino ſe hiziera vna calçada ancha y muy fuerte, que los Ingas mandaron hazer, con ſus paredes de vna parte y otra, tan fixas q̃ durarã muchos tiempos. Saliendo de la calçada ſe camina por vnos pequeños collados y laderas, haſta llegar a la ciudad del Cuzco. Antiguamente fue todo eſte valle muy poblado y lleno de ſementeras, tantas y tan grandes que era coſa de ver, por ſer hechas cõ vna orden de paredes anchas: y con ſu compas algo deſuiado ſalian otras: auiendo diſtãcia en el anchor de vna y otra para poder ſembrar ſus ſemẽteras de mayz y de otras rayzes q̃ ellos ſiembran. Y aſſi eſtauan hechas d̃ eſta manera, pegadas a las haldas de las ſierras. Muchas deſtas ſementeras ſon de trigo: porque ſe da bien. Y ay en el muchos ganados de los Eſpañoles vezinos de la antigua ciudad del Cuzco. La qual eſta ſituada entre vnos cerros de la manera y forma que en el ſiguiente capitulo ſe declara.

¶ Capitulo. xcij. De la manera y traça con que eſta fundada la ciudad d̃l Cuzco: y d̃ los quatro caminos reales que de ella ſalen: y de los grãdes edificios que tuuo: y quiẽ fue el fundador.

La ciudad d̃l Cuzco eſta fundada en vn ſitio biẽ aſpero y por todas partes cercado de ſierras, ẽtre dos arroyos pequeños, el vno de los quales paſſa por medio, porque ſe ha poblado de entrambas partes. Tiene vn valle a la parte de Leuante que comiença deſde la propia ciudad: por manera q̃ las aguas de los arroyos que por la ciudad paſſan corren al poniẽte. En eſte valle por ſer frio d̃maſiado

Fig. 2. View of Cuzco, from Pedro Cieza de León, *Parte Primera de la Crónica del Perú* (Seville, 1553). Library of Congress.

Figs. 3–5. Schematic depictions of the evolution of the city of Rome, from Boissard, I Pars Romanae urbis topographiae (Frankfurt, 1597). Getty Center, Resource Collections.

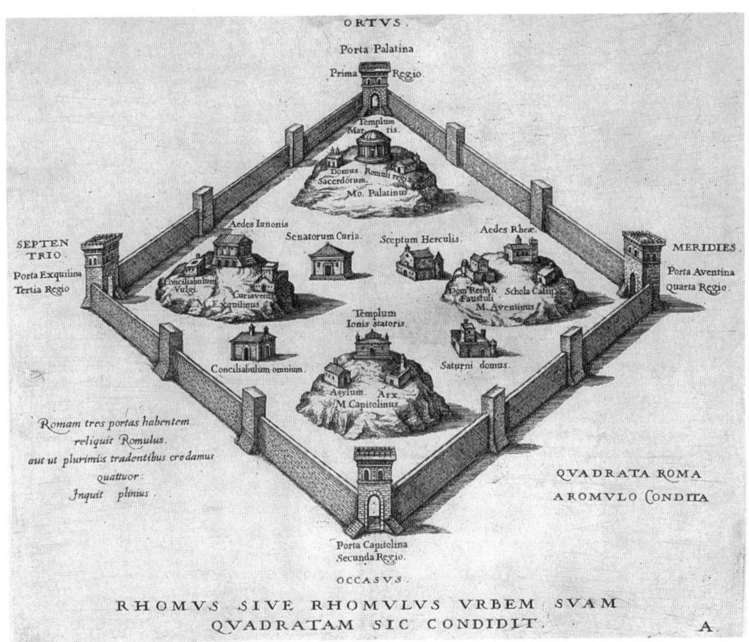

Fig. 3. "Rhomus or Rhomulus founded his square city in this way."

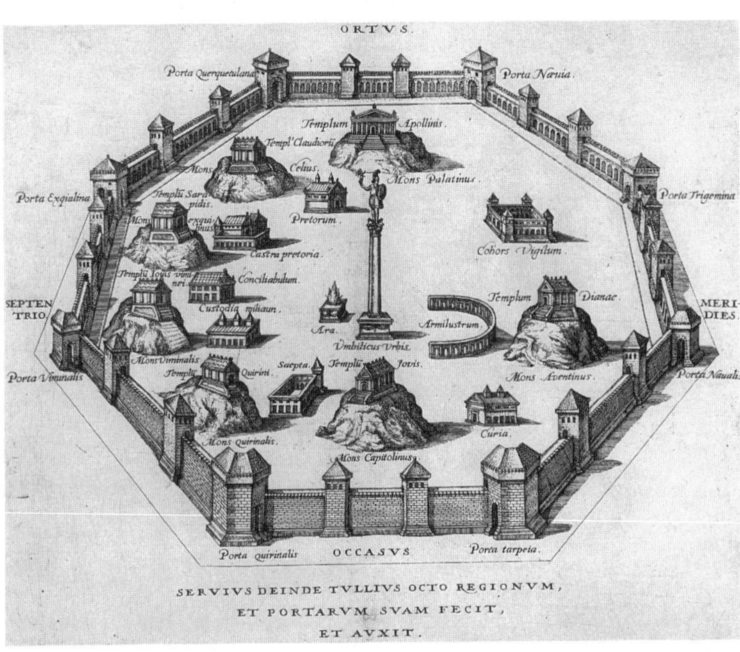

Fig. 4. "Later, Servius Tullius raised his city with eight regions and gates, and increased it."

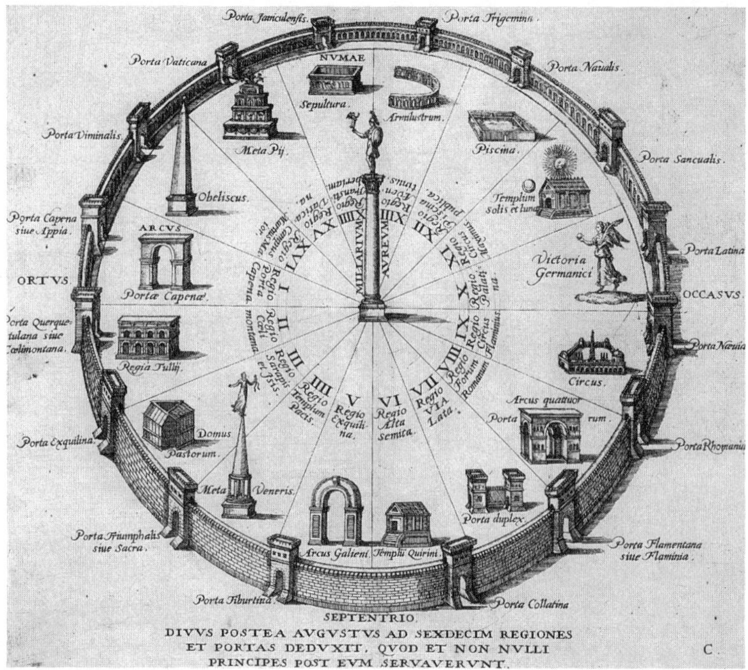

Fig. 5. "Finally, the divinized Augustus increased it to sixteen regions and gates. And after him, several emperors preserved it in this form."

ancient sources. De Bry's accompanying images, however, do not describe Roman topography in any realistic sense.

De Bry's primary aspiration in designing these plates was not to create a naturalistic representation of different phases of construction in ancient Rome, but rather to make clear to the viewer certain principles in the city's evolution. To supplement these schematic images, de Bry produced two spatially accurate perspective maps of ancient and contemporary Rome (figs. 6 and 7).[9] Spatially accurate maps and views of Cuzco and other American and European cities proliferated in the later sixteenth and seventeenth centuries (fig. 8). Indeed, realism in the representation of cities in due course prevailed over schematization and became the norm.[10]

Nonetheless, these parallels in the depiction of Rome and Cuzco should not be taken too far, because the archaeological and historical study of the two cities diverged radically. While from the sixteenth century onward Roman streets and buildings have been subjected to an ever more detailed antiquarian and archaeological scrutiny, this has not been the case in Cuzco. The labors of a small number of local *eruditi* investigating the Inca past of Cuzco is not comparable to the passionate professionalism of generations of scholars and archaeologists who spent

Figs. 6 and 7. Topographical maps of Rome in different eras, juxtaposed, from Boissard, *I Pars Romanae urbis topographiae* (Frankfurt, 1597). Getty Center, Resource Collections.

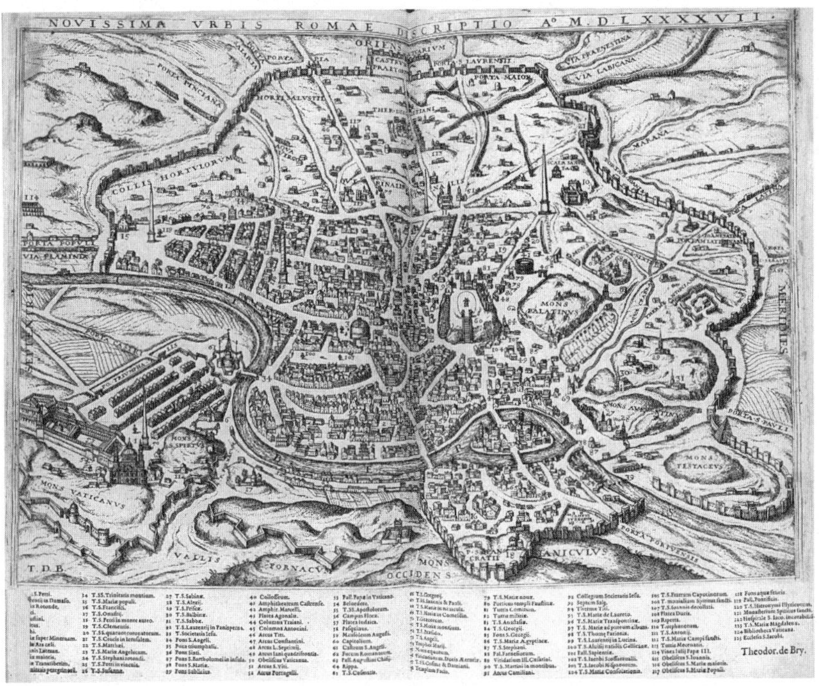

Fig. 6. Rome in the late sixteenth century.

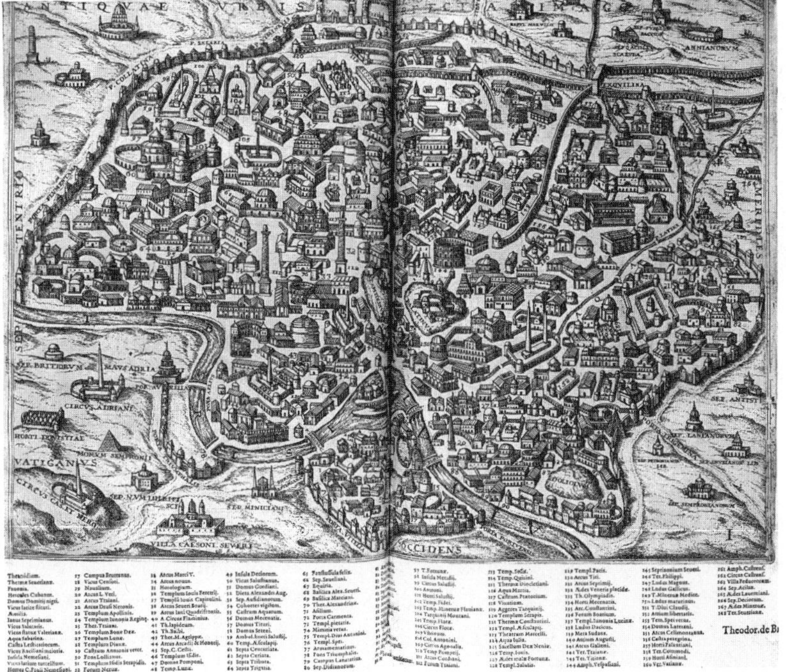

Fig. 7. Ancient Rome.

Fig. 8. The center of Cuzco in 1650, viewed from the cathedral, the roof of which appears at the lower edge. A procession headed by the image of Christ of the Earthquake appears in the main square. Church of El Triunfo, Cuzco.

their lives scouring texts and sites for details of the Roman past (figs. 9 and 10).[11] Cuzco, for all its splendor during almost three centuries of Spanish rule in Peru, was the capital of a defeated civilization. More important, unlike Rome, Cuzco represented a civilization that was not accessible to Europeans through a long-established learned tradition. Put differently, what Europeans might learn about Cuzco in particular and about America in general had to be translated or transposed into a familiar framework before it could be understood and absorbed.

One such framework was classical antiquity, which existed not only in the minds of scholars: Pedro Sancho, hardly a hero of the pen, compared the edifices of Cuzco to the Roman aqueduct of Segovia, which he thought had been built by the demigod Hercules, and to the Roman fortifications of Tarragona.[12] And Pedro Cieza de León, one of the greatest of all Inca experts, who was familiar with the writings of classical historians, was reminded in the Andes of exemplary European buildings and sometimes resorted to Roman religious institutions to explain those of the Incas. He thus thought that the women who were chosen by the Incas to serve the Sun resembled the Roman vestal virgins.[13] This same suggestion was later taken up by scholars, among them Justus Lipsius.[14] Historians other than Cieza likewise found in the Americas various reminders of the ancient Mediterranean.

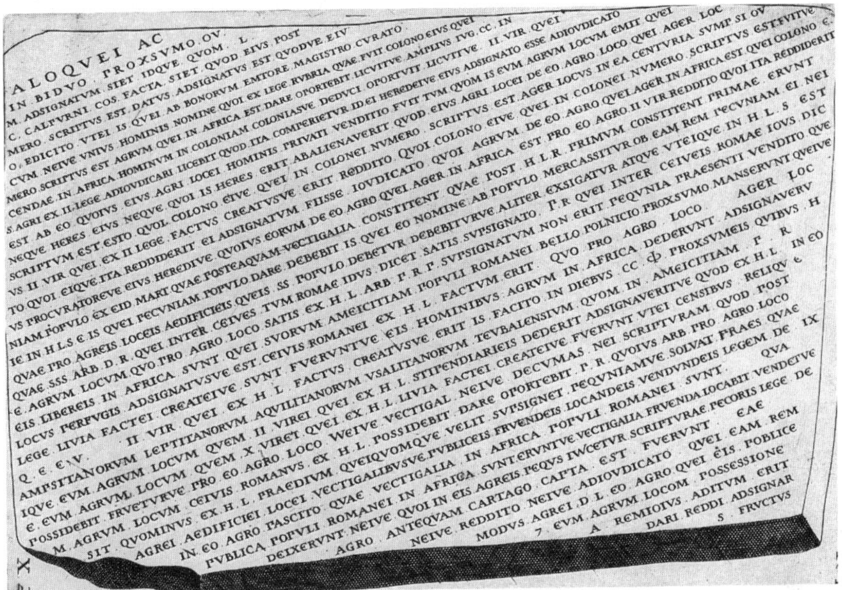

Fig. 9. Part of the Roman agrarian law of 111 B.C.E., engraving of a bronze tablet that is now lost. This copy from Boissard, *I Pars Romanae urbis topographiae* (Frankfurt, 1597), constitutes a crucial part of modern reconstructions of the inscription. Getty Center, Resource Collections.

Comparisons between Inca or Aztec and Greco-Roman deities, between Greco-Roman architecture and religious celebrations and their counterparts in the American present, and between Greco-Roman and American burial customs and modes of sacrifice all multiplied in the course of the sixteenth and seventeenth centuries, and not only in works focusing specifically on America.[15]

In 1556, for example, Vincenzo Cartari published in Venice an illustrated manual of the deities of classical antiquity for the use of writers and painters. He mentioned in passing the idols of peoples inhabiting the "islands" recently found by the Spanish but for the rest adhered to his main theme.[16] The new edition of Cartari's work that was published in 1615, however, contained a short supplement by Lorenzo Pignoria about the gods of Mexico and Japan. As Pignoria pointed out, the illustrations were derived from Mexican codices and from Japanese religious images that had reached Italian collections.[17] The engraver, moreover, studied his models carefully and thus succeeded in conveying a realistic impression of them (figs. 11 and 12).[18] Nonetheless, these foreign deities, for all their distinct visual identity, did not supply Pignoria with any significantly new information about hitherto unknown religions but instead confirmed what was already known. Vincenzo Cartari had accepted from Herodotus and Plato the widely approved opin-

In domo Card. Cæsij
47
L. CORNELIVS SCIPIO OREITVS
V. C. AVGVR TAVROBOLIVM
SIVE CREOBOLIVM FECIT
DIE III. KAL. MART.
TVSCO ET ANVLLINO COS.
G

Fig. 10. Altar honoring the mother of the gods, Cybele, riding a lion chariot, and her lover, Attis, standing under a tree. The altar is now in the Vatican Museum. Boissard, *I Pars Romanae urbis topographiae* (Frankfurt, 1597). Getty Center, Resource Collections.

ion that the Greeks had learned about their gods from the Egyptians. For Pignoria it followed that the gods of Mexico and Japan were also, somehow or other, derived from those of Egypt.[19]

These opinions regarding the common origin of all pagan deities in remote antiquity converged with a related theory regarding their meaning. Like many of his contemporaries,[20] Cartari thought that the gods of classical antiquity, their appearance, powers, and doings, however strange, were so many pointers to hid-

Fig. 11. Lorenzo Pignoria's portrait of the Aztec deity Tonacatecuhtli, inspired by an illustrated codex from Mexico that had reached Rome during the sixteenth century. Pignoria in Vincenzo Cartari, *Le vere e nove imagini* (Padua, 1615). Getty Center, Resource Collections.

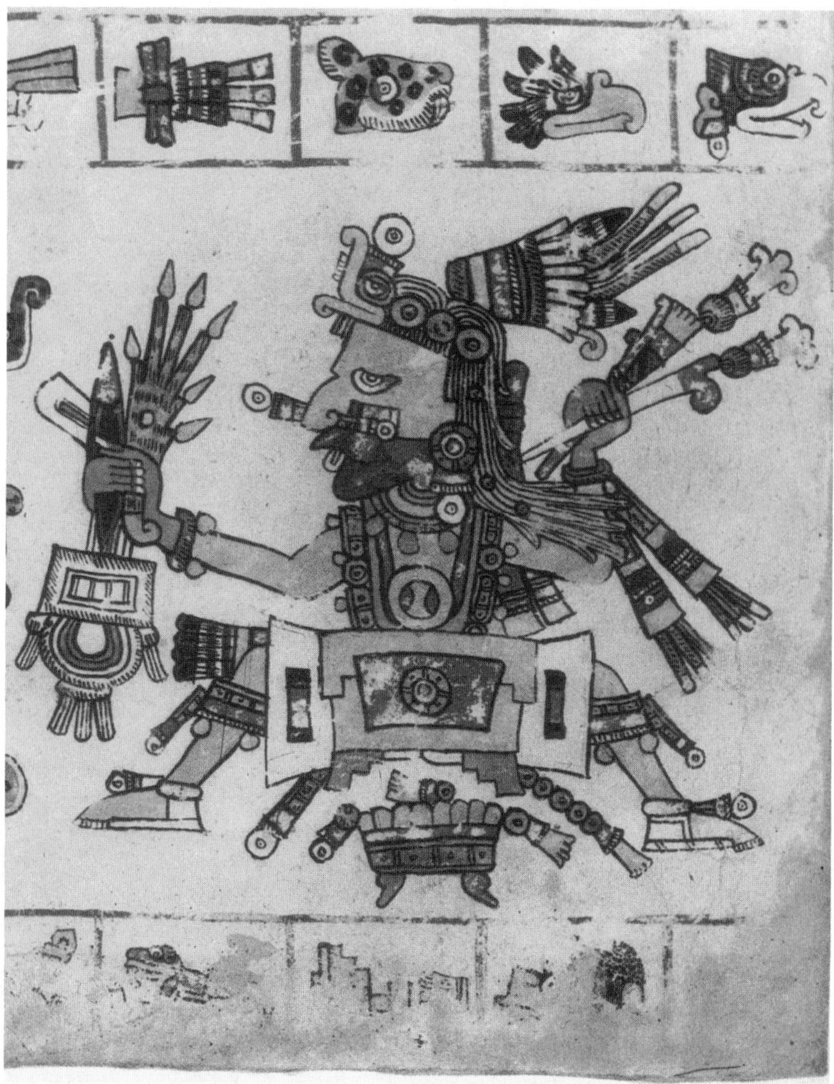

Fig. 12. Tonacatecuhtli, the Aztec lord of life and nourishment, as depicted in the Codex Borgia, fol. 61.

den theological and philosophical truths. The two-faced Janus of the Romans (fig. 13) was thus a representation of the natural and divine intelligences that live in the human soul, while the Roman Juno not only was goddess of sky and air and mistress of kingdoms but also embodied virtue (fig. 14).[21] Pignoria extended this theory regarding the theological significance of the gods of classical antiquity to the gods of Mexico and Japan, who also enshrined, for all that they were false gods, aspects of true religion. The Mexican creator was some kind of triad and adum-

De gli Antichi 35

Imagini diGiano inteſo ancora per il Sole, per il Tempo, per il Dio dell'anno, & della pace, ſignificano ancora li duoi lumi dell'anima noſtra, il lume diuino & il lume naturale.

C 2

Fig. 13. "Images of Janus, which by virtue of also representing the Sun, Time, the God of the year and peace, furthermore represent the two lights of the human soul, the divine light and the light of nature." Vincenzo Cartari, *Le vere e nove imagini* (Padua, 1615). Getty Center, Resource Collections.

De gli Antichi. 161

Imagini di Giunone Lucina & della Dea Siria de Hieropoli nell'Assiria, che è vn'istessa con Giunone, & delli vccelli à lei sacrati, significanti Giunone esser regina del Cielo, dominatrice dell'aria, signora de regni, & delle ricchezze. Questa fù intesa ancora per la virtù .

L

Fig. 14. "Images of Juno Lucina and of the Syrian goddess from Hierapolis in Assyria, who is one and the same as Juno, and of the birds sacred to her, which show that Juno is queen of the sky, rules over the air, and is mistress of kingdoms and of riches. She also represented virtue." Vincenzo Cartari, *Le vere e nove imagini* (Padua, 1615). Getty Center, Resource Collections.

Figs. 15–19. The hidden truths to be discovered in religions from all parts of the world.

Fig. 15. Divine messenger announcing the birth of the Aztec deity Quetzalcoatl. Lorenzo Pignoria in Vincenzo Cartari, *Le vere e nove imagini* (Padua, 1615). Getty Center, Resource Collections.

brated the Christian Trinity. The birth of the god Quetzalcoatl had been announced to his virgin mother by a figure who reminded Pignoria of the angel Gabriel (figs. 15 and 16). And the Japanese venerated a statue which evoked in Pignoria a sense of "reverence and I do not know what kind of devotion," because this statue conjured up in his mind's eye representations of the Virgin Mary (figs. 17, 18, and 19).[22]

Pignoria's speculations rested on precedents both ancient and recently formed. In late antiquity, Christian exegetes of the Bible had been faced with the task of explaining stories recounted in the book of Genesis to readers of Homer and the classical historians, who presented profoundly divergent ideas of humanity's origins and early history. Given that from a Christian vantage point the Bible was in the first instance to be interpreted literally or historically, Christian apologists insisted that all human beings were descendants of Adam and of the sons and

Fig. 16. Fra Angelico, *Annunciation.* Note the gesture of the angel Gabriel, which is replicated in Lorenzo Pignoria's depiction of the Aztec divine messenger (fig. 15). Museo Diocesano, Cortona.

Fig. 17. Personification of one of the aspects of a Buddha making the gesture of enlightenment. Twelfth century, painted wood. Chuson-ji, Hiraizumi, Iwate Prefecture, Japan.

Fig. 18. Japanese religious image, brought to Rome by missionaries, as depicted by Lorenzo Pignoria. The Buddhist gesture of enlightenment (seen in fig. 17) was reformulated by Pignoria into the Christian gesture of hands joined in prayer. Aureoles of flames and disk halo, customary in Buddhist iconography, appear to have reminded Pignoria of the mandorla of flaming rays that often surrounded images of the Virgin Mary (as in fig. 19, for example). The crown worn by Pignoria's figure can be compared to both the Buddha's crown and that worn by Mary as queen of heaven. Vincenzo Cartari, *Le vere e nove imagini* (Padua, 1615). Getty Center, Resource Collections.

Fig. 19. Virgin Mary standing on the moon and "clothed" in the sun, as seen by John in Rev. 12:1. Woodcut from Augsburg, ca. 1480. National Gallery of Art, Washington D.C.

daughters of Noah who peopled the earth after the Deluge. Other, nonbiblical accounts of floods and first origins were integrated into a chronology that began with the Creation, while subsequent events of biblical and gentile history figured in parallel chronological tables.[23] In this context, at the same time, Christians interpreted the writings of pagan philosophers, in particular those of Plato, as a *praeparatio evangelica*, a preparation for Christ.[24]

This late antique theory of the religious evolution of humanity was reaffirmed in the sixteenth century, although in a modified form. Spanish friars discovered in Mexico and Peru, so they thought, fragments of the story of Creation and of Noah's Flood as told in Genesis. Similarly, the Calvinist missionary Jean de Léry considered the myths that the Tupinamba of Brazil told him in about 1557 regarding a primal flood to contain traces of the story of Noah. Rather than attempting to devise chronologies correlating such events with what happened in the Old World, Europeans instead resorted to the thesis that the Indians had forgotten all but a few episodes in their history, but that these episodes were sufficient to prove their descent from Adam and Noah. Journeying from their original habitat in the eastern Mediterranean, so the theory ran, human beings had gradually forgotten their history and the worship of one God, which Adam, who had beheld his creator face to face, bequeathed to his descendants.[25] True religion was thus contaminated by idolatrous accretions, while the memory of historical events recorded in Genesis was transformed into myths of first origins such as Europeans heard in Mexico, Peru, and Brazil.

Before long, a New Testament supplement to this schema of American history and religion emerged, in that Europeans believed they were finding in the Americas traces of the preaching of one of Christ's original apostles.[26] Crosses were discovered in Mexico, Yucatan, and Peru. Jean de Léry likewise believed that the Christian message had reached America at some earlier time, in fulfillment of the psalmist's saying that "their sound has gone out to all the earth, and their words to the ends of the world."[27] In Peru, half a century later, the Augustinian friar Antonio de la Calancha explicitly included the Indians in biblical history and prophecy and argued that their conversion had been anticipated by Christ himself, who was facing westward, toward America, when he died on the cross.[28] Pignoria's parallels between Christian iconography and the religious imagery of Mexico and Japan thus rested on a broad basis of missionary experience. Indeed, in the course of the seventeenth century an entire scholarly industry came into existence tracing the ancestries of strange deities, including those of America, back to deities who had been worshipped in the ancient Mediterranean, and especially in Egypt (fig. 20).[29] So, far from modifying or compromising the long-established diffusionist theory of human social, cultural, and religious evolution throughout the world, the emergence of America on European intellectual horizons reinvigorated this theory and endowed it with much greater range.

Fig. 20. A set of deities of the Old World, which, according to François Lafitau, were related to each other and corresponded to deities also found in the Americas: an Egyptian Isis seated on a lotus flower; Chinese "Isis" on a heliotrope (compare the lotus of the Egyptian Isis); statue of the sun god, purportedly from the Via Appia in Rome; and another Chinese "Isis" with a solar face reminiscent of the face of the sun god from the Via Appia. Lafitau, *Moeurs des sauvages Amériquains* (Paris, 1724). Getty Center, Resource Collections.

From an American vantage point, however, the theory had shortcomings, because it could not accommodate the full complexity of the continent's history. The different chronologies of Mexico and Peru, the sheer diversity of American languages, and the difficulty of accounting for the manner in which Amerindians might have reached their different habitats were hard to fit into a unitary world history. Much of the American evidence thus had to be reshaped if it was to match the diffusionist scheme of things.

In Peru, for example, Francisco Pizarro's Spaniards encountered a religious world that had changed profoundly in the wake of recent Inca expansion and was to be transformed even further in the course of Spanish conquest and settlement. The invaders learned quickly that the Incas worshipped both the Sun and a group of creator deities described as Viracocha. There was also the god Pachacamac, "maker of the world," whose huge sanctuary on the coast near Lima was despoiled in 1532 by one of the Pizarro brothers. Finally, Spaniards in Peru noticed the prevalence of sacred objects described in Quechua as *huaca* that fitted the Christian conception of an idol only with difficulty.[30]

Within less than a generation, however, the Andean supernatural universe had been reformulated to match European conceptions of early human history. Around 1550 the conquistador Juan de Betanzos heard Andean accounts of first beginnings in which, as he understood it, both the Sun and Viracocha figured as creators. He resolved the contradiction he perceived in these accounts by suggesting that the Indians told the story of creation confusedly, having with passage of time forgotten its monotheistic import.[31] Among the several Spaniards to interpret Andean myths of creation according to these same guidelines was the great Dominican missionary Bartolomé de Las Casas.[32] But he evaluated Amerindian contributions to religious understanding in a much more positive light than many of his contemporaries and viewed Inca religion in particular in the late antique sense as a *praeparatio evangelica*, or preparation for the gospel. In his eyes, therefore, the Inca Sun cult, focused as it was on the most exalted of God's visible creatures, augured the worship of Christ the Sun of Justice in the Andes.[33] A few years later, the Italian Girolamo Benzoni published an account of his travels in Peru, where Andeans atop a classically inspired pyramid are depicted worshipping the Sun (figs. 21 and 22).[34] In such an interpretative context, it was not possible to think about the changing and often conflictive relationships between Viracocha, the Inca Sun, Pachacamac, and other Andean deities that resonated through the myths that Spaniards were told in Cuzco and on the Pacific coast of Peru in the mid-sixteenth century.[35]

In visual terms also, European concepts supplanted Andean concepts of deity. The Inca cult statue of the Sun which was revered in Cuzco's temple of the Sun known as Coricancha[36] was sculpted in gold and represented a young boy. The

Fig. 21. Andean worshippers of the Sun stand on a small pyramid, the prototype of which was to be found not so much in the Andes as in Europe. Girolamo Benzoni, *La historia del Mondo Nuovo* (Venice, 1565). Getty Center, Resource Collections.

invading Spaniards who visited Cuzco in 1533 saw this statue being placed on a gold throne in the courtyard of Coricancha and receiving sacrifices of food and drink. They also observed that at night the statue was "put to bed" in a room set aside for this purpose.[37] Later the Spaniards learned that inside the statue were preserved the hearts of deceased Inca rulers.[38] Las Casas, however, thought that the Inca Sun consisted of a golden disk representing a face with rays, "exactly as we depict it ourselves."[39] Some fifty years later, the Inca Garcilaso de la Vega repeated this assertion in his influential *Comentarios reales de los Incas.* The visualization of the Inca Sun as a golden face with rays found many supporters down to the eighteenth century, when Bernard Picart, in his encyclopedic work on the world's religions, published an engraving of an Inca ruler making his sacrifice to precisely such a sun (fig. 23).[40] This transformation of the Inca Sun into an image with a European iconographic ancestry underpinned its integration into a European hierarchy of worshipful beings that had its roots in Greco-Roman astrology (fig. 24).[41] Inca nobles in colonial Peru were aware of this new dimension in the character of their

117
Ad portam Oſtienſem
e regione montis TEſtacci.
annexum monibus.
C. CESTIVS L. F POB. EPVLO. P.R.
TR. PL. VII. VIR EPVLONVM.
OPVS ABSOLVTVM E TESTAMENTO DIEB. XXX
ARI ITRATV
PONTI PF. CLAMILAE HEREDIS ET POSTHI L.
D M
C. TERENTIO
C L S CORONI

Fig. 22. Funerary pyramid of Cestius, Rome. Boissard, *I Pars Romanae urbis topographiae* (Frankfurt, 1597). Getty Center, Resource Collections.

Tom. VI. N° 29
L' YNCAS consacre son VAZE au SOLEIL.

Fig. 23. Inca ruler dedicating a pitcher to the Inca Sun, which is represented by an image of European, not Andean, origin. Bernard Picart, *Cérémonies et coûtumes réligieuses des peuples idolâtres* (Amsterdam, 1735). Getty Center, Resource Collections.

ancestral deity and deployed the solar face as an emblem of their privileged status in Christian society (fig. 25). Even the Inca cult statue of the Sun appears to have been remembered, although in a new, Europeanized guise (figs. 26 and 27).[42]

These Peruvian developments were far from unique, in that evidence from all parts of the Americas appeared to lend support to the theory of primitive monotheism and the dispersion of all human beings from a single center after Noah's Flood.[43] Some aspects of Amerindian religious history and practice, however, constituted a tacit challenge to this theory.

Cieza de León, Las Casas, and Garcilaso all thought that the Incas had implemented a radical religious reform. Before the Incas, they maintained, Andean people had lived in a primitive polytheism, worshipping rocks, plants, and animals. Chaos in ideas about the nature of deity went hand in hand with social chaos, in that these early Andeans knew nothing of cities but lived in caves and on mountain tops in continuous fear of each other and the environment. This state of nature was brought to an end by the first Inca, who organized village settlements, introduced agriculture, and instituted the worship of an invisible creator alongside the worship of the Sun, whom he claimed as his own progenitor and protector.[44]

Fig. 24. Sun in the center of the zodiac. Sixth-century floor mosaic from the synagogue of Beth Alpha, Israel.

Such an account of early Andean religious history was incompatible with the supposition that the original knowledge of one God that Adam had passed on to his descendants had gradually been supplanted by the worship of idols.

To this difficulty Garcilaso added another. He was familiar with classifications of Andean idols in a hierarchy—ranging from the lower forms of being, such as rocks, plants, and animals, to the moon, sun, and stars—that missionaries had derived from the Bible and from classical philosophy. This order of being, Garcilaso felt, was not applicable to Inca and Andean ideas of the holy.[45] Instead, he produced a classification of Andean holy objects that was quite independent of European antecedents. There was in Inca religion no such thing as an idol in the European sense, Garcilaso argued. Rather, the Quechua term *huaca*, describing inter alia holy objects and places, referred in general to any exceptional thing, irrespective of whether its distinguishing feature was beauty, excellence, or ugli-

Fig. 25. Inca couple and attendants, from colonial Peru. The illustrator has slightly modified the attire worn by aristocratic Andeans of the colonial period, but the solar disk adorning the chest of the Inca lord also appears in colonial portrait paintings from Cuzco. Amédée François Frézier, *A Voyage to the South Sea* (London, 1735). Getty Center, Resource Collections.

Fig. 26. The captivity of Inca Tupa Amaru as depicted by the Andean historian Guaman Poma de Ayala, ca. 1613. The Inca is preceded by Spaniards, one of whom carries the cult image of the Inca Sun, represented both as a simple statuette and as a statuette circled in solar rays. As Guaman Poma appears to have understood, the original Inca cult image had no rays. But he thought it necessary to add a radiate version of the cult image, in order to depict its identity more explicitly and in accord with European conceptions. Guaman Poma de Ayala, *Nueva Crónica y buen Gobierno*. Royal Library, Copenhagen.

Fig. 27. Bronze statuette from colonial Peru. The gesture of the figure, hands clutched to the chest, recalls precolonial Inca statuettes, but the solar headgear reflects colonial ideas and iconographies. Peabody Museum, Harvard University. Photograph by Hillel Burger.

ness, holiness or the opposite.[46] To polarize the world into the sacred and the secular, and into sharply delineated boundaries between truth and error in the manner of many sixteenth-century Christians, was, so Garcilaso implied, to miss the point of Andean concepts of religion.

Finally, Garcilaso reviewed Andean and Inca myths of origins. In the opinion of some Spaniards, he observed, the four Inca brothers and their sisters who figured in the foundation myth of the Inca empire were proof that the story about Noah, his wife, and his three sons and their wives—about the four couples, that is, whom God had saved in the ark—was in some sense remembered in the Andes. Indeed, a set of quite detailed parallels could be constructed to correlate the Inca with the biblical story. Garcilaso enumerated these parallels, or as he termed them, "allegories," while at the same time questioning their validity. The Andean stories, he suggested, had best be accepted in their own right without reinterpretation.[47]

Garcilaso thus challenged—if only by implication—some key positions in European interpretations of Amerindian religions: first, the idea that an original monotheism of the first human beings had gradually declined into polytheism and idolatry; and second, the idea that, thanks to humanity's common origin after the Flood, basic religious concepts and some outline of the story of Genesis were remembered throughout the world. Yet, as Garcilaso knew very well, it was on the basis of precisely these propositions that early modern scholars and theologians affirmed the purposeful quality, uniqueness, and unity of God's creation.

Garcilaso countered the impact of the potentially heretical rejoinders that he formulated against these propositions in the preface of his work. Philosophers had considered the possibility of a plurality of worlds since classical antiquity,[48] and arguments favoring plurality had gained new force in the sixteenth century thanks to the discovery of America. But in theological terms the plurality of worlds was problematic because it compromised the uniqueness of salvation, which, in the aftermath of the Reformation, Catholics and Protestants reasserted with equal passion. This was why affirmations of the unity and uniqueness of the universe became a commonplace in American historiography,[49] and, in the preface to his *Comentarios reales*, Garcilaso added his voice to the chorus: "We begin by affirming that there is only one world, and although we speak of the Old World and the New World, it is because the latter has only recently been found, and not because there are two. . . . Those who persist in imagining that there are many worlds require no further reply beyond our allowing them to abide in their heretical imaginations until they are undeceived of them in hell."[50]

Garcilaso's history of the Incas became one of a handful of books about America that were translated into French and English and regularly consulted throughout Europe.[51] Among its many readers was, in the later seventeenth century, the

Parisian savant Bernard Fontenelle, who commented, as so many scholars had done earlier, on the similarity between Greek or Roman and Amerindian myths.[52] Nonetheless, there was a novel aspect to Fontenelle's point, in that he made explicit assertions that Garcilaso had only implied, and he did so even though they constituted a direct challenge to established Christian teaching.

Earlier historians of the Americas had selected for comment those Amerindian myths that invited comparison with stories from Genesis: myths about primal darkness being supplanted by light, about the creation of human beings, and above all, about deluge and restoration. Fontenelle, by contrast, drew attention to myths explaining causation in the course of nature, as, for example, the cause of rain and thunder. He thus compared Greek stories of nymphs and river gods, who in classical art were depicted pouring water from pitchers,[53] to an Inca myth explaining the cause of rain that he had read in Garcilaso. According to this myth, a princess living in the sky was wont to play with her little brother. From time to time the brother upset and broke the water pitcher that the princess carried, and this was when it rained on earth.[54] The prevalence in all places and periods of myths of this kind, which explained causation in the natural world,[55] drew Fontenelle's attention away from foundation myths supposedly documenting memories of humanity's common origins. The entire theory, he felt, had to be discarded.

Instead, according to Fontenelle, the beginnings of human history had to be considered in the light of "the ignorance of those first human beings" and their lack of "politesse."[56] It was only very gradually that humans were able to devise accurate explanations of natural and social events and to avoid divinizing forces of nature by endowing them with human characteristics so as to render them intelligible. A "Descartes of that distant age" of humanity would thus be satisfied that a river really did proceed from the water pitcher held by a deity, and in the stories that parents recounted to their children, observed reality fused spontaneously with reality created by the imagination.[57] It was in this way, not thanks to some long, drawn-out process of forgetting, that "human imagination created false divinities,"[58] who could only be discarded in the slow process of learning by experience.

What was true of the Greeks and Romans in classical antiquity was true of Amerindians, Lapps, and Africans in Fontenelle's own day.[59] Here also, Fontenelle reiterated a point that had been made before, but once again with a difference. Earlier writers had referred to classical antiquity to elucidate the Amerindian present or recent past, but Fontenelle made explicit the conclusion that had so far remained latent in these comparisons: that not all people originated in remote antiquity after the Deluge. Instead there were, as Fontenelle expressed it, "new peoples" such as the American Indians, whose spiritual and cultural development would unfold according to the same rules as that of the Greeks and Romans had done earlier.[60] It was due to this parallel development, whereby the effects of ignorance were always and everywhere the same,[61] rather than to the dispersion of peoples from a single center after Noah's Flood, that Amerindian religious ideas and practices resembled Greco-Roman ones.

In accord with his ideas on the origin and nature of pagan religions, Fontenelle was prepared to contemplate the possibility that there existed not only many autonomously evolving human cultures on earth but also many worlds, that planets and stars other than the earth were inhabited by intelligent beings. Such a proposition arose very cogently out of the knowledge of new planets and uncountable numbers of fixed stars at great distances from the earth that Galileo had sighted in his telescope. Fontenelle's speculation about other inhabited stars thus went hand in hand with the idea of an infinite universe that had been debated, on the basis of Galileo's discoveries, by Descartes and others not long before he was writing.[62] Here, however tentatively formulated, was the very cosmology that historians of the Americas, among them Garcilaso de la Vega, had sought to set aside for the preceding 150 years. In other respects also, the framework for understanding pagan religions that had been established by generations of scholars and biblical exegetes was being questioned during the later seventeenth century. In a work published in 1655 that Fontenelle may have known, Isaac La Peyrère argued that Adam had been the ancestor of the Jews only and that human beings had existed before Adam, even though the Bible had said almost nothing about them.[63] La Peyrère's thesis, topical as it was, generated much interest but was condemned by Jewish, Catholic, and Protestant authorities alike.[64] Among those to agree with it was Baruch Spinoza, who for reasons different from La Peyrère's viewed the Bible as a historical document comparable to other documents produced in societies similar to ancient Israel, and not as a text of universal history.[65]

Much erudition was deployed during subsequent decades to disprove propositions of this kind, and students of Amerindian religions continued to discover in these religions evidence of the historical accuracy and the divinely inspired quality of the Pentateuch and the Bible in general, and also of the unity and uniqueness of the world. It was with precisely this purpose that in 1724 the Jesuit François Lafitau, who had worked as a missionary in Canada for five years, published two illustrated volumes comparing the customs of American Indians to those of early humanity, especially in Egypt, Greece, and Rome.[66] The crux of his argument was that the pagan religions of the ancient Mediterranean, exactly like those of the Americas, reflected both the historical events and the God-given religious observances that had been described in the Bible.[67]

On the surface of things, Lafitau's was a deeply conservative book. Like Spanish missionaries in South and Central America who had written so as to render intelligible the beliefs and practices of the peoples to whom they were preaching, he rested much of his case on an analysis of myth. He collected, for example, a myth of origins told by the Iroquois, among whom he had worked as a missionary. In the beginning, when there was no earth, a woman living in the sky was seduced by the wolf-man, who lay in wait for her under a tree, and she was therefore expelled by the lord of heaven (fig. 28). Her fall from the sky was arrested by a sea turtle and an island came into existence, where the woman gave birth to two sons. In due course, the more warlike of these sons killed his brother. The woman was the ancestress of the Hurons and Iroquois. Kindred versions of this myth came, Lafitau believed, from Peru and Brazil. But more important in his mind were the myth's resonances with the Old World. "Through this myth," he wrote, "one seems to encounter the truth despite the thick darkness that envelops it. . . . One distinguishes the woman in the terrestrial paradise, the tree of the knowledge of good and evil (and) the temptation to which she had the misfortune to succumb. . . . One discovers here the wrath of God, who expelled our first ancestors from the garden of delights. . . . And finally one believes one finds here the murder of Abel killed by his brother Cain."[68] Lafitau also recognized in the Iroquois myth the expulsion of Ate or Strife from Mount Olympus as described in Homer's *Iliad*, while the Iroquois sea turtle represented the floating island of Delos on which the Greek goddess Leto had given birth to Apollo and Artemis. Moreover, the sea turtle led Lafitau to adduce evidence involving turtles from Indian and Egyptian religious monuments. All this demonstrated, he urged, the fact that the Iroquois, like Amerindians in general, shared historical memories—however much these were shrouded in legend—with the ancient nations of the Old World. This in turn was proof of the diffusion of humanity from one center, as suggested by a literal interpretation of Genesis.[69]

Amerindian customs and rituals told the same story, in Lafitau's eyes, as did the American continent's myths. Cults of a sacred fire among the Natchez Indians of Louisiana matched such cults in ancient Iran and elsewhere and constituted some reminiscence of the true God, who had been described in the Bible as a "consuming fire." This topic in turn led Lafitau to juxtapose, in the customary fashion, the vestal virgins of ancient Rome with the women chosen for the service of the divine Sun of the Incas, who in his mind resembled the "Virgins of the State" kept by the Iroquois.[70]

Lafitau was a careful reader of Garcilaso. The episodes he selected for comment included Garcilaso's account of Inca observances designed to bring lunar eclipses to an end. The Incas believed the moon to be fond of dogs, Garcilaso had written, because of "a certain service they had rendered her." During lunar eclipses, dogs were therefore tied up and beaten, in the hope that their lament would awaken the moon from the diseased sleep into which she was thought to have fallen, and which had brought about the eclipse. This story in turn reminded Lafitau of the Greek moon goddess, Diana, who also had dogs. According to another theory that

Fig. 28. The diffusion of religious ideas according to François Lafitau: the ancestress of the Iroquois, expelled from the sky, lands on a sea turtle; image of the Egyptian Harpocrates, from Rome, with turtle between his feet; the Greek goddess Venus on a sea turtle, an image Lafitau claimed to have derived from the Greek scholar-traveler Pausanias; Vishnu, from India, metamorphosed into a tortoise; "hieroglyphic hand," with a tortoise as a symbol of earth; Chinese dragon engendered by a tortoise. Lafitau, *Moeurs des sauvages Amériquains* (Paris, 1724). Getty Center, Resource Collections.

Lafitau encountered, the moon was swallowed up by a dragon when in eclipse (figs. 29 and 30). This creature evoked in his mind the seven-headed monster which the author of the book of Revelation saw threatening the lady clothed in the sun and standing on the moon; she, in turn, according to Catholic exegesis of the passage, represented the Virgin Mary (see fig. 19).[71] Once more, pagan ritual mysteriously enshrined the doctrine of the true religion.

Resemblances of this kind between Amerindian and ancient European pagan religions had been observed by historians of Amerindian religions from the beginning. Lafitau's work is thus firmly rooted in a stable scholarly tradition that in his day was already over two centuries old. During this period, the American continent had remained deeply permeable to those comparisons with Europe that made it possible to incorporate America within preexisting cognitive categories. Amerindian myth thus tended to be described in the framework posited by the Bible, while the study of ritual followed the categories established by humanist scholars investigating Greco-Roman paganism.[72] Nonetheless, for all Lafitau's conservatism, his work opened a new phase in understanding Amerindian religions.

Lafitau's insistence on the god-given origin of all religious belief and practice, his search for hidden traces of divine precept within the customs of the Huron and Iroquois Indians whom he sought to serve as a missionary, heightened his acumen as an observer. He was therefore less inclined than his predecessors to find among Indians further examples of a theme that was already well understood, namely, the corruption of original truths by idolatrous accretions. Hence, even if a certain religious practice did not fit into his scheme, he was capable of giving it detailed scrutiny. Topics such as transvestism among the Sioux, the possibility of matriliny among the Iroquois and Hurons, the Carib ritual of initiating diviners, and the interpretation given by members of different North American Indian nations to their dreams thus engaged Lafitau's curiosity and interest.[73]

Earlier missionaries had observed Amerindian religious customs and beliefs the more effectively to replace them with Christianity. Lafitau also was a missionary, but his fascination with deciphering the human record of divine precept appears to have circumscribed his commitment to the project of evangelization.[74] Indeed, he regretted the presence of Europeans among the Indians whom he studied because it disrupted their customs and traditions. Authentic traditions, Lafitau noted, could only be recorded from evidence collected among "peoples newly discovered."[75]

Lafitau might have paused at Fontenelle's idea that there existed recently formed peoples whose culture and religion matched that of nations of the past at an early phase of their development.[76] For this idea compromised the old hypothesis that all humans were descended from Adam and Noah but had, for the most part, forgotten this fact, thus devoting themselves to false worship. Lafitau did, however,

Fig. 29. American Indians during a lunar eclipse (top) according to François Lafitau; a dragon is waiting to swallow the moon, while Indians make noise to alert the moon to her danger. Lafitau thought this observance was ultimately derived from the vision of John in Revelation (bottom), according to which the lady (representing the Virgin Mary) who stood on the moon and was clothed in the sun was threatened by a seven-headed dragon, while her child was being removed to heaven. Lafitau, *Moeurs des sauvages Amériquains* (Paris, 1724). Getty Center, Resource Collections.

Fig. 30. A dragon about to devour the moon in eclipse. Woodcut from the collection of the German physician and humanist Hartmann Schedel. The image demonstrates that the belief that the moon in eclipse is devoured by a dragon, attributed by Lafitau to Amerindians, was in effect at home in Europe.

formulate his thesis of the nature of paganism in such a way as to take stock of the kind of objection against the established view that was raised by Fontenelle. This was why he repeatedly explained how, by means of cross-cultural comparisons, the divine precepts that with lapse of time had come to be encoded in all manner of religious observances could be discerned and deciphered.[77] The errors contained in the pagan religions of America and the Old World therefore interested Lafitau much less than did the multifarious traces that these religions revealed of God's original behests to his creatures. His ideas in this regard closely resembled those of the early Christian apologists who believed that pagan religion and Greek philosophy, in particular Platonism, had in some respect prepared the way for Christ's gospel. But the late antique legacy did not pass to the eighteenth century unchanged, for where in late antiquity human insight in philosophy and theology was conceptualized as part of a converse between God and human beings, Lafitau was more inclined to view human expressions of worship and belief in their own right and in isolation from divine initiatives. The idea that divine providence was actively engaged in guiding human beings to the truth was thus beginning to be transformed into a theory of natural religion, into the idea that, with due allowance being made for a certain skeptical reserve, human cognition could arrive at the fact that the deity exists.[78]

Lafitau was one of the first Europeans to interest himself in primitive humanity in its own right, or almost in its own right. A century earlier, the Indians of North America and Brazil, those beyond the frontiers of the former Aztec and Inca empires, had often been viewed as utter barbarians unworthy of attention were it not that, in accord with divine precept, their souls also deserved to be saved.[79] Lafitau, by contrast, did not discern a lack of civilization among the Indians whom he sought to convert, and he did not think of a hierarchy of American cultures, with Incas and Aztecs at the peak and the Indians of Brazil, Florida, and Canada at the bottom. Instead, he tended to conflate into one single whole what he read about Aztec and Inca religion and what he observed himself in Canada.

Although such conflation had occurred earlier—for example, in Theodore de Bry's famous volume about America—it became much more prevalent in the eighteenth century. Myths and rituals, customs and costumes of the Incas and Aztecs were assimilated into those of North American Indians. As a result, the Incas and Aztecs came to be imbued with an aura of the primitive they had not possessed earlier. In the engravings of Bernard Picart, published in 1735, we thus see scantily dressed Incas beating their dogs and raising a cacophony in order to terminate a lunar eclipse (fig. 31). The accompanying text paraphrases the account of such events by Garcilaso de la Vega that Lafitau had also used. Elsewhere, Picart depicted half-naked Incas in leaf skirts with feathers on their heads attending funerals (fig. 32).[80] The first Spaniards in Peru, by contrast, had commented on the excellent cloth worn by Andean people. Like the Incas, so Aztecs mourning the passing of one epoch and rejoicing at the inauguration of another are clothed in feathers and leaf skirts (fig. 33) which bear little resemblance to the garments they did wear, and, it must be added, not much resemblance to the attire of North American Indians.[81]

What Picart's engravings do illustrate, however, are European concepts of primitive human beings and their religious practices that did so much to motivate subsequent ethnographic inquiries (fig. 34). By now, the idea that polytheism was humanity's original religion was coming to be taken for granted. As Hume stated in his *Natural History of Religion*, first published in 1757, "The savage tribes of

Figs. 31–33. Bernard Picart's vision of Amerindian dress. Note especially leaf skirts, loin cloths, and feather headdresses, invented by earlier European illustrators on whose work Picart relied. Picart, *Cérémonies et coûtumes réligieuses des peuples idolâtres* (Amsterdam, 1735). Getty Center, Resource Collections.

Fig. 31. Half-naked Incas bewailing a lunar eclipse.

America, Africa and Asia are all idolaters. Not a single exception to this rule." By way of refuting the earlier theories of humanity's first religion which we have examined, Hume continued: "Adam, rising at once, in paradise, and in the full perfection of his faculties, would naturally, as represented by Milton, be astonished at the glorious appearances of nature, the heavens, the air, the earth, his own organs and members; and would be led to ask, whence this wonderful scene arose. But a barbarous necessitous animal (such as man is on the first origin of society), pressed by such numerous wants and passions, has no leisure to admire the regular face of nature, or make enquiries concerning the cause of those objects to which from his infancy he has been gradually accustomed."[82] The development of religion was thus seen to go hand in hand with that of society and culture, without the need to postulate the existence of a rational and monotheistic religion at the beginning of history when, according to the book of Genesis, Adam saw God.

As a result, the development of human societies could be examined independently of the constraints of revealed religion, as Fontenelle had begun to do.

Tom VI. Nº 34
HONNEURS FUNÉBRES, rendus aux GRANDS, du Perou apres leur mort.

Fig. 32. Incas, again mostly unclothed, attending funerals.

Desolation des MEXICAINS *à la fin du* SIECLE.

Rejouïssances des MEXICAINS, *au commencement du* SIECLE.

Fig. 33. Aztecs mourning the passing of the old era (top) and greeting the new one (bottom).

LE GRAND SACRIFICE des CANADIENS à QUITCHI-MANITOU
ou le GRAND ESPRIT.

Fig. 34. Indians from Canada making sacrifice to the Great Spirit. The image conveys the nobility and simplicity of outlook that many eighteenth-century Europeans saw manifest in primitive religion. Bernard Picart, *Cérémonies et coûtumes réligieuses des peuples idolâtres* (Amsterdam, 1735). Getty Center, Resource Collections.

Theories about the nature of human understanding continued to play a role in these inquiries, although, as we have seen, the content and purpose of these theories changed. The study of Greco-Roman antiquity, on the other hand, progressed, as it had done in the sixteenth and seventeenth centuries, much less speculatively. What mattered here was the recovery and analysis of the physical remains of classical antiquity, and, increasingly, philology.[83] The reasons for juxtaposing and comparing Greco-Roman and Amerindian religions during the sixteenth and seventeenth centuries had been for the most part theological. With the abeyance of those reasons in the eighteenth century, the two branches of scholarship drew apart, each defined by its own distinct traditions of inquiry and methods of proof. And finally, it must be said with a certain sadness that Cuzco, the Rome of its world as Garcilaso had described it,[84] was no match in the world of learning, as construed during the period here surveyed, for the Rome of the Romans.

ACKNOWLEDGMENTS

I would like to thank Amos Funkenstein for discussing some of the themes of this essay with me and for helping me to see—so I hope—the forest as well as the trees.

NOTES

1. This assessment differs from that of Frank Manuel, who in a now classic book argued that information from the Americas did lead Europeans to reconsider their own ancient past; see Frank Manuel, *The Eighteenth Century Confronts the Gods* (Cambridge, 1956), 18–20: "The juxtaposition of ancient and modern cults gave birth to a new perception of Greco-Roman religion," so that "pagan religion became a living flesh and blood reality which was mirrored in contemporary barbarism" in the Americas. See also ibid., 28, 43.

2. J. H. Elliott, *The Old World and the New, 1492–1650* (Cambridge, 1970); see also his "Renaissance Europe and America: A Blunted Impact?," in *First Images of America: The Impact of the New World on the Old*, ed. Fredi Chiappelli, 2 vols. (Berkeley, 1976), 1:11–26. See, further, Anthony Grafton, with April Shelford and Nancy Siraisi, *New Worlds, Ancient Texts: The Power of Tradition and the Shock of Discovery* (Cambridge, Mass., 1992), whose nuanced discussion of the uses to which ancient texts were put sheds new light on the complexity of the "canon" on which the European learned tradition was built; cf. below, note 83.

3. However, one should note that some good bibliographical tools were available to seventeenth-century scholars interested in the Americas. In 1629 the first of several editions of Antonio León Pinelo's *Biblioteca* appeared, listing manuscripts and printed books bearing on the Americas. Other bibliographic compilations followed, so that we are relatively well informed as to what was available in Europe about American themes at what time, where, and to whom. See *El Epitome de Pinelo: Primera bibliografía del Nuevo Mundo*, ed. A.

Millares Carlo (Washington, D.C., 1958). The modern literature is growing fast. See T. R. Adams, "Some Bibliographical Observations about the Relationship between the Discovery of America and the Invention of Printing," in Chiappelli, *First Images*, 2:526–36; R. Hirsch, "Printed Reports on the Early Discoveries and Their Reception," in ibid., 537–60; see also Julie Greer Johnson, *The Book in the Americas: The Role of Books and Printing in the Development of Culture and Society in Colonial Latin America, Catalogue of an Exhibition* (Providence, 1988). John Alden and Dennis Channing Landis, eds., *European Americana: A Chronological Guide to Works Printed in Europe Relating to the Americas, 1493–1750* (New York, 1980–94), is a most valuable guide.

4. See, on these authors, Philip Ainsworth Means, *Biblioteca Andina* (New Haven, 1928; Detroit, 1973). This useful book has still not been superseded.

5. See Bernadette Bucher, *Icon and Conquest: A Structural Analysis of the Illustrations of de Bry's Great Voyages* (Chicago, 1981).

6. Pedro Sancho's account of the conquest of Peru survives only in the Italian translation that appeared in Gian Battista Ramusio, *Navigationi et Viaggi*, vol. 3 (Venice, 1606; Amsterdam, 1967), 333–45. It is here that our illustration appears, facing p. 344. For a similar view of Cuzco, related to the preceding, see J. H. Parry, "Depicting a New World," in *The Early Illustrated Book: Essays in Honor of Lessing Rosenwald*, ed. S. Hindman (Washington, D.C., 1982), 136–48, at 141 with fig. 2, reproducing Braun and Hogenberg's rendering of Cuzco in their *Civitates Orbis Terrarum*. Parry does not mention Ramusio's picture. He highlights "the vast visual indifference of the New World Spaniards. They could not even—town dwellers as they were by preference—describe the appearance of Amerindian towns." The problem, however, lay with illustrators working in Europe who had never seen Amerindian cities and could thus form no appropriate visual image to match the often quite detailed Spanish descriptions, which have guided much subsequent topographical and archaeological research; see, in particular, E. George Squier, *Peru: Incidents of Travel and Exploration in the Land of the Incas* (London, 1877). Ramusio's picture, despite its fictional quality, was influential; versions of it are reproduced by Theodore de Bry, *Americae Pars sexta* (Frankfurt, 1596), 13, and unfoliated fold-out plate following 108; similar versions appear in the English translation of Garcilaso de la Vega, *The Royal Commentaries of Peru in Two Parts . . . Illustrated with Sculptures . . . Rendered into English by Sir Paul Rycaut Kt.* (London, 1688), facing pp. 13 and 550. Arnoldus Montanus, *De Nieuwe en onbekende Weereld: of Beschryving van America en't Zuid-land . . .* (Amsterdam, 1671), unnumbered engraving captioned "Cusco," had also seen Ramusio's picture or a copy of it.

7. Pedro Cieza de León, *Parte Primera de la Crónica del Perú* (Seville, 1553), ed. F. Pease under the title *Crónica del Perú: Primera parte*, 2d ed., corrected (Lima, 1984), chap. 92 on Cuzco, which contains the woodcut depicting Cuzco with Pizarro and Manco Inca.

8. Ianus Iacobus Boissardus, *I Pars Romanae urbis topographiae at antiquitatum quae succincte et breviter describuntur omnia quae tam publice quam privatim videntur animadversione digna. Topografia antiquae urbis Romae ex Io. Bartolomaeo Marliano Patritio Mediolanense praesenti instituto accomodata* (Frankfurt, 1597), pls. A, B, and C. Note also pl. D, a circular Rome, but showing the Tiber and its island by way of some approximation to physical geography.

9. Ibid., unnumbered map following pl. C and fold-out map, pl. I; note also the schematic maps of the different *regiones* of Rome.

10. See, for example, Richard L. Kagan, ed., *Spanish Cities of the Golden Age: The Views of Anton van den Wyngaerde* (Berkeley, 1989). On the painting of Cuzco's main square, showing processions to avert the earthquake of 1650, in the Church of El Triunfo, Cuzco, reproduced in figure 8, see José de Mesa and Teresa Gisbert, *Historia de la Pintura Cuzqueña* (Lima, 1982), 291–92.

11. For Cuzco, see Diego de Esquivel y Navía, *Noticias Cronológicas de la Gran Ciudad del Cuzco*, ed. Felix Denegri Luna, 2 vols. (Lima, 1980), an annalistic history of Cuzco from its pre-Inca beginnings to 1749 (i.e., the author's own day). On the author's manuscript sources, see Denegri Luna's introduction, lxxif. Esquivel y Navía also used published sources, especially Garcilaso. One of the new departures in sixteenth-century scholarship dealing with the classical past affected the study of inscriptions and coins, which were both perused as historical evidence for the first time. On Roman inscriptions in Spain, see Ambrosio Morales, *Las antiguedades de las ciudades de España que van nombradas en la Corónica . . .* (Cordoba, 1585; reprint, Madrid, 1792). The work is a documentary appendix of sorts to the author's history of Roman, Visigothic, and early medieval Spain. Another Spaniard, Antonio Agustín, wrote an authoritative treatise on Roman coins, *Antiquitatum Romanarum Hispanarumque in nummis veterum dialogi XI Latine redditi ab Andrea Schotto* (Antwerp, 1653). See, further, Sabine MacCormack, "History, Memory, and Time in Golden Age Spain," *History and Memory* 4 (1992): 36–68. For the text of the Lex Agraria of 111 B.C.E., reproduced in figure 9, see *Corpus Inscriptionum Latinarum* (Berlin, 1862), vol. 1, pt. 2, no. 585, where Boissard is cited as a source; note also Boissard, *I Pars Romanae urbis topographiae*, pl. 47, the altar of Lucius Cornelius Scipio Orfitus, reproduced in figure 10, which correctly renders the unusual spelling of the name in the inscription, OREITVS; see, further, Maarten J. Vermaseren, *Cybele and Attis: The Myth and the Cult* (London, 1977), 58f. and pl. 42.

12. Classical analogies were used to explain aspects of American reality almost from the beginning; see, on Peter Martyr and others, Antonello Gerbi, *Nature in the New World: From Christopher Columbus to Gonzalo Fernández de Oviedo* (Pittsburgh, 1985), 60ff. On Tarragona, see Kagan, *Spanish Cities*, 174–80.

13. On Cieza's comparisons of things Inca with things European, see Sabine MacCormack, *Religion in the Andes: Vision and Imagination in Colonial Peru* (Princeton, 1981), 106f.

14. On the vestal virgins, see Justus Lipsius, *De Vesta et Vestalibus Syntagma* (Antwerp, 1603), chap. 15, citing for authority Cieza and Agustín de Zárate.

15. Claude Guichard, *Funérailles et diverses manières d'ensevelir des Romains, Grecs et autres nations, tant anciennes que modernes* (Lyon, 1581), contains a long section on funerals in Africa, India, and the Americas, 336–42. The sources on America are Cieza, Gómara, Benzoni, Jean de Léry, and Thevet, and the information is reproduced with a sprinkling of misunderstandings and plain errors. In Francisco Peruzzi, *Pompe funerbri de tutte le nationi del mondo Raccolte dalle Storie Sagre e profane* (Verona, 1646), 125–27, by contrast, the Peruvian information is both brief and garbled. Gerardus Vossius, *De Theologia gentili et physiologia Christiana sive de origine idololatriae . . . Liber I et II* (Amsterdam, 1641), is for the most part about theological and philosophical ideas. The information about Peru in bk. 1, chap. 4, comes from Acosta.

16. See J. Seznec, *The Survival of the Pagan Gods: The Mythological Tradition and Its Place in Renaissance Humanism and Art* (New York, 1953), 251ff.; for idols of the "islands" found by the Spanish, see Vincenzo Cartari, *Le vere e nove imagini de gli dei delli antichi Di Vincenzo Cartari Reggiano . . . e altre memorie antiche . . . da Lorenzo Pignoria . . .* (Padua, 1615), XIVff. passim. Cartari added a number of medieval accretions to the classical pantheon, for example, the deity Demogorgon, who appears only in G. Boccaccio (who quotes an otherwise unknown source, Theodontius), *Genealogie deorum gentilium libri*, ed. V. Romano, 2 vols. (Bari, 1951), vol. 1, bk. 1, pp. 12ff. Boccaccio's *Genealogie* was much studied in Spain. For the copy of the Marqués de Santillana, see Mario Schiff, *Bibliothèque du Marquis de Santillane* (Paris, 1905), 333–39, 345. There are two early Latin editions of the *Genealogie* (Venice, 1472, and Cologne, ca. 1472), apart from numerous editions in Italian, French, and English. Bartolomé de Las Casas (see discussion below) consulted the work; see Bartolomé de Las Casas, *Apologética Historia*, ed. Edmundo O'Gorman (Mexico City, 1967), chap. 80, p. 417; chap. 103, p. 541; chap. 115, p. 607.

17. Cartari, *Imagini*, XXIII, mentions pictures of Mexican idols in the possession of Cardinal Amulio and in the "galleria de Sereniss. de Barviera." Another idol in this collection, also from Mexico, in which the devil was thought to have spoken, had been acquired from Cardinal Ximenez, archbishop of Toledo (see ibid., XXVII). See also ibid., XXXVII, for the origin of the design of the Japanese idol in the possession of Cardinal Girolamo Aleandro, who acquired the object from Jesuits.

18. Lorenzo Pignoria in ibid., V (fig. 11 in this essay), depicts a Mexican deity who is to be identified with Tonacatecuhtli, the lord of life and nourishment. This deity appears in the Codex Borgia (now in the Vatican Library), which was in Italy already in the sixteenth century; see Eduard Seler, *Comentarios al Codice Borgia*, 3 vols. (Mexico City, 1963), 1:9, 64–67; 2:173–76, 3: pl. 9, lower right, and pl. 61, lower right (fig. 12 in this essay). Possibly the manuscript that Pignoria consulted was the Vatican Codex 3738; see Seler, *Comentarios al Codice Borgia*, 2:175, with fig. 208a.

19. On Herodotus and Plato, and on the Greeks learning from the Egyptians, see Cartari, *Imagini*, 1ff. See Pignoria in Cartari, *Imagini*, IV, gods of Mexico, and XXIX, gods of Japan.

20. See Edgar Wind, *Pagan Mysteries in the Renaissance* (London, 1967); P. D. Walker, *Spiritual and Demonic Magic from Ficino to Campanella* (London, 1958).

21. Cartari, *Imagini*, 18, 35 (Janus), 161 (Juno).

22. Pignoria in Cartari, *Imagini*, VI, Mexican trinity; XIV, annunciation to mother of Quetzalcoatl; XXXVIII, Japanese statue. The identifications of the parallels involving the angel Gabriel and the Virgin Mary are my own; Pignoria only hints at them. For depictions of Mary such as Pignoria appears to have thought of, see Richard S. Field, *Fifteenth Century Woodcuts and Metalcuts from the National Gallery of Art* (Washington, D.C., n.d.), nos. 158, 160, 161–65, 170–73, 179. A fine engraving by Michael Wolgemuth was in the collection of Hartmann Schedel; see F. G. Kaltwasser, *Die Graphiksammlung des Humanisten Hartmann Schedel* (Munich, 1990), no. 29. Examples could be multiplied. See Nishikawa Kyōtarō and Emily J. Sano, *The Great Age of Japanese Buddhist Sculpture: A.D. 600–1300* (Seattle, 1982); nos. 16 and 18 in this catalog are examples of the type of figure on which Pignoria modeled his engraving.

23. See Alden Mosshammer, *The Chronicle of Eusebius and Greek Chronographic Tradition* (Lewisburg, 1979).

24. Werner Jaeger, *Early Christianity and Greek Paideia* (Oxford, 1961); Henry Chadwick, *Early Christian Thought and the Classical Tradition: Studies in Justin, Clement, and Origen* (Oxford, 1966); Jaroslav Pelikan, *Christianity and Classical Culture: The Metamorphosis of Natural Theology in the Christian Encounter with Hellenism* (New Haven, 1993).

25. On Peru and the Incas, see Pedro Cieza de León, *Señorío de los Incas*, ed. C. Aranibar (Lima, 1967), chaps. 3, 5; Francisco López de Gómara, *Historia general de las Indias* (Zaragoza, 1552), chap. 122; Las Casas, *Apologética Historia*, chap. 126; see also ibid., chap. 74, p. 383, on the confusion of languages. On the Tupinamba, see Jean de Léry, *History of a Voyage to the Land of Brazil, Otherwise called America*, trans. Janet Whatley (Berkeley, 1990), chap. 16, p. 144. Jean de Léry was in Brazil between 1556 and 1558. The method of accounting for perceived similarities between pagan and Christian belief by speculating about contacts in the remote past and by assuming a common ancestor for all human beings originated in late antiquity. Augustine was one of several Christians who believed that Plato had some familiarity with the Hebrew scriptures and found inspiration there for what Augustine understood to be Plato's monotheism. See Augustine, *De civitate dei*, ed. B. Dombart and A. Kalb (Turnhout, 1955), 8.11; Augustine, *De doctrina Christiana*, ed. J. J. Vogels (Bonn, 1930), 2.28.43, citing the authority of Ambrose of Milan. See also Clement of Alexandria, *Stromata* 1, ed. and trans. M. Caster (Paris, 1951), chap. 22; Origen, *Contra Celsum*, trans. Henry Chadwick (Cambridge, 1965), 4.39; Eusebius, *Praeparatio Evangelica* 11, ed. E. des Places, French translation by G. Favrelle (Paris, 1982), chap. 9, sec. 2. Don Cameron Allen, *The Legend of Noah: Renaissance Rationalism in Art, Science, and Letters* (Urbana, 1949). It is perhaps no accident that one of the most gripping representations of Adam seeing God at the very moment when his frame is embued with life—Michelangelo's *Creation of Adam* in the Sistine Chapel—was created at a time when humankind's direct knowledge of God began to be debated with regard to the Americas. See Rudolf Kuhn, *Michelangelo. Die sixtinische Decke: Beiträge über ihre Quellen und zu ihrer Auslegung* (Berlin, 1975), 23–29.

26. See L.-A. Vigneras, "Saint Thomas, Apostle of America," *Hispanic American Historical Review* 57 (1977): 82–90.

27. Léry, *Voyage*, 148. Characteristically, Léry, a Protestant, thought of the Christian message in scriptural terms, while Catholics were more likely to find relics, such as crosses and footprints of the apostle in the New World; see Jacques Lafaye, *Quetzalcoatl and Guadalupe: The Formation of Mexican National Consciousness, 1531–1813* (Chicago, 1974), 153ff., 180, 184ff.

28. See Sabine MacCormack, "Antonio de la Calancha: Un Agustino del siglo XVII en el Nuevo Mundo," *Bulletin Hispanique* 84 (1982): 60–94, at 84. Calancha had studied Adricomius's topography of the Holy Land, and he derived the idea that Christ at his death was looking westward from Adricomius's illustrations.

29. Of fundamental importance in this field is the three-volume work (which regrettably I have not been able to consult) of Athanasius Kircher, *Oedipus Aegyptiacus. Hoc est Universalis Hieroglyphicae Veterum Doctrinae Temporum Abolitae Instauratio* (Rome, 1652–55). For a short description, see B. L. Merrill, *Athanasius Kircher (1602–1680), Jesuit Scholar: An*

Exhibition of His Works in the Harold B. Lee Library Collection at Brigham Young University (Provo, 1989), 20–25. For the images of Isis and the Sun, in François Lafitau, *Moeurs des sauvages Amériquains comparées aux moeurs des premiers temps*, 2 vols. (Paris, 1724), vol. 1, pl. 6 (figure 20 in this essay), see also Athanasius Kircher, *China monumentis qua sacris qua profanis nec non variis naturae et artis spectaculis . . . illustrata* (Amsterdam, 1667), 140, depicting the lotus deity that Lafitau reproduced at the lower left; the lotus deity on the upper left also comes from this work by Kircher, unnumbered plate with the heading, "Typus Pussae seu Cybelis aut Isidis Sinensium" (Image of Pussa, or the Cybele or Isis of the Chinese).

30. MacCormack, *Religion in the Andes*, chaps. 2–3.

31. Juan de Betanzos, *Suma y narración de los Incas*, ed. M. del Carmen Martin Rubio (Madrid, 1987), bk. 1, chap. 11, p. 49: "unas veces tienen el Sol por hacedor y otras veces dicen que el Viracocha."

32. The *Apologética Historia* was completed in 1559; see, for this date, Edmundo O'Gorman in Las Casas, *Apologética*, xci. For Las Casas's interpretation of Andean religion, for example, on Viracocha the Creator in conflict with an opposing deity, see *Apologética*, chap. 126, where Las Casas interprets an Andean myth as a version of the story of the conflict between the Christian God and Lucifer. The *Apologética Historia*, not published until the nineteenth century, was liberally excerpted by Jerónimo Román, *Repúblicas del mundo* (Medina del Campo, 1575; revised, Salamanca, 1595), so that Las Casas's ideas about pagan religion did reach a wider public.

33. Las Casas, *Apologética*, chap. 126, p. 659. See, further, MacCormack, *Religion in the Andes*, 212–25.

34. Girolamo Benzoni, *La historia del Mondo Nuovo de m. Girolamo Benzoni Milanese.; laqual tratta dell'isole, e mari nuovamente ritrovati, e delle nuove citta da lui proprio vedute, per acqua e per terra in quattordeci anni* (Venice, 1565), plate facing p. 167. For the pyramid of Cestius, a funerary monument of early Augustan Rome, depicted by Boissard, *Romanae urbis topographiae*, pl. 117 (figure 22 in this essay), see L. Richardson, Jr., *A New Topographical Dictionary of Ancient Rome* (Baltimore, 1992), 353f.

35. Although my focus here is primarily on myth, let me note that Las Casas was more interested in ritual action, reading widely on this topic in the ancient sources and citing them extensively. But he selected and organized his information independently of these sources, according to methods that had been developed by humanist scholars in Italy during the preceding generation, in particular by Lilius Gregorius Giraldus. Giraldus's influential *De deis gentium varia et multiplex historia* (Basel, 1548; later editions, Basel, 1560, and Lyons, 1565; the treatise was also included in the numerous printings of Giraldus's collected works) begins by recounting the ancient stories of the gods in the fashion of medieval and renaissance manuals such as those by Boccaccio and Cartari (see above, note 16). But even here, ritual and philological details abound. Giraldus was less interested in the deeds of the gods than in how they were worshipped and how they had come into being in human minds. These themes dominate the concluding part of the *Historia*, consisting of a survey of ancient religious festivals, sacrifices, purifications, holy sites, and the like. Here Giraldus was guided not by the traditional manuals but by the ancient authorities them-

selves, in particular by the Roman antiquarian Marcus Terentius Varro; see Varro's *Antiquitates rerum divinarum*, ed. B. Cardauns, Akademie der Wissenschaften und der Literatur Mainz, Abhandlungen der geistes- und sozialwissenschaftlichen Kl. (Wiesbaden, 1976), 130f. Giraldus's source for the arrangement of Varro's *Antiquitates*, of which only fragments survive, perhaps was Augustine, *De civitate dei* 6.2–9. Just as in Varro's *Antiquitates*, temples, priesthoods, sacrifices, the festival calendar, and the divine personages addressed in cult were discussed under separate headings, so also in the works of Varro's Renaissance successors.

36. Quechua "enclosure of gold."

37. MacCormack, *Religion in the Andes*, 63ff., 249–50.

38. For a colonial rendering of this image, see fig. 26, Guaman Poma de Ayala, *Nueva Crónica y buen Gobierno*, ed. J. V. Murra and R. Adorno (Madrid, 1987), 449.

39. Las Casas, *Apologética Historia*, chap. 126, p. 660, quoted by Jerónimo Roman, *Republicas del Mundo. Republica de los Indios Occidentales* (Medina del Campo, 1575), bk. 1, chap. 5, fol. 361r, col. a. P. Duviols, "Punchao, Idolo Mayor del Coricancha: Historia y tipologia," *Antropologia Andina* 1, no. 2, Cuzco (1976): 156–83.

40. Bernard Picart, *Cérémonies et coûtumes réligieuses des peuples idolâtres*, vol. 1, pt. 1, *Qui contient les cérémonies religieuses des peuples des Indes occidentales* (Amsterdam, 1735), 123–30. The illustration of the worship of the solar disk (figure 23 in this essay) is Picart's pl. 29 (labeled, like all other plates in this volume, as belonging to volume 6). Picart's principal source on the Incas was Garcilaso de la Vega, whose *Comentarios reales de los Incas* (Lisbon, 1609), here cited in the edition by Carmelo Saenz de Santa Maria (Madrid, 1963), he consulted in the French translation. On the image of the Sun in Coricancha, see Garcilaso, *Comentarios reales*, bk. 3, chap. 20, p. 112: "la figura del sol, hecha de una plancha de oro . . . con su rostro en redondo, y con sus rayos y llamas de fuego, todo de una pieza, ni mas ni menos que la pintan los pintores." See, further, MacCormack, *Religion in the Andes*, 217, 324, 339.

41. The hierarchy of worshipful creatures of God in the Renaissance and Baroque periods was more than a theoretical convenience, because the belief that the planets and stars were guided by angelic forces was still widely held, even by astronomers. See Harry Wolfson, "The Problem of the Souls of the Spheres from the Byzantine Commentaries on Aristotle through the Arabs and St. Thomas to Kepler," *Dumbarton Oaks Papers* 16 (1962): 65–93; on the sun at the center of the zodiac, Giuliana Guidoni Guidi, "La rappresentazione dello Zodiaco sui mosaici pavimentali del Vicino Oriente," in *III Colloquio internazionale sul mosaico antico, Ravenna, 6–10 Settembre 1980*, ed. Raffaella Farinoli Campanati, 2 vols. (Ravenna, 1983), 1:253–62.

42. The series of paintings in the Museo de Arte Religioso in Cuzco, ca. 1675, depicting the procession of Corpus Christi shows several members of the Inca nobility, each wearing a golden solar disk on his chest; see Mesa and Gisbert, *Pintura Cuzqueña*, 177ff., with pls. 229–42. This ornament also appears in the depiction of Inca nobility in A. F. Frézier, *A Voyage to the South Sea and along the Coast of Chili and Peru, in the Years 1712, 1713 and 1714* (Paris, 1716; London, 1735), pl. 31 (figure 25 in this essay). Thomas B. F. Cummins, "We Are the Other: Peruvian Portraits of Colonial *Kurakakuna*," in *Transatlantic Encounters: Europeans and*

Andeans in the Sixteenth Century, ed. Kenneth J. Andrien and Rolena Adorno (Berkeley, 1991), 203–31. The Peabody Museum's early colonial bronze statuette of a male figure wearing a headdress of some kind surmounted by a solar disk is to my knowledge unique. It represents perfectly the convergence between certain Andean and European religious ideas in the early colonial Andes. See G. Bawden and G. W. Conrad, *The Andean Heritage* (Cambridge, Mass., 1982), 101 (figure 27 in this essay).

43. If the Indians, as was widely believed in the sixteenth and seventeenth centuries, had migrated to the Americas from the Old World, then (so the early modern reasoning went) one ought to be able to learn how they accomplished this migration and ought, furthermore, to find traces of Adam's monotheistic religion in the Americas. See Gregorio García, *Orígen de los Indios de el Nuevo Mundo e Indias Occidentales* (Valencia, 1607); the expanded version published in Madrid in 1729 was reprinted with a useful preface by F. Pease (Mexico City, 1981). See the excellent article by Joan-Pau Rubies, "Hugo Grotius's Dissertation on the Origin of the American Peoples and the Use of Comparative Methods," *Journal of the History of Ideas* 52 (1991): 221–44.

44. Garcilaso, *Comentarios reales*, bk. 1, chaps. 9–16.

45. Garcilaso cited as one of his authorities José de Acosta, *Historia natural y moral de las Indias* (Seville, 1590), ed. Edmundo O'Gorman (Mexico City, 1962); see bk. 5, chap. 2, on different kinds of idols. Acosta begins with idols of a general kind that he thought were derived from aspects of nature, such as the celestial bodies and the elements; next come aspects of nature of a particular kind, such as rivers and mountains. A second major group of idols had been created by human invention, and this group also was divided into two categories: objects of pure fiction, such as statues of deities, on the one hand, and objects "that truly were and are something," such as remains of the dead, on the other hand. In all, there were four classes of idols. See also bk. 5, chaps. 3–10, on examples of these four classes of idols in the Americas. Acosta's classification of objects of worship was an elaboration of the types of idols mentioned in the famous invective against idolatry in the book of Wisdom, chap. 14. See MacCormack, *Religion in the Andes* 219, 265–66, 268.

46. Garcilaso, *Comentarios reales*, bk. 2, chap. 4, pp. 47f.

47. Ibid., bk. 1, chap. 18, p. 30b, on Spanish reinterpretations of the Inca myth of the Ayar brothers who emerged from the cave at Pacaritambo at the beginning of time. The "window" in this cave, through which the Ayar brothers emerged, supposedly matched the window of the ark, while the Andean divinity who divided the world among the four brothers was thought to be the God of the Bible. On the Andean context of the myth, see Gary Urton, *The History of a Myth: Pacariqtambo and the Origin of the Inkas* (Austin, 1990).

48. See Amos Funkenstein, *Theology and the Scientific Imagination from the Middle Ages to the Seventeenth Century* (Princeton, 1986), 140–43.

49. See, for example, the opening chapter of Francisco López de Gómara's influential *Historia general de las Indias.*

50. Garcilaso, *Comentarios reales*, bk. 1, chap. 1, p. 7b.

51. Also in this group were, in order of importance, Gómara's *Historia general de las Indias*, Acosta's *Historia*, and Cieza's *Crónica del Perú.*

52. Fontenelle did not explicitly quote Garcilaso, but it is certain that he read the *Com-*

entarios reales, because he quotes a version of the Inca myth about the cause of rain and thunder which only appears in this work. Compare Garcilaso, *Comentarios reales*, bk. 2, chap. 27, p. 80, with Bernard Le Bovyer de Fontenelle, *De l'origine des fables*, in his *Oeûvres completes*, ed. A. Niderst, vol. 3 (Paris, 1989), 197.

53. An example of such a depiction survives in the lower right corner of the apse mosaic in Santa Maria Maggiore, Rome; see Walter Oakeshott, *The Mosaics of Rome from the Third to the Fourteenth Century* (London, 1967), pl. xiv, facing p. 95. Fontenelle would have had access to works about the antiquities of Rome such as Boissard's *Romanae urbis topographiae*, which included engravings of ancient sculptures, in this case both of a river god and of a nymph. The relief of the nymph sleeping next to her spring in pl. 25 of Boissard's work is graced with an inscription which suggests that not all the sculptures are quite accurately depicted—and some of them appear to have been fakes:

HUIUS NYMPHA DOCI BACRI [meaning LOCI SACRI] CUSTODIA FONTIS
DORMIO DUM BLANDAE SENTIO MURMUR AQUAE
PARCE MEUM QUISQUIS TANGIS CAVA MARMORA SOMNUM
RUMPERE SIVE BIBAS SIVE LAVERE TACE.

54. See above, note 52. For the river gods and their pitchers, see Fontenelle, *Fables*, 189, and Fontenelle, *Sur l'histoire*, in *Oeûvres completes*, 3:169–85, at 170. Fontenelle also compared Amerindian and Greek myths about punishments after death and about the origin of society; see *Fables*, 197.

55. Fontenelle, *Fables*, 198, citing a Chinese myth about one hundred princesses who cause the ebb and flow of the sea.

56. Ibid., 187, 196.

57. Ibid., 189 (Descartes); Fontenelle, *Histoire*, 171–72. See also M. Skrzypek, "La contribution de Fontenelle à la science des religions," in *Fontenelle: Actes du colloque tenu à Rouen du 6 au 10 octobre 1987*, ed. A. Niderst (Paris, 1989), 657–66, at 661; S. Berti, "La religion des anciens au debut du XVIIIe siècle. Deux exemples: Fontenelle et Ramsay," in ibid., 667–74, at 668f.

58. Fontenelle, *Fables*, 190; for the further development of the proposition that polytheism preceded monotheism, see David Hume, *The Natural History of Religion*, ed. A. Wayne Colver (Oxford, 1976), chap. 1, p. 26: "Polytheism or idolatry was, and necessarily must have been, the first and most ancient religion of mankind." Among the idolatrous peoples, he cites those of classical antiquity and "the savage tribes of America, Africa and Asia" (26f).

59. Fontenelle, *Fables*, 187, "les Cafres, les Lappons ou les Iroquois."

60. Fontenelle, *Histoire*, 174; *Fables*, 197f.

61. Fontenelle, *Fables*, 197.

62. Bernard Le Bovyer de Fontenelle, *Conversations on the Plurality of Worlds*, trans. H. A. Hargreaves (Berkeley, 1990). On Galileo's reflections on an infinite or a finite universe, see Alexander Koyré, *From the Closed World to the Infinite Universe* (Baltimore, 1957), 91–99.

63. See R. Popkin, *Isaac la Peyrère (1596–1676): His Life, Works, and Influence* (Leiden, 1987); see also A. Grafton, *Defenders of the Text: The Traditions of Scholarship in an Age of Science (1450–1800)* (Cambridge, Mass., 1991), chap. 8.

64. See R. Popkin, *La Peyrère*, 89ff.

65. Spinoza owned a copy of La Peyrère's *Prae-Adamitae*, published in Amsterdam (1655); see A. J. Servaas van Rooijen, *Inventaire des livres formant la bibliothèque de Benedict Spinoza, publié d'après un document inédit* (The Hague, 1889), 154, no. 28.

66. Lafitau mentions his five years in Canada in his *Moeurs des sauvages Amériquains comparées aux moeurs des premiers temps*, 1:2, along with his debt to the old Jesuit missionary Julien Garnier, whom he consulted and who had lived in Canada for sixty years.

67. See especially Lafitau, *Moeurs*, 1:10–15; here, Lafitau argued that religious practices were instituted from the beginning by God, and that all religious practices at all times and everywhere reflect in some respect this divine origin. As Lafitau points out, this argument militates against missionaries such as Acosta, who stressed the demonic origin of pagan religion.

68. Lafitau, *Moeurs*, 1:95; pl. 1, illustrating this myth, faces p. 95 (figure 28 in this essay).

69. For turtles on monuments from Egypt and India, see Lafitau, *Moeurs*, vol. 1, description of pl. 1. For Ate and Leto, see ibid., 95–96.

70. Ibid., 151–63 on fire cults, 168–77 on Vestal virgins, Inca chosen women of the Sun, and Iroquois virgins "serving the state."

71. Ibid., 249–52, with pl. 13, facing p. 250 (figure 29 in this essay); the passage from Garcilaso that Lafitau had in mind is *Comentarios reales*, bk. 2, chap. 23, p. 74a. The idea that the moon when in eclipse is swallowed by a dragon is depicted in a fifteenth-century woodcut; see F. G. Kaltwasser, *Die Graphiksammlung des Humanisten Hartmann Schedel* (Munich, 1990), fig. 90 (fig. 30 in this essay); similarly, fig. 77, the sun when eclipsed is also swallowed by a dragon. For Mary, see above, note 22.

72. See above, note 35.

73. See Lafitau, *Moeurs*, 1:52ff., 69ff., 344ff., 363ff.

74. Ibid., 5: a missionary goes overseas out of "zèle de religion," but also so as to "mettre au jour les découvertes qu'il y a faites et les connaissances qui'il y a acquises."

75. Ibid., 49, 339ff.

76. See ibid., 6ff., polemic against atheists who maintain that savages have no religion, or that it is manmade. The idea that religion is manmade is implied by Fontenelle in his *Fables*, which, however, Lafitau did not quote explicitly.

77. See, in particular, Lafitau, *Moeurs*, 1:7ff., 41.

78. See David Hume, *Dialogues Concerning Natural Religion*, ed. Stanley Tweyman (London, 1991), pt. 12, p. 172, where Philo professes his adoration for the "divine Being" on the basis of "natural religion." But note Hume's conclusion to the *Dialogues*, stating, p. 185, that "Philo's principles are more probable than Demea's but those of Cleanthes approach still nearer to the truth." Cleanthes throughout supports a more skeptical line of argument. The nature of Hume's skepticism has been a subject of much debate; see P. Russell, "Skepticism and Natural Religion in Hume's *Treatise*," *Journal of the History of Ideas* 49 (1988): 247–65; also, Tweyman in his introduction to the *Dialogues*, 1ff., and John W. Davis, "Going out the Window: A Comment on Tweyman," in ibid., 196–209. In the *Dialogues*, Hume appears to leave his own position deliberately opaque, given that the conclusion is a slightly adjusted translation of the conclusion of Cicero, *De natura deorum*, on which the *Dialogues* are modeled; see A. S. Pease, *M. Tulli Ciceronis De natura deorum*, vol. 2 (Darmstadt, 1968),

1227–28. No educated eighteenth-century reader would have missed this allusion. On what can be learned by human beings, see also *Dialogues*, pt. 2, p. 107: "The question is not concerning the *Being* but the *Nature of God*. This I affirm, from the infirmities of human understanding, to be altogether incomprehensible and unknown to us."

79. See, for this point, José de Acosta's much consulted *Historia*, bk. 6, chap. 7; see also José de Acosta, *De procuranda Indorum salute*, ed. and trans. L. Perena et al. (Madrid, 1984), bk. 1, chaps. 5–8. But note as well the view that in the Caribbean and Brazil, people followed an innocent, apparently imageless, and pure worship, devoid of ritual, expressed by Las Casas, *Apologética Historia*, chap. 166, p. 173; for a different view of such cultures, Léry, *Voyage*, chap. 16, pp. 146–48. For the general background, see Anthony Padgen, *The Fall of Natural Man: The American Indian and the Origins of Comparative Ethnology* (Cambridge, 1982).

80. Picart, *Cérémonies*, vol. 1, pt. 1, pl. 32, lunar eclipse. Ibid., pl. 34, Inca funeral, where the top picture is copied from Montanus, *De Nieuwe en onbekende Weereld*, unnumbered plate; the bottom picture is copied from de Bry, *Americae pars sexta*, 26, or possibly from the English translation of Garcilaso, *Royal Commentaries*, plate facing p. 182. Picart, *Cérémonies*, pl. 21, end of old and beginning of new Mexican epoch.

81. See Paul Hulton and David Beers Quinn, *The American Drawings of John White, 1577–1590*, 2 vols. (London, 1964), 1:37–47. The watercolor of the North American Indian priest wearing a simple cloak that was reproduced by Theodore de Bry in his *Americae pars sexta*, pt. 1, appears in Hulton and Beers Quinn, vol. 2, pl. 124. On Inca dress, of which, however, Picart is unlikely to have seen any examples, see J. H. Rowe, "Standardization in Inca Tapestry Tunics," in *The Junius B. Bird Pre-Columbian Textile Conference*, ed. Ann Pollard Rowe, Elizabeth P. Benson, Anne-Louise Schaffer (Washington, D.C., 1979), 239–64; R. Tom Zuidema, "Guaman Poma and the Art of Empire: Toward an Iconography of Inca Royal Dress," in Andrien and Adorno, *Transatlantic Encounters*, 151–202.

82. David Hume, *The Natural History of Religion*, ed. H. E. Root (Stanford, 1957), sec. 1, pp. 23, 24. See also sec. 4, pp. 32–33, on the natural inclination toward idolatry, whereby Christians in medieval Europe believed in "fairies, goblins, elves, sprites"; on the idolatries of Chinese, Laplanders, and others, see Donald T. Siebert, "Hume on Idolatry and Incarnation," *Journal of the History of Ideas* 45 (1984): 379–96.

83. J. H. Rowe, in a learned and lucid article that is still worth consulting, "The Renaissance Foundations of Anthropology," *American Anthropologist* 67 (1965): 1–20, sees a closer connection than the one outlined here between classical scholarship and the study of American cultures. Rudolf Pfeiffer, *History of Classical Scholarship from 1300 to 1850* (Oxford, 1976).

84. Garcilaso, *Comentarios reales*, proemio al lector: Garcilaso describes himself as "natural de la ciudad del Cozco, que fue otra Roma en aquel imperio." See, on this topic, Claire and Jean-Marie Pailler, "Une Amerique vraiment Latine: Pour une lecture 'Dumezilienne' de l'Inca Garcilaso de la Vega," *Annales: Economies, Societes, Civilisations* 47 (1992): 207–35.

ROLAND GREENE

Petrarchism among the Discourses of Imperialism

Whatever might be the other gains out of the rush of scholarly and popular discussion of 1492 and its consequences, we seem to be moving toward imagining those unprecedented events in a newly critical perspective: that is, toward recovering the complexity of early modern attitudes about such intersecting matters as economics and religion, or race and gender; toward treating the history of European imperialism as something other than a story of certain men's careers; and toward keeping in mind the important differences between the imperialist projects of Spain, Portugal, England, France, and the rest. One of the indispensable elements of such a critical perspective will be to understand what might be called the discourses of imperialism. At least since the important work of Irving A. Leonard and John Leddy Phelan, it has been understood—in theory, if not always in practice—that the European conquest depended on texts.[1] More recently, Tzvetan Todorov and Stephen Greenblatt have elaborated this proposition by applying literary methods to historical materials, and the results, while not uncontroversial, are proving to be central to a New World–oriented history and criticism of the 1990s.[2] Still, many historians and literary scholars alike have treated the writings and utterances of early modern imperialist actors as spontaneous, literal, and unmediated—even where, as in the case of Christopher Columbus, there has always been abundant evidence that the thoughts and acts for which he is now alternately celebrated and reviled come out of the available matrix of his era. While it is certainly easier to treat of people than of discourses, to detach actors from their contexts—to assign them full agency, responsibility, even authorship—one is often left no closer to discerning how and why events took place. Out of fashion as a strictly literary concept, character proves to be a crude instrument with which to address large-scale historical phenomena. It is perhaps even a distorting mirror that in the name of fixing personal and social responsibility finally obscures these facts behind the mystery of individual motivation.

The study of discourses, imperialist or otherwise, tends to come alive at sites of paradox: historical and literary junctures, for example, where a mode of writing gets decisively appropriated, seemingly out of its conventional usage, in ways that call for explanation. The classic early modern instance of this sort of crossing occurs around pastoral writing, which—as William Empson shows in a collaterally classic argument—has everything to do with the wishes of aristocrats and the bourgeoisie, and little or nothing to do with the experiences of the country people who are ostensibly its subjects.[3] More germane to the topic at hand, a singular coincidence figures in the shape and content of the sixteenth-century imperialist archive: why does the lyric writing derived from Petrarch's *Canzoniere* or *Rime sparse*, as well as the issues it entails, appear at many crucial points in the definition and administration of what Europeans knew as the New World?[4] How do several of the recorders of colonial American events—such as Francisco López de Gómara and Gonzalo Fernández de Oviedo y Valdés—come at their historical subject out of earlier careers as Italianate courtiers and sonneteers?[5] Why should the first published work by a *mestizo* writer of colonial Peru be a translation, and not the first in Castilian, of Leo Hebraeus's neo-Platonic, neo-Petrarchan *Dialoghi d'amore*?[6] What do love and empire—and not so much these occupations as the discourses that, in the sixteenth and seventeenth centuries, define and maintain them—have to do with each other?

One approach to these questions is to entertain the possibility that amatory and imperialist writing in this period share a discursive stream: that with certain exclusions understood, to write and read of unrequited love in the sixteenth and early seventeenth centuries is often to treat geopolitical conquest—though generally not the other way around. Early modern European culture recognizes a one-way channel that opens from the convention of Petrarchan lyric poetry onto the less acutely defined space of writing about the Americas. The former provides terms and attitudes for the latter; somehow it prepares *conquistadores*, *encomenderos*, and chroniclers for their American careers. At the same time, the imperialist canon lends contemporaneity, even urgency, to a poetic convention that can often seem frayed even in its most accomplished productions. The hint of cannibalism that appears in, say, Shakespeare's first sonnet ("Pitty the world, or else this glutton be, / To eate the worlds due, by the graue and thee") indicates something of how the amatory mode draws vividness and relevance out of imperialist preoccupations—here, perhaps out of Walter Ralegh's awareness in the contemporaneous *Discoverie of Guiana* (1595) that Englishmen may sooner be mistaken for "men eaters, and *Canibals*" than encounter actual cannibals (who "vnfortunatly passed by vs as we rode at ancor in the port of *Morequito*").[7] Where Ralegh often imagines—mostly with a fascinated horror—such humanist categories as conqueror, cannibal, cacique, and queen dissolving into one another, Shakespeare's speaker warns his young addressee of deserving the name of cannibal, against bringing the horror on himself as readily as any savage would ("thy selfe thy foe, to thy sweet selfe too cruell").

The international appeal of Petrarchism in the sixteenth century is largely political, or to be more specific, imperialist; because of its engagement with such political issues as the distribution of power among agents, the assimilation of difference, and the organization of individual desires into common structures of action and reaction, Petrarchan subjectivity becomes newly immediate in the age of Europe's discovery and administration of the New World. Further, in the first phase of colonization, until about 1600, Petrarchism operates as an original colonial discourse in the Americas, perhaps the first highly conventional language brought over from Europe that adequately expresses colonial experience as a set of relations between individual standpoints, that treats the frustrations as well as the ambitions of Europeans, and that allows Americans the capacity to play out their roles as unwilling (or, at most, deeply ambivalent) participants in someone else's enterprise. This revision of our notion of Petrarchism's place in the world calls for several adjustments in the conventional wisdom. To think of colonial discourse as potentially informed by Petrarchism means that the "Petrarchans" that concern us should be, for example, not only poets such as Thomas Wyatt, Louise Labé, and Philip Sidney, but explorers and *conquistadores* such as Christopher Columbus and Hernán Cortés, who tend to treat Petrarchan writing as a sort of handbook of attitudes in ambiguous situations; it relocates poet-imperialists such as the soldier and apologist Luís de Camões, the second marquis of the Valley of Oaxaca and would-be emperor Martín Cortés, and the failed entrepreneur Ralegh at the center of the convention, where the fictional and practical aspects of Petrarchism often meet in single texts written under both imperatives, such as Camões's lyric *Rimas* (ca. 1560) and Ralegh's *Discoverie of Guiana*.[8] To think of Petrarchism as colonial is to reconsider many amatory lyrics of the sixteenth century as engaged in an international, transgeneric dialogue—an exchange of perspectives with the literally colonial texts, such as Columbus's diaries and Hernán Cortés's *relaciones*, that gives these poems an external politics while the colonial texts take emotional meaning in return. For sixteenth-century poets and readers, in fact, the boundaries between these kinds of writing may not be as decided as much of the work on them by literary critics and historians has indicated.

In this essay, I can only indicate how Petrarchism shapes colonial experience as we know it, and as the sixteenth century knew it, in certain canonical texts. There is a model of colonial experience as first-person fiction, what might be called a representative anecdote, that runs disconnectedly through many of these texts and can be recovered and assembled out of them.[9] Columbus's diaries and letters mark the original site of material transmission between Old and New World cultures and, especially, the first texts in which the role of explorer of the Americas is defined and put into action. Columbus invents a first-person orientation to the New World that generations of travelers, conquerors, and colonizers will accept and adapt—and he does so out of attitudes, assumptions, and scraps of text that are heavily invested with the intellectual and emotional conditions we call Petrarchan. But if Columbus is the prototypical subject in this fiction of colonial experience, Brazil is its quintessential object; the texts concerning its discovery and founding draw on the same cultural and literary reserve of Petrarchan humanism, specifically from the areas where the fictional woman of Petrarch's lyrics, Laura, and other desired objects are loaded with semantic ambiguity, celebrated and deplored as epitomes of the speakers' and their societies' polarized values. The import of the laurel for Petrarch and some of his successors—a mythic tree that stands in for the lover's complex motives, and as the laurel crown, a material product that compensates for his imaginative and emotional suffering without making Laura herself at all accessible or attainable—recurs in the first chapter of Brazilian history through the cultural role of *pau-brasil*, or brazilwood, the first commodity of the New World. I will glance at some of the many sixteenth-century texts in which a clerical observer laments the Europeans' covetous "amor" or "love" of brazilwood, an empirical event that goes to constitute the founding myth of Brazil, and beyond it, of the New World, as colonial object.

To show the other side of the mutual involvement of Petrarchan ideas and colonial practice, I will look at one poem by Thomas Wyatt (1503–42), who appears at the historical juncture in which Petrarchism enters English literature. Wyatt's poetry has been limited by parochial interpretations, especially by criticism that thinks of the court as the only important political site in his work. I believe that nearly as much of his importance ought to be tied to the international cohort of speculative thinkers on love and politics to which he was exposed throughout his career, and to which much of his poetry speaks; therefore I will place his poems in an approximation of such a context, including lyrics by the French poet Louise Labé (1520–66) and the Spaniard Gutierre de Cetina (?1520–57).[10] Finally, I will address a text that falls on both sides of the perhaps anachronistic divide between lyric writing and historical narrative—namely, the *Quinquagenas* of the General Chronicler of the Indies, Fernández de Oviedo (1478–1557). This little-known work in poetry and prose, unpublished in the sixteenth century, represents something like textual fallout from Oviedo's official *Historia general y natural de las Indias* (1535). Composed between 1546 and 1556, the *Quinquagenas* seems to exist in order to expose the drives overwritten in the *Historia* and in Oviedo's career: first-person rather than institutional, emotional instead of detached, and extravagantly Petrarchan in place of the scriptural, classical, and medieval sources to which the *Historia* continually refers. The *Quinquagenas* amounts to a retrospective disclosure of not quite hidden sources, perspectives, and values. For us it ought to matter as a corroboration of the sometimes fugitive textual currents that run through the events and archives of the European conquests of America, and an incitement to a new mode of reading.

The career of Christopher Columbus marks the first obvious point of contact between a fifteenth-century Romance culture in which certain notions about de-

"Prima Columbi in Indiam navigato. Anno 1492. VII," from Johann Theodor de Bry, *Grands Voyages*, pt. IV (Latin) (Frankfurt, 1594). John Carter Brown Library.

sire and difference were under discussion and the emergent reality of the desired and different New World. Too often, the conventional history of the early Americas tends to naturalize Columbus out of his specific national background, his complicated career in several enterprises, and the highly determined ideological and emotional template he brings to his work as discoverer. Like Cabot and Vespucci, Columbus was a trans-Romance figure who probably absorbed much from the intellectual formations that were under way in European culture in the years around 1492. Consider the international dimensions of his language: he knew Latin; he read but barely spoke Italian, while he spoke but probably did not write his native dialect of Genoese; he read Landino's Italian translation of Pliny's *History* and made marginal notes in Spanish, the adopted language of his adulthood; he spoke Portuguese but probably did not write it (although he sent a letter to Ferdinand and Isabella in a Castilian laced with Portuguese idioms); and he seems to have written a language that few spoke, a "Genoese Latin" that served commercial men throughout the European economy.[11] One is obliged, I think, to protest the assumptions of those historians who treat Columbus's seemingly naive texts as though they have no antecedents.[12] We should recognize that the perceptible humanisms in Columbus's writing, Petrarchan and otherwise, come out of his exposure to a post-Latin, countermedieval culture that by the end of the fifteenth century had become established across the national and linguistic borders he regularly crossed. Columbus had a large, diverse, and intellectually cognate set of vernacular models for the discursive representation of his experience that would have been unimaginable to a forerunner such as Marco Polo or the factitious Mandeville, but that he duly received and adapted as a pragmatic Romance humanist. Petrarchism, which appears prominently in Spain in the middle of the fifteenth century and consolidates its authority between the 1490s and the mid-sixteenth century, and which seems always to adopt a hegemonic relation to other cultural texts, is one of these models—and probably the one that makes possible Columbus's work of inventing a first-person experience within the colonial enterprise.[13]

In the body of Columbus's writing dating from his original landfall, the emotional dimension to his New World experience is quite clear: "Esta es para desear, e vista, es para nunca dexar" ("This is a land to desire, and seen, it is never to be left").[14] Each of the elements in this formula is important in turn. Before the first landfall, while he and his crew are still at sea, Columbus conceives an erotics of nature that might have been extracted from any number of lyrics like *Canzoniere* 52, in which the crucial act is the speaker's attempted seeing of the woman, and the thematic element is the figurative relation between veil and breeze.

> Non al suo amante più Diana piacque
> quando per tal ventura tutta ignuda
> la vide in mezzo de le gelide acque,
>
> ch' a me la pastorella alpestra et cruda
> posta a bagnar un leggiadretto velo
> ch' a l'aura il vago et biondo capel chiuda;
>
> tal che mi fece, or quand' egli arde 'l cielo,
> tutto tremar d'un amoroso gielo.
>
> (Diana did not please her lover more
> when by such a chance he saw her
> all naked among the gelid waters
>
> as did me the cruel alpine shepherdess
> set to wash a pretty veil
> that encloses her lovely blonde head from the breeze,

> so that she made me, now when the sky burns,
> tremble all over with an amorous chill.)[15]

In this madrigal, the veil (*velo*) not only encloses the woman's head from the breeze (*l'aura*) but effectively hides her from all sight in the poem, ours as well as the speaker's. Moreover, the breeze carries the speaker's desire, concretizing—but not entirely, because breezes are invisible, and dissipate—the current that runs from subject to object, and returning the subject's passions back onto him when the veil counters the chill of the breeze.[16] Densely packed with allusions to the Ovidian-Petrarchan myth of Actaeon and Diana, the madrigal celebrates the erotic charge of not seeing, of awaiting the undressing, of experiencing love as an auto-reflexive circuit that (perhaps) does not engage the woman at all.

For the relatively inexperienced Columbus, who is still imagining his Indies from shipboard, the figurative bond between the wind (usually "el viento" or "los aires") and the emotions is strong and mutual: the wind, "calm" or "contrary" or even "amorous," is continuous with feelings, and often corresponds exactly to the psychic condition of the crew. Meanwhile, the sails ("velas") stand in figuratively for everything that turns the emotions one way or another—in manipulating them, Columbus often catalyzes the feelings of his volatile crew—but most often they ensure that the Spanish ships are engulfed in their own longings, are emotionally (and sometimes literally) floundering without resort to an available object. The erotic highlight of this episode comes with what seems to be the first sighting of land on 11 October 1492, a voyeuristic moment in which the desire to see turns back on the seer while true seeing is thwarted:

> The admiral being on the sterncastle at ten o'clock at night, saw light, although it was a thing so closed that he did not want to affirm it was land. But he called Pero Gutiérrez the steward of the king's dais and told him that it appeared to be light: that he should look and so he did it and saw it: he also told Rodrigo Sánchez de Segovia, whom the king and queen were sending in the armada as overseer, the which saw nothing because he was not in a place where he could see. After the admiral said it, it was seen once or twice: and it was like a little wax candle that rose and levitated, the which seemed to few an indication of land. . . . The admiral admonished them they should keep a good lookout on the forecastle and look well for land: and that to whomever should say first that he saw land he would give later a silk jacket: apart from the other rewards that the rulers had promised to whomever first saw land.[17]

Like Laura's hair, this first light is "[en]closed" off from the subject's vision, but like the Petrarchan lover, Columbus makes a satisfying experience of its absence. Burning with the compulsion to see his object, Columbus turns his sailors into a cohort of gazers who keep each other afire without engaging the object at all. The most urgent acting-out of the Petrarchan undercurrent in this passage comes with the appearance of Sánchez, the overseer or comptroller of the expedition (but literally, the "veedor"): in his desire to see, Columbus strips the institutional abstractions from his crew, taking the comptroller as what he literally should be, the seer, and demanding that Sánchez participate in this exercise of witness.[18] But Sánchez "saw nothing because he was not in a place where he could see," and the New World's fugitive quality, its resistance to being seen and apprehended, seems almost deliberately parabolized here. It will tease Columbus and his crew several more times before finally yielding its reality to their interpretations.

With the landfall, however, Columbus begins to dismantle his original symbolic apparatus. Where the *figura* of the sails had controlled the metonymic bond between the wind and the emotions, such instruments must be put away here because, representationally speaking, his desire is no longer ineffable but highly immediate; with real "naked people" interrupting the mythology of Ovid and Petrarch, there is no distance or inaccessibility for sails, or veils, to mediate. The people encountered in the Caribbean will not hold still for his erotic abstractions, however impeccable the sources from which he adapts them. And while at sea Columbus constructed satisfaction out of frustration, on land he turns the presence of his object into the lack of gratification—he continually pushes away the margin of success and the recognition of totality, even to the point of reinventing the physical world as he goes. Because he thinks of desire as a Petrarchan does, he must keep the exploratory urges and emotions alive, and his colonial project unfulfilled, even when the land and people of the Caribbean are manifestly under his control. In fact, the Columbian experience in the New World includes the first exercise in what will be periodic rewritings of Petrarchan ideology (and, of course, the poetry it produces) to accommodate empirical events—a regular cycle of adjustment as the conquests of the Indian societies develop, gold and silver become less idealized and more palpable, and otherness gains a face. As the known world expands and changes, I will suggest, the Petrarchisms of both imperialists and poets—and the discursive common space that holds texts of both sorts—change in measurable reaction.

As Columbus reports, his native Americans seem addicted to the pleasures of sex, of eating, of cruelty—and in some cases, such as the persistent legend of cannibalism, of all these acts at once.[19] They are a "people of love" ("gente de amor") who can be "on the verge of going crazy" with desire for bells and other trinkets—but who, when they are the givers, can be utterly "desirous" of pleasing others.[20] Pleasure in the Columbian New World is never final, however, but is heavily overwritten by unrequitedness and unfulfillment. There is always more to see, taste, imagine; and the supposed hedonism of the Americans brings out the

Europeans' own heavily glossed and justified desires, making them even more ardent for sex, food, and conquest. With the arrivals of the Europeans at Hispaniola, Jamaica, and other Caribbean landfalls, a standard sort of reception occurs. On seeing and being seen, the natives recognize themselves as objects and flee like figures in Ovidian-turned-Petrarchan myth, which casts the explorers in culturally appreciable roles—as Apollos or Actaeons—that they are entirely willing to play; or the Indians unknowingly act out a scene of literalized cupidity, shooting arrows, and drawing the Europeans into shooting back, in reciprocal stagings of blood lust. In the Columbian accounts, certain episodes are almost generic: the Indians are either fierce Cupids or frightened prey, ambiguous pronouns serve as a crude correlative for the blurred colonial situation, and the two parties become identified, merging in a continual interchange of the roles of subject and object, hunter and hunted. Accordingly, Europeans such as Columbus can scarcely represent the New World without treating these intimations or accusations of their own (often grotesque or excessive) desires.

The need to keep oneself at the center of the project as the unsatisfied first person—in Columbus's own case, as the supremely disappointed lover whose unfulfillment seems to increase as he accomplishes more—is the basis of the Columbian fiction within the literature of discovery. Perhaps the most daring move in this fiction is the idea Columbus articulates in 1498: that the world itself, which he is in danger of knowing more extensively than any other living geographer, is

> not round in the form [Ptolemy and others] have written, but it is in the form of a pear, which is round all over, except where it has the stalk, which rises higher, or as though one had a ball that were very round but in one place it were like a woman's nipple, and this part with the stalk is the highest and nearest to the sky. . . . In the other hemisphere I have no difficulty with it as a round sphere as they have said. But this hemisphere, I say is like half of a very round pear, which would have a raised stalk, as I have said, or like a woman's nipple on a round ball. So that of this half, neither Ptolemy nor the others who wrote about the world had knowledge, being very ignorant of it. They only based themselves on the hemisphere where they were, which is a round sphere.[21]

He goes on to argue that this summit is the site of the Earthly Paradise, "whereto no one can come save by the will of God."[22] Like the love poets of the early sixteenth century who turn female persons into collections of parts, and for whom the female breast becomes a canonical sign of incompleteness and unknowability (recall Clément Marot on the breast as a ball of ivory, "au milieu duquel est assise / Une Freze, ou une Cerise / Que nul ne veoit, ne touche aussi" ["in the middle of which is seated / a strawberry or a cherry, / that no one sees or touches"]),

"XVI Gualtherus Ralegh amicitiam contrahit cum rege Arromaia," from Johann Theodor de Bry, *Grands Voyages*, pt. VIII (Latin) (Frankfurt, 1599). John Carter Brown Library.

Columbus keeps his and his society's geopolitical ambition or desire alive, and his political position compelling, by undoing the totalizing work of exploration.[23] He puts himself—and all explorers of the hemisphere to date—back at the beginning of the project. He will keep going; he will not have to reckon with completion or satisfaction. In the largest sense, that is both the source of his continuing appeal as an imaginative standard through the sixteenth century—recall Ralegh's enthusiastic but anachronistic imitation of Columbus as eager lover in the *Guiana* tract of 1595—and the occasion of his political downfall. If Petrarch's work can be charged with idolatry, Columbus's project is inevitably attacked as slippery rhetoric that produces neither a reliable supply of gold nor a credible victory for Christianity but simply moves the signs of these presences around in journals and letters as the project drags on forever.

Columbus's cultural role is obviously part of, but not limited to, his geopolitical one. In discovering a continent for Spain and Europe, he invents the explorer and *conquistador* as the first-person register of culturally legible events and produces a narrative history that will be repeated and glossed by many later figures, but never superseded or replaced. From Petrarch and other sources at hand, he organizes a complex of colonial ideas and emotions for a European community that has its

Ovid, its Lucian, its Pico della Mirandola, and its romances but will shortly need an adaptable, synthetic fiction to explain the work of discovering, reconnoitering, and governing. Even when his political and commercial career is threatened, Columbus finds the textual resources to empower his persona as lover of the Indies. An example is the *Lettera rarissima* from Jamaica of 1503, in which he justifies his failures as governor of Hispaniola and recounts his redundant fourth voyage to the skeptical king and queen. Columbus asks for pity and pardon in the approximate words—and the exact emotions—of the retrospective first sonnet of the *Canzoniere*, an unmistakable borrowing: "Yo estoy tan perdido como dixe. . . . Llore por mí quien tiene caridad, verdad y justiçia" ("I am as lost as I have said. . . . Weep for me, whoever has charity, truth, and justice").[24] His biographer Samuel Eliot Morison, who is not often sensitive to the discursive currents that run through Columbus's texts, calls the letter "an incoherent screed" from "a man suffering both in mind and in body; incoherent, exaggerated, interspersed with discussions" of contrary things. He admires only the "noble and eloquent peroration"—in other words, the Petrarchan plea that closes the letter.[25] While the *Lettera rarissima* did nothing for Columbus's material fortunes and might have made things worse, it was published at Venice in 1505 and went directly into his internationally recognized identity, to join the accumulating stock of European colonial attitudes: the colonizer as prodigal of his own life for the sake of society. In a letter of the same time, Vespucci, who often seems to expose Columbus's subtexts deliberately, announces himself to Pietro Soderini in the literal words of the same sonnet. If he were a better Christian than a traveler, Vespucci writes, "if it had pleased God that I had followed [a good life]: as Petrarch says I should have been another man from what I am now."[26] The intersection of amatory and colonial discourses is never more substantial than in these self-conscious apologies, with which the original discoverers of the Americas give their positions affect and urgency—and above all, a clearly articulated personal and social value—that will draw others into the enterprise.

But the Petrarchan colonial anecdote I am following is not written exclusively with an emphasis on the first person: in the case of the Brazilian discovery and the subsequent colonial literature, one sees a version of European experience in the New World that is more preoccupied with the imaginative construction of the object. Brazil was a legendary idea long before Pedro Alvares Cabral's sighting on 22 April 1500, of the place we know by that name. Since the map of Angelino Dalorto of 1325, geographers had faithfully believed in an island called Brasil that would be found "not far west of Ireland."[27] Over time the name migrated, staying always a few steps ahead of contemporary knowledge, and expeditions were regularly mounted to find it, including several of the 1480s and 1490s. The most notorious of these voyages—the Englishman John Day wrote a famous letter about it to Columbus—is John Cabot's of 1498, which landed in a "Brazil" that might have been anywhere between Cape Breton to the north and Long Island to the south. The name Brazil does not settle onto the present-day place with Cabral's encounter, as we will soon see; only in Duarte Pacheco Pereira's *Esmeraldo de situ orbis*, begun about 1505, does the name attach to its present-day site, as Pereira abandons the notion of Brazil as an island for the observation that it is "a very large landmass" of "such greatness and length that on either side its end has not been seen or known, so that it is certain that it goes round the whole globe."[28]

Among the many conceivable reasons that kept the name Brazil at large for many years, there is the semantic complex of the name itself, and the significance it held for the European imagination. One medieval conception of the undiscovered Brazil is as an especially hot or ardent place, from an etymology its name shares with the modern English word *brazier* and the Romance equivalents. A complementary idea of the place involves the abundance of *pau-brasil*, or brazilwood, the plant of great commercial value that was resolved into a vivid red dye for the clothes of courtly ladies and gentlemen: the Brazilian historian Cândido Mendes calls the crimson or vermilion of *pau-brasil* the most "famous and predilected" color of the age, "as much with Christian peoples as with their rivals."[29] A customary medieval color of desire, as in the fabliau "Du chevalier a la robe vermeille," this red itself became restlessly desired across the higher class strata and sites of privilege in early modern Europe.[30] Finally, there is the superintending idea of Brazil as an island, which participates in the Renaissance convention of seeing islands and fictions as mutually revealing models, and practically warrants that such a place cannot be found, much less conquered, until it escapes from the imaginative category it shares with utopia and the "isla" governed by Sancho Panza.[31] The settling of the name on present-day Brazil depended in part, I think, on the emergence of a place large enough, inexhaustible enough, to serve as the stage for European desire, a place properly hard to subdue to the imagination; in part on the sheer abundance of brazilwood there; and in part on the inevitable relaxation or surrender of the impulse to dream ahead of the culture's collective gains, especially as the number of voyages quickly multiplied.

Like Columbus in his subjective interpretations of the wind, the early chroniclers of Brazil owe much of their understanding of the name, the wood, and the place to the interventions of Petrarchism. Since the founding of a tradition of learned commentary, most attentive readers of the *Canzoniere* have recognized that Petrarch condenses semantic ambiguities and contrary ideological forces into the term *Laura*, the proper name of his speaker's amatory object. A poem such as *Canzoniere* 5 gives us that name as a material fetish: taking it apart as though reaching for the origins and nature of his passion, the speaker discloses properly sacred values ("laudare et reverire," "praise and reverence") to which his poems sometimes nominally attend, but he really lusts after the Apollonian glory of the laurel.

> Quando io movo i sospiri a chiamar voi
> e 'l nome che nel cor mi scrisse Amore,
> LAU-dando s'incomincia udir di fore
> il suon de' primi dolci accenti suoi;
>
> vostro stato RE-al che 'ncontro poi
> raddopia a l'alta impresa il mio valore;
> ma "TA-ci," grida il fin, "ché farle onore
> è d'altri omeri soma che da' tuoi."
>
> Così LAU-dare et RE-verire insegna
> la voce stessa, pur ch'altri vi chiami,
> o d'ogni reverenza et d'onor degna;
>
> se non che forse Apollo si disdegna
> ch'a parlar de' suoi sempre verdi rami
> lingua mor-TA-l presuntuosa vegna.

> (When I move my sighs to call you and the name that Love wrote on my heart, the sound of its first sweet accents is heard without in LAU-ds.
>
> Your RE-gal state, which I meet next, redoubles my strength for the high enterprise; but "TA-lk no more!" cries the ending, "for to do her honor is a burden for other shoulders than yours."
>
> Thus the word itself teaches LAU-d and RE-verence, whenever anyone calls you, O Lady worthy of all reverence and honor;
>
> except that perhaps Apollo is incensed that any mor-TA-l tongue should come presumptuous to speak of his eternally green boughs.)[32]

In the cultural onomastics of Brazil, where the European colonial cohort is put into the role of subject, an equivalent construction of this geopolitical object takes place. Like the laurel of Ovidian and Petrarchan myth, *pau-brasil* has a sacred meaning and devotional applications. On Cabral's landing at Porto Seguro, according to most accounts, his first official acts were to build an enormous cross of brazilwood, and to name the country Santa Cruz after the cross. Here is the version by the early historian João de Barros:

> Several days had gone by in which the weather was unsuitable due to rain, when it came to pass on the third of May that Pedro Alvares wanted to depart, in order to give a name to that newly found land: he ordered that there be raised up a

huge cross on the highest point of a tree, & at its foot a Mass was said, which was arranged with the solemnity of blessings by the priests; giving this name to the land, Santa Cruz. Almost as though out of reverence for the sacrifice that was celebrated at the foot of that tree, & as the result of what was erected in it with so many blessings and prayers, all that land was dedicated to God. . . . By that name of Santa Cruz the country was called in those first years: and the cross raised there lasted for some years. However, as the Devil by the raising of that cross lost the dominion he had had over us, through the passion of Jesus Christ consumed in it: so when the red wood called *pau-brasil* began to come from that land, he worked to make this other name stick in the mouth of the people, and to have the name Santa Cruz become lost. As though the name of a wood for dyeing cloth were more important than that of the wood that gave color to all the sacraments by which we are saved, through the blood of Jesus Christ that was spilled on it. And since there is no other way for me to wreak vengeance on the Devil, in the name of Jesus Christ I admonish all those who read these words to give back to this land the name that with so much solemnity was given it, on the pain of that same cross that will be revealed to them on the Day of Judgment, accusing them of being more devoted to *pau-brasil* than to it.[33]

This is an indispensable episode in colonial Brazilian history. One commentator, Frei Antonio de Santa Maria Jaboatão, attributes the change in name from the divine Santa Cruz to the amatory and commercial Brazil to "the unfaithful politics of men, or their imprudent ambitions."[34] The most succinct of all is Fernão Lopes de Castanheda, writing in 1552: "In this land Pedro Alvares ordered set down a base of stone with a Cross, and through this was bestowed the name of Land of Santa Cruz, and later this name was lost and the name of Brasil remained instead on account of the *amor* of *pau-brasil*."[35]

Though historical and latter-day narrators naturally do not use the word, the issue here, as in *Canzoniere* 5 or any number of early modern lyrics, can be called autoreflexivity—the property that characterizes Petrarch's poems as more modern than medieval, and that in the fifteenth and sixteenth centuries brings constant recriminations against his work on Christian grounds. While much medieval poetry is more or less allegorical in the Augustinian sense that "as all desire is ultimately a desire for God, so all signs point ultimately to the Word," Petrarch's achievement is to write an "autonomous universe of . . . signs without reference to an anterior logos," a self-contained and necessarily idolatrous fiction, a circuit of meaning.[36] Of course the autoreflexive dimension of Europe's interest in the colonial Americas is already legible in Columbus: many commentators, most recently Todorov, have noticed that the Columbian project seems to be about its own continuation, that Columbus himself is concerned as much with the endless discovery of beauty as with the material goals of the Spanish crown.[37] Brazil's standing in the colonial anecdote implies that the hot place, the red place, the country consecrated to commercial desire for its own sake, is a reification of this idea of autoreflexivity: an ideological necessity, perhaps, that is not overwhelmed by the official Christianity of the Portuguese but continues to struggle with that standpoint in a sort of staged confrontation that abstracts the contradictory impulses of the entire project. A recent rendition of these impulses appeared in the exhibit by the United States of Brazil at Expo 92 in Seville. The entrance to the exhibit in the Pavilion of the Americas was framed by two enormous panels bearing the alternate names of the place, Vera Cruz and Brasil. Just before entering, one is implicitly invited to choose the rubric under which Brazilian reality is to be understood. In fact, however, the older, allegorical concept is all but impossible to maintain under the pressure of modernity, and becomes a marker for a vanished world view at the literal threshold of what supplanted it.

Because of Brazil's vitality as the canonical American object, and the commercial rather than colonial emphasis of its early reconnaissance by the Portuguese, the literature of its explorers is oddly impersonal, and objectification—its successes, its hazards, its political significance—is often under discussion there. The canonical instances are the narrative of Hans Staden, a German mercenary who was captured by the Tupinamba Indians in 1552 and made the article of an elaborate cannibalistic ritual before he escaped, and the story of the less fortunate Bishop Sardinha, whom the Caeté Indians found after a shipwreck in 1556; as Simão de Vasconcellos tells it, "they hit the holy prelate with a sacrificial club and split his head open in the middle . . . [and] carried [him] off to become a choice provision for their stomachs, [his] bones to be insignia of such a great deed. And that was the end of the first bishop of Brazil."[38] In the twentieth century, a residual emphasis on Americans as the unwilling objects of colonial experience produces several highly outspoken schools of Brazilian modernism, notably two movements led by the poet Oswald de Andrade, *Pau-Brasil* and *Antropofagia*, the latter of which takes the consumption of Bishop Sardinha as the founding date of a revolution of "cultural cannibalism" against European ideology and aesthetics.[39] A central motive of these vanguards is to exploit the (sometimes latent) anxiety of Europeans that their objectification of Brazil might turn back on them, making Old World bodies and texts into mere insignia. For these artists and their successors down to the present in Brazil, the objective orientation of Luso-American culture is a given—and it was given in large part, I believe, by the imperialist redaction of Petrarchism.[40]

Having examined briefly how Petrarchan motives condition the colonial discourse of the New World, I aim to look at certain poetic texts that respond to the American presence in the European view of the world, and that continue the process (begun by Columbus and others) of scripting colonial ideas and emotions. Thomas Wyatt's version of *Canzoniere* 102 ("Cesare, poi che 'l traditor d'Egitto") is a translation with an agenda: it indicates that the selection and transmission of the poem in English, circa 1540, can make a type of political statement in itself. What is for Petrarch a classicist gesture, an affirmation that ancient models still define and circumscribe modern conduct, becomes for Wyatt a topical reflection on—more than anything else—the relations of "passion" and "color," the incommensurability of human insides and outsides, and the helplessness of the first person within a warped system of communication. Most of these elements are potentially available in Petrarch's original, but in Wyatt's adaptation they come forward, loosening their subjection to the logical structures around them. The poet touches certain commonplaces of the moment, allows them to regroup around their shared urgencies and contradictions, and lets them remain as the central problem of the (ostensibly translated, but now updated) poem.

Here is *Canzoniere* 102, and after it, Wyatt's version:

Cesare, poi che 'l traditor d'Egitto
li fece il don de l'onorata testa,
celando l'allegrezza manifesta
pianse per gli occhi fuor, sì come è scritto;

et Anibàl, quando a l'imperio afflitto
vide farsi Fortuna sì molesta,
rise fra gente lagrimosa et mesta
per isfogare il suo acerbo despitto;

et così aven che l'animo ciascuna
sua passion sotto 'l contrario manto
ricopre co la vista or chiara or bruna.

Però s' alcuna volta io rido o canto,
facciol perch' i' non ò se non quest'una
via da celare il mio angoscioso pianto.

(Caesar, because the traitor of Egypt
made him a gift of that honored head,
hiding his obvious joy,
wept outwardly with his eyes, as it is written;

and Hannibal, when to the afflicted empire
he saw Fortune become so troublesome,
laughed among a sad and tearful people,
to let out his bitter spite;

and thus it happens that each soul
covers its passion under the contrary mantle,
with a view now clear, now dark.

But if some time I laugh or sing,
I do it because I have no way but this one
to hide my anguished tears.)

Cesar when that the traytor of Egipt
with thonourable hed did him present
covering his gladness did represent
playnt with his teeres owteward as it is writt
and Hannyball eke when fortune him shitt
clene from his reign & from all his intent
laught to his folke whom sorrowe did torment
his cruell dispite for to disgorge and qwit.
So chaunceth it oft that every passion
the mynde hideth by color contrary
with fayned visage now sad now mery.
Whereby if I laught any tyme or season
it is for bicause I have not her way
to cloke my care but vnder sport & play[41]

Wyatt receives from Petrarch a lyric that poses an amatory situation in terms of martial and perhaps colonial relations: the anecdotes of Caesar in Egypt and Hannibal in Zama compare conquerors who dissemble to their peoples and lovers who dissemble to their beloveds. In this period, which sees "an indubitable consciousness that Spain is repeating the destiny of Rome," Caesar is the conventional epithet for Charles V, Hannibal is a standard comparison for Cortés, and this poem seems about to cast its first person in the role of the next cunning conqueror—until the word "color" appears in the third quatrain to turn the poem's structure of relations around, to subjugate the speaker to the unmentioned woman.[42] The chief site of revisionary activity in Wyatt's poem is that quatrain, where Petrarch's shift (in his first tercet) to the contemporary outcome of classical precedents becomes the English poet's account of a more complicated set of events. Wyatt's rearrangement of these lines puts "every passion" at the front, subjects "the mind" emotionally—and perhaps grammatically—to it, and joins passion to the notions of feigning and "color contrary" in order to depict, in the end, a freshly contemporary setting of emotional indeterminacy. Does the mind hide passion or vice versa? Does passion indicate color or the other way around? What is the relation between "color" and "visage," which in *Canzoniere* 102 seems to be the simpler unanimity of a certain "manto" ("mantle") or attitude and a corresponding facial expression ("or chiara or bruna," "now clear, now dark")? What is the political standing of a person who may be colored by passion, or passionate because colored, or both? With these questions, Wyatt's "Cesar" quietly displays its situation in a much larger world than Petrarch inhabited, and for that a world in which a synchronic, geopolitical axis of difference emerges to inflect the active diachrony of Petrarchan humanism. I would guess that Wyatt saw the phrase "or chiara or bruna"—which can easily be read as "now plain/straightforward/pale, now brown"—and decided to work with the half-articulated conceit of love as changing one's color. Emerging from this revision is not Petrarch's enactment of the mind's covering passion with a cloak, but a more volatile confrontation between these factors that overthrows the received poem's logical order and brings "passion" and "color" forward. Speaking through the poem in broadcast is a complex of beliefs that sees passion and color as collaborators against the rational mind.

In English as well as several other western European languages, the matter of racial difference comes into the word *color* during the early modern period, especially through the history of international exploration. The idea of blackness with reference to Africans was long established by the fifteenth century, of course, but more elaborate predications about something between the symbolic extremes of black and white—a racial "color" that exists as much in the minds of observers as in physical fact—largely depend on the perceived ambiguity of the Indians' appearance and identity.[43] The *Oxford English Dictionary* finds the earliest such usage of *color* in the Egerton manuscript of Mandeville's *Travels*, which was probably translated from French in the fifteenth century, while in Spanish and Portuguese the racial sense of *color* and *cor*, respectively, became commonplace after the dissemination of texts by the first generation of travelers to the Americas.[44] Columbus and the early chroniclers of Brazil virtually invent, and rely on, a modern notion of "color" to indicate the arresting and indeterminate nature of the Indians. The former's first usage of 1492 compares the people of Guanahaní with "the color of the Canary Islanders, neither black nor white";[45] and in 1500, in an episode that personifies the legendary idea of Brazil, Pero Vaz de Caminha observes, next to (and presumably under) a red paint that cannot be washed away, a "côr" with which the natives are born: "There was one there who spoke much to the others, telling them to go away, but they did not, in my opinion, have respect or fear of him. This one who was telling them to move carried his bow and arrows, and was painted with red paint on his breasts and shoulder blades and hips, thighs, and legs, all the way down, and the unpainted places such as the stomach and belly were of their own colour, and the paint was so red that the water did not wash away or remove it, but rather when he came out of the water he was redder."[46]

With its canonization in the earliest *relaciones* from the Americas, this mode of observation and description becomes an almost invariable element in the chronicles of such colonial centers as Mexico and Peru. By mid-century, color is one of the most semantically weighted categories in European writing about the New World—a sort of staging area for many theoretical and practical issues concerning the Indians, including questions of their humanity and their capacity for European-directed improvement. The first two or three generations of narrators of the New World typically imagine a continuity between the colors of the Indians and those of their places, foods, plants, and animals. Even so, the matter of color often threatens the certainties of these commentators, insisting on ambiguity and inflecting the continuing discussions about such comparatively abstract issues as law and governance. López de Gómara, in the first part of his *Historia general de las Indias* (1552), wants to see racial color as one more indication of the New World's uniqueness and bounty, and as a motive for the objectification of the Indians. But as he records their colors with deliberate precision, Gómara cannot help making his way intellectually from one race to another, and thus bridging the theoretical difference between Europe and the Americas: "There are white men of many manners of whiteness, and reds of many manners of redness, and blacks of many manners of blackness; and white goes to red by degrees of pale ['descolorido'] and blond, and to black by ashcolored, swarthy, chestnut, and tawny, like our Indians, the which in general are all tawny or like cooked quince, or bilious yellow or nut-brown, and this color is by nature."[47] The more the Americans are represented as colored, the more their color is treated as graded and ambiguous; and the more ambiguous their color, the more their claims as subjects gain in volume and urgency.

In fact, those claims were increasingly urgent, in both moral and legal terms, at the time of Wyatt's "Cesar." The debates of the 1530s and 1540s generally admit the Indians' indeterminate color as an index, perhaps unspoken but nonetheless evident, in the continuing adjustments of the American social order. In a *cédula* of 1541, Prince Philip of Spain excludes *negros* (blacks) from the *encomiendas* on the grounds that they corrupt the *indios*, who are closer to whites and therefore the necessary objects of this ostensibly benevolent system of exploitation. Whatever instability between colors might have been produced by the decree is addressed in another, one year later, that affirms that "no mestizo or mulatto" may possess Indians without a special dispensation.[48] In the legal and symbolic terms of the era, the Indians' volatile identity is preserved partly by maintaining the borders to black and white against incidentally articulated openings, for the sake of still other charged openings that enable the Spanish administration to rehearse the correlations of difference and enfranchisement. J. H. Elliott has suggested that "the colour of the Indians . . . lacked the historical and emotional overtones which were beginning to be associated with the more familiar black."[49] Without disagreeing, I would insist that their color had a set of emotional overtones of its own for

Europeans, a complex of identification and anxiety that can be read, for instance, through the many attempts to improve the treatment of the Indians while shoring up the structures that kept them in place.

All of this may seem far afield of a translated love poem like Wyatt's "Cesar," even one in an explicitly political register, but I believe the connection is a live one. Love poetry is one of the available discourses—for sheer volume in this period, perhaps the most available—in which the concerns of power, selfhood, and difference can be figured with shadings of particularity and ambiguity. Moreover, the experience occasioned by European involvement in the Americas has an impact on these concerns even where a poet may not be willfully using poetry as a medium for imperialist issues. The fact of European domination in the Americas tends to make Petrarchism—already international, already political—respond with a fresher and more contemporary investment in these matters. In this case, the poet's choices of charged words, ambiguous grammatical structures, and commonplace associations gain purchase on an intellectual and cultural dialogue of great contemporary import.[50] One might gloss Wyatt's lyric by saying that the natural dissemblings of love have now reddened, now darkened the speaker's face; but instead of showing mastery and strategy, this transformation circa 1540 typifies the mock-colonial situation between these lovers. How did he become her victim, and a naked one too?

> Whereby if I laught any tyme or season
> it is for bicause I have not her way
> to cloke my care but vnder sport & play
>
> (12–14)

Instead of laughing and crying strategically, this lover probably never laughs, and laughing would be his only defense against showing his naked emotions. Having entered the poem as a potential conqueror, he leaves it as a self-denying wretch who can either cavort like a savage or go naked like a savage. Some drastic shift in the distribution of power is a common event in Wyatt's poems, inseparable from his notion of Petrarchism, but here it is enacted as a shift in cultural and political situation, where the lover turns from possible conqueror to practically conquered, seemingly on the basis of color. He is easily susceptible to misunderstanding by the woman, for the sexual difference between them, always a formidable barrier in a poem by Wyatt, has been overlaid with a kind of social difference—conqueror against conquered, civilized versus barbarian—that can be found within love itself.

By way of suggesting a context around what I consider Wyatt's historically particular work in "Cesar," I will briefly treat two other poems that reimagine Petrarchism in contemporary terms, namely, the twenty-first sonnet from the series by Louise Labé and the sonnet "Si de Roma el ardor" ("If the ardor of

Rome") by Gutierre de Cetina. Recent scholarship has done much to reintroduce Labé. From her unusual vantage as a female poet working within an overwhelmingly male convention, she typically identifies with both the subject and the object in Petrarchan fiction and allows her speaker to articulate her desires in comparatively direct, unveiled fashion. Sonnet 21 raises the issue of color in a series of questions about the ideal lover.

Quelle grandeur rend l'homme venerable?
Quelle grosseur? quel poil? quelle couleur?
Qui est des yeus le plus enmieleur?
Qui fait plus tot une playe incurable?

Quel chant est plus à l'homme convenable?
Qui plus penetre en chantant sa douleur?
Qui un dous lut fait encore meilleur?
Quel naturel est le plus amiable?

Je ne voudrois le dire assurément,
Ayant Amour forcé mon jugement:
Mais je say bien et de tant je m'assure,

Que tout le beau que lon pourroit choisir,
Et que tout l'art qui ayde la Nature,
Ne me sauroient acroitre mon desir.[51]

(What height makes a man venerable?
What breadth? what hair? what color?
Who honeys eyes the most?
Who gives the most incurable wound?

What song is most appropriate for a man to sing?
Who best penetrates by singing his sadness?
Who makes a sweet lute sound best?
What type of naturalness is most amiable?

I do not wish to say for certain,
For Love has forced my judgment:
But I know well and I am sure of this much:

That all the beauty anyone could choose,
And all the art that improves nature,
Could not increase my desire.)

Labé's Sonnet 20, which precedes this one in the series, closes with the lines: "Je croy qu'estoient les infernaus arrets, / Qui de si loin m'ourdissoient ce naufrage" ("I think it was orders from Hell / That arranged the shipwreck of my life"), which leaves the speaker well-placed for this American excursion. In fact, Sonnet 21 is an open channel for the sorts of concerns that New World–oriented Europeans often articulate in mid-century. According to Elliott, these include certain "creatively disturbing" questions: "What were the essential characteristics of humanity? What constituted a civilized man, as distinct from a barbarian? In what respects were certain peoples of the world deficient, and how best could their deficiencies be remedied?"[52] In Labé's poem, the experience of love works to undo her speaker's settled European perspective, and discloses what is savage about this man as well as what is potentially civilized about savages. Starting with the unexpected word "couleur" in line 2, the poem strikes an especially broad, disinterested position for its humanist interrogation. If anything, the questions seem to favor savagery, and what begins as a possible American theme becomes more emphatic as the lyric wears on. The question of "color" might mean "what shade of (white European) complexion looks best"—in fact, I am unable to find a published scholar who thinks it means anything else—but by the end of the second quatrain, one has to recognize that racial "color" and other New World–oriented matters make a wedge that widens her poem's field of concern, that poses international against interpersonal politics.[53] There are a number of potential crossings between the two sonnets: Labé's eighth question, for example, is cognate with Wyatt's assumption that savages (including conquered peoples) convert their emotions directly into song while civilized peoples, including conquerors, dissemble. For Wyatt, that was the last disempowering blow that finished the poem—his speaker had no way to dissemble but to mimic a savage—while for Labé the same question becomes part of an audition. This poem's man is virtually invited to enact the role of savage, instead of having it forced on him unawares.

The concluding tercet blurts out the insight that occasions the poem, and that sometimes breaks out of other sixteenth-century texts in this unguarded way: that the Petrarchan and the colonial experiences replicate each other; that from the first-person European vantage one feels very much like the other; and that the crucial homology occurs in their modes of provoking, articulating, and organizing desire. To strip away the man's protective layers of civilization and see him in his "natural" state is to incite desire of the American kind—a highly immediate, self-perpetuating condition that is programmatically unrequited—and, of course, that property, the fact that its desires cannot be fulfilled, is the factor in Europe's imperialist experience that inspires Labé's American conceit in the first place. One of this sonnet's most interesting considerations is that the speaker declines to accept a stock colonial role in her own conceit as either conqueror or vassal. The gesture at the poem's turn ("I cannot say for sure") is really her refusal to overstate her position as creatively disturbed European. It is enough for Labé's strategically ahistorical speaker to register some typical continental emotions around the idea of the Americas. To introduce a logic of geopolitical domination here would undermine the relative equality of lovers on which many of her poems insist, and which makes her version of Petrarchism compelling.[54]

The other poem at hand is Cetina's sonnet, which is probably a little later than Wyatt's mature work.

Si de Roma el ardor, si el de Sagunto,
de Troia, de Numancia, y de Carthago;
si de Iherusalén el fiero trago,
Belgrado, Rodas y Bizancio junto;

si puede piedad moveros punto
quanto ha avido de mal del Indo al Tajo,
¿por qué del fuego que llorando apago
ni dolor, ni piedad en uos barrunto?

Pasó la pena déstos, y en un hora
acabaron la vida y el tormento,
puestos del enemigo a sangre y fuego.

Vos dais pena inmortal al que os adora;
y así vuestra crueldad no llega a cuento
romano, turco, bárbaro ni griego.[55]

(If the ardor of Rome, if that of Sagunto,
of Troy, of Numantia, and of Carthage,
if the fierce calamity of Jerusalem,
Belgrade, Rhodes and Byzantium together;

if pity can move you at all,
given the evil that has happened from the Indus to the Tagus,
why does neither the fire I put out by crying,
nor my pain, nor pity for me affect you?

The pain of all these has passed, and at once
life and torment come to an end,
put by their enemy to blood and fire.

You give immortal pain to your adorer:
and thus your cruelty cannot be measured as
Roman, Turk, barbarian, or Greek.)

Cetina was a member of the second generation of Spaniards in Mexico, joining in the transplantation of peninsular culture after the conquest; he seems to have visited Mexico twice, in 1546 and 1550, and died there in 1557.[56] "If the ardor of Rome" belongs to a compendium of religious and amatory poetry by various Spanish and Spanish-American poets, entitled *Flores de varia poesia*, that was copied into a manuscript in Mexico City in 1577 and may have been compiled by Cetina himself. Perhaps another revision of *Canzoniere* 102, the sonnet raises the political stakes from where Wyatt leaves them.

It begins with a catalog of sieges inflicted by imperial geopolitics, including the histories of Petrarch's Caesar and Hannibal, but without always specifying the sides at issue; that is, the "ardor" of Rome is the repertory of emotions it experiences and provokes in an international context, not something particular to either of its roles as conquering or conquered state—the loser to (but later the winner over) Carthage, say, or the eventual victor against Numantia. For this poem, the sensation of ardor or zeal is presented in its martial sense, as belonging chiefly to wars and politics, and the speaker asks the woman: If you understand the ardors of nations under political stresses, if you are moved by the history that has passed between one society and another, why are you unaffected by my scaled-down feelings of volatility and abjectness? As in Labé's sonnet, the implicit understanding here is that the amatory and imperialist experiences reflect each other; why is the woman alive to one but not the other?

The speaker casts himself as a participant in an imperialist enterprise, then: perhaps as a prospective conqueror in his relations with the woman, one who now experiences different and unaccustomed emotions as the conquered party. International undertakings in politics and war and interpersonal ventures in love, he reminds her and us, will often escape their agents' intentions; the roles of victor and vanquished are highly fluid. But what sort of conqueror is she? The first tercet conveys a turn in the argument, in which the woman's crimes against the speaker are described, if not detailed, for the first time. While in other contexts it can stand for classical sieges, "blood and fire" is practically a technical term in sixteenth-century New Spain for the uncompromising savagery of some Indian groups—what Cortés calls "horrid and abominable custom[s]"—and their resistance to Spanish notions of civilization, as well as for the *conquistadores*' answering suppression of the Indians by any means. In other words, the term denotes a kind of war that makes Europeans feel and seem as savage as the Indians.[57] Until the dissemination of facts about the very different Inca regime, some version of this term invariably figures in descriptions of American barbarism and Spanish responses to it. One of its functions in colonial discourse seems to be as a metonymy of deliberately uncertain reference. Like some tropes in Petrarchan poetry, "blood and fire" becomes a meeting site for its two potential subjects, the Spaniards and the Indians, in which they join and become indistinguishable: the Spanish answer to the "blood and fire" barbarity of the tribes is to kill them and burn their towns, and before long, even in the sight of a practical-minded *conquistador* like Cortés, "que casi no nos conocíamos unos a otros, tan revueltos y juntos andaban con nosotros" ("we could hardly distinguish between ourselves and them, so fiercely and so closely did they fight with us").[58] The Third Provincial Council of 1585 convened a *consulta*, in fact, explicitly to determine whether "blood and fire" was a licit means of warfare against the Chichimecas, who had been in continual rebellion since about 1550.[59] In Cetina's poem, because of the speaker's passivity, the woman's temporally specific, perhaps ritualistic murder of him ("in one hour" or "at one time") and the dissolution of his identity into blood and fire becomes their closest encounter. He will never be more to her than the elemental remains of her cruelty.

But something in this poem is more than merely topical, and might even be urgent. In representing the speaker as a conquered people, Cetina asks his readership to imagine the barbarians or Indians as victors against the Spanish, and to occupy the first-person position of the loser in such an outcome. Despite the historical jumps of the first stanza, the sonnet has a clear geopolitical and historical itinerary: it is a record of Spanish struggles against imperialism that suddenly imagines the war against New World "barbarian[s]" as another chapter in this history, and that proposes to think politically through the emotions of unrequited love. What if the "ardor" of the New World enterprise proves impossible to satisfy? What if its object cannot be possessed? What if, in this sense, the barbarians conquer Spain and produce another Sagunto or Numantia? In their way, these questions are no more direct or radical than those raised by Bartolomé de Las Casas, Francisco de Vitoria, or any number of mid-century chroniclers and critics of the empire. All of these texts, including amatory sonnets, might be understood together as part of a continuing interrogation of the imperialist enterprise by its own ostensibly humanist ideology.

Questions like these undergird—and, I think, redeem—the somewhat flat, generic assertions of the poem's conclusion, where Cetina's anticipation of an imperial unraveling, of a new, but old, chapter in the history of Spanish capitulation, is written out only in the insertion of a new adjective ("bárbaro") in the list of conquering nations. "Barbarian" has an immense topical resonance here: in *De indis* (1539), for example, it is Vitoria's usual term for the New World peoples, living under Spanish dominion, whose rights he reasons and defines.[60] In the later 1550s, as an epilogue to his *Apologética historia sumaria*, Las Casas produced a detailed account of the types of barbarism and the ways in which the Indians might be considered barbarians.[61] In spite of the dismissal of mere barbarism as a description of this woman, Cetina's poem seems to foreground that epithet, the only contemporary one, as the likeliest approximation of her cruelty and puts the present-day Spanish engagement with barbarians into an uncomfortable historical context. Is it possible that the woman has no sensation of Spain's historical suffering because she is another of its conquerors? Can the speaker's unrequitable desire for a barbaric woman be seen as an interpersonal rendition of Spain's desires for unattainable conquests—and are both equally likely for defeat?

The Petrarchan current in imperialist writing often carries questions such as these, even admitting them to texts where such considerations might seem out of place, overly speculative, perhaps subversive. Oviedo's *Quinquagenas* is such a text. Composed in Santo Domingo on the island of Hispaniola, this voluminous work—so entitled because each of its three sections has fifty stanzas, and each stanza has fifty lines—is announced as a tribute to "the generous and illustrious and no less famous kings, princes, dukes, marquises, and counts and gentlemen and notable persons of Spain."[62] For this project Oviedo invents (or better, names) a verse form, "segunda rima," after the *terza rima* of Dante and Petrarch.[63] The fifty-line stanzas are interrupted often and at irregular intervals for prose commentaries on Oviedo's elliptical poetry. In spite of its claims to treat particular persons, the character of the whole work is that of a scattered, impulsive meditation on the Spanish national and imperial condition from Oviedo's vantage as *alcaide* of Santo Domingo. Its aggressively first-person stance seems obviously part of the design: with it, the *Quinquagenas* becomes a repository for the obsessions, judgments, and emotional displays that the official chronicler of Spanish imperialism had been obliged to discipline in his *Historia general y natural de las Indias* of a decade earlier.[64] While the most frequently cited authorities in the *Historia* are perhaps Pliny and Isidore of Seville, the texts most often invoked in the *Quinquagenas* come out of a different register of experience: the tales of Giovanni Boccaccio and other writers of romance and fabliaux; the verses of Italian poets such as Giovanni Pontano and Serafino della Aquila, both of whom Oviedo had known in Naples at the turn of the century; and most of all, the poetry of Petrarch.

It is not that these latter models go unmentioned in the *Historia*. Much to the contrary, they often supply moral exempla, anecdotes, and raw verbal material for the institutional chronicle, as where Oviedo cites Pontano's opinion as to which emperor Pliny addressed in his own *Natural History*, where he extracts a moral concerning life in the Indies from the first lines of *Canzoniere* 7, or where he brings a verse from Serafino to bear on Cortés's dispute with the *adelantado* Diego de Velázquez.[65] One of the most typical and revealing appropriations of amatory matter in the *Historia* occurs in the sixth book of the first part, where Oviedo is committed to discussing the mineral wealth and especially the mines of gold supposed to be found in Hispaniola. He digresses from this account before it properly begins in order to tell of "a collar of gold," perhaps a relic from Roman times, found in 1496 by a shepherd in Asturias.[66] The manifest purposes of this episode are to profess the continuities between the speculative riches of Hispaniola, the slightly less fanciful hidden wealth in present-day Spain, and the wealth of the Caesars mentioned by Pliny and others and, perhaps more important, to distract us from a direct statement of Hispaniola's resources, whether prophecy or record, by lingering over the qualities and appearances of this collar—in much the same way that an amatory lyric's speaker will often dwell on surfaces out of stupefaction or oblivion.[67] In the middle of this digression, Oviedo adduces the famous lines that open the octave and sestet of *Canzoniere* 190, in which Petrarch's speaker encounters a lovely white doe wearing a collar of diamond and topaz,

> Una candida cerva sopra l'erba
> verde ma parve . . .
>
> (A white doe on the green grass
> appeared to me . . .)

with the inscription: "Nessun mi tocchi. . . . libera farmi al mio Cesare parve" ("Let no one touch me. . . . it pleases my Caesar to make me free").[68] The quotation from Petrarch by Oviedo,

> Nessun mi tocchi, al bel collo dintorno
> Scripto havea . . .
>
> (Let no one touch me, around her beautiful neck
> she wore the writing . . .)

including ellipses, breaks off just before mentioning the diamonds and topazes, implying that the supposedly historical collar of Asturias stands in for the symbolic one of *Canzoniere* 190. Here, as in many passages of the *Historia*, Oviedo's anecdote extracts or mines meaning from Petrarch's verses: that the gold, collar, and deer all belong unproblematically to Caesar, and that the collar discovered some forty years earlier compels attention to the survival of imperial power. If the emotional sense of *Canzoniere* 190 entails much more than this Caesarian interpretation—if it is about the deer's being out of reach and the man's lack of satisfaction, if Caesar is less the subject of Petrarch's poem than a nonpresence represented by his oppressive label—one is hardly encouraged to notice any such dross or residue of Oviedo's appropriation. In this case, the specificity of the collar ("I had [it] in my power . . . I held it in my hands") tends to distract us from its own merely symbolic character, its job as a marker for a gold supply that is much less definite, much more inchoate and hard to locate.[69] The Petrarch of the *Historia*, scarcely at odds with Pliny, Isidore, or any other authority, is ostensibly a sloganeer in the service of Oviedo's official, institutional agenda. In episodes such as this, it is as though the Oviedo of the *Historia* lives within a Petrarchan lyric, records its natural history in Plinian terms, takes its symbols and effects as real and telling, and repeats with conviction the often hollow words of the unrequited lovers who are his models.

The answer to this mode of appropriation comes, I believe, in the *Quinquagenas*. Following on the twentieth and twenty-first stanzas, which treat things that are "inútil" ("useless") to attempt—to bring iron to Biscay, to expect merchants to tell the truth, to ask ducks and shrimp to be chaste—Oviedo continues the list of futilities with the following instances:

Ni que canten anadones
Según cantan ruyseñores;
Ni escusarse los amores
En la gente del palaçio;
Ni que tenga vn topaçio
Mas valor quel dïamante.[70]

(That ducks should be expected
To sing like nightingales;
That courtly people
Should do without love;
That a topaz should be worth more
Than a diamond.)

He goes on almost cynically: "Some things that are naturally inclined and formed for different effects cannot be separated from their customs, nor is human art or ingenuity enough to make them rebel from or contradict their nature. And to want to do otherwise would be to flail at the wind."[71] At first reading, the passage might seem not very different from those in which bits of Petrarch and other poets are cited in the *Historia*; but the critical difference, of course, is that in the earlier work the principal stream of meaning runs through the prose, while in the *Quinquagenas* the prose glosses serve merely to explicate Oviedo's often oblique verses. Accordingly, in the latter work, poetry is treated as though by a serious amateur poet: as being constituted by a bringing together of discourses, and as having a franchise for ambiguity, differentiation, and irony. Oviedo's own verses in this stanza insist on qualifying the sort of writing and reading he depended on in the

Historia: all discourses cannot be mined of meaning and reduced to a single substance, desire will out, and—in case these cautions seem too vague—the diamond and the topaz of the classic Petrarchan collar are, he emphasizes, two real and distinct material objects with their respective values and associations. With this last, Oviedo interjects his own verse exactly where his past quotation of *Canzoniere* 190 broke off, rippling the tapestry of the *Historia*: "One has to understand that a churl does not speak like a discreet courtier, nor a vile creature like a discreet and polite person and so forth. . . . Although love tempts one and all, its exercises are very separate and different. . . . Love makes each of them speak his own language. . . . If the reader pays attention and is a man of understanding, he will understand from the verse of these *Quinquagenas* other, deeper, and more exquisite things than what the letter says."[72] Further, by way of explaining the lines quoted above, Oviedo peels away a layer of text to show another famous lyric from the *Canzoniere* as his model, namely, the canzone numbered 105. The relevant lines out of Petrarch, which Oviedo quotes as a lesson in reading his own verses, are these:

> Forse ch'ogni uom che legge non s'intende;
> et la rete tal tende che non piglia;
> et chi troppo assotiglia si scavezza.[73]
>
> (Perhaps every man who reads does not understand,
> And he who casts the net does not always catch,
> And he who is too subtle breaks his neck.)

Disturbing the surface he assembled in the official text, and challenging us to read for the particular modulations in which desire gets expressed, Oviedo allows here and elsewhere in the *Quinquagenas*, in poetry, what the *Historia* scarcely admits in prose, that unrequitedness is part of our encounters with persons, societies, and texts. One may read too intensely or too casually, one may dull or ignore the implications of certain passages, or one may simply impose one's will on a text, but desire—ours, that of which the text speaks, and that of our objects—will always leave something unconverted into meaning or value. In this important sense, persons, societies, and texts are finally unconquerable; but it is only through this realization that one can begin to recover deeper and more exquisite things that lie hidden beneath the surfaces. Such is the half-articulated conclusion that an old Petrarchist, imperial factotum, and chronicler discloses near the end of his life. Exposing the seams of the official account in a dense poetry fashioned for that purpose, and stripping that poetry in turn to reveal its Petrarchan subtexts, Oviedo anticipates something of the foregoing readings in this essay of Columbus, Wyatt, and the rest. His combined works, with their mutual commentaries and different degrees of textual consciousness, tend to confirm what the informed reader of both amatory and imperialist writing might already have suspected: that the latter is seldom far from recognizing the exploratory, interrogative motions of Petrarchism. As historians and literary scholars—as readers of early modern discourses—we are perhaps closer than ever to recovering what Oviedo and many others of his time understood.

ACKNOWLEDGMENTS

This essay was originally delivered as a lecture at the English Institute in August 1990 and was revised for the conference on America in European Consciousness at Brown University. I thank Kathryn Burns, Jennifer Carrell, and Curtis Perry for their advice and criticism.

NOTES

1. Irving A. Leonard, *Books of the Brave: Being an Account of Books and Men in the Spanish Conquest and Settlement of the Sixteenth-Century New World* (Cambridge, Mass., 1949; rev. ed., Berkeley, 1992); John Leddy Phelan, *The Millenial Kingdom of the Franciscans in the New World: A Study of the Writings of Gerónimo de Mendieta (1525–1604)*, University of California Publications in History, no. 52 (Berkeley, 1956).

2. Tzvetan Todorov, *The Conquest of America: The Question of the Other*, trans. Richard Howard (New York, 1982); Stephen Greenblatt, *Marvelous Possessions: The Wonder of the New World* (Chicago, 1991).

3. William Empson, *Some Versions of Pastoral* (London, 1935; New York, 1974), 3–23.

4. Recent critical writing on Petrarchism has been rich; several of the most influential books and essays of the last twenty years will be cited below in connection with particular issues. For overviews of the phenomenon from very different standpoints, see Thomas P. Roche, Jr., *Petrarch and the English Sonnet Sequences*, AMS Studies in the Renaissance, no. 18 (New York, 1989), and my *Post-Petrarchism: Origins and Innovations of the Western Lyric Sequence* (Princeton, 1991).

5. In his introduction to Francisco López de Gómara, *Annals of the Emperor Charles V*, ed. and trans. Roger Bigelow Merriman (Oxford, 1912), x, Merriman notes that Gómara lived in Italy for ten years from 1531. On the Italian background to Oviedo's career, see the editor's introduction to Gonzalo Fernández de Oviedo, *Historia general y natural de las Indias*, ed. Juan Pérez de Tudela Bueso, Biblioteca de Autores Españoles, nos. 117–21 (Madrid, 1959), 1:xxxi, and Oviedo's own testimony in the abridgment of the *Quinquagenas* entitled *Las memorias de Gonzalo Fernández de Oviedo*, ed. Juan Bautista Avalle-Arce, North Carolina Studies in the Romance Languages and Literatures: Texts, Textual Studies, and Translations, nos. 1–2 (Chapel Hill, 1974), 1:76, 200, 254; 2:544, 639–40.

6. Sabine MacCormack, *Religion in the Andes: Vision and Imagination in Early Colonial Peru* (Princeton, 1991), 332–82, relates the Inca Garcilaso's ideas of Incaic religion with close reference to Leo Hebraeus's philosophical dialogues. In " 'This Phrasis Is Continuous': Love

and Empire in 1590," *Journal of Hispanic Philology* 16 (Winter 1992): 237–52, I discuss Garcilaso's translation of the *Dialoghi* as a political and personal statement from his standpoint as a *mestizo*.

7. William Shakespeare, *Sonnets*, ed. Stephen Booth (New Haven, 1977), 4; Walter Ralegh, *The Discovery of the Large, Rich, and Beautiful Empire of Guiana*, ed. Robert H. Schomburgk, Hakluyt Society, 1st ser., no. 3 (London, 1848), 60, 57. Philip P. Boucher, *Cannibal Encounters: Europeans and Island Caribs, 1492–1763* (Baltimore, 1992), 13–30, and esp. 25, identifies the materials on which the European idea of cannibalism was based in about 1590.

8. Lesley Byrd Simpson, *Many Mexicos*, 4th ed. (Berkeley, 1971), 130–35, describes, sometimes in colloquial language that unwittingly allows latent Petrarchisms to emerge ("the Marqués blew hot and cold," 133), the abortive rebellion around the Marquis, the legitimate son of the *conquistador* Hernán Cortés. Margarita Peña, in her edition of *Flores de baria poesía* (Mexico City, 1980), 28–30, accounts for Cortés's career as a poet.

9. Kenneth Burke, *A Grammar of Motives* (New York, 1945; reprint, Berkeley, 1969), 59–61, treats the need for a "representative anecdote" on which to establish a critical vocabulary and the terms of analysis itself.

10. For a more extensive discussion of Wyatt's poetry in these terms, see my "The Colonial Wyatt: Contexts and Openings," in *Rethinking the Henrician Era: Essays on Early Tudor Texts and Contexts*, ed. Peter C. Herman (Urbana, Ill., 1994), 240–66.

11. Ramón Menéndez Pidal, *La lengua de Cristóbal Colón* (Madrid, 1942), 9–30, treats the various sources of Columbus's spoken and written languages. Perhaps the best study of the latter is Virgil I. Milani, *The Written Language of Christopher Columbus* (Buffalo, 1973). On "latin genovisco" or Lingua Franca, see Keith Whinnom, "The Context and Origins of Lingua Franca," in *Langues en contact—Pidgins—Creoles—Languages in Contact*, ed. Jürgen M. Meisel, Tübinger Beiträge zur Linguistik 75 (Tübingen, 1977), 3–18, abridged as "Lingua Franca: Historical Problems" in *Pidgin and Creole Linguistics*, ed. Albert Valdman (Bloomington, 1977), 295–310.

12. In general, historians of navigation and exploration participate in this sort of omission more often than scholars with other interests. Two highly visible examples are the introductions to *The Four Voyages of Columbus*, ed. and trans. Cecil Jane, Hakluyt Society, 2d ser., nos. 65 and 70 (London, 1930–33; reprint, New York, 1988), esp. 1:cvi–cx and 2:xix–xx. More recently, a note of agnosticism can be detected in William D. Phillips, Jr., and Carla Rahn Phillips, *The Worlds of Christopher Columbus* (Cambridge, 1992), 127, where the authors allow that Columbus "made use of the wealth of printed material available in the late fifteenth century as he planned his voyages and speculated on religious matters" but leave the reader to imagine what (besides Pliny, Marco Polo, and Pierre d'Ailly) these texts might have been, in what spirit they were read, and what difference they made.

13. On the rise of Petrarchism in Spain, see Joseph G. Fucilla, *Estudios sobre el petrarquismo en España* (Madrid, 1960), xiii–25: "It is evident from this sketch we have presented that there was an intensification of interest towards the *Canzoniere* in the last years of the fifteenth century and in the first years of the sixteenth" (xv).

14. Christopher Columbus, *Textos y documentos completos*, ed. Consuelo Varela (Madrid, 1982), 143. Here as throughout this essay, the translations are mine unless I indicate otherwise. For an alternate translation, compare Jane, *Four Voyages*, 1:12.

15. All quotations of the *Canzoniere* in the original Italian are from Gianfranco Contini's edition (Turin, 1964).

16. John Freccero, "The Fig Tree and the Laurel: Petrarch's Poetics," in *Literary Theory/ Renaissance Texts*, ed. Patricia Parker and David Quint (Baltimore, 1987), 30–31, is the defining instance of this argument, though Freccero emphasizes the veil's and the breeze's roles as fetishes that operate on different levels (the latter, on the level of the poem's material language, as a pun on Laura). See also Giuseppe Mazzotta, "The *Canzoniere* and the Language of the Self," *Studies in Philology* 75 (1978): 283–84. On the veil as a traditional figure for the material sign that covers a referent, see Erich Auerbach, "Figura," in his *Scenes from the Drama of European Literature* (New York, 1959; Minneapolis, 1984), 49–51, and D. W. Robertson, Jr., *A Preface to Chaucer* (Princeton, 1962), 280, 291–92, 319–20.

17. Christopher Columbus, *The Diario of Christopher Columbus's First Voyage to America, 1492–1493*, ed. Oliver Dunn and James E. Kelley, Jr., American Exploration and Travel Series, no. 70 (Norman, Okla., 1989), 58–62.

18. As Dunn and Kelley point out (ibid., 59), Samuel Eliot Morison, in his edition of the *Journals and Other Documents on the Life and Voyages of Christopher Columbus* (New York, 1963), 63, translates "veedor" as "comptroller." They also remark a note in Cecil Jane, ed. and trans., *The Journal of Christopher Columbus*, rev. L. A. Vigneras, Hakluyt Society, extra ser., no. 38 (London, 1960), 204, which indicates that the *veedor* "was to keep a record of all the gold, precious stones and spices, and to make sure that the Crown would not be cheated out of its share."

19. "La Carta del Doctor Chanca," in Jane, *Four Voyages*, 1:30–33.

20. Columbus, *Diario*, 280, 282, 254.

21. Columbus, *Textos y documentos*, 213–14; compare Jane, *Four Voyages*, 2:28–33. Continuing in their agnostic vein, Phillips and Phillips, *Worlds of Columbus*, observe that "Columbus's speculations about the earthly paradise and his blending of the Bible, Ptolemy, and his own experience would not have seemed as odd to his intended audience as they seem to us" (221).

22. Columbus, *Textos y documentos*, 216; compare Jane, *Four Voyages*, 2:36–37.

23. Clément Marot, "Le Beau Tétin," in *Poètes du XVIe siècle*, ed. Albert-Marie Schmidt (Paris, 1953), 331–32. The translation is by Nancy Vickers, who has written several influential studies of such physical imagery, including "Diana Described: Scattered Woman and Scattered Rhyme," in *Writing and Sexual Difference*, ed. Elizabeth Abel (Chicago, 1982), 95–109, and " 'The blazon of sweet beauty's best': Shakespeare's *Lucrece*," in *Shakespeare and the Question of Theory*, ed. Patricia Parker and Geoffrey Hartman (New York, 1985), 95–115.

24. Columbus, *Textos y documentos*, 329.

25. Samuel Eliot Morison, *Admiral of the Ocean Sea: A Life of Christopher Columbus*, 2 vols. (Boston, 1942), 2:391–92.

26. Amerigo Vespucci, *Lettera delle isole nuouamente trouate in quattro suoi viaggi* (Florence, 1505–06), aiv–aiir. Compare the modern edition in *Il Mondo Nuovo di Amerigo Vespucci*, ed. Mario Pozzi (Milan, 1984), 126, and in English, *The Letters of Amerigo Vespucci*, trans. Clements R. Markham, Hakluyt Society, 1st ser., no. 90 (London, 1894), 1–2. Frederick J. Pohl, *Amerigo Vespucci* (New York, 1944), 150–55, presents the case for this letter's being a

forgery, while Stefan Zweig, *Amerigo*, trans. Andrew St. James (New York, 1942), 43–46, assumes that it is not. The former is a much more reliable book, though a standard biographical-cultural account of Vespucci remains to be written.

27. James A. Williamson, *The Cabot Voyages and Bristol Discovery under Henry VII*, Hakluyt Society, 2d ser., no. 120 (Cambridge, 1962), 10.

28. Duarte Pacheco Pereira, *Esmeraldo de situ orbis*, trans. George H. T. Kimble, Hakluyt Society, 2d ser., no. 79 (London, 1937), 12; the aforementioned naming of Brazil is on 136.

29. Cândido Mendes de Almeida, introduction to José da Silva Lisboa (Visconde de Cayrú), *Principios de direito mercantil e leis de marinha*, 6th ed., 2 vols. (Rio de Janeiro, 1874), 1:cccxliii.

30. Anatole de Montaiglon and Gaston Raynaud, eds., *Recueil général et complet des fabliaux des XIIIe et XIVe siècles*, 6 vols. (Paris, 1872–90), 3:36.

31. On the ideological content of islands, see Fredric Jameson, "Of Islands and Trenches: Neutralization and the Production of Utopian Discourse," in *The Ideologies of Theory: Essays 1971–1986*, Theory and History of Literature, nos. 48–49 (Minneapolis, 1988), 2:75–101.

32. The translation is by Robert M. Durling, from his edition and translation of *Petrarch's Lyric Poems* (Cambridge, Mass., 1976).

33. Joam de Barros, *Ásia: Dos feitos que os portugueses fizeram no descobrimento e conquista dos mares e terras do oriente, primeira decada* (1552–53), ed. António Baião, 4th ed. (Coimbra, 1932), 173–75.

34. Fr. Antonio de Santa Maria Jaboatam, *Novo orbo serafico brasilico, ou chronica dos frades menores da provincia do Brasil*, 5 vols. (1761; Rio de Janeiro, 1858–62), 1:5.

35. Fernão Lopes de Castanheda, *História do descobrimento & conquista da India pelos portugueses, Livro I e II* (1551), 3d ed., ed. Pedro de Azevedo (Coimbra, 1924), 73.

36. The argument originates in Freccero's indispensable "The Fig Tree and the Laurel," 23, 27.

37. Todorov, *Conquest of America*, 3–13, 24–25.

38. Hans Staden, *Wahrhaftige Historie und Beschreibung eyner Landtschafft der Wilden, Nacketen, Grimmigen, Menschfresser Leuten, in der Newen Welt America gelegen* (Marburg, 1557), trans. Albert Tootal and Sir Richard F. Burton, Hakluyt Society, 1st ser., no. 51 (London, 1874); Simão de Vasconcellos, *Chronica da companhia de Jesus do estado do Brasil* (1663; Lisbon, 1865), 186.

39. Haroldo de Campos, "The Rule of Anthropophagy: Europe under the Sign of Devoration," trans. Maria Tai Wolff, *Latin American Literary Review* 27 (1986): 54.

40. Any number of Brazilian cultural phenomena, from Carmen Miranda to concrete poetry, might be taken as evidence of this trend. On the former, see Caetano Veloso, "Caricature and Conqueror, Pride and Shame," trans. Robert Myers, *New York Times*, 20 October 1991, sec. 2, 34, 41; on the latter, Charles A. Perrone, "The Imperative of Invention: Brazilian Concrete Poetry and Intersemiotic Creation," *Harvard Library Bulletin*, n.s., 3 (Summer 1992): 44–53.

41. Richard Harrier, *The Canon of Sir Thomas Wyatt's Poetry* (Cambridge, Mass., 1975), 99–100.

42. Jaime González Rodríguez, *La idea de Roma en la historiografía indiana (1492–1550)* (Madrid, 1981), 92. As González Rodríguez indicates, the work of López de Gómara is perhaps the most influential of those "destined to exalt the hero Cortés in the classical mode" (122). Francisco Cervantes de Salazar, "Túmulo Imperial de la Gran Ciudad de Mexico" (1560), in *México en 1554 y Túmulo Imperial*, ed. Edmundo O'Gorman (Mexico City, 1963), 190, treats Cortés's fealty to "Caesar" (Charles V) as a latter-day improvement on the successes of Hannibal and other famous generals; compare Bernal Díaz del Castillo, *Historia verdadera de la conquista de la Nueva España*, ed. Joaquín Ramírez Cabañas (Mexico City, 1970), 33, trans. J. M. Cohen as *The Conquest of New Spain* (London, 1963), 47, where Díaz briefly traces Cortés's four lines of descent and goes on to liken him to Alexander the Great, Julius Caesar, and Hannibal, among others.

43. Frank M. Snowden, Jr., *Before Color Prejudice: The Ancient View of Blacks* (Cambridge, Mass., 1983), mounts a survey of classical attitudes toward race and color and demonstrates that the coordination between physical facts and symbolic constructions differs widely across times and places, so that for social and cultural purposes Africans can be variously "black," "colored," or even "white." The standard study of the black and white extremes in European and North American thought is Winthrop D. Jordan, *White over Black: American Attitudes toward the Negro, 1550–1812* (Chapel Hill, 1968), 3–43, in which the announced purpose of the project enforces a certain oblivion toward the question of color where Indians are concerned (as, for instance, at 27).

44. Sir John Mandeville's *Travels*, ed. Malcolm Letts, Hakluyt Society, 2d ser., nos. 101–2 (London, 1953), 1:33. The word "colour" leads Mandeville into a highly reiterative passage on the "black[ness]" of the Numidians. As Letts explains, however, the word "colour" and the passage around it do not appear in all manuscripts of the *Travels*.

45. Columbus, *Diario*, 66.

46. *A Carta de Pero Vaz de Caminha*, ed. Jaime Cortesão (Rio de Janeiro, 1943), 215. The translation, by William Brooks Greenlee, appears in *The Voyage of Pedro Alvares Cabral to Brazil and India*, Hakluyt Society, 2d ser., no. 81 (London, 1937), 18.

47. Francisco López de Gómara, *Primera parte de la historia general de las Indias*, ed. Enrique de Vedia, Biblioteca de Autores Españoles, no. 22 (Madrid, 1852), 289–90. J. H. Elliott, "The Discovery of America and the Discovery of Man," in *Spain and Its World, 1500–1700* (New Haven, 1989), 48, adduces a similar description of a generation later by Juan López de Velasco, *Geografía y descripción universal de las Indias* (1574), ed. Marcos Jiménez de la Espada, Biblioteca de Autores Españoles, no. 248 (Madrid, 1971), 14, where accounts of the Indies themselves, their weather, winds, lands and soils, trees, grains and seeds, animals, birds, mines, and metals precede the discussion of the color of the people.

48. *Cedulario indiano*, comp. Diego de Encinas, ed. Alfonso Garcia Gallo, 2 vols. (Madrid, 1945–46), 2:225–26.

49. Elliott, "The Discovery of America," 48.

50. Compare Magnus Mörner, *Race Mixture in the History of Latin America* (Boston, 1967), 6: "Prior to 1500 differential valorization of human races is hardly noticeable. . . . It seems as if Western man was made conscious of racial characteristics, above all, by Renaissance curiosity."

51. Louise Labé, *Oeuvres complètes*, ed. François Rigolot (Paris, 1986), 132–33.

52. Elliott, "The Discovery of America," 43.

53. Conventional (that is, nonpolitical) assessments of the sonnet are offered by Enzo Giudici in his edition of Labé's *Oeuvres complètes* (Geneva, 1981), 191, n. 124, where he comments on the lack of an obvious source, and in his essay *Louise Labé* (Rome, 1981), 78, where he remarks on the "traces of realism" in this and other sonnets.

54. Compare the discussion of Sonnet 21 in Ann Rosalind Jones, *The Currency of Eros: Women's Love Lyric in Europe, 1540–1620* (Bloomington, 1990), 168–69, which remarks the poem's celebration of "feminine subjectivity" and its depreciation of the logic of the *blason*—elements I would connect through its muted but insistent political register.

55. Peña, *Flores de baria poesía*, 506.

56. Begoña López Bueno, *Gutierre de Cetina, poeta del Renacimiento español* (Seville, 1978), 66–75, gathers information about Cetina's first voyage to Mexico in 1546; his possible relations with Cortés; his return to Spain in 1548 via Italy, where he received a letter that he carried to the future Philip II; his return to Mexico; his commercial activities there; and his death following an argument over a woman.

57. For an early anecdote in which "blood and fire" characterizes the religious practices of the Indians, see Hernán Cortés, "Primera Carta-Relación" (1519), in *Cartas de Relación*, with an introduction by Manuel Alcalá (Mexico City, 1983), 21–22, translated as "The First Letter," in *Letters from Mexico*, ed. and trans. Anthony Pagden (New Haven, 1986), 35.

58. Hernán Cortés, "Segunda Carta-Relación" (1520), in *Cartas de Relación*, 85, trans. Pagden in *Letters from Mexico*, 142. Cortés means his confusion between the Spaniards and the Otomi Indians literally: that is, there were so many Indians that the Spaniards could not tell their own men. But I read the sentence as the outcome of the entire letter, in which the level of Spanish barbarism is continually rising to meet that of the Indians.

59. José A. Llaguno, SJ, *La personalidad jurídica del indio y el III Consilio Provincial Mexicano (1585)* (Mexico City, 1963), 70–87. As indicated on the last page of this discussion, the council concluded that "we neither find nor feel justification for making open warfare, to blood and fire, as has been and is being sought."

60. See, for instance, the first sentences of *De indis*, in *Las relecciones De Indis y De Iure Belli*, ed. Javier Malagón Barceló (Washington, D.C., 1963), 4: "Et tota disputatio & relectio suscepta est propter barbaros istos novi orbis, quos Indos vulgò vocant, qui ante quadraginta annos venerunt in potestatem Hispanorum, ignoti prius nostro orbi" ("And all of the disputation and relection concern those barbarians of the New World, vulgarly called Indians, who, previously unknown in our country, for forty years have come under Spanish power").

61. Fray Bartolomé de Las Casas, *Apologética historia sumaria* (1559), ed. Edmundo O'Gorman, 2 vols. (Mexico City, 1967), 2:637–54.

62. Avalle-Arce, *Memorias*, 1:19. Avalle-Arce's edition, under the title of his devising, is an abridgment of the *Quinquagenas* proper. The only previous publication of Oviedo's manuscript is *Las Quinquagenas de la Nobleza de España*, ed. Vicente de la Fuente (Madrid, 1880), the first volume of a projected but incomplete set of three. For a recent study that offers more summary than interpretation, see Antonello Gerbi, *Nature in the New World: From*

Christopher Columbus to Gonzalo Fernández de Oviedo, trans. Jeremy Moyle (Pittsburgh, 1985), 378–84; compare Gerbi's useful account (157–63) of Oviedo's usage in the *Historia* of Petrarch, Dante, and other poets and humanists of the fourteenth and fifteenth centuries.

63. Avalle-Arce, *Memorias*, 1:18, 36–38.

64. For a useful study of the *Historia*, see Stephanie Merrim, "'Un *Mare Magno* e Oculto': Anatomy of Fernández de Oviedo's *Historia General y Natural de las Indias*," *Revista de Estudios Hispánicos* (Puerto Rico) 11 (1984): 101–19. For an overview of Oviedo's life and writings, see Juan Bautista Avalle-Arce, "Oviedo a media luz," *Nueva Revista de Filologia Hispánica* 29 (1980): 138–51. Daymond Turner reconstructed Oviedo's library in two articles: "Biblioteca Ovetense: A Speculative Reconstruction of the Library of the First Chronicler of the Indies," *PBSA* 57 (1963): 157–83, and "Los libros del Alcaide: La biblioteca de Gonzalo Fernández de Oviedo y Valdés," *Revista de Indias* 125–26 (1971): 139–98.

65. Oviedo, *Historia general y natural*, 1:14, 222; 2:149.

66. Ibid., 1:155.

67. Examples include *Canzoniere* 126, ll. 40–65, in Contini, *Canzoniere*, 168–69.

68. Ibid., 246.

69. Oviedo, *Historia general y natural*, 1:155.

70. Avalle-Arce, *Memorias*, 1:117.

71. Ibid.

72. Ibid., 119.

73. Contini, *Canzoniere*, 139.

DAVID QUINT

A Reconsideration of Montaigne's *Des cannibales*

At a fairly early point in *Des cannibales* (*Essais* 1.31) comes the passage that has greatly contributed to the idea of the noble savage, and that has caused the essay to be read as an encomium of the natural way of life of the New World inhabitants. It is the passage cited and imitated in Shakespeare's *The Tempest* (2.1.143–64), when the old courtier Gonzalo envisions the utopian commonwealth he would build if he could rule Prospero's island. Montaigne asserts that the life of the cannibals surpasses in happiness not only the mythical golden age but the ideal polities projected by Lycurgus and Plato, who were unable to imagine maintaining society "with so little artifice and human solder" ("avec si peu d'artifice et de soudeure humaine") (153;204),[1] that is, without the intervention of culture. The essay goes on to define this state of nature by listing those cultural institutions that it lacks: no trade, no writing or arithmetic, no juridical or political offices, no servitude or class division between rich and poor, no business or testamentary settlements, no kinship relations, no agriculture or metallurgy. This impressive chain of privatives reaches its rhetorical climax as the cannibals' language itself proves devoid of the terms of a European culture that lacks their simplicity:

> The very words that signify lying, treachery, dissimulation, avarice, envy, belittling, pardon—unheard of. (153)
>
> (Les paroles mesmes qui signifient le mensonge, la trahison, la dissimulation, l'avarice, l'envie, la detraction, le pardon, inouïes.) (204)

These terms suggest that what the cannibal lacks, above all, is the self-consciousness and self-division of the European. A familiar dialectic here shapes the perception of the "primitive" or the "natural" human being that will become a constituent feature of romanticism and of Rousseau's noble savage two centuries later. The cannibal cannot tell a lie, not knowing what one is, or betray, or dissemble, and the integrity and single-mindedness of his contented existence is witnessed by his lack of desire of more for himself or of less for others: envy is here a middle term between avarice and detraction.

So far so good, but it is the last not-so-innocent term, "pardon," that should give us pause. "In cauda venenum" ("the sting is in the tail"), or, as Montaigne himself in *Des livres* describes the technique of the epigram that ends with a reversal of what has preceded it, "the stings with which Martial sharpens the tails of his" ("les esguillons dequoy Martial esguise la queuë des siens) (299;391). The whole essay of *Des cannibales* ends with a spectacular instance of this technique: "They don't wear breeches," says the essayist, seemingly dismissing the whole subject. But here the unsettling final term, "pardon," as it already anticipates the ensuing description of the central, horrifying event of the cannibals' culture, cannot help but evoke the issue of clemency that has already been placed front and center in the *Essais*. In the B-text of 1588, the opening essay, *Par divers moyens on arrive a pareille fin*, introduces as Montaigne's first citation of classical authority a reference to Seneca's *De Clementia* (2.4.4–2.5.1), and the answering essay 1:24, *Divers evenemens de mesme conseil*, is structured around the well-known story of Augustus and Cinna from the same Senecan moral treatise. Where the first essay begins by taking the vantage point of the defeated seeking to find mercy from their conquerors when these have "vengeance in hand" ("la vengeance en main") (3;11), the latter addresses the perspective of the victorious rulers and advises them that the best policy is always to forgo revenge and to pardon: "It was clearly finer and more generous in the man who had received the offense to pardon it than to do otherwise" ("Il n'y a point de doubte, qu'il ne fut plus beau et plus genereux à celuy qui avoit receu l'offence, de la pardonner, que s'il eust fait autrement") (93–94;127). The cannibals' warfare is described as "wholly noble and generous" ("toute noble et genereuse") (156;208). Yet they do not pardon their captives, but eat them instead "to betoken an extreme revenge" ("pour representer une extreme vengeance") (155;207). In this case the cannibals' single-mindedness, which prevents any deviation from their goal of vengeance, becomes bloody-mindedness.[2]

The way that the epigrammatic sting of "pardon" concludes and calls into question the glowing, idealizing description of the cannibals' society that has come before provides a cautionary glimpse at the structures of reversal that will run through *Des cannibales*—including, as Edwin M. Duval has pointed out, the opposition of nature and culture.[3] The further we read the essay the more questions it poses about the virtue of the cannibals. Despite the disavowals of this passage, the cannibals' culture is to be understood not only as the negation of European mores, but by its own positive, if peculiar and horrific, institutions that the essay confronts and describes in some detail. The essay finally focuses on the treatment of prisoners and raises questions about the relationship of noble martial valor, Stoic resolve, cruelty, and revenge: these issues link it to other essays in Montaigne's collection and suggest that, in spite of its exotic subject, it needs to be understood in their larger context. In what follows, I shall try to embed *Des cannibales* in the *Essais*, noting how it echoes and is echoed by a group of essays that are interrelated among themselves. From this cross-referencing I shall return to a reading of the essay's analysis of the cannibals' culture. This analysis, in turn, will be juxtaposed with Montaigne's examination of another culture of military virtue, the gladiatorial Roman culture described in 2:23, *Des mauvais moyens employez à bonne fin.* Both cultures are explicitly compared to Montaigne's France, torn apart by the Wars of Religion, and I shall finally argue that this calamitous historical situation of civil war, where the refractory French nobleman and the intransigent Huguenot martyr share a common Stoicism with the Brazilian cannibal and the Roman gladiator, governs the cultural analysis of *Des cannibales.*

My argument—that Montaigne's essay on the cannibals turns out to be at least equally about his own France and that the terms with which it discusses the Brazilian natives are deeply rooted in his own historical and political preoccupations—runs counter to the traditional and still prevalent critical reception of *Des cannibales* that congratulates Montaigne for his freedom from ethnocentric prejudice. The essayist does indeed state his preference for the unbiased, objective ethnographic detailing of *topographers* over the interpretative reporting of *cosmographers* who always add something of their own in the telling, and he insists that he has received his information about the cannibals from an eyewitness, a servant of his who had spent some time among them.[4] Gérard Defaux, in an important polemical article, has suggested the extent to which this version of Montaigne as proto-anthropologist is untenable. He doubts the very existence of the servant and points out that all of Montaigne's descriptions of the cannibals derive from the works of those cosmographers he professes not to have consulted. Moreover, he notes how Montaigne himself interprets the cannibals and shapes his description of their culture according to preexisting European typologies; for instance, he connects the passage I began with to conventional Ovidian descriptions of the Golden Age, the same golden age that the cannibals are said to surpass. Defaux concludes that the essay ends in an aporia; its true subject is not an escape from ethnocentrism but rather just the opposite: the impossibility of ever acknowledging—achieving knowledge of—the foreign other because the would-be knower cannot escape the terms of his own language and culture.[5]

As helpful as Defaux's arguments are in demystifying the claims of the essay to an impartial, factual account of the cannibals and their society, his conclusions are unnecessarily drastic. The ideal of an objective or transparent reporting of the practices of an alien culture—just the facts, please—is indeed utopian. There are no "facts" without interpretation, since "facts" are constituted by the language that describes them, in this case the language and cultural codes of the European observer of the New World peoples. But it does not follow that *everything* gets lost in the translation, that *nothing* of the cannibals' culture can get through the interpretive accounts made of it both by the cosmographers and by Montaigne himself, however distorting those accounts may be. Even the most confirmed structuralist is conscious that alien cultures do communicate with each other, with greater and lesser degrees of understanding and accommodation of their discursive systems to the challenge of the new—just as the individual discursive systems of a given culture change and develop across time and become capable of expressing new concepts and ideas.

Even if Montaigne's essay may not tell us much about the Brazilian cannibals—and it may tell us more than Defaux is inclined to think—it can tell us something about Montaigne's France, at least as seen through the essayist's eyes. Poststructuralist anthropology has particularly emphasized a "linguistic turn" toward self-consciousness and has targeted for examination the ethnographer's own discursive practice and cultural makeup as much as the culture that is his or her declared object of study.[6] *Des cannibales* invites this approach, for at the famous moral high point at the center of the essay, Montaigne declares of the Brazilians' cannibalism,

> I am not sorry that we notice the barbarous horror of such acts, but I am heartily sorry that, judging their faults rightly, we should be so blind to our own. I think there is more barbarity in eating a man alive than in eating him dead; . . . (155)

> (Je ne suis pas marry que nous remerquons l'horreur barbaresque qu'il y a en une telle action, mais ouy bien dequoy, jugeans bien de leurs fautes, nous soyons si aveuglez aux nostres. Je pense qu'il y a plus de barbarie à manger un homme vivant qu'à le manger mort, . . .) (207)

and goes on to condemn the European use of torture, especially that which he and his fellow Frenchmen have recently seen for themselves during the Wars of Religion. It has always been a humanistic article of belief that one studies other cultures in order better to understand one's own. It should then come as little surprise that the cannibal society that Montaigne describes should serve as a model for his France.

For the cannibal society to do so, however, its barbaric horror needs in fact to be noticed. The traditional reading of *Des cannibales* that praises Montaigne's impartial objectivity toward the New World peoples is tacitly based on the approval of them he voices in such passages as the comparison to the Golden Age—as if objectivity and approval were the same, and as if it were impossible for a European to disapprove of the cannibalism of non-Europeans without revealing an incurable ethnocentrism or, even worse, a colonialist ideology. The ideological stakes that may lie behind these latter kinds of assumptions need not concern us, but in its perpetuation of the idea of the noble savage, it seems to reverse Montaigne's concern: it recognizes all too well the barbarity of the European while it seems blinded to that of the cannibals. This hardly seems to be the essay's fault, for while Montaigne continues to praise the virtue and abilities of the Brazilians throughout *Des cannibales,* its second half draws the reader closer and closer to the war and cannibalism in which such virtue results, from the initial image of an age of gold to images of dismembered limbs and roasted flesh.

Cannibal Cruelty

The cannibals, according to the essay, fight their wars merely for glory and to demonstrate their superiority in valor over their enemies—the cannibals from the other side of their mountains. They are, it seems, willing to let the prisoners they take in battle go, a pardon of sorts, providing "that they confess and acknowledge their defeat" ("la confession et recognoissance d'estre vaincus") (156;209), and they threaten the prisoners with torture and dismemberment and remind them of the feast that will be made of their flesh "for the sole purpose of wringing from their lips some weak or base word, or making them want to flee, so as to gain the advantage of having terrified them and broken down their firmness" ("pour cette seule fin d'arracher de leur bouche quelque parole molle ou rabaissée, ou de leur donner envie de s'en fuyr, pour gaigner cet avantage de les avoir espouvantez, et d'avoir faict force à leur constance") (156;209). The cannibals attempt to break down the constancy of their adversaries and make them say uncle; when that fails, as it almost always does for reasons that will be examined below, they eat them.

In the 1588 addition to the end of the first essay, *Par divers moyens,* Montaigne inserts a classical anecdote that replays a very similar scenario. After conquering the city of Gaza, Alexander the Great berates the opposing commander, Betis:

> "You shall not die as you wanted, Betis: prepare yourself to suffer every kind of torment that can be invented against a captive." The other, with a look not only confident, but insolent and haughty, stood without saying a word to these threats. Then Alexander, seeing his proud and obstinate silence: "Has he bent a knee? Has any suppliant cry escaped him? I'll conquer your muteness yet, and if I cannot wring a word from it, at least I'll wring a groan." And turning his anger into rage, he ordered Betis' heels to be pierced through and had him thus dragged, alive, torn and dismembered, behind a cart. (5)
>
> ("Tu ne mourras pas comme tu a voulu, Betis; fais estat qu'il te faut souffrir toutes les sortes de tourmens qui se pourront inventer contre un captif." L'autre, d'une mine non seulement asseurée, mais rogue et altiere, se tint sans mot dire à ces menaces. Lors Alexandre, voyant son fier et obstiné silence: "A-il flechi un

Cannibals taunting their victim, from Johann Theodor de Bry, *Grands Voyages*, pt. III (Latin) (Frankfurt, 1592). John Carter Brown Library.

> genouil? luy est-il eschappé quelque voix suppliante? Vrayment je vainqueray ta taciturnité; et si je n'en puis arracher parole, j'en arracheray au moins du gemissement." Et tournant sa cholere en rage, commanda qu'on luy perçast les talons, et le fit ainsi trainer tout vif, deschirer et desmembrer au cul d'une charrete.) (14)

This addition—which now, however, sets the tone and scene for the entire *Essais* that follow it—clearly echoes *Des cannibales*: the conqueror's exasperated, vain effort to wring a word ("arracher parole") of supplication from his imperturbable captive leads to his vindictive dismemberment of the captive's body. It makes a difference that the body in this case is still alive, and the language—"tout vif, deschirer et desmembrer"—is also reminiscent of the essay's already cited condemnation of modern European torture, particularly the cruelties practiced "on the pretext of piety and religion" ("sous pretexte de pieté et religion") (155;208) by the Catholic and Huguenot sides in the French civil wars: "I think that there is more barbarity in eating a man alive than in eating him dead; and in tearing by tortures and the rack a body still full of feeling" ("Je pense qu'il y a plus de barbarie à manger un homme vivant qu'à le manger mort, à deschirer, par tourmens et par geénes, un corps encore plein de sentiment") (155;207–8).[7] Alexander's action not only mimics, but exceeds the barbarity of the cannibals and—as another internal echo of the *Essais* suggests—virtually defines cruelty itself. So Montaigne, again speaking in the context of the civil wars in France, writes in *De la cruauté* (2:11):

> I could hardly be convinced, until I saw it, that there were souls so monstrous that they would commit murder for the mere pleasure of it; hack and cut off other men's limbs; sharpen their wits to invent unaccustomed torments and new forms of death, without enmity, without profit, and for the sole purpose of enjoying the pleasing spectacle of the pitiful gestures and movements, the lamentable groans and cries, of a man dying in anguish. For that is the uttermost point that cruelty can attain. (315–16)

> (A peine me pouvoy-je persuader, avant que je l'eusse veu, qu'il se fut trouvé des ames si monstrueuses, qui, pour le seul plaisir de meurtre, le voulussent commettre: hacher et détrencher les membres d'autruy; esguiser leur esprit à inventer des tourmens inusitez et des morts nouvelles, sans inimitié, sans profit, et pour cette seule fin de jouïr du plaisant spectacle des gestes et mouvemens pitoyables, des gemissemens et voix lamentables d'un homme mourant en angoisse. Car voylà l'extreme point où la cruauté puisse atteindre.) (411–12)

Promising Betis all the tortures that can be invented and seeking to wring groans ("gemissement") if not a plea for mercy from him, Alexander reaches the very height of tyranny and cruelty—"our ordinary vices" ("nos fautes ordinaires") (156;208), remarks Montaigne in *Des cannibales.* But the customary behavior of the Brazilian cannibals, too, is echoed and implicated in this passage from *De la cruauté,* for it is with the promise of similar "torments" and "the cutting up of their limbs" ("des tourmens . . . du detranchement de leurs membres") (156;209) that they try to break the wills of their captive foes.

The cannibalism of the New World peoples is thus related to the essayist's examination and critique of cruelty. While the cannibals may be easily excelled by Old World practitioners, they are cruel nonetheless and have readily adopted the even more sadistic Portuguese mode of executing prisoners in place of their own (155;207). It has recently been suggested by Judith Shklar that Montaigne's abhorrence of cruelty is the overriding ethical concern of the *Essais* as a whole;[8] it is certainly a recurrent issue in a series of essays. In *Couardise mere de la cruauté* (2:27), Montaigne argues against killing as an act of vengeance because the real aim of revenge is to make itself felt on the victim, to make the victim repent of his offense.

> “He will repent it,” we say. And because we have given him a pistol shot in the head, do we think that he repents it? On the contrary, if we consider it, we will find that he makes a face at us as he falls. He does not even hold it against us, so far is he from repenting. (524)

> (“Il s’en repentira,” disons nous. Et, pour luy avoir donné d’une pistolade en la teste, estimons nous qu’il s’en repente? Au rebours, si nous nous en prenons garde, nous trouverons qu’il nous faict la mouë en tombant: il ne nous en sçait pas seulement mauvais gré, c’est bien loing de s’en repentir.) (672)

An analogous scene in *Des cannibales* describes the final moments of the captive cannibal before his enemies kill and eat him as the sign of extreme vengeance.

> Those that paint these people dying, and who show the execution, portray the prisoner spitting in the face of his slayers and making a face at them. Indeed to the last gasp they never stop braving and defying their enemies by word and look. Truly here are real savages by our standards; for either they must be thoroughly so, or we must be; there is an amazing distance between their character and ours. (158)

> (Ceux qui les peignent mourans, et qui representent cette action quand on les assomme, ils peignent le prisonnier crachant au visage de ceux qui le tuent et leur faisant la mouë. De vray, il ne cessent jusques au dernier souspir de les braver et deffier de parole et de contenance. Sans mentir, au pris de nous, voilà des hommes bien sauvages; car ou il faut qu’ils le soyent bien à bon escient, ou que nous le soyons: il y a une merveilleuse distance entre leur forme et la nostre.) (211)

The repentance of the victim sought by the avenger in *Couardise mere de la cruauté* is closely related to the confession of having been vanquished sought by the cannibals and by Alexander, but neither is forthcoming in any of these cases.[9] The defiance of the cannibal, sticking out his tongue at his captors at the instant of his death, is thus not so unique as *Des cannibales* here proclaims it to be, although it is exemplary of the emptiness of a vengeance that rarely brings any satisfaction to the avenger—and may, for that very reason, turn all the more lethal. But the behavior of the cannibals seems purer—more natural—because it is so deeply inculcated by their culture, because, knowing “how to enjoy their condition happily and be content with it” (“sçavoir heureusement jouyr de leur condition et s’en contenter”) (156;209), the cannibals cannot imagine behaving otherwise. It is they, rather than the European observers castigated earlier in the essay for judging according to the standards of their own countries (152;202), who are caught up in—we might say the victims of—their ethnocentrism.

Cannibal Culture

The essay, in fact, repeatedly emphasizes the fertility of the cannibals' region, which abounds in fish and flesh (153;205), and their contentment with the necessities of nature: "Anything beyond that is superfluous to them" ("Tout ce qui est au delà est superflu pour eux") (156;208). Spending their whole days dancing (154; 205), the cannibals live in a land of Cockaigne—and they certainly do not need to eat each other to make up a protein deficiency in their diets.[10] Their cannibalism and the warfare that literally feeds it are superfluous products of a culture that, however simplified, possesses its own logic. Its essentials, which are twofold, are stated twice in a short space of the essay:

> He [the cannibal prophet] recommends to them only two things: valor against the enemy and love for their wives. . . . their whole ethical science contains only these two articles: resoluteness in war and affection for their wives. (154)

> (Il ne leur recommande que deux choses: la vaillance contre les ennemis et l'amitié à leur femmes. . . . toute leur science ethique ne contient que ces deux articles, de la resolution à la guerre et affection à leurs femmes.) (206)

These two injunctions of cannibal ethics turn out to be related, for in this polygamous culture "the higher their reputation for valor the more wives they have" ("en ont d'autant plus grand nombre qu'ils sont en meilleure reputation de vaillance") (158;211). By their number, the wives become the badge of their husbands' valor, and the "jealousy" with which they contend to obtain more companions for the "honor" of their spouse mirrors the "jealousy in valor" ("jalousie de la vertu") (156;208) that is the basis of the cannibals' warfare with their neighbors.

For otherwise, the cannibals have little way of telling one another apart. In a passage that appears to owe more to Plato's *Republic* than to his ethnographic sources, Montaigne relates that "they generally call those of the same age, brothers; those who are younger, children; and the old men are fathers to all the others" ("ils s'entr'appellent generalement, ceux de mesme aage, freres; enfans, ceux qui sont au dessoubs; et les vieillards sont peres à tous les autres") (156;208), and they leave their property to all in common.[11] In a society where all are alike, martial valor becomes the only mark of identity, and the invincible courage of the cannibal warrior is perhaps less marvelous when it and it alone defines who he is. Cannibal society thus appears intensely competitive—all the more so because there is but one focus of competition and because the cannibals are identical one with another. Their striving one and all to distinguish themselves in battle in the same culturally prescribed manner only makes them seem more alike.

Here, then, is an example, at the level of a whole society, of that crisis of likeness that René Girard has described as the crisis of culture itself and the source of its violence.[12] Among the cannibals this violence is apparently displaced from within the society of similar males—competing to establish their dissimilarity—onto the foreign enemy, but the pattern of likeness only reinstates itself when the enemy turns out to be another cannibal tribe with an identical culture from the other side of the mountains. The reciprocity is spelled out by the essayist's laconic sentence, "These on this side, do the same in their turn" ("Autant en font ceux-cy à leur tour") (156;209), and, most remarkably, in the song of the cannibal captive before he is executed and devoured:

> I have a song composed by a prisoner which contains this challenge, that they should all come boldly and gather to dine off him, for they will be eating at the same time their own fathers and grandfathers, who have served to feed and nourish his body. "These muscles," he says, "this flesh and these veins are your own, poor fools that you are. You do not recognize that the substance of your ancestors' limbs is still contained in them. Savor them well; you will find in them the taste of your own flesh." (158)

> (J'ay une chanson faicte par un prisonnier, où il y a ce traict: qu'ils viennent hardiment trétous et s'assemblent pour disner de luy: car ils mangeront quant et quant leurs peres et leurs ayeux, qui ont servy d'aliment et de nourriture à son corps. "Ces muscles," dit-il, "cette chair et ces veines, ce sont les vostres, pauvres fols que vous estes; vous ne recognoissez pas que la substance des membres de vos ancestres s'y tient encore: savourez les bien, vous y trouverez le goust de vostre propre chair.") (211)

"An invention that certainly does not smack of barbarity" ("Invention qui ne sent aucunement la barbarie"), Montaigne immediately comments, playing in this gustatory context on the connotation of "sent" and, perhaps of the *essai* itself, as a kind of tasting. Wit aside, Montaigne might well congratulate the invention of the cannibal's song, because it is his own, as a philological comparison to his source in André Thevet's *Les Singularitez de la France antarctique* demonstrates. There the cannibal captive sings:

> The Margageas our friends are valiant, strong, and powerful in war, they have taken and eaten a great number of our enemies, just as these enemies will eat me

some day when it will please them to do so: but for my part, I have killed and eaten the relatives and friends of him who holds me prisoner: with many similar words.[13]

(Les Margageas noz amis sont gens de bien, forts & puissans en guerre, ils ont pris & mangé grand nombre de noz ennemis, aussi me mangeront ils quelque iour quand il leur plaira: mais de moy, j'ay tué & mangé des parens et amis de celuy qui me tient prisonnier: avec plusieurs semblables paroles.)

The inventive essayist has supplied the other similar words the cosmographer has left out, and he should be credited for the alimentary conceit—not at all barbarous—that the cannibals are eating not only the flesh of their fathers and grandfathers that has gone into nourishing the captive they eat in turn, but, as the captive says, their own flesh.

Montaigne, that is, deliberately revises Thevet's account in order to depict a cannibal society and larger culture that, even as it directs its violence outward in war against its enemy, is literally devouring itself. Not only is the enemy another identical cannibal, not only does the perfect reciprocity of vengeance between the two enemy tribes reinforce their similarity and promise an unending chain of violence that turns the victory of today into tomorrow's defeat, but the competition of valor *within* the society fuels the warfare in the first place and, even as it seeks to differentiate one cannibal from another, leads them all to the same end: killed or eaten by an enemy that will be killed or eaten in turn. At the end of the essay, Montaigne asks a cannibal who has been brought to France, a cannibal captain or king, one who had thus succeeded in distinguishing himself in an otherwise egalitarian and virtually anonymous culture, what advantage he gained from his superior position. "He told me that it was to march foremost in war" ("il me dict que c'estoit marcher le premier à la guerre") (159;213): designated the first in bravery, but also the first to be killed.

A Roman Analogue

The cannibal culture, in which we may now discern as many dystopian as utopian features, is not an isolated case in the *Essais*. Some of its patterns, in particular its emphasis on military prowess and valor, its collapse of difference between foreign war and intrasocietal competition and violence, its ultimately self-defeating and self-consuming mechanisms, are found in Montaigne's analysis of ancient Rome in the short essay, *Des mauvais moyens employez à bonne fin* (2:23). The evil means of the title are twofold—the foreign wars the Romans fought and the gladiatorial games they held in their arenas—and these are interrelated. The essay begins with the conceit of the body politic, whose superabundance of health needs on occasion to be purged by a bloodletting: by sending out a part of the population to conquer new territory, as the ancient Franks first came to France or as the Romans founded their colonies. The conceit somewhat shifts its meaning as Montaigne describes a second Roman strategy:

> Sometimes also they deliberately fostered wars with certain of their enemies, not only to keep their men in condition, for fear that idleness, mother of corruption, might bring them to some worse mischief—
>
> We bear the evils of long peace; fiercer than war,
> Luxury weighs us down
>
> Juvenal
>
> —but also to serve as a bloodletting for their republic and to cool off a bit the too vehement heat of their young men, to prune and clear the branches of that too lustily proliferating stock. (517)

> (Par fois aussi ils ont à escient nourry des guerres avec aucuns leurs ennemis, non seulement pour tenir leurs hommes en haleine, de peur que l'oysiveté, mere de corruption, ne leur apportast quelque pire incovenient,
>
> Et patimur longae pacis mala; saevior armis,
> Luxuria incumbit;
>
> mais aussi pour servir de saignée à leur Republique et esvanter un peu la chaleur trop vehemente de leur jeunesse, escourter et esclaircir le branchage de ce tige foisonnant en trop de gaillardise.) (663)

Here the metaphor of bloodletting becomes literalized in a sinister way, for the hot-blooded valorous Roman youth who threaten the Republic and who are purged from its body in fact shed their own blood on enemy soil. The overly healthy and abundant population of Rome is kept in check by periodic wars, and the essay goes on to acknowledge, as Montaigne thinks of his contemporary France, that a foreign war is a lesser evil than a civil one (518;664). Yet the Roman wars are also said to keep the young men of the city "in condition" ("en haleine") (517;663), and the same metaphor of military or athletic training crops up when the essay turns explicitly to its titular subject of means and ends and describes how "the Romans trained the people to valor and contempt for dangers and death by those furious spectacles of gladiators" ("les Romains dressoient le peuple à la vaillance et au mespris des dangiers et de la mort par ces furieux spectacles de gladiateurs") (518;664). The chicken-and-egg paradox of the essay lies in the question of whether the military virtue and prowess instilled by the gladiatorial games was the response to or the cause of Rome's foreign wars: whether those wars required a hot-blooded citizenry trained up in valor or whether the games created the hot blood in Rome's youth that then required war in order to be purged in foreign climes. The distinction of means and ends collapses in any event, for while both the wars and gladiatorial games are means supposedly conducive to the end that is the health of the Roman republic, they in fact feed off one another in an endless cycle. Even the distinction between the gladiators and the citizenry collapses by the end of the essay:

> The early Romans used criminals for such examples; but later they used innocent slaves, and even freemen who sold themselves for this purpose; [B] finally Roman senators and knights, and even women. (519)

> (Les premiers Romains employoient à cet exemple les criminels; mais dépuis on y employa des serfs innocens, et des libres mesmes qui se vendoyent pour cet effect; [B] jusques à des Senateurs et Chevaliers Romains, et encore des femmes.) (665)

Thus the potential civil violence that Rome tried to avoid by fighting wars against external enemies returns—as a kind of double—in the combat of the arena, which, with the 1588 (B) addition to the essay, finally includes all sectors of the population. Even Rome's foreign wars were partly directed at her own citizens, and here the society trained up in military valor is seen manifestly warring against itself.

In their brave composure the gladiators whose behavior educated the Romans in valor closely resemble the cannibals. Verbal echoes link the descriptions of these similarly self-destructive cultures:

> It was in truth an admirable example, and very fruitful for the education of the people, to see every day before their eyes a hundred, even a thousand pairs of men, armed against one another, hack each other to pieces with such extreme firmness of courage that they were observed never to let slip a word of weakness or commiseration, never to turn their back or make even a cowardly movement to avoid their adversary's blow, but rather to extend their neck to his sword and offer themselves to the blow. (518)

> (C'estoit, à la verité, un merveilleux exemple, et de tres-grand fruict pour l'institution du peuple, de voir tous les jours en sa presence cent, deux cens, et mille couples d'hommes, armez les uns contre les autres, se hacher en pieces avecques une si extreme fermeté de courage qu'on ne leur vist lâcher une parolle de foiblesse ou commiseration, jamais tourner le dos, ny faire seulement un

mouvement lâche pour gauchir au coup de leur adversaire, ains tendre le col à son espée et se presenter au coup.) (665)

Montaigne prefaces this combat in which the gladiators cut each other to pieces with an implicit comparison to the ancient practice of allowing the vivisection of criminals. His phrase "cut up alive" ("déchirez tout vifs") (518;664) links *Des mauvais moyens* both to the condemnation of torture in *Des cannibales* and to Alexander's treatment of Betis ("tout vif, deschirer") in *Par divers moyens.* The marvelous, instructive example of the gladiators' fighting is like the firmness of the cannibals' warfare—"C'est chose emerveillable que de la fermeté de leurs combats" (155;207)—in which retreat and fear are unknown. And as both the cannibals and Alexander sought in vain to wring suppliant words from their captives—"quelque parolle molle ou rabaissée" as *Des cannibales* (156;209) has it—the gladiators will not let a word of weakness escape their lips. Similarly, Montaigne writes of the cannibal captives, "There is not one in a whole century who does not choose to die rather than to relax a single bit, by word or look, from the grandeur of an invincible courage" ("il ne s'en trouve pas un, en tout un siecle, qui n'ayme mieux la mort que de relascher, ny par contenance, ny de parole, un seul point d'une grandeur de courage invincible") (156;209). At the center of both the cannibal and Roman cultures is a ritualized spectacle of bravery, where the defeated demonstrate their refusal to give in to their conquerors or to the prospect of death. Their stubborn silence and unmoved countenances are the signs of a rigid virtue that will not bend—compare "relascher . . . de parole" and "lâcher une parolle"—unless, in the case of one cannibal captive, to sing a song of defiance or, of another, to make a face at his captors. In both cultures this unyielding valor—which in Rome the gladiatorial spectacle is supposed deliberately to inculcate in the citizenry—produces a state of permanent warfare, both without and, as it turns out, within the society.

The Cannibals and France: Noble Stoics

Des mauvais moyens ends with a second evocation of the civil wars in the France of Montaigne's day. In a final ironic twist of the essay's terms, France has become a kind of fighting arena and a dumping ground where other countries can send their excess of hot-blooded young soldiers to do combat as mercenaries (i.e., gladiators). For if the cannibal culture that consumes itself finds an analogy in the equally self-destructive mechanisms of Roman culture, both, in turn, are looked at as models for France. At the end of *Des cannibales* the cannibals who have been brought to France express their wonder at the class hierarchy of its society, having noticed "that there were among us men full and gorged with all sorts of good things, and that their other halves were beggars at their doors, emaciated with hunger and poverty" ("qu'ils avoyent aperçeu qu'il y avoit parmy nous des hommes pleins et gorgez de toutes sortes de commoditez, et que leurs moitiez estoient mendians à leurs portes, décharnez de faim et de pauvreté") (159;213). But for all the difference that the cannibals see between French society and their own, the wording suggests instead the *similarity* between the two. In France the rich are eating off the poor, literally stripping their flesh ("décharnez") away by starving them. It is a more mediated kind of cannibalism, but cannibalism nonetheless. The cannibal visitors express surprise that the poor do not strike back. But peasant revolts and class warfare were, in fact, endemic to sixteenth-century French society. And as both the closing remark of *Des mauvais moyens* and the condemnation of cruel religious strife at the center of *Des cannibales* attest, the Roman and cannibal societies, societies where foreign war collapses into internal war, point specifically to the France of the Wars of Religion.

In relating the cannibals' unbending martial valor both to modern civil strife and to the violence of the gladiators, Montaigne makes *Des cannibales* part of a critique of Stoicism that is a central and continuing project of the *Essais*, and he also suggests the political dimension of this critique.[14] For Montaigne Stoicism was the language of virtue of an embattled sixteenth-century aristocracy. The old *noblesse d'épée*, Catholic and Protestant, clung to its traditional military ethos and provided the chief antagonists of the French civil wars; they fought both against the crown and amongst themselves, both to maintain their old feudal prerogatives and to support their religious causes.[15] In a shrewd observation upon *Des cannibales*, Michel de Certeau asks, "Does not this detour into the New World reconnect with a medieval model that was then in the process of disappearing?"—the model of a feudal warrior society where, as de Certeau puts it, "speech and weaponry coincided in 'honor.' "[16] I would suggest, where de Certeau probably would not, that this model could not disappear fast enough for Montaigne the royalist *politique*. He demonstrates the consequences of the Stoic postures and martial values of the belligerent French nobility by attributing them to the cannibals and by observing how they then play themselves out, turning the cannibals' otherwise idyllic existence into a constant state of warfare and revenge.

Montaigne depicts the cannibals as perfect Stoics, so perfect that they call Stoicism itself into question. In a digression in *Des cannibales*, the essayist notes that

> it is a trick of art and technique, which may be found in a worthless coward, to be an able fencer. The worth and value of a man is in his heart and his will; there lies his real honor. Valor is the firmness, not of legs and arms, but of heart and soul; it consists not in the worth of our horse or our weapons, but in our own.

> He who falls obstinate in his courage, [C] *if he has fallen, he fights on his knees* [Seneca]. [A] He who relaxes none of his assurance, no matter how great the danger of imminent death; who, giving up his soul, still looks firmly and scornfully at his enemy—he is beaten not by us, but by fortune; he is killed, not conquered. (157)

> (c'est un tour d'art et de science, et qui peut tomber en une personne lasche et de néant, d'estre suffisant à l'escrime. L'estimation et le pris d'un homme consiste au coeur et en la volonté; c'est là où gist son vray honneur; la vaillance, c'est la fermeté non pas des jambes et des bras, mais du courage et de l'ame; elle ne consiste pas en la valeur de nostre cheval, ny de nos armes, mais en la nostre. Celuy qui tombe obstiné en son courage, [C] "*si succederit, de genu pugnat*"; [A] qui, pour quelque dangier de la mort voisine, ne relasche aucun point de son asseurance; qui regarde encores, en rendant l'ame, son ennemy d'une veuë ferme et desdaigneuse, il est battu non pas de nous, mais de la fortune; il est tué, non pas vaincu.) (209–10)

The citation from Seneca's *De Providentia* added in the 1595 (C) edition is inserted into a passage that already recalls Seneca's *De Constantia* and is an inventory of Stoic commonplaces. The captive sage's confrontation with his conqueror in the fortunes of war and with the threat of torture is a favorite Stoic scenario—and, as a third term that further joins *Des cannibales* with *Des mauvais moyens*, Seneca frequently illustrates Stoic indomitability with the behavior of gladiators in the arena.

Montaigne elsewhere (1:39:177;235) cites another story recounted in *De Constantia* (5.6–7). After the fall of his city, Megara, and the loss of his wife, children, property, and the freedom of his country, the philosopher Stilpo calmly told the victorious Demetrius Poliorcetes that he had lost nothing of his own, that is, his personal virtue. So, Seneca writes, "he wrested the victory from the conqueror, and bore witness that, though his city had been captured, he himself was not only unconquered but unharmed." And Seneca introduces the anecdote by describing the nature of virtue itself: "Virtue is free, inviolable, unmoved, unshaken, so steeled against the blows of chance that she cannot be bent, much less broken. Facing the instruments of torture she holds her gaze unflinching, her countenance changes not at all."[17] Montaigne's cannibals entirely live up to this Stoic precept: theirs is a society of virtue—and cannibalism.

The implacable behavior of the cannibals, among whom neither captive nor captor is willing to give an inch, in fact brings out the element of political resistance that is already implicit in the Senecan virtue to which their constancy is compared. There is an easy slide from an apparently passive Stoic composure that appears not to care at all about the external blows of fortune to an active defiance of the conquering enemy. In a world of never-say-die Stoics, there can be no relenting and no pardon. The aim of revenge, according to *Couardise mere de la cruauté*, was to force an admission of repentance from the enemy, but to be a Stoic or a cannibal means never having to say you're sorry.

The remark about fencing that opens the Senecan digression in *Des cannibales* ties this Stoic virtue to traditional noble values. For fencing, as the remark implies, was considered in the sixteenth century to be a new Italian art—something that could be learned and not inherited by blood lineage—and thus tied to an emerging court culture.[18] A 1588 (B) addition to *Couardise mere de la cruauté* appears to echo these conservative aristocratic sentiments:

> But this [fencing] is not properly valor, since it draws its support from skill and has its basis in something other than itself. The honor of the combat consists in the jealousy of courage, not of craft. And therefore I have observed a friend of mine, renowned as a grand master in this exercise, to choose in his quarrels weapons that deprived him of the means of this advantage, and which depended entirely on fortune and assurance, so that his victory should not be attributed to his fencing skill rather than his valor. And in my childhood the nobility avoided the reputation of good fencers as insulting, and learned it furtively, as a cunning trade, derogating from true and natural valor. (527)

> (mais ce n'est pas proprement vertu, puis qu'elle tire son appuy de l'addresse et qu'elle prend autre fondement que de soy-mesme. L'honneur des combats consiste en la jalousie du courage, non de la science; et pourtant ay-je veu quelqu'un de mes amis, renommé pour grand maistre en cet exercice choisir en ses querelles des armes qui luy ostassent le moyen de cet advantage, et lesquelles dépendoient entierement de la fortune et de l'asseurance, affin qu'on n'attribuast sa victoire plustost à son escrime qu'à sa valeur; et, en mon enfance, la noblesse fuyoit la reputation de bon escrimeur comme injurieuse, et se desroboit pout l'apprendre, comme un mestier de subtilité desrogeant à la vraye et naifve vertu.) (676)

With its appeal to the *mos maiorum*, this passage describes the "natural valor" of the nobility—the valor that one is born with and that cannot be taught—in Stoic terms of a reliance on "soy-mesme" or, as *Des cannibales* puts it, on "la nostre." The friend of Montaigne who forgoes the advantage of his fencing skill seeks to depend on fortune and assurance, or, again to compare it to the earlier passage, on an assurance that will acknowledge only fortune as its conqueror. The observation that the honor of combat consists in a "jalousie de courage" recalls the warfare of the cannibals, whose only basis is a "jalousie de la vertu," and is paralleled in turn by still another passage of *Des cannibales*, this a later (C) addition: "The role of true victory is in fighting, not in coming off safely; and the honor of valor consists in combat, not in victory" ("Le vray vaincre a pour son roolle l'estour, non pas le salut; et consiste l'honneur de la vertu à combattre, non à battre") (157;210). The idea of a natural or native valor ("naifve vertu") further links the old European warrior aristocracy to the New World natives, whose own martial valor is, at least initially, declared by *Des cannibales* to be so close to an "original naturalness" ("naifveté originelle"). But this link, which de Certeau suggests bathes the natives in a kind of nostalgic afterglow of a vanishing feudal order, may not be so flattering to Montaigne's contemporary aristocrats, who, in seeking to perpetuate that order and its ethos of Stoic defiance and revenge, have plunged France into a civil war even more terrible than the retaliatory warfare that wracks the cannibals' society. *Des cannibales*, that is, may not so much create the figure of the noble savage as disclose the savagery of the nobility.

The Cannibals and France: Stoic Huguenots

If the cannibals embody the Stoic and martial values embraced by the aristocratic antagonists on *both* sides of the French Wars of Religion, it was nonetheless the Protestants who most explicitly identified their "constancy" in the face of persecution as a superior form of Seneca's "constantia." In *Feux*, the middle book of his epic poem *Les Tragiques*, Agrippa d'Aubigné, the Huguenot poet and Montaigne's contemporary, describes the tortures and martyrdom to which his coreligionists were subjected and the resolution they displayed, a *constance* that, he concludes at the end of the book, was a God-given sign of their election.[19] One of the Huguenot martyrs, Richard de Gastines, a precocious child and a "fair mirror of constancy" ("beau mirouer de constance") (l. 722), gives a long speech in which he cites Seneca and the ancient Stoics as models from whom a contempt for death can be learned (ll. 789–810); when he sheds natural tears at the sight of his father condemned with him on the scaffold, Richard nonetheless declares that his soul remains unmoved ("pas esmeuë") (l. 937). And d'Aubigné includes another anecdote about two girls tortured by their Catholic aunt and uncle, who try to turn them back to the worship of "idols": "For thirty days these girls, torn by whips and hot irons, retain their assurance."

> (Par trente jours entiers ces filles, deschirees
> De verges et fers chauds, demeurent asseurees.)
>
> (ll. 1013–14)

Obstinacy against torture and death becomes in this Protestant vision a divinely inspired religious experience that is to be aligned with the martyrdom of the saints of the early church. And it has a direct political application, encouraging other Huguenots in their intransigence.

Montaigne predictably takes a dim view of such behavior. In the essay *Defence de Seneque et de Plutarque* (2:32), he notes that if one asked the participants "in these civil wars, there will be found acts of patience, obstinacy, and stubbornness in this miserable age of ours and amid this rabble" ("en ces guerres civiles, il se trouvera des effets de patience, d'obstination et d'opiniatreté parmy nos miserables siecles et en cette tourbe molle") (547;702) equal to the examples of antiquity. "How many of them have been seen patiently letting themselves be burned and roasted for opinions borrowed from others, unknown and not understood!" ("Combien en a l'on veu se laisser patiemment brusler et rotir pour des opinions empruntées d'autruy, ignorées et inconnues!") (548;702). The peasants being roasted for religious tenets they do not understand are less constant than merely stubborn. Where Montaigne in *Des cannibales* condemned the use of torture, of roasting victims bit by bit, especially under the pretext of piety and religion, he here looks, with no less disapproval, at the other side, the victims' own behavior. The peasants are dying for "opinions" and thus are examples of "opiniastreté," a kind of blind obstinacy. The (B) addition to the essay goes on to compare their conduct to the storied stubbornness of women. "And stubbornness," it concludes, "is the sister of constancy, at least in vigor and firmness" ("Et est l'opinastreté soeur de la constance, au moins en vigueur et fermeté") (548;703). The sister is the inferior female version or false double of constancy: Montaigne seems concerned to discredit religious obstinacy by differentiating it from Stoic firmness. The suspicion remains, however, that he sees both kinds of inflexibility as self-destructive. The unwillingness to relent and compromise is an exasperating provocation, inviting from the wielders of power the violence and cruelty they are only too willing to deal out. Like d'Aubigné's exemplary witnesses to their faith, these peasants, presumably also Protestants, seek out martyrdom, and martyrdom is what they get. But in the process they have engulfed France in civil war.

The moderate Catholic Montaigne distrusts religious fanaticism on either side of the Wars of Religion. He nonetheless appears especially critical of a Huguenot intransigence that has appropriated the language and gestures of Stoicism. His aversion to such obstinate faith and its political consequences lies behind one final passage from the *Essais* that I want to juxtapose with *Des cannibales*: a condemnation or questioning of the behavior of the early martyrs of the faith themselves in *De l'yvrongnerie* (2:2). This essay moves from its ostensible subject of drunkenness to an attack on the idea of Stoic constancy. Even the sage has to blink at a threatening blow, the essayist remarks with some satisfaction, and he concludes that "all actions outside the ordinary limits are subject to sinister interpretation" ("toutes les actions hors les bornes ordinaires sont subjectes à sinistre interpretation")

(250;329). The 1580 (A) version of the text goes immediately on to illustrate the point:

> Our martyrs were heard crying out to the tyrant in the midst of the flame: "It's roasted enough on that side, chop it up, eat it, it's cooked, start on the other side!" And that child in Josephus, all torn by biting pincers and pierced by the awls of Antiochus, still defied him, crying out with a firm and steady voice: "Tyrant, you're wasting your time, here I am still at ease; where is that pain, where are those torments, with which you were threatening me? Is this all you know how to do? My constancy gives you more pain than I feel from your cruelty. O cowardly wretch, you are giving up, and I am growing stronger; make me complain, make me bend, make me yield, if you can; give your satellites and your executioners courage; see, they have lost heart, they can do no more; arm them, goad them!" When we hear such defiance, surely we must confess that in these souls there is some alteration, some frenzy, however holy it be. (250)

> (Quand nous oyons nos martyrs crier au Tyran au milieu de la flamme: "C'est assez rosti de ce costé là, hache le, mange le, il est cuit, recommance de l'autre"; quand nous oyons en Josephe cet enfant tout deschiré des tenailles mordantes et persé des aleines d'Antiochus, le deffier encore, criant d'une voix ferme et asseurée: "Tyran, tu pers temps, me voicy tousjours à mon aise; où est cette douleur, où sont ces tourmens, dequoy tu me menassois? n'y sçais tu que cecy? ma constance te donne plus de peine que je n'en sens de ta cruauté; ô lache belistre, tu te rens, et je me renforce; fay moy pleindre, fay moy flechir, fay moy rendre, si tu peux; donne courage à tes satellites et à tes bourreaux; les voylà defaillis de coeur, ils n'en peuvent plus; arme les, acharne les";—certes il faut confesser qu'en ces ames là il y a quelque alteration et quelque fureur, tant sainte soit elle.) (329)

It is a coincidence, though I think a telling one, that d'Aubigné's rhyme words, "deschiree" and "asseuree," reappear in Montaigne's quite free adaptation of a passage from *On the Martyrdom of the Maccabees* (8–16) attributed to Josephus, itself an elaboration of the famous story of the martyrdom of the seven brothers in 2 Macc. 7. In the scriptural version, the first of these brothers, all of whom affirm their faith in God and defiance of Antiochus Epiphanes, is, at the tyrant's orders, cooked alive in a frying pan (4–5), linking these Jewish witnesses to "our [i.e., Christian] martyrs," in this case St. Lawrence, martyred on the grill, whose words are reported by Prudentius in the second hymn (ll. 401–8) of the *Book of Crowns* (*Peristephanon*). Both of these culinary martyrdoms, of course, evoke the vengeful rites performed by the New World cannibals—and the modern-day French practice of roasting the living flesh of religious enemies. The defiant words of the martyrs to their tyrannical persecutors match the song of the cannibal prisoner toward his captors: all exhibit the highest Stoic virtues of firmness, assurance, constancy. The Jewish child of Maccabees explicitly reveals the element of aggression in this constancy: it is meant to cause pain in the tyrant Antiochus, to reciprocate his cruelty.

But constancy also summons cruelty into action. The child literally asks for it—make me bend, make me yield—just as in Montaigne's opening essay the "mine . . . asseurée" of the captive Betis makes his conqueror Alexander ask, "Has he bent a knee?" ("A-il flechi un genouil"), and to tear Betis limb from limb ("deschirer et desmembrer") behind his chariot. Montaigne labels the behavior of the martyrs, as well as the "Stoic sallies" ("saillies Stoiques") that immediately follow them in *De l'ivrongnerie*, as forms of frenzy. It is a holy madness, but nonetheless madness, and he remarks at the original end of the essay that it "transcends our own judgment and reason; inasmuch as wisdom is an orderly management of our soul, which she conducts with measure and proportion and is responsible for" ("surpasse nostre propre jugement et discours. D'autant que la sagesse c'est un maniment reglé de nostre ame, et qu'elle conduit avec mesure et proportion, et s'en respond") (251;330). Montaigne wants none of it: this religious conviction that is so easily confused with opinionated stubbornness, this passive-aggression that makes the martyr complicit with his own torture and turns a Stoic contempt for the body into cruelty against one's own limbs. The trouble with would-be martyrs, and Montaigne doubtless has the intransigent Huguenots in mind, is that they will not listen to reason and that they positively demand to be killed: their constancy becomes interchangeable with the cruelty with which it is met. As interchangeable as a cannibal prisoner from one identical tribe defying his cannibal captors from another, all of them one flesh.

Montaigne the Cosmographer

The obstinate valor that Montaigne praises in the cannibals is their culture's version of the virtue that he consistently condemns in its European forms, whether mediated by Stoic philosophy, by an aristocratic code of martial honor, or by sectarian religious fanaticism. It is a virtue, we might say, of rugged individualism, of an autonomous self that would rather destroy itself than accept any limitation imposed on it from the outside: there is a clear link between the Stoic who stands up to the torture of the tyrant and the Stoic who commits suicide as an act of political resistance. Montaigne sees this suicidal constancy operating at the heart of the French civil wars, and I would suggest that the self-portrait of the *Essais*—the skeptical, flexible, hopelessly inconstant essayist who bows before the higher authority of church and state—is an attempt to find an alternative, less politically threatening model of virtue and selfhood.[20] And while Montaigne may praise the indomitable courage of the individual cannibal, his essay demonstrates how a society where everyone possesses this same virtue, and no one is willing to yield or to pardon, must ultimately consume itself. The Stoic individualism of the cannibals is similarly self-defeating; its endless cycle of reciprocal vengeance, of interchangeable victors and victims, finally confuses the individual identities of the belligerents themselves. Shaped as it is by Montaigne's political experience, *Des cannibales* provides an admonitory object lesson for his contemporary France.

But if the essay is directed toward—and determined by—the current distress of France, if the cannibals' society holds up a dark mirror to Montaigne's own, what happens to its claims to present the New World natives on their own terms? By demonstrating the relation of *Des cannibales* to other essays in the collection, I have tried to suggest that these terms belong not so much to the cannibals as to recurring preoccupations of the *Essais* that tell us more about the essayist and his response to the specific historical circumstances of the French civil wars.

And yet it may be precisely because Montaigne sees the cannibals through the terms of the crisis of his own society that he may come to understand something central about their culture.[21] The Tupinamba of Brazil were, of course, far removed culturally from the Aztecs, and it may not be legitimate to compare or link the two. But the Aztecs did produce written records that preserve some of the rituals of their warrior culture. In a magnificent reconstruction of this culture, Inga Clendinnen has argued that the Aztec warrior had to "strive to desire, or at least to embrace" not only the idea of capturing captives for sacrifice—which included cannibalism—but also the prospect that he would himself be captured and sacrificed by his enemies in turn. That is, the warrior and his captive were finally interchangeable: dying in the correct sacrificial way was as much a test and expected part of the warrior's bravery as his prowess on the battlefield. As Clendinnen describes the elaborate ritual of the feast of Xipe Totec, the captor of the chief sacrificial victim

> was given the cane and a bowl of blood which he carried throughout the city, daubing the blood on the mouths of the stone idols in all the temples. The circuit completed, he went to Moctezuma's palace to return the magnificent regalia of he who offers a victim at the gladiatorial stone, and from there went back to his local temple to flay and dismember his captive's body. And then, later in the day, he watched his lamenting kin eat the maize stew and the flesh of his captive, while they wept for their own young warrior. He did not participate, saying "Shall I perchance eat my very self?" . . . Behind the desperate excitements of battle lay the shadow of the killing stone, and a lonely death among strangers. This is why the captor, in the midst of the adulation accorded him for having

taken a victim for the sun, wore at the cannibal feast of his kin the chalk and down of the victim; why the kin lamented; why he could not eat of what was indeed his "own flesh," for he too, ideally, would die on the stone, and his flesh be eaten in another city.[22]

Here, if Clendinnen's compelling analysis is correct, was another cannibalistic New World society that ate its own flesh—and acknowledged as much. But we should recall that the "invention" of the cannibal's defiant song in Montaigne's essay, the song where he tells his captors that they will be enjoying the taste of their own flesh when they feast off his body, belonged to Montaigne himself, the humanist sitting in his study, not to the eyewitness testimony of his ethnographic sources. It may be nothing more than coincidence, but this juxtaposition of the sixteenth-century essayist and the modern scholar suggests a pleasing paradox: perhaps only by confronting the New World culture from the vantage point and preoccupations of his own could Montaigne put the right words in the mouth of his valiant cannibal.

NOTES

1. Citations of Montaigne's text are drawn first from Donald Frame's English translation, *The Complete Essays of Montaigne* (Stanford, 1958), then from the edition of Albert Thibaudet and Maurice Rat, *Oeuvres complètes* (Paris, 1962). Respective page references are given in parentheses. In some cases I have slightly altered Frame's translation to emphasize key words that are repeated from essay to essay.

2. The issue of pardoning may be prompted by a passage in one of Montaigne's principal "cosmographic" sources, the *Histoire d'un voyage faict en la terre du Brésil* (1578) by the Protestant Jean de Léry, who describes the unrelenting nature of the cannibals' hatred and draws, as Montaigne will also draw, an analogy to the civil wars in France, with a particular accusation against the French disciples of Machiavelli—that is, the Florentine Catherine de' Medici and her Catholic party: "De plus, sitôt que la guerre est une fois déclarée entre quelques-unes de ces nations, tous allèguent que, puisque l'ennemi qui a reçu l'injure s'en ressentira à jamais, c'est agir trop lâchement que de le laisser échapper quand on le tient à sa merci: leurs haines sont donc tellement invétérées qu'ils demeurent perpétuellement irréconciliables. A ce propos on peut dire que Machiavel et ses disciples (dont la France pour son malheur est maintenant remplie) sont les vrais imitateurs des cruautés barbaresques: car ces athées, contrairement à la doctrine chrétienne, enseignent et pratiquent aussi que les nouveaux services ne doivent jamais faire oublier les vieilles injures: *c'est-à-dire que les hommes, tenant du naturel du diable, ne se doivent point pardonner les uns aux autres*" (my emphasis). I quote from the modern edition of M.-R. Mayeux, *Journal de bord de Jean de Léry en la terre du Brésil 1557* (Paris, 1957), 296. David Lewis Schaefer notes that the cannibals' lack of a word for pardon is a sign of their cruelty; see *The Political Philosophy of Montaigne* (Ithaca and London, 1990), 187.

3. Edwin M. Duval, "Lessons of the New World: Design and Meaning in Montaigne's 'Des Cannibales' [I:31] and 'Des coches' [III:6]," in *Montaigne: Essays in Reading*, ed. Gérard Defaux, *Yale French Studies*, no. 64 (New Haven, 1983), 95–112.

4. For suggestive remarks on the class-inflected role of the servant in the essay, see Stephen Greenblatt, *Marvelous Possessions: The Wonder of the New World* (Chicago, 1991), 146–50.

5. Gérard Defaux, "Un Cannibale en haut de chausses: Montaigne, la différence et la logique de l'identité," *MLN* 97 (1982): 919–57. For Defaux's discussion of the rhetoric of the golden age, see 951–56.

6. See, for example, the essays collected by James Clifford and George E. Marcus in *Writing Culture* (Berkeley, Los Angeles, and London, 1986); James Boon, *Other Tribes, Other Scribes* (Cambridge, 1982); Karl-Heinz Kohl, *Exotik als Beruf* (1979; 2d ed., Frankfurt and New York, 1986).

7. For episodes of real cannibalism and of the role of cannibalism in the polemical rhetoric of the struggle between French Catholics and Protestants, see Frank Lestringant, "Le Cannibale et ses paradoxes: Images du cannibalisme au temps des Guerres de Religion," *Mentalities/Mentalités* 1, no. 2 (1983): 4–19.

8. Judith Shklar, *Ordinary Vices* (Cambridge, Mass., 1984). See also Schaefer, *The Political Philosophy of Montaigne*, 227–36.

9. In his *Cosmographie universelle* (Paris, 1575), bk. 21, chap. 15, p. 945, André Thevet writes of his conversation with the cannibals' captives: "Que si je leur parlois de les delivrer, et racheter, des mains de leurs ennemis, ils prenoient tout en mocquerie, me faisans la mouë, disoient que nous *Aiouroiou* (ainsi nous nomment ils, combien que ce soit un nom d'une espece de gros Perroquets), n'estions point hommes de coeur: . . ." See the modern edition of Thevet's text in *Les Français en Amérique pendant la deuxième moitié du XVIe siècle: Le Brésil et les Brésiliens par André Thevet*, ed. Suzanne Lussagnet (Paris, 1953), 198.

10. On Montaigne's care to identify the cannibalism of the Brazilians as a ritual of revenge rather than as a necessary dietary supplement, see the two-part article of Frank Lestringant, "Le canibalisme des 'cannibales,'" *Bulletin de la société des amis de Montaigne*, 6th ser., nos. 9–10 (1982): 27–40, and nos. 11–12 (1982): 19–38.

11. Compare Plato, *Republic* 461d. See also Léry, *Histoire*, 348.

12. The influence of Girard's thought on my reading of Montaigne's essay will be obvious. See René Girard, *La Violence et le sacré* (Paris, 1972).

13. André Thevet, *Les Singularitez de la France antarctique . . .* (Antwerp, 1558), 74v. Compare another version of this song in the *Cosmographie universelle*, 945 (*Les Français en Amérique*, 198): "Nos amis les Margageaz sont gens de biens, fortz et puissants en guerre: ils ont prins et mangé plusieurs de voz parents noz ennemis, et de ceux qui me tiennent pour me faire mourir: mais ils vengeront bient tost ma mort, et vous mangeront quand il leur plaira, et voz enfans aussi: quant à moy j'ay tué et mangé plusieurs amis de ce malin Aignan, qui me tient prisonnier. Je suis fort, je suis puissant: c'est moy qui ay mis en route plusieurs fois vous autres coüards, qui n'entendez rien à faire guerre, et plusieurs autres parolles disent-ils, qui monstre le peu de compte qu'ils ont de la mort, et que la crainte d'icelle ne peut en rien esbranler leur plus que brutale asseurance." Compare as well analogous words of defiance by a cannibal captive in Léry, *Histoire*, 311: "Avec une audace et une assurance incroyables, il se vantera de ses prouesses passées, et dira à ceux qui le tiennent lié: 'Le premier j'ai moi-même, vaillant que je suis, lié ainsi et garotté vos parents.' Puis, s'exaltant

toujours de plus en plus, avec la contenance de même, il se tournera de côté et d'autre, et dira à l'un: 'J'ai mangé ton père,' à l'autre: 'J'ai assommé et boucané tes frères'; 'Bref, ajoutera-t-il, j'ai en général tant mangé d'hommes et de femmes, voire des enfants, de vous autres *Toüoupinambaoults*, pris en guerre, que je ne saurais en dire le nombre. Et au reste ne doutez pas que pour venger ma mort, les *Margaias* de la nation d'où je suis n'en mangent encore plus tard autant qu'ils en pourront attraper.' " Léry's passage may be slightly closer to Montaigne's text, but it is in Thevet that the cannibal's defiance takes the form of a song. There is, however, no notion in these texts that the cannibal invites his enemies to eat the flesh of their own relatives.

14. Pierre Villey, in *Les Sources et l'évolution des "Essais" de Montaigne* (Paris, 1908) and in the concise and elegant *Les Essais de Michel de Montaigne* (Paris, 1932), proposed an influential and still powerful reading of the *Essais* in which he traced Montaigne's philosophical journey in stages from an early attachment to Stoicism through a skeptical crisis to a later acceptance of epicurean precepts. Villey's view has been challenged, quite correctly in my opinion, by Schaefer, who sees the *Essais* engaged in a polemic against Stoicism from their inception; see *The Political Philosophy of Montaigne*, esp. 29–30, 201–26. In keeping with its Straussian approach, Schaefer's book largely ignores the historical and political context of this opposition to Stoicism and the diehard postures of its adherents.

15. Gerhard Oestreich argues that the neostoicism preached by Justus Lipsius—whom Montaigne admired and with whom he corresponded—helped to create the ethos of the bureaucratic ministers and functionaries of the modern nation-state—in France, the members of the *noblesse de robe*. See *Neostoicism and the Early Modern State*, trans. David McLintock (Cambridge and London, 1982), 45. Yet Oestreich also shows, 76–89, how Lipsius assimilates Stoic virtues with the military virtues of a warrior nobility, the *noblesse d'épée*. This latter, soldierly Stoicism appears to be the target of Montaigne's critique. His own class snobbery, precisely that of the recently ennobled aristocrat of the *robe* trying to adopt the manners and attitudes of the *noblesse d'épée*, produces professions of admiration for the "vacation militaire": "La forme propre, et seule, et essencielle de noblesse en France, c'est la vacation militaire" (2:7, 363). But insofar as the militarism of the French nobility posed a threat to the civil order of France that, for Montaigne, was represented by the monarchy, it was to be condemned. Montaigne similarly seems to have flirted with Stoicism before engaging in the quarrel with it that fills the *Essais*, and he was misread as a Stoic by Lipsius himself: see Hugo Friedrich, *Montaigne*, trans. Robert Rovini (Paris, 1968), 77–78. For a good discussion of the new class to which Montaigne belonged, see George Huppert, *Les Bourgeois Gentilshommes* (Chicago and London, 1977), esp. 85–102. Both Jean-Pierre Boon and James J. Supple link Montaigne's interest in Stoicism to the military culture he professed to admire and take part in; see Boon, *Montaigne, gentilhomme et essayiste* (Paris, 1971), 38–39, and Supple, *Arms versus Letters* (Oxford, 1984), 203–4. Supple, 195–97, connects the cannibals of Montaigne's essay to this culture and notes that "his admiring description of the Cannibals' methods of war does not seem to be ironic." I suggest the contrary. But an attraction/repulsion toward Stoic tenets, partly determined by the essayist's class position, may help to explain how Montaigne can praise the cannibals for their exemplary martial valor and Stoicism and simultaneously demonstrate how that valor and

Stoicism are root causes of the warfare and cannibalism that continuously wrack their society. For a richly suggestive linking of Renaissance Stoicism to the "crisis of the aristocracy" and to the question of revenge raised by *Des cannibales*, see Gordon Braden, *Renaissance Tragedy and the Senecan Tradition* (New Haven and London, 1985), esp. 107–14.

16. Michel de Certeau, *Heterologies: Discourse on the Other*, trans. Brian Massumi (Minneapolis, 1986), 77.

17. *De Constantia* 5.4–5: "Libera est, inviolabilis, immota, inconcussa, sic contra casus indurat, ut ne inclinari quidem, nedum vinci possit; adversus adparatus terribilium rectos oculos tenet, nihil ex vultu mutat." Seneca, *Moral Essays*, trans. John W. Basore, Loeb Classical Library (Cambridge, Mass., and London, 1935), 1:61.

18. Castiglione's *Book of the Courtier* itself links fencing to the courtier's art: see the crucial passage in bk. 2, sec. 40. For an Elizabethan attack on Italian fencing and the rapier and a defense of the old English short sword, see George Silver, *Paradoxes of Defense* (London, 1599), collected and reprinted in *Three Elizabethan Fencing Manuals*, ed. James L. Jackson (Delmar, N.Y., 1972).

19. I cite *Les Tragiques* from Agrippa d'Aubigné, *Oeuvres*, ed. Henri Weber (Paris, 1969).

20. In the *Apologie de Raimond Sebond* (2.11), Montaigne twice invokes the authority of Epicurus and the specter of cannibalism to argue for obedience to higher authority: "J'en diray seulement encore cela, que c'est la seule humilité et submission qui peut effectuer un homme de bien. Il ne faut pas laisser au jugement de chacun la cognoissance de son devoir; il le lui faut prescrire, non pas le laisser choisir à son discours: autrement, selon l'imbecillité et varieté infinie de nos raisons et opinions, nous nous forgerions en fin des devoirs qui nous mettroient à nous manger les uns les autres, comme dit Epicurus" (467); "Epicurus disoit des loix, que les pires nous estoient si necessaires que, sans elles, les hommes s'entremangeroient les uns les autres" (541). The *Apologie* ends famously in its (C) version by reminding humanity of its dependence "à nostre foy Chrestienne, non à sa vertu Stoïque" (584).

21. That understanding is interested, reflecting the desires, situation, and needs of the understander—who is still capable of self-criticism and not condemned to a merely relativistic vantage point—is a guiding tenet of Frankfort School thought; see Jürgen Habermas, *Knowledge and Human Interests*, trans. Jeremy J. Shapiro (Boston, 1971). See also, from a different perspective, David Bromwich, "The Genealogy of Disinterestedness," in Bromwich, *A Choice of Inheritance* (Cambridge, Mass., and London, 1989), 106–32.

22. Inga Clendinnen, "The Cost of Courage in Aztec Society," *Past and Present* 107 (1985): 72–74; this argument has been incorporated into Clendinnen's *Aztecs* (Cambridge, 1991), 94–98.

Part III

America and European Aspirations

LUCA CODIGNOLA

The Holy See and the Conversion of the Indians in French and British North America, 1486–1760

The idea of the conversion of the heathen to Christianity is a fundamental concept of the Christian church, whose expansionist drive can thus be traced back to its very origins.[1] From their early Mediterranean enclave, deep in the land of the Jews, the followers of Jesus Christ moved north toward Rome, the capital of a vast empire, organized a church led by the pope and his bishops, and made Rome the pope's Holy See and the center of the Christian church. From Rome the church moved south, toward Muslim lands, east, and farther north. Christianity became the religion of Europe, and when some Europeans left their continent in the fifteenth century to "discover" the rest of the world, their religion went with them to Africa, Asia, and the Americas.[2] Shortly before the 1492 voyage of Christopher Columbus, Pope Innocent VIII (1432–92, reigned from 1484), in the *incipit* of his bull *Orthodoxe fidei propagationem* (13 December 1486), clearly defined the duties of the Roman church in the presence of European expansion: "Our chief concern and commission from heaven is the propagation of the orthodox faith, the increase of the Christian religion, the salvation of barbarian nations, and the repression of the infidels and their conversion to the faith."[3] Conceived for a conquered Moorish kingdom, these guidelines were confirmed by Innocent VIII's successor, Alexander VI (1431–1503, reigned from 1492), immediately after Columbus's return in 1493. In his two bulls *Inter cetera* (3 and 4 May 1493), the new pope stated that the work most "pleasing to the Divine Majesty" was "that the Catholic faith and Christian religion be particularly exalted in our day and everywhere spread and enlarged, so that souls be saved and barbaric peoples be humbled and brought to the faith."[4] The bull *Inscrutabili divinae providentiae* (22 June 1622), by which Pope Gregory XV (1554–1623, reigned from 1621) established the Sacred Congregation "de Propaganda Fide," was based on the same principles of *Inter cetera* and the following bulls.[5] French Capuchin Pacifique de Provins (René de L'Escale, 1588–1648), a missionary with a long experience in the Middle East, France, and the Americas, would thus, more simply, express the general purpose of missionary endeavor: "[T]o spread the net of the Gospel over the most remote countries and nations of the earth" and "bring these savage peoples back to the knowledge of the true God that we adore."[6] The missionary principles of the Catholic church have changed little over the years. According to the latest encyclical issued by Pope John Paul II (1978–), *Redemptoris missio* (7 December 1990), "No believer in Christ, no institution of the Church can avoid this supreme duty: to proclaim Christ to all peoples." The final aim is conversion through baptism, because "the Church is the ordinary means of salvation" and its missionary mandate must be carried "unto the uttermost part of the earth" and "into all the world . . . to every creature."[7]

The belief that the rest of the world had to be reclaimed to Christianity did not belong to ecclesiastics only. Private entrepreneurs and crown administrators alike carried crosses on the side of their weapons, bibles and gospels along with their administrative papers. Ships from Spain, Portugal, France, England, the Netherlands, and Sweden brought soldiers and settlers to the New World together with priests and nuns of all sorts. Charters and commissions always mentioned, among the grantee's duties, the conversion of the pagan natives to the True Faith, and so did the propaganda literature promoting the opportunities of the New World.[8] When the Reformation split Western Christendom into two parts, Catholics and Protestants immediately began to compete in a race against time. At stake were the souls of multitudes of idolaters who inhabited lands still unknown. In the one hundred years immediately following the Council of Trent (1545–63) this missionary drive became an overwhelming impulse for many members of the Christian community. On the Catholic side, the Chilean lawyer Juan Luis Arias (fl. 1590–1609) warned his countrymen against "English and Dutch heretics, instigated by the devil . . . sowing with great zeal and speed the infernal poison of their heresy, infesting thus those millions and millions of good people who dwell" in Florida, New Spain, New Mexico, the kingdom of Quivira, the Californias, Virginia, and Bermuda. On the Protestant side, Richard Hakluyt (1552?–1616) was a man of the church, and for him the importance of English expansion was in direct proportion to its capacity for extending the divine plan for the universe over the whole world.[9] Compared to the Iberian experience, and even to the more modest French success, whereby New France was virtually kept alive as a colony until the 1650s by the church itself, the practical influence of religion on early English expansion was small and marginal, and Protestant efforts achieved little.[10]

Whether the original inhabitants of America were human beings was a question that certainly never crossed the collective mind of either the officials of the Holy See, who were based in Rome and delegated their spiritual powers, or of the missionaries in the Americas, who were granted such spiritual powers and used them with the non-Christians. This meant, in effect, that the Indians were worthy of such attention and of such an overwhelming effort, and that they were, in principle, able to understand and willing to learn. The extent of the humanness of the American Indians and their rank within human society was the subject of a long debate among Europeans; in fact, the "dispute of the new world," which involved a discussion of the origins of the Indians and of the physical nature of the new continent, raged from the time of the discovery well into the nineteenth century.[11] To be sure, the Christian doctrine as expressed by the popes was clear enough. In his bulls *Inter cetera*, Alexander VI quickly declared that Indians were indeed capable of being Christianized.[12] After the first generation of Spanish domination had clearly shown the ravages of the conquest upon the Indian peoples, Pope Paul III (1468–1549, reigned from 1534) issued the bull *Veritas ipsa* (2 June 1537), otherwise known as *Sublimis Deus* (4 June 1537), that stressed the view of his predecessor.[13]

This was, however, a theoretical debate that only affected the early days of the Iberian conquest. It had no impact on European expansion in North America, as most of those who took part in it were "university intellectuals who had never left Europe and never set eyes upon an American Indian."[14] It had even less impact on the practice of missionary work, in spite of the fact that most intellectuals who took part in the debate were members of the church. Recourse to classical authorities, from Aristotle to Plato to Pliny the Elder, or to the Old and New Testaments, is sometimes to be found in the various dedicatory letters, prefaces, and introductions to some of the more ambitious printed literature. But this was nothing more than a literary device and was not related to the debate on the nature of the Indians or the nature of the New World.[15] A telling example is the uncommonly long preface to the *Voyage des isles camercanes* (1652), in which its erudite author, the Discalced Carmelite Maurile de Saint-Michel (d. 1669), assembled forty-two pages of classical and biblical citations because he felt he had to prove that, in spite of dealing with a foreign land, his narrative would entertain the reader. Yet not a single sentence was meant to explain the nature of the Indians or to justify the worthiness of his missionary endeavor.[16] Furthermore, references to supportive authorities seem to be almost completely absent in the manuscript correspondence between the missionaries and their superiors at the Holy See or in the headquarters of the regular orders.[17]

The sterility of this theoretical debate does not come as a surprise. Whereas European intellectuals had a purely philosophical interest in the matter and knew they would never be personally involved either in field work or in missionary administration, the high officials of the Holy See and of the regular orders were administrators, not intellectuals. The Holy See was rather more than the pope, although the pope was its absolute leader. On the one hand, it was a source of mystical power, belonging "to the charismatic dimension of human experience."[18] On the other hand, it was also a sophisticated bureaucracy, inspired by a common ideology, refined by centuries of trials and adjustments, made up of cardinals, nuncios, prefects, secretaries, and the scores of clerks comprising the various sacred congregations. They extended their authority throughout the Catholic world and routinely met with the hundreds of agents of the foreign crowns, the clergy, and the missions, and with the procurators of the many regular orders, all of whom deemed it necessary to reside in Rome in order to better press their case.[19] It was this Holy See which was responsible for planning, coordinating, and implementing the defense of the faith within the Old World and the attack upon the heathen in the New. This Holy See, as British historian Peter Partner explains for the sixteenth century, was made of secretaries and chamber clerks who "were either men of business or men of letters; they were not . . . church thinkers or reformers."[20] These men were too busy with pending business to devote any significant portion of their time to discuss the overall meaning of their task. After all, their faith was there to provide all the answers. Together with the missionaries in the field whom they coordinated, by taking their habit they had espoused the idea that all humankind could and indeed must be converted, and they would not be bothered by intellectual diatribes.[21] For the Holy See bureaucrats, then, almost immediately the question was not whether to perform their apostolic duties toward the Indians, but how best to do it.[22]

Within the Christian world, spiritual jurisdiction was exercised by the pope through his bishops. A bishop, however, could only enjoy his ordinary jurisdiction within the territorial limits of his diocese. Thus, territories that were outside the Christian world were not comprised in any diocese. They consequently were reserved to the sole jurisdiction of the pope and were considered mission territories. In the early age of European expansion, the pope delegated some of his spiritual powers to a number of regular orders, who were thus exempted from episcopal jurisdictions and would report only to the pope himself.[23] Theoretically, this system applied to the Americas in 1492. To be sure, long before Columbus the Holy See had extended its dominion over the American territory. On 6 January 1053 Pope Leo IX (1002–54, reigned from 1049) had invested Adalbert, archbishop of Hamburg-Bremen (ca. 1000–1072), with spiritual authority over the whole of Scandinavia, which explicitly included Greenland. The first residential bishop of Greenland, Arnald (fl. 1105–50), had reached his see at Gardar, in the East Settlement, in 1126. Although at the time no distinction was made between European Greenlanders and the Inuit population, there is no reason to believe that they would have been regarded by Rome as separate entities, their only difference being that some of the Greenlanders had already been converted.[24] We are not aware, however, of any Greenlanders' lasting influence on Inuit or Indian cultures.[25]

Although it had not been forgotten in 1492, when contact between the Old World and the New was renewed,[26] the Greenland precedent proved to be ineffective in shaping structures of the Christian church in the New World. At the time, the Holy See and the Iberian crowns were in the process of negotiating and concluding a new and somewhat original system of relations. This included the transfer upon the crowns of most of the pope's spiritual and administrative privileges and duties relating to residents (native and European) of their territories. The pope had no adequate resources to undertake the conversion of the Indians and was wholly dependent on the conquering European nations even for the most elementary knowledge of the New World. By 1508, through the *patronato real* (royal patronage), the Spanish crown assumed responsibility to promote the conversion of the Indians and to support the colonial church. It also controlled all financial matters relating to the church and ecclesiastical appointments and payments. By 1514, through the *padroado*, the Portuguese crown exercised the same control over religion and evangelical efforts in their colonies.[27] The patronage system did not prevent the Holy See from occasionally intervening in American matters, nor did it sever its relations with Iberian America. This included regions such as California, New Mexico, and Florida that were later annexed to the British colonies or conquered by the United States. However, it certainly made these relations very special well into the nineteenth century. Because of the effectiveness of the royal patronage system, then, any discussion of the modes of the religious conquest of the Americas must make a clear distinction between Iberian and non-Iberian America, as two very different systems of relations applied.

Contrary to Iberian America, in what would become French and British America the Indians came under the direct spiritual jurisdiction of the pope, as no system of royal patronage applied. This does not mean that the pope was always in control. In fact, the little evangelical action that was taken in the course of the sixteenth century and the early seventeenth century came independently of the Holy See. As early as 1497 some priests seem to have accompanied navigator John Cabot (fl. 1461–98) during his last voyage. Raimondo de Raimondi di Soncino, the Milanese ambassador in London, wrote: "I . . . believe that some poor Italian friars will go on this voyage, who have the promise of bishoprics."[28] In 1504 "a preste" reportedly went "to the new Ilande," evidently Newfoundland.[29] In 1535 Guillaume Le Breton and Anthoine, possibly two Benedictine monks, accompanied French explorer Jacques Cartier (1491–1557) in his second voyage to Canada.[30] Around 1540 religion became a label to be used in conjunction with the French foreign policy.[31] The letters patent prepared for Cartier's third and last voyage (17 October 1540) declared that one purpose of the expedition was to collect information on the "savage peoples who live without knowledge of God and without use of reason" and "to have them instructed in the love and fear of God and of the holy Christian law and doctrine."[32] Similar declarations were contained in the 1541 charters granted to Cartier's superior, the Protestant Jean-François de La Rocque de Roberval (ca. 1500–1560), although there is no evidence that either Cartier or Roberval took clergy with them or that missionary efforts were really contemplated.[33] Somewhat later, two more Catholic priests and one Huguenot minister accompanied French Lieutenant-General Pierre Du Gua de Monts (1558?–1628) during the first attempt to establish a French settlement in Acadia in 1604.[34]

The scanty information on religious activity in North America during the sixteenth and the early seventeenth centuries certainly mirrors the limited number of exploring and colonizing initiatives. Yet there is little doubt that an unknown number of priests accompanied the fishing ships when these left the coastal towns of France in the spring bound for the North Atlantic banks. This may indeed have happened several times during the sixteenth and the seventeenth centuries. In fact, from the mid-sixteenth century onward French and Basque fishing ships numbered several hundred per summer. In 1604 King Henri IV (1553–1610, reigned from 1589), through the agency of the Jesuit Pierre Coton (1564–1626), asked Claudio Aquaviva (1543–1615), the General of the Society of Jesus, to provide two of his missionaries to accompany the fishing fleet to the Grand Banks.[35] We also know, for example, that in the second half of the 1660s French secular priest Pierre de Neufville (fl. 1650–69) went to Newfoundland every summer for four years to minister to the fishermen. He had been granted permission by François de Ville-Montée (d. 1670), the bishop of Saint-Malo, and neither he nor his superior had realized that in order to perform pastoral duties in the New World one needed special permission from the Holy See.[36] The fishing fleet, however, was regarded as a simple extension of the crew's home territory. The priests received their "faculties" (spiritual powers) from the bishops of their ports of provenance, and these maintained personal jurisdiction over their diocesans even outside their diocese of residence.[37] The pattern seems clear enough. On the one hand, several priests probably accompanied French and Basque ships to the New World and returned home with them. Like the crews they ministered to, however, they hardly had any interest in the Indians of North America. Neufville, for example, mentioned them ("savages . . . who live without law or knowledge of God") only because they preyed upon the fishermen while these were arranging their catch.[38] On the other hand, the general conversion of the Indians was a proclaimed objective of all exploring and colonizing expeditions, and yet systematic plans to carry over to the Americas "our holy Christian faith and Holy Mother the Catholic church" were not implemented or even attempted in the course of the sixteenth century.[39] Furthermore, in neither case was the presence of the Holy See acknowledged or the necessity of a New World church organization mentioned.

Not until 1610, the date of the arrival of French secular priest Jessé Fléché (d. 1611?) in the Port-Royal colony (present-day Annapolis Royal, Nova Scotia), did a priest cross the North Atlantic in order to attempt the conversion of the Indians.[40]

Fléché's departure was also the occasion for the earliest open acknowledgment of the Holy See's overall spiritual jurisdiction over the original inhabitants of North America. According to French lawyer and traveler Marc Lescarbot (ca. 1570–1642), Fléché had asked and obtained faculties enabling him to minister to the Micmacs from Roberto Ubaldini (1578–1635), bishop of Montepulciano and papal nuncio in France, who had granted them on behalf of Pope Paul V (1552–1621, reigned from 1605). "Not that a French bishop could not do it," remarked Lescarbot, "but, once that choice was made, I believe that said mission is as good [as approved] by him, who is bishop, as it would be by another, although he [the nuncio] is a foreigner."[41] The beginning of French permanent settlement in the Americas must have entailed a new awareness of the Holy See's jurisdiction, because in 1611 the Jesuit Pierre Biard (1567/68–1622) and Énemond Massé (1575–1646) asked and obtained similar powers from the nuncio. As they were members of a regular order, and one of the importance of the Society of Jesus (founded in 1534, approved in 1540), they could probably have gotten away without the Holy See's special permission. Yet the sponsors of Biard and Massé felt that their explicit responsibilities over the Indians required an extension to North America of the special faculties the society enjoyed "in Peru and in the other Indies," the "privileges of the Indies."[42] Furthermore, in 1618 Guido Bentivoglio (1577–1644), archbishop of Rhodes and Ubaldini's successor at the French nunciature, authorized the Franciscan Recollet provincial of Saint-Denys (Paris), Jacques Garnier de Chapouin (d. 1620), to establish a mission of his order in Canada. Upon the petition of King Louis XIII (1601–43, reigned from 1614) that the friars were to "teach and instruct those poor Savages in the things of the Faith," their superior, Joseph Le Caron (ca. 1586–1632) was granted the necessary faculties on behalf of his companions.[43]

Further special authorizations meant for the conversion of the Indians would have been granted somewhat at random, as in the case of Fléché, Biard and Massé, and Le Caron, had not the Sacred Congregation "de Propaganda Fide" been established in 1622. The congregation was founded to spread the True Faith among the infidels, to protect it where Catholics lived side by side with non-Catholics, and ultimately to achieve union with the Protestant and Orthodox churches. Propaganda was meant to pursue these goals by coordinating all missionary activities and centralizing information on foreign lands.[44] At the time, European settlement in North America was beginning to take shape. Port-Royal had been founded in 1605, Jamestown in 1607, Québec in 1608, Cuper's Cove in 1610, Bermuda in 1612, and Plymouth in 1620. From its very inception, then, these new settlements and the land around them, with all their inhabitants, Indian and European, came under the jurisdiction of the new congregation.[45] Indeed, everyone in Rome seemed to be aware that North America was Propaganda's responsibility and duly forwarded any matter pertaining to the New World to its officials. Furthermore, most

LA

CONVERSION

DES SAVVAGES

QVI ONT ESTE' BA-

PTIZE'S EN LA NOVVELLE

France, cette annee 1610.

AVEC VN BREF RECIT

du voyage du Sieur DE

POVTRINCOVRT.

A PARIS,

Chez IEAN MILLOT, tenant sa boutique sur les degrez de la grand' Salle du Palais.

Avec Priuilege du Roy.

1610.

Title page of Marc Lescarbot, *La Conversion des sauvages* (Paris, 1610). John Carter Brown Library.

decisions made by Propaganda did not require anyone's approval. When the pope or other congregations had to be consulted, Propaganda's decisions or suggestions were never reversed. It may well be said, then, that as far as North America was concerned, and at least until the 1830s, Propaganda alone spoke for the Holy See, whereas other Roman agencies and even the pope himself had only occasional relations with the New World. (The relationship between Propaganda and the regular orders was, however, far more difficult and complex, and, to say the least, not all information that reached the orders' headquarters in Rome was forwarded to the congregation.) In short, the Holy See's policy toward North America was Propaganda's policy, which in turn was shaped over the years by a handful of Roman officials who dealt with North America as part of their duties covering the entire world.[46]

Theoretically, from 1622 onward Propaganda enjoyed jurisdiction over seculars and regulars alike, and both needed to refer to it for faculties necessary to operate in mission territories. Yet regular orders, such as the Society of Jesus, the Recollets, and the Capuchins, both branches of the Order of Friars Minor (Franciscans), had been involved in missionary work long before the establishment of Propaganda.[47] This meant that the officials of Propaganda had much to learn from them, and their common objective, the conversion of the heathen, would certainly have been negatively affected by a lack of cooperation. The Jesuits, however, refused to comply. For a long time they fought for their independence, while in fact carrying out the colonization of New France almost by themselves, not to mention their very successful apostolate among the Hurons.

One must admit that the Jesuits had well earned their prominent place in Canadian society and had left Propaganda with little alternative. Francesco Ingoli (1578–1649), the intelligent and hardworking first secretary of Propaganda, hoped that by sending to Canada the priest Charles Camus Duperon, a nobleman from Lyons he hoped to make into the first Canadian bishop, he could be informed of any theological infringement on the part of Jesuits in their relationship with the Indians, because "in these far-away places, in order to make conversions easier, regular priests allow to use theology and to preach the Gospel in a way that this Holy See has not approved, as we know it happened in Japan."[48] Yet, in the absence of any significant intervention on the part of the French crown and contrary to the overall failure of all private entrepreneurs who had attempted to invest in the New World, the Jesuits had managed to raise enough money and to send enough priests to the colony to keep it going during the early, most delicate phase of its history. By bringing over indentured servants, they had also succeeded in offering the colony enough settlers—an enterprise that had again witnessed the utter failures of both the crown and the private entrepreneurs, whose interests in the fur trade were in direct opposition to the peopling of the colony and to the church's attempt at

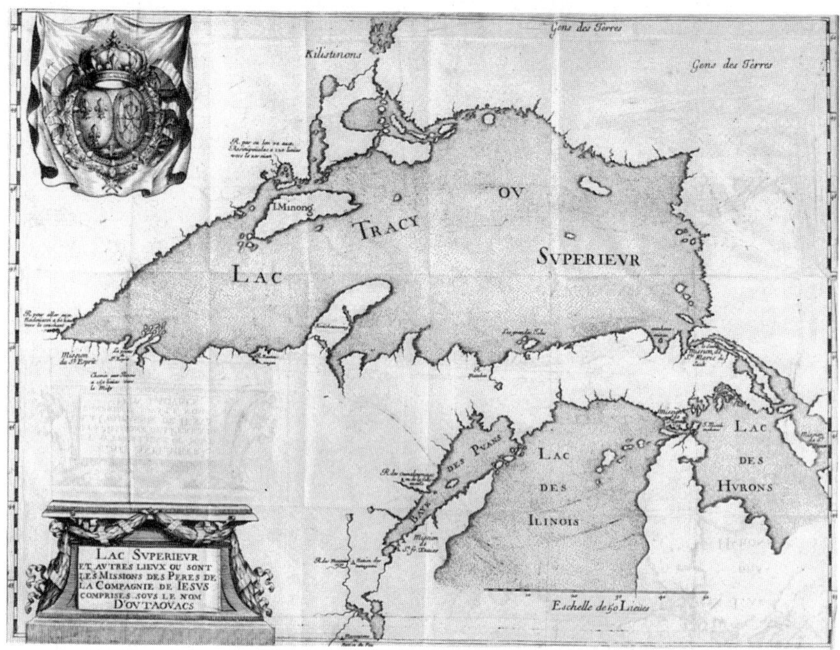

"Lac Superieur," from Claude Dablon, *Relation . . . les Années 1670 et 1671* (Paris, 1672). John Carter Brown Library.

converting the Indians. Without the church, still mainly represented by the Jesuits, it is very unlikely that Canada would have survived through the 1650s.[49]

In the early years of missionary endeavor, North America was considered important for its savage and barbarous inhabitants, not for the few English and French who had settled there—soldiers, bureaucrats, merchants, fishermen, fur traders, settlers. The basic assumptions were that this was a land almost empty of Europeans but availing a native population ripe for conversion, or, in the words of a missionary, "full of peoples that never heard the news of the Holy Gospel."[50] These peoples were the targets of the missions of the secular priest Fléché, of the Jesuits Biard and Massé, of the Recollet Le Caron, and of their companions. They had been granted papal authorizations, somewhat at random, for "pagan lands" and for reclaiming the Indians "from idolatry to the Catholic religion."[51] These Indians were invariably described as good-natured, docile, willing to listen and to learn. Consequently, conversions would have been quick and numerous.[52] These preconceptions did not apply to Indians only but were also applied to Africans, that is, in principle, to all "primitive" peoples outside of Europe and of the sophisticated Arab and Asian civilizations.[53] Gregorio Bolivar (1580–1631), a Recollet with twenty years' experience in South America but who had never set foot in

North America, reported that "those poor and unsophisticated Indian barbarians" showed great facility in "learning all that is taught to them."[54] Almost at the same time, the Discalced Carmelite Simon Stock (Thomas Doughty, 1576–1652) warned of the diffusion of Protestantism among the Indians "who dwell between Florida and the Land of Bacalaos," who were all called "Canadians." According to Stock, these peoples were "innumerable," "of an excellently benign and human disposition," and "desirous to be Christians."[55] A petition that some unnamed English priests, possibly Jesuits, addressed to Pope Urban VIII (1568–1644, reigned from 1623) in 1634 suggested that a mission be established in Catholic Maryland, where Leonard Calvert (1610/11–47) had recently been appointed governor. They explained that the Indians who were under Spanish domination hated their masters so much that "whenever they felt the desire to embrace the Christian Religion," they traveled to Protestant Virginia or New England to be instructed and baptized in the Christian faith. A mission in Maryland, which they believed bordered on Spanish territories, would then have welcomed these pious Indians and prevented them from unwittingly embracing Protestantism.[56] In the 1640s Pacifique de Provins spent the last years of his restless missionary life yearning for those "lands of northern America" with "innumerable and docile peoples," "well disposed to receive our holy Faith," who had never "seen a Christian but for the occasional passages." He had been told that they lived in a land that was neither Spanish nor French, English nor Dutch, and the enterprise had "not been attempted for 500 years."[57] In their enthusiasm, sometimes missionaries would ask to be sent to "America and Africa" at the same time.[58] And it was the same Pacifique de Provins who reported that the king of Comando, a nation on the Gulf of Guinea, had offered "the most beautiful of his palaces" to the missionaries and had allowed his son to be "instructed and cathechized." Madagascar, he also reported, was a place where "all are easy to convert," possibly too much so, since "some Mohameddan priests" had built nine mosques and the Dutch Protestants were threatening to "rot a thousand of these poor souls."[59] In 1659 François de Laval (1623–1708), bishop of Petraea and vicar apostolic of Canada, who had then just reached his new post in Québec, still believed that only the "barbarous Iroquois . . . stand before the salvation of all the peoples of this new world."[60]

None of these preconceptions were based on actual field experience.[61] In fact, the candid hopes of many prospective missionaries were often severely tried by the acquaintance with real human beings, Indian or African. Those who survived the impact of contact justified their failure by citing external causes—the selected savage nation was too small, the climate was unbearable, missionaries should have been more numerous, epidemics killed off the converts, Christian leaders exploited them, Protestant encirclement and Indian enemies were constant threats. Others would simply show their deception or lower their visionary dreams to more realistic statistical figures. In 1635 the Catholic promoters of the Maryland colony were not enthusiastic about their Indians but admitted that it was "much more Prudence and Charity, to Civilize, and make them Christians, then to kill, robbe, and hunt them from place to place, as you would doe a wolfe."[62] Madame de Brice (fl. 1644–52), a widow from Auxerre, was sent to Port-Royal with the plan to establish a school for ten or twelve Indian girls. This was the number one could hope for in a desolate land where "woods and forests [are] so confused, that when the snow falls it does not melt for six full months," and Indians were reckoned as only five hundred scattered in an area of two to three hundred leagues. In ten years, only five or six of them had been baptized.[63] The Capuchin mission on the Guinea coast was destroyed by tropical disease, as most missionaries died "of terrible infirmities and dreadful pains caused by the intemperate air and the poisonous rains," which lasted three to four months every year and provoked "worms in the legs, arms and other parts, very big and long."[64] Climate (the "intemperate air") was also said to be one of the main causes of illness and death among the Jesuits of Maryland in the 1660s, besides "cruelty of heretics" and "fatigue." When their provincial reported twenty Indians converted, thirty-two baptized, eleven confessions on point of death, and eight married couples reunited as the colony's record for 1664, the historian knows that these are hard figures, not European wishful thinking.[65] Charles Poncet de Brétigny (ca. 1610–44), French governor of the Cap-du-Nord colony at the border between Brazil and Guyana, was accused of "madness and cruelty" toward his Indians, who were fully justified, given their "simplicity" and their "great disposition . . . to come to God," for having "killed and eaten him." There, English secular priest Christopher of the Holy Trinity ([Christopher?] Gardiner, d. 1646) had managed to baptize 140 of them, whereas 146 was the record for Pacifique de Provins's stay in the West Indies.[66]

In North America, visionary schemes and wishful thinking are typical of the first half of the seventeenth century, when the drive of the Catholic Reformation coincided with the missionaries' lack of field experience. Yet this pattern regularly resurfaced during frontier conditions—that is, whenever a new territory or people was discovered or simply imagined, in the west and the north, for example, or in a hostile human environment, in Protestant areas such as Maryland (from 1645) or Virginia, for example. In 1660 Laval mentioned the departure for the west of Jesuit René Ménard (1605–ca. 1661), sent to convert "innumerable peoples who to date have no instruction whatsoever of the Christian faith."[67] In 1671 the Dutch captain Laurens van Heemskerk (ca. 1632–99) enlisted the support of the Holy See for a plan to establish a mission and a seminary in Hudson Bay (renamed by him Northern Florida). He maintained that the local natives were "of mild features, docile, weak" and "easy to convert, . . . this nation being very simple, and easy to persuade."[68] Later, in 1703, when the vast territory of Mississippi had just been discovered, the French Jesuits announced the presence of "multitudes of peoples, who have never heard of [the Christian] Religion."[69] And after the Seven Years' War, in 1766, Canadian secular priest Joseph-André-Mathurin Jacrau (ca. 1698–1772) reported on rumors he had heard from *coureurs-de-bois* of innumerable peoples living even further west. They were "good, sweet and full of reciprocal charity . . . hav[ing] no king but only village chiefs who enjoy very little authority." Jacrau was hopeful that Providence was "prepar[ing] the means to enlighten these peoples."[70] In fact, the earliest negative view of Indians with whom contacts had not yet been made was received by Propaganda in 1820, when the bishop of Québec, Joseph-Octave Plessis (1763–1825) filed a report on his diocese that defined the Indians living west of the Rocky Mountains as "nomadic and very ferocious peoples" that should be left to the care of priests from Russia or California.[71]

The officials of Propaganda lived in Rome and seldom had any opportunity to see the faraway places they administered. Given the distance between the Holy See and North America, none of these officials went there, and rarely did they meet anybody who came from there. This meant that, at least until the end of the eighteenth century, their vision of the New World very much mirrored that of their correspondents—the nuncios, the bishops, the vicars apostolic, the superiors of the missions, and the individual missionaries. Little by little, Propaganda came to share their correspondents' ideas, viewpoints, perceptions, images of the New World,[72] including their attitude toward the American Indians. To be sure, North America was never a top priority in the agenda of the cardinals of Propaganda. For example, when its cardinals met for the first time on 8 March 1622 to share among themselves jurisdictional responsibility for the various parts of the world, only Brazil and the West Indies were mentioned, both as appendages of their mother lands, Portugal and Spain. Even later, their interest in North America or the Americas in general was not comparable to the time they spent, for instance, on Germany, Illyria, Albania, the East Indies, or France.[73]

Yet, within North America, Propaganda officials at first believed, just like anybody else, that their apostolic duty should be directed toward the Indians. There was little they could do, however, except grant faculties to those who asked for them, constantly solicit fuller reports from their correspondents, or make their best of contradictory geographical information. Ingoli, who was an intelligent and hardworking bureaucrat, supported Pacifique de Provins in all his mental wanderings. In 1647 he suggested that the Capuchin friar was to abandon his mission on the coasts of Acadia, "where the people are more barbarous and more difficult to reduce to civilized life and then to the knowledge of the true God." Pacifique de Provins should instead devote his efforts to the peoples of the interior of the continent, "who live a more civilized life than the coast peoples because they are in a more temperate climate, that is, at the same latitude as Constantinople." From there, Ingoli continued, Pacifique de Provins might be able to communicate with the Recollets of New Mexico, whose Indians, "very civilized" because they too lived at the same latitude, knew a way to the western Indian nations.[74] It was Ingoli again who, in 1635, suggested that the priest Camus Duperon use only Latin as his working language with the Indians of Canada, so that these could learn to read books and communicate more easily with the Holy See.[75] In fact, their entire correspondence, no matter how unrealistic some of their proposals, shows that the American Indians, not the society of European origin, were the subject of interest for the Holy See officials.

In the 1650s and 1660s New France changed substantially. The Hurons ceased to be an important factor in Canadian society after the Iroquois destroyed them in 1649. In 1650 the French in the St. Lawrence valley were more numerous than the Indians for the first time. New land opened up for agriculture, new opportunities favored immigration from France, and the population of the colony more than doubled in ten years (from 1,206 to 2,690 between 1650 and 1660), reaching the 10,000 mark in the 1680s. At the same time, the centralizing project of Louis XIV (1638–1715, reigned from 1643) and of his principal minister, Jean-Baptiste Colbert (1619–83), began to take shape. Crown initiative replaced what had been, until that time, mostly private entrepreneurship. An orderly institutional development was required from the colonies, modeled along the patterns of the provinces of France. The governor, the intendant, and the bishop[76] would represent the military, administrative, and religious symbols of power, all of them present in the crown. By and large, by the end of the 1660s Canada had become a full-fledged, albeit small, colony, which from the St. Lawrence valley extended into a vast interior through a network of Indian alliances.[77]

By the mid-seventeenth century, except for Acadia, the Indians had ceased to be an important factor in the east and had been relegated to the margins of the society of European origin. As for the west, in the late seventeenth century the French colonial authorities continued to allow Canadians to engage in the fur trade, despite the fact that it had ceased to be profitable, in order to exploit the Indian nations as military allies against the encroaching British colonies. The Anglo-Americans, however, had no use for the Indians, except for those interested in the fur trade. Their presence blocked their road to further expansion, and their military alliance with the French made them outright enemies. This trend was coupled by a general disillusionment with the Indians' ability to assimilate the better part of European "civility." According to both the French and the English, over the years Indians had in fact remained "primitive" societies with little to offer to Europeans. Although their material imprint over European life was far from negligible (maize, tobacco, moccasins, and the lightweight bark canoe being among the New World's most celebrated additions), their intellectual influence was regarded as next to nothing, if not negative altogether.

The notorious and scandalous instances of the "white Indians," Anglo-Americans who had actually elected to live among the Indians, often after having been taken forcibly from their own families and settlements, has been well described by American historian James Axtell.[78] The French attitude toward intermarriage and miscegenation is another good case in point. In the early days both were encouraged, as such unions were deemed to favor Indian cultural and religious adaptation to the European ways and to increase the colony's population. In practice, not many such marriages took place. According to Canadian historian Cornelius John Jaenen, only seventeen intermarriages were recorded in Canada between 1664 and 1700. Mixed unions were much more numerous in the Illinois and Lower Louisiana settlements, where French women were scarce and relations with the Indians an everyday occurrence. The available records show an average of one French-Indian legal marriage for each French couple.[79] Yet the early expectations of the French crown officials soon gave way to disillusionment and prejudice against such unions, since the offspring, in their eyes, manifested the worst features of both races.[80] By the mid-seventeenth century, in French and even more so in English America, Indian and European societies were clearly developing along different, and all too often contrasting, paths.

As far as religious structures were concerned, Laval's appointment as bishop and vicar apostolic of Canada in 1658 signaled the beginning of a new era. Laval replaced the Jesuit superior as the highest religious authority in the colony[81] with the full support of the French crown, of the Holy See, and of the regular orders, including the Jesuits. The thousands of Hurons that the Society of Jesus claimed to have converted or baptized before the nation's collapse were indeed part of the rationale for the erection of the new vicariate apostolic in Canada.[82] Yet the new stability of the colony had the effect of shifting the attention from the Indians to the growing European population. Slowly, but surely, the need to maintain the True Faith amongst the French community replaced the earlier enthusiasm for missionary work and the ill-placed hope for an easy evangelization of all North American Indians.[83]

In New France, this shift from the spiritual well-being of the Indians to the needs of the European community owed much to the end of Huronia in 1649, although it became more evident during Laval's mandate as vicar apostolic. Laval's changing attitude during his administration clearly demonstrates this shift in focus. Laval was not at all uninterested in the Indian missions. He had been selected in a particularly devout French entourage, consisting of a number of

LE GRAND
VOYAGE DV PAYS
des Hurons, situé en l'Amerique uers la mer douce
ez dernieres confins de
la nouuelle France
Ou il est traicte de tout
ce qui est du pays & du
gouuernement des Sauuages
Auec un Dictionnaire
de la Langue huronne
Par Fr. Gabriel Sagard
Recollect de S.t Francois
de la prouince S.t Denis

A. PARIS Chez Denys
Moreau rue S.t Jacques à
La Salamandre 1632

Title page of Gabriel Sagard, *Le Grand Voyage du pays des Hurons* (Paris, 1632). John Carter Brown Library.

young prelates who had devoted their lives to missionary endeavor in foreign countries. Among his companions were Pierre Lambert de La Motte (1624–79), François Pallu (1626–84), and Ignace Cotolendi (1630–62), who were appointed respectively vicars apostolic in Cochinchina, Tonkin, and Nankin. Laval ended up in Canada, because he had openly declared his preference for "a savage country, rather than . . . a civilized one."[84] In August 1659, less than two months after his landing in Québec, the new vicar apostolic wrote to Alexander VII (1599–1667, reigned from 1655) and to the general of the Society of Jesus, Goswin Nickel (1584–1664), praising the latter's missionaries "for reclaiming the new Christians from their barbarity to the worship and religion of God."[85] With the passing of time, however, he became increasingly conscious of the difficulties his church encountered in dealing with the Indians. At first, he nurtured some hopes toward the Iroquois. He then became convinced that there was no other way to deal with them but outright annihilation and asked Louis XIV for military intervention.[86] The restructuring of his European-Canadian church soon began to take most of his time. The founding of the seminary, the collection of the tithes, the administration of his French abbeys, Rouen's interference with his jurisdiction, the dispute with the governor (mainly over the brandy trade with the Indians), and the Recollets' behavior became Laval's main concerns. At first, the information he sent to Rome provided abundant information on the Indians and could take the form of a separate report.[87] His later letters to the Holy See show a progressive loss of interest for the Indian missions, which increasingly became the subject of a distinct but rather short paragraph near the end.[88]

The Ursulines and the Augustines Hospitalières de la Miséricorde de Jésus debated at length whether to return to France when their failure at educating the Indian children had become all too evident. Eventually, they decided to stay on but to devote themselves to the community of European origin.[89] Little interest in the Indian missions was shown by Laval's five immediate successors,[90] and after the British conquest of Canada (1760), Bishop Jean-Olivier Briand (1715–94, bishop 1766–84) informed the Holy See that he had some hope of being authorized to use former Jesuits for the Indian missions, "for which Canadians have absolutely no taste, but that I should take care of."[91] It is, then, quite clear that, at least by the end of the 1660s, for the bishops of Canada and for the rest of the French clergy the spiritual well-being of the Indians had ceased to be the focus of their religious interest in the New World. Coincidental with the waning importance of the missionary church was the growing importance of the *routinière* church, that is, of the church whose main aim was to keep the faith among Catholics, not to convert heretics and pagans. Bishop, chapter and vicars general, parish priests, seminaries, and female and male members of the regular orders were all there to provide the European population with the same services they performed in France—baptisms, marriages, funerals, confessing, praying, preaching, counseling, teaching, caring for the sick and the poor, and maintaining and raising moral standards.[92] Indian missions did not disappear altogether. In fact, they continued to exist and, in some cases, to thrive, and there was an important revival of missionary work in the nineteenth century.[93] But after the 1660s missionaries became the imperial agents of the crown, employing different means than the soldier and the merchant, but certainly serving the same purpose—to keep the allegiance of the Indian nations in order to assure the French crown's control over North America and to fend off British expansionism.[94]

This was not, however, a peculiar Canadian trend. One must note that a similar shift took place in the French West Indies, where the relationship between the French and the Indians had not substantially changed since the early days of colonization. The charter of the Compagnie des Isles de l'Amérique, established in 1635 by Louis XIII and his principal minister, Armand-Jean du Plessis, cardinal de Richelieu (1585–1642), included the clause for the company to bring over to the islands "a number of priests and members of the regular orders in order to instruct the Indians and their inhabitants . . . in the Catholic, Apostolic and Roman religion."[95] Yet thirty-odd years of missionary efforts did not produce any encouraging result, as "Carib resistance to Christianity was nearly total."[96] In 1668 the Dominican Pierre La Forcade (d. 1673) would maintain that the West Indians were pagan and savage peoples, "almost beasts," who were not to be converted and persisted in their errors. Conversely, his confrère Philippe de Beaumont (1620–80) admitted that little had been accomplished until then but stressed that "it is a work that requires perseverance."[97] In fact, La Forcade had become interested in the French community only, whereas Beaumont still regarded his role as primarily devoted to the Indians. In spite of the space that the West Indian missionaries devoted to the Indians in their published accounts, La Forcade's point of view would eventually prevail, just as in Canada.[98]

In this general framework, there is very little room for the British continental colonies. There, Catholics were rare and the "Romish religion" was more a flag to rally against than a real threat.[99] Penal laws forbade the free exercise of the Catholic religion, except, for a short time, in Maryland. Moreover, the American Catholic community did not surface until the mid-eighteenth century, when their numbers, though still small, became noticeable. In 1750 they were but a fraction of the 1,206,000 inhabitants, and only in a limited number of colonies did they exist at all. They were 3,000 in Maryland in 1708 and had risen to between 5,000 and 7,000 fifty years later. Meanwhile, the Catholics of Pennsylvania had grown to 2,000. In the rest of the colonies they were virtually nonexistent. Richard Challoner (1691–1781), bishop of Debra and vicar apostolic in the London district, wrote in 1745 that there was no hope for proselytizing there, "until the exercise of the Catholic religion be tolerated in England."[100] On the eve of American independence, the Catholics of the thirteen colonies numbered between 20,000 and 25,000, or about 1 percent of a population of 2,300,000—the same percentage they constituted in Britain. They were clearly only a fraction of the entire Catholic population of the New World—although the great waves of emigration of the post-Napoleonic era would soon change all that.[101]

The British continental colonies were, until 1756, in the hands of the London province of the Society of Jesus.[102] Reports on the state of religion were occasional, information scanty, and the overall picture one of little hope amidst much suffering.[103] The only known clue that some information managed to reach Rome on the Jesuit mission in Maryland (1634–45), the only real attempt on the part of the British Catholics to convert the Indians, is the translation into Italian of excerpts of the *Declaratio Coloniae* of 1633, written by Jesuit Andrew White (1579–1656), later superior of the mission, and revised by Cecil Calvert, the second baron Baltimore (1605–75), besides a request for missionaries that the latter had forwarded to Rome via Carlo Rossetti (1614–81), archbishop of Tarsus, the former nuncio in England.[104] There followed a solid silence, at least until the American West opened up for colonization after the War of American Independence.[105] That early Indian evangelization was, however, "ultimately wasted effort" is the opinion of American historian Thomas W. Spalding. According to his most recent official history of the archdiocese of Baltimore, the colonists "pushed the natives beyond the fringe of the settlement," that is, out of the overall picture of Catholic expansion.[106] There is little wonder, then, that the shift that had occurred within the Catholic church in New France, from the Indians to the population of European origin, could not and did not take place in the British colonies.

As we have seen, Rome had initially mirrored a general attitude on the part of the local clergy that emphasized missionary work among the Indians. It continued to follow its correspondents when they shifted their attention toward the European population of North America. To be sure, the Holy See officials had never reneged on their duties toward those who had left Europe for the New World. As early as 1504 Pope Julius II (1443–1513, reigned 1503–13) had issued the bull *Illius fulciti praesidio* (15 November 1504), in which Spain's duties in the New World were defined as twofold—to "preach the word of God, convert the . . . infidels and barbarous peoples, instruct and teach the converts in the true faith," and to minister to them "and to all other Christians for the time being living there."[107] As for North America, in 1635 Ingoli got his facts garbled but, at the same time, showed his awareness of a de facto double responsibility in Canada. According to him, both the Recollets and the Jesuits were in charge of the "new Christians," whereas only the former were assigned to the Indians.[108] This idea of a double responsibility seemed to apply whenever frontier conditions were met. For example, in Acadia around 1650, the Capuchins were said to minister to the Indians who lived close to Port-Royal as well as to the French soldiers who defended the colony from enemy raids.[109] And in 1684, during the immediate aftermath of the discovery of Louisiana, Recollets were employed to preach the gospel to the Indians they might encounter and also to the members of the French exploring expedition.[110]

It so happened, however, that in the 1650s and the 1660s most of Propaganda's customary North American sources dried up. The disappearance of Pacifique de Provins on the Guyana coast in 1648 was followed almost immediately by the end of the Capuchin missions in Acadia (1655).[111] Except for a detailed and yet puzzling report of the late 1680s on Chedabouctou,[112] the Micmacs of Acadia did not resurface until the mid-1750s.[113] But even more deceiving must have been Laval's virtual disappearance from the list of the regular informers of Propaganda. The Holy See's success in reaching an agreement with the French crown for the erection of a full bishopric in Québec had in fact consigned the Canadian church into the hands of the Gallican church.[114] Very rarely did Laval's successors correspond with the Holy See, and never did they volunteer information on the state of their diocese, let alone of their Indian flock.[115]

Clearly, after the 1660s there were for the Holy See two North Americas. For opposite reasons, both of them were unmanageable: Canada, because its very success had been the cause of the severance of its relationship with Rome; and the British continental colonies, because anti-Catholic penal laws and the small number of the faithful made sheer survival the only real issue at stake. In both cases the issue of the conversion of the Indians had lost its relevance. In the almost one hundred years that intervened between the erection of the bishopric of Québec (1672) and the military conquest of Canada (1760), some pieces of news with reference to the Indians continued to be sent from North America to the Holy See; most of them concerned the newly discovered territories of Louisiana and Mississippi and their alleged multitudes of heathen.[116] These were, however, pale reminders of the heroic age of the Indian missions in the first half of the seventeenth century. What was even more important, the Indian missions, or, for that matter, the Indians themselves, had become marginal to the development of North America. They were now picturesque introductions to a world that had become fully European, albeit different from the Europe of its origins. In the two general reports of the state of the world that were written in 1678 and 1709 by Urbano Cerri (d. 1679) and Niccolo' Forteguerri (1674–1735), both sometime secretaries of Propaganda, the focus was on the development of the European colonies. The Indians had reverted back to their traditional role as "fond of eating human flesh, inconstant, deceitful, malicious, vindictive, cruel, and thieving, . . . very strong and very tall, idolaters in religion."[117]

French showing Christian images to the Indians, from Louis Armand de Lom d'Arce, baron de Lahontan, *Memoirs de l'Amerique Septentrionale* (Paris, 1722). John Carter Brown Library.

Once again, the Holy See followed in the general negative trend. There were two main reasons for this. First, converting the Indians proved to be a very difficult task, no matter how enthusiastic the missionaries could be. Even for the better trained and most successful among them, such as the Jesuits, to simply learn and use the Indians' languages proved to be a demanding task. Not only did Indians lack words for salt, leaven, castle, pearl, prison, mustard seed, casks of wine, lamp, candlestick, torch, kingdom, king, shepherd, flock, and sheepfold,[118] but concepts like the Holy Trinity or Mary's virginity were mysteries that could not be explained even to Europeans, let alone to the Hurons. A refined Jesuit linguist, Charles Garnier (1606–49), would complain that "our mysteries are completely new to them; their language provides us with very few of the words that would be necessary."[119] Even the most successful Indian mission, such as Jesuit Huronia was before its destruction, was indeed "very far away from the ten million souls that our confrères have baptized . . . in the East and West Indies," as French Recollet Gabriel Théodat Sagard (fl. 1614–36) lamented in 1632 after his own experience in the New World.[120] Secondly, given the nature and the final end of the church's involvement in North America, intellectual disillusionment also played a major part. Although the missionaries came to realize that Indians were not as savage as they were at first described, they found little in the Indian world attractive.[121] Their efforts to adapt to the Indian intellectual environment, by learning the native languages and understanding their culture, were simply means to better implement their overall plans. Probably the only temptations for the missionaries came from the easiness of the Indians' sexual habits.

Yet room for cultural compromise would have been available, had Indian society proved to be less "primitive" and more of an enviable alternative to European civility. Cultural compromise, in fact, did take place in the church's relationship with the sophisticated Asian societies and their religions. There, the borderline between using local cultural modes and accepting local religions was, at times, extremely thin. Some missionaries adopted the uniforms, the appearances, the ceremonies, the language, the vocabulary, and often the concepts of Confucianism and of other Asian religions for the purpose and to the extent of making themselves indistinguishable from local dignitaries and clergymen. In theory, this apparent openness was a means to change local societies from within without sacrificing the principles of Christian religion. Among the most notable advocates of these methods were Matteo Ricci (1552–1610) in China, Roberto de Nobili (1577–1656) in India, Alessandro Valignano (1539–1606) in Japan, Alexandre de Rhodes (1591–1660) in the Tonkin, and Antonio de Andrade (1580–1634) in Tibet, all members of the Society of Jesus. Strongly opposed were the Dominicans (Order of Friars Preacher) and the Franciscans. The debate whether this attitude was acceptable raged within the Catholic church for two centuries, and what came to be known as the Chinese Rites and the Malabar Rites controversies were eventually resolved, by Pope Benedict XIV (1675–1758, reigned from 1740) in 1742 and 1744, by closing the door to any compromise.[122] In his 1636 relation from Huronia, written at the height of Jesuit success in New France, the Jesuit Jean de Brébeuf (1593–1649) made it very clear: "I do not suggest . . . that our savages can be made to compare with the Chinese, the Japanese and the other nations which are perfectly civilized, but [it is my] only [wish] to raise them from the condition of beasts in which the opinions of some have reduced them, to give them their rank within humankind, and to show that some kind of political and civil life are extant amongst them."[123] Asian societies could, and at times did, represent an interesting diversion for the European intellectual curiosity, while Indian societies were deemed to be too primitive to arouse much interest among Europeans.

The "primitiveness" of Indian societies, from which they seemed unable to reclaim themselves, had another negative effect on the efforts aimed at the conversion of their members. It made it almost impossible to implement the Holy See's own directions regarding the creation of a local clergy. In principle, as Indians had been declared members of the human race, they could also become members of the clergy, provided that certain intellectual requisites were met. In 1628 Ingoli, the secretary of Propaganda, clearly stated that "the Indians being men, they are consequently able of [understanding and practising the Catholic] Religion, and among them there must be some who are apt to be promoted to priesthood."[124] In practice, were the Indians thought to be "apt" enough?

On 7 March 1646, an "early fruit of . . . the mission of Canada" was baptized in Paris, "solemnly and before a large gathering of people."[125] Upon the insistence of the queen regent, Anne of Austria (1601–66), the twenty-two-year-old West Indian was named after the future king of France, Louis. A duke and a duchess acted as his godparents, and only unfavorable circumstances prevented the archbishop of Paris, Jean-François-Paul de Gondy (d. 1679), from being present in person. Louis had been sent to France in order to win more support for Pacifique de Provins's mission in Guadeloupe.[126] During his stay in France (December 1645–April 1646), where he "live[d] with great edification of all," Louis became somewhat more proficient in the French language and was returned to his country.[127] Unfortunately, he died only one year after his return. Whether Louis was able to lead "other pagan savages" to the True Faith, as Cardinal Rainaldo d'Este (d. 1672), a member of Propaganda, expected from him, we do not know.[128]

In sending this "early fruit" of his mission to Paris, Pacifique de Provins had in fact complied with a long-established practice, of which the baptism on European soil of these native Americans was usually regarded as the climax.[129] The most spectacular of these ceremonies took place in 1613, when French Capuchin Claude d'Abbeville (Firmin Foullon, d. 1632) accompanied six Brazilian Tupinambas to Paris for baptism and the king, Louis XIII, and the queen regent, Marie de' Medici (1573–1642), served as prominent godparents.[130] In 1637 two Montagnais girls, renamed Marguerite Thérèse and Marie-Magdelène, were baptized in the Carmelite convent in Paris. Charlotte-Marguerite de Montmorency, princess of Condé (d. 1650), Chancellor of France Pierre Séguier (1588–1672), Marie-Madeleine de Combalet (later duchess of Aiguillon, 1604–75), and Secretary of State François Sublet des Noyers (1588–1645) acted as godparents.[131] The main idea, as in the case of Pacifique de Provins's Louis, was to have them trained as Christians and sent back home, where they were supposed to set higher moral standards amongst their compatriots, to assist the missionaries, and to become themselves propagators of their faith, sometimes as *dogiques* (catechists).[132] On this procedure, both Holy See officials in Rome and field missionaries entertained no doubts. As to whether these same Christians could be promoted to priesthood, the deep gap between theory and practice proved that within the church the same consensus had not been reached on that point.

Since its early days, Propaganda officials showed themselves to be the least Eurocentric agency of the church. A polyglot printing press was established as early as 1626 especially to prepare books in foreign languages to be used in the missions. A year later the Urban College (Collegio Urbano) was founded to train secular missionaries destined for mission countries or originally from there. Meanwhile, the study of foreign languages was encouraged at all levels.[133] The creation of a local clergy, however, ranked first and foremost among Propaganda's officials and certainly was Secretary Ingoli's own priority.[134] It had become all too evident that the clergy of European origin strongly opposed the ordination of native priests, on the rationale that the native candidates' external behavior or intellectual potential were not appropriate or sufficient to make good priests out of them. Over the years, Ingoli did his utmost to demolish their case. "European priests do not want that local [candidates] be promoted [to priesthood], lest they be driven thence, thus losing their rule, and the great gains that they extract from the Indies," he accused.[135] Reason alone ("nature") would dictate that among the multitudes of human beings living in Europe, Asia, Africa, and America some would be eligible for the priesthood.[136] Indians who had gone to Rome from Iberian America had proved their aptness, and so had "the Brahmins, the Chinese, the Cochinese, the Tonkinese, and all Indians born of a Spanish father who are very apt to become priests."[137] Furthermore, Ingoli countered the accusations that South American Indians were prone to drunkenness and inconstancy by explaining that the drunkenness of many Europeans did not bar them from priesthood, and that wine had been introduced and was sold by the Spaniards. Lapses into idolatry and the absence of any sentiment of shame for their errors were due to the fact that Europeans had withheld full instruction from them. Yet, if Indians were reputed to make good magistrates, military commanders, bureaucrats, and chaplains, why could they not become good priests?[138] Ingoli's views were indeed the views of the newly founded congregation, which in 1630 decreed that, concerning the ordination of the natives of the Indies, "the best among the Indians . . . be promoted to the sacred orders, including priesthood."[139] Europeans were treated no differently. Seventy-five years later, in 1705, former Propaganda archivist William Lesley (1621–1707) submitted to Pope Clement XI (1649–1721, reigned from 1700) a new plan to coordinate better the administration of the missions. According to the experienced Scot, three procurators each for Asia, Africa, and America should be appointed, who were to live in Rome and possibly be "a local [priest] or a qualified person."[140]

Although the Holy See seemed to make no distinction between converts, or candidates to priesthood, in the Far East and in Iberian America, the attitude of the church at large toward the native inhabitants of these two faraway worlds was markedly different. Political diffidence on the part of the field missionaries, rather than a negative judgment on the nature of the natives' minds, seemed to slow the creation of a local clergy in Asia. Although the Japanese converts were reputed to be "able to become priests," the first two Japanese priests (Sebastian Kimura, ca. 1566–1622, and Luis Niabara, d. 1618) had been ordained as recently as 1601, and the ordained Japanese only numbered fourteen by 1614. The first Chinese priest, the Dominican Gregorio Lo Wen-tsao (renamed Lopez, 1616–91), waited until 1654. In Goa local candidates were ordained but not given positions of responsibility. As shown by the debate within Catholicism caused by the Asian rites, these were sophisticated societies with well-developed philosophies and theologies. The danger was that a sudden influx of foreign clergy might contaminate Christian doctrine from within.[141] As for the Indian societies of the Americas, their "primitiveness" made such an occurrence impossible. In Spanish America, the provincial councils of Lima and Mexico (1552, 1555, 1557) had openly excluded the possibility that Indians be promoted to priesthood, and it was only in 1583 that the provincial council of Lima reversed that decision. In practice, however, in spite of the millions of proclaimed conversions, not a single Indian was ordained until the end of the eighteenth century, not even in the *reducciones* of Paraguay, where the most successful Jesuit experiment lasted from 1610 to 1768. In Brazil the situation was no better. As shown by American historian Stuart B. Schwartz, "With rare exceptions none of the Brazilian religious houses opened their membership to persons of Indian, black or mixed origins unless these were obscure or quite distant in time."[142]

Within the Americas, North America was long considered the most "primitive" area, mainly because it was reckoned to be almost empty of Indians, the few ones living there being mostly nomadic peoples.[143] There again, two centuries of missionary work among the Indians elapsed without a single North American Indian having been promoted to the priesthood. To be sure, in 1668 Laval welcomed the election of Pope Clement IX (1600–1669, reigned from 1667) with the news that some Indians had joined six French and Canadian minor clerics in the Québec seminary. According to the vicar apostolic, the newcomers "shall be available for promotion to priesthood, if sometime they prove to be qualified, as the case may be." Between that year and 1677, all the European seminarians were ordained, but not one of their Indian companions.[144] And, as far as we know, North American Indians waited until 1832 to be admitted to the Urban College in Rome, where they were supposed to become priests and be trained so that they might return, as missionaries, to their peoples. Two Ottawas from northern Michigan, William Mackawdebenessy (ca. 1814–33) and the *métis* Augustin Kiminitchagan Hamelin (ca. 1814–after 1840), signed in at the college in July 1832. The former died, still in Rome, one year later, whereas the latter left for health problems in 1834 and never became a priest.[145]

In conclusion, available evidence seems to prove that, when confronted with the issue of the conversion of the North American Indians, the Holy See shared most experiences, and, indeed, the same reality, with the other European countries that were directly involved in the New World. In the sixteenth and early seventeenth centuries, a general consensus on the moral necessity of converting all heathens to Christianity was virtually unmatched by practical initiatives. In the first half of the seventeenth century, both the Holy See (with Propaganda) and France (with the Jesuits, the Recollets, and the Capuchins) produced their greatest efforts at evangelization, as the conversion of the Indians remained a primary objective of colonization and, indeed, made colonization possible. After the 1660s the increased size and needs of the European community relegated the Indians and missionary endeavor to a marginal role within the colony. As far as the Holy See's attitude was concerned, this trend applied to both New France and the French West Indies. As for the British continental colonies, the minimal information that reached Rome, coupled with the minuscule size of the Catholic community there and its legal status, made it almost impossible for the Holy See to distinguish between Indians to be converted and Europeans to be maintained in the True Faith. Furthermore, the Holy See soon shared with the other European countries a general disillusionment with the ease of evangelization and with the stubborn "primitiveness" of the Indians. Although within the church there was plenty of room for cultural compromise with non-European societies, such as the Asian ones, North American societies showed no attractive features for European missionaries. Thus, the Eurocentric attitude of the church, no matter how strongly denied in theory, especially on the part of the Holy See proper, was all the more evident in the Americas, where local converts were refused admission to the clergy until well into the nineteenth century.

ACKNOWLEDGMENTS

The author wishes to thank Giovanni Pizzorusso (formerly a doctoral student with the Università di Genova), Ileana Pagani (Università di Salerno), and Matteo Sanfilippo (Università della Tuscia) for their comments on an earlier version of this essay.

NOTES

The following abbreviations are used in the notes:

AA	America Antille
AAQ	Archives de l'Archidiocèse de Québec, Québec
AC	America Centrale
ACU	Archives of Collegio Urbano, Rome
AN	Archives Nationales, Paris
APF	Archives of the Sacred Congregation "de Propaganda Fide," Rome
ARSI	Archivum Romanum Societatis Iesu, Rome
AS	America Settentrionale
ASV	Vatican Secret Archives, Vatican City

BAV Biblioteca Apostolica Vaticana, Vatican City
C Congressi
CP Congregazioni Particolari
FV Fondo Vienna
MD Miscellanee Diverse
MV Miscellanee Varie
OCD Order of the Discalced Brothers of the Blessed Virgin Mary of Mount Carmel (Discalced Carmelites)
OFM Order of Friars Minor (Franciscans)
OMI Oblates of Mary Immaculate
OP Order of Friars Preacher (Dominicans)
OSB Order of St. Benedict (Benedictines)
PF Sacred Congregation "de Propaganda Fide"
SJ Society of Jesus
SOCG Scritture Originali riferite nelle Congregazioni Generali
SS Segreteria di Stato
WDA Westminster Diocesan Archives, London

1. This essay is mostly based on a number of guides and calendars of Vatican material that were prepared during the past decade. See Finbar Kenneally, OFM, ed., *United States Documents in the Propaganda Fide Archives: A Calendar*, 1st ser., 7 vols. and Index (Washington, 1966–81); Monique Benoit and Gabriele P. Scardellato, *A Calendar of Documents of North American Interest in the Series Francia, Archives of the Secretary of State of the Holy See*, Finding Aid in microform (Ottawa, 1984), and *A Calendar of Documents of North American Interest from Various Series and Sub-Series of the Archivio Segreto Vaticano*, Finding Aid in microform (Ottawa, 1984); Giovanni Pizzorusso, "Archives of the Sacred Congregation 'de Propaganda Fide': Calendar of Volume I (1634–1760) of the Series *Congressi America Antille*," *Storia nordamericana* 3, no. 2 (1986): 117–64, and "Roman Ecclesiastical Archives and the History of the Native Peoples of Canada," *European Review of Native American Studies*, 4, no. 2 (1990): 21–26; Luca Codignola, *Guide to Documents Relating to French and British North America in the Archives of the Sacred Congregation "de Propaganda Fide" in Rome, 1622–1799/Guide des documents relatifs à l'Amérique du Nord française et anglaise dans les Archives de la Sacrée Congrégation "de Propaganda Fide" à Rome, 1622–1799* (Ottawa, 1991), to be used in conjunction with its calendar (Finding Aid no. 1186, 5 vols.); and Luca Codignola, "The Casanatense Library," *Annali Accademici Canadesi* 7 (1991): 99–104.

2. For a very general overview and chronology of Christian missions, see Simon Delacroix, ed., *Histoire universelle des missions catholiques*, 4 vols. (Paris and Monaco, 1956–59); Stephen Charles Neill, *A History of Christian Missions* (Harmondsworth, 1964); Josef Metzler, OMI, ed., *Sacrae Congregationis de Propaganda Fide Memoria Rerum*, 3 vols. in 5 tomes (Rome, Freiburg, Vienna, 1971–76); Willi Henkel, OMI, ed., *Ecclesiae Memoria: Miscellanea in onore del R.P. Josef Metzler O.M.I. Prefetto dell'Archivio Segreto Vaticano* (Rome, Freiburg, Vienna, 1991). For the pre-Columbian concerns of the Holy See, see Jean Richard, *La Papauté et les missions d'Orient au Moyen Age (XIIIe-XVe siècles)* (Rome, 1977);

James Muldoon, *Popes, Lawyers, and Infidels: The Church and the Non-Christian World, 1250–1550* (Philadelphia, 1979); John Webster Grant, *Moon of Wintertime: Missionaries and the Indians of Canada in Encounter since 1534* (Toronto, 1984), 9–10.

3. The original Latin version is in William E. Shiels, SJ, *King and Church: The Rise and Fall of the Patronato Real* (Chicago, 1961), 277 ("Orthodoxe fidei propagationem nostre cure celitus commissam et Christiane religionis augmentum et animarum salutem barbararum quoque nationum et aliorum infidelium quorumlibet depresionem et ad fidem conversionem supremis desiderantes affectibus"). Translations into English are in ibid., 66, and in John Horace Parry, Robert G. Keith, and Michael Jimenez, eds., *New Iberian World: A Documentary History of the Discovery and Settlement of Latin America to the Early 17th Century*, 5 vols. (New York, 1984), vol. 1, *The Conquerors and the Conquered*, 373.

4. The original Latin version is in Frances Gardiner Davenport and Charles O. Paullin, eds., *European Treaties Bearing on the History of the United States and Its Dependencies, 1455–1815*, 4 vols. (Washington, 1917–37), vol. 1, *To 1648* (1917), 58, 72–73; in Shiels, *King and Church*, 283; and now in Josef Metzler, OMI, ed., *America Pontificia Primi Saeculi Evangelizationis, 1493–1592: Documenta pontificia ex registris et minutis praesertim in Archivo Secreto Vaticano existentibus*, 2 vols. (Vatican City, 1991), 1:71–75, and "Specimina quaedam no. 1" ("fides catholica et christiana religio nostris praesertim temporibus exaltetur, ac ubilibet amplietur et dilatetur, animarumque salus procuretur, ac barbarae nationes deprimantur et ad fidem ipsam reducantur" [Shiels version]). The translation into English used here is in Shiels, *King and Church*, 78; other translations are in Davenport and Paullin, *Treaties*, 1:61, 75–76, and in Parry, Keith, and Jimenez, *New Iberian World*, 1:272.

5. APF, MD, vol. 22, fols. 1^{rv}–4^{rv}; reprinted in Metzler, *Memoria Rerum*, 3/2, *1815–1972* (1976), 662–64.

6. APF, SOCG, vol. 144. fols. 183^{rv}, 195^{rv}, Pacifique de Provins to Bernardino Spada, Paris, 25 October 1646 ("respandre les retz de l'evangile dans les plus eslonguées contrées et nations de la terre"); Pacifique de Provins, *Le voyage de Perse et Brève relation du voyage de l'Amérique*, ed. Godefroy de Paris and Hilaire de Wingene (Assisi, 1939), 5* ("ramener ces peuples sauvages à la connaissance du vrai Dieu que nous adorons"). Some theologians believed that "savages" were to be "brought back" to Christianity as God had revealed himself to all peoples, although some had simply lost most of their knowledge of him and of their own history. By this time, however, the concept of a "return to the Faith" is very much a rhetorical device only. On this point, see the thorough essay by Sabine MacCormack in this volume. On Pacifique de Provins, see Luca Codignola, "A World Yet to Be Conquered: Pacifique de Provins and the Atlantic World, 1629–1648," in *Canada ieri e oggi. Atti del 6o Convegno Internazionale di Studi Canadesi. Selva di Fasano, 27–31 marzo 1985*, ed. Luca Codignola and Raimondo Luraghi (Fasano, 1985), vol. 3, *Sezione Storica*, 59–84, and "Pacifique de Provins and the Capuchin Network in Africa and America," in *Proceedings of the Fifteenth Meeting of the French Colonial Historical Society, Martinique and Guadeloupe, May 1989/Actes Du Quinzième Colloque De La Société d'Histoire Coloniale Française, Martinique et Guadeloupe, Mai 1989*, ed. Patricia Galloway and Philip Poulin Boucher (Lanham, 1992), 46–60. Pacifique de Provins was active in present-day Turkey, Syria, Lebanon, Jordan, Israel, Egypt, Iraq, and Iran (1621–23, 1626–29); he lived in Guadeloupe from 15 May 1645 to

June 1646, visiting Martinique, Dominica, and Marie Galante. He died on the Guyana coast in 1648. See also Raoul de Sceaux, OFM Cap, *Histoire des Frères Mineurs Capucins de la Province de Paris (1601–1660)*, 2 vols. (Blois, 1965–?), vol. 2, [*1626–1660*] (n.d.), 437–38.

7. John Paul II, *Encyclical Letter Redemptoris Missio of the Supreme Pontiff John Paul II on the Permanent Validity of the Church's Missionary Mandate*, [7 December 1990], (Rome, 1991), 8, 9. New Testament citations are from the Authorized King James Version of Acts 1:8 and Mark 16:15; *Redemptoris Missio*, 33, uses another version, and its citations are slightly different.

8. Neill, *History*, 140–41; Cornelius John Jaenen, *The Role of the Church in New France* (Toronto, 1976), 22–23; Robert T. Handy, *A History of the Churches in the United States and Canada* (Oxford, 1976), 1; Robert F. Berkhofer, Jr., *The White Man's Indian: Images of the American Indian from Columbus to the Present* (New York, 1978), 115–25; John Parker, "Religion and the Virginia Colony, 1609–1610," in *The Westward Enterprise: English Activities in Ireland, the Atlantic, and America, 1480–1650*, ed. Kenneth R. Andrews, Nicholas P. Canny, and Paul E. H. Hair (Detroit, 1979), 245–70; Karen Ordahl Kupperman, *Settling with the Indians: The Meeting of English and Indian Cultures in America, 1580–1640* (London, 1980), 159–88 (mainly on the English Protestant attitude); James Axtell, *The Invasion Within: The Contest of Cultures in Colonial North America* (New York, 1985), 23–32.

9. British Library (Department of Printed Books), 4745.f.11 (8), sig. A, *Papeles Tocantes la Iglesia Espanola*, Juan Luis Arias, "Señor. El Doctor Iuan Luis Arias dize," [1609] ("los Hereges Ingleses, y Olandeses, a quienes el demonio instiga . . . tan afectuosa, y aceleradamente . . . el sembrar . . . el infernal veneno de su Heregia, y inficionar con el los millones de millones, de may buena gente que habitan"). A translation into English is given in Richard Henry Major, ed., *Early Voyages to Terra Australis, now Called Australia: A Collection of Documents, and Extracts from Early Manuscript Maps* (London, 1859). On the Protestant-Catholic race, see Francis Jennings, *The Invasion of America: Indians, Colonialism, and the Cant of Conquest* (Chapel Hill, 1975), 53. For a short discussion, based on the Newfoundland example, see Luca Codignola, *Terre d'America e burocrazia romana: Simon Stock, Propaganda Fide, e la colonia di Lord Baltimore a Terranova, 1621–1649* (Venice, 1982), 36–37, translated, with revisions, as *The Coldest Harbour of the Land: Simon Stock and Lord Baltimore's Colony in Newfoundland, 1621–1649* (Kingston and Montreal, 1988), 18–19.

10. See a good discussion on this point in Loren E. Pennington, "The Amerindian in English Promotional Literature, 1575–1625," in Andrews, Canny, and Hair, *Westward Enterprise*, 175–94. See also Louis Booker Wright, *Religion and Empire: The Alliance between Piety and Commerce in English Expansion, 1558–1625* (Chapel Hill, 1943); David Beers Quinn, *England and the Discovery of America, 1481–1620, from the Bristol Voyages of the Fifteenth Century to the Pilgrim Settlement at Plymouth: The Exploration, Exploitation, and Trial-and-Error Colonization of North America by the English* (London, 1974), 312; Bernard W. Sheehan, *Savagism and Civility: Indians and Englishmen in Colonial Virginia* (Cambridge, 1980), 116–43; author's interview with D. B. Quinn, "English Discoveries and Explorations to 1607," *Storia Nordamericana* 4, no. 1–2 (1987): 197–98.

11. The latest summary (based on Spanish sources) of the debate is J. H. Elliott, *Spain and Its World, 1500–1700* (New Haven, 1989), 42–64, which follows the same author's *The Old*

World and the New, 1492–1650 (Cambridge, 1970). See also Cornelius John Jaenen, *Friend and Foe: Aspects of French-Amerindian Cultural Contact in the Sixteenth and Seventeenth Century* (Toronto, 1976), 12–40; Berkhofer, *White Man's Indian*, 1–49; Harry Culverwell Porter, *The Inconstant Savage: England and the North American Indian* (London, 1979), 3–180; Laura Schrager Fishman, "How Noble the Savage? The Image of the American Indian in French and English Travel Accounts, ca. 1550–1680" (Ph.D. diss., City University of New York, 1979); Olive Patricia Dickason, *The Myth of the Savage and the Beginnings of French Colonialism in the Americas* (Edmonton, 1984), 27–40 (she mainly uses French sources but explains the general diatribe well), and "Old World Law, New World Peoples, and Concepts of Sovereignty," in *Essays on the History of North American Discovery and Exploration*, ed. Stanley H. Palmer and Dennis Reinhartz (College Station, Tex., 1988), 52–78. The "dispute of the New World" theme is best described in Antonello Gerbi, *La disputa del Nuovo Mondo: Storia di una polemica, 1750–1900* (Milan and Naples, 1955; rev. ed., ed. Sandro Gerbi, 1983), trans. Jeremy Moyle as *The Dispute of the New World: The History of a Polemic, 1750–1900* (Pittsburgh, 1973); Antonello Gerbi, *La natura delle Indie Nove: Da Cristoforo Colombo a Gonzalo Fernández de Oviedo* (Milan and Naples, 1975), trans. Jeremy Moyle as *Nature in the New World: From Christopher Columbus to Gonzalo Fernández de Oviedo* (Pittsburgh, 1986); and Antonello Gerbi, *Il mito del Perù*, ed. Sandro Gerbi (Milan, 1988). Unfortunately, available only in Italian are Giuliano Gliozzi, *Adamo e il Nuovo Mondo: La nascita dell'antropologia come ideologia coloniale, dalle genealogie bibliche alle teorie razziali (1500–1700)* (Florence, 1977); Sergio Landucci, *I filosofi e i selvaggi, 1580–1780* (Bari, 1972); Piero Del Negro, *Il mito americano nella Venezia del '700*, rev. ed. (Padua, 1986), 24–27; and Federica Ambrosini, *Paesi e mari ignoti: America e colonialismo europeo nella cultura veneziana (secoli XVI-XVII)* (Venice, 1982), esp. 284–94. Of great value are Lewis Hanke, *The Spanish Struggle for Justice in the Conquest of America* ([Washington], 1949); Henri Baudet, *Paradise on Earth: Some Thoughts on European Images of Non-European Man* (Middletown, 1988), a translation of the original book in Dutch, published in Den Haag in 1959; and Anthony Pagden, *The Fall of Natural Man: The American Indian and the Origins of Comparative Ethnology* (Cambridge, 1982).

12. According to Alexander VI, Indians "believe that the one God and Creator is in heaven and that the Catholic faith should be embraced and good morals practiced" ("credunt unum Deum Creatorem in coelis esse ac ad fidem catholicam amplexandum et bonis moribus imbuendum satis apti videntur" [Shiels version]). The original Latin version is in Davenport and Paullin, *Treaties*, 1:59, 73; in Shiels, *King and Church*, 284; and in Metzler, *America Pontificia*, 1:73. The translation into English used here is in Shiels, *King and Church*, 79; other translations are in Davenport and Paullin, *Treaties*, 1:62, 72, and in Parry, Keith, and Jimenez, *New Iberian World*, 1:272. See also Dickason, *Myth*, 29.

13. Paul III stated that the Indians were "truly men . . . not only capable of understanding the Catholic faith but . . . desir[ing] exceedingly to receive it." For that reason, they should be converted "by preaching the word of God and by the example of good living." The Latin original of *Sublimis Deus* is in Mariano Cuevas, *Documentos inéditos del siglo XVI para la historia de Mexico* (Mexico, 1914), 84–86. The translation into English used here is in Parry, Keith, and Jimenez, *New Iberian World*, 1:387–88; another is in Lewis Hanke, "Pope Paul III

and the American Indians," *The Harvard Theological Review* 30, no. 2 (April 1937): 71–72. The Latin original of *Veritas ipsa* is in Metzler, *America Pontificia*, 1:364–66. According to Metzler, *Veritas ipsa*, *Sublimis Deus*, and *Excelsus Deus* are variants of the same bull ("vero homines, non solum christianae fidei capaces existere, sed . . . ad fidem ipsam promptissime currere"; "verbi Dei praedicatione et exemplo bonae vitae"). See also Gliozzi, *Adamo*, 291–92; Dickason, *Myth*, 32; Elliott, *Spain*, 47.

14. Pagden, *Fall*, 4.

15. A good discussion is Jack Warwick, "L'antiquité dans le cadre référentiel du 'sauvage,' " in *Les figures de l'Indien*, ed. Gilles Thérien (Montréal, 1988), 107–18. See also Michel Bideaux, "Culture et découverte dans les Rélations des Jésuites," *XVIIe Siècle* 112 (1976): 3–30; Pagden, *Fall*, 7. For examples of this recourse to classical and sacred authorities, see Dickason, *Myth*, 17–22, 280–81. It might be appropriate to note that the index to the seventy-three volumes improperly known as the *Jesuit Relations* contains only five references to the great philosophical authority of the classical age, Aristotle. See Reuben Gold Thwaites, ed., *The Jesuit Relations and Allied Documents: Travels and Explorations of the Jesuit Missionaries in New France, 1610–1791*, 73 vols. (Cleveland, 1896–1901).

16. Maurile de Saint-Michel, OCD, *Voyage des isles camercanes. En l'Amériqve. Qvi font partie des Indes Occidentales, et Vne Relation Diversifiee de plusieurs Pensées pieuses, & d'agreables Remarques tant de toute l'Amerique que des autres Païs. Avec l'etablissement des RR.PP. Carmes Reformez de la Province de Touraine esdites Isles: Et un discours de leur Ordre. Composé par F. Mavrile de S. Michel Religieux Carme de la mesme Prouince: Partie pendant son voyage: Partie depuis son retour* (Le Mans, 1652). On Maurile de Saint-Michel, see Jacques de Dampierre, *Essai sur les sources de l'histoire des Antilles françaises (1492–1664)* (Paris, 1904), 128–29; Philip Poulin Boucher, *Les Nouvelles Frances: France in America, 1500–1815, An Imperial Perspective* (Providence, R.I., 1989), 38.

17. This impression is mostly based on Thwaites, *Jesuit Relations*; Lucien Campeau, SJ, ed., *Monumenta Novae Franciae*, 6 vols. to date (Rome, Québec, and Montréal, 1967–); and on the works cited in note 1 above.

18. Peter Partner, *The Pope's Men: The Papal Civil Service in the Renaissance* (Oxford, 1990), 5. As one North American bishop, Joseph-Octave Plessis, defined it in the late 1810s, the Holy See was the "center of the light" ("centre de la lumière"), "the rich source whose waters descend over all corners of the Catholic Universe" ("la source féconde dont les eaux se répandent sur toutes les parties de l'Univers Catholique"). See APF, C, AS, vol. 2, fols. 305^{rv}–306^{rv}, Plessis to Francesco Fontana, Rome, 4 January 1820; APF, C, AC, vol. 3, fols. 564^{rv}–565^{rv}, Plessis to Lorenzo Litta, Québec, 26 April 1817. Plessis was bishop (1806–19) and archbishop (1819–25) of Québec.

19. For a general overview of the Holy See's bureaucracy, see Niccolo' Del Re, *La curia romana: Lineamenti storico-giuridici* (Rome, 1952; rev. ed., 1970). Pope convincingly argues that the bureaucracy of the Holy See was able to to go "out of court," that is, to think and act independently of the strong central authority, at least since the early sixteenth century, a proper attitude of a "modern" bureaucracy. See Partner, *Pope's Men*, 3–5.

20. Partner, *Pope's Men*, 135. Note also the general attitude on the part of the Roman intellectuals, at least in the eighteenth century, who "wanted to play it safe" and limited their

inquiries to such "innocuous sciences" such as astronomy, theology, sacred history, and archaeology (see Hanns Gross, *Rome in the Age of Enlightenment: The Post-Tridentine Syndrome and the Ancien Régime* [Cambridge, 1990], 268).

21. This point is further explained in Luca Codignola, "Rome and North America, 1622–1799: The Interpretive Framework," *Storia Nordamericana* 1, no. 1 (1984): 5–33, reprinted with revisions in Codignola, *Guide*, 1–24.

22. In order to describe the church in this essay, I have used neither the modern definition given by the Second Vatican Council (1962–65), a community of bishops, secular priests, male and female members of regular orders, and laity, each with their own functions and importance (James J. Hennesey, SJ, *American Catholics: A History of the Roman Catholic Community in the United States* [New York, 1981], 3), nor the more traditional definition by John Dawson Gilmary Shea (1824–92), the father of American Catholic history, "the duly consecrated hierarchy and activities sanctioned by them" (Henry Warner Bowden, "John Gilmary Shea: A Study of Methods and Goals in Historiography," *The Catholic Historical Review* 54, no. 2 [July 1968]: 251). Rather, I have used the definition Partner used for the years 1417–1527, which seemed to apply also to the early modern era: namely, "a single body of Christians, held together under God's guidance by the sacraments" administered by a "divinely ordained priesthood" (Partner, *Pope's Men*, 5).

23. With special reference to early North America, this system is well described in Lucien Campeau, SJ, "Les initiatives de la S. Congrégation en faveur de la Nouvelle-France," in Metzler, *Memoria Rerum*, 1/2, *1622–1700* (1972), 729–30; and expanded in the same author's *L'Éveché de Québec (1674): Aux origines du premier diocèse érigé en Amérique française* (Québec, 1974), 1–8, where the concept of personal jurisdiction of the bishops is also briefly explained.

24. Wolfgang Seegrün and Theodor Schiffer, *Germania Pontificia sive Repertorium Privilegiorum et Litterarum a Romanis Pontificibus ante Annum MCLXXXXVIII Germaniae Ecclesiis Monasteriis Civitatibus Singulisque Personis Concessorum*, vol. 6, *Provincia Hammarburgo-Bremensis* (Gottingen, 1981), 56–57 ("in omnibus gentibus Sueonum seu Danorum, Noruuechorum, Islant, Scrideuinnum, Gronlant et universarum septentrionalium nationum"). See also Finn Gad, *The History of Greenland*, 3 vols. (Kingston and Montreal, 1971–82), vol. 1, *Earliest Times to 1700* (1971), 60–63, a translation from the original work in Danish, published in Copenhagen in 1967–75. According to Gad, Iceland had its bishop in 1056 and the Faeroe Islands at the end of the eleventh century. See also Tryggvi J. Oleson, *Early Voyages and Northern Approaches, 1000–1632* (Toronto, 1963), 7; Olafur Halldorsson, "The Conversion of Greenland in Written Sources," in *Proceedings of the Eighth Viking Congress, Aarhus, 24–31 August 1977*, ed. Hans Bekker-Nielsen, Peter Foote, and Olaf Olsen (Odense, 1981), 203–16; Stefan Weinfurter et al., comp., *Series episcoporum Ecclesiae Catholicae occidentalis ab initio usque ad annum MCIIC*, ser. 5, *Germania*, vol. 2, *Archiepiscopatus Hammerburgensis sive Bremensis* (Stuttgart, 1984), 30–33.

25. Bruce Graham Trigger, *Natives and Newcomers: Canada's "Heroic Age" Reconsidered* (Kingston and Montreal, 1985), 119.

26. Louis Rey, "The Evangelization of the Arctic in the Middle Ages: Gardar, the 'Diocese of Ice,'" *Arctic: Journal of the Arctic Institute of North America* 37, no. 4 (December 1984): 324–33.

27. The Spanish patronage derived from papal bulls issued from 1486 through 1508, of which the *Inter cetera* were the most important. The Portuguese patronage derived from bulls issued between 1456 and 1514. On this point, see the latest and very good summary in Martin A. Burkholder and Lyman L. Johnson, *Colonial Latin America* (New York, 1990), 83–96; also Josep M. Barnadas, "The Catholic Church in Colonial Spanish America," in *The Cambridge History of Latin America*, ed. Leslie Bethell, 5 vols. to date (Cambridge, 1984–), vol. 1, *Colonial Latin America* (1984), 511–40; and Eduardo Hoornaert, "The Catholic Church in Colonial Brazil," in ibid., 541–56. Specifically on the Spanish patronage, see Shiels, *King and Church*, and Parry, Keith, and Jimenez, *New Iberian World*, 1:372–90. On the Portuguese patronage, see Giuseppe Sorge, *Il "Padroado" Regio e la S. Congregazione "de Propaganda Fide" nei secoli XIV–XVII* (Bologna, 1985), and "La polemica giuspatronale tra la S. Sede e la Monarchia portoghese nella seconda metà del secolo XVII," in *S. Sede e corona portoghese: Le controversie giuspatronali nei secoli XVII e XVIII*, ed. Giuseppe Sorge et al. (Bologna, 1988), 15–65. The latest survey of Iberian Catholicism is Stafford Poole, "Iberian Catholicism Comes to the Americas," in Charles H. Lippy, Robert Choquette, and Stafford Poole, *Christianity Comes to the Americas* (New York, 1992), 1–129.

28. Archivio di Stato, Milano, Potenze Estere, Inghilterra, Raimondo de Raimondi di Soncino to Giovanni Maria Visconti, Duke of Milan, London, 18 December 1407, published in Henry Percival Biggar, *The Precursors of Jacques Cartier, 1497–1535* (Ottawa, 1911), 18 ("Credo . . . andarano cum questo passagio alcuni poveri frati italiani, li quali tutti hanno promissione di vescovati"); translated into English in *Calendar of State Papers and Manuscripts Existing in the Archives and Collections of Milan*, ed. Allen B. Hinds (London, 1912), 1:338, no. 552; James Alexander Williamson, *The Cabot Voyage and Bristol Discovery under Henry VII* (Cambridge, 1962), 211; D. B. Quinn, Alison M. Quinn, and Susan Hillier, eds., *New American World: A Documentary History of North America to 1612*, 5 vols. (New York, 1979), 1:97. We do not know who had informed and invited them to go, nor do we know whether they really went with Cabot.

29. Robinson Trust, Phillips MSS 4, 104, fol. 53^{v}, King's Daybook, 7–10 April 1504, quoted and reproduced in Quinn, *England and the Discovery of America*, 124 and following 294.

30. Campeau, "Initiatives," 728; Campeau, *Éveché*, 3.

31. Marcel Trudel, *Histoire de la Nouvelle-France*, 3 vols. in 4 tomes to date (Montréal, 1963–83), vol. 1, *Les vaines tentatives, 1524–1603* (1963), 129–31. See also Boucher, *Nouvelles Frances*, 3–24.

32. "Commission délivrée à Cartier (17 octobre 1540)," in Jacques Cartier, *Relations*, ed. Michel Bideaux (Montréal, 1986), 233 ("gens sauvaiges vivans sans congnoissance de Dieu et sans vsaige de raison," "instruire en l'amour et craincte de Dieu et de sa saincte loy et doctrine chrestienne"). See also Trudel, *Histoire*, 1:130–31; D. B. Quinn, "Religion in North America," in Codignola and Luraghi, *Canada ieri e oggi*, 3:36.

33. Letters patent to Jean-François de La Rocque de Roberval (15 January 1541, 18 February 1541) are in *A Collection of Documents Relating to Jacques Cartier and the Sieur de Roberval*, ed. Henry Percival Biggar (Ottawa, 1930), 178–85, 207–9. See also D. B. Quinn, "Religion in North America," 36.

34. Nicolas Aubry (fl. 1604–11) was one of the two Catholic priests. The other Catholic

priest and the Huguenot minister died at Port-Royal during the winter of 1605–6. See Campeau, *Monumenta*, vol. 1, *La première mission d'Acadie (1602–1616)* (Rome and Québec, 1967), 11; Dominique Deslandres, "Séculiers, laïcs, Jésuites: Épistèmes et projets d'évangelisation et d'acculturation en Nouvelle France. Les premières tentatives, 1604–1613," in Serge Gruzinski, ed., "Anthropologie et histoire," special section of *Mélanges de l'École Française de Rome* 101, no. 2 (1989): 763–64.

35. Pierre Coton, SJ, to Claudio Aquaviva, SJ, Fontainebleau, 25 October 1604, printed in Campeau, *Monumenta*, 1:4–6. See also William John Eccles, "The Role of the Church in New France," in his *Essays on New France* (Toronto, 1987), 26.

36. APF, SOCG, vol. 418, fols. 234^{rv}–235^{rv}, Pierre de Neufville to Clement IX, [Rome, 1668/69] (reporting fifty-three ships from southern France in 1667 or 1668, one ship carrying almost one hundred men); APF, SOCG, vol. 419, fol. 390^{rv}, Neufville to PF, [Rome, 1669]; APF, SOCG, vol. 418, fols. 233^{rv}, 236^{rv}, PF's summary of Neufville's petition, Rome, 26 May 1669 (containing further information). On Neufville, see Codignola, *Guide*, 5–6. On the fishing fleet, see Laurier Turgeon, "Le temps des pêches lointaines: Permanences et transformations (vers 1500–vers 1850)," in *Histoire des pêches maritimes en France*, ed. Michel Mollat du Jourdin (Toulouse, 1987), esp. 136–38. On the volume of the French North Atlantic fishing fleet, Canadian historian Laurier Turgeon maintains that, with some five hundred ships and twelve thousand men employed every year after the mid-sixteenth century, "les terre-neuviers français représentent . . . une de plus importantes flottes d'Europe," with nothing "à envier à la prestigieuse flotte espagnole du commerce hispano-américain qui compte à peine la moitié de ce tonnage et de ces équipages" (ibid., 138).

37. On spiritual jurisdiction on ships, with special reference to North America, see Campeau, "Initiatives," 729; Campeau, *Éveché*, 4. A more spiritual and sociological approach is Alain Cabantous, *Le ciel dans la mer: Christianisme et civilisation maritime (XVe–XIXe siècle)* (Paris, 1990), 213–29.

38. APF, SOCG, vol. 418, fols. 234^{rv}–235^{rv}, Neufville to Clement IX, [Rome, 1668/69] ("sylvestr[es] . . . sine lege et cognitione Dei uiuent[es]").

39. Commission to Roberval (18 February 1541), in Biggar, *Collection*, 207 ("nostre saincte foy chrestienne et Saincte Mère eglise catholicque"). See also Trudel, *Histoire*, 1:132; and Leslie Claude Green, "Claims to Territory in Colonial America," in Leslie Claude Green and Olive Patricia Dickason, *The Law of Nations and the New World* (Edmonton, 1989), 27–34 (but Green's portion of the collective book is less satisfactory).

40. "[D]u moins autant qu'on sache," according to Canadian Jesuit historian Lucien Campeau, the recognized authority in this field (Campeau, "Initiatives," 729).

41. Marc Lescarbot, *Relation derniere de ce qvi s'est passé av voyage dv sievr de Povtrincovrt en la Nouuelle-France depuis 20. mois ença* (Paris, 1612), 10; also reprinted in Campeau, *Monumenta*, 1:176 ("Non qu'un évêque françois ne l'eust peu faire, mais ayant fait ce choix, je croy que la dite mission est aussi bonne de lui, qui est évêque, que d'un autre, encore qu'il soit étranger"). On the controversy over the powers of the nuncio in France at the time, see Pierre Blet, SJ, *Histoire de la Représentation Diplomatique du Saint Siège des origines à l'aube du XIXe siècle* (Vatican City, 1982), 373–74.

42. ASV, SS, Francia, vol. 54, fol. 131^{r}, Roberto Ubaldini to Scipione Borghese, Paris,

29 October 1610, printed in Campeau, *Monumenta*, 1:96 ("nel Perù e nell'altre Indie"). A similar request is made by the Jesuit procurator general, Lorenzo de Paoli, in APF, Informazioni, vol. 136, fol. 570[rv], de Paoli to Paul V, [Rome, 1610/11]. The two Jesuits obtained their faculties, but not the "privileges of the Indies" they had requested. The best discussion of this matter is in Campeau, "Initiatives," 729–30; specific documents are in Campeau, *Monumenta*, 1:103–4, 320–406 (367).

43. ASV, SS, Francia, Misc. Arm. I, vol. 34. fol. 196[rv], Denys-Simon de Marquemont to Paul V, [Rome, November 1617] ("insegnar et instruire quelli poveri Selvagii nelle cose della Fede"); APF, SOCG, vol. 259, fols. 190[v], 195[rv], Guido Bentivoglio to Joseph Le Caron, Paris, 20 March 1618; both documents edited in Conrad-Marie Morin, OFM, "Le Saint-Siège et l'établissement de l'Église au Canada sous le régime français d'après les archives romaines: L'affiliation au Saint-Siège ou la mission apostolique (1615–1658)" (Laurea diss., Universitas Gregoriana, 1942), 232–35. See also Conrad-Marie Morin, OFM, "La naissance de l'Église au Canada," *Revue d'histoire de l'Amérique française* 1, no. 3 (December 1947): 331–35. The most updated summary of the early Recollet years in Canada is in Trudel, *Histoire*, vol. 2, *Le comptoir, 1604–1627* (1966), 210–36, 317–51. On the papal authorization, see Campeau, "Initiatives," 732–34.

44. Codignola, *Guide*, 25. Attempts to establish such an agency had been made since the time of Paul V's pontificate. See Nikolaus Kowalski, OMI, and Josef Metzler, OMI, *Inventory of the Historical Archives of the Sacred Congregation for the Evangelization of Peoples or "de Propaganda Fide,"* new enl. ed. (Rome, 1983), 11–13. Metzler, *Memoria Rerum*, is the major starting point for any historical work dealing with Propaganda. On the intellectual climate behind the establishment of Propaganda, see the illuminating essay by John M. Headley in this volume.

45. Pius X (1835–1914, reigned from 1903) withdrew most of the United States and Canada, together with Newfoundland, Great Britain, Scotland, the Netherlands, and Luxembourg, from the jurisdiction of the Propaganda by issuing the bull *Sapienti consilio* (29 June 1908). See Del Re, *Curia romana*, 193; Codignola, *Guide*, 25.

46. Codignola, *Guide*, 4.

47. As for North America, the Recollets were in Acadia from 1611 to 1613 and in Canada from 1615 to 1629 and again from 1670 to 1849. The Capuchins were in Acadia only from 1632 to 1655 and again from 1785 to 1827. Their relations with Propaganda went smoothly enough.

48. APF, SOCG, vol. 402, fols. 200[rv], 202[rv], Francesco Ingoli's comments, [Rome, February 1641] ("in cotesti luoghi lontani, li Religiosi per facilitar le conuersioni seruendosi della theologia condescendono nella predicat.e del Uangelo à cose, che da questa Sta Sede non sono state approuate come s'è ueduto nel Giapone"). The words "seruendosi della theologia" are syntactically unclear. The reference to Japan in these comments shows a clear preoccupation with the "rite controversy." Ingoli was secretary of Propaganda from 1622 to 1649.

49. For a survey of the relationship between Propaganda and the orders, see Codignola, *Guide*, 7–8. On the controversy with the Jesuits and the question of the privileges of the Indies, see Campeau, *Monumenta*, vol. 4, *Les grandes épreuves (1638–1640)* (Rome and Montréal, 1989), 14, 20, 251, 254, 446. Among the most important related documents, see

APF, SOCG, vol. 397, fols. 31[rv], 38[rv], Muzio Vitelleschi to Urban VIII, [Rome, before 23 March 1637], printed in Campeau, *Monumenta*, vol. 3, *Fondation de la mission huronne (1635–1637)* (Rome and Québec, 1987), 482–83; and APF, SOCG, vol. 399, fols. 119[rv], 132[rv], Joseph-Marie Chaumonot to Antonio Barberini, [Canada, March 1638], published in Campeau, *Monumenta*, 4:13–16. As for the importance of the Jesuit efforts in the early colonization of New France, Canadian historian William John Eccles explains: "The agency mainly responsible for the development and expansion of the colony during these years [1632–63] was the Church" (*France in America*, 2d ed. [Toronto, 1990], 39).

50. APF, SOCG, vol. 131, fol. 342[rv], Simon Stock to [PF], London, 28 July 1628 ("plen[a] di populi che non hanno mai senti[to] novo del Santo Evangelio"). Stock's letter is translated into English in Codignola, *Coldest Harbour*, 112–14; the Italian original is in Codignola, *Terre d'America*, 152–54. The best recent discussion of the contemporary vision of an "American emptiness" is in Jennings, *Invasion of America*, 15–42.

51. APF, SOCG, vol. 259, fols. 190[v], 195[rv], Bentivoglio to Le Caron, Paris, 20 March 1618 ("ad partes tantum paganorum pro illorum ab idolatria ad catholicam Religionem conversione"), edited in Morin, "Saint-Siège," 233.

52. Luca Codignola and Giovanni Pizzorusso, "Luoghi, metodi e fonti dell'espansione missionaria tra medioevo ed età moderna: L'affermarsi della centralità romana," in Stefano Pittaluga, ed., *Relazioni di viaggio e conoscenza del mondo fra medioevo e umanesimo. Atti del V Convegno internazionale di studi dell'Associazione per il Medioevo e l'Umanesimo Latini (AMUL). Genova, 12–15 dicembre 1991*, special issue of *Columbeis* 5 (1992): 1–19, rev. and enlarged as Luca Codignola and Giovanni Pizzorusso, "Les lieux, les méthodes et les sources de l'expansion missionnaire du moyen-age au XVIIe siècle: Rome sur la voie de la centralisation," in *Transferts culturels en Amérique et ailleurs (XVIe–XIXe siècle)*, ed. Laurier Turgeon, Réal Ovellet, and Denis Delage (Québec, 1994).

53. For a recent anthropological approach to the issue of the relationship between Christianity and non-European cultures, see the twelve articles collected in Gruzinski, "Anthropologie et histoire," 733–1035 (dealing with America, Africa, the Middle East, India, Borneo, China, and Mongolia).

54. APF, MV, vol. 6, fol. 194[rv], Relaçion de la Virginia por fr. Gregorio de Bolivar menor observante Predicator de la Yndia Ocidental. The original Spanish text is published in Josef Metzler, OMI, "Der alteste Bericht über Nordamerika im Propaganda-Archiv: Virginia 1625," *Neue Zeitschrift für Missionswissenschaft* 25 (1969): 35–37 ("simples y miseros yndios barbaros," "aprénder lo que les ensenan"). See also Codignola, *Coldest Harbour*, 21.

55. APF, SOCG, vol. 347, fols. 253[rv], 266[rv], Simon Stock, OCD, to [PF], London, 13 September 1625 ("qui inter Floridam et terram Bacalaos habitant," "Canadenses," "prae caeteris benigni et humani"); APF, vol. 132, fol. 251[rv], Stock to [PF], London, 28 April 1630 ("innumeri," "desideranno essere Chistiani [*sic*]"). Stock's letters are translated into English in Codignola, *Coldest Harbour*, 85–88, 119–20; the Italian original is in Codignola, *Terre d'America*, 127–29, 159–60.

56. APF, SOCG, vol. 394, fols. 75[rv]–76[rv], English clergy to Urban VIII, [1634] ("quando incenduntur desiderio Christianam Religionem amplectendi").

57. APF, vol. 259, fols. 205[rv]–206[rv], Pacifique de Provins to [Francesco Ingoli], Paris,

9 March 1644 ("paesi dell'America settentrionale," "disposti a ricevere nostra Santa Fede," "da cinquecento anni non si è tenta[ta]"); APF, vol. 141, fols. 108^{rv}, 113^{rv}, Pacifique de Provins to Ingoli, Paris, 17 October 1641 ("populi infiniti et domesticati"); APF, vol. 141, fols. 107^{rv}, 114^{rv}, Pacifique de Provins to Ingoli, Paris, 12 December 1641 ("veduto christiano se non per qualche sorte et passagio"). See Codignola, "World to Be Conquered," 70–73. The five-hundred-year interval must be read within the concept of the "return" to the faith (see note 6 above).

58. APF, vol. 141, fols. 23^{rv}, 29^{rv}, Christopher of the Holy Trinity to Ingoli, Paris, 10 January 1642; APF, vol. 142, fols. 51^{rv}, 60^{rv}, Mathieu Darcelle to Ingoli, Paris, 13 March 1643.

59. APF, vol. 141, fols. 56^{rv}–57^{rv}, Pacifique de Provins to Ingoli, Paris, 25 April 1642 ("il più bel de suoi palazzi," "ammaestrare et catechisare"); APF, SOCG, vol. 259, fols. 205^{rv}–206^{rv} ("tutti sono facili a convertirsi"); APF, vol. 141, fols. 39^{rv}–40^{rv}, Pacifique de Provins to Ingoli, Paris, 14 March 1642 ("qualche sacerdoti mahumetani"); APF, vol. 141, fols. 105^{rv}–116^{rv}, Pacifique de Provins to [Ingoli], Paris, 7 November [1641] ("guastaranno un milliaro di queste anime"). See Codignola, "World to Be Conquered," 74–76.

60. ASV, SS, Lettere dei Vescovi, vol. 44, fols. 244^{rv}–245^{rv}, François de Laval to Alexander VII, Québec, 31 July 1659 ("Barbar[i] Iroquae[i] . . . nimirum soli sese opponunt saluti omnium gentium huius noui orbis"). Laval was the first vicar apostolic of Canada, with the title of bishop of Petraea *in partibus infidelium* (1658–74), and later the first bishop of Québec (1674–88). He resigned in 1688, and until his death in 1708 he was referred to as Monseigneur l'Ancien.

61. See Roy Harvey Pearce, *Savagism and Civilization: A Study of the Indian and the American Mind*, 2d ed. (Berkeley, 1988), 3–49, and Sheehan, *Savagism and Civility*, 9–64, for the English passage from a preconceived ideal of "Paradise" to the field experience with the "Ignoble Savagism." For the French, see Cornelius John Jaenen, *The French Relationship with the Native Peoples of New France and Acadia* ([Ottawa], 1984), 59–63, and Pierre Berthiaume, "Les *Relations* des jésuites: Nouvel avatar de la Légende dorée," in Thérien, *Figures*, 121–39 (an interesting literary interpretation). For Brazil, John Hemming, *Red Gold: The Conquest of the Brazilian Indian* (London, 1978), 98–118.

62. *A Relation of Maryland; Together With A Map of the Countrey, The Conditions of Plantation, His Majesties Charter to the Lord Baltemore, translated into English* ([London], 1635), 37.

63. APF, SOCG, vol. 141, fols. 107^{rv}–114^{rv}, Pacifique de Provins to Ingoli, Paris, 12 December 1641 ("selve et boschi, tanto confusi che, cascando la neve, resta sei mesi intieri senza liquefarse"); APF, SOCG, vol. 259, fols. 205^{rv}–206^{rv}, Pacifique de Provins to [Ingoli], Paris, 9 March 1644; APF, SOCG, vol. 199, fols. 397^{rv}–398^{rv}, 407^{rv}–408^{rv}, Pacifique de Provins to PF, Paris, 24 June 1644. See Codignola, "World to Be Conquered," 68–69.

64. APF, SOCG, vol. 259, fols. 205^{rv}–206^{rv}, Pacifique de Provins to [Ingoli], Paris, 9 March 1644 ("malattie terribile di dolori acuti causati dall'intemperia de l'aria et delle piogge venenose," "vermi nelle gambe, brachi et altre parte, grossissimi et longii"). See Codignola, "World to Be Conquered," 66. On the tropical disease environment, see Kenneth Gordon Davies, *The North Atlantic World in the Seventeenth Century* (Minneapolis, 1974), 250–52; Alfred W. Crosby, *Ecological Imperialism: The Biological Expansion of Europe, 900–1900*

(Cambridge, 1986); Philip D. Curtin, *Death by Migration: Europe's Encounter with the Tropical World in the Nineteenth Century* (Cambridge, 1989).

65. APF, FV, vol. 12, fols. 71^{rv}–72^{rv}, [Edward Courtenay] to [Gian Paolo Oliva and PF], [London, 31 May 1662] ("uel coeli intemperie, uel Haereticorum saeuitiâ, uel grauissimis laboribus"); APF, FV, vol. 12, fols. 110^{rv}–111^{rv}, [John Clark] to [PF], [London, 16 May 1664]; APF, FV, vol. 12, fols. 121^{rv}–122^{rv}, [Clark] to [PF], [London], 7 April 1665; APF, FV, vol. 12, fols. 144^{rv}–145^{rv}, [Clark] to [PF], [Ghent?], 15 June 1667.

66. APF, vol. 144, fols. 176^{rv}–177^{rv}, Pacifique de Provins to Ingoli, Guadeloupe, 20 September 1645 ("pazzia et crudeltà," "amazzato et mangiato"); APF, SOCG, vol. 145, fols. 100^{rv}, 108^{rv}, Pacifique de Provins to Ingoli, Paris, 23 October 1646; APF, SOCG, vol. 144, fols. 183^{rv}, 195^{rv}, Pacifique de Provins to Bernardino Spada, Paris, 25 October 1646 ("simplicité," "grande disposition qu'elles [*sic*] ont à devenir à Dieu"). See Codignola, "World to Be Conquered," 77–78.

67. APF, SOCG, vol. 256, fols. 19^{rv}–20^{rv}, Laval to Alexander VII, Québec, 29 October 1660 ("ad gentes numerosissimas quae de fide christiana nihil hactenus edocta sunt").

68. AN, Fonds des Colonies, C11A, vol. 3, fols. 120^{rv}–122^{rv}, Laurens van Heemskerk to [Jean-Baptiste Colbert], Porchemut, 12 March 1670 ("de douce complexion et d'humeur docile, faible," "Cette nation estant fort simple, et facile à persuader"). Also APF, SOCG, vol. 427, fols. 363^{rv}–364^{rv}, A person of importance and some pious ladies to Pietro Bargellini, [Paris, February? 1671]; APF, SOCG, vol. 427, fols. 362^{rv}–365^{rv}, Bargellini to [Antonio Barberini], Paris, 27 February 1671. See Codignola, "Laurens van Heemskerk's Pretended Expeditions to the Arctic, 1668–1672: A Note," *The International History Review* 12, no. 3 (August 1990): 519, 523–25.

69. APF, SOCG, vol. 546, fols. 155^{rv}–156^{rv}, French Jesuits to Fabrizio Paolucci, [1703] ("une infinité de peuples qui n'ont jamais entendu parler de la Religion").

70. APF, C, AS, vol. 1, fols. 224^{rv}–225^{rv}, Joseph-André-Mathurin Jacrau to Pietro Pamphili Colonna, Québec, 20 August 1766; copy in AAQ, 1 CB, IV, 188, the latter published in [Ivanhoë Caron, ed.], "Pierre de La Rue, abbé de L'Isle-Dieu: Lettres et mémoires de l'abbé de L'Isle-Dieu," *Rapport de l'Archiviste de la Province de Québec* (1937–38), 242–44 ("bons, doux et charitables les uns envers les autres; il n'ont point de Roi mais seulement des Chefs de village qui n'ont que bien peu d'autorité," "prépare les moyens pour éclairer ces peuples").

71. APF, CP, vol. 146, fols. 676^{rv}–679^{rv}, Plessis to PF, Rome, 17 November 1819 ("vagas et ferocissimas gentes"); copies in APF, SOCG, vol. 937, fols. 689^{rv}–692^{rv}, and in AAQ, 10 CM, III, 151.

72. Codignola, *Guide*, 13–15. Also Massimo Petrocchi, *Roma nel Seicento* (Bologna, 1970), 151–52.

73. APF, Acta, vol. 3, fols. 3^{rv}–5^{rv}, Proceedings of the General Congregation of 8 March 1622; published in Metzler, *Memoria Rerum*, 3/2:659–61. See Codignola, *Guide*, 3.

74. APF, Lettere, vol. 25. fol. 25^{rv}, [Ingoli] to Pacifique de Provins, Rome, 11 February 1647 ("oue il popolo è piu Barbaro, e più difficile da ridurre alla vita Ciuile p[rim]a e poi alla cognit[io]ne del vero Iddio," "che uiuono con maggiore Ciuiltà delle Littorali per esser quelle in Clima più temperato, cioè nel parallelo di Cons[tantin]op[o]li," "assai Ciuili").

75. APF, SOCG, vol. 402, fols. 200^{rv}, 202^{rv}, Charles Camus Duperon to PF, [Lyons, January 1641] (Camus Duperon's letter with Ingoli's comments on its verso); APF, Lettere, vol. 9, fols. 136^{rv}–137^{rv}, [Ingoli] to Camus Duperon, Rome, 4 May 1641 (final version of the answer sent to Camus Duperon). Camus Duperon seems not to have gone to North America. See Conrad-Marie Morin, OFM, "Les tentatives du secrétaire François Ingoli pour l'érection d'un évêché au Canada (1631–1641)," Société Canadienne d'Histoire de l'Église Catholique, *Rapport* (1944–45), 69–82. This might have been a "technical" suggestion, as Ingoli was very much in favor of the use of local languages; furthermore, Paul V's brief *Romanus Pontifex* (27 June 1615) had allowed the use of literary Chinese in the local liturgy, thus formally opening the door to the use of the vernacular.

76. Eccles, *France in America*, 75. See also note 60 above.

77. John J. McCusker and Russell R. Menard, *The Economy of British America, 1607–1789* (Chapel Hill, 1985), 112; Brian Young and John Alexander Dickinson, *A Short History of Quebec: A Socio-Economic Perspective* (Toronto, 1988), 29–30, 37–39, 40–42, 47–51; Eccles, *France in America*, 63–94.

78. James Axtell, "The White Indians of Colonial America," *The William and Mary Quarterly* 32, no. 1 (January 1975): 55–88, reprinted in James Axtell, *The European and the Indian: Essays in the Ethnohistory of Colonial North America* (New York and Oxford, 1981), 168–206.

79. Jaenen, *Role*, 28–29, 32, 155; Charles Edwards O'Neill, SJ, *Church and State in French Colonial Louisiana: Policy and Politics to 1732* (New Haven, 1966), 16, 72, 83, 87–88, 92, 98, 107, 158, 246–55, 288.

80. See James Axtell, "Colonial America without the Indians: Counterfactual Reflections," *The Journal of American History* 73, no. 4 (March 1987): 981–96, reprinted in James Axtell, *After Columbus: Essays in the Ethnohistory of Colonial North America* (New York, 1988), 222–43; William John Eccles, "The Frontiers of New France," in *Essays on Frontiers in World History*, ed. George Wolfskill and Stanley Palmer (College Station, Tex., 1983), 49.

81. Before the appointment of a bishop, "le R. Père Supérieur de la Mission [faisait] ici les fonctions Ecclésiastiques, comme les Mariages, les Baptêmes et autres semblables," according to the Ursuline Marie Guyart, known as Marie de l'Incarnation (1599–1672). See Marie de l'Incarnation to Claude Martin, Québec, 22 October 1649, printed in Marie de l'Incarnation, *Correspondence*, ed. Guy Oury, OSB (Solesmes, 1971), 371–83 (quote at 378).

82. APF, SOCG, fols. 119^{rv}, 126^{rv}, Celio Piccolomini's answers to Alexander VII's questionnaire, [Rome, 1567/68]. There is an open debate on the meaning of these conversions and, consequently, on the number of converts, although most scholars seem now to agree on the ten thousand figure. See Codignola, "Historians against Contact: Indians and Europeans in the Early Northeast," *International Journal of Canadian Studies/Revue internationale d'études canadiennes* 5 (Spring 1992): 168.

83. A recent overview of the French religious experience is in Robert Choquette, "French Catholicism Comes to the Americas," in Lippy, Choquette, and Poole, *Christianity*, 131–242.

84. ASV, SS, Lettere dei Principi, vol. 81, fol. 15^{rv}, Louis XIV to Alexander VII, Paris, 26 January 1657 ("plustôt . . . un païs Sauvage, qu' . . . un civilizé"), published in Ferdinando Antonelli, ed., *Quebecen: Beatificationis et canonizationis Ven. Servi Dei Francisci de Mont-*

morency-Laval Episcopy Québecensis (+1708) (Rome, 1957), 17. See APF, SOCG, vol. 226, fols. 104^{rv}, 109^{rv}, Carlo Vittori Roberti to PF, Paris, 9 April 1666 (for a later report on the four prelates' activities). See also Raoul-Scipion-Philippe Allier, *La cabale des dévots, 1627–1666* (Paris, 1902), 140–58; Guillaume de Vaumas, *L'éveil missionnaire de la France (d'Henri IV à la fondation du Séminaire des Missions Étrangères)* (Lyon, 1942), 368–73, 399–415; Noël Baillargeon, *Le Séminaire de Québec sous l'épiscopat de Mgr de Laval* (Québec, 1972), 10–15; Massimo Marcocchi, *Colonialismo, cristianesimo e culture extraeuropee: L'Istruzione di Propaganda Fide ai Vicari apostolici dell'Asia Orientale (1659)* (Milan, 1980), 48–51; Nadia Pardini, "François de Laval (1623–1708): Dalla Francia alla Nuova Francia (1623–1673)" (Laurea diss., Università di Pisa, 1988), 21–28; Louis Châtellier, *L'Europe des dévots* (Paris, 1987), 84–123.

85. ARSI, Gallia 109/II, fols. 436^{rv}–437^{rv}, Laval to Goswin Nickel, Québec, August 1659 ("neophytos . . . christianos quos a barbaria sua Revocarunt ad dei cultum et Religionem"), published in Antonelli, *Quebecen*, 34–35; ASV, SS, Lettere dei Vescovi, vol. 44, fols. 244^{rv}–245^{rv}, Laval to Alexander VII, Québec, 31 July 1659.

86. ARSI, Gallia 103/II, fols. 343^{rv}–344^{rv}, Laval to Nickel, Québec, 21 April 1663. This is the first of many letters in which Laval openly admitted his choice.

87. See, for example, APF, SOCG, vol. 256, fols. 33^{rv}–36^{rv}, Laval to [PF], [Québec, 26 August 1664], published in Antonelli, *Quebecen*, 94–98.

88. Roberta Profetti, "L'esperienza canadese di François de Laval (1623–1708), primo vescovo di Québec, 1659–1688" (Laurea diss., Università di Pisa, 1989), lists Laval's known manuscript letters to Rome for the years 1658–86 and edits the most interesting. Profetti's dissertation must be consulted together with Pardini, "Laval," and with Benoit and Scardellato, *Calendar from Various Series*. On Laval's changing attitude toward the Indians, see Jaenen, *Role*, 31–32.

89. Denys Delâge, *Le pays renversé: Amérindiens et européens en Amérique du nord-est, 1600–1664* (Montréal, 1985), 333. On the very special experience of the nuns in New France, see the recent enlightening article by Leslie Choquette, "'Ces Amazones du Grand Dieu': Women and Mission in Seventeenth-Century Canada," *French Historical Studies* 17, no. 3 (Spring 1992): 627–55.

90. Furthermore, Laval and Jean-Baptiste de La Croix de Chevrières de Saint-Vallier (1653–1727, bishop from 1688) respectively spent twelve and seventeen years in Europe during their mandate at Québec; Louis-François Duplessis de Mornay (1663–1741, bishop from 1728 to 1733) never set foot in North America; and Pierre-Herman Dosquet (1691–1777, bishop from 1733 to 1739) spent only one year out of six in Canada.

91. APF, Udienze, vol. 11, fol. 51^{rv}, Jean-Olivier Briand to Giuseppe Maria Castelli, Québec, 29 October 1769 ("pour les quelles les Canadiens n'ont guères de goût mais que devrois-je faire").

92. A good summary of the functions of the church in Canada is in Marcel Trudel, *Initiation à la Nouvelle-France* (Montréal and Toronto, 1968), 249–77. See also Jaenen, *Role*, 95–157 (Jaenen clearly distinguishes the two Canadian churches, as he titled the two parts of his book "The Missionary Church" and "The Colonial Church"); Luca Codignola, "Church and State—The French Colonies" and "Roman Catholicism—The French Colonies," in

Encyclopedia of the North American Colonies, ed. Jacob Ernest Cooke et al., vol. 3 (New York, 1993), 517–20 and 543–53.

93. Lucien Lemieux, *Les années difficiles (1760–1839)* (Montréal, 1989), 235–54, shows the marginalization of the Indians in the late eighteenth and nineteenth centuries.

94. Jaenen, *Role*, 34; author's interview with William John Eccles, "New France and the History of North America," *Storia nordamericana* 2, no. 2 (1985): 66.

95. Jean-Baptiste Du Tertre, OP, *Histoire générale des Antilles habitées par les Francois. Divisée en deux tomes, Et enrichies de Cartes & de Figures*, 4 vols. (Paris, 1667–71), vol. 1, *Contenant tout ce qui s'est passé dans l'establissement des Colonies Françoises. Par le R.P. du Tertre, de l'Ordre des FF. Prescheurs, de la Congrégation de S. Louis, Missionnaire Apostolique dans les Antilles* (1667), 12–13 ("nombre de Prestres & de Religieux, pour instruire les Indiens & habitans d'icelles . . . en la Religion Catholique, Apostolique, & Romaine").

96. Davies, *North Atlantic World*, 267. See also Philip Poulin Boucher, *Caribbean Encounters: Europeans and Island Caribs, 1492–1763* (Baltimore, 1992).

97. APF, C, AA, vol. 1, fols. 245^{rv}–248^{rv}, Pierre La Forcade to [Giovanni Battista De Marinis], Martinique, 13 May 1668 ("quasi belluae"); APF, C, AA, vol. 1. fols. 228^{rv}–234^{rv}, Philippe de Beaumont to Claude-André Leclerc de Château du Bois, Saint-Christophe, 8 April 1668 ("[c]'est un ouvrage qui demande perseverance"). These documents are summarized in Pizzorusso, "Archives," 132–33. On this dispute, see Giovanni Pizzorusso, " 'Due sorte d'infedeltà': La conversione degli indiani e dei negri nelle Antille francesi nel XVII secolo," in *Europa tra Oriente e Occidente*, ed. Gabriella Airaldi (Genoa, 1992), 93–109. On Beaumont and La Forcade, see Bernard David, *Dictionnaire biographique de la Martinique (1635–1848): Le clergé*, 3 vols. (Fort-de-France, Martinique, 1984), 1:14–16, 145–46.

98. See, for example, André Chevillard, OP, *Les Desseins de son Eminence de Richelieu pour l'Amérique. Reproduction de l'édition de 1659* (Basse-Terre, Guadeloupe, 1973), first published in 1635; and Raymond Breton, OP, *Relations de l'île de la Guadeloupe*, 1 vol. to date (Basse-Terre, 1978–), written between 1647 and 1657. For a general overview of the relationship between Indians and missionaries in the early-seventeenth-century French West Indies, see Giovanni Pizzorusso, "Alla ricerca della centralità romana: Le missioni cattoliche nelle Antille e in Guyana (1635–1675)" (Ph.D. diss., Università di Genova, 1993); Pizzorusso, "Archives," 119.

99. See the latest overview in Charles H. Lippy, "Christianity Comes to British America," in Lippy, Choquette, and Poole, *Christianity*, 243–365, which devotes very little room to Catholicism (287–88, 290–94, 359–60).

100. APF, SOCG, vol. 729, fols. 47^{rv}–48^{rv}, Benjamin Petre and Richard Challoner to PF, [London], 3 September 1745 ("si semel Catholicae Religionis in Angliâ toleraretur"). The report was drafted and handwritten by Challoner.

101. Robert V. Wells, *The Population of the British Colonies in America before 1776: A Survey of Census Data* (Princeton, 1975), 46–47, 49, 61, 147, 284; McCusker and Menard, *Economy of British America*, 54, 136, 203. For contemporary estimates of American Catholics and a general discussion, see Luca Codignola, "The Policy of Rome towards the English-speaking Catholics in British North America, 1750–1830," in *Creed and Culture: The Place of English-Speaking Catholics in Canadian Society*, ed. Terrence Murphy and Gerald Stortz (Montreal,

1992), 101. See also Charles H. Metger, *Catholics and the American Revolution: A Study in Religious Climate* (Chicago, 1962), 138–53; Hennesey, *American Catholics*, 42, 55. Catholics in England and Wales numbered 80,000 in 1770, with an overall population of 6.5 million in 1750 and 9.4 million in 1780. See John Bossy, *The English Catholic Community, 1570–1850* (London, 1975), 185; Ian R. Christie, *Wars and Revolutions: Britain, 1760–1815* (London, 1982), 3, 158–59.

102. The problem of spiritual jurisdiction over the British colonies was not raised by the Holy See until 1745, although formally, from "time out of mind," it apparently belonged to the vicar apostolic of the London district of England (WDA, B, vol. 45, no. 135, Fisher [*vere* Challoner] to [Christopher Stonor], [London], 14 September 1756). The vicar apostolic mentioned for the first time the Jesuit de facto jurisdiction over the British colonies in APF, SOCG, vol. 729, fols. 47^{rv}–48^{rv}, Petre and Challoner to PF, [London], 3 September 1745. Jurisdiction was formally granted to the vicar apostolic in 1756 (APF, Acta, vol. 126, fols. 352^{v}–358^{r}, Rome, Proceedings of the General Congregation of 6 December 1756). See also Peter Keenan Guilday, *The Life and Times of John Carroll, Archbishop of Baltimore (1735–1815)* (New York, 1922), 142–46; Francis O. Edwards, *The Jesuits in England: From 1580 to the Present Day* (Tunbridge Wells, 1985), 123–25, 130; Codignola, "Policy of Rome," 101–3.

103. APF, FV, vol. 12, fols. 71^{rv}–72^{rv}, [Courtenay] to [Oliva], [London, 31 May 1662]; APF, FV, vol. 12, fols. 110^{rv}–111^{rv}, [Clark] to [PF], [London, 16 May 1664]; APF, FV, vol. 12, fols. 121^{rv}–122^{rv}, [Clark] to [PF], [London], 7 April 1665; APF, FV, vol. 12, fols. 144^{rv}–145^{rv}, [Clark] to [PF], Ghent, [15 June 1667]; APF, C, Anglia Miscellanee, vol. 1, 137–72, Claudio Agretti to [Clement X], Bruxelles, 14 December 1669; APF, SOCG, vol. 597, fols. 329^{rv}–330^{rv}, The English Jesuits in Maryland to PF, [1714].

104. APF, SOCG, vol. 347, fols. 376^{rv}–377^{rv}, Excerpts from *Declaratio Coloniae*, [London, 10 February 1633]; APF, SOCG, vol. 84, fols. 112^{rv}–113^{rv}, Carlo Rossetti to [PF], Ghent, 17 August 1641; APF, SOCG, vol. 84, fols. 110^{rv}, 114^{rv}, Rossetti to [PF], Ghent, 24 August 1641; APF, SOCG, vol. 141, fols. 346^{rv}, 351^{rv}, Rossetti to [PF], Ghent, 7 September 1641; APF, SOCG, vol. 141, fols. 347^{rv}, 350^{rv}, [Rossetti] to [PF], [Ghent, 7 September 1641]; APF, SOCG, vol. 141, fols. 348^{rv}–349^{rv}, [Rossetti] to [PF], [Ghent, 7 September 1641], copy in BAV, Cod. Barberini Lat. 8690, fols. 173^{rv}–174^{rv}. On the Jesuit mission, see Thomas Aloysius Hughes, *History of the Society of Jesus in North America, Colonial and Federal: Text and Documents*, 4 vols. (London, 1907–17), vol. 1, *Text: From the First Colonization till 1645* (1907), 246–52; Oskar Arnold Meyer, ed., "The Catholic Mission in Maryland, 1641," *The American Historical Review* 12, no. 3 (April 1907): 584–87; and the most exhaustive article by James Axtell, "White Legend: The Jesuit Missions in Maryland," *Maryland Historical Magazine* 81, no. 1 (Spring 1986): 1–7; reprinted in Axtell, *After Columbus*, 73–85. A modern edition of White's *Declaratio* is in Edwin A. Dalrymple, ed., *Relatio Itineris in Marylandiam. Declaratio Coloniae Domini Baronis de Baltimore. Excerpta ex Diversis Litteris Missionariorum Ab Anno 1635, ad Annum 1638. Narrative of a voyage to Maryland, By Father Andrew White, S.J. An Account of the Colony of the Lord Baron of Baltimore. Extracts from Different Letters of Missionaries, From the Years 1635 to the Year 1677* (Baltimore, 1874).

105. One should add that the disproportionate interest shown by the English press in the Indians of the British colonies, for example, in the years 1685–1715, was mainly due to their

being exotic and picturesque elements of the New World. Their actual size was, in fact, described as minimal. See Kenneth R. MacDonald, Jr., "The Image of America: America in the English Press, 1685–1715" (Ph.D. diss., West Virginia University, 1976), 49–50.

106. Thomas W. Spalding, *The Premier See: A History of the Archdiocese of Baltimore, 1789–1989* (Baltimore and London, 1989), 3. The marginal place of the Indians in the early history of American Catholicism is all the more evident in Spalding's book, as it is in Hennesey, *American Catholics.*

107. The original Latin version is in Shiels, *King and Church,* 304, and in Metzler, *America Pontificia,* 1:91–94 and "Specimina quaedam n. 9" ("verbum Dei predicent . . . [et] infideles et gentes barbaras ad fidem Christi convertant et conversos in eadem fide instruant et doceant," "ac omnibus aliis Christianis in illis pro tempore degentibus"). Translations into English are in ibid., 102, and in Parry, Keith, and Jimenez, *New Iberian World,* 1:378. Contrary to Shiels, I prefer "for the time being" to "now" as a translation of "pro tempore."

108. APF, SOCG, vol. 259, fols. 182^{rv}, 188^{rv}, Ingoli to Giuseppe Ceva, [Rome], 19 January 1635 ("nuovi cristiani," "gentili"). At the time, the Recollets were still hoping to be sent back to Canada, although they only returned there in 1670. The meaning of "nuovi cristiani" is somewhat obscure. It probably meant "Indian converts" in opposition to "gentiles" (heathen). In this case, the Indian converts would be considered full-fledged members of the Christian community of European origin.

109. APF, CP, vol. 6, fols. 277^{rv}, 294^{rv} [unknown provenance, possibly from the Capuchin Order, ca. 1650].

110. APF, SOCG, vol. 491, fols. 334^{rv}–335^{rv}, Hyacinthe Lefèvre to PF, [Paris?, 1684].

111. The best summary to date of the Capuchin activities in Acadia is in Trudel, *Histoire,* 3/1, *La seigneurie des Cent-Associés, 1627–1663: Les événements* (1979), 108–13, who uses all available sources, except for those documents of the archives of Propaganda that were still unknown in 1979 and for the "official" history of the Paris province of the Capuchin order. The pertinent volume (albeit only partially printed) is Raoul de Sceaux, *Histoire,* 2:313–14, 523–24. Pacifique de Provins's death is described in ibid., 437–38, and in Codignola, "Pacifique," 59–60.

112. APF, SOCG, vol. 495a, fols. 363^{rv}–364^{rv}, Chrysostome de la Passion to PF, [1686]; another copy in SOCG, vol. 495b, fols. 161^{rv}–162^{rv}. See also APF, Acta, vol. 56, fol. 67^{rv}, Rome, Proceedings of the General Congregation of 26 March 1686; APF, Lettere, vol. 75, fols. 85^{v}–86^{rv}, Edoardo Cibo to César d'Estrées, [Rome], 26 March 1686. Chrysostome de la Passion's report describes the needs of the mission of the province of St. Yves (Paris), of the Third Order Regular of St. Francis, in the new colony of Chedabouctou, Acadia, where the missionary "Massimiliano Sanvaleriano" resided two years, learned the native language, and, with the assistance of one or more companions, baptized many gentiles. To my knowledge, these documents are the only available reference to this colony.

113. APF, FV, vol. 58, Index, fol. 32^{r}, PF's note, [Rome], 16 July 1755. The Jesuit Pierre Audran (1721–after 1784) had submitted to the Holy See his doubts concerning the formula of baptism used by the missionaries among the Micmacs. A number of documents in the archives of Propaganda refer to this case, but this seems to be the earliest one.

114. Of his last known twenty-one letters for the period 1673–86, only three are addressed

to Propaganda. Out of forty-eight letters for the period 1658–72, only eleven are not to be found in the archives of Propaganda. See Profetti, "Esperienza," 302–4.

115. With almost no exceptions, Saint-Vallier, Mornay, Dosquet, and François-Louis de Pourroy de Lauberivière (1711–40, bishop from 1739) only wrote to Propaganda to request their faculties or to ask for various kinds of practical assistance, whereas Henri-Marie Dubreil de Pontbriand (1708–60, bishop from 1741) never even bothered to do so. Saint-Vallier wrote twice, the first time when he was informed of his appointment, and the second upon his arrival in Québec. Dosquet, however, was consulted on Canadian matters after he had resigned from Québec. See the above instances in Codignola, *Guide*; Benoit and Scardellato, *Calendar in Series Francia*; and in Benoit and Scardellato, *Calendar from Various Series.*

116. For a quick overview of the Christian missionary revival toward the Indians in the late eighteenth and early nineteenth centuries, see Handy, *History*, 157–59; Codignola, *Guide*, s.v. "Natives, American."

117. APF, MV, vol. XI, fols. 1^{rv}, 48^{rv}–179^{r}, Relazione di Mgr Urbano Cerri alla Santità di NS. PP. Innocenzo XI dello Stato di Propaganda, [Rome, 1678] (a complete version, of many preserved in European archives); Niccolo' Forteguerri, *Memorie intorno alle missioni*, ed. Carmen Prencipe Di Donna (Naples, 1982), written between 1706 and 1709, first published in 1828 ("vaghi di mangiare carne umana, incostanti, ingannatori, maligni, vendicativi, crudeli, e ladri, . . . dotati di gran forza ed altissimi di statura; di religione idolatri"). The citation is Forteguerri's and refers to New England only, but it well expresses the stereotypical view of all Indians of the two officials. Urbano Cerri had been secretary of Propaganda from 1675 to 1679, Forteguerri from 1730 to 1735.

118. Jérôme Lalemant, SJ, to Paul Le Jeune, SJ, Des Hurons, 27 May 1640, reprinted in Campeau, *Monumenta*, 4:736. On Jesuit education, see Axtell, *Invasion Within*, 71–90.

119. Charles Garnier, SJ, to Henri de Saint-Joseph, OCarm, Immaculée-Conception, 28 April 1638, printed in Campeau, *Monumenta*, 4:32 ("Nos mystères leur sont tous nouveaux; leur langue ne nous fournit que bien peu des mots qui nous seroient nécessaires" [1638]). See also Dickason, *Myth*, 254–58; Urs Bitterli, *Cultures in Conflict: Encounters between European and Non-European Cultures, 1492–1800* (Stanford, 1989), 100–102 (a translation from the original book in German, published in Munich in 1986).

120. Gabriel Théodat Sagard, *Le Grand Voyage du Pays des Hurons*, ed. Réal Ovellet and Jack Warwick (Montreal, 1990), p. 72 ("le christianisme est . . . bien loin des dix millions d'âmes que nos Religieux ont baptisées . . . dans les Indes orientales et occidentales"). Gabriel Théodat Sagard's *Grand Voyage* was originally published in 1632.

121. See Wilcomb Washburn, "The Clash of Morality in the American Forest," in *First Images of America: The Impact of the New World on the Old*, ed. Fredi Chiappelli, 2 vols. (Berkeley, 1976), 1:335–50 (a good summary of Indian virtues and vices); Berkhofer, *White Man's Indian*, 74 (on Jesuit influence on Noble Savage theories); James Talmadge Moore, *Indian and Jesuit: A Seventeenth-Century Encounter* (Chicago, 1982), 50–58; Dickason, *Myth*, 267–68 (the last two authors emphasize Jesuit admiration for Indian culture); Bitterli, *Cultures in Conflict*, 98 (a balanced summary of Huron vices and virtues as seen by the Jesuits).

122. See Jaenen, *Friend and Foe*, 50–51, and by the same author, "Missionary Approaches to Native Peoples," in *Approaches to Native History of Canada: Papers of a Conference Held at the National Museum of Man, October 1975*, ed. D. A. Muise (Ottawa, 1977), 10 (both on the rite controversy in relationship with Canada); Axtell, *Invasion Within*, 111–12 (on Jesuit adaptation). The controversy is also briefly touched on in relation to the western United States in the nineteenth century in Hennesey, *American Catholics*, 132. In general, see Henri Chappoulie, ed., *Aux origines d'une église: Rome et les missions d'Indochine au XVIIe siècle*, 2 vols. (Paris, 1943–48); E. Jarry, "La querelle des rites," in Delacroix, *Histoire*, vol. 2, *Les missions modernes* (1957), 337–52 (a useful insider's view); Paolo Beonio Brocchieri, "Il Giappone e la cultura europea nel Seicento," in Dino Pastine et al., *L'Europa cristiana nel rapporto con le altre culture nel secolo XVII. Atti del Convegno di studio di Santa Margherita Ligure (19–21 maggio 1977)* (Florence, 1978), 455–66; Sergio Zoli, "La Cina nella cultura europea del Seicento," in ibid., 85–164; Marcocchi, *Colonialismo*, 28–40 (the best short account in the international context); François Lebrun and Elizabeth Antébi, *Les Jésuites ou la gloire de Dieu* ([France], 1990), 60–84 (a telling visual history).

123. Jean de Brébeuf, SJ, "Relation de ce qui s'est passé dans le pays des Hurons en l'année 1636, envoyée à Kebec au R.P. Paul Le Jeune, Supérieur de la mission de la compagnie de Jésus en la Nouvelle-France," Saint-Joseph-des-Hurons (Ithonatiria), 16 July 1636, reprinted in Campeau, *Monumenta*, 3:371 ("Je ne prétends pas icy mettre nos sauvages en parallèle avec les Chinois, Japonnois et autres nations parfaitement civilisées, mais seulement les tirer de la condition des bestes, où l'opinion de quelques-uns les a réduits, leur donner rang parmy les hommes et faire paroistre qu'il y a mesme parmy eux quelque espèce de vie politique et civile"). On Europe's imitation of China in the seventeenth and eighteenth centuries, see also Lewis Adams Maverick, *China: A Model for Europe* (San Antonio, 1946), 1–61.

124. APF, SOCG, vol. 189, fols. 163^{rv}, 171^{rv}, Ingoli's memorandum, [Rome], 1628 ("essendo gl'Indiani huomini, sono conseguentemente capaci di Religione: e in essi è forza che ve ne siano degl'idonei al Sacerdotio"), published in Metzler, *Memoria Rerum*, 3/2:678–79. This is based upon Session 23 of the Council of Trent, "Vera, & Catholica doctrina de Sacramento Ordinis ad condemnandos errores nostri temporis" (15 July 1563).

125. APF, SOCG, vol. 144, fols. 174^{rv}, 179^{rv}, Louis-François de Paris to Ingoli, Paris, 8 March 1646 ("primitia della sua [Pacifique de Provins's] missione di Canada" [words written by a Propaganda copyist]); APF, Lettere, vol. 24, fols. 62^{v}–63^{r}, [Propaganda] to Pacifique de Provins, Rome, 7 May 1646 ("primitia della med:ma miss:ne," "con grande solennità, e concorso di Popolo"). Pacifique de Provins's official title was prefect of the mission of Canada; hence the error in Louis's origin.

126. APF, SOCG, vol. 139, fols. 174^{rv}, 179^{rv}, Louis-François de Paris to Ingoli, Paris, 8 March 1646.

127. APF, SOCG, vol. 144, fols. 175^{rv}, 178^{rv}, Louis-François de Paris to Ingoli, Paris, 27 April 1646; APF, Lettere, vol. 24, fols. 62^{v}–63^{r}, [PF] to Pacifique de Provins, Rome, 7 May 1646 ("uiue con grande edificat:ne di tutti").

128. APF, Acta, vol. 17, fol. 112^{v}, Rome, Proceedings of the General Congregation of 11 June 1646 ("alios gentiles syluaticos"); APF, Lettere, vol. 24, [PF to Louis-François de Paris],

Rome, 11 June 1646; APF, SOCG, vol. 260, fols. 88rv, 98rv, [Joachim de Corbeil and Alexis d'Auxerre] to [Dionisio Massari], Paris, 20 February 1650; another copy in APF, vol. 260, fols. 114rv, 121rv.

129. Dickason, *Myth*, 205, 213, 217–21; Axtell, *Invasion Within*, 55–56; Bailey Wallis Diffie, *A History of Colonial Brazil, 1500–1792* (Malabar, 1987), 32.

130. Hemming, *Red Gold*, 206; Dickason, *Myth*, 217. On these Tupinambas, see Archivio di Stato, Turin, C.J.b.VI.5, fols. 1rv–5rv, La navigation des frencois aux payis des Topinamboux et Margaias situés dans le Bresil entre les deux rivières de Maregnon et des Amazones [after 1613]. This little-known document was published in Corradino Astengo, "La France Equinoxiale," *Studi e Ricerche di Geografia* 5, no. 1 (1982): 64–88.

131. Campeau, *Monumenta*, 3:457–59, 465–67, 544–46, 638.

132. Cornelius John Jaenen, "Amerindian Responses to French Missionary Intrusion, 1611–1760: A Categorization," in *Religion/Culture: Comparative Canadian Studies*, ed. William Westfall et al. ([Ottawa], 1985), 194–95. The word "dogique" comes from the Japanese "dojuku," literally meaning "living together." See Neil S. Fujita, *Japan's Encounter with Christianity: The Catholic Mission in Pre-Modern Japan* (New York and Mahwah, N.J., 1991), 74.

133. Maksimilian Jezernick, "Il Collegio Urbano," in Metzler, *Memoria Rerum*, 1/1, *1622–1700* (1971), 465–82; Marcocchi, *Colonialismo*, 45. As for languages, see s.v. "Lingue e missione" in the index to Metzler, *Memoria Rerum*, 1/2.

134. See Josef Metzler, OMI, *Mezzi e metodi per l'evangelizzazione dei popoli secondo Francesco Ingoli* (Rome, 1969); "Francesco Ingoli und die Indianerweihen," *Neue Zeitschrift für Missionswissenschaft* 25, no. 4 (1969): 262–72, and "Francesco Ingoli, der erste Sekretär der Kongregation (1578–1649)," in Metzler, *Memoria Rerum*, 1/1:197–243.

135. APF, SOCG, vol. 189, fols. 175rv–176rv, Ingoli's memorandum, [Rome], 1628 ("Li Sacerdoti europei, non vogliono che siano promossi li Nationali, per non essere di là poi cacciati e non perder quel dominio, e li guadagni grandi, che dall'Indie cavano"), published in Metzler, *Memoria Rerum*, 3/2, *1815–1972* (1976), 677–78. For the debate on the local clergy, see the documents published in ibid., 675–90; Marcocchi, *Colonialismo*, 43–48; Chappoulie, *Aux origines d'une église*, 1:383–90.

136. APF, vol. 189, fols. 163rv–171rv, 224rv–225rv, Ingoli's memorandum, [Rome], 1628 ("natura"), published in Metzler, *Memoria Rerum*, 3/2:678–79.

137. APF, SOCG, vol. 189, fols. 231rv–232rv, Ingoli's memorandum, 1628 ("Li Bracmani, li Chinesi, li Cocinesi, li Tonquinesi e tutti gl'Indiani nati di padre spagnolo sono attissimi al Sacerdotio"). Quoted in Chappoulie, *Aux origines d'une église*, 1:387–88, and in Marcocchi, *Colonialismo*, 47. "Cocinesi" ("Cochinese") were the Christians of the diocese of Cochin in India.

138. APF, SOCG, vol. 189, fols. 163rv, 171rv, Ingoli's memorandum, [Rome], 1628, published in Metzler, *Memoria Rerum*, 3/2:678–79.

139. APF, Acta, vol. 7/I, fols. 172v–173r, Rome, Proceedings of the General Congregation of 28 November 1630 ("qui ex Indis fuerint magis habiles . . . ad sacros ordines usque ad sacerdotium inclusive promoveantur"), published in Metzler, *Memoria Rerum*, 3/2:690.

140. APF, SOCG, vol. 560, fols. 154rv–163rv, William Lesley to Clement XI, [Rome, January 1705] ("nazionale o soggetto idoneo"). Also APF, SOCG, vol. 560, fols. 139rv–152rv, Motiui, e

Raggioni, che mostrano le obligationi di tutti i Cattolici, e particolarmente de Romani à concorrere con la Santa Sede Apostolica à procurare la Conuersione degli Scismatici, Eretici, et altri Infedeli, e La Propagatione della Fede di Giesù Christo per tutto L'uniuerso Mondo proposto al Sommo Pontefice Clemente XI nel mese di Gennaro, 1705.

141. APF, SOCG, vol. 189, fols. 175^{rv}–176^{rv}, 216^{rv}–217^{rv}, Ingoli's memorandum, [Rome], 1 August 1628 ("capaci del Sacerdotio"), published in Metzler, *Memoria Rerum*, 3/2:677–78. See also Charles Ralph Boxer, *The Christian Century in Japan, 1549–1650* (Berkeley, 1951), 72–90, 188–247; Hubert Cieslik, *Kirishitan Jinbutsu No Kenkyu/Studies on Christian People: Japanese Priests in Historical Perspective* (Tokyo, 1963), 20 (Cieslik's own source is Italian Jesuit Daniello Bartoli); Dino Pastine, "Il problema teologico delle culture non cristiane," in Pastine et al., *Europa cristiana*, 1–22; Charles Ralph Boxer, "European Missionaries and Chinese Clergy, 1654–1810," in *The Age of Partnership: Europeans in Asia before Dominion*, ed. Blair B. King and M. N. Pearson (Honolulu, 1979), 97–121; Marcocchi, *Colonialismo*, 35–37; Jacques Gernet, *Chine et christianisme*, 2d ed. (Paris, 1991); Giuseppe Sorge, *L'India di S. Tommaso: Ricerche storiche sulla chiesa malabarica* (Bologna, 1983), 78–85, and *Matteo de Castro (1594–1677)* (Bologna, 1986); Derek Massarella, *A World Elsewhere: Europe's Encounter with Japan in the Sixteenth and Seventeenth Century* (New Haven, 1990), 43–44; Fujita, *Japan's Encounter*, vii, 91, 98–99.

142. Marcocchi, *Colonialismo*, 26–27. See also Robert Ricard, *La "conquête spirituelle" du Mexique: Essai sur l'apostolat et les méthodes missionnaires des Ordres Mendiants en Nouvelle-Espagne de 1523–24 à 1572* (Paris, 1933), 260–81; Sorge, *Matteo de Castro*, 31 (on different approaches to Japan, Mexico, and Brazil); Stuart B. Schwartz, "The Formation of a Colonial Identity in Brazil," in *Colonial Identity in the Atlantic World, 1500–1800*, ed. Nicholas P. Canny and Anthony Pagden (Princeton, 1987), 41–44 (quote at 44).

143. Historians have yet to agree on the size of the Indian population at the time of first contact, as well shown in John D. Daniels, "The Indian Population of North America in 1492," *The William and Mary Quarterly* 49, no. 2 (April 1992): 298–320.

144. ASV, SS, Lettere dei Vescovi, vol. 53, fols. 505^{rv}–606^{rv}, Laval to Clement IX, Québec, 26 October 1668 ("quos . . . ad sacerdotium promouere, si idonej aliquando euaserint, si videbitur, promptum erit"); copy in APF, C, AS, vol. 1, fols. $1[c]^{rv}$–$1[d]^{rv}$; the latter published in Antonelli, *Quebecen*, 117–18. Jean Caignet (fl. 1663–70) was ordained in 1668, Louis Petit (d. 1709) in 1670, Charles-Amador Martin (1648–1711) in 1671, Pierre de Francheville (1648–1713) in 1676, Pierre-Paul Gagnon (1649–1702) in 1677, and Louis Soumande (1652–1706) in 1677. See Joseph Le Caron, "Liste des prêtres séculiers et religieux qui ont exercé le saint ministère en Canada (1604–1690)," *Le Bulletin des Recherches Historiques* 47, no. 8 (August 1941): 225, 227, 232, 234; Baillargeon, *Séminaire*, 44.

145. ACU, Registro, VII/2, 233 B; ACU, Giuramento, VIII/3, 81–84; ACU, Elenco, VI/2, 13. I am grateful to Giovanni Pizzorusso for making me aware of this important, albeit small, repository. These documents were completely unknown to date. For all known details of their story, see Robert Frederick Trisco, *The Holy See and the Nascent Church in the Middle Western United States, 1826–1850* (Rome, 1962), 212–15. One should add that Americans and Canadians of European origin waited almost as long as the two Indians. The first two young Americans admitted to the Urban College were Felix Dougherty (1774–after 1798) and Ralph Smith (ca.

1773–after 1798), who arrived in January 1788 from the diocese of Baltimore, whereas Norbert MacEachern (1809–34) and Eugene MacEachern (1810–1839), from the diocese of Charlottetown, Prince Edward Island, waited until January 1829. Norbert died in Rome, and Eugene died during his return voyage to Prince Edward Island. See *sub voce* in Codignola, *Guide.* On these archives and on the Canadian students at the Urban College, see Giovanni Pizzorusso, *Documents d'intérêt canadien dans les Archives du Collège Urbain*, Finding Aid in typescript (Rome and Ottawa, [1992]).

JOHN M. HEADLEY

Campanella, America, and World Evangelization

Insofar as Tommaso Campanella is known at all today beyond the immediate circle of Renaissance scholarship, he is remembered as the author of *The City of the Sun*, arguably the most famous utopia after that of Thomas More. Yet to the seventeenth century he was known rather for his political writings, preeminently the *Monarchy of Spain* (*Monarchia di Spagna*), which ran during this period to eleven editions in German, Latin, and English; as a late Renaissance magus and philosopher, through his *On the Sense of Things and of Magic* (*Del senso delle cose e della magia*), his *Metaphysics*, and *Astrology*; and even earlier as a poet, for his rough-hewn, but intensely powerful sonnets. Among all the philosophers of the day Campanella alone hastened to the defense of Galileo in 1616 and in the resulting *Defense of Galileo* (*Apologia pro Galileo*) presented the first reasoned defense for *libertas philosophandi* (the principle of free philosophizing).[1]

But if Campanella was a philosopher of encyclopedic range, he lacked the characteristic prudence, even physical timidity, of a philosopher. Indeed, forever consumed by a unitary vision of human society and impelled by astrological, apocalyptic, and messianic signs, this Dominican friar as radical prophet and world reformer led a popular revolt in Calabria against the Spanish viceregal authority which landed him in prison. Between Campanella's apprehension in the autumn of 1599 and his endurance of thirty-six hours of dreadful torture in June 1601, Giordano Bruno—fellow Dominican, Neapolitan, and poet-philosopher—would suffer the spectacular death of being burned at the stake in the Campo dei Fiori in Rome. By courage, cunning, and above all by writing, Campanella survived to see at last the light of freedom and become an intimate of Pope Urban VIII and later of Richelieu.

The imprisonment that began in 1600 represented no new experience for Campanella, nor would this present detention be the last occasion for his confinement, yet it certainly proved to be the longest—a period of twenty-six years. Shifted among Naples's worst dungeons, sometimes in chains, often in darkness, the man survived. His very survival, not to mention his immense productivity, remains a monument to the will's triumph and the mind's freedom, whatever the obscurities and tergiversations of his formal philosophy. The astonishing literary output of these years attests to a prodigious memory and a comprehensive, questing mind as well as to the porous nature of seventeenth-century European prisons. In his own soaring affirmation of the mind's power and place Campanella reveals a transcendent confidence:

> Man lives in a double world: according to the mind he is contained by no physical space and by no walls, but at the same time he is in heaven and on earth, in Italy, in France, in America, wherever the mind's thrust penetrates and extends by understanding, seeking, mastering. But indeed according to the body he exists not, except in only so much space as is least required, held fast in prison and in chains to the extent that he is not able to be in or to go to the place attained by his intellect and will, nor to occupy more space than defined by the shape of his body; while with the mind he occupies a thousand worlds.[2]

If we are to understand the world of America revealed to the thrust of Campanella's mind, we need first to apprise ourselves of that intellectual world which he had brought with him into his dreadful confinement as well as the intellectual currents and institutional developments operative in Europe and the Catholic church at the turn of the sixteenth century. To what extent does he participate in and partake of them? What does it mean to be a Dominican of Neapolitan stamp, mesmerized by the global imperialism of Spain and the Counter-Reformation dynamics of papal Rome in the period initiated by Columbus and by Luther? Just how far down the road can one go in the dilution and extension of an inevitably Eurocentric Christianity in order to engage in a single net, all the peoples, both old and new, of humanity?

Intellectual and Institutional Background

In several major respects the sixteenth century emerges as the most revolutionary in the Western experience. The increasing impact of printing, Copernicanism as a delayed action bomb, and the discovery of America, together with the encompassing of the globe, all introduced a new instability as well as opportunity. More immediately and narrowly, within the European encampment the Protestant Reformation had shattered the medieval catholic unity of the church, creating in its wake at Lambeth Palace, Wittenberg, Geneva, and in numerous state churches a polycentric ecclesiastical landscape. Nevertheless, the general persistence of that arrangement, inherited from the Emperor Theodosius and the late Roman Empire, whereby the single true religion is axiomatic for political unity and the sole basis for social order and ethical conduct, now had the effect of maximizing hostility between differing dogmatic/political constructs and throttling dissent within these same polities. With the crystallization of dogmatic positions and confessional camps, the last half of the sixteenth century saw a destabilized, polycentric Europe thrusting into the poorly perceived, yet tantalizing, other worlds present on a suddenly expanded, if slowing shrinking, planet.

Any assessment of the intellectual context at the end of the century needs to take into account the currents stemming from the Italian Renaissance. As a preeminently cultural and intellectual movement promoted by a new elite, the Renaissance would in its later stage take its revenge upon that essentially religious, popular movement of the Reformation which it had earlier done so much to sire. Both revived Stoicism and Florentine Platonism would have the effect of dissolving the rigidities and sharp edges of confessional positions and the exclusiveness of dogmatic Christianity into a more comprehensive and general rationalism or naturalism. For its part, the Stoic current advanced ideas of a rational, natural law that provided a potential basis of equality and community not simply for Europeans but for all humans insofar as they were rational creatures. On the other hand, Renaissance Platonism, multiform and hybrid, diffuse and all too often turbid, would nevertheless advance the notion of a universal theism, a *prisca theologia* that emphasized the fundamental unity of all religions whatever their different guises. The frequent resort to the legendary figure of Hermes Trismegistus as an authority reminds us of the importance, in the universalizing process, of astrology, magic, and the occult as the science of the day. In the course of the later sixteenth century the Hermetic influence leaves its trail in the work of the great French orientalist, Guillaume Postel, of the Protestant apologist and friend of Henry of Navarre, Philippe de Mornay, and of the Platonist Francesco Patrizi, whose works were condemned by Rome.[3]

Projecting forward into the seventeenth century, we can assess the fruit of these forces in Lord Herbert of Cherbury's *On Truth* (*De veritate*), first published in 1625. In his reductive theology Lord Herbert claimed the reality of five common notions regarding religion that were natural and thus accessible to all people. Significantly, he almost never mentions Christ, and the doctrinal importance of the Incarnation and the Crucifixion is virtually ignored. The Christian God as Creator, insofar as it is Christian at all, is thus easily reinterpreted in terms of the Platonist One. Herbert is unable to subscribe to a literal need for redemption through a special act of grace. Considered by some the forerunner of deism, Herbert remains broadly indebted to Ficino, and specifically to the Florentine philosopher's *De christiana religione* I, 4, which posits a single universal religion in a diversity of rites and forms.[4] It is noteworthy that when this statement of easy optimism regarding a universal access to the Creator God was republished in 1633, Herbert, who possessed some of Campanella's works and apparently admired him, arranged to have the Dominican receive a copy of *De veritate.* Although we cannot be sure of the reaction, it seems to have been favorable.[5]

Given the exuberant speculation in prophecy evinced by Lutheranism, English puritanism, and even in the radical edges of mendicant Catholicism, it is hardly surprising that early-seventeenth-century theologies should seek to enlist the current sciences of astrology and magic for calculating the universal end as well as renovation of all things. Contemporary cosmologies reveal a further important ingredient constituting the intellectual background to the age: namely, the sense that the present planetary system was not likely to persist and would shortly come to an end.[6] Indeed, Campanella had melded prophecy and magic with an astronomy proclaiming the sun's approach to the earth. Those apocalyptic as well as astronomical predictions for the year 1600 had proved disastrously false for Campanella and his followers. But failure and long imprisonment did not prevent him from continuing to celebrate new comets, new stars, and new continents as heralding Isaiah's new world.[7]

To appreciate the institutional base for world evangelization, we need first to remind ourselves of those traditional mendicant religious orders, the Augustinians, Franciscans, and Dominicans, which had been in the business of missionary endeavor and conversion of the infidel in north Africa and China since the thirteenth century. Acquisitive of the new techniques of argumentation provided by the universities and precocious in learning the necessary Asian and oriental languages, the friars served as the happy combatants in extending the faith.[8] With a flair for publicity, the Jesuits, the best known of the new religious orders produced by the Counter-Reformation, would appear to outstrip their rivals in energy and effectiveness. Operating within that arrangement known as the Patronato Real, whereby the organization and directives for the church in Spain's American holdings came not from Rome but from the Spanish king and his Council of the Indies, the Jesuits experienced no inner tension nor division; they believed that the best interests of Roman Catholicism and the Spanish empire coalesced and that in good conscience they could act as agents of both the faith and its temporal champion.[9] The collective achievement of Catholic religious orders in promoting missions, learning the native languages, developing grammars, and laying out new dioceses presents a stunning contrast to the quiescence of Protestantism in this respect. Admittedly, the Catholic world continued to nurse a universal outlook and dynamic that now allowed it to mount a global effort to convert all peoples of the earth. Perhaps most awesome in this enterprise was the immense and ultimately impossible task of seeking to Christianize the most sophisticated and oldest civilization on earth—that of China.[10]

Because of the tight control of state churches over their colonial empires, Rome appeared slow to create an administrative arm that might preside over the task of universal conversion. Indeed, a congregation for missions was not to be found among the fifteen established by Sixtus V in the reorganization of the papal curia in 1588. Not until Gregory XV in June 1622 did the papacy take the fateful step with the creation of the sixteenth, the Congregatio de Propaganda Fide, constituting a panel of thirteen cardinals charged as much with the task of regaining the heretic in Europe as with winning the infidel beyond. The universal outreach of Rome in these decades, the vision of the commitment to a vast enterprise of global evangelization, the winning of new peoples and cultures to the faith, can best be measured by the fact that the printing office of the congregation had at its command fifteen different fonts for various scripts and, by 1643, twenty-three different languages.[11]

The driving force in the newly established congregation was its talented, high-minded secretary, Francesco Ingoli. Largely to him fell the task of defining the nature and effectiveness of this new administrative arm of the papacy. A contemporary described him as the head, the body, and the feet of the new congregation. Blocked from entering into the Patronato Real of the Catholic king, Ingoli, insofar as the Portuguese patronal system allowed, promoted a Roman presidency over efforts to implement a native clergy and a locally organized system of examination for the missionaries.[12] From Paris, Campanella would address five letters to him in the last years of the Dominican's life (1635–37), in one of which he felt free to urge that the mumbled mass must be spoken in the vernacular and that the clergy might be married and the laity allowed to communicate in both kinds.[13]

Campanella's own commitment to global missionary endeavor was deeply rooted in his being and integral to his total thought. The Dominican partook generously of the heady intellectual atmosphere of the late Renaissance and fervently espoused the current magical and astronomical pursuits that seemed to lend support to the universal realization of biblical prophecy and apocalyptic. Although his passionate concern for evangelization penetrated all his works, the most specific dealing with this issue remained his *Quod reminiscentur et convertentur* (Ps. 21:28, Douai: "All the ends of the earth shall remember, and shall be converted to the Lord and all the kindreds of the Gentiles shall adore in his sight"),[14] composed largely in the first months of 1618, if conceived two years before. Campanella always considered it, along with the *Metaphysics*, as one of his two most important works and in fact spent the last years of his life in Paris vainly trying to obtain Rome's permission for its publication. In the ecumenical impulses and missionary enthusiasm that constitute the genesis of this work and become evident in the larger enterprise of his *Theology* (1614 to 1624), there is a climate that anticipates the founding of the Propaganda.[15]

In the development of a theology that sought to be accessible to all peoples and promotive of the efforts of missionaries, Campanella avails himself of those same currents of Stoicism and Florentine Platonism that were shaping the discourse of Lord Herbert. Yet while the latter manifested no clear commitment to Christianity, Campanella did not part company from the Christian tradition. His position is certainly ambiguous and much more complicated than that of his English contemporary. As one who wished to use the power and universal structure of the church as an instrument for an ecumenical religion, he could only benefit from identifying with the papacy. As an ardent Dominican and admirer of St. Thomas Aquinas, he loudly claimed to be adherent to the Angelic Doctor's teachings. In fact, some modern interpreters, in emphasizing his formal theology, will urge its orthodoxy.[16] Yet in his reshaping of Christianity into a missionary doctrine to engage the varied populations for an abruptly enlarged jurisdiction, Campanella inevitably responds to the possibilities afforded by astrology and magic, Stoicism, and Platonism in order to dissolve the more exclusive features of the Christian faith and open it up to the community of humankind. In a sense Nicola Badaloni is right when he suggests that, like Grotius for Protestantism, Campanella sought to develop the *communitas* of Christianity, while dismantling the traditional concept of God in order to make way for science and human power.[17]

In his construction of a natural theology that perilously presents the features of a naturalistic religion, Campanella affirms the universality of the religious instinct.[18] The human mind is itself a divine remembrance (*Dei memoriale*) and in the image of God.[19] So far this is quite traditional and acceptable. With the scriptural support of Eccles. 1:16, he asserts that in the womb has been created the fear of the Lord which constitutes religion.[20] But the major springboard for his universal religious naturalism derives from specific recourse to the stock text provided by Ficino in *De christiana religione* I, 4, that peoples do not disagree in religion but *in ritu* and in the notion of the divine.[21] Beginning with the definition of religion in Eccles. 1:16 and ascending through the fathers to St. Thomas, Campanella comes to rest with Ficino, *Theologia platonica* XIV, 9: "I understand religion to be itself an instinct common and natural to all people whereby everywhere and always a certain ruling (*regina*) of the world is recognized and honored which first by natural sagacity we know, then by philosophical reasons, and afterwards by prophetic words and miracles."[22] From here it is a short Stoic step to claiming that one natural law in the hearts of all defies whatever diversity might exist.[23]

Central and decisive to any form of Christianity is its understanding of Christ—the aspects and features it chooses to emphasize and those it seeks to minimize or suppress. Such is certainly the case with Campanella. In his formal theological statements he can appear quite orthodox, but peeping out from the interstices of his writings, especially those of an "aphoristic" sort, a number of dissident themes present a distinctly less orthodox picture of Christ. In the course of Campanella's trial following the abortive conspiracy of 1599, evidence emerged to the effect that he was scandalized by the scandal of Christ. In short, he espoused Christ in glory; the Christ of the Passion and Crucifixion left him uneasy, even upset.[24] One of Campanella's more moving sonnets deriving from the period of his early imprisonment explicitly challenges a piety that makes so much of the six hours on the cross and yet fails to do justice to Christ in glory, *Christus triumphans*, ruling heaven in splendor and soon to bring his glory to earth.[25] Here we find a conscious rejection of that late medieval piety, persisting into the Counter-Reformation, that emphasizes Christ's agony to the neglect of his lordship and rule. Faced with a need similar to that of Lord Herbert to provide a blander Christianity to a more universal public, Campanella emotionally shuns the very cross that gives distinctive force to Christian thought and piety. In order to appreciate the curious affinities and tensions in his position, we may recall Blaise Pascal's Fifth Letter, where it is claimed that a Dominican, a member of Campanella's own order, will complain to Rome and to the Propaganda that the Jesuits in China specifically suppress the offense of the cross and preach only a glorious, and not a suffering, Christ.[26] While notable, the congruence of the Dominican Campanella with the Jesuits on properly confessional matters, excepting education, is hardly surprising.[27]

Less emotional and more philosophical is Campanella's emphasis upon Christ as the prime Reason to which all people as rational beings give their assent.[28] Early in his imprisonment he had identified Christ as the purest expression of the law of nature, to which Christianity had simply added sacraments, thereby distinguishing Christ and the Christian.[29] In one of his most important works, the later *Atheism Conquered* (*Atheismus Triumphatus*), composed first in Italian in 1605, then in Latin in 1607, but not published until 1631 (then to be immediately sequestered, censured, revised, and only finally republished in Paris in 1636), Campanella defined more explicitly the identification of Christ as Reason: All peoples recognize Christ as the Primal Reason (*Deum primam Rationem*), and all peoples are Christian when they live according to reason, even though they may not know Christ. In Christianity alone is perfect rationality as the early church fathers had urged. Christ is the head of all rational creatures. While supportive of a comprehensive natural law, Christ also manages to embody a supernatural *magiam* imparted through the sacraments.[30] In the more formal treatment of this issue provided by his *Theologia*, Campanella will recognize the need to keep in balance Christ as Redeemer and Christ as Legislator, yet he will associate Protestantism with a single-minded plumping for the former, while he himself gravitates toward a Christ as King, as Doctor, but preeminently as Legislator.[31]

The thorny issue of predestination and free will reveals the direction and intent of Campanella's theologizing. Once again formally orthodox and apparently Thomistic, he will nevertheless build up a sediment of preference in his recourse to authorities that will weight the scales in favor of the general rationality of the early Greek fathers, especially the Alexandrian school and John Chrysostom, and away from Augustine, particularly the later Augustine. He contrasts the Augustinian tradition, whereby predestination seems to follow from an invincible decree, with that of the Greek fathers—Origen, Chrysostom, Theophylact, Athanasius, Basil, Cyril, Cassian, and Justin Martyr—which he claims takes into account a divine foreknowledge of human merits.[32] Campanella presses a distinction between

God's antecedent will, whereby all are saved, and his consequent will, whereby divine predestination and reprobation follow according to the most secret foreknowledge of our merits and demerits.[33] Campanella continues to take as his basic premise and guide 1 Tim. 2:4, that God wants all to be saved. Thus among several reasons for his continuous recourse and reference to Origen is the great Alexandrian's doctrine of the total restoration of all things (*apokatastasis panton*), whereby ultimately the whole of God's Creation, including Satan himself and the fallen angels, will be taken up into a universal reconciliation with God.[34] Nevertheless, he seeks to distance himself from Origen's most distinguished modern promoter, Erasmus, as too Pelagian, while claiming for his own position a Catholic middle way defined by the Councils of Orange (529) and of Trent.[35] For his broad, generous view of the soterial process, Campanella has frequent recourse to St. John Chrysostom, who is in fact his favorite church father. God is not an accounter of persons, but to all he has wanted to offer and does offer grace.[36]

Throughout his life Campanella remained profoundly troubled, on the one hand, by the multitude of peoples on the earth and, on the other, by the limited number of the saved even within the Christian camp. The magnitude of this problem—namely, the number of peoples, populations, and cultures that remain in idolatry and ignorance, removed from a European Christ and his salvation—can be found in his *Theologia* of the period 1614–24.[37] Earlier, in his *Atheismus Triumphatus*, he had expressed the belief that it is absurd to think that only Christians, a small part of humanity comparable to a finger on the entire human body, will be saved. Here he had asked how God can be a good father to all people and yet neglect the Tartars, the Japanese, the Chinese, the Arctic, and Antarctic peoples.[38] In the review of the work by the Roman censors, the new master of the Sacred Palace, Niccolò Riccardi, had apparently not objected at first, and indeed, a Dominican consultor attached to the Holy Office deemed the study "surely a golden work . . . worthy . . . to be brought to light for the benefit of the entire Christian community." The book duly appeared from a Roman press in 1631. Shortly, however, the shine began to wear off; doubts beset Il Mostro, as Riccardi was called, and he managed a reversal of the decision, to be repeated more momentously the following year in the case of Galileo's *Dialogue*.[39]

Riccardi would rapidly become the most bitter, deceitful, and dangerous of Campanella's enemies. Campanella had to meet the doubts of the master of the Sacred Palace with specific replies as well as by recasting the *Atheismus Triumphatus* in a more patristic mold. In the process he revealed his all too liberal propensities regarding salvation as well as further indebtedness to Chrysostom and an open world far more sensitive to engaging and winning the Jew or uncommitted Gentile, pagan or infidel. Thus we encounter the following positions: that one is damned to hell to suffer physical punishments there only for one's own sins, not for original sin; that all children are spared;[40] that, although baptism is necessary, some may be saved by recommending themselves to God;[41] and that, according to our native endowment (*facere quod in se est*) and 1 Tim. 2:4, God wants all to be saved. In defending his own words, *Salvabitur ad regnum* (He will be saved for the Kingdom), Campanella also sought to include the unbaptized so long as they serve the natural law.[42] His last years in Paris would be convulsed by the ongoing *De auxiliis* controversy between the Jesuits and his fellow Dominicans over the operation of divine grace. In this conflict over the perennial and now obsessive issue of predestination and salvation, it is noteworthy that Campanella aligned his own position and sympathies perilously close to the Jesuits and granted a greater role to human merits and effort in the process of salvation than the hardliners, his own Dominicans, would allow.[43]

The problem of how to adjust a Eurocentric Christianity to a global arena made all the more pressing the definition and recognition of a universalized religion. In the explicit task of missionary endeavor, quite apart from the thorny debates back home in Europe on predestination, Campanella as a Dominican participated in a rich and most influential tradition. Almost a century earlier Francisco de Vitoria and the Spanish natural law school of theologians had revamped Stoic notions of rationality and natural law in a revival of Thomism that would make a parochially hardened Christianity more supple and accessible. When Vitoria came to examine the reasons and justification for the Spanish presence in the New World, he found none except for a narrow, tenuous, but ultimately most vital one, derivative from natural law: the right of peoples to communicate. This right of commerce among peoples most immediately provided the justification for Christian missionaries to have free access to possible converts and also the right of all races to move freely from one community to another. The impelling right and need for communication, the power of the word and of the tongue, and the triumph of Spanish navigation in encircling the globe are all of capital importance to Campanella's program and total vision. From his Dominican as well as his magical perspective, the new devices of printing press, compass, and arquebus possess an almost sacral quality in affirming this right of communication.[44]

Nevertheless, for our Dominican it is always language, the tongue, the preached word that enjoys ascendancy. This right, indeed imperative, to communicate achieves its best expression in one of the "legationes" or commissions serving as chapters to the later sections of Campanella's formidable presentation of Rome's current apostolate, the *Quod reminiscentur*. Acting upon the commonly held European attitude, recently reaffirmed by Botero, that China had arrogantly turned away from all external associations and looked inward upon herself, Campanella abjures her emperor in his legation to the monarch of the Chinese. He resorts to the image of the cheese and the worms, which was broadly current in his own time and has been recently made familiar to a modern audience by Carlo Ginzburg. But here, as elsewhere in the Dominican's writings, he uses it for epistemological and political purposes rather than in the cosmogonic sense of Menocchio. Campanella admonishes the emperor:

> Those men [your subjects] are lacking in aspiration (*parvis contenti*); they seem not men but like worms born inside a cheese, who reckon nothing more nor better there to be in the world beyond their own cheese from which they are nourished, sustained, hidden, or as worms born in man's stomach who know nothing of man, nor his mind, cocooned away, not wanting to be disturbed. So, oh king, you seem to be to us. . . . Stick your head out beyond your cheese, beyond the stomach of your land.[45]

Laced now with Western *curiositas*, the passage distills much of that immense Christian dynamic, experienced so deeply by the imprisoned friar.

Against such an intellectual and institutional background, the operation of Campanella's thought on a world and, specifically American, hemispheric scale can now be examined.

The American Indian in the Developing Imperial/Global Evangelization

If Campanella's thought possessed a single informing figure, it was probably that of Christopher Columbus. Columbus's name appears in the vast majority of Campanella's works, for he never tires of showing how the actual experience of encountering another hemisphere brought to naught the traditional authority of respected church fathers asserting that no antipodes could exist. In the preface to his immense *Metaphysics*, he leads off with Christopher Columbus as providing the supreme evidence for experience over authorities, for empirical testimony over opinions. For this world as the codex of God, the Book of Nature we learn to read through the external senses. And where we cannot directly read all of it ourselves, we must credit the testimony of others. But not all others are to be credited, for too many falsely transcribe their own books from the divine codex and represent their books as the original autograph and not as copy. Whereas *opinio* becomes the reading from our own self-devised books, *testimonium* is the direct reading from God's book. Thus what better confutation of the authoritative opinions of Lactantius and Augustine in their negation of antipodes than Columbus's testifying by his own navigation into another hemisphere?[46] Direct experience displaces venerable opinion.

Early in his Neapolitan imprisonment (1603) Campanella had identified Columbus as providing the bridge between Christ and Caesar. He had hailed this "audacious genius," and prior to the notoriety of Galileo he had included Columbus with two other Italians, Vespucci and Telesio, as having exceeded in action and performance what the Greeks could only fabulate.[47] In his earlier Italian *Poetics*, composed in 1596, and in the later Latin *Poetics* Campanella pursued his lonely war against the poetry of fables—Homer, the Greeks in general, and now the currently fashionable Ariosto, Boiardo, and Tasso—all in the interest of advancing a poetry of power and utility. Throughout he insists on the majesty and import of Columbus's achievement as being the very stuff of great epic, although his own age had failed to accept this challenge. For what is suitable to Jason is not so to Columbus or Caesar: not all wars or grand enterprises are just and marvelous, "only those that bring great utility to posterity and give laws to the conquered . . . thereby producing a change of empire and religion, itself the soul of empire, and the innovation of a new age."[48] In the later Latin *Poetics* of 1613 Campanella includes among the truly marvelous, suitable for serious poetic celebration, "the new discoveries such as that of the New World, of artillery, of a new heaven and new planets by my friend Galileo, the astronomic hypothesis of Copernicus, of Timaeus and Philolaus, and of all that is not ordinary." Human actions ushering in a new epoch of the world commend themselves to epical exposition: for example, the arrival of Aeneas in Italy, Joshua's entry into Palestine, the landing of the Spaniards in America with Columbus beggaring all other human enterprises.[49] Whoever will write this long overdue epic of Columbus "will record what happened to him in the voyage with respect to his crew, what he experienced from the sea, from the weather, from monsters, and from the inhabitants of the new continent and whatever served to retard or hasten the occupation of the New World."[50]

Columbus has a cultural, moral, and ultimately religious significance. Never unmindful of the apocalyptic dimensions to America's discovery, Campanella sees Columbus not only as bearing Christ to the New World but as establishing the Columbian church (*Columbam ecclesiam*).[51] For good reason Campanella had begun his huge *Theologia* by asserting the principal causes impelling his work; the first three were the heresies associated with the Protestant movement, the discovery of the New World with its unknown and unknowing people, and the discovery of new stars and a new construction of the world, requiring incorporation into a new theology.[52] He would go on to observe that Luther and Columbus had shaken philosophers and theologians from a sleep of ignorance and negligence.[53] If the impact of Luther would impel Rome to a closing of ranks and a definition of doctrine, in short, to clarification and defensiveness, that of Columbus drove Rome toward meeting the challenge and the opportunities of a globe without walls and to the true realization of her universalism. What before had seemed unnatural Columbus had now made natural. In his wake Spain had girdled this globe with her navigation, introducing religion and polity where there had been barbarism.[54]

In short, Columbus creates for Campanella—and for succeeding European generations—a more ample and comprehensive vision of the physical, moral, and religious world.

The discovery of new stars and a new understanding of the universe, of course, brings Galileo into focus. Both Christopher Columbus and Galileo Galilei release two distinct cognitive, conceptual processes of immense, transforming influence for Campanella as well as for his age. Here the Dominican seems to have maintained a more balanced comparison than will later develop largely at the hands of Galileo's Tuscan admirers, who, in comparing the Genoese admiral to the Florentine astronomer, will exalt the latter as producing accomplishments more intellectual and celestial.[55] Although for Campanella the Galilean issue came into focus only after 1611, he engaged most meaningfully but in different ways during the rest of his life the implications of both men's accomplishments. And in this ongoing interpretation of each, profound as well as revealing, Galileo never displaces Columbus in the friar's estimation.

A child of Galileo, Vitoria, and yes, Machiavelli, but always with a Dominican voice, Campanella has drawn the essential conclusion from the event of Christopher Columbus: the construction of the greatest empire in history and the achievements of Spanish navigation had created not simply an American theater but a global context. In the *Monarchia Messiae*, dating from 1605 but not published until 1633, we read:

> If all the world were ruled by one, knowledge would be increased on account of all the land and sea traffic, the trade and communication; those subjects known hitherto by individual peoples might be better observed and known in others, especially astronomy, astrology, physics and politics, which require much observation,—and what one does not know, the other knows. But the devil, envying us such opportunity (*bonum*), would want that we all remain within our own boundaries, as worms within a cheese, so that he may render us all ignorant and deceive us. Likewise he desires that we do not communicate with one another what we observe and know, nor journey to investigate the works of God in foreign regions, in order that we might not know and see one another but rather that language and religion be diversified so that what would [otherwise] be admitted through common knowledge, nurturer of mutual love among us, we would introduce piecemeal only through wars and death in continuous fear, without charity in God our Father and in our all being sons of the same. But in order that the necessary commerce and communications of this type may be accomplished God permits wars, famines, plagues whereby . . . we might be compelled by his flails to set forth and seek the sciences and contemplate the world, its parts and the works of God, seeking remedies for our evils and entreating the favor of God who brings forth all wealth. . . . Thus we

may transport religion and polity, and the seeds are planted in the warm southern parts of the world or the frigid northern parts or elsewhere. . . . The discovery of the new hemisphere has produced marvels amidst our sciences; indeed we may surpass the ancient philosophers, unless mutual envy buries us.[56]

The possibilities for a new world order, a Spanish/papal amalgam, afford opportunities commercial, epistemological, and scientific.

Campanella's universalism is inevitably and unashamedly Eurocentric: he does not hesitate to exploit ostensible American resources, but always for maintaining the larger universalizing purposes of Spain. In the *Monarchia di Spagna*, his most widely read work during the seventeenth century, Campanella had early indicated his sensitivity to problems of demography. He considered the decline of Spain's population to be her greatest problem. To correct this matter he sought to convince Philip III that his greatest riches from America should be people, not gold. He then proceeded to urge the transporting of Indians to Spain for training in agriculture, artisanry, and other pursuits. He would even go so far as to coopt the more intelligent for bishoprics, abbacies, and baronicies. Campanella recommends that a gifted Indian convert can be educated as a priest and serve in converting his own people or that a converted Indian chieftain be rewarded with a Spanish barony as a means of engaging his affections. In actual fact, however, the entire native population of America becomes a vast quarry for resolving the problem of labor in Spain's global empire. Apparently ignorant of the ghastly loss of population suffered by the Indians through disease during the course of the sixteenth century and unaware of their increasingly evident unsuitability for hard labor, Campanella urges that the unconverted serve as a recruitment pool for use in the galleys and that the converted participate in global resettlement and repopulation. Transported to the shores of Africa, Asia, and Spain, they will establish colonies and be trained in agriculture, artisanry, and manufacture. In being Hispanicized, some may become soldiers and even members of religious orders (*religiosi*), but the main point would be to relieve the Spaniards of labor and free them for concentrating upon soldiery.[57] Weird as this suggestion appears and impossible as it would have proved in contending with existing social prejudices and the social structure, it was part of a much larger concept for the resuscitation of Spain: namely, that as with the Romans in the process of Romanizing their subject peoples during the Empire, the Spanish must learn to Hispanicize their diverse populations and thereby make them a living, functional part of their empire.[58] In urging this solution, Campanella struck a vital chord for the survival of any polity or system. Here he seems to have preceded the swelling chorus of alarm spread by the *arbitristas* and the later fatal remedial action undertaken by Philip IV's great minister Olivares to de-Castilianize the Spanish *monarquía*.[59]

THOMAS CAMPANELLA
An Italian *FRIAR*
And
Second *MACHIAVEL.*

His advice to the *King* of *Spain* for attaining the univerſal *Monarchy* of the World.

Particularly concerning *England*, *Scotland* and *Ireland*, how to raiſe Diviſion between KING and PARLIAMENT, to alter the Government from a Kingdome to a Commonwealth. *Thereby* embroiling *England* in Civil war to divert the *Engliſh* from diſturbing the *Spaniard* in bringing the *Indian* Treaſure into *Spain*.

Alſo for reducing *Holland* by procuring war betwixt *England*, *Holland*, and other Sea-faring Countries, affirming as moſt certain, that if the King of *Spain* become maſter of *England* and the Low Countries, he will quickly be Sole *Monarch* of all Europe, and the greateſt part of the new world.

Tranſlated into Engliſh by *Ed. Chilmead*, and publiſhed for awakening the Engliſh to prevent the approaching ruine of their Nation.

With an admonitorie Preface by WILLIAM PRYNNE *of* Lincolnes-Inne *Eſquire.*

LONDON,
Printed for *Philemon Stephens* at the Gilded Lyon in St. *Pauls* Church-Yard.

Title page of Tommaso Campanella, *Advice to the King of Spain* (London [1659], the second English edition of the *Monarchia di Spagna*). John Carter Brown Library.

Equally unsettling to traditional European parochialism appears his plan for the relocating of the Holy City to Jerusalem, not Rome. Again in the *Monarchia di Spagna*, he broaches this idea as something occurring after the fall of the Antichrist and involving the establishment of his ideal state, presumably of a thousand years' duration.[60] Following a revelation of St. Bridget and the prophecies of Isaiah and Zechariah, he seeks to reconstitute a sacred center of space where Jews, Moslems, and Christians may commune as one; he prophesies that in the first Resurrection the Roman church will migrate to the New World, being first in Spain, later in Peru, afterward in Japan, circling the earth from the Occident into the Orient, and from Japan coming along the shores of Asia, into the Red Sea, and finally to the Jews, who will be converted.[61] Presumably Campanella was fully aware of the canonical maxim *ubi papa, ibi ecclesia Romana* (wherever the pope, there the Roman church), for from Jerusalem the king of Spain and the pope would rule the divine empire.

Columbus and the new technology evinced by Spanish navigation changed everything, opening up the world and requiring mental adjustments and relocations of every sort. Possibly among the oddest to the twentieth-century imagination, but real enough to Campanella's contemporaries, is one appearing in the immense lumberyard of his *Theologia*: namely, that Columbus and subsequent Spanish navigators have proved that purgatory, paradise, and even the Elysian Fields are no longer to be located in that other hemisphere. In the process of their relocation, Campanella follows Augustine in reassigning hell to the center of the earth.[62] Yet, as he ponders, the friar is aware that the Spanish oceanic power has by no means penetrated all shores. Writing in 1606, he is correct in his belief that Spanish navigators are pressing on to the Antarctic, if not to the Arctic, pole.[63]

Only rarely does Campanella provide any specific recommendations regarding the tactics of his missionaries. Of the possible missionary methods outlined by José de Acosta in his *De Procuranda Indorum Salute* (How the salvation of the Indians is to be achieved)—the apostolic, with no military force even for protection; the missionaries to be preceded by a military force, as advocated by Sepúlveda; the missionaries proceed to evangelize under military protection—Campanella could agree with Acosta in adopting the last.[64] Yet Campanella will credit the contemporary missionary with a special gift. After reading the histories of present-day evangelizers in Japan and China, he claims them to be specially endowed with the same miracles as those of the apostles, the saints, and the martyrs. He can even provide a principle for the availability of miracles: where Catholics are *in possessione*, no miracles occur; but with heathen or heretic, whether it be St. Francis preaching to Moslems in Egypt, or Dominic being tested in Toulouse, or Campanella, as he imagines himself at Wittenberg, challenging the Lutherans to the ordeal by fire, miracles are forthcoming according to need.[65]

Following St. Bernard as well as Vitoria, he urges that evangelization be by persuasion, not by force: Christ sent his apostles as sheep among wolves; he did not equip them with bombards.[66] While the realities of the American context would compel him more frequently to violate the limits of persuasion and find justification for the use of force, in his more formal, systematic work, the *Theologia*, he could promote a broader, comprehensive, and inclusive set of practices. On the critical matter of baptism, and specifically the baptism of infant children, heretic or infidel, he considers the option of relying upon the authority of the church in possible opposition to the will of the parents, only to reject it. Instead he adheres to St. Thomas in requiring that the law of nature be observed and that sons be recognized as being under the will and power of their parents. If the son is an adult and proves willing and well-instructed, baptism is enjoined, for in returning to his parents, he may convert them.[67] As early as his *Monarchia di Spagna* (1600), Campanella had manifested dissatisfaction and impatience with what he understood to be the prevailing practices of missionaries, arguing that catechisms should be in the native language and that brief histories should be composed after the fashion of the early fathers who converted the gentiles, and not the verbose stuff of the moderns. He even advocates the nurturing of a native clergy, whose preachers might be sent into the less accessible mountainous areas to convert their brethren.[68]

Of all his works, Campanella's *Quod reminiscentur et convertentur*, invoking the summons of Ps. 21:28 to conversion, stands among those most esteemed by the Dominican. Long contemplated and planned, but not composed until the period 1616–18, during his return engagement to the dreadful dungeon of San Elmo,[69] the work captures that sense of Rome's universal pastoral outreach which would shortly find institutional expression in Gregory XV's establishment of the Congregatio de Propaganda Fide in 1622. Dedicated in turn to Popes Paul V, Gregory XV, and Urban VIII, the work, much to Campanella's disappointment in his last years, would not see publication until the mid-twentieth century. The very word *reminiscentia*, recollection, suggests the Platonic assumption that knowledge is simply the conscious recovery of something already latent in the mind. As a promise to conversion, *reminiscentia* represents a powerful invocation to a universal response. Indeed, the time for this intellectual/spiritual recovery (*tempus huius reminiscentiae*), for the realization of that one universal sheepfold under one pastor, according to John 10:16, had now arrived.[70]

In his memorial of 22 December 1618 to Paul V, Campanella presented a distillation of the total work, providing the pattern and plan of a fourfold composition.[71] Although the tract would be divided into four books—the first being directed to the Catholic European rulers, schismatics, and Protestant heretics; the second to the outer world of heathenism stretching over the greater part of the globe in Asia, Africa, and America; the third to the Jews; and the fourth to the Moslems—like the

Propaganda itself, it made no essential distinction between the apostolate to the heretic and that to the Indians, both Western and Eastern. The breathtaking scope of the work captures the dynamic of Rome at this time as well as the irrepressible energy and confidence of the Dominican friar. Notable in the general program of world evangelization is the calling of an assembly to Rome that would include all peoples and rulers—Persians, Africans, Jews, Christians, Moslems, pagans—whereby their legates and learned might be engaged in persuasive *disputatio*.[72] Campanella experiences the temporal crunch: on the one hand, why has a benevolent God withheld his remedies and doctrine from the better part of the world for so long (referring thereby to the peoples of Africa, the Far East, and southern Asia, the supposedly innumerable peoples of the Arctic and Antarctic, as well as the inhabitants of the New World)?[73] On the other hand, the calculations of both prophecy and astrologic time would announce that the moment for the convoking of all peoples had struck.

In such a vast global enterprise, it is still somewhat startling that the problem of the conversion of the American Indian occupies less than 20 percent of the space devoted to the gentiles in book 2 and less than 2 percent of the total work. Nevertheless, the passage presenting the American legation is more compressed, intense, and less rambling than many of his other treatments. While aware of the ethnological question as it bears upon the prevailing theory of the general diffusion of humankind from a single Noachian source, Campanella refuses to be much troubled by the problem that was coming to convulse some of the best minds of the age.[74] Regarding the spatial problem of transmigration, Campanella answers those who would ask how people in another hemisphere are able to migrate from our parents in Phoenicia to a place so remote without memory or method (*ratio*) by arguing that from the Chinese coast to Japan is but a hop and from Japan to the American mainland (*Quiviram*) in the other hemisphere seems equally simple; likewise simple is the same sort of stepping stones from European islands in the Atlantic to the latent American shore.[75] Temporally, apart from his earlier rhetorical question, he will observe that it has been 2,300 years since the prophet Isaiah predicted the coming of Christ (Isa. 42:8) and that in several ages after his advent his doctrine would come to Japan. Now 1,600 years have passed since its arrival for the instruction of Europeans by word and example in the ways of God, who has sent those Europeans to bear witness to that truth throughout the entire world before he returns to judge humankind.[76]

Campanella subscribes to that early anthropological notion perhaps best evident in his fellow Dominican Las Casas, but also voiced by other European minds of the sixteenth and seventeenth centuries, that in the beginning all peoples were barbarians—except, apparently for Campanella, the Greeks and the Hebrews, with a special assist from his native Calabrians:

As when Greece flourished almost 2,000 years ago, refined by wisdom and the arts, all peoples that were not conversant with her polity and philosophy they called barbarians, as if beasts living without human virtue. Then when diffused through the world by the domination of the Latins, Greece having been conquered, the Romans as partakers of virtue were no longer called barbarians. Truly the Romans themselves did not consider all Italians, nor Greeks as barbarians. For from the Greeks still not conquered in war, they accepted laws and philosophy. And in Italy that province now called Calabria was then called Magna Graecia and the Greeks recognized it [as the source of their] philosophy and religious rites. . . . According to Diogenes Laertius, therefore the Greeks and Italians mutually communicated. In such wise also the Hebrews perhaps by a higher law labelled all peoples non-Judaic as Gentiles, denoting the multitude, the untaught race, and good for nothing according to Isaiah and Esdras. . . . For barbarian and Gentile signify him who is ignorant of divine wisdom, untaught by God, as a son but alienated as a slave, enemy, brute. And thus we have all been Gentiles and barbarians. . . . God however, rich in mercy, . . . dissolving the walls separating us from each other, has incorporated us into one family, visiting us and calling us into his school and inheritance; and he has adopted them as sons by means of legates, sent throughout the world; by a certain divine wisdom, attested by miracles, virtues and the deification of man, they have reduced us to the one God.[77]

Thus Campanella explains at the outset of book 2 the twin labels of barbarian and gentile, distinguishing the great mass of humanity and the twofold process of Greeks and Hebrews in bringing this latent dross of humanity to God.

Once outside of Catholic Europe, Campanella organizes his great work on missions in terms of a series of "legationes" or commissions. On the issue of cannibalism presumably present in central Africa, the Dominican moves easily from his sole heathen African legation to that single legation directed to the American continent.[78] Here his known sources for treating America will be Las Casas, Girolamo Benzoni, and Botero.[79] He begins the legation by reminding his Indian audience of the gospel delivered to them almost 130 years ago, a gospel from which they had withdrawn "just as we and almost the entire human race with the exception of a few (*exceptis paucis*) from the stock of Noah" survived the Flood, "as our histories and your traditions in Mexico, Peru, and China attest." His wording is almost intentionally ambiguous in including the American Indian in the original Noachian dispensation and, as with many contemporary ethnographers, in exhibiting the presumed similarities betraying the desired common origin.[80] In his *Theologia* he confidently affirms that there was circumcision in Yucatan as there had been in Egypt, Africa, and with the Hebrews. He goes on to speculate that possibly by force of the winds, ships have been driven from Africa to the New

World, where memory of the event came to be lost for lack of writing.[81] Indeed, whatever his heterodox hesitations, Campanella's Christian universalism and program of world evangelization dictate adherence to the monogenetic-biblical derivation for the *Americani.* The single-source Adamic origin of humankind necessarily serves to reinforce the universal order envisaged.[82] Quite uncharacteristically for his own more compromising, Jesuit-like approach to the problem of converting the Indian, but quite in keeping with the hard-sell tactics of his own fellow Dominicans, Campanella pitches his evangelizing to lead off with the Incarnation, Passion, and Resurrection of Jesus Christ—in other words, he does not hesitate to present the true *scandalon* for both rational as well as illiterate people.[83]

It is of course the Genoese Italian, Christopher Columbus, who as a *columba* has brought the Christian faith to the shores of the New World. Yet while celebrating the wondrous achievements of Spanish navigation and Spanish arms, Campanella can give voice to the conquered and subjected Indians, articulating their alienation and suffering:

> Our leaders have reckoned you Spanish to be the sons of God descending from the clouds in ships and with thundering cannon, as God himself, superior beings, as if centaurs, immortal warriors. . . . But now we are aware that you are as mortal as we, avid for gold and silver, killing our kings against your own pledged word; and we know that the art of artillery, the clock, of letters, and horsemanship to be human inventions, not divine and that you exterminate us cruelly and hold us in servitude. We understand fully you Spanish to be men, rapacious, cunning, ambitious, who under the false pretext of proclaiming the gospel have subjected and pillaged the kingdoms of others. Wherefore we do not reckon your religious practices (*religiones*) to be better than ours, which we now find similar in many things, in many preferable. Nor has God abandoned us at such a time, caring nothing for us, if he is the one God of all, if many [gods, then] each cultivates his own.[84]

Thus Campanella, despite his preoccupations with power and order, assumes a position in the Lascasian tradition of protest in defense of the American Indian. Among the very last words that he will write at the end of his life, in notes explicating his eclogue to the dauphin, shortly Louis XIV, he will remember the Indians in their sufferings and sing of a New World in which they are liberated from their crucifixion in the mines, for which the Americans, justly, hate the Christians.[85]

Yet, expectably, the grand purpose of evangelization will justify all such base actions. As he had written a decade earlier, Spain's only justification for being in the New World was evangelization.[86] Whatever the presumed common origin and perceived parallels and connections between Indian and Christian religions, he can dismiss the former as being arrogantly sunk in deviltry, depravity, and the tyranny of false gods.[87] The devil is able to move all bodies locally[88] and has introduced sodomy, whereby semen is misspent, polygamy, whereby love is dissipated, and cannibalism, whereby murder prevails and safety evaporates.[89] Because of such depravity, it is only the great mercy of God that has sent to them the Spanish liberators. Liberation from idolatry by means of the gospel and introduction to sciences and arts will ultimately justify fully for Campanella the enormities of the Spanish presence in the newfound hemisphere.[90] In short, it is the American Indian's violation of the natural law by sodomy and cannibalism, idolatry, and cultivation of the diabolic that warrants and even justifies the harsh action of the Spanish conquest. The desperate nature of the situation required the shift from persuasion to force: "We were compelled to resort to iron as a doctor in desperately mortal cases."[91]

Actually, elsewhere in his *Theologia* and in a sermon constituting the appendix to his *Monarchia Messiae*, both stemming from this same period of 1618, Campanella presented his argument in conscious opposition to the great Thomists of the previous century. Cajetan, De Soto, and Vitoria were wrong in claiming that Christian rulers have no right to use force, even if their missionaries are attacked. Indeed, insofar as possible one should proceed by persuasion and not by force. If first received, then attacked, the preachers should be able to expect armed defense. The blatant violation of natural law by cannibalism, idolatry, and sodomy demands that the pope send not only doctors of the gospel but also soldiers to exterminate the crime and punish the criminals. Campanella cites as example Alexander the Great, who founded his empire on this law: he subjected the barbarians and introduced civilization, for his preceptor, Aristotle, taught that those violating the laws of nature ought to be subjugated like so many beasts. And if De Soto believes the king of Spain hardly to be a competent judge for such very different peoples, Campanella refers to the pope and invokes the power of the keys.[92] More specifically, in the *Theologia* he argues that the pope may have the material sword and is able, when persuasion proves ineffective, to constrain the entire human race to rationality. The Americans had dishonored humankind and merited being subjected as beasts and compelled to humanity (*cogi ad humanitatem*).[93] If a harsher justification of force by a churchman can hardly be found, the majesty of the cause summoned. As an apparent product of third generation missionary attitudes regarding the American Indian, Campanella here reflects the prevailing mood of pessimism and ethnic prejudice which had come to settle on the Spanish colonial bureaucracies, both secular and ecclesiastic, in contrast to the earlier Franciscan optimism.[94] When aligned with the *conpelle intrare* (Luke 14:23) of an earlier church, the imperative of the apostolate in his own age would suggest that the sheepfold of salvation must be transformed and expanded to apply to a comprehensive, global assemblage, distinguished by European principles of humanity and rationality.

Conclusion

In conclusion, it can be said that Campanella deeply partook of the principles driving that great preaching order, the hounds of the Lord, of which he was a member. He shared that immense momentum of the age stemming from Rome and from the mendicant tradition—the natural theology of St. Thomas and his *Summa contra Gentiles* to convert. But Campanella brought his own peculiarly torqued and radical perspective that would abandon the dominant Aristotelianism of the day, capture the prophetic and eschatological, and seek to enlist the new, the innovative, the expansive, promoted by the terrestrial and celestial discoveries of his age. He strains to mobilize the innovations implicit in the work of Columbus and Galileo in order to reinforce the interests of a universal papal theocracy, Eurocentric essentially, but capable of making huge compromises and dilutions in current orthodoxy that it might extend to the pagan, the heretic, and the infidel an often unrecognizable Christianity in the form of a naturalistic religion, presided over by papal Rome.

What, then, did America finally signify for Campanella? In the first place, America possessed epistemological significance, for its very discovery by the Europeans attested to the authority of direct experience and thus the displacement of long-esteemed authors, venerable *auctoritates.* Secondly, America had immense eschatological significance for Campanella, who shared the prevalent conviction most deeply experienced by the religious orders themselves, that only when the evangel had been preached to all people would the end occur. In the light of Matt. 24:14 and comparable texts, the fact of America and her peoples provided enormous stimulus to missionary activity. Intimately associated with the sense of the end's imminence loomed the impressive intellectual activity and achievements of his own age—achievements that a later period would identify with the rapidly maturing Scientific Revolution. Indeed, Dan. 12:4 had prophesied that there would be great concourse and increase of knowledge, and the ship that passes through the pillars of Hercules in the frontispiece of Bacon's *Magna Instauratio* reminds us of this contemporary reality.

Still, there remains a third level of significance, less clear and evident, but perhaps ultimately more important and distinctively Campanellan. America served as a summons to world community, calling Europeans forth from the parochial to the global, the universal, envisaging a world without walls, a global order nurtured by unhampered commerce, communication, and intellectual exchange.[95] In short, America impelled Europe toward a growing sense of global interconnectedness.

Just as in the previous generation Giordano Bruno had grasped the meaning of Copernicus by positing the reality of an infinite universe, so Campanella now struggled to adumbrate for his own generation the meaning of Columbus by dimly discerning a truly global world order.

Yet we must not exaggerate. Such a suggestion of global interconnectedness would seem to fall short of a true transformation of consciousness or even a transposition of perspectives directly attributable to the impact of America. Like other Europeans, Campanella was unable to accept or understand America on its own terms; rather, America came to serve and to confirm existing needs, perceptions, and aspirations. Campanella does not escape an inevitable Eurocentrism, but it is one opened up, extended, and universalized to realize now a global enterprise.

Nevertheless, because such a world order can only be of God's making, the figure of Columbus ultimately possesses apocalyptic and broadly eschatological significance. And whatever the global scope of evangelization, it can only be properly seen as one among several signs confirming this world's oncoming end and the church's subsequent renewal in the thousand years of a golden age, constituting its seventh state. For our Dominican, the narrow shoal of present time dwindles before the fulfillment of all the prophesied signs. Not in the current temporal course but only in a new aeon will the fellowship of a cleansed humanity and Christianity be realized.

NOTES

For the present subject the following basic studies may be recommended: Giovanni di Napoli, "Ecumenismo e missionarismo in Tommaso Campanella," *Euntes docete* 22 (1969): 265–308; A. J. Marquis, "Le traité missionnaire 'Quod Reminiscentur' de Tommaso Campanella," *Neue Zeitschrift für Missionswissenschaft* (Supplementa) 17 (1971): 331–60; Rosario Romeo, "Le scoperte americane nella coscienza italiana del cinquecento," *Rivista Storica Italiana* 65 (1953): 326–79; Romano Amerio, "L'opera teologico-missionaria di T. Campanella nei primordi di Propaganda Fide," *Archivum Fratrum Praedicatorum* 5 (1935): 174–93.

The following abbreviations are used in the notes for the cited works of Campanella:

AP — *Articuli prophetales*, ed. Germana Ernst (Florence, 1977).

AT — *Atheismus Triumphatus seu Reductio ad religionem per scientiarum veritates . . . contra Antichristianismum Achitophellisticum* (Rome, 1631).

AV — *Antiveneti*, ed. Luigi Firpo (Florence, 1945).

CS — *La Città del Sole/The City of the Sun*, ed. Daniel J. Donno (Berkeley, Los Angeles, London, 1981).

DPI — *Discorsi ai principi d'Italia*, ed. Luigi Firpo (Turin, 1945).

Lett. — *Tommaso Campanella: Lettere*, ed. Vincenzo Spampanato (Bari, 1927).

Meta. — *Metafisica*, ed. Giovanni di Napoli, vols. 1–3 (Bologna, 1967).

MM	*Monarchia Messiae*, ed. Luigi Firpo (Jesi, 1633; Turin, 1960).
MN	"Le monarchie delle nationi . . . ," in L. Amabile, *Fra T. Campanella ne' Castelli*, vol. 2 (Naples, 1887), 299–347.
MS	*De monarchia hispanica* (Amsterdam, 1653).
Op. in.	*Opusculi inediti di Tommaso Campanella*, ed. Luigi Firpo (Florence, 1951).
P^{1-3}	P^1 = "Poesie," P^2 = "Poetica," P^3 = "Poëtica," in *Tutte le opere di Tommaso Campanella*, ed. Luigi Firpo (Verona, 1954).
QR	*Quod reminiscentur et convertentur ad dominum universi fines terrae* (Ps. 21), ed. Romano Amerio, bks. 1 and 2 (Padua, 1939); bk. 3, *Per la conversione degli Ebreii* (Florence, 1955); bk. 4, *Legazioni ai Maomettani* (Florence, 1960).
T	*Teologia*, ed. Romano Amerio, vol. 1 (Milan, 1936); vols. 2–30 (Rome, 1955–80).

1. On the bibliography of Campanella, see Luigi Firpo, *Bibliografia degli scritti di Tommaso Campanella* (Turin, 1940). On the first appearance of *libertas philosophandi*, see R. B. Sutton, "The Phrase *libertas philosophandi*," *Journal of the History of Ideas* 14 (1953): 310–16.

2. *Meta.* III, 156.

3. On this last point, see R. D. Bedford, *The Defense of Truth: Herbert of Cherbury and the Seventeenth Century* (Manchester, 1979), 218–24.

4. Ibid., 177, 218.

5. D. P. Walker, *The Ancient Theology: Studies in Christian Platonism from the Fifteenth to the Eighteenth Century* (Ithaca, 1972), 168, 188.

6. Charles Webster, *From Paracelsus to Newton: Magic and the Making of Modern Science* (Cambridge, 1982), 48.

7. For example, see his letter to Galileo, 5 August 1632, *Lett.*, 241.

8. Berthold Altaner, "Sprachstudien und Sprachkenntnisse im Dienste der Mission des 13. und 14. Jahrhunderts," *Zeitschrift für Missionswissenschaft* 21 (1931): 113–36.

9. Peggy K. Liss, "Jesuit Contributions to the Ideology of Spanish Empire in Mexico," *The Americas* 29 (1973): 322–23.

10. See the extensive, illuminating introduction of J. S. Cummins to his edition of *The Travels and Controversies of Friar Domingo de Navarrete, 1618–1686*, vol. 1 (Cambridge, 1962); also the same author's "Two Missionary Methods in China: Mendicants and Jesuits," *Archivo Ibero-Americano* 38 (1978): 33–108.

11. Willi Henkel, "The Polyglot Printing-Office of the Congregation," *Sacrae Congregationis de Propaganda Fide Memoria Rerum: 350 anni a servizio delle Missioni* (Rome, 1972), 335–50, esp. 337, 343.

12. On the important figure of Francesco Ingoli, see Josef Metzler, "Papstlicher Primat als pastorale Verantwortung und missionarischer Auftrag in frühen Dokumenten der Progaganda-Kongregation," in *Konzil und Papst: Historische Beiträge zur Frage der höchsten Gewalt in der Kirche*, Festgabe für Hermann Tüchle, ed. Georg Schwaiger (Munich/Paderborn/Vienna, 1975), 373–86, esp. 375–78; and also by the same author, the several articles on the Propaganda and Ingoli appearing in *Sacrae Congregationis de Propaganda Fide memoria rerum*, vol. I/1 (Rome, 1971); Jean Beckmann, "La Congrégation de la Propagation de la Foi

face à la politique internationale," *Neue Zeitschrift für Missionswissenschaft* 19 (1963): 241–71, esp. 245–51; P. Nicola Kowalsky, "Il testamento di Mons. Ingoli, primo segretario della Sacra Congregatione 'de Propaganda Fide,' " ibid., 272–83; Josef Grisar, "Francesco Ingoli über die Aufgaben des kommenden Papstes nach dem tode Urban VIII. (1644)," *Archivum Historiae Pontificiae* 5 (1967): 289–324.

13. *Lett.*, 326.

14. All biblical references will be to the Vulgate—*Biblia Sacra iuxta vulgatam versionem*, ed. Robert Weber (Stuttgart, 1969)—and in this particular instance to the Gallican version of the Psalms. Their English equivalents follow Douai-Rheims.

15. Luigi Firpo, "A proposito del *Quod Reminiscentur* di T. Campanella," *Giornale Critico della Filosofia Italiana* 21 (1940): 271–75. See also Firpo's *Bibliografia*, 153–57.

16. Here see especially the study by the editor of the *Theologia*, Romano Amerio, *Il sistema teologico di Tommaso Campanella* (Milan/Naples, 1972), and Giovanni di Napoli, *Tommaso Campanella filosofo della restaurazione cattolica* (Padua, 1947). While Amerio admits an earlier period of incredulity on Campanella's part, ending with a conversion in 1603, Di Napoli argues persuasively for his orthodoxy throughout and specifically against any juvenile period of waywardness. See his "L'eresia e i processi Campanelliani" in *Tommaso Campanella (1568–1639): Miscellanea di studi nel 4° centenario della sua nascita* (Naples, 1969), 169–258.

17. Nicola Badaloni, *Tommaso Campanella* (Milan, 1965), 284.

18. *Meta.* III, 110.

19. *QR*, 8.

20. *Meta.* III, 184.

21. *Meta.* III, 112.

22. *Meta.* III, 212.

23. *AT*, 109.

24. Luigi Amabile, *Fra Tommaso Campanella: la sua congiura, i suoi processi e la sua pazzia, narrazione con molti documenti . . .*, vol. 1 (Naples, 1882), 166n.

25. P[1], 37, sonnet 22, "Nella resurrezione di Cristo."

26. Blaise Pascal, *Les provinciales* (Cinquième Lettre) in *Oeuvres complètes*, ed. Jacques Chevalier (Paris, 1954), 705–6. See also Cummins, *Navarrete*, lxi, for the Jesuit reluctance to press the cross in their catechizing. And yet in America the great José de Acosta, SJ, will urge the teaching of the mystery of Christ first and foremost—Christ and *hunc crucifixum*. See *De procuranda indorum salute libri sex* (Cologne: Birckmann, 1596), 451.

27. Noteworthy is the measure of agreement shared by the Dominican Campanella with the Jesuits on many theological matters and on missionary practices. See Di Napoli, "Ecumenismo," 271–72, 283; *AV*, 118–19; *MS*, 148–49; *QR*, 55; and the citations of N. Bobbio in his edition of the *Città del sole* (Turin, 1941), 113. Their most significant disagreement is on education, where Campanella in his defense of the Piarists found the Jesuit program too "elitist." See his "Liber apologeticus contra impugnantes institutum scholarum piarum," ed. K. Jensen and A. K. Liebreich, *Archivum Scholarum Piarum* 8 (1984): 29–76, esp. 48–57.

28. *Lett.*, 93–95.

29. Ibid., 63.

30. *AT*, 72–75, 109, 126; *Meta.* III, 296.

31. *T*, XVIII, 168; cf. *T*, XXI, 10, 14, 32, 38.

32. *Meta.* III, 356, 358. Campanella continues to attribute to Justin Martyr the spurious *Confutatio dogmatum quorundam Aristotelicorum* (Migne P.L.6:1491–1564), wrongly assigned to San Giustina da Fozio but possibly the work of Diodorus of Tarsus. See *Op. in.*, 41, n. 4. For another example of Campanella's specific opting for the fathers prior to St. Augustine, see *MS*, 236.

33. *T*, XVIII, 106, 108; I, 357–59.

34. *Meta.* III, 346; but cf. *T*, XXX, 238 for a more orthodox statement.

35. *T*, XIII, 42, 44, 50, 58, 64, 70, 74.

36. Ibid., I, 364–66.

37. Ibid., XVIII, 30; XXVII, 16, 48, 50, 52, 110.

38. *AT*, 9–10; "Risposte alle censure dell 'Ateismo triunfato,'" in *Op. in.*, 12.

39. "Risp.," 11, n. 4: "opus certe aureum . . . dignum . . . quod ad totius reipublicae Christianae utilitatem in lucem prodeat."

40. Ibid., 16.

41. Ibid., 20.

42. Ibid., 31.

43. "Compendium" in *Op. in.*, 128–30.

44. On Vitoria and the *titulus naturalis societatis et communicationis*, see Anthony Pagden, "The School of Salamanca and the 'Affair of the Indies,'" *History of Universities* 1 (1981): 71–112, esp. 85; also the same author's "Dispossessing the Barbarian" in *The Languages of Political Theory in Early Modern Europe* (Cambridge, 1987), 79–98, esp. 81, 86–87, which shows how this capacity for communication, rooted in natural law, provides both *jus peregrinandi* and *jus praedicandi*. On Campanella's concept of language as an expansive, magical force in the service of both terrestial and celestial discovery, see the suggestive article by Dennis Costa, "Poetry and Gnosticism: The 'Poetica' of Tommaso Campanella," *Viator* 15 (1984): 405–18 at 409. *CS* (120–21) declares compass, press, and arquebus as the great *segni* of the imminent unification of the world.

45. *QR*, 221; *Meta.* I, 144, and *T*, XXIX, 89, for the philosophy of Aristotle as the proverbial worm in the stomach of man. Cf. also *Lett.*, 100, and the present author's "Tommaso Campanella and the End of the Renaissance," *Journal of Medieval and Renaissance Studies* 20 (1990): 172, n. 35. For a permutation of this important and recurring image, conveying a sense of the human condition as one of isolation and noncommunication, see sonnet 4, P^1, 16. For a similar contemporary view of China's isolation by a fellow Dominican, see Fr. Gregorio Garcia, OP, *Predicacion del evangelio en el nuevo mundo* (Baeça: Pedro de la Cuesta, 1635), who explains that Chinese edicts prohibited trade and communication with other nations, which accounts for the Chinese being unknown in the world and as if totally absconded *en su nido* until the navigation of the Portuguese and Castilians (fol. 49^v). It is interesting to note that by "New World" he understands China as well as America, *ambas Indias*, Oriental and Occidental (fol. 15^v). I am using here the John Carter Brown Library copy of this work.

46. *Meta.* I, 78–84. Geoffrey Atkinson, *Les nouveaux horizons de la Renaissance française*

(Paris, 1935), 255–61, quotes twenty-four separate European authors from the sixteenth century who cite the confirmation of antipodes, but largely either to celebrate the superiority of moderns to ancients or superior navigation. While there is a trace of the epistemological importance in N. Le Huen and Acosta, only Jacques Cartier in his *Brief Récit et succinte narration* (1545) specifically makes the point: "Experientia est rerum magistra." None apparently refer to Columbus and none sustain this appeal to experience and to Columbus as does Campanella in too many instances to cite. For an interesting analysis of some of the issues raised by the problem of the antipodes, see Valerie I. J. Flint, "Monsters and the Antipodes in the Early Middle Ages and the Enlightenment," *Viator* 15 (1984): 65–80. On Campanella's association of the eighth-century bishop of Salzburg with Columbus regarding the antipodes, see *T*, X/2, 198.

47. P[1], 100–101.

48. P[2], 353, 358.

49. P[3], 1037–38.

50. Ibid., 1128.

51. *MM*, 87.

52. *T*, I, 3.

53. Quoted in Amerio, *Il sistema teologico*, 140: " . . . in artibus humanis et scientiis fiunt quotidie homines sapientiores ob inventionem novarum rerum, unde excitamur in studiis ad profectus maiores. Profecto Lutherus et Columbus excitarunt philosophos et theologos de somno ignorantiae et negligentiae."

54. *T*, XXVII, 90, 92.

55. On the contemporary comparison of Columbus with Galileo, see the interesting article by Andrea Battistini, "'Cedat Columbus' e 'Vicisti, Galilaee!': due esploratori a confronto nell'immaginario barocco," *Annali d'Italianistica* 10 (1992): 116–32.

56. *MM*, 15.

57. *MS*, 279–80. The Amsterdam 1653 edition, used here for convenience, conforms to Elzevir's earlier 1640 and 1641 editions of this work.

58. *MS*, 71, 90, 162.

59. Perhaps J. H. Elliott's most succinct statement on these matters can be found in his *Revolt of the Catalans* (Cambridge, 1963), 179–87, 249–51.

60. *MS*, 271; cf. also *AP*, 40–41, 144, 232; *T*, XXVII, 128.

61. *T*, XXVII, 118–28. For the transfer of the Roman church to the New World and several other ideas that seem to parallel as well as anticipate Campanella, see Marcel Bataillon, "La herejía de Fray Francisco de la Cruz y la reacion antilascasiana," in *Études sur Bartolomé de Las Casas* (Paris, 1965), 309–24.

62. *T*, XXIX, 52. Cf. also ibid., IV/2, 186–88, and on the location of Abraham's bosom, ibid., XXI, 8, 44.

63. *AP*, 289–90. Given the fact that Pedro Fernández de Quirós was at this very time pursuing abortive efforts to define and claim *Terra Incognita Australis* for Spanish Catholicism (see note 64), Campanella was almost uncannily *au courant.*

64. *De procuranda Indorum salute* (Salamanca: Guillelmu[s] Foquel, 1589), bk. 2, chap. 8, 235–36. See also *La Australia del Espíritu Santo: The Journal of Fray Martin de Munilla*

O.F.M. and other Documents relating to the Voyage of Pedro Fernández de Quirós to the South Sea (1605–06) and the Franciscan Missionary Plan, ed. and trans. Celsus Kelly, OFM, vol. 1 (Cambridge, 1966), 17–18.

65. *QR*, 130, 179. The continuance and, even more specifically, the resumption of miracles in a missionary context find confirmation in the contemporary Catholic theology of Bellarmine and his associates, who consciously point to the contrasting evangelical quiescence of the Protestants, sitting by the fireside or lying in their warm beds "whilest the Jesuits go into barbarous countries to worke miracles." See D. P. Walker, "The Cessation of Miracles," in *Hermeticism and the Renaissance*, ed. Ingrid Merkel and Allen G. Debus (London and Toronto, 1988), 111–24, esp. 117–18.

66. *T*, X/3, 58.

67. Ibid., XXIV/1, 200–204. Although the American reference here is not specific, nevertheless it is fair to believe, given the centrality of children in the missionary practices of the religious orders in the New World, that the passage pertains as much to Amerindians as any heathens. On such evangelical tactics, see Richard Trexler, "From the Mouths of Babes: Christianization by Children in Sixteenth-Century New Spain," in *Religious Organization and Religious Experience*, ed. J. Davis (London and New York, 1982), 115–35.

68. *MS*, 282.

69. See note 15 above.

70. *QR*, 8–9, 14–15; Marquis, "Le traité missionnaire," 347–48. It is interesting to note that in his scholastically constructed *Theologia* he can take these same texts, John 10:16 and Ps. 21:28, and present a darker, more realistic appraisal of the world scene for missionaries as a scholastic objection to be eschatologically demolished: the greater part of the globe remains in ignorance of God and in idolatry; the same Hebrews continue to be apostate; the foul Moslems lord it over thirty kingdoms; the interiors of Asia, Africa, and all of America walk in darkness; while if the church has acquired much power over secular princes since its victory over the Roman Empire, still that power is not so great that it is able to subject without resistance all the realms of the earth. *T*, XXVII, 16.

71. *Lett.*, 191–92; Luigi Firpo, "Un memoriale inedito e un indice delle opere di Tommaso Campanella," *Rivista di Filosofia* 38 (1947): 213–29.

72. *QR*, 30; cf. also *Lett.*, 15–17; *AP*, 284–85. Emeric Crucé in his *Le nouveau Cynée* (Paris, 1623), 73, has been recognized as recommending a Society of Nations seated at Venice, convoking all monarchs of the earth, including the Great Turk. Campanella would seem to have anticipated Crucé in such a notion.

73. *QR*, 37.

74. On this issue, see Margaret T. Hodgen, *Early Anthropology in the Sixteenth and Seventeenth Centuries* (Philadelphia, 1964), 218ff. Robert Brerewood in his *Enquiries touching the diversity of languages and religions* (1614) observes the same quadripartite division of world religions as does Campanella. For the most recent comprehensive study of the theological implications, see Giuliano Gliozzi, *Adamo e il Nuovo Mondo* (Florence, 1977).

75. *QR*, 202–3. For *Quivira*, see Botero's *Le relatione universali*, which presents America under two headings—"Peninsula septentrional" and "Peninsula Austral" (fols. 217, 223, 238). With the former, Botero claims that Francisco Coronado in his northernmost explorations

in 1579 penetrated *El reyno de Quivira*, which would be identified broadly with the midwestern United States today. He describes this area as being not as populated and united as others (fols. 234ᵛ–235ᵛ). None of the Italian editions being available to me, I used a Spanish rendition: *Descripcion de todas las provincias y reynos del mundo* (Gerona: Caspar Garrich, 1622). On this Spanish translation and abridgment, see *European Americana*, ed. John Alden and Dennis C. Landis, vol. 2 (New York, 1982), 205 (#622/21).

76. *QR*, 217–18.

77. Ibid., 199–200. On the Lascasian parallel, see J. H. Elliott, *The Old World and the New, 1492–1650* (Cambridge, 1970), 48–50.

78. *QR*, 256.

79. In his "Documenta ad Gallorum Nationum" (1635), *Op. in.*, 95, Campanella specifically recommends the writings of Las Casas and Benzoni in order to appreciate the reduction of a people to ashes. Cf. also MN, 311–12. For evidence of his knowledge of Botero's *Relationi universali*, which he would have read before his long imprisonment, see *CS*, 129, n. 2, and 139, n. 72.

80. *QR*, 256. On presumed similarities among peoples, see Hodgen, *Early Anthropology*, 297–337.

81. *T*, IV/1, 16.

82. Gliozzi, *Adamo*, 356–67, esp. 361–63.

83. *QR*, 256–57; on the tougher evangelizing practices of the Dominicans, see Cummins's article cited in note 10 above.

84. *QR*, 258.

85. P^1, 308.

86. *DPI*, 158.

87. *QR*, 258–60.

88. Ibid., IV, 132.

89. Ibid., 260–61. On the devil as responsible for messing up the biblical monogenetic scheme in America especially and most of Africa, see *T*, XXVII, 48–52. For reiterations of this explanation by Robert Burton and by José de Acosta, see Hodgen, *Early Anthropology*, 219, 267, 302.

90. *QR*, 262. In a most curious passage, *QR*, 88, while addressing the non-Catholic Christian rulers, Campanella claims that the kingdom of Abyssinia, lacking iron and the art of smelting, shows a willingness to have armaments and ironware imported, hence as a means of promoting reunion since "petietis magistros in fide catolica et in arte ferraria et in caeteris, quibus Europaei abundamus." According to my colleague David Newbury, Meroe, near the Abyssinian capital of Axum, smelted and forged iron since the eighth century B.C., although the earlier productivity could well have fallen into desuetude by Campanella's time. Of the absence of iron, its manufacture, and use, however, in the pre-Columbian societies of America, we hear nothing!

91. *QR*, 263; cf. also *MM*, 36.

92. *MM*, 84–87.

93. *T*, X/3, 58.

94. On the harder mood at the end of the sixteenth century, see C. R. Boxer, *The Church*

Militant and Iberian Expansion, 1440–1770 (Baltimore and London, 1978), 18; see also J. H. Elliott, "Renaissance Europe and America: A Blunted Impact?," in *First Images of America: The Impact of the New World on the Old*, ed. Fredi Chiappelli, 2 vols. (Berkeley, 1976), 1:15–16. On contrasting models and strategies for conversion—persuasion versus coercion—entertained by the early and the sixteenth-century church, and the decisive presence of the state in opting for coercion, see Sabine MacCormack, " 'The Heart Has Its Reasons': Predicaments of Missionary Christianity in Early Colonial Peru," *Hispanic American Historical Review* 65 (1985): 443–66, esp. 463–64.

95. *MM*, 15.

KAREN ORDAHL KUPPERMAN

The Beehive as a Model for Colonial Design

Colonization of America forced English backers to think about the essential ingredients of their society in unprecedented ways, because successful planting required replication. Promoters of the earliest colonies, Roanoke in 1585 and the initial Virginia colonies in Maine and on the Chesapeake in 1607, had not anticipated such pressure because they had not expected true transplantation. The first projects were organized along military lines; planners assumed that army discipline could be transferred wholesale to the new environment. Promoters expected colonists to seek products of value, largely from trading with Indians, while living within a highly regimented society. What they learned was that such a regime could not be maintained except with the harshest discipline, and that if the rules were applied rigorously, no lucrative trade could be generated.

Investors learned, some more quickly than others, that only true colonies, re-creations of English society, could accomplish their goals. They were then forced to confront the most difficult questions of all: What were the fundamental elements of their own familiar society? What must be present in order for transplanted English men and women to work together effectively and contentedly? How could one create a commonwealth?

During the first fifty years of English colonization, from Ralegh's initial steps toward founding Roanoke in the early 1580s to the successful establishment of the puritan colony of Massachusetts Bay in 1630, promoters grappled with these questions. The early colonies provided plenty of examples of failure, but drawing their lessons, separating the fundamental from the merely accidental and seeing how to prevent recapitulation of mistakes, was far more difficult. In some cases later ventures dropped elements of earlier plans that we can now see were essential to success and included aspects that doomed their planters to suffering or failure. Only very slowly, largely through trial and error rather than theoretical advance, were the strands separated and the grounds of success made clear. These elements then stood out very starkly, rendering the colonies stripped-down versions of the parent society.

As they began to think about creating new societies, some theorists turned to the natural world for models of social organization. Early modern English men and women found raw nature uncongenial; the word "natural" meant undeveloped or, in the human case, a simpleton. "Artificial" was a word of highest praise.

One image from the natural world recurs again and again in the colonization literature, but this one, the image of the beehive as the perfect society, was beloved precisely because it presented a civil, unnatural model from nature. The beehive was an example of artifice in nature. It became a much-used metaphor for colonization because, although its meaning seemed clear, it was an extremely flexible model that contained many levels of meaning. The beehive was a model that could express what everybody knew to be true, even as knowledge was changing, thus creating a spurious sense of common assumptions.

Not only nature but the ancients as well pointed to this example. Ancient writers had originally cited the hive as the model for a perfect human society. Philemon Holland translated Pliny's natural history at the beginning of the seventeenth century, offering a detailed portrait of a regimented order. Pliny described the hive as waking together to "three big hums or buzzes," like the sound of a trumpet, and described the ordered industry of the hive: "Some are busie in building, other in plaistering and overcasting, to make all smooth and fine: some be at hand to serve the workemen with stuffe that they need; others are occupied in getting ready meat and victuals out of that provision which is brought in: for they feed not by themselves, but take their repast together, because they should both labour and eat alike, and at the same houre."[1] Virgil likewise celebrated these "great souls in little bodies" in their "miniature state."[2]

Endorsed by both ancient wisdom and nature, the hive seemed to offer a perfect model for colonization. Bee behavior provided a defense against the argument that colonization involved novelty. Just as bees swarmed from the overfull hive, English men and women should leave England, groaning under its heavy burden of overpopulation, for the good of the commonwealth. As John Cotton wrote: "Nature teacheth bees to doe so, when as the hive is too full, they seeke abroade for new dwellings: So when the hive of the Common-wealth is so full, that Tradesmen cannot live one by another, but eate up one another, in this case it is lawfull to remove."[3] Richard Hakluyt similarly pointed to the example of the "Grecians and Carthaginians of olde time" but wrote that, if his readers were still unconvinced of the lawfulness of colonization, "yet let us learne wisdome of these smal weake and unreasonable creatures."[4]

This unnatural example from nature did not endorse haphazard activity or individualistic striving. Bees moved out of the overfull hive in orderly swarms under the leadership of their "Captains," as Hakluyt pictured it. Strong leaders, predestined to that role by birth, and iron discipline kept the "painfull" bees to their appointed tasks. Thus, as Richard Eburne wrote in 1624, nature taught the "Amazonian Bees" and human beings alike "that we shall transgress the very order of Nature and neglect that instinct which is engraffed in all if we shall make such a removal without the conduct of such men as for their place and power, birth and breed, may be fit to order and rule, to support and settle the rest."[5]

THe Parliament is held, Bils and Complaints
Heard and reform'd, with ſeverall reſtraints
Of uſurpt freedome ; inſtituted Law
To keepe the Common-Wealth of Bees in awe

Frontispiece of John Day, *A Parliament of Bees* (London, 1641). The Pierpont Morgan Library, New York. PML 17571.

Without such strong leadership, the hive, like human society, would degenerate; the drones would multiply and devour the work of the others. England, for these writers, provided an example of just such a situation. Overpopulation and lack of opportunities for productive work had converted the people into drones, mere consumers, and "a Drone will in short space devoure more hony than the Bee can gather in a long time."[6] Such degeneration, a tragedy for the commonwealth, was social, not personal, in origin. As Sir William Vaughan wrote, "without Discipline, Our Bees turne Drones" and decline from "vertuous Thrift, To idlenesse, and basest shift."[7]

Bees thus provided a complex example; the hive was a society in which each painful (painstaking) member played a role. When all worked together the bees were rich in honey and the population swelled. The little commonwealth prospered. Order underlay all: the drones, though essential, must be controlled, and the workers must pursue their search steadily. Strong leadership was the key to this insect society's success; without "Master Bee" holding absolute authority, even the most populous hive would decline and fail.[8] Captain John Smith was celebrated as the man who saved the newly planted Jamestown by forcing every colonist, gentle or base, to work. He began the dedication of his *Description of New England* (1616) with this metaphor: "If the little Ant, and the sillie Bee seek by their diligence the good of their Commonwealth; much more ought Man. If they punish the drones and sting them steales their Labour; then blame not Man. Little hony hath that hive, where there are more Drones then Bees: and miserable is that Land, where more are idle then well imployed."[9]

Gabriel Plattes suggested the English should go to school with bees to understand how to erect a "well-ordered and flourishing Common-wealth."[10] The hive, as Richard Remnant wrote, was "a feminine Monarchy, and orderly Commonwealth, consisting of an amiable, loving and gentle Queen, and of proper, comely, able, attentive and diligent guard and commanders, with loyall and laborious, provident and valorous Commons: all worthy admiration, and serious observation."[11]

The regimentation of the hive, then, with all inhabitants going about their assigned tasks at the direction of central authority, seemed a perfect model for new societies in America; these new hive/commonwealths could even provide correctives for the ills of England itself.

The hive seemed to define the commonwealth: "They may well bee said to have a Common-wealth, since all that they doe is in common, without any private respect."[12] Plantation designers expected all the colonists to work in communal enterprises "without any private respect." Unfortunately, the early colonies did not thrive during the period of common work; backers thought the problem lay in colonists' lack of purpose. The solution that seemed obvious to promoters was to send great men, leaders with sufficient stature to overawe settlers and command

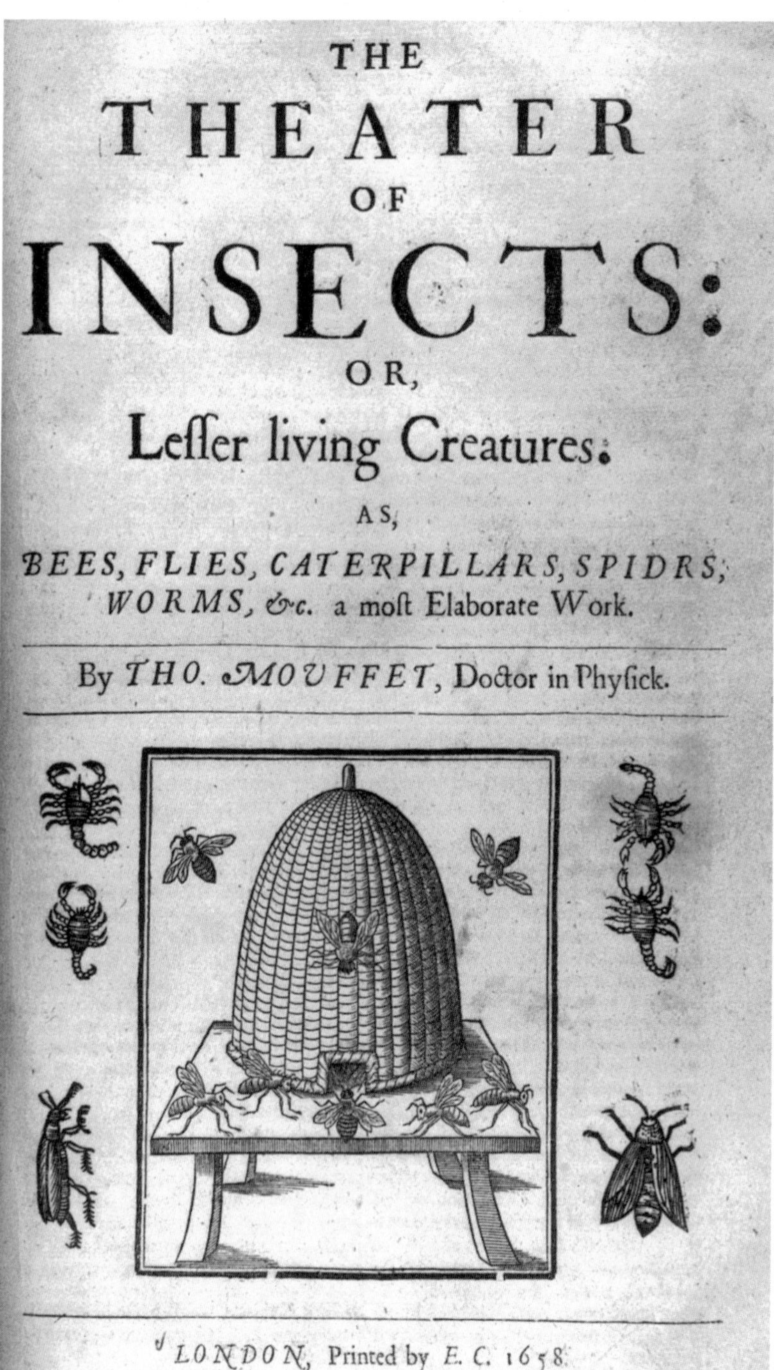

THE

THEATER

OF

INSECTS:

OR,

Leſſer living Creatures:

AS,

BEES, FLIES, CATERPILLARS, SPIDRS, WORMS, &c. a moſt Elaborate Work.

By *THO. MOUFFET*, Doctor in Phyſick.

LONDON, Printed by *E. C.* 1658.

Title page of Thomas Moffett, *The Theater of Insects* (London, 1658). Courtesy of the Trustees of the Boston Public Library.

obedience as the monarch of the hive does. Breeding set such men apart just as bees destined for positions of command were distinguished from "the vulgar" by special marks.[13] On such reasoning the Virginia Company sent Lord de la Warr to the floundering Jamestown colony in 1610. De la Warr, who traveled with "many gentlemen of quallety," no sooner landed than he "sett all things in good order."[14]

Unfortunately, life in the colony was too rough for one of de la Warr's gentle breeding. He described his encounter with the American environment as a series of hostile confrontations: he was "welcomed by a hote and violent Ague," after which "the Flux surprised me . . . then the Cramps assaulted my weak body with strong paines and afterwards the Gout," which so weakened his constitution that it "drew upon me the disease called the Scurvy; which though in others it be a sicknesse of slothfulnesse, yet was in me an effect of weaknesse, which never left me, till I was upon the point to leave the world."[15] Lord de la Warr returned to England and died in attempting to go back to Virginia in 1618. In 1619 the earl of Warwick, leader of one of the warring factions in the Virginia Company, was rumored to be considering going himself to Virginia to govern the colony; the report specified that not only had the colonists been warned, but Opechancanough, overlord of many tribes around the Chesapeake, had also been informed of the projected arrival of such a great noble.[16]

The assumption that the presence of a noble leader would save a venture by imparting a sense of purpose and focusing the people's energies pervades the early colonial period. Members of the Providence Island Company, when their West Indian experiment was at a low ebb in the later 1630s, decided that only the presence of leading puritan laymen could save that disordered society; the earl of Warwick again announced his intention to embark for America. The government of Charles I was so persuaded by this logic that it promised special favors to any Providence Island Company member who emigrated. In the event, however, none did.

Linked to the notion that great men could save the colonies was the assumption that disorder must be met with severe laws strictly enforced. Again the beehive provided the model. John Levett wrote: "These Master Bees are absolute in their authorities and commands, and out of a regall power or civill discipline answerable to our Marshall lawes, and as having a supreame prerogative above all the rest, he over-vieweth all that are within the compasse of his squadrons, he administreth Justice unto all, correcting the lazie, sloathfull, and disobedient, and giving honour and incouragement to those which are painefull, laborious and diligent."[17]

The Jamestown colony, begun in 1607, exemplified the difficulties of transplantation. Problems created by divided and wavering authority led to irresolution in the men; they died in alarmingly large numbers amidst the confusion. The problem was seen as inherent in the settlement's design. John Rolfe described the situation in early Virginia:

> The begynning of this Plantacion was governed by a President & Councell Aristocratycallie. The President yerely chosen out of ye Councell, which consisted of twelve persons. This government lasted above two yeres: in which tyme such envie, dissentions, and iarrs were daily sowen amongst them, that they choaked ye seedes and blasted the fruits of all mens labors. If one were well disposed and gave good advisement to proceed in the Busines: others out of the malice of their hartes would contradict, interdict withstand and dashe all. Some rung out and sent home to loud prayses of the riches & fertilenes of the Country, before they assaied to plant, to reape or search the same. Others sayd nothing; nor did any thing thereunto. All would be Keisars, none inferior to other. Some drew forward, more backward. The vulgar sort looked for Supplies out of England, neglected husbandry. Som wrote home, there was no want of food, yet sought for none. Others that would have sought could not be suffered: in which confusion, much confusion yerely befell them, and in this goverment happened all the mysery. Afterward a more absolute goverment was graunted Monarchally, wherein it still contynueth.[18]

Rolfe looked back from a time when early disorder had been replaced by control. His analysis was not unlike Richard Remnant's description of the fate of a hive that lost its queen: "Without one they cannot subsist, but are distract, disperst, wander and worke not, but come to nought and perish."[19] The most serious problem was motivating and controlling a large population of young men cut off from their own society and placed in a situation where no riches were forthcoming. Ralph Hamor described the improvident migrants as "no more sensible then beasts, would rather starve in idlenesse (witnesse their former proceedings) then feast in labour, did not the law compell them thereunto." Sir Thomas Dale, he wrote, had arrived in Jamestown in May 1611 to find the men at "their daily and usuall workes, bowling in the streets."[20]

In analyzing why Jamestown's settlers had failed so badly at replicating English society abroad, the Virginia Company concluded that the problem was diffusion of authority, their own failure to lodge adequate power in a leader of undeniable stature. As Robert Gray said in his 1609 book, *A Goodspeed to Virginia*, the "Magistrate must correct with al sharpenesse of discipline those unthriftie and unprofitable Drones, which live idly."[21] Arguing that under the original charter the settlement had degenerated "from civil Propryety to Naturall, and Primary Community," company members redesigned the colony's government along military lines, even for civilian colonists, and authorized harsh punishments for all violations. During the colony's "infancie," Virginia was to be ruled by a soldier-governor armed with "sole and absolute" power. The council was reduced to an advisory role. David Konig writes of the company's instructions to Governor Sir Thomas Gates that they were "a magna carta for baronial tyranny." Gates was urged "for capitall and

English sporting life in the New World, from Johann Theodor de Bry, *Grands Voyages*, pt. X (German) (Oppenheim, 1618). John Carter Brown Library.

Criminal Justice in Case of Rebellion and mutiny and in all such cases of present necessity, [to] proceede by Martiall lawe according to your commission as of most dispatch and terror and fittest for this governement and in all other causes of that nature as also in all matters of Civill Justice you shall finde it properest and usefullest for your governement to proceede rather as a Chauncelor then as a Judge rather uppon the natural right and equity then uppon the nicenes and letters of the lawe [(]which perplexeth in this tender body) rather then dispatcheth all Causes." Lord de la Warr was given similar instructions to follow "a Summary and arbitrary way of Justice mingled with discreet formes of Magistracy."[22]

The Virginia code of "Lawes Divine, Morall and Martiall" written under this regime called for a society of perfect regimentation, such as writers fancied the beehive to be. All colonists were to report to work at a drumbeat signal, akin to Pliny's three great hums or buzzes that alerted the hive, and were to continue working until the drum sounded again. Resistance was to be punished swiftly and severely. Colonists condemned once were "to lie upon the Guard head and heeles together all night, for the second time so faulting to be whipt, and for the third time to be condemned to the Gallies for a yeare." Every occupation was to be pursued with the same degree of dedication. Gardeners, cooks, bakers, or laundresses were slated to receive the most severe punishments for deviation from duty, and private trading with mariners carried the death penalty. Even hygiene was to be regulated; anyone failing to keep his house and the street before it "sweete and cleane" or whose bedstead was less than three feet off the ground would "answere the contrarie at a martiall Court."[23] Ralph Hamor, like John Rolfe, wrote in support of this regime, approving Dale's campaign to "reduce" the people "to good order, being of so il a condition as may well witnesse his severe and strict imprinted booke of Articles, then needefull with all severity and extremity to be executed."[24] But although stalwarts celebrated the harsh restoration of order, under this martial law Virginia barely held on for almost a decade, and the death rate remained high. The colony survived but did not flourish.

In calling for emigration of a noble leader whose presence alone could command respect, adventurers were implicitly conceptualizing a colony as analogous to an English county, the governor being comparable to the lord lieutenant. The lieutenants were the principal link between the counties and the central government in England. Operating under the royal prerogative, they carried out royal directives and maintained the peace. They were the link connecting the king and his privy council with the counties; information and opinions were gathered and disseminated by them and their deputies. Governors occupied a similar linking role between the colonists and the sponsoring company. Like the lieutenants, colonial governors were authorized to impose martial law in case of rebellion or invasion.

The analogy was problematic, however, because of discontent at home over the role of the lords lieutenant. Gentlemen throughout England viewed the Stuart monarchs' increasing reliance on the lieutenancy as usurping the local government roles of the gentry, and as symptomatic of the growth of prerogative government.[25] In conceptualizing their colony as a perfectly ordered beehive under the command of a strong ruler governing through martial law, the Virginia Company was defying the lessons of contemporary English experience, particularly popular resistance to regimentation. They sought a kind of orderliness in the colonies that was unrealistic for any English society.

Martial law was a particular irritant in England, especially as the government of Charles I imposed a military presence on the counties through forced billeting in the later 1620s. When Parliament met in 1628, members came with their pockets full of complaints about the soldiers billeted throughout the country and their flouting of the law. Claiming that the civil law had no jurisdiction over military men, the veterans recognized no authority but their own officers. In parliament Sir Edward Coke argued that martial law was not allowed in time of peace, "which is when the courts of Westminster are open." To those like Sir Henry Marten, who argued that common law and martial law could exist together, one for the civilian, the other for the soldier, Coke answered, "It is impossible: . . . If the soldier and the judge should sit both of one bench the drum would drown the voice of the crier."[26] The House of Lords debated the question of the relationship between the soldiers and the townspeople of Banbury, with the puritan colonial promoter William Fiennes, Lord Saye and Sele, pressing the case of the civilians. The debate culminated in a ruling by the Lord Keeper: "The soldiers . . . are not to be governed by a distinct lawe, but by the Law of the Kingdom and [he] charge[d] them to live Orderly according to the Law."[27] The Petition of Right summed up the nation's grievances in 1628, and it focused on four issues: forced loans, arbitrary imprisonment, billeting of soldiers on citizens, and the use of martial law.[28] Rank and file subjects hated these impositions. The gentry also disliked them because the entire military structure rested on the royal prerogative rather than on laws made by Parliament. English subjects resisted such concentration of power and the enforced orderliness that was its goal.

Promoters originally conceived overseas plantations as simplified versions of English society; they could be more orderly than the parent because they would not bring unproductive people and the complicating remnants of past social forms. Jamestown's experience demonstrated that a colony conceived as a regimented beehive could hold on, but also that such a model could never lead to creation of a genuinely thriving settlement in America as in England. That lesson was clear when, at the end of the 1620s, political and economic pressures combined to revive interest in attempting large-scale transplantation to America. What was still not obvious was just how English society should be constructed abroad.

The beehive offered models beyond regimentation. In fact, study of bees provided sophisticated lessons that might have prevented some of the early English failures in America and much of the misery. All English colonies before Massachusetts Bay in 1630 were founded with about one hundred settlers. That number may have been chosen in part because it resonated with ancient precedents—the Roman centurion and the ancient English administrative unit of the hundred. When the Virginia Company later introduced the possibility of privately owned and run settlements under the company umbrella, these "particular plantations" were called hundreds.[29] These small early colonies all experienced great hardship; some, such as those at Roanoke and Sagadahoc, failed entirely, and contemporaries blamed in part their small size. Richard Eburne argued in 1624 that ten or twelve thousand settlers should be sent annually to America in the founding period; the example of bees demonstrated that "the smallest swarms do seldom prosper but the greatest never lightly fail."[30]

Similarly, the society of the hive refuted the other fallacy of early colonization. Sending young men exclusively, mainly soldiers, doomed the plantations. In a seventeenth-century "newe plantation," wrote John Pory, secretary of the Virginia

Assembly, to the sponsoring company in London, "it is not knowen whether man or woman be more necessary."[31] Eburne, footnoting Charles Butler's treatise on bees, *The Feminine Monarchy* (1609), pointed out that the age profile of the swarm paralleled that of the parent hive. Eburne went on to argue that families made superior settlers. Six years later Massachusetts Bay, populated immediately by large numbers of all ages and both genders, would prove Eburne's arguments.[32] What participants and observers began to understand as they surveyed the first fifty years of English colonization was that only settlements that replicated essential structures of English life and offered prospective migrants incentives not available at home would succeed.

Two puritan colonies were founded in 1630: Massachusetts Bay in cold, rocky New England and Providence Island on a semitropical island off the coast of Nicaragua. The Massachusetts Bay Company was led by London merchants and county gentlemen, whereas the Providence Island Company comprised the greatest lay puritans in the land, puritan nobles and leading gentry. The founders of each, convinced that earlier ventures had been perverted by poor design and unworthy settlers, sought to create plantations that would avoid the mistakes of all previous plans. Each group of investors contained veterans of earlier companies, who knew the pitfalls. The design of the two colonies thus represents the culmination of fifty years of experience, but these adventurers drew quite different lessons from that experience.

As they studied the existing examples, neither group of puritan leaders found much worthy of emulation in planning their own settlements. We know the thinking of the Massachusetts Bay Company founders because of the various analyses that circulated to interested parties during the winter of 1629–30. John Winthrop's own statement has survived in his "Reasons to be considered for justifieinge the undertakeres of the intended Plantation in New England." In countering those who pointed to "the ill successe of other Plantations," he delineated their three "great and fundamentall errors": "their mayne end was Carnall and not Religious"; "they used unfitt instrumentes, a multitude of rude and misgovernd persons the very scumme of the Land"; "they did not establish a right forme of goverment."[33] The Providence Island investors agreed wholeheartedly with Winthrop's analysis.

Both puritan colonies believed that they had eliminated the first problem; both were established to secure the true reformed religion. They disagreed on the solution to the third, and neither could fully deal with the second. Massachusetts as much as Providence Island attracted undesirable elements, or found that uncertain circumstances brought out the worst in people. John Winthrop in Massachusetts complained in a letter to his wife, Margaret, about the behavioral changes in his colonists: "I thinke heere are some persons who never shewed so much wickednesse in England as they have doon heer." James Hopkins, vicar of

Great Wenham, Suffolk, advised Winthrop to ignore criticism and not to be discouraged by his colony's "hard beginninges," which represented God's testing, his urging to "cleve the closser unto him." Hopkins asserted that all plantations were "meane at the first," so New England's apparent failure at that early stage need not erase all hope. Even after five years of settlement, Reverend Nathaniel Ward of Ipswich, Massachusetts, wrote despairingly to John Winthrop, Jr., of the "multitudes of idle and profane young men, servants and others" that plagued the colony, so that many said "with greif we have made an ill change, even from the snare to the pitt."[34] Providence Island Company member Sir Benjamin Rudyerd wrote describing the situation in that colony at the same time that James Hopkins wrote to John Winthrop: "Wee well hoped (according to our Intentions) That wee had planted a Relligious Collonye in the Isle of Providence, instead whearof wee fynd the roote of bitterness plentifullye planted amongst you, an industrious supplanting one of another, and not a Man theare of Place (a straunge thinge to consider) but hee doth both accuse, and is accused; these are uncomfortable fruites of Religion."[35] Both settlements were plagued in their early years by disruptive colonists and unmet hopes.

Nothing is more strikingly different than the solutions the two groups of puritans offered to this key problem of how to control, focus, and motivate people in the colonial setting, how to make people behave as English men and women. The Massachusetts Bay Company planners differed from the Providence Island investors in that many of them intended to emigrate themselves. They argued that only cutting the colony off from supervision from England could allow it to begin to create an improved version of English society. Leaders made their own emigration conditional on the promise that the charter would be surrendered to them and company meetings would be held in New England.[36]

Events proved that decentralization, transferring control to America, led to success. Transportation of the Massachusetts Bay Company's charter had broken the link with the sponsors through the governor, who was no longer a lieutenant. Further devolution of authority occurred in the colony as the headright system, under which individuals who emigrated received land from the company, was transformed into a system in which land grants were made to towns, who then allotted land to their inhabitants.[37]

Where the Massachusetts Bay planters sought to correct the undeniable problems seen in Virginia and other colonies through transfer of control to America, the Providence Island adventurers argued that the only way to prevent perversion of purpose was to manage every aspect of the colony's life from London. They believed that the disorders and dereliction of previous colonists were the result of inattention or divided counsel among investors. For this reason, they refused merchants admission to their ranks, believing that only oversight by the right kind of people, whose eyes were always fixed on lofty goals rather than immediate gain, could lead to creation of a godly and purposeful English society abroad.

Colonies had to achieve two goals. One was to re-create the web of relationships on which government rested in England; the other was to instill a sense of purpose in the planters. The Providence Island Company believed these could be accomplished by sending the right kind of settlers, all committed to building a godly society, and by unified and enlightened guidance from London. In their desire to prevent the subversion of purpose they saw in other ventures, they disastrously misjudged the avenues leading to a strong and well-knit society. Massachusetts Bay's success would demonstrate how wrong the Providence Island Company had been.

The key to getting people to work together on common goals, paradoxically, was to allow them to work for themselves and their families. All first-generation English colonies that survived into the 1630s and became thriving enterprises—Virginia, Maryland, Bermuda, Barbados, Plymouth, Connecticut, Massachusetts Bay—promised land to settlers in something approaching outright ownership and allowed for protection of that property in a representative assembly to allocate general obligations. Families, made possible by the emigration of women, rendered individual efforts meaningful; passing an estate on to one's children was the goal of hard work and deferred gratification. Successful colonies also firmly placed the colonial militia under the control of leading planters. To those who feared military weakness, William Wood of New England answered with the hope that "when the Bees have Honie in their Hives, they will have stings in their tailes."[38] Once these institutional arrangements were in place, colonial development quickly and assuredly entered an accelerating phase that led to economic success and a strong sense of purpose.[39]

Virginia had begun to take the steps that would lead to such institutions after 1618, as the headright system guaranteed land to every emigrant and to those who imported them, and the Virginia Assembly held its first meeting in 1619. Soon, wrote Patrick Copland, the colonists were "busied in their Vocations as Bees in their Hives."[40] The Virginia militia was reorganized under civilian control after the great Indian attack of 1622. Although observers in England still saw only disarray as the death rate for newcomers remained high and the Virginia Company succumbed to a royal investigation in 1625, the ground had been prepared for Virginia's establishment; the pace of immigration increased and planters fell to tobacco cultivation with single-minded dedication.[41] Thereafter, every successful English colony followed this pattern.

Providence Island was the only colony that as late as the 1630s tried to adhere to a system based on direction from the top. Even more fundamental to Providence Island's failure was the system of landholding and government ordained by the adventurers. They insisted that colonists remain tenants—in the early years they were tenants at will—and that they share their proceeds with the investors. Under the first arrangement, half of their product was owed to the backers. Tenancy at halves had seemed an obvious arrangement to all colonial backers, who needed to find some way to repay the enormous costs of founding a colony, and it was tried in all settlements before 1630. It was always hated by settlers, and every successful colony moved to eliminate it; no colony was secure until tenancy was abandoned. In some colonies, such as Virginia, Bermuda, and Plymouth, the system was legislated away. In others, such as Maryland and Barbados, tenancy remained on the books, but the planters operated as freeholders because backers were too weak to enforce the arrangement.

Only in Providence Island, because of the investors' meticulous attention to detail and commitment to control, did the tenancy arrangement continue. The company did slowly retreat from the original terms and made the sharecropping arrangement more favorable to the planters, while also agreeing to offer leases. The investors were disgusted by endless wrangling among the leading planters, and this confirmed them in their belief that autonomy for the colony would lead to chaos. But they never understood that the conflict for which they felt such scorn was actually the inevitable outcome of their control of the colony's economic and political life. In England, as Cynthia Herrup has shown, most disputes or even minor crimes never entered the legal system; they were settled by a process of arbitration in which gentry acted as mediators.[42] Because the leading planters on Providence Island were kept in a dependent status, they were unable to act in that character. Thus the company denied the planters the attributes of leaders while demanding that they fulfill the obligations of that role. The grandees in England never understood that the purposeful activity of the hive must be generated from within it.

What is fascinating about this denial is that the Providence Island adventurers are the famous "Middle Group" in the Long Parliament.[43] The principal members were well known in their own time and to history because of their roles in Parliament and in the English Civil War of the 1640s: John Pym and Oliver St. John, the earls of Warwick and Manchester, Sir Benjamin Rudyerd, Sir Nathaniel Rich, Sir Thomas Barrington, Lord Saye and Sele and Lord Brooke, and Richard Knightley. Conrad Russell has demonstrated that these men sought not just to protect their own ability to live and worship as puritans, but to establish the reformed religion securely in England and to give the monarch the resources to take up England's historic destiny at the head of the Protestant nations.[44] They are the men traditionally credited with destroying a tyrannical monarchy and attempting to create the foundations of a liberal order in England. More recently, historians such as Ann Hughes, Richard Cust, and William Hunt have demonstrated that they were extremely effective political leaders in their counties and seemed to understand better than most the bases of English government.[45]

In their resistance to Stuart attempts at unparliamentary taxation, they demonstrated clear understanding that the subjects' right to independence and security as property holders underlay the English system of government. Sir Nathaniel Rich's House of Commons speech on the forced loan forcefully enunciated the association between a sound economy and rights of ownership: "No propriety, no industry; no industry, all beggars; no propriety, no valor; no valor, all in confusion." John Pym made this connection in speeches before and after Parliament's suspension during the 1630s, the decade through which the Providence Island colony struggled: "For who will contend, who will endanger himself for that which is not his own?"[46] But the Providence Island colony occupied an ambiguous position. Although it was designed as a replica of English society, the island and its resources were owned by the investors, whose own property rights required protection. Moreover, company members never understood that, in fearing the consequences of devolution and in resisting settlers' demands for autonomy, they undermined the colonists' natural urge to create a productive society.

Providence Island Company investors avoided transfer of control to colonists because they continued to believe that plantations left to their own devices would degenerate. They did not learn the lessons from experience that led to success in other settlements. Thus their colony barely held on through the decade in which English settlements in America became secure through massive emigration. Once the basic institutions that seemed to ensure an independent sufficiency for planters and their families were in place, thousands of English men and women were prepared to remove across the ocean; some sixty-nine thousand emigrated during the crucial decade after 1630.[47] Economic distress and a lack of places on English land coincided with fear that the royal government intended to force the nation into a dramatically restricted range of religious experience. The combination created willingness to take the drastic step of removal.

Adverse economic conditions had been building in England from the late sixteenth century. William Symonds, in a very influential sermon sponsored by the Virginia Company, had spoken movingly of his England, where the "mightier like old strong bees thrust the weaker, as younger, out of their hives." He painted a heartrending picture of a countryside devoid of opportunity, where enclosing landlords converted thriving townships "to a shepheard and his dog," and rich shopkeepers ground the faces of the poor. To all the dispossessed he recommended America: "Take the opportunity, good honest labourers which indeede bring all the hony to the hive, God may so blesse you, that the proverbe may be true of you, that *A May swarme, is worth a kings ransome.*"[48]

As experience accrued, colonial promoters increasingly began, like Symonds, to write of the hive as a society in which workers willingly engaged in productive activity rather than being compelled to orderly labor. This theme focused on America's attraction for ordinary English men and women frustrated by lack of opportunity at home and even stressed the deleterious role played by some great men. All these books, with their analyses of England's problems and hopes for formation of perfected old world societies abroad, were published in England for English consumption. In this way the colonial venture taught lessons to Europe.

Some writers even questioned the scorn heaped on the drones and saw them instead as victims of an unproductive society. Charles Butler devoted the third chapter of his *Historie of Bees* to the drones. Although they were usually thought to be mere consumers, putting on a great show but performing no useful function, he wrote, the drone is actually the male bee, necessary for breeding. Pliny, available in English translation from 1601, had argued that the drones, "unperfect bees, and the last fruit of such old ones as are weary and able to do no more good," are forced to do all the "drudgery" for the hive and are "to say a truth, no better than slaves to the right bees indeed." Yet, Pliny argued, the drones added to the increase of the hive and were valuable.[49] Modern studies have delineated the drones' reproductive role. All the disciplined gathering, storing, and building by bumblebee workers, according to Bernd Heinrich, is directed to one aim, the hive's product: the queens and drones who will allow the hive to reproduce itself. Without the drones, and the capacity to replicate itself, the hive is a failure.[50]

Only a trickle of colonists answered Symonds's early call, but the analogy of colonization to emptying the over-full and unproductive hive continued to seem relevant. Richard Ligon urged men with strength and resources to come to Barbados, where they could build their own fortunes and help other poor men and women, rather than stay unproductively at home: "Every drone can sit and eate the Honey of his owne Hive."[51] William Bullock urged planters not to rely on servants tricked or pressed into emigrating, "which sends Drones to the Hive, in stead of Bees." Rather, they should take "stout Labourers and good Worke-men" and pay them wages—£3 to £10 a year. The ability to create a stake "keeps a servant in heart," and Bullock calculated that even at the lower wage a servant in Virginia could invest in a cow and some vendible commodities and have £60 by the time his term was up. Then "he may see himselfe fit to wooe a good man's daughter."[52]

As England's economic situation worsened, and as the opportunities offered ordinary emigrants became more secure, this reasoning was irresistible to many. Even within the colonies the process of hiving off, forming new societies, continued. Cotton Mather wrote in his *Magnalia Christi Americana* of the ironic effects of Massachusetts Bay's success: "It was not long before the Massachuset Colony was become like an Hive overstock'd with Bees; and many of the new Inhabitants entertained thoughts of swarming into Plantations extended further into the Country."[53]

But for those who planned colonies and those who went to them the beehive's conceptual role had changed, and with it basic notions about how government worked in England. Although it continued to be a rhetorical device, the regimentation of the hive receded as a model and was replaced by a new, more sophisticated reading that derived from American experience. Just as bees swarmed from the over-full hive to take up productive roles in a new model of the old hive, a new plantation was indeed like a swarm.[54] As a replica of the parent hive it was not an extension, but a separate society. Legitimacy within these communities was not the product of transferred status from English hierarchies but grew out of relationships within the colony. Investors who allowed this devolution to happen, or were too weak to prevent it, sponsored successful colonies. Crèvecoeur, writing at the close of the colonial period, renewed these themes, remarking of his bees, "It is in freedom that they work." He argued that America attracted Europe's "poor and middling" and that "here they are become men." Comparing the diligence and productivity of Nantucket's householders to a well-ordered hive, he remarked on the absence of "the servility of labour which I am informed prevails in Europe."[55] Rank and file settlers, given the chance to be productive and to keep the product of their labor, took on the dedication and industry of the worker bees. The drones of England became the workers of America.

NOTES

1. Pliny, *The Historie of the World: commonly called the naturall Historie of C. Plinius Secundus*, trans. P. Holland (London, 1601), published as *Pliny's Natural History: A Selection from Philemon Holland's Translation*, ed. J. Newsome (Oxford, 1964), 125–26.

2. Virgil, *The Georgics*, trans. Robert Wells (Manchester, 1982), Georgic 4, 79–82. I thank Sabine MacCormack for calling the ancient tradition of beehive as model to my attention.

3. John Cotton, *God's Promise to His Plantation* (London, 1630), 9.

4. Richard Hakluyt, "Epistle Dedicatorie" to Philip Sidney, in *Divers voyages touching the discoverie of America* (London, 1582). See also Richard Eburne, *A Plain Pathway to Plantations* (1624), ed. Louis B. Wright (Ithaca, 1962), 32, 41.

5. Hakluyt, "Epistle Dedicatorie" to *Divers voyages*; Eburne, *Plain Pathway*, 102.

6. Robert Gray, *A Goodspeed to Virginia* (London, 1609), D3^{v}.

7. Sir William Vaughan, *The Newlanders Cure* (London, 1630), 103.

8. John Levett, *The Ordering of Bees* (London, 1634), 66–69. Timothy Raylor points out the difficulties posed by the absolutist implications of this analogy in mid-seventeenth-century England; see "Samuel Hartlib and the Commonwealth of Bees," in *Culture and Cultivation in Early Modern England: Writing and the Land*, ed. Michael Leslie and Timothy Raylor (Leicester, 1992), 91–129, esp. 105–15. See also J. P. Somerville, *Politics and Ideology in England, 1603–1640* (London, 1986), 46–48. I thank Walter Woodward for bringing Raylor's essay to my attention.

9. John Smith, *Description of New England* (1616), in *The Complete Works of Captain John*

Smith, ed. Philip L. Barbour, 3 vols. (Chapel Hill, 1986), 1:311. "Sillie" meant simple or unsophisticated.

10. Gabriel Plattes, *A Discovery of Infinite Treasure, Hidden Since The Worlds Beginning* (London, 1639), sig. C2v, 60–62 (62 is erroneously labeled 66).

11. Richard Remnant, *A Discourse or Historie of Bees; Their Nature and usage, and the great profit of them* (London, 1637), chap. 3. The gender of the commanding bee was in dispute in the early modern period.

12. Charles Butler, *The Historie of Bees. Shewing Their admirable Nature, and Properties, Their Generation, and Colonies; Their Government, Loyaltie, Art, Industrie, Enemies, Warres, Magnanimitie, &c.*, 2d ed. (London, 1623), Bv. This book was originally published under the title *The Feminine Monarchy* (London, 1609). On its political implications, see Kevin Sharpe, *Politics and Ideas in Early Stuart England: Essays and Studies* (London and New York, 1989), 52–54.

13. Butler, *Historie of Bees*, B2v–B3.

14. George Percy, "A Trew Relacyon of the Procedeinges and Ocurrentes of Momente which have hapned in Virginia from the Tyme Sir Thomas Gates was shippwrackte uppon the Bermudes anno 1609 untill my departure outt of the country which was in anno Domini 1612," *Tyler's Quarterly Historical and Genealogical Magazine* 3 (1922): 270.

15. Lord de la Warr, *The Relation of the Right Honourable the Lord De-La-Warre, Lord Governour and Captaine Generall of the Colonie, planted in Virginea* (London, 1611), A4–A4v. On the belief that scurvy proceeded from moral weakness and laziness, see Karen Ordahl Kupperman, "Apathy and Death in Early Jamestown," *Journal of American History* 66 (1979): 24–40.

16. "A Declaracion made by the Counsell for Virginia and Principall Assistants for ye Sumer Ilandes," 7 May 1623, in *Records of the Virginia Company of London*, ed. Susan Myra Kingsbury, 4 vols. (Washington, D.C., 1906–35), 2:404–5.

17. Levett, *Ordering of Bees*, 68.

18. John Rolfe, *A True Relation of the state of Virginia lefte by Sir Thomas Dale Knight in May last 1616* (New Haven, 1915), 34–35.

19. Remnant, *Discourse of Bees*, chap. 3.

20. Ralph Hamor, *A True Discourse of the Present Estate of Virginia* (London, 1615), 2, 26.

21. Gray, *Goodspeed*, D3v.

22. Virginia Company, *A True and Sincere Declaration of the Purpose and End of the Plantation Begun in Virginia* (London, 1610), 6–12; "Instructions orders and constitucions by way of advise sett downe declared and propounded to Sir Thomas Gates knight Governor of Virginia and of the Colony there planted," May 1609, in Kingsbury, *Records of the Virginia Company*, 3:15; and "Instructions orders and constitucions by way of advise sett down declared propounded and delivered to Sir Thomas West knight Lo. La Warr Lo. Governor and Capten Generall of Virginea," [1609/10?], ibid., 27–28. David Konig, "Colonization and the Common Law in Ireland and Virginia, 1569–1634," in *The Transformation of Early American History: Society, Authority, and Ideology*, ed. James A. Henretta, Michael Kammen, and Stanley N. Katz (New York, 1991), 70–92, quote 83.

23. William Strachey, *For the Colony in Virginea Britannia. Lawes Divine, Morall and*

Martiall, etc. (London, 1612), 2, 12–15, 17, 32. Strachey says the laws were established in early summer of 1610 and were "exemplified and enlarged" by Sir Thomas Dale on 22 June 1611. See also Darrett B. Rutman, "The Virginia Company and Its Military Regime," in *The Old Dominion: Essays for Thomas Perkins Abernethy*, ed. Darrett B. Rutman (Charlottesville, 1964), 1–20, and Warren M. Billings, "The Transfer of English Law to Virginia, 1606–1650," in *The Westward Enterprise: English Activities in Ireland, the Atlantic, and America, 1480–1650*, ed. K. R. Andrews, N. C. Canny, and P. E. H. Hair (Liverpool, 1978), 217. A particularly illuminating discussion is offered by Stephen Greenblatt, "Martial Law in the Land of Cokaigne," in his *Shakespearean Negotiations: The Circulation of Social Energy in Renaissance England* (Berkeley, 1988), 129–63, esp. 148–55.

24. Hamor, *True Discourse*, 27. See the discussion of the ambiguity embedded in the word "reduce" in the introduction to this volume.

25. On these issues, see Anthony Fletcher, *Reform in the Provinces: The Government of Stuart England* (New Haven, 1986).

26. *Commons Debates, 1628*, ed. Robert C. Johnson et al. (New Haven, 1977), 449–50, 545, 554–55, 558–60.

27. *Lords Debates, 1621, 1625, 1628*, ed. Frances Helen Relf, Camden Society 42 (London, 1929), 72–78; Conrad Russell, *Parliaments and English Politics, 1621–1629* (Oxford, 1979), 335–37, 359. See also Richard Cust, *The Forced Loan and English Politics, 1626–1628* (Oxford, 1987), 57.

28. The Petition of Right is printed in *The Stuart Constitution, 1603–1688: Documents and Commentary*, 2d ed., ed. J. P. Kenyon (Cambridge, 1986), 68–71. On the grievances stirred by billeting and martial law, see Russell, *Parliaments and English Politics*, 344–46, 380; Lindsay Boynton, "Martial Law and the Petition of Right," *English History Review* 79 (1964): 255–84; Lois G. Schwoerer, *"No Standing Armies!": The Antiarmy Ideology in Seventeenth-Century England* (Baltimore, 1974), chap. 2; and E. S. Cope, "Politics without Parliaments," *Huntington Library Quarterly* 45 (1982): 272.

29. James Muldoon pointed out to me the ancient precedents for one hundred as an effective unit.

30. Eburne, *Plain Pathway*, 110.

31. John Pory, "A Reporte of the Manner of Proceeding in the General Assembly convened at James City," 31 July 1619, in Kingsbury, *Records of the Virginia Company*, 3:160.

32. Eburne, *Plain Pathway*, 142. Butler's treatise was reissued in 1623 with the title *The Historie of Bees. Shewing Their admirable Nature, and Properties, Their Generation, and Colonies; Their Government, Loyaltie, Art, Industrie, Enemies, Warres, Magnanimitie, &c.* His description of the swarm's composition in this second edition occurs at sig. I3–I3[v]. Like John Levett, Butler praised bees for their loyalty to their rulers and their willingness to work at their appointed tasks for the good of the commonwealth; see B[v], B3, C4.

33. John Winthrop, "Reasons to be Considered," 1629, in *Winthrop Papers*, 6 vols. to date (Boston, 1929–92), 2:138–45, quotes 142–43.

34. John Winthrop to Margaret Winthrop, 23 July 1630, *Winthrop Papers*, 2:303; James Hopkins to John Winthrop, 25 February 1633, ibid., 3:105–7; Nathaniel Ward to John Winthrop, Jr., 24 December 1635, ibid., 215–17.

35. Sir Benjamin Rudyerd to Providence Island Governor Philip Bell, 1633, Bermuda Archives, Acc. 51.

36. Winthrop, "Reasons to be Considered," *Winthrop Papers*, 2:142–43; "The true coppie of the Agreement of Cambridge, August. 26. 1629," ibid., 151–52.

37. Darrett B. Rutman, *Winthrop's Boston: A Portrait of a Puritan Town, 1630–1649* (Chapel Hill, 1965), 40–46; Virginia Anderson, *New England's Generation: The Great Migration and the Formation of Society and Culture in the Seventeenth Century* (Cambridge, 1991). On the definition of the term "inhabitants," see John Frederick Martin, *Profits in the Wilderness: Entrepreneurship and the Founding of New England Towns in the Seventeenth Century* (Chapel Hill, 1991), 218–24, 277–85.

38. William Wood, *New Englands Prospect* (London, 1634), 54.

39. For the transition to landownership and participatory government in contemporary colonies, see Karen Ordahl Kupperman, *Providence Island, 1630–1641: The Other Puritan Colony* (Cambridge, 1993), 123–26.

40. Patrick Copland, *Virginia's God Be Thanked* (London, 1622), 10.

41. See W. F. Craven, *The Dissolution of the Virginia Company: The Failure of a Colonial Experiment* (New York, 1932), chap. 3, and Edmund S. Morgan, *American Slavery—American Freedom: The Ordeal of Colonial Virginia* (New York, 1975), chap. 5.

42. Cynthia Herrup, *The Common Peace: Participation and the Criminal Law in Seventeenth-Century England* (Cambridge, 1987), 54, 85–88.

43. On the Middle Group, see J. H. Hexter, *The Reign of King Pym* (Cambridge, Mass., 1941); Christopher Thompson, "The Origins of the Politics of the Parliamentary Middle Group, 1625–1629," *Transactions of the Royal Historical Society*, 5th ser., 22 (1972): 71–86; and Valerie Pearl, "Oliver St. John and the 'Middle Group' in the Long Parliament," *English Historical Review* 81 (1966): 490–519.

44. Conrad Russell, "The Parliamentary Career of John Pym," in *The English Commonwealth, 1547–1640*, ed. Peter Clark, Alan G. R. Smith, and Nicholas Tyacke (New York, 1979), 147–65; Russell, *Parliaments and English Politics.*

45. Ann Hughes, *Politics, Society, and Civil War in Warwickshire, 1620–1660* (Cambridge, 1987); Cust, *Forced Loan*; and William Hunt, *The Puritan Moment: The Coming of Revolution in an English County* (Cambridge, Mass., 1983).

46. Sir Nathaniel Rich, Speech of 26 March 1628, BL Stowe MS 366, fols. 20^{v}–21. The Pym quote is from his Speech on the Impeachment of Roger Manwaring, 4 June 1628, in Kenyon, *The Stuart Constitution*, 15–16; see also John Pym, Speech to the Short Parliament, 5 April 1640, *A speech delivered in parliament, by a worthy member thereof, and a most faithfull well-wisher to the church and common-weale; converning the grievances of the kingdome* (London, 1641), 36 (incorrectly numbered 26).

47. Henry A. Gemery, "Emigration from the British Isles to the New World, 1630–1700: Inferences from Colonial Populations," in Paul Uselding, ed., *Research in Economic History: A Research Annual*, no. 5 (1980): 179–231, esp. 215.

48. William Symonds, *Virginia. A Sermon Preached at White-Chappel* (London, 1609), 19–22. Richard Eburne also compared inmates, those living in the houses of others rather than setting up for themselves, to drones (*Plain Pathway*, 92–93).

49. Newsome, *Pliny's Natural History*, 127.

50. Bernd Heinrich, *Bumblebee Economics* (Cambridge, Mass., 1979), 16–17, 95–97, 144–45; C. R. Ribbands, *The Behaviour and Social Life of Honeybees* (London, 1953), 64–65, 142–43, 255–59.

51. Richard Ligon, *A True and Exact History of the Island of Barbadoes* (London, 1657), 108.

52. William Bullock, *Virginia Impartially examined, and left to publick view* (London, 1649), 52–53.

53. Cotton Mather, *Magnalia Christi Americana* (London, 1702), 23.

54. On colonization as a swarming, see Alfred W. Crosby, "Ecological Imperialism: The Overseas Migration of Western Europeans as a Biological Phenomenon," *The Texas Quarterly* 21 (1978): 10–22.

55. J. Hector St. John Crèvecoeur, *Letters From an American Farmer* (London, 1782), 33, 50, 72, 172. In a note to the first letter, he remarks that many of the essays were written before the beginning of the rupture between England and its American colonies (ibid., 7).

Part IV

America and the Scholarly Impulse

HENRY LOWOOD

The New World and the European Catalog of Nature

Introduction

Managing new information has been a challenge for naturalists since the first stirrings of the Scientific Revolution. By the beginning of the seventeenth century, trickles of scientific news swelled to a flood bearing everything from new stars to strange beasts and exotic plants. The danger of drowning under these discoveries could have been approximately measured in botany, to take one example, by a sounding of the plant kingdom in terms of its growing number of types. In the middle of the sixteenth century, the German herbalist Leonhart Fuchs listed roughly five hundred plants in his great herbal; this was about the number Dioscorides knew.[1] Fuchs recorded the existence of more than one hundred plants found in Germany, although he continued to work with the catalog of Mediterranean plants established by the ancient writers. Just eighty years later, the University of Basel's assiduous professor of anatomy and botany, Caspar Bauhin, described some six thousand plants in his *Pinax*, a twelvefold increase over Fuchs's compilation.[2] After another eighty years had passed, the English botanist John Ray compiled his catalog of nearly twenty thousand plants at the end of the seventeenth century, thereby summarizing the current state of botanical knowledge. The flow of new discoveries and observations thus multiplied the botanical inventory by forty in about 150 years. This impressive rate of growth made it difficult for many botanists to cope with the augmentation of knowledge in their field. Ray's able contemporary, Joseph de Tournefort, concluded that botanists would have to reorganize their subject in the face of such fecundity; he proposed a *retranchement* of botanical systematics reorienting it toward a higher taxonomic unit, the genus, in order to once again reduce the number of basic types to about six hundred.[3] Eighteenth-century naturalists sought systems of nomenclature and taxonomy primarily as a means of intellectually harnessing nature's plenitude.

Looking backward from our vantage point, it is evident that exploration of the New World added momentum to the accelerating pace of knowledge about the natural world. The French botanist Alphonse de Candolle considered the discovery of America to be "the last great event which caused the diffusion of cultivated plants into all countries," a sentiment shared by many naturalists concerned, like Candolle, with the "dispersion of useful plants" around the globe.[4] Knowledge was dispersed as well. Activities such as collecting, describing, naming, and cultivating New World plants left many traces in the typical botanical garden or *hortus siccus*, and they touched every kind of botanical writing. It is not difficult to find illustrations of several varieties of tobacco, tomatoes, peppers, maize, and other plants in the sixteenth century, beginning with the first picture of maize in a botanical book, the splendid woodcut made from a living specimen for Fuchs's herbal of 1542. Animals from the New World did not have the same impact on European zoological activity that its potentially useful plant life had on herbalists and botanical writers, but neither were they neglected, and sloths, alligators, armadillos, and many kinds of fish and fowl can all be found lurking in books published before 1600. The European writers who turned their attention to American plants and animals extracted original observations from various sources and then sought to interpret and organize them by adapting the methods with which they edited, revised, and commented upon the botanical and zoological writings of antiquity.[5] The steady inflow of reports from present-day Turkey, the Middle East, North Africa, and Asia also contributed novel observations to these projects. It is safe to say that these parts of the world were in fact more familiar than America to European writers of the sixteenth century, given the economic importance of Eastern overland trade and the steady Portuguese intrusion along the African coast into Asia. A few of them had traveled far and wide themselves in order to get a glimpse of plants noticed by Pliny or Dioscorides or had spent time at remote colonial outposts.[6] The quantitative explosion of information from all these sources challenged writers, illustrators, and printers to compile the catalog of nature, that is, to find techniques for presenting timely accounts of recent discoveries, while also assimilating and organizing a vast, rapidly growing body of reports. Books would gradually change accordingly, both in appearance and content, as verbal precision became more precious and folios crammed with full-page illustrations grew more expensive with each new discovery.[7]

Despite all of this activity and interest, the assimilation of early accounts of nature in the New World lagged behind other efforts to gather and digest information about the living world. Those who crossed the ocean occasionally remarked upon the flora and fauna they saw, sometimes even recording observations with purpose and clarity, but the authoritative descriptions of plants and animals generally appeared only in the works of authors who had never been to America. The greatest concentration of images and texts communicating information about nature in the New World appeared in the *res herbaria*, the scholarly writings of the Renaissance herbalists. The economic importance of medicinal herbs, spices, edible plants, and foodstuffs; the relative ease of transporting botanical specimens and planting preserved seeds; and the centrality of herbal writings in the medical literature were among the factors that turned the attention of medical doctors, in particular, to the world inventory of plants.[8] And in these writings, particularly in the well-defined botanical tradition of the herbalists, sixteenth-century Europeans rarely confronted the New World head-on. They hardly cited the literature of exploration and passed over the voyages of discovery in silence. Descriptions of American plants, even those accompanied by lifelike woodcuts, often failed to mention New World habitats and origins. Sometimes they relocated these plants to better-known parts of the world. The prefaces and dedications of herbals mentioned humanists like Fuchs, Gesner, and Ruelle, whose task had been "elucidating Hippocrates, Dioscorides, Galen"; praised the founders of botanical gardens, such as Luca Ghini, for creating places where one could find an "infinity of rare plants"; and extolled the virtues of patrons willing to sponsor these enterprises.[9] But for the most part, these paeans to the achievements of contemporaries were silent on the exploration of the New World. Unconsciously perhaps, the acknowledged geographical expansion of nature could be assimilated in terms of the spatially confined local activities of European writers; chronicles of the exploration of America, let alone the act of discovery itself, seemed to have no place in the mainstream of the Renaissance *res herbaria*, judging from the herbalists' condensed versions of its history. The relationship among original eyewitness accounts, what they reported, and reports derived from them in European books remains to be sorted out for the botanical and zoological catalogs of nature in the first century or so after the discovery, but it is not too early to raise a few historical issues. How were observations recorded, preserved, and transported to Europe? Were they typically published in their original form, and if so, how rapidly? What means existed for the rapid printing of new observations and their integration into systematic works? What roles were played by publishers, as well as compilers and artists chosen by them, in depicting, summarizing, and presenting these observations? Were illustrations an important part of this process of communication? While I do not propose to answer all of these questions in this essay, perhaps I can sketch out a few relevant themes.

Scott Atran, in his illuminating study of the cognitive foundations of natural history, has located the important innovations of the Italian, German, and Flemish botanists of the sixteenth and early seventeenth centuries in a rejuvenated respect for local data and folk knowledge of plants. Until then, according to Atran, scholastic naturalists took it for granted that local flora and fauna could be fully described in terms of the types fixed by ancient writers to deal with Mediterranean plants and animals. Fuchs, Otto Brunfels, Jerome Bock, and other herbalists active in the sixteenth century broke away from this tradition by paying attention to local flora, sometimes retaining ancient names and types, sometimes noting differences, while generally easing the constraint that plants enumerated by Theophrastus or Dioscorides ought to be represented in central Europe. It was, argues Atran, precisely the search for a new correspondence of ancient and local data that "prodded the herbalists to fix a medium of communication and to establish a shared repository of data about the living world."[10] This program meant transcribing local knowledge and communicating it across time and space through a variety of techniques and technologies: herbaria, gardens, woodcuts, and printed books. Atran's important contribution is the notion that systematic taxonomy grew gradually out of local discoveries followed by the comparison and integration of empirical data. In other words, he recasts the usual opposition of folk knowledge and system, concluding that the goal of an overarching "worldwide system" rose out of efforts to express local material more or less uniformly for the purposes of comparison and identification.

Atran's thesis strikes me as plausible and stimulating. Extended to New World natural history, it suggests that the incorporation of American beasts and plants into the catalog of nature repeated a problem European naturalists encountered for the first time in dealing with disparities between their own local data—principally direct observations—and the ancient corpus, except that New World observations, as they joined those gathered from Africa, Asia, Turkey, and other areas, presented a different set of incongruities by setting foreign types, rather than ancient writings, against knowledge rooted in familiar local data. The central problem remained that of naming and describing new types in nature, and naturalists intuitively persisted in the commonsense method of working from affinities with recognizable European forms. Fuchs, Brunfels, and the herbalists who followed them referred their observations to ancient paragons; New World observers were more likely to use European types known to them as points of reference.[11] The difference between the two situations was one of attitude and perception. The newly appreciated local data, such as plants they could inspect personally, were real for the central European herbalist. They were the stuff of carefully prepared woodcuts "from life" and personal, ocular inspection; eventually, the assumption that ancient types must be present would appear to conflict with empirical facts. In this light, the development of precise techniques for recording and communicating novel observations proceeded confidently, despite the bypassing of venerated authorities. For reports from the New World, the dilemma was reversed. These observations—from the perspective of European writers trying to identify herbs and animals—were mediated, at best by more or less reliable printed and personal witnesses, but just as often by crude or faulty illustrations (sometimes of unclear origin), suspect editions, or excerpts from otherwise unavailable manuscript reports. Techniques for communicating facts about nature thus functioned differently when European naturalists considered American types. Compared to their increasing perception and appreciation of direct evidence such as plants flowering in their own gardens or growing in the countryside near their homes, the evolving relationship between experienced and mediated knowledge was inverted as they sought to extend their catalogs of nature to the New World.

Authorities and Authors

The absence of eyewitness accounts of American plants and animals in the burgeoning scholarly literature of natural history does not seem to have disturbed the authors of botanical and zoological treatises. Was this simply a case of blissful ignorance masquerading as satisfaction? On the one hand, it is true that the "processing" of scientific information from the new World did not proceed as quickly as it might have. The 1,300 or so plants inventoried by Francisco Hernández in Mexico during the 1570s, for example, would not be represented in the botanical literature until the second half of the seventeenth century.[12] The full impact of detailed and reliable reports from America did not reach Europe until the eighteenth century. Yet, despite large gaps in their knowledge, sixteenth-century naturalists were not ignorant of the importance of traveler's accounts, nor of the New World. They had witnessed and participated in the production of a more systematic accounting of the flora and fauna of the greater Mediterranean region, an achievement that had benefited immensely from new information drawn from travel narratives such as Pierre Belon's observations throughout Greece, Judaea, Egypt, and Arabia on his journeys between 1546 and 1560 or Prospero Alpini's studies of exotic plants he observed on trips to Crete and Egypt in the early 1580s. European writers cited the published chronicles of these travelers, weighed their value as sources, and used them to settle controversial or confusing matters.[13] There does not seem to have been any prejudice per se against eyewitness accounts.

As for the New World, in some respects it had become too familiar, at least with respect to its plant life. Seeds and dried specimens from America were by the end of the sixteenth century readily available in Europe, and living, flowering specimens could be found in gardens or, in some cases (maize, for example), even in the countryside. Pressed flowers, collected assiduously, were preserved in bound volumes and placed on library shelves, while the skins of animals were brought back to Europe and saved with other artifacts. All of these sources could potentially be used to describe plants or animals and, through devices like the pantograph, to make images of them for printed books.[14] The widespread availability of some New World plants may explain the paucity of references to their original habitat in the sixteenth-century botanical literature and the occasional downright confusion as to their provenance. These plants tended to be useful or edible—maize, squash, tomato, tobacco—so it should not be surprising that herbalists dwelled on their cultivation, medicinal properties, and preparation as food, rather than the context of their discovery.

Maize provides an excellent example of the provenance problem.[15] Discovered for Europeans by Columbus, it was described by dozens of eyewitnesses in the New World, some of whom were capable and reliable observers. The Spanish royal official Gonzalo Fernández de Oviedo y Valdés gave a careful account, in which he speculated that this plant was the "millet of India" mentioned by Pliny, despite some discrepancies.[16] Not long after Oviedo published this version (the second) of his description of maize in 1535, Indian corn began to appear in Old World herbals, first in the *Kräuterbuch* (1539) of Jerome Bock and then in Fuchs's illustrated herbal of 1542.[17] Neither Bock nor Fuchs mention the New World origins of the plant. Bock starts out by noting that "our Germany will soon be known as *Felix Arabia*, because from day to day we take in so many foreign plants from foreign lands, among which the large foreign grain [groß Welsch korn] is the least." His description is limited to the grain "we have," meaning that he probably investigated it much as he would any other locally available plant, though he also speculated, on the basis of his own research and passages in Pliny and Dioscorides, that it had come to Europe from India. For this reason, he dubbed it "Frumentum Asiaticum."

Fuchs rarely ventured beyond Bock in originality. His treatment of maize was no exception, although he did offer a splendid woodcut of the plant (the first in a European herbal). He called it "Turcicum Frumentum" or "Türckisch Korn." Considering that the title page of *De historia stirpium* advertised original illustrations directly "from nature," Fuchs's comment that the Turkish grain "is now growing in all gardens," and his conclusion that it had come originally from Turkey (i.e., Asia), we should not be surprised that the New World origins of maize were not appreciated until 1570, when Pietro Mattioli asserted that "it ought to be called *Indicum*, not *Turcicum*, for it was first brought from the West Indies, not out of Turkey or Asia, as Fuchs believed."[18] Mattioli apparently did know of Oviedo's account. Despite Mattioli's argument, confusion about the provenance of maize persisted. Matthias de L'Obel, for example, presented a thin case for two distinct types, Indian and Turkish corn, in his *Kruydtboeck* of 1581; he disputed Mattioli's solution to the problem by recalling that Pliny had never been to America, so logic dictated that the two types of grain could not possibly be the same plant.[19] John Gerard was content with one kind of maize but suggested in his herbal that it had come to Europe from both Asia and America. He also studied it locally, noting that he had grown it in his own garden. It is quite possible that his rather implausible reasoning rested on a mistranslation or misunderstanding of L'Obel.[20] The 1636 revision of Gerard's herbal by Thomas Johnson followed Mattioli and returned maize to its habitat of "America and the Islands adjoining."[21] Most of the herbalists recognized between 1583 (Dodoens) and 1605 (L'Obel) that some form of maize

Turcicum frumentum, from Leonhard Fuchs, *De historia stirpium* (Basel, 1542). John Hay Library, Brown University.

had come from the New World, but not always at the expense of Asian corn, which one important work published as late as 1658 still mentioned.[22]

This quick summary of a complicated matter suggests that the interlinked accounts of the herbalists paid little attention to the literature of exploration for decades after published versions of accounts such as those of Oviedo were available. Even after information derived from eyewitnesses penetrated scholarly discussions in print, most European writers continued to generate descriptions and names from locally available sources such as gardens and specimens, and illustrations were also prepared from them. Perhaps, as Finan has suggested, there actually were two types of maize available to the herbalists.[23] More important, this example of the reception of information about the New World in scholarly discourse of the sixteenth century suggests that the common language of European contributors to the inventory of nature, built on a foundation of local knowledge and classical sources, appears to have been capable of sealing out New World testimony for a long period of time. Why should this have been so?[24]

The Catalog of Nature

By 1600 fairly current scientific news about the New World circulated in Europe through a variety of sources, ranging from printed narratives to dockyard gossip. Printers eager to benefit from readers' appetite for news had begun to publish timely shorter pieces on the exploration of the New World much earlier, of course, such as the initial reports of the use of Guaicum as a cure for syphilis appearing in dispatches published within the first few decades after Columbus's voyages. Early printed recipes, observations, and letters carried titles that conveyed brevity or clarity and a focus on one piece of information.[25] They also kept the presses going in order to add chronicles and news to longer works, including reprints of books with an established reputation.[26] Such brief intelligences, in whatever form, often presented useful news. At the same time, much of what was divulged in larger academic treatises touching these same topics drew on correspondence or even hearsay that had never been and would never be published separately. The constant arrival and assessment of information in these various forms led herbalists and other compilers of observations and descriptions to bring out a steady stream of new editions of their works, in which they "retracted, changed, invented, and replaced" passages.[27] The ways in which they received and edited news for publication would provide a foundation for their construction of a catalog of nature.

Consider the Flemish naturalist Carolus Clusius (Charles de L'Ecluse), who often included reports from other naturalists in his own works and utilized a range of techniques for dealing with new sources of information. He was perhaps the most conscientious editor and translator of travel narratives toward the end of the sixteenth century and thus played an important role in writing the natural history of many distant lands. Indeed, his *Exoticorum libri decem* of 1605, ostensibly a collected edition of his own writings, included quite a few reports and exploration accounts that he had already translated or prepared for publication one or more times earlier in his career, only to edit and bring them up to date once again for this important compendium. The *Exoticorum* thus included observations and commentary from many sources: Belon's *Observationes*, Garcia de Orta's materia medica of India, and works by José de Acosta and Nicolas Monardes, such as the latter's *Libri tres*, *Libellus de Rosa*, and *Dissertatiuncula de citriis*. At first glance, this compilation may have seemed like another anthology gathering editions of time-worn favorites, but nothing could be further from the truth. Clusius's botanical works joined those of two other Flemish naturalists, Rembert Dodoens and Matthias de L'Obel, also issued at the press of their publisher and countryman, Christopher Plantin, to set a new standard for the integration of specific reports with the developing corpus of natural history information, and for the pooling of textual and visual information across editions, titles, and even authors. Clusius and Plantin collaborated to insert late-breaking news into books in press, usually in the form of dated appendices. Writers and compilers working with Plantin honed this technique. The cosmographical works of Abraham Ortelius, for example, also included many addenda, usually based on information submitted by correspondents.[28] Clusius proceeded similarly. He inserted many such bulletins in the *Exoticorum libri*, sometimes in notes, more often in addenda based on new information provided to him and including woodcuts of plants and animals drawn from fresh sources—a flower from a physician in Vienna or an animal skin from a merchant in Holland perhaps. He frequently added communications confirming that this or that plant had at last flowered in a European garden and justified last-minute additions posting new discoveries (such as an appendix to an appendix added after the *Exoticorum* had been printed) by noting that "I happened to see certain plants that nobody has mentioned yet."[29] As editor and translator of several works of natural history by other authors—all published by Plantin or his son-in-law Raphelengius—Clusius found many opportunities to compare reports and add or supplement commentary clarifying issues. In the Plantin edition of Belon's *Observationes*, for example, Clusius provided notes that were set off both typographically and by special marks from Belon's original text. He referred his readers to a discussion of the *tatou*, or armadillo, in his own edition of Monardes.[30] In the *Exoticorum libri*, he juxtaposed printed accounts of the American sloth from Oviedo and André Thevet, adding his own evaluation of a skin obtained by a correspondent in Amsterdam along with a new woodcut of the beast; at the last minute, he added another report in an addendum offering yet another image based on a new specimen. This final version of the sloth would become "the

AVCTARIVM. 373

dem ex America delatum, quodque non multis diebus ante quàm nauis Amſtelredamum appelleret, in itinere extinctum fuiſſet. Quum verò figura illa cap. xvi. libri v. exhibita, mihi minimè ſatisfaceret, ut quæ ad animalis exuvium vetuſtate jam valde corruptum delineata: illum orabam, ut ſuum illud animal ad paucos dies mihi concederet, quo commodiùs ejus formam obſervare poſſem: quod ſanè lubens fecit: nam brevi poſt, illud ad me mittebat cum avium Paradiſearum majoris generis Rege. In tabella itaque ejus iconem ſtatim exprimendam curabam: & quia ad Oviedi deſcriptionem magis accedere videbatur, quàm illa quæ cap. xvi. lib. v. poſita, in hoc Auctarium inferendam cenſebam cum brevibus quibuſdam ipſius animalis notis, quales videlicet in arida animalis pelle ſufſulta obſervare licuit, ut cum alia icone conferri queat.

IGNAVVS.

A collo ad extremam dorſi partem, paullò plus quàm quatuordecim uncias longum erat ejus corpus, craſſitudo verò ſive ambitus pænè totidem continebat: in vivo autem animali longè majorem fuiſſe, non eſt dubium: collum ipſum ſex uncias longum erat, & quatuor craſſum, comprehenſis etiam ipſis villis: anteriora crura ad pedum (quos planos habebat inſtar urſorum aut ſimiarum) uſque flexuram, ſeptem unciarum longitudinem ſuperabant: poſteriora autem, ſex cum ſemiſſe dumtaxat longa, ut anterioribus ferè integrâ unciâ eſſent breviora: anteriores pedes à flexura ad ungues uſque, tres uncias erant longi; poſteriores autem ejuſdem pænè longitudinis, utrique tamen valde anguſti, licet plani, ut mirum videri non debeat, ſi cum difficultate ſubſiſtere & progredi queat: ſinguli verò tribus contiguis unguibus binas uncias cum ſemiſſe longis, albis, & valde mucronatis præditi, pronâ quidem parte arcus inſtar elatis, ſupinâ autẽ ſive infernâ carinatis: univerſum corpus à ſummo capite ad ungues uſque, denſiſſimis iiſque prolixis villis erat obſitũ, coloris partim nigri, partim cineracei, pænè ut meles, quem vulgus taſſum ſive taxum appellat, mollioribus tamen, atque à collo ſecundum dorſi longitudinem uſque ad poſteriora ferè crura, nigrorum pilorum quadam ſerie erat inſignitum: totum collum à cervice ad anteriora uſque crura veluti jubâ quadam nigrorum crinium in utrumque latus propendentium tectum habebat: caput exiguum, brevibus pilis ſubrufis obſitum, cum mento & gutturis parte: roſtro ſimiam quodammodo referebat; breve enim, glabrum, & obtuſum, ſimiſque naribus erat præditum, exiguis etiam dentibus, ſatis tamen latis: quùm verò rictum amplum non habeat, hoc animal vix mordere poſſe, mihi perſuadeo.

ad calcem cap. XVIII. *lib.* V. *Exoticorum.*

Poſtea tamen intelligebam ex eorum ſerpentum eſſe genere, qui in interiore Braſilianorum regione reperiuntur, atque in arboribus plerumque verſari ſolent, ut hominibus per ſilvas iter facientibus inſidientur: nam iſtam habent conſuetudinem, ut aliquem ſibi vicinum conſpicientes, illico in eum inſiliant, & corpus ejus atque brachia multiplici nexu ligantes (ut nudi incedunt iſti Braſiliani) ſuum os in illorum anum inſerant, adeoque valenter ſugant, ut ſpirandi facultatem ipſis adimant, & niſi cultrum aut aliud ferreum inſtrumentum apud ſe habeant, quo ſerpentes qui tali ratione illos ligatos detinent, conficere queant, ipſis haud dubiè pereundum eſt.

Ii 3 LACER-

Icnavus, from Charles L'Ecluse, *Exoticorum libri decem* (Antwerp, 1605). John Hay Library, Brown University.

most persistent image of all."[31] Clusius encouraged the interweaving of observations made in different times and places through these editorial practices.

These techniques made it indeed possible for a clever editor—if, like Clusius, the beneficiary of correspondence, specimens, gardens, and a benevolent publisher—to update, integrate, and revise descriptions and images of sloths, tobacco plants, tomatoes, and other objects without leaving home.[32] Converting this raw material into a coherent version of the catalog of nature called for writers and compilers to sift sources, compare known and unknown, and balance venerated authorities against ocular witnesses. I have already noted that observers of local flora or fauna in Europe or America named and described what they saw by a process of comparison, whether a German herbalist matched a local plant to a description in Dioscorides, or a New World naturalist put into words his impression of an oak tree or a sloth with reference to a like form in England or Spain. European writers collating and summarizing reports relating to New World forms often joined these tendencies by a chain of reasoning linking observations to antecedent references in the classical texts of antiquity. The confusion about the origins of maize, for example, might be interpreted as demonstrating the herbalist's tendency to rely on the freshly recovered texts of Dioscorides and Pliny. It may seem, therefore, that the orientation of bookish scholars working in Europe toward ancient opinions separated them from an empirical outlook prevailing among eyewitnesses working in the New World, and that this intellectual vantage point suppressed a clear and rapid evaluation by European writers of firsthand accounts from America.

As appealing as this argument may be, I do not think that it is very powerful in explaining the slow integration of the New World into the catalog of nature, for observers active in America also tended to cite the opinions of the ancients, or at least to know them well enough as authorities in natural history. Oviedo called Pliny "the foremost of all natural historians" and "a very accurate scholar."[33] Acosta's *Historia natural y moral de las Indias* is virtually a gloss on Pliny in the introductory sections and contains references to him throughout, while Hernández went so far as to edit Pliny's encyclopedic *Natural History*.[34] Oviedo admired his classical predecessor, however, more as a model to be followed than as a guide to what he saw. Still, he compared his observations both to what he knew from Spain and to ancient authorities. For example, his discussion of the jaguar in the *Sumario* focused on whether this New World beast deserved the Old World name of tiger. He called upon the writers of antiquity generally and to Pliny in particular to define the qualities of the tiger, while also recalling such an animal that Columbus had transported to Toledo and given the name. He wondered if the New World tiger were swift enough to deserve the appellation but then noted simply that animals, humans, or plants can have one quality here and a different, or even opposite, one somewhere else, such as people of different skin color, plants that are poisonous in one place and benign elsewhere, and so on. The verdict? "All these things, and many others that could be said in this connection, can easily be proved, and should be believed when they have been related by men who have read widely or who have traveled about the world. Their own experience has proved what they said." He concluded this discussion with the possibility that the American beast might be a slower version of the tiger known in antiquity, but he doubted it, for "the many animals that exist in the Indies that I describe here, or at least most of them, could not have been learned about from the ancients, since they exist in a land which had not been discovered until our own time."[35] Oviedo took the ancient sources into account but was not willing to reject what his own eyes and reasoning told him. Still, his references and mode of reasoning could easily have been accepted by scholars writing in Paris or Amsterdam.

The important point is that naturalists working from their desks in Europe did not have the same options as Oviedo when it came to resolving a confusing issue raised by observations in the New World. They could not question a native as to the medicinal properties of a strange herb, for example. Nonetheless, they had a good deal more than books available to them, and furthermore, they could ask for specimens they did not have. Clusius boasted of the progress that would be made if material collected from "India, Ethiopia, and America" were sent back to Europe, providing his successors with "ample material" for natural history.[36] By the end of the sixteenth century, it was not unusual for voyagers sent off from the Old World to carry with them wish lists provided by naturalists, ranging from instructions to count fish or carefully observe the land to requests for seeds, dried plants, or other specimens.[37] Journals, such as the one kept by Thomas Hariot in Virginia, also functioned as registers of plant and animal life.[38] The artist Thomas Bavin was told before heading off to New England in 1582 that he should document "birdes beastes fishes plantes hearbes Trees and fruictes" by drawing one of each kind "that is strange to us in England."[39] The gardens used by herbalists like Gerard, Mattioli, or Clusius and the collections of minerals and dried specimens consulted by Conrad Gesner and Ulysse Aldrovandi filled out the range of sources available in Europe to those writers who used ocular evidence to adjudicate unresolved questions.

Typographic Culture and New World Natural History

Printed books in the sixteenth century were often publishing projects shaped by what I will call typographic culture, a term that refers to the system of relationships and practices through which typographers, publishers, authors, and illustrators produced books. The realities and exigencies of sixteenth-century book production complicate any assessment of the communication of information during this period and, in particular, how books were used as sources for New World natural history. A full appreciation of published texts must take into account that authors and editors did not often determine alone what actually went into a printed book, and sometimes their participation in the process was virtually expendable. Printers and publishers obviously played a role in the physical production of books, but they often shaped context and content as well, especially when, as so frequently occurred, printer-publishers as a routine aspect of their business acquired the means to produce editions without having to solicit new manuscripts or illustrations. Most of the major sixteenth-century printed sources of information about plants and animals evolved through a series of editions under an editor or sequence of editors, such as Mattioli, Clusius, or Joachim Camerarius; authorial and editorial control, which usually required a sympathetic publisher, was a crucial element in the continuity and reliability of these editions. But if a publishing project requiring this kind of guidance fell into the hands of a printer eager to exploit an attractive set of woodcuts in his possession or to rearrange texts creatively for the purposes of an anthology or abridgment, its trustworthiness diminished rapidly; scholarly writers paid little attention to such texts, unless to draw the attention of readers to their shortcomings.[40] It turns out that many of the primary accounts of nature in the New World either were not printed at all or, if published, appeared in editions that seemed suspect to academic writers working in the humanist tradition of editorial practice. Other locally available means for acquiring knowledge—herbaria, gardens, *Wunderkammern*, and the like—provided sources that European herbalists preferred to these mediated, often dubious sources of information in print.

One way to approach these issues of preferred modes of scholarly communication and the printing of scientific news from the New World is through the question of how and by whom control was exercised over the publication of early modern science. The deployment of this control and the ways in which it was wielded carried implications for the production, reproduction, and integrity of knowledge about nature generally and for the entrance of New World observations into the European catalog of nature specifically. For more than two centuries after Gutenberg's invention, authors rarely governed the publication of their own ideas.[41] Their limited measure of control usually evaporated altogether once a manuscript was in a printer's hands. Consistent legal concepts of authorship and the printed book as a form of intellectual property did not even begin to take shape until around the end of the seventeenth century. Printers were capable of interpreting manuscripts correctly, as well as preserving text and images given over to their care, but the point is that authors themselves could do little—short of independently printing their works themselves—to insure that their books accurately expressed the information and views that they sought to convey. Manuscripts, drawings, woodcut illustrations, and even previously published material—in other words, the raw material of printed books in the sixteenth century—circulated freely and could be acquired or appropriated by publishers with great freedom.

Naturalists active in the New World were doubly disadvantaged, as authors of potentially useful firsthand accounts, by remoteness from the European publishing centers. The writings of the Spaniard Gonzalo Fernández de Oviedo provide a telling example of their difficulties in bringing original observations into the mainstream of European writing and publication. Oviedo was the first of the early chroniclers to owe a large part of his literary reputation to writing about nature in the New World, and not just to his tales of conquests and riches. He appears to have been a careful observer, offering clear descriptions of rubber trees, maize, tobacco, cinnamon, and other useful plants. He published his first book on the New World, the so-called *Sumario*, in 1526 at his own expense.[42] The circuitous course of his manuscript notes on the way to publication goes a long way to explain their limited impact in the European catalog of nature in the sixteenth century. The *Sumario* provided information about the plants and animals of Hispaniola and the mainland around the isthmus of Panama. Oviedo composed this little book in Spain at the request of Emperor Charles V under what were hardly ideal circumstances. He had already started work on a more comprehensive treatise, but when he was called upon to write the summary, his longer manuscript was still at his residence at Santo Domingo. As he explained in the introduction to the *Sumario*, he was writing the shorter tract "from memory" to provide his sovereign with a "little pleasure" and to summarize new information about the West Indies.[43] The more substantial contribution to New World natural history would only be partially published in his lifetime. Its first part was issued in 1535 and again in 1547, with the first book of a second part seeing print in 1557. It appears that Oviedo did not personally oversee any part of the printing of this *General and Natural History of the West Indies* completed after 1535.[44] The remainder of the second part and all of the third part were not published in their entirety until the edition of the Real Academia de la Historica of Madrid in the nineteenth century.[45]

As for Oviedo's succinct *Sumario*, it was not issued again in Spanish until the eighteenth century. It appeared at least three times in Italian between 1535 and 1565, once in French in 1545 (in a translation from the Italian), and in an English version translated by Richard Eden and published in 1555 and again in 1577, "a partial but unsatisfactory translation and summary."[46] The *Historia general y natural* fared even worse at the mercy of the unrestrained print community. It appears to have been published only in the abridged forms of the partial publication already mentioned, then three times as part of G. B. Ramusio's *Navigationi et viaggi* between 1556 and 1606, and in a French translation published in 1555.[47] Most of these translations and excerpts came out in a concentrated period between 1555 and 1565, that is, long after Oviedo seems to have taken even a limited personal interest in the publication of his manuscript. In other words, the *Sumario* and *Historia general y natural* became ordinary commodities of typographic culture, available to interested printers for republication in abridged, altered, or translated forms, but by virtue of these changes not dependable in any particular version as a source of authoritative information. Perhaps this is why there has been persistent confusion about the relationship of Oviedo's two works and, more important, why even naturalists who were able to visit the New World seem generally not to have consulted them.[48]

It is not difficult to conjure up other examples of sluggish passage from manuscript to print, uncontrolled editions, and the dilution of original narratives in poor excerpts and translations. These common occurrences made it difficult to assess the value of some of the most important eyewitness accounts of nature in the New World. Another significant case in point would be the Spanish physician Francisco Hernández, who compiled the earliest extensive treatment of American plants, animals, and minerals. The authoritative edition of his remarkable pandect of New World medicinal simples was not published until almost seventy-five years after Hernández had traveled through Hispaniola, Cuba, and central Mexico between 1570 and 1577. His manuscript notes, including drawings and paintings, sat in the library of the Escorial (where they would be destroyed by fire in 1671), while a copy remaining in Mexico yielded two printed abridgments that almost certainly did not circulate widely in Europe, if at all. Notes made from the Escorial copy by Leonardo Recchi provided a textual basis for the edition prepared by the Lincean Academy in Rome and printed in 1628, but due to the death of its patron, Prince Cesi, it was not issued in its ultimate published form until 1651.[49] The pattern of desultory publication exemplified by the works of Oviedo and Hernández differed markedly from the orderly sequence of carefully prepared editions and intertextual relationships linking the work of European writers compiling inventories of plants and animals, especially the herbalists. After the 1540s or so, dynamic catalogs of nature admitted modification and improvement through commentaries, addenda, vivid illustrations, or critical revisions, as I have already shown for Clusius. It is not that typographic culture always worked to the detriment of rapid and faithful publication, but only that scientific texts in particular did not fare well when careful authorial or editorial control gave way to the inclinations of printers free to do as they wished. The example of Hernández is also a reminder that many manuscripts began to gather dust before ever reaching the beaten path of publication. For these reasons, eyewitness accounts from America remained hidden from the view of most European naturalists writing in the sixteenth century, and, as a result, these mainstream writers did not work from a comprehensive list of New World plants and animals until the end of the seventeenth century.

The New Book of Nature

As we have seen, the difficulties associated with bringing reliable firsthand accounts to print and then insuring the integrity of printed texts and images were acute in the sixteenth century. Authors and editors faced them head-on in fields of learning measured by the incremental evolution of a body of writings and commentary, like the *res herbaria.* While the term *auctor* (author) could mean a guarantor as well as a creator of knowledge, even a living author of early printed books was often powerless to guarantee that a published book reflected his intentions. Printers and publishers (usually the same person) controlled the production of books and owned the final product, as well as the materials, such as woodcuts and engravings, that they used to produce it. But even without this complex of relationships among authors, artists, and printers, printing technology mediated substantially between original observations and their record in printed form, particularly with respect to visual information.[50] Countless sixteenth- and seventeenth-century examples of corrupt printed texts, inferior reprints, poorly copied woodcuts and engravings, and complaints about them testify to a gap between the theoretical capabilities of printing and the achievement in practice of fixity and reliable communication.

Early botanical books, for example, contain ample evidence of problems arising from the printer's control of book production and ownership of printed information in its material forms. An author, an artist, and a blockcutter might take great pains in working together to make illustrations for a particular edition of a botanical work, but typographical routines favored the degradation rather than the improvement or even fixity of these images in subsequent editions. If original woodcuts or engravings survived, they almost always belonged to the printer-publisher, as was often true even of the original drawings. If the printer could not lay his hands on the originals, he had copies made from previously printed images, which could then be reduced, combined, recombined, and altered with astonishing ease to suit a certain readership or fill a program of publication. Among the herbals, for example, even the most magnificent editions were subject to corruption.[51]

Such compromises of what Elizabeth Eisenstein has called the "preservative powers of print" were not necessarily capricious.[52] Printers with specific linguistic, scholarly, and educational markets in mind usually had good reasons for adding, subtracting, or changing images and even text, as in the addition of indices, commentaries, or appendices. More economical editions were sometimes in order, and neither intellectual ownership nor copyright infringed upon the printer's freedom to make the necessary changes. Original combinations of previous works were created with ease, particularly anthologies and collections of illustrations. In the latter case, for example, sets of woodcuts, engravings, or plates might be readily available through circulation, inheritance, or outright sale. The printer merely reached into the pool of available images and arranged for them to be mixed into new combinations. These were not cases of printing piracy, if the printer owned the images, though we might see the books produced as conflicting with an author's intentions. Authors merely furnished the raw materials; once a printer had a manuscript and suitable images to put alongside it, the author, for all practical purposes, had relinquished control over the project, and he owned nothing when it was completed.

I have argued previously in a paper with my colleague Robin Rider that with regard to the concepts of authorial control and intellectual ownership in science, important changes in the publishing landscape did not take place until the later seventeenth century, especially in England. Practical changes in the relationship between scientific authors and the typographic community resulted from the prestige of individual authors, such as Robert Boyle and Sir Isaac Newton, agents such as Henry Oldenbourg, and, above all, the collective power and privilege of new scientific institutions led by the Royal Society of London and the Paris Academy of Sciences, who, emboldened by royal charters and rights of imprimatur and censorship, dared tread on the toes of printers and publishers. The changes resulting from this shift in control of printing technology put limits on the autonomy of the typographic community in matters relating to the printing of the new book of nature and also led to a pattern of relying on collaboration and new institutional muscle to deal with the problems of publishing scientific reports in rapidly expanding spheres of scientific knowledge.[53]

These matters, so removed in time and space from the first explorers of the New World, nevertheless provide a rough framework for understanding the evolving nature of the communication of knowledge realized within the constraints of typographic culture. In the sixteenth century, environments conducive to authorial or editorial control of the printed catalog of nature existed only when favorable relationships among writers, their sources, and printers governed the process of publication, and these situations were local, rather than universal. (Of course, this abridgment of the system of communication does not even begin to address its most variable element, the reader.) Writers of books on plants and animals, who were particularly dependent on the flow of new information, had few options for constructing forms of authorial control and managing the editorial process governing revisions of the standard catalogs of nature. Their situation magnified the importance of collective projects as counterweights to the aspects of typographical culture leading to the dissipation of reliable information. Collaboration, by promoting the sharing of texts and images, strengthened the endurance of information, while it also encouraged continuity in revisions of the catalog of nature through new editions and thus extended authorial control over time; finally, the strength in numbers achieved by cooperation raised consciousness among at least a few printers of the need to increase their attention to the stability of conventions for the publication of knowledge. The editorial tradition of the *res herbaria et animalia*, of the living world, best exemplified by Clusius, his colleagues, and the support they received from the publishing house of Plantin, presaged the positive effects on scientific publication of more formal modes of cooperative activity in the seventeenth century. New World natural history penetrated this tradition with difficulty, however. Eyewitness naturalists, such as Oviedo and Hernández, were unable to find dependable ways of publishing their work. It is significant that the first breakthrough of American natural history into the mainstream of European writing occurred as a result of a collaborative undertaking sponsored by one of the first scientific societies in the seventeenth century.

The expanding scope and volume of information about New World plants and animals only gradually stimulated cooperative enterprises centered on printing books. By contrast, compilers of the catalog of nature in Europe started by developing techniques for the public communication of knowledge, as well as its continuous revision and extension. The herbalists and botanical writers, for example, fell into a small number of interlinked projects organized around revisions of a well-defined set of texts. Mattioli's *Commentarii*, first published in 1554, provided such a text, and it appeared in new editions throughout the remainder of the sixteenth century.[54] The foremost example of intertextual linkages would be the long sequence of Plantin editions supervised by the herbalists Dodoens, L'Obel, and Clusius. These projects worked within the humanist framework of diligent editorial work and the inclusion of classical sources, but they also relied upon careful attention to locally available empirical knowledge. With respect to what Atran has called the "shared repository of data about the living world," two important changes occurred by the end of the sixteenth century: first, it became an increasingly collaborative enterprise; and second, the utility of a given publication began to hinge on its reliability and currency. Both of these developments encouraged close working relationships between editors (and authors), on the one hand, and printers, on the other. In this context, isolation and distance from European centers of publishing, such as Antwerp or Venice, was more of a liability than direct experience of nature in exotic places could overcome, even with regard to the accumulation of new information. Monardes in Spain or Clusius in Flanders could accomplish more to introduce New World plants and animals to Europe than Oviedo or Hernández from the other side of the Atlantic. Without links to the natural history traditions exemplified by active publishing projects, manuscripts and drawings brought back to Europe gathered dust in archives or, even worse perhaps, fell prey to dissipative practices of typographic culture.

Gerald Strauss, writing about Ortelius and popular cosmography, has called the process of soliciting criticism, revising, and reprinting such works "a sort of cooperative enterprise on an international basis";[55] the task of organizing a vast array of specimens, objects, and observations certainly lent itself to a division of labor at the European end. In the matter of cooperation between publishers and compilers of the catalog of nature, the house founded by Plantin stood second to none in publishing books offering information about nature in the New World, beginning in the 1560s. The enormous store of more than two thousand images prepared for these books in the Plantin shop appeared together in the *Plantarum seu stirpium icones*, first published separately in 1581, and were used over a period of decades for the herbals by Dodoens, Clusius, and others published by Plantin.[56] This pool of illustrations provided many familiar images of New World plants, such as the first printed version of *nicotinia rustica L.* prepared for Dodoens's herbal, the two sloths in Clusius's *Exoticorum libri*, and the Indian puffing away alongside a tobacco plant made for L'Obel and Pena's *Nova stirpium adversaria*, as well as woodcuts appearing in the Plantin editions of Monardes.[57]

The House of Plantin (Christopher Plantin himself, followed by his son-in-law Raphelengius and the Moretus family) in fact produced several important books relevant to American natural history, besides the herbals already mentioned, and they carried the marks of the publisher, his editors, and his artists. Consider the Plantin editions of Garcia de Orta's *Coloquios dos simples*,[58] which consisted of dialogues between de Orta, then the senior physician in India, and a newly arrived colleague occupied with the Indian materia medica. This book was first printed at Goa and was probably suppressed after it was determined that Orta had secretly practiced Judaism. The transformation of these *Coloquios* occurred about the time of de Orta's death and before his family's difficulties with the Holy Office. Clusius found a copy in Lisbon and, having taken extensive notes on it, prepared a Latin summary, published by Plantin in 1567.[59] He had done this sort of work before, and, as we have seen, it was his bent to substantially modify and add to the works he abstracted or edited. In this case, he added material from the New World, and in so doing he became one of the first herbalists to take notice of the accounts of Oviedo and Thevet previously mentioned. Plantin and his heirs reissued this book at least four times, and each time Clusius added text and illustrations. The fourth edition of 1593, published by Plantin's widow and Jan I. Moretus, included Monardes's *Simplicium medicamentorum ex Novo Orbe delatorum*, first published by Plantin in 1579, and Cristóbal da Costa's follow-up to de Orta's work on Indian simples.[60]

Despite the existence of such texts as those published by the House of Plantin, the publication that introduced a systematic, firsthand inventory of nature in the New World into the European catalog of nature was the edition of Francisco Hernández prepared by the Lincean Academy. Founded at Rome in 1603, this academy had, by the time several of its members began work on this project,

Title page of Francisco Hernández, *Rerum medicarum* (Rome, 1651). John Carter Brown Library.

already sponsored the publication of such important scientific works as Galileo's *Istorio e dimostrazioni intorno alle macchio solari* (1613), his *Saggiatore* (1623), and, in natural history, the famous *Apiarium* (1625), in which perhaps the first illustrations produced from microscopic images were published. Not only had the *Apiarium* appeared under the auspices of the Lincean Academy, but its observations of bees and their behavior had also been the result of a collaboration of several academy members.[61] The publication of Hernández's *Rerum . . . Novae Hispaniae thesaurus* was also a joint undertaking. Members of the academy edited the manuscript of Recchi's digest, and the small group divided the labor that augmented the text and prepared illustrations for this edition. The commentary by the capable Fabio Colonna and other *Lincei* and the "phytosophical tables" on issues of classification and nomenclature by Prince Cesi himself were particularly important in updating Hernández's observations.[62] Although, as previously noted, the path of the manuscript to published book was not completed until 1651, this edition would be taken up by botanists seeking a full treatment of the New World for the catalog of nature.

This acceptance occurred when John Ray fully utilized the Lincean edition of Hernández's inventory in his *History of Plants*, published between 1686 and 1704.[63] For evidence of the importance of Hernández's published observations, one need only refer to the bibliography in Ray's incarnation of the catalog of nature. He conceived the *History* as an undertaking "not merely [to] catalogue but describe, which should not be confined to Britain or Western Europe but include all known species."[64] In the preface, he explained that he had worked through a vast literature. Fortunately, it had not been necessary to inspect all the various "Historias, Theatra, Pandectas, Adversaria, Observationes, Illustrationes, Commentarios" describing plants, thanks to the industry already shown by compilers of earlier catalogs, such as Johann and Caspar Bauhin, Fabio Colonna, and Clusius, in sifting through these sources. Ray followed closely the editorial traditions of the Plantin editions and the *Lincei*, whose efforts had cut his own project down to size.[65] His bibliography of sources included all the renowned sixteenth-century herbalists, from Brunfels and Fuchs through the Plantin publications and on to John Gerard and Ray's own contemporary, Rudolf Camerarius. He also included a few of the peripatetic naturalists, such as Jakob de Bondt, whose *Historia Naturalis Indiae orientalis* drew upon firsthand knowledge of Batavia and India, Prospero Alpini, and, for America, Georg Marcgraf on the natural history of Brazil, where he had traveled in the 1640s.[66] But Hernández stood alone as the representative of the sixteenth-century Americanists. Ray cited the 1651 edition by the *Lincei* of the *Plantas y Animales* and referred to Hernández throughout the *Historia plantarum.* At the end of book 2, after appendices and other addenda, Ray added a complete list of plants from Hernández's inventory that he had not been able to identify.[67]

Perhaps, as Hernández's biographer has argued, Ray was not alone in transcribing this information, only in fully acknowledging its source in Hernández's work.[68] Nonetheless, Ray's inclusion of this New World inventory is significant, because it represented nothing less than the inclusion of Hernández's observations and notes in what Cuvier later called "the most complete treatise which had yet appeared on vegetation in general."[69] In Ray's adoption of Hernández's observations, as they had been rescued and preserved by the *Lincei* project, the European catalog of nature opened up at the end of the seventeenth century to include the New World.

Conclusion

It would appear that the reports of explorers and firsthand observers of American plants and animals such as Oviedo merged only slowly and incompletely with the efforts of European writers on natural history to begin a catalog of the world's plant and animal life in the sixteenth and early seventeenth centuries. The European catalog of the living world took little account of the literature of exploration until much later, partly because very few of the most valuable firsthand reports were printed in a timely or reliable fashion during their authors' lifetimes, partly because other kinds of sources were available in Europe, and partly because the eyewitness-authors seem to have been both physically and intellectually isolated from the dominant lines of editing and publication. A Monardes or Clusius could preside over the accumulation of descriptions and images of New World plants and animals without setting foot on the American continent. A few writers, Mattioli and Clusius, for example, apparently did use information culled from Oviedo's printed works, but these occasional references did as much to confuse as to clarify. José de Acosta, who mentions Monardes as a source for his *Historia natural y moral de las Indias*, published in 1590, seems to have been the first writer even to know about the inventory completed by Hernández. Yet he did not try to integrate the original observations found there (if he had read them), or those of anyone else, for that matter, with the prevailing traditions of European natural history literature.[70]

European writers from Fuchs on had taken notice of New World plants and animals, but the forms displayed and discussed in the European catalog of nature of the sixteenth century owed rather little to a direct confrontation with original accounts. Eyewitness descriptions such as those by Oviedo and Hernández infiltrated the lines of herbalists and other writers by the 1570s, but their impact was intermittent and indirect, usually to be bypassed altogether when usable New World specimens were available for inspection. Maize, for example, seems to have been so familiar to European writers that their texts pulled it out of the New World altogether.[71] Matthias de L'Obel boasted, in a book published in 1576, that plants from all over the world could be found in innumerable Belgian gardens.[72] With so many opportunities to bypass exploration accounts, which even when published did not seem to offer reliable information, the naturalists turned to evidence they themselves could directly experience and their artists could illustrate "from life." New World origins were sometimes lost when European writers turned exclusively to these sources.

It appears that the "common language" described by Atran may have insulated the emerging literature of natural history from eyewitness accounts in America until the rediscovery of original sources in the seventeenth century. By then a new wave of expeditions—such as Marcgraf's travels to Brazil—offered many more observations and thus gave a new urgency to projects surveying and cataloging these data. For more than a century after Columbus's first voyage to America, European naturalists working on the catalog of nature relied on their familiarity with locally available flora and fauna, while printers channeled original accounts of the New World into the domain of unrestrained typographic culture or ignored them altogether; both tendencies discouraged the careful appraisal of New World observations within the dominant traditions of natural history writing in Europe. In time, the honing of editorial practices, the proliferation of expeditions, and the concentration of effort made possible by collaborative projects combined to wear down this insulation. In the first instance, however, the European discovery of America was for natural history, as indeed for other scholarly subjects of the sixteenth century, at most a marginal event.[73]

NOTES

1. Leonhart Fuchs, *De historia stirpium* (Basel, 1542). This is not far from the six hundred plants in Middle English manuscript herbals identified by Tony Hunt, *Plant Names of Medieval England* (Cambridge, 1989). The number known to Dioscorides has been estimated at 550; see Jerry Stannard, "P. A. Mattioli: Sixteenth Century Commentator on Dioscorides," *Bibliographical Contributions of the University of Kansas Library* 1 (1969): 61.

2. Caspar Bauhin, *Pinax theatri botanici* (Basel, 1623).

3. J.-P. Tournefort, *Elémens de botanique* (Paris, 1694), 3.

4. Alphonse de Candolle, *Origin of Cultivated Plants* (New York, 1892), 20.

5. The historical literature on this subject is scattered. The best starting point is probably the work of Antonello Gerbi, *Nature in the New World: From Christopher Columbus to Gonzalo Fernández de Oviedo*, trans. Jeremy Moyle (Pittsburgh, 1985), and, for the later period, *The Dispute of the New World: The History of a Polemic, 1750–1900*, trans. Jeremy Moyle (Pittsburgh, 1973). For the herbalists, Edward Lee Greene's *Landmarks of Botanical History*, ed. Frank N. Egerton, 2 vols. (Stanford, 1983) is indispensable. A recent guide to the primary literature is Anita Guerrini, *Natural History and the New World, 1524–1770: An Annotated Bibliography of Printed Materials in the Library of the American Philosophical Society* (Philadelphia, 1986).

6. This group included Pierre Belon, Garcia de Orta, Prospero Alpini, and Leonhard Rauwolf.

7. Even when such books were published, the expense and difficulty was noted by authors or printers, and sometimes in privileges. Cf. "Exemplum Privilegii Senatus Veneti" in Pietro Andrea Mattioli, *Commentarii in libros sex Pedacii Dioscorides Anazerbei* (Venice, 1554), [þ8]^{r}.

8. On the characteristics and interests of late medieval and Renaissance botanists, see Karen Meier Reeds, *Botany in Medieval and Renaissance Universities* (New York, 1991).

9. Pietro Andrea Mattioli, "Il Matthioli a gli studiosi Lettori," in *I Discorsi . . . ne i sei libri della materia medicinale di Pedacio Dioscoride Anazarbeo* (Venice, 1557), ß3^{v}–[ß4^{v}].

10. Scott Atran, *Cognitive Foundations of Natural History: Towards an Anthropology of Science* (Cambridge, 1990), 128.

11. "Consequently, the process for incorporating new species seems to function in reverse. Instead of attempting to match foreign species to local types, it is more often a matter of matching local species to foreign types, although the principle is basically the same." Atran, *Cognitive Foundations*, 130. It should, however, be noted here that Oviedo, Acosta, and most of the other systematic observers in the New World frequently cited classical writers, especially Pliny, in their notes.

12. It is interesting to compare this number to major additions in print of the same period. Prospero Alpini, for example, added fifty-seven plants and trees in *De plantis Aegypti* (Venice, 1592), including coffee arabica and the banana, and then another 145 plants (85 from Crete) in *De plantis exoticis libri duo* (Venice, 1627).

13. An example is the treatment of the hippopotamus in Mattioli's Dioscorides commentaries. In the 1557 edition cited above, this section was brief and almost bereft of contemporary information (as was the 1554 edition upon which this one was based). By 1565 Mattioli had reviewed numerous pieces of evidence and critically assessed Belon's observations, first published as *Les observations plusieurs singularitez et choses memorables trouvés en Grece, Asie, Iudée, Arabie, & autres pays estranges . . .* (Paris, 1553); see Pietro Andrea Mattioli, *Commentarii . . .* (Venice, 1565), 328. He generally augmented his commentary substantially (also adding woodcuts) in this 1565 edition, and I assume that this is when he brought in his treatment of Belon. Marginal notes and index entries in the 1558 edition do refer to Belon's "errors" and "absurd opinions," but I have not looked for the hippopotamus entry in this earlier edition. In any event, Mattioli clearly used Belon's observations within a few years of their publication.

14. The Felix Platter collection at the Botanical Institute Library in Bern provides a well-preserved example of a sixteenth-century herbarium. On Fabio Colonna's use of the pantograph to etch flattened specimens directly onto the copperplate, see A. Hyatt Mayor, *Prints and People: A Social History of Printed Pictures* (New York, 1971), item 103.

15. Except where citing primary works, my discussion of maize draws on the fine article by John J. Finan, "Maize in the Great Herbals," *Annals of the Missouri Botanical Garden* 35 (1948): 149–91.

16. Gonzalo Fernández de Oviedo, *Historia general y natural de las Indias*, 3 pts. in 4 vols. (Madrid, 1851–55), 1:268. Finan gives the relevant Pliny citation as *Naturalis Historiae Libri XXXVII*, bk. 18, chap. 7.

17. Hieronymus Tragus (Jerome Bock), *New Kreütter Buch von underscheydt, würckung, und namen* (Strasbourg, 1539), fol. xxi–xxii; Fuchs, *De historia stirpium*, 824–25 (the woodcut takes up all of 825).

18. Finan, "Maize," 164.

19. Ibid., 163.

20. On Gerard's debt to the Flemish botanists and particularly to L'Obel, see Robert H. Jeffers, *The Friends of John Gerard (1545–1612): Surgeon and Botanist* (Falls Village, Conn., 1967).

21. John Gerard, *The Herball; or, generall historie of plantes* (London, 1636), 82.

22. Finan, table 2, "Place of Origin of Maize according to the Herbals," in "Maize," 169.

23. Ibid., 183.

24. While I am not ready to detail the argument, I believe that maize was not an exception. Judging from discussions of tobacco and the tomato in the sixteenth-century herbals, the pattern held of relying on classical sources and locally available seeds and specimens, while losing New World origins (or at least not discussing them). One wild card in these discussions was the role played by Monardes in clarifying some unclear issues by virtue of the sources available to him, but he was silent on the origins of maize.

25. Examples include Lorenz Fries, *Ein clarer bericht wie man alte scheden, löcher und bülen heylen soll mit dem holtz Guaiaco* (Strasbourg, 1525), 11 pages; *Eyn bewert Recept wie man das holtz Gnagacam fur die Frantzosen brauchen sol* ([Nuremberg?], 1518), 4 leaves; *Capitulo over Recetta delo arbore over legno detto Guiana: remedio contra el male gallico* (Venice, 1520), 7 leaves.

26. The *Coronica de las Indias* provides one example: the copy at the Bancroft Library includes the *Conquista del Peru* of Francisco de Xerez, also printed in 1547 (it was first published in 1534); see *Coronica de las Indias: La hystoria general de las Indias agor nueuamente impressa corregida y emendata con la conquista del Peru* (Salamanca, 1547). An important study of printed reports pertaining to the discovery generally is Rudolf Hirsch, "Printed Reports on the Early Discoveries and Their Reception," in *First Images of America: The Impact of the New World on the Old*, ed. Fredi Chiappelli, 2 vols. (Berkeley, 1976), 537–60.

27. Pietro Andrea Mattioli, *Commentaires . . .* (Lyon, 1572), [alpha]1[v].

28. Elizabeth L. Eisenstein, *The Printing Press as an Agent of Change: Communications and Cultural Transformations in Early-modern Europe* (Cambridge, 1979), 110, cites an unpublished study by Gail Bossenga indicating that Ortelius preferred such addenda to making corrections in previously published material.

29. Carolus Clusius, *Exoticorum libri decem* ([Antwerp], 1605), [***1][r].

30. *Petro Bellonii . . . plurimarum singularium & memorabilium rerum in Graecia, Asia, Aegypto, Iudaea, Arabia, aliisque . . . Observationes* (Antwerp, 1589), 495.

31. William B. Ashworth, Jr., "The Persistent Beast: Recurring Images in Early Zoological Illustrations," in *The Natural Sciences and the Arts: Aspects of Interaction from the Renaissance to the 20th Century*, ed. Allan Ellenius (Uppsala, 1985), 60.

32. The same applies to Nicolas Monardes, who never left Spain while producing his much-quoted accounts, later edited again by Clusius, brought together in the *Primera y segunda y tercera partes de la historia medicinal de las cosas que se traen de nuestras Indias*

occidentales que sirven en medicina (Seville, 1574). Plantin publications—the 1553 edition of Dodoens's herbal and the *Stirpium adversaria nova* of Pena and L'Obel—joined Monardes as the original sources for the iconography of the tobacco plant.

33. Gonzalo Fernández de Oviedo, *A Natural History of the West Indies*, trans. Sterling A. Stoudemire (Chapel Hill, 1959), 3. It should be noted that travelers to other parts of the world also balanced attention to classical sources with an insistence on following ocular evidence. Belon discusses this issue in his account of his travel through Asia Minor and the Middle East; see *Observations*, 1^{v}–3^{r}, 77^{v}.

34. José de Acosta, *Historia natural y moral de las Indias* . . . (Seville, 1590); Francisco Hernández, ed. and trans., *Historia natural de Cayo Plinio Segundo* (Madrid, 1624).

35. Oviedo, *Natural History*, 45–47.

36. Clusius, *Exoticorum libri*, $+3^{v}$.

37. For example, such instructions were provided by Richard Hakluyt and John Dee to Arthur Pet and Richard Jackman, who took off in 1580 for the Northwest Passage. Cf. J. R. Hale, *Renaissance Exploration* (New York, 1968), 76–77.

38. Thomas Hariot's journal was published as the *Briefe and True Report . . . of Virginia* (Frankfurt am Main, 1590).

39. Paul Hulton, *America 1585: The Complete Drawings of John White* (Chapel Hill, 1984), 9.

40. One example of the distance herbalists sought to put between themselves and printer's editions was the dispute between Leonhart Fuchs and the German printer Christian Egenolff. See Greene, *Landmarks of Botanical History*, 1:275, 487, n. 18.

41. A useful recent summary of this issue is provided by Adrian Johns, "History, Science, and the History of the Book: The Making of Natural Philosophy in Early Modern England," *Publishing History* 30 (1991): 5–30.

42. *Oviedo de la natural hystoria de las Indias* (Toledo, 1526). The colophon offers the information that "the present treatise . . . was printed at the expense of the author"; Oviedo, *Natural History*, 121. On Oviedo generally, see Gerbi, *Nature in the New World*. For more information on bibliographical matters, see Daymond Turner, *Gonzalo Fernández de Oviedo y Valdés: An Annotated Bibliography*, University of North Carolina Studies in the Romance Languages and Literatures, no. 66 (Chapel Hill, 1966).

43. Oviedo, *Natural History*, 4.

44. Gonzalo Fernández de Oviedo, *La historia general de las Indias* (Seville, 1535); *Coronica de las Indias* (see note 26); Libro XX, *Dela segunda parte dela general historia delas Indias* (Valladolid, 1557). Cf. Turner, *Gonzalo Fernández de Oviedo y Valdés*, xiv–xvi.

45. Oviedo, *Historia general y natural de las Indias*.

46. Sterling A. Stoudemire, foreword to Oviedo, *Natural History of the West Indies*, v.

47. Turner, *Gonzalo Fernández de Oviedo y Valdés*, 12–13.

48. Summarized in Gerbi, *Nature in the New World*, 214–15; Stoudemire, "Editor's Introduction," in Oviedo, *Natural History of the West Indies*, ix–x. As for ignorance of his work, I am referring to Hernández and Thevet; see Gerbi, *Nature in the New World*, 132, and Ashworth, "The Persistent Beast," 60.

49. Francisco Hernández, *Rerum medicarum novae Hispaniae thesaurus, seu plantarum, animalium, mineralium mexicanorum historia. Nova plantarvm, animalivm et mineralivm*

Mexicanorvm historia a Francisco Hernandez primum compilata, dein a Nardo Antonio Reccho in volvmen digesta, a Io. Terentio, Io. Fabro, et Fabio Colvmna Lynceis . . . notis, & additionibus longe doctissimis illustrata. Cui demum accessere, aliqvot ex principis Federici Caesii frontispiciis Theatri naturalis phytosophicae tabulae vna cum quamplurimis iconibus ad octingentas, quibus singula contemplanda graphice exhibentur . . . (Rome, 1651). The publishing history is covered in detail in Germán Somolinos D'Ardois, *Vida y obra de Francisco Hernández* (Mexico City, 1960), 296–303, 409–17.

50. As William M. Ivins, Jr., pointed out in his important studies of prints, causes for distrust inhered in the production and reproduction of illustrations, since as printed they were necessarily "second-hand." William M. Ivins, Jr., *Prints and Visual Communication* (Cambridge, Mass., 1953).

51. Fuchs's *De historia stirpium* is a good example of a book that fell prey to corruption after the first edition.

52. Eisenstein, *The Printing Press as an Agent of Change*, 686. The move from script to print meant, in her words, that "with proper supervision, fresh data could at long last be duplicated without being blurred or blotted out over the course of time."

53. Henry Lowood and Robin Rider, "The New Book of Nature: Communities and Control" (Paper read at the annual meeting of the History of Science Society, October 1990).

54. Pietro Andrea Mattioli, *Opera quae extant omnia: hoc est, Commentarij in VI. libros Pedacij Dioscoridis Anazerbie medica materia*, ed. Caspar Bauhin ([Frankfurt], 1598). In the preface, Bauhin recalls eleven editions published between 1554 and 1586; see **4^r^. The *Commentarii in libros sex Pedacii Dioscorides . . . de materia medica* (Venice, 1565) was the first folio edition with the familiar woodcut illustrations that would be reused into the eighteenth century. Bauhin continued the task of revising and improving Mattioli's commentaries and adding new information to them. Joachim Camerarius provided a German edition, *Kreutterbuch deß . . . Herrn D. Petri Andreae Matthioli* (Frankfurt, 1600) in the third edition. He had seen Gesner's manuscript of the Opera Botanologica and was eager to merge his own observations with those of Gesner and Mattioli; thus several lines of development in natural history merged in what began as a commentary on Dioscorides.

55. Gerald Strauss, "A Sixteenth-Century Encyclopedia: Sebastian Münster's Cosmography and Its Edition," in *From the Renaissance to the Counter-Reformation*, ed. C. H. Carter (New York, 1965), 158.

56. *Plantarum seu stirpium icones* (Antwerp, 1581). A second edition appeared in 1591, with additional indexes but otherwise unchanged. It appears that the job of arranging the more than two thousand images fell to Matthias de L'Obel, though the accomplishment has also been attributed to the reputable Prussian physician Severin Göbel the Elder. As far as I have been able to ascertain, however, Göbel never worked alongside the Flemish botanists or ever set foot in Antwerp. On Göbel, see *Deutsches Biographisches Archiv*, fiche 400 (from Christian Gottlieb Jöcher, *Allgemeines Gelehrten Lexikon* (Leipzig, 1750–51); *Dictionary of Scientific Biography*, vol. 9 (New York, 1974), s.v. Michael Maier. It has been traditional to credit L'Obel with the compilation, because the illustrations refer to entries in his botanical works published by Plantin. There is nothing in the Plantin correspondence that seems to

indicate otherwise. For the attribution to Göbel (presumably the Elder), see *Plant, Animal & Anatomical Illustration in Art & Science: A Bibliographical Guide from the 16th Century to the Present Day*, ed. Gavin D. R. Bridson and James J. White (Winchester, 1990), 39.

57. For the Dodoens image, see the reprinted French translation by Clusius, *Histoire des plantes de Rembert Dodoens* (Brussels, 1978), 305 (*Hyoscyamus luteus*). The illustration of the smoking native is in Matthias de L'Obel and Pierre Pena, *Nova stirpium adversaria . . .* (Antwerp, 1576), 252. For a sense of how important the Plantin pool of images was for New World iconography, see the relevant sections in Ernst and Johanna Lehner, *How They Saw the New World* (New York, 1966).

58. This was originally published as Garcia de Orta, *Coloquios dos simples, e drogas he cousas medicinais da India* (Goa, 1563). The first Plantin edition was the *Aromatum, et simplicium aliquot medicamentorum apud Indos nascentium Historia* (Antwerp, 1567). On Orta, see A. G. Keller, "Garcia d'Orta," in *Dictionary of Scientific Biography*, vol. 10 (New York, 1974), 236–38

59. As indicated on the title page, "nunc verò primùm latina facta, & in epitomen contracta à Carolo Clusio."

60. The Plantin editions were published in 1567, 1574, 1579, and 1593, the latter by Plantin's widow and J. Mourentorff. One or more Italian translations also appeared at least six times between 1576 and 1616 at Venice. The additions by Monardes and Acosta were continuously paginated with Orta's text, though with separate title pages. Clusius's Latin translation and abridgment of Acosta's work was entitled *Aromatum & medicamentorum in Orientali India nascentium* and was printed in 1582, 1593, and 1605 by Plantin and his successors; in the third edition of 1605, it was included in Clusius's collected works as part of the *Exoticorum libri decem.*

61. See Peggy Sue Kidwell, "The Accademia dei Lincei and the *Apiarium*: A Case Study of the Activities of a Seventeenth Century Scientific Society" (Ph.D. diss., University of Oklahoma, 1970).

62. See note 31 and, for full bibliographical details, the excellent bibliography and notes in Somolinos D'Ardois, *Vida y obra de Francisco Hernández.* The title of Cesi's contribution to the 1651 edition was "Phytosophicarum tabularum ex frontispiciis naturalis theatri principis." On Cesi, see Stillman Drake, "Federico Cesi," *Dictionary of Scientific Biography*, vol. 3 (New York, 1971), 179–80.

63. John Ray, *Historia Plantarum*, 3 vols. (London, 1686–1704).

64. C. E. Raven, *John Ray: Naturalist* (Cambridge, 1986), 202.

65. John Ray, "Praefatio," in *Historia Plantarum*, 1:[A4][r].

66. John Ray, "Historiae rerum naturalium Brasiliae libri octo," in *Historia naturalis Brasiliae*, ed. Jan de Laet (Leiden, 1648).

67. John Ray, "Compendium Historiae Plantarum Mexicanorum Francisci Hernández," in *Historia Plantarum*, 2:1929–43.

68. Somolinos D'Ardois, *Vida y Obra de Francisco Hernández*, 417–18.

69. Quoted in Raven, *John Ray*, 221.

70. José de Acosta, *Obras*, Biblioteca de Autores Españoles, no. 73 (Madrid, 1954), 3. On Acosta and Hernández, see Somolinos D'Ardois, *Vida y obra de Francisco Hernández*, 289–

96. See also the reprint of the 1590 edition of Acosta's *Historia natural y moral*, with an introduction by Barbara G. Beddall, published as *Historia natural y moral de las Indias* (Valencia, 1977).

71. Mattioli says about cactus that "peregrinus in Europa est arbor, & in Italia à multis in hortis colitur," in *Compendium de plantis omnibus . . .* (Venice, 1571), 160.

72. Matthias de L'Obel, *Plantarum seu stirpium historia* (Antwerp, 1576), 3.

73. Here I am paraphrasing from David Armitage's contribution to this volume.

CHRISTIAN F. FEEST

The Collecting of American Indian Artifacts in Europe, 1493–1750

History of Research

Five centuries after Europe began to invent and discover America, the question of the role that American Indian artifacts played in the shaping of this New World in the European consciousness must remain largely unanswered. Although such artifacts have supplied tangible evidence for the human nature of the indigenous inhabitants of the lands across the Atlantic ever since Columbus returned from his first voyage, serious interest in their study—and in the study of their collecting—has significantly lagged behind the critical examination of other sources available for an understanding both of native America and of its European perception.

This situation is itself an artifact of the history of research, and it illustrates in part the insignificant role and undeservedly minor academic status that ethnographic museums and their collections have played in anthropological and historical research. On the other hand, an understanding of the often now unique documents collected in the sixteenth and seventeenth centuries has suffered not only because they were separated from their original cultural context and meaning, but also due to the European contexts in which they were preserved.

The date of 1750, which marks the end of the period under consideration, coincides rather closely with a paradigmatic change in the collecting of non-European artifacts in Europe. Spurred by the development of the new taxonomic systems of nature, the great voyages in the Age of Enlightenment (for which those by James Cook stand as the type specimen) returned with a rich harvest not only of natural history specimens, but also of ethnographic objects. While there was hardly a taxonomic system for the ethnographic material (other than a slowly emerging classification by "race"—i.e., "culture" in modern terminology—of the peoples who had produced these artifacts), there was at least a conscious effort to document some of the cultural context (however little understood) from which the artifacts were taken.

These new collections formed the basis for the first separate ethnographic departments within natural history cabinets or natural history museums, and ultimately ethnographic museums. What had remained of the collecting activities of earlier ages languished more or less forgotten as oddities in the art collections which had become the heirs of the old Kunst- and Wunderkammern.

The restructuring of the museum world in the second half of the nineteenth century and the development of professional anthropology within the framework of natural history museums led to the "discovery" of the early pieces for the new museums. Much like that of America, it was a discovery only in terms of a new paradigm, because these pieces had been there all along, often recognizably published in the catalogs of their former repositories, which the new curators of the ethnographic collections had never read and often continued to ignore.[1]

What was discovered were, of course, only the pitiful remnants of once much larger groups of objects. Under the most favorable conditions, such as those obtaining in Vienna, for example, the artifacts were then still part of integral collections, whose documentary history could be traced through a continuous succession of catalogs.[2] Elsewhere, especially in northern Italy, these objects had partly become divorced from their history, were sold to passing visitors, who rarely kept sufficient records, and were finally often disposed of in auction sales.[3]

Of the objects which ended up in ethnographic collections, not all received the same amount of attention. Not unexpectedly, the pieces of featherwork and turquoise mosaic from Mexico were given the greatest prominence in displays and publications; Brazilian featherwork and weapons were noted at least in part, whereas the rest of the material was often at best recataloged. The small number of objects recovered was often seen as an indication of their unique nature, a view which influenced their interpretation and frequently led to rash attributions of provenance and meaning. Further contributing to many of the early misperceptions was the fact that the historical ethnography of the Americas of the sixteenth and seventeenth centuries was then still badly understood.

Professional ethnology and archaeology, which increasingly moved away from the museums to the universities, were concerned with the contextual information to be derived from field work and controlled excavations. The period between prehistory and the present, especially in its relation to the study of material documents, quickly reverted to the status of a Dark Age dominated by the myths created by curators who lacked historical training and proliferated by historians who lacked ethnographic expertise.

It is only within the last three decades that a new approach to the study of these objects has taken shape. The rise of ethnohistory, the emergence of non-European art history, and a renewed interest in the history of museums and of collecting have all contributed to a different appreciation of sixteenth- and seventeenth-century ethnographic objects as documents illuminating the histories of both the cultures which had produced them and which had collected them.

The European culture of collecting, which fully emerged in the sixteenth century from the tradition of late medieval treasuries, is generally associated with the term "Kunst- and Wunderkammern." Assembled by princes and scholars, the encyclopedic nature of these collections was built on their representation of both the natural and the artificial, the works of God and the works of Man. In the absence of modern taxonomic models, the most outstanding principle of selection of the items to be included was their "rarity," which might be based on the individual genius or skill of their maker, or on an origin far distant in time or space. In the course of their development, the princely collections tended to focus increasingly on "art," whose emergence as a separate domain paralleled and was in part caused by the growth of the culture of collecting, yet some princely collections continued to include "natural curiosities."[4]

Kunst- and Wunderkammern were unlike modern museums not only because of the different nature of their selective principles, but also because a focus on public education was generally absent. This does not necessarily mean that they were inaccessible to the public. One may recall the display in 1520 in Brussels of the treasures sent to Charles V from the "new golden land," made famous by Dürer's often-quoted diary entry;[5] one may also refer to the description of a visit to a princely Kunstkammer by the picaresque hero in Grimmelshausen's novel *Simplicissimus*.[6] Travel guide books alerted visitors to the more notable collections and their contents.[7] Sometimes, and more often in the case of scholarly collections, catalogs provided a fairly complete discussion of the objects. By the late seventeenth century, books began to be published in which readers were advised on how to organize their own collections. Obviously, the culture of collecting had spread to the middle class.

Space prevents a full listing of these collections,[8] but at least some of the major Kunst- and Wunderkammern, which also contained American material, should be noted here in an attempt to convey some sense of the distribution and the typological range of such collections. Among the colonial powers, the kings of Spain[9] and France[10] (but not of England) owned significant collections of this kind, none of which was published in catalogs at the time. The latter is also true of the Austrian Habsburg collections in Prague, Graz, and Ambras Castle near Innsbruck,[11] of the extensive Medici collections in Florence,[12] and of the equally important collection of the Bavarian kings in Munich.[13] A fairly cursory published catalog exists for the royal collection in Dresden,[14] and a very complete one for the royal Danish collection in Copenhagen.[15] Gottorp Castle in Schleswig housed the Kunstkammer of Friedrich, duke of Gottorp, which had absorbed the Dutch collection of Bernhard Paludanus, and which would in turn be absorbed by the royal Danish collection.[16] Copenhagen also included the collection of Ole Worm, one of the most important scholarly collections north of the Alps.[17] In northern

Ole Worm's museum as illustrated in the frontispiece of Olaus Worm, *Museum Wormianum sue Historia Rerum Rariorum* (Leiden, 1655). John Carter Brown Library.

Italy the collections of Antonio Giganti, Ulisse Aldrovandi, and later Ferdinando Cospi of Bologna and that of Manfredo Settala of Milan were published in catalog form or to illustrate tracts of natural history.[18] Two printed catalogs also exist for the Jesuits' Musaeum Kircherianum in Rome, but none is available for that of the Congregation de Propaganda Fide, which included material sent back from the American missions.[19] In England a catalog of the extensive collection of John Tradescant was published before its acquisition by Elias Ashmole;[20] only a manuscript catalog exists for that of Sir Hans Sloane, which became the founding collection of the British Museum.[21] Another collection which ultimately became part of the British Museum was that of the Royal Society of London.[22] Published catalogs also exist for the Theatrum Anatomicum of the University of Leiden and of the collection of Levinus Vincent in Amsterdam.[23] For France, the collections of the Bibliothèque Sainte-Geneviève in Paris and of Paul Contant of Poitiers may be mentioned as examples of institutional and individual collecting.[24]

Much of the work of reevaluating the American materials in these collections in terms of their meaning for the European culture of collecting and their importance for our understanding of the cultures they partly represent remains to be done. But at least there is a growing awareness of the agenda for future research. It may thus be useful, first of all, to survey the sources and discuss some of their problems before attempting to present some ideas on the collecting of American Indian artifacts in Europe before 1750, much of which will of necessity be highly anecdotal.

Sources and Problems

Understandably, most of the past research has centered on the specimens surviving in European collections. It should be noted at the outset that the assignment of artifacts to this group may be based on two criteria. One, preferably, is the availability of records documenting the presence of such items in a European repository before a given cutoff date. The second is based on typological grounds, whenever there is reason to believe that an artifact of a certain type or style could not possibly have been made after a given date. Examples for such groups of objects would be Mexican turquoise mosaics, which should date from the sixteenth century, or Tupinamba clubs, which are unlikely to have been available after the seventeenth century. In many cases, assignments on the basis of type or style are presently still impossible.

In 1985 a survey of Mexican and South American artifacts surviving from sixteenth- and seventeenth-century European collections (exclusive of pictorial manuscripts)[25] listed as coming from Mexico more than thirty pieces of featherwork (one headdress, four shields, one fan, and a group of pictures, trypitcha, and bishops's miters of colonial origin),[26] twenty-three turquoise mosaics, about twenty small lapidary works, one wooden figurine, one amber figurine, three spear throwers,[27] two obsidian mirrors,[28] one shell-beaded skin apron,[29] and several groups of colonial pottery.[30] To these should be added a Mixtec golden finger ring and a colonial golden figurine.[31] The Mexican items add up to just above ninety objects in a more or less pre-Cortesian tradition plus a substantial number of colonial artifacts.

From the West Indies, just five Taíno pieces (at least two of them early colonial) can lay claim to a sixteenth- or seventeenth-century pedigree. It is conceivable that some, especially wooden, objects that have survived without a clear history may have been collected during the same period, but others have been recovered archaeologically, such as the cotton *zemi* (a Taíno term for supernatural beings and their representations) mistakenly included among the presumed Kunstkammer objects.[32]

Brazil is represented in the same survey by ten Tupinamba,[33] three Tarairiu, and more than a dozen long, square clubs from the Brazilian/Guyana borderlands,[34] nine anchor axes,[35] and a few bows;[36] about twenty pieces of featherwork; and more than a dozen miscellaneous items, including hammocks,[37] musical instruments, ornaments, and other implements. To these should now be added a spear thrower, four oars, two trumpets, a necklace, a circular object, and a quiver.[38] These add up to more than ninety artifacts from lowland South America.[39]

From the Andean highlands comes a fairly well documented group of five wooden objects from Colombia, but virtually nothing else. Excluding the colonial Mexican pottery and some other artifacts which technically represent more of a Spanish than an indigenous tradition, the total number for Middle and South America comes to close to two hundred objects.[40]

Apart from the scarcity of Andean and the lack of Central American material in this group,[41] the absence of weapons from Mexico and of clothing other than featherwork is remarkable.

The evidence for objects from native North America in pre-1750 European collections was published more recently.[42] The Arctic is well represented by a group of perhaps a dozen kayaks, with the earliest two dated to 1606 and 1612, some paddles and oars, hunting gear, a woman's parka, a man's kayak shirt, snow goggles, drums, and a few ivory carvings. Objects from the Southeast include at least one basket, a rattle, and a few tobacco pipes. The majority of North American objects, however, originated in the northeastern Woodlands, from the Atlantic seaboard to the western Great Lakes and the eastern Subarctic, with a few Plains items interspersed. Weapons include more than a dozen ball-headed clubs and two bladed weapons, at least one quiver, but no bows and arrows; clothing is represented by one shell-beaded and several painted skin robes, a few quilled and/or painted coats and shirts, some pairs of quilled moccasins, and quilled and other ornaments; means of transportation are illustrated by at least one birchbark canoe model, one or two pairs of snowshoes, and a number of burdenstraps; among the objects of domestic and personal use are a bone comb, a bone spoon, a set of quilled birchbark bowls and some quilled bark boxes, one shell-beaded and several painted pouches with quilled fringe, a number of pouches and a basket decorated with false moose-hair or porcupine quill embroidery; items of at least partly ceremonial significance include two artificial wolf heads, two wooden staffs, several wampum belts and strings, and a number of tobacco pipes. The total number of approximately one hundred items would be substantially increased if all undocumented material that may have predated 1750 were included.

This select group of three hundred or so specimens, representing the nonarchaeological survival of the material heritage of the native Americas in European repositories, however, is only the tip of the iceberg formed by the documentary evidence relating to European collecting of Native American specimens before 1750. Manuscript inventories and published catalogs exist both for collections that have maintained some sort of continuous existence as well as for those that were dispersed or destroyed.[43] Most of these descriptive sources have been used primarily for the purpose of establishing a pedigree for surviving objects, whereas the study of these lists with a view toward the history of ethnographic collecting has been sadly neglected.[44] There is substantial variation in the value of these documents. In some cases, descriptions are barely sufficient to help the reader recognize an object even if it has survived, but there are instances where the written records even provide ethnographic information not available in other sources.[45] On the whole, the usefulness of catalogs and inventories increases with a detailed knowledge of the artifacts that might be described, which is why they are of minor interest to art historians who work with them more regularly—while they are often unknown to the curators of ethnographic collections.

Supplemental information on American objects displayed in Europe before 1750 is contained in travel books of the time and in the writings of visitors. The better guide books list and describe the more interesting objects either on the basis of now lost labels or of information offered by the collector or curator. Visiting savants rarely cover the ground as systematically as the books but often add insights based on their special interests.[46] There are also some eighteenth-century guide books to museums, which partly draw on published catalogs and descriptions but sometimes add new information.[47]

The majority of the catalogs and inventories are not illustrated,[48] although some catalogs offer at least an overall view of the collection as displayed,[49] while others picture a highly selected group of items in the form of woodcuts or engravings.[50] Since most of these collections were available at least to the scholarly public, illustrations of some of their contents occasionally also were published in other connections.[51] In a number of cases, pictures supply the only evidence for objects which must have been exhibited in European collections. The American drawings by and attributed to Burgkmair and Dürer, as well as some of the earliest woodcuts showing American Indians, were obviously based on artifacts which had become separated from their makers or owners, but which cannot presently be identified on inventories or lists of specific collections.[52] Illustrations of specimens likewise turn up in the correspondence and general papers of individual collectors, mostly in connection with objects offered them for sale and irrespective of whether they were ultimately bought.[53] Images of such artifacts may be of help in clarifying the identity of ambiguously described items, but they may likewise add to the ethnographic record when depicting now lost objects.

Documentation of the transfer from the American field to the European collection or between collections within Europe[54] are not at all common. On a history-of-collecting level, the latter situation is of significant interest for a better understanding of the mechanics of the early European market in Native American artifacts and of the mobility of the objects. Shipping lists, which exist for some of the earliest collections to be sent from Mexico,[55] may not only establish the final link between today's museum object and its American cultural matrix, they also vividly illustrate how few of the items sent were ever entered into the inventories of collections.[56]

Reports on field collecting, the most critical juncture in the history of the cultural alienation of material documents, have received even less attention than some of the other sources. The most likely explanation is that only in a very few exceptional cases can surviving reports on collecting activities be matched with surviving objects. The documentary chain of evidence of what happened in the transfer from the original cultural context to another must therefore of necessity generally remain incomplete. Still, much needs to be learned about the principles involved in early field collecting if we want to arrive at a considered opinion either of the objects we would like to regard as important sources of Native American cultures or of the collection of American Indian artifacts in Europe.

One frequently overlooked type of collecting, for example, involved native peoples carried to Europe for a variety of reasons.[57] In some cases it might be said that the people themselves were collected, which is especially true of those Eskimos forcibly brought to England, to Denmark, or to the Netherlands, whose kayaks, other artifacts, and even bodies were deposited in collections after their death.[58] In late-seventeenth-century Paris, a North American visitor was flayed after his death at the Hôtel-Dieu in order to preserve his nicely tattooed skin.[59] But even natives who had not come as objects of curiosity were apparently approached by collectors wishing to add to their cabinets. The Four Kings of Canada, who in 1710 had come to London on a political errand, not only were made to contribute to the entertainment of the public but also left some of their baggage to British collectors. John Pointer's Museum Pointerianum included not only the "Indian Kings' Speech to Queen Ann" but also "An Indian Prince's Cane. Given me Richard Dashwood Esqr. of the Inner Temple, who beg'd it of the Prince for me."[60] The Thoresby collection in 1712 claimed to have received as a gift from John Cookson of London "a knife taken from one of the Mohawks at London, An. 1710." And among the objects assembled by Sir Hans Sloane, there were at least three thought to have been obtained from the distinguished visitors: a burden strap, a prisoner tie "from the Iroquois by the Indian kings," and "a long thin piece of wood . . . which one of the Indian kings thrust down his throat. 'tis used as a remedy to cause vomiting as a proang tho it did not cause him to vomit."[61]

The artifacts sent in 1519 by Cortés to Charles V as part of the royal fifth due to the sovereign included—unknown to the Spanish—the costumes used in the impersonation of four gods, which Moctezuma, prompted by a series of omens, had forwarded to the conquistadors who landed in Vera Cruz.[62] Other artifacts were delivered as part of ceremonial exchanges, and still others were obtained as loot. Often artifacts were collected primarily as evidence for the presence of natural

Drawing attributed to Hans Burgkmair, ca. 1520, showing an African model wearing presumably South American featherwork and carrying an "anchor ax" from Brazil. Department of Prints and Drawings, British Museum.

resources in the New World, and this is as true of the golden ornaments from the civilizations of Mexico and the Andean highlands as of the belts of silk grass or the necklace of mountain lion claws taken from Virginia to England by William Strachey.[63] The demonstration of the possible usefulness of native crafts for Europeans was another reason for obtaining samples of such products. William Wood praised the New England natives' stone pipes and noted that "they be much desired of our English Tobaconists, for their rarity, strength, handsomenesse, and coolnesse."[64] Missionaries would preserve at least sample specimens of idols to document the need to spread the word of the gospel.[65] On the other hand, they might also encourage their new converts to show their gratitude to the European benefactors of the missions (and thus of their own salvation) by producing appropriate native gifts. In 1654 the French Jesuit Father Le Mercier supervised the manufacture of a wampum belt by the Catholic Hurons of St. Mary, which carried the inscription "Ave Maria Gratia Plena"; it was sent to the Congregation of Our Lady in the Professed House of the Society of Jesus in Paris and may have ended up in the Jesuits' museum in Rome, where the same or a similar belt was described in 1709.[66]

When field collecting was done upon the request of European correspondents, it was not necessarily for a cabinet or museum. In 1687 William Byrd, a Virginian trader, sent to a gentleman in England "an Indian habitt for your boy, the best I could procure amongst our neighbour Indians."[67] But by the late sixteenth century, a market had developed in which dealers or agents in Europe supplied the owners of collections with whatever was needed. Hannibal of Hohenems, who sent what was believed to be Moctezuma's battle ax to Ferdinand II of Tyrol, was as much Ferdinand's agent as Johann Christoph Khevenhüller, who also supplied Rudolf II and Archduchess Maria of Graz with American items, or Philipp Hainhofer, who worked for several German princes. These dealers were in turn furnished with the needed objects by sources in America, which especially included missionaries.[68]

The survey of the types of sources to be used has already indicated that the history of collecting American Indian artifacts in Europe may be described as a history of losses: losses of the primary documents—the objects—and losses also of the secondary documentation that somehow links an artifact with its former context.

The loss of objects in actual numbers is staggering. Of approximately one hundred items of Americana listed in Tradescant's 1656 catalog, just over twenty have survived.[69] Only one of about twenty-five American and Greenlandic ethnographic specimens belonging to Ole Worm at the time of his death in 1654 can be today identified beyond doubt in the Danish National Museum, and a weaker case can be made for another three.[70] Of the extensive American section of the

Kunstkammer of Albrecht V of Bavaria, only a single piece has come down from the early seventeenth century.[71] Around thirty pieces present in Prague in the 1620s have been reduced to three now in Vienna.[72] A higher survival rate is indicated for the thirteen items listed on the 1596 Ambras inventory of Ferdinand of Tyrol, of which ten remain in Vienna today, but nothing has survived of a somewhat smaller number of American objects in neighboring Ruhelust also belonging to Ferdinand.[73] The situation is not much different with respect to early-eighteenth-century collections: of about 250 American pieces in the Sloane collection, about thirty can be identified in the British Museum today.[74] Nothing seems to be left of Ralph Thoresby's collection in Leeds, which in 1712 included at least sixteen American artifacts.[75]

The case is obviously even worse when a survival rate is calculated on the basis of shipping lists. Of the hundreds of objects described on the very detailed lists available for objects sent to Spain from Mexico in the first years after the conquest, only two can be identified with some certainty among the survivors.[76] There were, of course, also substantial losses on the way from the New World to the Old, and even in the Americas. It is a well-documented fact that objects of pagan worship were indeed collected for the explicit purpose of being destroyed, although the claim that "more than 170,000 statues of this kind of idols [*zemis*] made of various kinds of materials were broken, destroyed, and burned by the priests of our order of Saint Benedict in the Island of Hispaniola alone" may be something of an overstatement.[77]

Whereas the wholesale destruction of items suspected of representing the work of the devil was more common in the Americas than in Europe, its influence on the low survival rate in places like late-sixteenth- and seventeenth-century Spain should not be underestimated. More important, however, were greed (in the case of works of precious metal, almost none of which has survived), negligence combined with changes in collectors' tastes (which doomed much of the featherwork), wars (in particular the Thirty Years' War), and the dispersal of collections. Mexican mosaics in Italian collections suffered terrible losses when lapidaries of the eighteenth and early nineteenth centuries used what now would be regarded as precious works of art as sources of raw materials.

One of the reasons that estimates of the survival rate will always remain at best rough approximations stems from the fact that catalogs and inventories are deficient as far as provenances are concerned. Some items are listed without any indication of their origin. The Mexican feather fan now in Vienna, for example, could not be clearly recognized as such on the Ambras inventory of 1596 if it had not survived; the description is specific enough to remove any doubts about its identity, however, and the actual piece clearly shows its Mexican origin. Once the identity is accepted, a similar origin may be guessed for similarly described items elsewhere.[78]

Almost as bad is the case whenever objects are designated as "Indian." This is particularly the case in German and English catalogs,[79] whereas Spanish lists often distinguish between "India" and "Las Indias,"[80] and the French generally use "Américains."[81] In the early sixteenth century, "Calicut" is sometimes used instead of "India" and carries the same ambiguity.[82] Whether such items can be unequivocally assigned to Asia or the Americas depends, again, upon the details supplied by the description. A similar problem is presented by the use of the term "Moorish" instead of "Mexican."[83]

More specific terms encountered in the written records are "West Indian," "American," "Brazilian," "Canadian," "Greenlandic," or "Floridian," "Virginian," "Mexican," or "Peruvian." These may sometimes be mistaken, but more often than not they at least point in the right direction. Specific peoples are rarely mentioned before the eighteenth century. A wampum belt is identified as "Huron" in the Musaeum Kircherianum, and several items from Surinam are attributed to the "Caraibs" in the catalog of a collection in the Alsatian Château de Ribeauville in the second half of the seventeenth century.[84] "Cherekee," "Mohawk," "Iroquois," and "Esquemo" appear in early-eighteenth-century English catalogs.[85]

Misattributions can sometimes be recognized because of the obvious contradiction between the description and the provenance, such as when a snowshoe from the North American subarctic is referred to as "Greenlandic."[86] Changes in the attribution from one inventory to another of the same collection are not always for the better: in Prague, an "Indian boat of leather" (most likely a kayak) became a "leathern Japanese little ship" between 1621 and 1737.[87] An Iroquoian pipe head in Ole Worm's collection was thought to be "Brazilian" in 1655, a "West Indian tobacco pipe called 'Calicot' " in 1673, and consequently "East Indian" in 1690; had this particular item not survived, it would have been difficult to guess its actual origin.[88] Further changes in the records made in the nineteenth century attribute some American objects to places such as Tahiti, New Zealand, China, or Madagascar.[89]

Whereas the attributions supplied by the catalogs are often of little help in identifying actual provenance, they do illustrate an early modern generalization of "otherness," which only gradually gave way to an awareness of the differences between the various cultures thus grossly equated. It was only by the mid-eighteenth century that specific "races" (however misconstructed themselves by even more specific contemporary standards) became the focal point for ethnographic collecting.[90]

Illustrations may, of course, be rather helpful in correcting misattributions: based on published images, we can be sure that a "West Indian" *zemi* from the Kunstkammer in Graz was indeed a Javanese kris.[91] This discovery, in turn, has led to the reconsideration of a "Mexican idol" in Kassel as a kris.[92]

American Representation

A German treatise of 1707 on how to organize a cabinet or museum offers specific suggestions as to which objects would be suitable to be included among the "Foreign Rarities," some of which are also illustrated on the accompanying plates. The section on clothing and implements might, for example, encompass a Brazilian feather crown and feather skirt, a Floridian feather crown, and a Mexican women's skirt, next to Cairene women's shoes, Egyptian women's shoes and bonnet, an Ethiopian sun shade, a Chinese Mandarin hat, a Japanese sun shade and women's bonnet, Japanese seals and writing implements, a Muscovite hat and whip, and a Laplander's skis. Exotic weapons and armor could include a Brazilian shield, a Greenlandic boat and paddle, a Singhalese fighting hat, as well as a Japanese helmet, shot pouch, standard, pike, saber, and halberd. To illustrate idolatry, Mexican idols of wood and "northern, malformed images from Greenland, decorated with furs, feathers, and fishbone" are suggested along with Indian idols of porcelain, ivory, clay, or metal, "called zemmes." Judging from the illustrations, American ethnography was also placed in the section on ancient weapons, where a Brazilian anchor ax is featured as an ancient sacrificial hatchet, and in the natural history section, where one of a pair of Brazilian garters made of fruit shells is used to illustrate the fruits.[93]

Whereas the selections reflect some of the things commonly found in collections of the day, the nice balance between American, Asian, and African objects reflected in it was hardly ever achieved. In part, the representation of the Americas was linked to colonial interests of the collectors' countries in the New World. Thus, it is not surprising that two-thirds of Sir Hans Sloane's ethnographic objects came from North America, and an even higher percentage of the Spanish royal collections derived from Spanish America.[94] In central European collections, on the other hand, the New World fared less well. Of 260 artificial curiosities in the Kundmann collection in Breslau, only three or four were American, one African, but sixty-one Asian (covering the continent from Turkey and Persia through India to China and Japan).[95] Even in the Netherlands, where there was no shortage of Brazilian and Arctic American material, a famous collection such as the Theatrum Anatomicum in Leiden listed twenty European and eighteen Asian artifacts next to just five from the Americas and one each from the Pacific and Africa—the latter in addition to seventeen Egyptian antiquities.[96]

There are, however, some similarities in how the Americas were represented in these collections beyond the local differences in access to specific groups of objects. The following survey is far from exhaustive and is based on only a small sample of the existing evidence.

Eskimo material, mostly from Greenland and usually referred to as such, was present in many of the early collections, from Sweden to Italy and from England to

Mexican deity with two horns, probably Mixtec. Listed on the 1590 inventory of the Kunstkammer in Graz as "a Moorish face with several turquoise and two large pearls, on it three precious stones and a large pearl lost," the origin of the object would be impossible to ascertain in the absence of the item itself. Museum für Völkerkunde, Vienna.

Bohemia. Apart from objects derived from Frobisher's voyages, Canadian Eskimo artifacts hardly occur much before 1700 and then primarily in British collections.[97]

The type specimen for "Greenlanders" was indeed, as the German treatise of 1707 suggests, the kayak, together with its paddles and, somewhat less commonly, hunting gear. Apart from the kayaks already noted among the surviving pre-1750 pieces, they can be documented for Prague, Copenhagen, Lambeth, Vlissingen, Gottorp, Leiden, Leipzig, London, Edinburgh, Burray, and Frankfurt.[98] John Davis is said to have collected five kayaks, and in 1656 Nicolas Tunes brought "a large number" of them to Vlissingen.[99]

Eskimo hunting gear and oars without kayaks are on record in Amsterdam and Leipzig, and clothing of fur, bird skin, and fish entrails in Copenhagen, Lambeth, and Amsterdam.[100] Although the sealskin garment in the Cospi collection had a label identifying it as a "coat of an Indian priest," Sturm's claim that a good museum should include fur and bone idols from Greenland is based on a single item described and illustrated from the Gottorp collection;[101] Sloane misidentifies a canoe fitting as "An Indian God of the Inhabitants about Hudsons Bay."[102]

North American boats also entered European collections at an early date. In 1599 Walter Cope had in his London house "A long narrow Indian canoe, with the oars and sliding planks, hung from the ceiling." In 1603 a group of "Virginians" paddled their boat on the River Thames in London, while three years later another one was brought back from Canada by the Sieur de Monts.[103] The latter was clearly described as a birchbark canoe, but the "Virginian" boat may have been a dugout. Contant's collection in Poitiers included a "boat called a Canoe, 18 foot long, from a single bark of an Indian tree called Ceiuas," which the accompanying illustration clearly shows to have been a Beothuk birchbark canoe. A century later, Bonanni illustrates a model of a birchbark boat from the Jesuit collections in Rome.[104]

Based on the pipes surviving in Copenhagen, identified as "Indian" and "Brazilian" on the early inventories,[105] it is tempting to think of several similarly described pipes as North American. Among them are the two "Brazilian" pipes of clay in the Cospi collection, three wooden pipes, "one of them very big," in the Theatrum Anatomicum in Amsterdam, three others with the images of "Indian idols" in the Roeter collection in Amsterdam, and yet three more in Leipzig as from northeastern North America.[106] An Iroquois provenance of a tobacco pipe "made of marble, very curious" recorded in 1670 in La Rochelle may be deduced from the context in which it occurs.[107] The Sloane collection included an "Indian Calumet or stone pipe of peace" from New England; the Thoresby collection in Leeds had the "head of a Calumet" of white stone, which had "embossed upon it three Heads of their Kings, or rather Deities."[108] Four Virginian clay pipes from the same collection, however, may not have been of native manufacture.

Apart from the surviving wampum belts and strings, Contant's "Belt of pieces of shell money," if indeed a wampum belt, may be the earliest known example to have entered a European collection. By 1669 the Royal Society had received three belts, two strings, and two pairs of bracelets as a gift from Governor John Winthrop of Connecticut. Similar to the belts preserved at Chartres and in Paris must have been one also made by Hurons and inscribed "Ave Maria Gratia Plena" in the Musaeum Kircherianum in Rome. Another wampum belt had survived in the collection of the Collegium Propaganda Fide in Rome, only to be lost within the last eighty years.[109] A wampum bracelet is on record in Thoresby's collection in Leeds. One belt each is illustrated in the description of the Bibliothèque Sainte-Geneviève and in the 1706 catalog of Levinus Vincent's collection. A whole "suit of clothes, with coat, trousers and sword belt, entirely of their money . . . threaded and worked with all kinds of animals" was made by some natives of New Sweden for Governor Printz, while William Byrd of Virginia sent to John Clayton in England "a cap of wampum."[110]

The most easily identified North American weapon is the ball-headed club, and it is also one that has survived in substantial numbers in England, Sweden, Denmark, the Netherlands, France, and Italy. A fine example, inlaid with shell, was seen among the objects brought by the Sieur Monts from Acadia in 1606 by Fabri de Peiresc.[111] An exquisite description is given of another one sent from North Carolina in Thoresby's catalog. The same catalog also lists a stone-bladed weapon inlaid with wampum and copper ("brass annulets") similar to the two surviving examples in Copenhagen and Stockholm.[112]

A bow was brought from Canada by the Sieur de Monts in 1606, and specimens from both Canada and Virginia were among the "Bowes, Arrowes, Quivers, Darts" in the Tradescant collection. An "Indian" bow and arrows owned by Thoresby may also have been from North America.[113]

Complete sets of men's and women's clothing from New France are illustrated by Bonanni; various Virginian "Match-coats" and habits and shoes from Canada are listed by Tradescant. But such artifacts were clearly not abundant in pre-1750 collections. Whether the "Indian girdle" in the Tradescant collection was North American cannot be ascertained; Thoresby had one that had belonged to the daughter of an Indian "queen" of Maryland, which was probably of the same type as the women's girdles of "silk grass" collected a century earlier in Virginia by William Strachey.[114] Not surprisingly, only English collections make reference to Virginia or other specific British colonies in North America.[115]

In 1670 the Sieur de Bernonville had in his collection in La Rochelle "the personal equipment of a savage chief," including moccasins, "two halters with which he bound poor Christian prisoners," and various trophies of "Christians slain in battle" and "of enemies whom the chief has eaten." The halters for prisoners in particular make an Iroquois attribution of this group very likely.[116]

Despite the prominence of Florida in Sturm's "ideal cabinet," objects bearing this designation are extremely rare in collection records. Aldrovandi shows a "queen from the island of Florida" wearing a feather wig from the Giganti collection, which is more likely to have been of Brazilian origin (see also below). Settala illustrates a spear from Florida and refers to a bow as coming from the same area. The wooden head of an idol, said to be from Florida, listed on the 1598 inventory of the Kunstkammer in Munich and illustrated by Pignoria in 1626 is certainly from Florida in a wide sense of the word. It is also one of the few North American "idols" in the early collections. Another one, also from "Florida," was in the seventeenth-century collection of Don Vicencia Juan de Lastanosa; yet another one was collected in early colonial Virginia by the Reverend Alexander Whitaker.[117]

Whereas the records frequently refer to the "West Indies," this cannot necessarily be understood as referring to the Caribbean islands, but generally as an attempt to specify an American rather than East Indian origin. A "West Indian" apron described and illustrated by Olearius has survived and can be identified as northwest Mexican or Californian. Some of the specimens called "West Indian" are in fact from Brazil, whereas none of the few surviving Taíno items was called anything specific on the inventories. A *zemi* made of shell beads in the Munich collection that can be identified as of Taíno origin was said to be from Mexico and a gift of Francisco Ximenes, the archbishop of Toledo, who had died in 1517, before the first Spanish contacts in Mexico. Petrus Martyr de Angleria writes of sending four cotton *zemis* to another churchman, and indeed many such pieces must have ended up in early collections. Finally, a Taíno *duho* (or wooden stool), is shown on a drawing among the papers of Nicolas Claude Fabri de Peiresc; it is not known whether this was in his collection, but it illustrates the fact that such items were available in Europe in the seventeenth century.[118]

"A boat with its oars, which is used by the inhabitants of the Antilles" in the cabinet of S. Victor in Brussels is one of the few explicit and believable references to the West Indies; a rush basket from the Barbados in the Thoresby collection is another.[119]

"Mexico" is also a relatively rare attribution encountered in the records. The mistaken provenance of the Taíno piece just mentioned is the only case where the Munich inventory, which includes many clearly identifiable Mexican objects, makes reference to Mexico.[120] Nor do any of the Spanish or Austrian Habsburg inventories from 1661 to the mid-eighteenth century use such a label. The only indirect reference, contained in the designation "Montezuma's battle ax," is again a mistake, since the surviving object is clearly Brazilian. A similar mistake involving an Indonesian kris described in Kassel as a "Mexican idol" has been noted above.[121]

The picture was different in Italy, where Aldrovandi, Cospi, and others do (and often correctly) refer to artifacts as Mexican. The fact that some of the surviving

Mexican objects can be traced through minor collections in the German provinces, however, may be taken as a clue that the problem of identifying Mexican material is not due to its rarity.[122]

This situation, however, makes it rather difficult to cull from the records information on which Mexican objects were favored by collectors. Based on the surviving specimens, it is obvious that featherwork, small stone sculptures of various kinds, and turquoise mosaics (including masks, sacrificial knives, and animal-shaped mirror frames) were the most common.[123] Textiles and gold jewelry were certainly also present, as indicated by the 1524 Mecheln inventory and the Spanish Habsburg lists, but are difficult to trace—partly because they were melted.[124] Two Mexican textiles are mentioned in the Musaeum Kircherianum, but only a maguey fiber thread in Ole Worm's collection.[125]

Most surprising is the absence of clearly identifiable Mexican weapons, especially when compared to the number of clubs from North America and Brazil. Apart from feather or turquoise mosaic shields and spear throwers, only one spear from Mexico survived into the nineteenth century, before it was destroyed at the Real Armería in Madrid. Even among the artifacts listed in 1524 in Mecheln there were only a few spears, but no clubs.[126]

By the end of the sixteenth century, one type of Mexican artifact, feather pictures, was greatly sought by collectors. These can be easily detected in the records, although they are hardly ever called Mexican (and, indeed, are sometimes labeled "Peruvian").[127] The reason for their popularity was the incredible technical perfection, which made viewers frequently touch them in order to make sure they were not painted.[128]

As far as Brazil is concerned, identification is made somewhat easier by more frequent references to a Brazilian origin, and by the assumption that we can recognize at least some Brazilian pieces on the basis of their description. Whether this assumption is really warranted is somewhat doubtful. There can be no doubt, however, that there was much featherwork from Brazil in pre-1750 collections. A number of Tupinamba feather mantles have survived and another one is clearly illustrated by Settala; Terzaghi's catalog of the Settala collection identifies this and other pieces of featherwork as belonging to "Indian priests."[129] An illustration in the catalog of Vincent's collection in Amsterdam shows what may be another one, as well as Tupinamba back ornaments and other likely Brazilian feather pieces. Contant lists "garments of various feathers," which are likely to have been of Brazilian origin. An "Indian mantle of various parrot feathers, lined with red cloth and decorated with golden borders" in Prague was perhaps Mexican rather than Brazilian. Another Prague inventory, however, describes a "large naked woman, formed of materia [plaster], with an Indian mantle of red feathers." It is not clear whether the two were the same item; if so, the second piece could be mistaken for a

Brazilian feather mantle.[130] The Royal Society of London likewise had an "Indian Mantle; also made of feathers," but a "Match-coat from Virginia of Feathers" in the Tradescant collection at least suggests an alternative provenance.[131]

Aldrovandi pictures a "savage" man and a "Floridian" woman both wearing feather hoods or wigs, which appear to relate in type to similar Brazilian pieces preserved in Copenhagen.[132] "An Indian Peruque, Made not of Hair, but Feathers" in the Royal Society and one almost identically described in Ralph Thoresby's collection may belong to the same group. Thoresby also had "The Crown of an Indian King, the inside is made of split cane," which is reminiscent of other Brazilian pieces in Copenhagen.[133] Most of the other featherwork, however, is described without sufficient precision to be attributed to Brazil. Some items may only be guessed to have been made of feathers, such as the "several crowns which the Queen in America has worn" in Walter Cope's collection, a "frontlet of the same feathers," and "several Indian capes made of parrot feathers" in the Lorenz Hoffmann collection in Halle, "an Indian belt plaited of feathers of various colors" in Ulm, or a "crown of a king of the savages of America"; others may not even have been American at all.[134]

Brazilian bark cloth, variously colored, is noted in Terzaghi's catalog of the Settala collection.[135]

Of weapons, a great number of Brazilian bows still remain from early collections. Of two bows illustrated from Settala's museum, one is covered with a plaited decoration similar to the surviving bow in Brussels. The same collection included arrows, one of them clearly a Brazilian whistling arrow. On the other hand, none of Tradescant's bows and arrows are listed as Brazilian, yet the surviving bow is thought to be of that origin. Grew lists a "West-Indian" bow, arrows, and quiver. No provenance is indicated for various arrows, spears, daggers, and a shield in Contant's collection.[136]

A Tupinamba club is recognizably described and called "Brazilian" on the Prague inventory of 1607–11; another, labeled "Indian," was in Ambras, either of which may be the piece now in Vienna. Contant's "Indian club of ebony" and "another club of Orobotan wood" as well as Settala's "Brazilian club of very hard wood" and "another Brazlian club" may also belong here.[137] Anchor axes were probably intended by descriptions in Munich and Halle. The Royal Society collection featured "A Tamahauke, or Brasilian Fighting-Club," but the generic term for clubs and hatchets does not allow a precise identification (Tradescant, however, did include the long square clubs from the Brazilian/Guyana region under this term).[138]

"Indian morris-bells of shells and fruits" in the Musaeum Tradescantianum are identifiable as Brazilian through an illustration in Johnson's edition of Gerard's *Herball*, which identifies the nuts as "Ahouay Theueti"; a similar item survives in

Copenhagen (probably from Gottorp, where Olearius describes and illustrates them). A pair of such leg rattles is illustrated by Aldrovandi; others were in Poitiers ("bundle of the fruit Auoay Indico"), Milano, and apparently in Prague. A "bunch of Indian wooden bells" in Ruhelust also may be related to this group. This artifact type very appropriately also figures in Sturm's "ideal" cabinet.[139]

Peru was rather poorly represented in the collections, especially outside of Spain. Various items, including idols of stone, textiles, and examples of metalwork, are listed in the collections of Charles V and Philip II, who had specifically requested the viceroy of Peru to send samples of that country's crafts. Some of these were preserved at the Palacio del Buen Retiro in 1667.[140] Peruvian shoes were a popular item also outside Spain; apart from Siamancas, we have records for the Tradescant collection and Leiden.[141] Otherwise, only isolated items show up: a bag in the Musaeum Kircherianum, bark cloth textiles in the Settala collection, a "passport which the King of Peru had given to the English, artificially written on wood" in Walter Cope's collection in 1602, or "two beautifully worked coconuts of the island Peru, from which the women use to drink" in the pre-1683 Lorentzen collection in Leipzig (and more likely of Brazilian origin).[142]

Settala's museum is almost unique in having several items attributed to Chile and Paraguay. Another reference to Chile occurs in the Gottorp collection in connection with the desiccated body of an Indian, formerly one of a pair owned by Paludanus.[143]

Apparently regarded as typical for America were stone lip plugs. One in Leiden is called a "West Indian Cassuwe stone, of greenish color, such as the kings of America put into the lower lip when they decorate themselves." Others are listed by Contant and Tradescant. No provenance is indicated in either case.[144]

A favorite item in pre-1750 collections were hammocks (see also above for surviving specimens). They were not only mentioned for the Brazilian Tupinamba by Montaigne in *Des cannibales* but are clearly recognizable in catalogs and inventories even where no provenance is supplied: "An Indian bed of netted work," 1596 in Ruhelust; five "Indian beds," four of them netted, one woven, 1598 in Munich; another one each, 1611 in Stettin, 1616 in Tours ("a piece of material from woven wood, in which forest people of the Indies sleep"), and 1650 in Prague; two in Milano, said to be from Brazil and Paraguay, respectively; a total of five, 1668 in Graz; "a Hamack or net, which the Americans tie between two trees and sleep therein," in Leiden; others in the Royal Society collection and in the Musaeum Kircherianum. An "Indian bed" is also mentioned in Strasbourg in 1618. The hammock in Rome was called Mexican; two now in Copenhagen were referred to in Gottorp as from the coastal regions of Brazil. The Ribeauville collection lists "a ball of cotton from Surinam, which the Caraib women spin on their spindles and of which they knit their hamac." It is indeed likely that various regions were represented in this group.[145]

The same is true of various kinds of bread found in several collections: Siamancas had "pan de las Yndias," Contant "bread of a floury tree, called Cassaui or Yucca," Christoph Weickmann in Ulm "bread of Yucca Canedana," Copenhagen "bread of Yuca Casavi," Tradescant "Cassava Bread 2 sorts," the Royal Society of London "Cassavi-Bread," the Musaeum Kircherianum "Brazilian bread called Mandioca," Levinus Vincent in Amsterdam "bread of the root Cassave," and Thoresby "Cassada-bread."[146]

Order and Appreciation

European collecting seriously began and developed during the 250 years following Christopher Columbus's first voyage across the Atlantic. While the discovery of the New World was not the cause of this development, the collecting of American Indian artifacts certainly profited from it. Within this period several types of collections emerged and established different paradigms for the organization of the material and for the place that American ethnographic material could possibly be assigned in it.[147]

Without wishing to simplify a complex matter, one may say that, apart from the distinction between the princely collections (which often reflected the ideas of domination and representation) and those of scholars (whose quest was for knowledge), there were distinctions according to the organization of the cabinets. The two major systematic principles involved in how a collection was set up were material and subject matter. Ferdinand of Tyrol's Kunstkammer in Ambras was displayed according to the material of the items: most of the American items were in the feather case, but there was also a case for lapidary work, or one for wooden objects. Ole Worm likewise organized his museum according the material from which the items were made, and in this he was certainly influenced by Aldrovandi, in whose collection the artificial rarities were inserted among the natural substances from which they had been made.[148]

The other principle may be illustrated by referring to the Kunstkammer in Copenhagen, which after 1680 was divided into such entities as the Heroic Cabinet (featuring the kings and great men), the Cabinet of Natural Objects, or the Cabinet of Medals, with most of the Americana in the Indian Cabinet.[149] In this connection "India" stands, of course, for exotic places in general. An Indian Cabinet which existed in Dresden, for example, was regarded as especially memorable for its "foreign Indian rarities and naturalia" and was located next to a "cabinet with many Turkish and other nations' weapons" and another one "wherein are sundry Turkish, Roman, Greek, and other nations' habits."[150] Tradescant's American ethnographic material was featured under five different headings: "Mechanick artificiall Works in Carvings, Turnings, Sowings, and Paintings," "Variety of Rari-

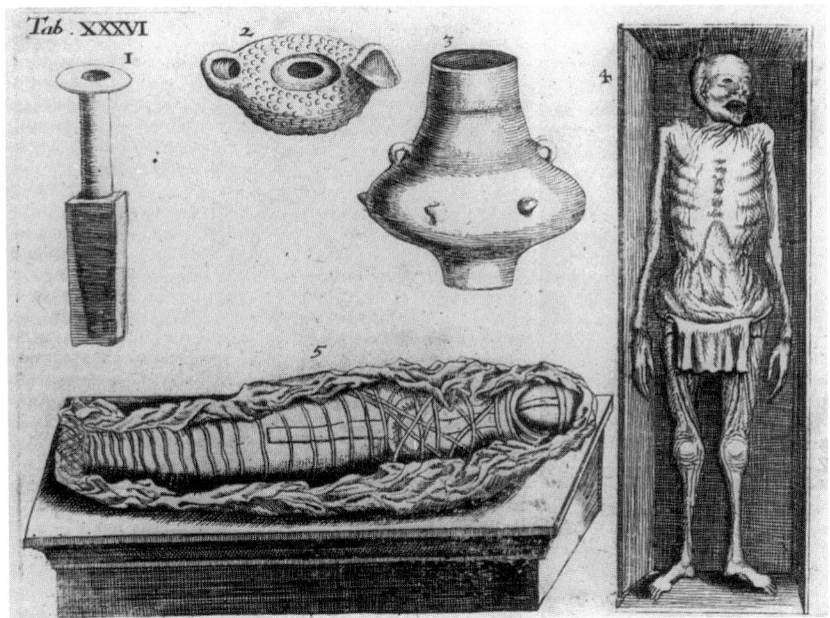

Mummy or "dried Indian," attributed to "Chili," from the collection of Bernhard Paludanus, later displayed in the Gottorp Kunstkammer. Adam Olearius, *Gottorffische Kunst-Kammer* (Schleswig, 1674), pl. xxvi. Österreichische Nationalbibliothek, Vienna.

ties" (which foreshadows Sloane's "Miscellanies" section as the appropriate place for ethnography), "Warlike Instruments," "Garments, Vestures, Habits, Ornaments," and "Utensils."

Few collectors probably followed the detailed outline of an ideal collection proposed by Sturm in 1707. Here the American objects would be in the third chamber, devoted to "Exotic Rarities," preceded by Antiquities and the Treasure, and followed by Naturalia, the Kunstkammer of European *artificiala* (including a special section on "Amateur and Women's Art"), Mathematical and Physical Curiosities, Garden, Orchard, and Zoo. "Exotic Rarities" were subdivided into four sections: "Clothing and utensils of foreign heathen nations," "Idols and sacrificial vessels of the heathen, who remain in our times," "Armory of all contemporary foreign nations," and "All kinds of rarities of the Turkish, Jewish, and Popish religion" ("Matters relating to the Romish superstition" also held a special place in Thoresby's museum).[151]

This classification also uses the term "Memorabilia" as a synonym for "Exotic rarities."[152] One important feature of collecting in general was indeed the stress on the memorable, which in turn frequently manifested itself in the presumed association of objects with notable events or persons. This also applied to Native

“Exotic rarities” in the “ideal cabinet.” Next to Japanese military equipment and dress items, an Egyptian ladies’ shoe, a Sami ski, and headgear from Egypt, Muscovy, and Sri Lanka are featured featherwork (nos. 19 and 20) and a shield (no. 23) from Brazil, a feather crown (no. 21) from Florida, a Mexican apron (no. 26), and a Greenlandic kayak and paddle (nos. 28 and 27). [J. C. Sturm], *Des Geöffneten Ritter-Plattes Dritter Theil* (Hamburg, 1707), pl. iv. Bildarchiv der Österreichischen Nationalbibliothek, Vienna.

American artifacts, although certain limitations were imposed by the small number of famous, named individuals. But designations like "Pohatan, King of Virginia's habit," "the sword of Quoniambec," "the mighty king Muttazuma of Mexico's battle ax," or "the costumes of Moctezuma" raised at least a few select items above the sea of American anonymity.[153]

Evidence for the perception of America and its native peoples in the context of early European collections as "savage" rather than "royal" is found in entries such as "two pipes made of the legs which have been eaten by the cannibals of America," "necklaces made by the American Indians from the teeth of their vanquished enemies," "a Brazilian field apron made from the skin of their killed enemies," "an American apron of the people who go naked there," or "a suchlike little pouch, wherein the Americans use to put the cut off heads of their enemies."[154] On the whole, however, the descriptions are neutral or appreciative of the workmanship of American artifacts, except in the case of "idols," which were often regarded as ugly.

But no matter how the collections were structured, it is obvious that with rare exceptions there was no separate representation of the Americas. Among the exceptions was the Mauritshuis in The Hague, where Johan Maurits of Nassau had assembled "many rarities from America." Aldrovandi kept catalogs according to the "regions and places from which various things have originated," but the organization of his published works seems to indicate that this was only a supplemental index.[155] If there was an organization by place, it followed the simple division of "domestic" versus "foreign" (the latter eventually including, as we have seen, both Native American artifacts and curiosities relating to the "Romish superstition").

Typical for pre-1750 collections was probably the definition of a "cabinet" by Neickelius: "But since a curious one finds his entertainment and pleasure as well in *Naturalibus* as in things of art, antiquities, coins, medals, and such like, he can very well so arrange his Chamber or Cabinet, that he may collect and preserve therein something of all of the above said: and since there are many different things in one case next to one another, so one calls such a receptacle a Chamber of Rarities or Cabinet."[156]

Given the organization of the ethnographic material in collections before 1750, it is obvious that the majority of the viewers were unlikely to differentiate between American objects and those from other far-off lands. What likely impressed visitors most was the very variety of strange and never-before-seen artificial rarities. Renward Cysat of Lucerne, who in 1613 inspected the cabinet of Felix Platter in Basel, expressed his amazement at the sight of "Heathen, Turkish, Moorish, Canibal, Indian, Japanese things ex antipodibus and from the New World, of their idols, habits, armor, arms, and suchlike, so that one is thereof smitten and forgets to shut the mouth."[157]

Gasping speechlessness before all those "marvellous artificial things" that caused reflection on the "subtle ingenuity of people in foreign lands" was not only experienced by Dürer in 1520 in front of the things sent to Charles V from the "new golden land"; it was a recurrent sensation for many who looked at the material evidence for the otherness defining the self that had been assembled in European collections.[158] As "Indian rarities," whether from the Americas or from elsewhere, their decontextualized and bewildering variety helped to construct in a visual and immediate mode the notion of the antipodal Other that was America.

ACKNOWLEDGMENTS

The author wishes to acknowledge his gratitude to all his colleagues, but especially to George R. Hamell, J. C. H. King, and William C. Sturtevant, who over the years have shared with him their knowledge of the collecting and the collections of American Indian artifacts in Europe.

NOTES

1. Cf., for example, Christian F. Feest, "Vienna's Mexican Treasures: Aztec, Mixtec, and Tarascan Works from Sixteenth Century Austrian Collections," *Archiv für Völkerkunde* 44 (1990): 4.

2. Franz Heger, "Altmexikanische Reliquien aus dem Schlosse Ambras in Tirol," *Annalen des k.k. Naturhistorischen Hofmuseums* 7 (1892): 379–400.

3. Elizabeth Carmichael, *Turquoise Mosaics from Mexico* (London, 1970).

4. See, for example, Barbara J. Balsiger, "The 'Kunst- und Wunderkammern': A Catalogue Raisonné of Collecting in Germany, France, and England, 1565–1750" (Ph.D. diss., University of Pittsburgh, 1970), 540–83; Elisabeth Scheicher, *Die Kunst- und Wunderkammern der Habsburger* (Vienna, 1979), 12–43; Arthur MacGregor, "Collectors and Collections of Rarities in the Sixteenth and Seventeenth Centuries," in *Tradescant's Rarities: Essays of the Foundation of the Ashmolean Museum*, ed. Arthur MacGregor (Oxford, 1983), 70–97; Oliver Impey and Arthur MacGregor, eds., *The Origins of Museums: The Cabinets of Curiosities in Sixteenth- and Seventeenth-Century Europe* (Oxford, 1985); Adalgsia Lugli, *Naturalia et Mirabilia: Il collezionismo enciclopedico nelle Wunderkammern d'Europa* (Milano, 1983); Ellinoor Bergvelt and Renée Kistemaller, eds., *De wereld binnen handbereill. Nederlendse Kunst- en rariteitenverzamelingen, 1585–1735*, 2 vols. (Amsterdam, 1992). For the relationship between collecting and the origins of "art" as a separate domain, see Joseph Alsop, *The Rare Art Traditions* (New Haven and London, 1982).

5. Cf. Christian F. Feest, "'Selzam ding von gold da von vill ze schreiben were': Bewertungen amerikanischer Handwerkskunst im Europa des frühen 16. Jahrhunderts," *Jahrbuch der Willibald-Pirckheimer-Gesellschaft* (1992), 105–26.

6. Siegfried Streller, ed., *Grimmelshausens Werke*, 4 vols., Bibliothek Deutscher Klassiker (Berlin and Weimar, 1977), 1:73–74.

7. See, for example, Martin Zeiller, *Itinerarium Germaniae Nov. Antiquae. Teutsches Reyssbuch durch Hoch und Nieder Teutschland* (Strasbourg, 1632); Christoph Abraham von Eyl, *Parisische Conferentzen Darinnen vorgetragen wird eine Historische nach dem Alphabet eingerichtete Namens-Tafel über die Provintzien, Städte, Vestungen und Oerter der vereinigten Niederlande* (Sultzbach, 1672). These guidebooks also provide some measure for the public interest (or lack thereof) in exotic American artifacts. Maximilian Misson, whose Italian tour guide was successfully published in many editions, describes the Museum Anatomicum in Leiden, Ambras Castle, the Medici collections in Florence, the Musaeum Kircherianum, the collections of Cospi in Bologna and of Settala in Milan, all of which included American material, yet he makes reference only to "des ouvrages des Indes" in Settala's museum. Cf. Maximilian Misson, *Voyage d'Italie de Monsieur Misson. . . . Cinquième édition* (Utrecht, 1722).

8. An extensive, yet incomplete list is supplied in the form of a "catalogue raisonné" by Balsiger, "The 'Kunst- and Wunderkammern,'" 32–507, 597–736. Although somewhat dated and covering a much larger field, David Murray's *Museums: Their History and Their Use* (Glasgow, 1904), is also still a useful reference tool with an extensive listing of catalogs. Some of the collections and the catalogs and inventories associated with them are discussed by various essays in Impey and MacGregor, *Origins.*

9. The manuscript inventory of the collection of Charles V (Carlos I) is in Rudolf Beer, ed., "Acten, Regesten und Inventare aus dem Archivo General zu Simancas," *Jahrbuch der Kunstsammlungen des allerhöchsten Kaiserhauses* 12 (1891): clxx–ccxxiii; for that of the collection of Philip II, see F. J. Sánchez Cantón, ed., *Inventarios Reales bienes muebles que pertenecieron a Felipe II,* Archivo Documental Español 11 (Madrid, 1956–59). American materials in these and other royal collections are discussed in María Paz Aguiló Alonso, "El coleccionismo de objetos procedentes de ultramar a traves de los inventarios de los siglos XVI y XVII," in *Relaciones Artisticas entre España y América* (Madrid, 1990), 107–49; Juan José Martin Gonzalez, "Obras artísticas de procedencia americana en las colecciones reales españolas: Siglo XVI," in *Relaciones artisticas entre la Península Ibérica y América,* Actas del V Simposio Hispano-Portugés de Historia del Arte (Valladolid, 1990), 157–62; Paz Cabello and Cruz Martínez, "Tres siglos de coleccionismo americanista en España," *Fragmentos* 11 (1987): 48–66. Virtually no object of a pre-Columbian tradition collected before 1750 survives in Spanish museums today.

10. Marie-Noëlle Bourguet, "The French Museum and America," *Journal of the History of Collections* 5, no. 2 (1993), in press. Two lists of ethnographic objects removed from the royal natural history cabinet in 1796, apparently the earliest such documents, may be found in E.-Th. Hamy, *Les origines du Musée d'Ethnographie du Trocadéro* (Paris, 1890), 81–83, 87–89. For a discussion of some of the surviving pieces, see E.-Th. Hamy, *Galerie Américaine du Musée d'Ethnographie du Trocadéro* (Paris, 1897), vol. 1, and "Note sur d'anciennes peintures sur peaux des indiens Illinois," *Journal de la Société des Américanistes de Paris* 2 (1897–98): 185–95; Anne Vitart Fardoulis, "Les objets indiens des collections royales," in *Le Canada de Louis XIV,* ed. Jean Palardy and Caroline Montel-Glenisson (Saint-Germain-en-Laye, 1980), 129–38, and "Les objets américains de l'Hôtel de Sérent ou une collection ethnographique au 18e siècle," *Archivio per l'antropologia e la etnologia* 113 (1983): 143–50.

11. For a general discussion of the Austrian Habsburg collections, see Scheicher, *Kunst- und Wunderkammern*; manuscript inventories of these collections were published in Rotraud Bauer and Herbert Haupt, eds., "Das Kunstkammerinventar Kaiser Rudolfs II, 1607–1611," *Jahrbuch der Kunsthistorischen Sammlungen in Wien* 72 (1976); Joseph Wastler, "Zur Geschichte der Schatz-, Kunst- und Rüstkammer in der k.k. Burg zu Grätz," *Mittheilungen der k.k. Central-Kommission zur Erforschung und Erhaltung der Kunst- und historischen Denkmale*, n.s., 6 (1880): xxix–xxxv, lv–lxii, xcvi–cv, cxlviii–cli; Heinrich Zimmermann, "Urkunden, Acten und Regesten aus dem Archiv des k.u.k. Ministerium des Innern," *Jahrbuch der kunsthistorischen Sammlungen des allerhöchsten Kaiserhauses* 7 (1888): xvii–xxxiii, and "Das Inventar der Prager Schatz- und Kunstkammer vom 6. Dezember 1621," *Jahrbuch der Kunstsammlungen des allerhöchsten Kaiserhauses* 25 (1904): xiii–lxxv; Wendelin Boeheim, "Quellen zur Geschichte der kaiserlichen Haussammlung und der Kunstbestrebungen des durchlauchtigsten Erzhauses. Urkunden und Regesten aus der k.u.k. Hofbibliothek," *Jahrbuch der kunsthistorischen Sammlungen des allerhöchsten Kaiserhauses* 7 (1888): ccxxvii–ccciv. Specimens surviving at the Museum für Völkerkunde in Vienna are discussed in Feest, "Vienna's Mexican Treasures."

12. For American objects that have survived in Florence and Rome from the Medici collections, see Detlef Heikamp and Ferdinand Anders, *Mexico and the Medici* (Florence, 1972); Detlef Heikamp, "Mexico und die Medici-Herzöge," in *Mythen der Neuen Welt*, ed. Karl-Heinz Kohl (Berlin, 1982), 126–46; Sara Ciruzzi, "Gli antichi oggetti americani nelle collezioni del Museo Nazionale di Antropologia e Etnologia," *Archivio per l'antropologia e la etnologia* 113 (1983): 151–65.

13. A discussion of American objects with extensive quotations from the 1598 Munich inventory may be found in Detlef Heikamp, "Mexikanische Altertümer aus süddeutschen Kunstkammern," *Pantheon* 28 (1970): 205–20.

14. Tobias Beutel, *Chur-Fürstlicher Sächsischer stets grünender hoher Cedern-Wald* (Dresden, 1671).

15. Oliger Jacobaeus, *Museum Regium, seu Catalogus* (Copenhagen, 1696). The 1737 inventory is reproduced with a complete account of the surviving pieces in Bente Gundestrup, *Det kongelige danske Kunstkammer 1737/The Royal Danish Kunstkammer 1737* (Copenhagen, 1991).

16. Adam Olearius, *Gottorffische Kunst-Kammer, worinnen allerhand ungemeine Sachen so theils die Natur, theils künstliche Hände hervorgebracht und bereitet. Vor diesem aus allen vier Theilen der Welt zusammengetragen* (Schleswig, 1674).

17. Olaus Worm, *Museum Wormianum sue Historia Rerum Rariorum* (Amsterdam, 1655); H. D. Schepelern, *Museum Wormianum* (Odense, 1971), supplies a concordance of the various catalogs of the Worm collection. The surviving American ethnographic specimens from Worm's and the other collections in Copenhagen are discussed in Torben Lundbæk and Bente Dam-Mikkelsen, *Etnografiske genstande i Det kongelige danske Kunstkammer 1650–1800/Ethnographic Objects in the Royal Danish Kunstkammer 1650–1800*, Nationalmuseets skrifter, Etnografisk række 17 (Copenhagen, 1980), 1–33; cf. Berete Due, "Early American Objects in the Department of Ethnography, the National Museum of Denmark, Copenhagen," *Archivio per l'antropologia e la etnologia* 113 (1983): 137–40.

18. Ulisse Aldrovandi, *Ornithologia hoc est avibus historiae libri XII* (Bologna, 1599), and *Museum Metallicum* (Bologna, 1648); Lorenzo Legati, *Museo Cospiano* (Bologna, 1677); Paulus Terzaghi, *Museum Septalianum* (Milan, 1664). For the Aldrovandi manuscript catalog, see Laura Laurencich Minelli, "Oggetti studiati da Ulisse Aldrovandi," *Archivio per l'antropologia e la etnologia* 113 (1983): 187–206; cf. also, by the same author, "L'indice del Museo Giganti: Interessi etnografici e ordinamento di un museo cinquecentesco," *Museologia Scientifica* 1 (1984): 191–242, "Museography and Ethnological Collections in Bologna during the Sixteenth and Seventeenth Centuries," in Impey and MacGregor, *Origins*, 17–23, and "Dispersione e recupero della collezione Cospi," *Atti e memorie della Deputazione di storia patria per le province di Romagna*, n.s., 33 (1983): 185–202; Laura Laurencich Minelli, ed., *Bologna e il Mondo Nuovo* (Bologna, 1992); Antonio Aimi, "Il Museo Settala: i reperti americani di interesse etnografico," *Archivio per l'antropologia e la etnologia* 113 (1983): 167–86; Vincenzo de Michele et al., *Il Museo di Manfredo Settala nella Milano del XVII secolo* (Milan, 1983).

19. Georgius de Sepi, *Romani Collegii Societatis Iesu Musæum Celeberrium* (Amsterdam, 1678); Philippus Bonanni, *Musaeum Kircherianum sive Musaeum a. P. Athanasio Kirchero incoeptum* (Rome, 1709); for material in the Propaganda Fide, some of which has since been lost, cf. David I. Bushnell, Jr., "North American Material in Italian Collections," *American Anthropologist*, n.s., 8 (1906): 250–53. For American material in early Italian collections, see Detlef Heikamp, "American Objects in Italian Collections of the Renaissance and Baroque: A Survey," in *First Images of America: The Impact of the New World on the Old*, ed. Fredi Chiappelli, 2 vols. (Berkeley, 1976), 1:455–82.

20. John Tradescant, *Musæum Tradescantianum: or, A Collection of Rarities Preserved at South-Lambeth neer London* (London, 1656). The history of the collection and the specimens surviving in Oxford (Ashmolean and Pitt Rivers museums) are discussed in detail in MacGregor, *Tradescant's Rarities.*

21. Cf. David I. Bushnell, Jr., "The Sloane Collection in the British Museum," *American Anthropologist*, n.s., 8 (1906): 671–85; H. J. Braunholtz, *Sir Hans Sloane and Ethnography* (London, 1970); J. C. H. King, "North American Ethnography in the Collection of Sir Hans Sloane," in Impey and MacGregor, *Origins*, 232–36. A detailed study of the Sloane collection by King is in preparation.

22. Nehemiah Grew, *Musæum Regalis Societatis, or a Catalogue & Description of the Natural and Artificial Rarities Belonging to the Royal Society and preserved at Gresham Colledge* (London, 1681); cf. also Thomas Birch, *The History of the R. Society of London* (London, 1756–57).

23. Gerard Blancken, *Catalogue de ce qu'on voir de plus remarquable dans la chambre de l'Anatomie publique, de l'université de la Ville de Leide* (Leiden, 1710); Levinus Vincent, *Elenchus Tabularum, pinacothecarum, atque nonnullarum cimeliorum in gazophylacio Levini Vincent* (Amsterdam, 1719).

24. Claude du Molinet, *Le Cabinet de la Bibliothèque de Sainte-Geneviève*, (Paris, 1692); for the specimens surviving at the library, see Françoise Zehnacker and Nicolas Petit, *Le Cabinet de curiosités de la Bibliothèque Sainte-Geneviève* (Paris, 1989). Paul Contant, "Exagoga Mirabilivm naturae è Gazophylacio Pauli Contanti Pictauensis Pharmacopaei," in *Les*

Oeuvres de Iacqves et Pavl Contant pere et fils maistres apoticaires de la ville de Poictiers (Poitiers, 1628), vol. 2.

25. Christian F. Feest, "Mexico and South America in the European Wunderkammer," in Impey and MacGregor, *Origins*, 237–44; the following notes add more recent references, notes on overlooked specimens, and some objects that date between 1700 and 1750, a period not covered in the original survey. For Mexican material, see also Christian F. Feest, "Das Erbe der Kunst- und Wunderkammern. Mexicana des 16. Jahrhunderts in europäischen Museen," in *Glanz und Untergang des Alten Mexiko*, ed. Arne Eggebrecht, 2 vols. (Mainz, 1986), 1:185–88. For Mexican pictorial manuscripts, some of which were also kept in Kunstkammer-type collections (others were in libraries), see John B. Glass, "A Survey of Native Middle American Pictorial Manuscripts," in *Guide to Ethnohistorical Sources*, vol. 3, ed. H. F. Cline, gen. ed. R. Wauchope, Handbook of Middle American Indians 14 (Austin, Tex., 1975), 3–80, and John B. Glass with Donald Robertson, "A Census of Native Middle American Pictorial Manuscripts," in ibid., 81–252.

26. Cf. also Christian F. Feest and Peter Kann, eds., *Gold und Macht: Spanien in der Neuen Welt* (Vienna, 1986), 393–95. To these should be added two (including the earliest dated) colonial feather pictures: see Pascal Mongne, *Trésors américains: Collections du Musée des Jacobins d'Auch* (Boulogne-Billancourt, 1988), 277–78, pl. 16, and Donna Pierce, "Bishop's Miter," in *Mexico: Splendors of Thirty Centuries* (New York, 1991), 260–63; Laura Laurencich Minelli and Alessandra Filipetti, "Per le collezioni americaniste del Museo Cospiano e dell'Istituto delle Scienze: Alcuni oggetti ritrovati a Bologna," *Archivio per l'antropologia e la etnologia* 113 (1983): 215–16.

27. Cf. also Ciruzzi "Antichi oggetti americani," 152.

28. To these should be added another obsidian mirror: see Eggebrecht, *Glanz und Untergang*, vol. 2, #354.

29. Due, "Early American Objects," 137, tav. 1.

30. Cf. Feest and Kann, *Gold und Macht*, 384–87.

31. Heikamp, "Mexikanische Altertümer," 213–17.

32. Feest, "Mexico and South America," 240; Jay A. Levenson, ed., *Circa 1492: Art in the Age of Exploration* (Washington, D.C., 1991), 579–81.

33. To these should now be added two other Tupinamba clubs (Zehnacker and Petit, *Cabinet de curiosités*, 81; one in the Museo de América, Madrid, seen in January 1986).

34. Another Brazilian/Guyana long, square club survives in Florence (Ciruzzi, "Antichi oggetti americani," 157–58), and an example of a broadly similar, but shorter (and generally later) type of club in Madrid (Feest and Kann, *Gold und Macht*, 355).

35. To these should be added another anchor ax (Otto Zerries, "Das außerandine Südamerika," in *Kunst der Naturvölker*, ed. Emmy Leuzinger, Propyläen Kunstgeschichte, Supplementband 3 (Frankfurt am Main, Berlin, Vienna, 1978), fig. 384a.

36. Another bow is in Brussels (Sergio Purin, personal communication, 1987), and four more are in Florence (Ciruzzi, "Antichi oggetti americani," 157–59).

37. Three more hammocks are found in Skokloster Castle (Christian F. Feest, "New Sweden: 350 Years Later," *European Review of Native American Studies* 3, no. 1 [1989]: 53–54) and Paris (Zehnacker and Petit, *Cabinet de curiosités*, 82).

38. Due, "Early American Objects," 137, tav. 1; Ciruzzi, "Antichi oggetti americani," 161–63, 164n; Zehnacker and Petit, *Cabinet de curiosités*, 82; Otto Zerries, "Drei alte figürlich verzierte Holztrompeten aus Brasilien in den Museen zu Kopenhagen, Leiden und Oxford," *Ethnologische Zeitschrift Zürich* 1 (1977): 77–89.

39. Feest, "Mexico and South America," 240–43.

40. Ibid., 243–44.

41. A beaded apron in Copenhagen (Lundbæk and Dam-Mikkelsen, *Etnografiske genstande*, 21; Due, "Early American Objects," 137, tav. 1) is thought to be Central American but could equally be from elsewhere. From the eighteenth century, a Miskito hatchet survives in the Sloane collection (Braunholtz, *Sir Hans Sloane*, 35).

42. Christian F. Feest, "North America in the European Wunderkammer," *Archiv für Völkerkunde* 46 (1992): 61–109.

43. In addition to the inventories of the Austrian and Spanish Habsburg collections noted above, see also the important inventory of the Mecheln collection of Archduchess Margarete in Heinrich Zimmermann, ed., "Urkunden und Regesten aus dem k.u.k. Haus-, Hof-, und Staatsarchiv in Wien," *Jahrbuch der kunsthistorischen Sammlungen des allerhöchsten Kaiserhauses* 3 (1885): cxix–cxx. Among the manuscripts catalogs that have been published, cf., for example, Werner Fleischhauer, "Die Kunstkammer des Grafen Ulrich von Montfort zu Tettnang, 1574," *Ulm und Oberschwaben* 44 (1982): 9–28, for the Montfort collection at Tettnang; Antonio Giganti's index in Laurencich Minelli, "L'indice del Museo Giganti," 228–42; or the microfiches of the 1685 Ashmolean catalog in MacGregor, *Tradescant's Rarities*.

44. Franz Heger's study of records of lost Americana in Habsburg collections ("Verschwundene altmexikanische Kostbarkeiten des XVI. Jahrhunderts, nach urkundlichen Nachrichten," in *Anthropological Papers Written in Honor of Franz Boas* [New York, 1906], 306–15) was aimed at the possible identification of the rediscovered Mexicana and perhaps also the discovery of others. Information on lost objects from inventories and published catalogs is included in Christian F. Feest, "Spanisch-Amerika in außerspanischen Kunstkammern," *Kritische Berichte* 20 (1992): 43–58, and Feest, "North America."

45. See, for example, Thomas Dunbar Whitaker, ed., *Musæum Thoresbyanum, or a Catalogue of the Antiquities, and of the Natural and Artificial Rarities Preserved in the Repository of Ralph Thoresby . . . A.D. MDCCXII*, 2d ed. (Leeds, 1816).

46. For early accounts of the Tradescant collection, see, for example, MacGregor, *Tradescant's Rarities*, 20–22.

47. See, for example, Michael Bernhard Valentini, *Museum Museorum oder vollständige Schaubühne Aller Materialien und Specereyen. Zweyte Edition* (Frankfurt, 1715); C. F. Neickelius, *Museographia oder Anleitung zum rechten Begriff und nützliche Anlegung der Museorum oder Raritäten-Kammern* (Leipzig and Breslau, 1727).

48. For the exceptions, Aldrovandi and Settala, see Laurencich Minelli, "Oggetti studiati," Aimi, "Il Museo Settala," and de Michele et al., *Museo di Manfredo Settala*.

49. For those showing American objects, cf. Worm, *Museum Wormianum*; Du Molinet, *Le Cabinet*; Terzaghi, *Museum Septalianum*; Vincent, *Elenchus Tabularum*.

50. Woodcuts appear, for example, in Aldrovandi's *Ornithologia* and *Museum Metalli-*

cum, or Legati's *Museo Cospiano*; engravings in Contant, "Exagoga Mirabilivm," Olearius, *Gottorffische Kunst-Kammer*, Jacobaeus, *Museum Regium*, Vincent, *Elenchus Tabularum*, Bonanni, *Musaeum Kircherianum*; of American objects, Worm, *Museum Wormianum*, 383, only illustrates a copy of a Mexican pictorial manuscript.

51. See, for example, Charles L'Ecluse, *Exoticorum Libri Decem: Quibus Animalium, Plantarum, Aromatum, aliorumque peregrinorum Fructuum historiae describuntur* (Antwerp, 1605); Honorius Philoponus, *Nova Typis Transacta Navigatio* (Linz, 1621); Johannes Neander, *Tabacologia: hoc est Tabaci seu Nicotinae descriptio* (Amsterdam, 1622); Lorenzo Pignoria, "Seconda parte delle Imagini de gli dei Indiani," in Vincenzo Cartari, *Seconda Novissima Editione delle Imagini de gli dei delli Antichi* (Padua, 1626); Fortunato Liceto, *Pyronarcha sive de fulminum nature deque felssium origine* (Padua, 1634); [César de Rochefort], *Histoire Naturelle et Morale des Iles Antilles de l'Amérique. . . . Seconde edition* (Rotterdam, 1665).

52. William C. Sturtevant, "First Visual Images of Native America," in Chiappelli, *First Images*, 1:420–22, figs. 2–4.

53. Cf. King, "North American Ethnography"; Henri Dubled et al., *Nicolas-Claude Fabri de Peiresc (1580–1637)* (Carpentras, 1981), plate after 31.

54. For the transfer of whole collections, for example, the Paludanus collection to Gottorp, and the Gottorp collection to Copenhagen, cf. Lundbæk and Dam-Mikkelsen, *Etnografiske genstande.*

55. Luis Torres de Mendoza, ed., *Coleccion de Documentos Ineditos relativos al descubrimiento, conquista, y organizacion de las antiguas posesiones españolas de América y Oceania*, vol. 12 (Madrid, 1869); cf. Marshall H. Saville, *The Goldsmith's Art in Ancient Mexico*, Indian Notes and Monographs, Miscellaneous 7 (New York, 1920).

56. Cf. Feest, "Vienna's Mexican Treasures."

57. Cf. Christian F. Feest, "Indians and Europe? Editor's Postscript," in *Indians and Europe*, ed. Christian F. Feest (Aachen, 1987), 613–20.

58. William C. Sturtevant and David Beers Quinn, "This New Prey: Eskimos in Europe in 1567, 1675, and 1577," in Feest, *Indians and Europe*; Peter J. P. Whitehead, "Earliest Extant Painting of Greenlanders," in ibid., 144; John Brand, *The Little Kayak Book* (Colchester, 1984), 3–4; Gerd Nooter, *Old Kajaks in the Netherlands*, Mededelingen van het Rijksmuseum voor Volkenkunde, Leiden 17 (Leiden, 1970), 10–11.

59. Sieur de Dièreville, *Relation of the Voyage to Port Royal in Acadia or New France*, Publications of the Champlain Society, no. 20 (Toronto, 1933), 170.

60. Catalogue of the Museum Pointerianum, St. John's College, Oxford, Ms. 252, fol. 161^{v}.

61. Whitaker, *Musæum Thoresbyanum*, 47. Braunholtz, *Sir Hans Sloane*, 34–35. Olearius, *Gottorffische Kunst-Kammer*, 5, reports that he questioned the Eskimos taken to Bergen in 1654 and later to Gottorp Castle about the meaning of an "idol" from Davis Straits in the collection.

62. Feest, "Vienna's Mexican Treasures," 33.

63. William Strachey, *The Historie of Travell into Virginia Britania* (1612), Hakluyt Society, 2d ser., no. 103 (London, 1953), 125; Louis B. Wright, ed., *A Voyage to Virginia in 1609* (Charlottesville, 1964), 89.

64. William Wood, *New Englands Prospect* (1634), Publications of the Prince Society, no. 3 (Boston, 1865), 39; cf. Christian F. Feest, "European Collecting of American Indian Artifacts and Art," *Journal of the History of Collections* 5 (1993): 1–11.

65. Samuel Purchas, *Hakluytus Posthumus, or, Purchas His Pilgrimes* (1625), Hakluyt Society, extra ser., nos. 14–33 (Glasgow, 1905–7), 19:110.

66. Reuben Gold Thwaites, ed., *The Jesuit Relations and Allied Documents*, 73 vols. (Chicago, 1896–1901), 41:165–75; Bonanni, *Musaeum Kircherianum*, 225.

67. Marion Tinling, ed., *The Correspondence of the Three William Byrds of Virginia, 1684–1776*, Virginia Historical Society Documents 12–13 (Charlottesville, 1977), 1:61.

68. David von Schönherr, "Urkunden und Regesten aus dem k.u.k. Statthalterei-Archiv in Innsbruck," *Jahrbuch der Kunstsammlungen des allerhöchsten Kaiserhauses* 14 (1893): clxvii; Christian F. Feest, "Zemes Idolum Diabolicum: Surprise and Success in Ethnographic Kunstkammer Research," *Archiv für Völkerkunde* 40 (1987): 189; Oscar Döring, *Des Augsburger Patriziers Philipp Hainhofer Beziehungen zum Herzog Philipp II von Pommern-Stettin*, Quellenschriften für Kunstgeschichte und Kunsttechnik, n.s., 6 (Vienna, 1894), 188.

69. Tradescant, *Musæum Tradescantianum*, 37, 41–54; MacGregor, *Tradescant's Rarities*, 108–39, 339–40.

70. Schepelern, *Museum Wormianum*, 340, 346–48, 352, 356, 362; Lundbæk and Dam-Mikkelsen, *Etnografiske genstande*, 18, 9, 11, 22.

71. Zeiller, *Itinerarium Germaniae*, 286–88; Heikamp, "Mexikanische Altertümer," 207–10, 213–15.

72. Zimmermann, "Inventar der Prager Schatz- und Kunstkammer," xx, xxxiii, xxxvi, lx–lxii; Ferdinand Anders, "Der Federkasten der Ambraser Kunstkammer," *Jahrbuch der Kunsthistorischen Sammlungen in Wien* 61 (1965): 130–32; Feest, "Vienna's Mexican Treasures," 32.

73. Boeheim, "Quellen zur Geschichte," ccxxxvii, cclx, ccxcv, ccciv; Feest, "Vienna's Mexican Treasures."

74. Braunholtz, *Sir Hans Sloane*, 20–21; King, "North American Ethnography," 233–34.

75. Whitaker, *Musæum Thoresbyanum*, 36–47.

76. Torres de Mendoza, *Coleccion de Documentos Ineditos*, 318–62; Saville, *The Goldsmith's Art*, 15–19, 21–35, 56–101; Feest, "Vienna's Mexican Treasures," 16–17, 24–25.

77. Philoponus, *Nova Typis Transacta Navigatio*, 49; Feest, "Zemes Idolum Diabolicum," 183.

78. Karl Anton Nowotny, *Mexikanische Kostbarkeiten aus Kunstkammern der Renaissance* (Vienna, 1960), 19; Feest "Vienna's Mexican Treasures," 18.

79. Tradescant, *Musæum Tradescantianum*; Whitaker, *Musæum Thoresbyanum*; Boeheim, "Quellen zur Geschichte"; Bauer and Haupt, "Kunstkammerinventar Kaiser Rudolfs II." The catalog of the Weickmann collection identifies as "Indian" some surviving objects that are known to be African, as well as others that may have been American: *Verzeichnus Unterschidlicher Thier/Vögel/Fisch/Meergewächs/Ertz= und Bergarten/Edlen und anderen Steinen/außländischem Holtz und Früchten/Kunst= und frembden Sachen . . .* ([Ulm], 1655), 23–24; cf. Richard Andree, "Seltene Ethnographica des städtischen Gewerbe-Museums zu Ulm," *Baessler-Archiv* 4 (1914): 36–37.

80. Cf. Sánchez Cantón, *Inventarios Reales.* Antonio Giganti's index distinguishes between "India" and "Mondo nuovo"; cf. Laurencich Minelli, "L'indice del Museo Giganti."

81. Du Molinet, *Le Cabinet.*

82. Cf. Feest, " 'Selzam ding,' " 116.

83. Cf. Feest, "Vienna's Mexican Treasures," 11–12. See also Theodor Hampe, ed., *Das Trachtenbuch des Christoph Weiditz von seinen Reisen nach Spanien (1529) und den Niederlanden (1531/2),* Historische Waffen und Kostüme 2 (Berlin and Leipzig, 1927), 24, for the use of "Moorish" instead of "Mexican" on a derivative of Christoph Weiditz's drawings of Aztecs. "Moors" is also apparently used for the indigenous inhabitants of the "West Indies"; cf. Valentini, *Museum Museorum,* vol. 2 (appendix), 35, 36.

84. Bonanni, *Musaeum Kircherianum,* 225; L. Baillet, "Curiosités exotiques rassemblées au château de Ribeauville d'après un inventaire su XVIIe siècle," *Bulletin de la Société d'Histoire et d'Archéologie de Ribeauville* 22 (1959/60): 17.

85. Whitaker, *Musæum Thoresbyanum,* 47; Bushnell, "Sloane Collection," 673, 675; Braunholtz, *Sir Hans Sloane,* 34.

86. Grew, *Musæum Regalis Societatis,* 375.

87. Zimmermann, "Inventar der Prager Schatz- und Kunstkammer," xxxiii; Karl Köpl, "Urkunden, Akten, Regesten und Inventare aus dem k.k. Statthalterei-Archiv in Prag," *Jahrbuch der Kunstsammlungen des allerhöchsten Kaiserhauses* 10 (1889): clxix.

88. Schepelern, *Museum Wormianum,* 352; Lundbæk and Dam-Mikkelsen, *Etnografiske genstande,* 18–19.

89. Cf. Ciruzzi, "Antichi oggetti americani," 159, 161; Feest, "Vienna's Mexican Treasures," 31, 32.

90. Cf. Feest, "Collecting American Indian Art."

91. Philoponus, *Nova Typis Transacta Navigatio,* pl. 8; Feest, "Zemes Idolum Diabolicum," 182–87.

92. Cf. Heikamp, "Mexikanische Altertümer," 206. [J. C. Sturm], *Des Geöffneten Ritter-Platzes Dritter Theil, worinnen zu noch mehreren galanten Wissenschaften Anleitung gegeben, und zwar besonders Unterricht ertheilet wird, was bey Raritäten- und Naturalien-Kammern . . . hauptsächlich zu bemerken vorfällt* (Hamburg, 1707), 41, pl. 4, also refers to an illustration of a kris as a representation of a *zemi* ("Zemme").

93. Sturm, *Geöffneter Ritter-Platz,* 4O–41, 34, 46, pls. 3, 4, 7.

94. King, "North American Ethnography"; Beer, "Acten, Regesten und Inventare"; Sánchez Cantón, *Inventarios Reales.*

95. Johann Christian Kundmann, *Sammlung von natür- und künstlichen Sachen, auch Münzen, welche dieses 1753 Jahr . . . verkaufet werden soll. Collectio rerum naturalium artificialium et nummorum quae hoc MDCCLIII. anno . . . distrahetur* (Breslau, 1753), 450, 468.

96. Blancken, *Catalogue.*

97. See, for example, Braunholtz, *Sir Hans Sloane,* 34.

98. See, for Prague, 1621: Zimmermann, "Inventar der Prager Schatz- und Kunstkammer," xxxiii; London, 1625: C. C. A. Gosch, ed., *Danish Arctic Expeditions, 1605–1620,* Hakluyt Society, nos. 96–97 (London, 1897), 1:36n; Copenhagen, 1642: Schepelern, *Museum Wormianum,* 356; Lambeth, 1656: Tradescant, *Musæum Tradescantianum,* 42, allegedly the

one collected by Frobisher in 1577; Vlissingen, 1697: B. de Monconys, *Beschreibung seiner in Asia und das Gelobte Land, nach Portugall, Spanien, Italien, in Engelland, die Niederlande und Teutschland gethanen Reisen* (Leipzig and Augsburg, 1697), 583, probably one of those brought back by Nicolas Tunes in 1656 (cf. Rochefort, *Histoire Naturelle et Morale*, 204, 219–20); Gottorp, 1666: Olearius, *Gottorffische Kunst-Kammer*, 5, tab. 3 (cf. Jacobaeus, *Museum Regium*, 54, tab. 12); Leiden, 1672: Eyl, *Parisische Conferentzen*, 343, and Blancken, *Catalogue*, 4; Leipzig before 1683: Valentini, *Museum Museorum*, vol. 2 (appendix), 31; London, 1681: Grew, *Musæum Regalis Societatis*, 364–65; Edinburgh, 1688: Dale Idiens, "Eskimos in Scotland: c. 1882–1924," in Feest, *Indians and Europe*, 171–72; Burray, 1700: Idiens, "Eskimos in Scotland," 162; Frankfurt, 1715: Valentini, *Museum Museorum*, vol. 2 (appendix), 133.

99. Gosch, *Danish Arctic Expeditions*, 1:36 and 36n; Rochefort, *Histoire Naturelle et Morale*, 219.

100. See, for Amsterdam, 1672: Eyl, *Parisische Conferentzen*, 155; Leipzig, 1715: Valentini, *Museum Museorum*, vol. 2 (appendix), 31; Copenhagen, 1642: Schepelern, *Museum Wormianum*, 356; Lambeth, 1656: Tradescant, *Musæum Tradescantianum*, 47, also boots and shoes, 48, 50; and Amsterdam, 1715: Valentini, *Museum Museorum*, vol. 2 (appendix), 54.

101. Olearius, *Gottorffische Kunst-Kammer*, 5, tab. 4.

102. Braunholtz, *Sir Hans Sloane*, 34.

103. David Beers Quinn, "Virginians on the Thames," *Terrae Incognitae* 2 (1970): 9, 7; Robert Le Blant and René Baudry, *Nouveaux Documents sur Champlain et son époque*, vol. 1, Publication des Archives Publiques du Canada 15 (Ottawa, 1967), 103–4.

104. Contant, "Exagoga Mirabilivm," 7, unnumbered plate; Bonanni, *Musaeum Kircherianum*, 229, fig. 9; cf. also the surviving model in Oxford: Feest, "North America."

105. Schepelern, *Museum Wormianum*, 352.

106. Legati, *Museo Cospiano*, 269; Eyl, *Parisische Conferentzen*, 113, 135; Valentini, *Museum Museorum*, vol. 2 (appendix), 35. Cf. also the drawings of three pipes, two of them with sculptured designs, illustrated by Neander, *Tabacologia*, which must have been based on specimens in Europe.

107. Murray, *Museums*, 1:95; Balsiger, "The 'Kunst- and Wunderkammern,' " 665; see also the other pieces in the Sieur de Bernonville's collection described below.

108. Bushnell, "Sloane Collection," 675; Whitaker, *Musæum Thoresbyanum*, 46.

109. Contant, "Exagoga Mirabilivm," 7; Birch, *History of the R. Society*, 2:418–19, summarily noted by Grew, *Musæum Regalis Societatis*, 370; Bonanni, *Musaeum Kircherianum*, 225, and note 66 above; Bushnell, "North American Material," 250, pl. 22, and Father J. Penkowski, personal communication.

110. Whitaker, *Musæum Thoresbyanum*, 43; Du Molinet, *Le Cabinet*, pl. 4; Vincent, *Elenchus Tabularum*, pl. 5; Peter Lindeström, *Geographia Americae with an Account of the Delaware Indians*, trans. Amandus Johnson (Philadelphia, 1925), 222; Tinling, *Correspondence of the Three William Byrds*, 1:61.

111. Le Blant and Baudry, *Nouveaux Documents sur Champlain*, 103; there is a slight possibility that this is the one now at the Bibliothèque Sainte-Geneviève in Paris.

112. Whitaker, *Musæum Thoresbyanum*, 36; cf. Lundbæk and Dam-Mikkelsen, *Etnografiske genstande*, 31, and Staffan Brunius, "North American Indian Collections at the

Folkens Museum-Etnografiska, Stockholm," *European Review of Native American Studies* 4, no. 1 (1990): 30.

113. Le Blant and Baudry, *Nouveaux Documents sur Champlain*, 103; Tradescant, *Musæum Tradescantianum*, 45; Whitaker, *Musæum Thoresbyanum*, 36.

114. Bonanni, *Musaeum Kircherianum*, figs. 7, 8; Tradescant, *Musæum Tradescantianum*, 47, 49; Whitaker, *Musæum Thoresbyanum*, 43; Wright, *A Voyage to Virginia*, 89.

115. Tradescant, *Musæum Tradescantianum*, 45, 47, 51, 53; David Sturdy and Martin Henig, *The Gentle Traveller: John Bargrave, Canon of Canterbury, and His Collection* (Abingdon, n.d.); Grew, *Musæum Regalis Societatis*, 370; Whitaker, *Musæum Thoresbyanum*, 36, 43, 45, 46; Braunholtz, *Sir Hans Sloane*, 35.

116. Murray, *Museums*, 1:95; Balsiger, "The 'Kunst- and Wunderkammern,' " 665.

117. Aldrovandi, *Ornithologia*, 1:657; Laurencich Minelli, "Oggetti studiati," 196–97, and "L'indice del Museo Giganti," 208–10, fig. 4; Aimi, "Il Museo Settala," 175–77; Terzaghi, *Museum Septalianum*, 92, 94; Heikamp, "Mexikanische Altertümer," 210; Feest, "Zemes Idolum Diabolicum," 190–91; Ronald Lightbown, personal communication, 1983; Purchas, *Hakluytus Posthumus*, 19:11O.

118. Olearius, *Gottorffische Kunst-Kammer*, 4, tab. 2; Lundbæk and Dam-Mikkelsen, *Etnografiske genstande*, 32; Heikamp, "Mexikanische Altertümer," 210; Feest, "Zemes Idolum Diabolicum," 190; Petrus Martyr de Angleria, *De Orbe Nouo* (Alcalá, 1530), reprinted in Petrus Martyr de Angleria, *Opera* (Graz, 1966), fol. xix^{v}; Dubled et al., *Nicolas-Claude Fabri de Peiresc*, after 31. "Moorish" weapons and shoes from the "West Indies" are listed in the catalog of the pre-1683 Lorentzen collection in Leipzig; cf. Valentini, *Museum Museorum*, vol. 2 (appendix), 35, 36.

119. Monconys, *Beschreibung*, 574; Whitaker, *Musæum Thoresbyanum*, 39.

120. That the others were known to be Mexican, however, is indicated by Zeiller, *Itinerarium Germaniae*, 287.

121. Feest, "Vienna's Mexican Treasures," 13, 49, 50.

122. Laurencich Minelli, "Oggetti studiati," 189; Laurencich Minelli and Filipetti, "Per le collezioni americaniste," 211; de Sepi, *Romani Collegii Societatis Iesu Musæum*, 34; Bonanni, *Musaeum Kircherianum*, 229, 232: cf. Feest, "Vienna's Mexican Treasures," 12–13.

123. Cf. Heikamp, "Mexikanische Altertümer," "American Objects," "Mexico und die Medici-Herzöge"; Feest, "Vienna's Mexican Treasures"; Martin, "Obras artísticas," 157.

124. Zimmermann, "Urkunden und Regesten," cxix–cxx; Beer, "Acten, Regesten und Inventare"; Sánchez Cantón, *Inventarios Reales*; Martin, "Obras artísticas," 159.

125. Bonanni, *Musaeum Kircherianum*, 232; Schepelern, *Museum Wormianum*, 346; cf. also the "West Indian thread" in Tradescant, *Musæum Tradescantianum*, 51.

126. Ross Hassig, *Aztec Warfare: Imperial Expansion and Political Control* (Norman, Okla., and London, 1988), 83; Zimmermann, "Urkunden und Regesten," cxix–cxx.

127. Cf. Terzaghi, *Museum Septalianum*, 91; Aimi, "Il Museo Settala," 179.

128. Cf. Ferdinand Anders, "Las Artes Menores. Minor Arts," *Artes de México* 137 (1971): 4–66; Christian F. Feest, "Koloniale Federkunst aus Mexiko," in Feest and Kann, *Gold und Macht*, 176–77. A feather mosaic miter and a small picture of the same style were in Antonio Giganti's collection in 1586: Laurencich Minelli, "L'indice del Museo Giganti," 211, 236, 238.

An unusual "Mexican purse of parrot feathers" was in the king of Denmark's Kunstkammer since at least 1696 but was sold in auction in 1824 and must be considered lost (Gundestrup, *Kongelige danske Kunstkammer*, 1:127).

129. Jacobaeus, *Museum Regium*, 49; Bonanni, *Musaeum Kircherianum*, 226; Aimi, "Il Museo Settala," 173; de Michele et al., *Museo di Manfredo Settala*, 13, 23; Terzaghi, *Museum Septalianum*, frontispiece, 91.

130. Vincent, *Elenchus Tabularum*, pls. 2, 5; Contant, "Exagoga Mirabilivm," 7; Bauer and Haupt, "Kunstkammerinventar Kaiser Rudolfs II," 34; Zimmermann, "Inventar der Prager Schatz- und Kunstkammer," xxxvi.

131. Grew, *Musæum Regalis Societatis*, 373; Tradescant, *Musæum Tradescantianum*, 47.

132. Aldrovandi, *Ornithologia*, 657; Laurencich Minelli, "Oggetti studiati," 194–200; Lundbæk and Dam-Mikkelsen, *Etnografiske genstande*, 27.

133. Grew, *Musæum Regalis Societatis*, 373; Whitaker, *Musæum Thoresbyanum*, 41; Lundbæk and Dam-Mikkelsen, *Etnografiske genstande*, 29.

134. Gottfried von Bülow, ed., "Diary of the Journey of Philip Julius, Duke of Stettin-Pomerania, through England in the year 1602," *Transactions of the Royal Historical Society*, n.s., 6 (1892): 25; Contant, "Exagoga Mirabilivm," 7; for Halle, 1625: cf. Balsiger, "The 'Kunst- and Wunderkammern,' " 262; *Verzeichnus Unterschidlicher Thier*, 23; Vincent, *Elenchus Tabularum*, 41, pl. 5.

135. Terzaghi, *Museum Septalianum*, 131.

136. Aimi, "Il Museo Settala," 177–78; Terzaghi, *Museum Septalianum*, 94; Tradescant, *Musæum Tradescantianum*, 45; MacGregor, *Tradescant's Rarities*, 120; Grew, *Musæum Regalis Societatis*, 367; Contant, "Exagoga Mirabilivm," 7.

137. Bauer and Haupt, "Kunstkammerinventar Kaiser Rudolfs II," 37; Feest, "Vienna's Mexican Treasures," 50; Contant, "Exagoga Mirabilivm," 7; Terzaghi, *Museum Septalianum*, 92.

138. Munich, 1598: Heikamp, "Mexikanische Altertümer," 209; Halle, 1625 ("a wooden American poleax"): cf. Balsiger, "The 'Kunst- and Wunderkammern,' " 262; Grew, *Musæum Regalis Societatis*, 267; Tradescant, *Musæum Tradescantianum*, 46.

139. Tradescant, *Musæum Tradescantianum*, 42; MacGregor, *Tradescant's Rarities*, fig. 179; the original source of this drawing is L'Ecluse, *Exoticorum Libri Decem*, 232, which is also the source for Gulielmus Piso, *De Indiae Utriusque Re Naturali et Medica Libri Quatuordecim* (Amsterdam, 1658), 1:308; Lundbæk and Dam-Mikkelsen, *Etnografiske genstande*, 26; Olearius, *Gottorffische Kunst-Kammer*, 27, tab. 18; Laurencich Minelli, "Oggetti studiati," 195–96; Contant, "Exagoga Mirabilivm," 7; Aimi, "Il Museo Settala," 170, 172; Bauer and Haupt, "Kunstkammerinventar Kaiser Rudolfs II," 19; Boeheim, "Quellen zur Geschichte," 67; Sturm, *Geöffneter Ritter-Platz.*

140. Sánchez Cantón, *Inventarios Reales*, 1:275, 2:252; Beer, "Acten, Regesten und Inventare," clxx; Martin, "Obras artisticas," 157; Ignacio Bernal, *A History of Mexican Archaeology* (London and New York, 1980), 131.

141. Beer, "Acten, Regesten und Inventare," clxx; Tradescant, *Musæum Tradescantianum*, 50; Blancken, *Catalogue*, 16.

142. Bonanni, *Musaeum Kircherianum*, 230; Terzaghi, *Museum Septalianum*, 132; Aimi, "Il

Museo Settala," 179; Bülow, "Diary of the Journey of Philip Julius," 25; Valentini, *Museum Museorum*, vol. 2 (appendix), 32.

143. Terzaghi, *Museum Septalianum*, 91, 92, 131; Aimi, "Il Museo Settala," 176, 177, 179–80; de Michele et al., *Museo di Manfredo Settala*, 23, Olearius, *Gottorffische Kunst-Kammer*, 71, tab. 36.

144. Eyl, *Parisische Conferentzen*, 347; Contant, "Exagoga Mirabilivm," 4; Tradescant, *Musæum Tradescantianum*, 37.

145. Boeheim, "Quellen zur Geschichte," ccxxxvii; Heikamp, "Mexikanische Altertümer," 209; Döring, *Philipp Hainhofer*, 158; Balsiger, "The 'Kunst- and Wunderkammern,'" 727; Köpl, "Urkunden, Akten, Regesten und Inventare," cxxxi; Aimi, "Il Museo Settala," 173; Wastler, "Geschichte der Schatz-, Kunst- und Rüstkammer," c, ci; Eyl, *Parisische Conferentzen*, 329; Grew, *Musæum Regalis Societatis*, 371–72; Bonanni, *Musaeum Kircherianum*, 229; Zeiller, *Itinerarium Germaniae*, 216; Lundbæk and Dam-Mikkelsen, *Etnografiske genstande*, 22–23; Baillet, "Curiosités exotiques," 17.

146. Beer, "Acten, Regesten und Inventare," ccxxii; Contant, "Exagoga Mirabilivm," 2; *Verzeichnus Unterschidlicher Thier*, 23; Schepelern, *Museum Wormianum*, 348; Tradescant, *Musæum Tradescantianum*, 43; Grew, *Musæum Regalis Societatis*, 371; de Sepi, *Romani Collegii Societatis Iesu Musæum*, 34; Vincent, *Elenchus Tabularum*, 41; Whitaker, *Musæum Thoresbyanum*, 40–41.

147. Cf. Impey and MacGregor, *Origins*; Alsop, *The Rare Art Traditions.*

148. Scheicher, *Kunst- und Wunderkammern*, 81, 85–131; Lundbæk and Dam-Mikkelsen, *Etnografiske genstande*, xx.

149. Lundbæk and Dam-Mikkelsen, *Etnografiske genstande*, xxi–xxii; Gundestrup, *Kongelige danske Kunstkammer*, 2:1–52. American objects also appeared outside Copenhagen's "Indian Cabinet": most Greenlandic material was featured in a special section of the "Chamber of Antiquities"; a few others were grouped with the naturalia.

150. Beutel, *Chur-Fürstlicher Sächsischer Cedern-Wald*, L3, M2, M3; cf. Neickelius, *Museographia*, 194.

151. Whitaker, *Musæum Thoresbyanum*, 49.

152. Sturm, *Geöffneter Ritter-Platz*, 40.

153. Tradescant, *Musæum Tradescantianum*, 47; Alain Parent et al., eds., *La Renaissance et le Nouveau Monde* (Québec, 1984), 102; Schönherr, "Urkunden und Regesten," clxvii; Bernal, *History of Mexican Archaeology*, 131.

154. Lundbæk and Dam-Mikkelsen, *Etnografiske genstande*, 21; Contant, "Exagoga Mirabilivm," 8; Kundmann, *Sammlung*, 450; Eyl, *Parisische Conferentzen*, 113.

155. Eyl, *Parisische Conferentzen*, 308; Laurencich Minelli, "Oggetti studiati," 188–89.

156. Neickelius, *Museographia*, 7.

157. Elisabeth Landoldt, "Materialien zu Felix Platter als Sammler und Kunstfreund," *Basler Zeitschrift zur Geschichte und Altertumskunde* 72 (1972): 245–306.

158. Feest, "'Selzam ding,'" 120–23.

RICHARD C. SIMMONS

Americana in British Books, 1621–1760

The nature, depth, and range of European knowledge and perceptions of America to be found in contemporary print culture has been a subject of historical study for many years.[1] Recent publications have provided systematic guides to European printed works relating to the Americas from the era of Columbus to the mid-eighteenth century, although it is still doubtful if as many finding aids and detailed guides exist for these as for manuscript sources. Preeminent among such publications is *European Americana*, which attempts to list all European imprints from 1493 to 1750 relating to the New World. The first volume, which appeared in 1980, covered the years from the first European contacts to 1600. Subsequent volumes have so far extended this cover to the years 1601–50, 1701–25, and 1726–50. *European Americana* is the central twentieth-century bibliographical contribution to its subject.[2]

Another current work, conceived and undertaken in a completely different fashion, is the *Eighteenth-Century Short Title Catalogue* (*ESTC*) of books in the English language. A first installment listed the holdings of the British Library and was published on microfiche. A second, much-expanded version, with about 300,000 entries, lists the holdings of libraries around the world.[3] For the historian this is a better finding aid, as is *European Americana*, than the great current catalogs of seventeenth-century imprints[4] precisely because it is not a short-title catalog. I suppose one may call it a medium-title catalog, since it abbreviates the longer titles without losing much relevant detail. In these days of increasingly used computer searches, it will probably be advisable for bibliographical guides to include complete titles in order to allow different search strategies. In the case of British imprints relating to the Americas, the intensive use of *ESTC* will allow *European Americana* to be supplemented and aid in the publication of a full British Americana down to 1800.

Over a considerable period, with the help of these major bibliographies, I have slowly put together my own checklist of British imprints relating to North America for the years 1621 through 1760.[5] It will become clear as this essay progresses that my own perceptions and strategies have diverged to some extent from those which guided the compilers of *European Americana* and that I have been able to add to the listings contained in it. One wish has been to make some more-or-less intensive searches in specific collections. Although the compilers of *European*

Americana were able to take excellent steps in this direction, they were forced by constraints of time and available resources to work mainly from information provided to them or accessible in printed catalogs. Guided by a particular wish to look closely at American references in cheap popular literature (chapbooks, garlands, and broadsides especially), which are under-cataloged, my special investigations have been made so far in superb but little-used collections of chapbooks and ballads in various libraries in England and Scotland, including the holdings not only of the Bodleian, of the British Library, and of Cambridge University Library but of the National Library of Scotland and of provincial English libraries in such cities as Manchester and Newcastle. (The Bibliographical Society of America has supported the extension of this research into the period after 1760, and important items for the period of the American Revolution have been found.) Of related interest is the penetration of a consciousness of America into popular entertainments. The *Compleat Country Dancing-Master . . .* (London, 1718, 1735) contains 364 dances, including "America," "Indian Queen," and other New World titles.

Other specific collections, especially Scottish ones, have also been looked at. Some of the sermons given before the Society in Scotland for Propagating Christian Knowledge and other printed Scottish Americana rest in the manuscript collections of the Scottish Register Office in Edinburgh and have not been recorded from that source in *ESTC* or *European Americana.* The location of printed items in collections of mainly manuscript materials in England and Scotland is something that presents a difficulty to historical bibliographers. Other items not listed in *European Americana* are in the National Library of Scotland. Among these, *A succinct view of the Society in Scotland for propagating Christian knowledge* . . . (Edinburgh, 1738) discusses the conversion of Indians in "our colonies in North-America," while various printed circulars plead for money from the Church of Scotland to support this and other missionary work.

There may also be a need for the further investigation of Americana in dramatic and quasi-dramatic works. While *European Americana* sometimes lists books of which no extant copies are known, its format precludes it from listing such lost plays and masques as the *Conquest of the West Indies* (1601/2), *The Masque of Amazons* (1618), or *A tragedy of the plantation of Virginia* (licensed for acting in August 1623),[6] and although it has an index entry under "poems," it has none to dramatic works. There were representations of the New World in masques and pageants as well as in plays in the later sixteenth and the seventeenth centuries, and these are probably under-recorded. Popular pageants, such as those forming part of the Lord Mayor's procession in London, may also have been important in providing a broad audience with depictions of New World themes. To cite only two examples, the theme of the pageant for Sir James Edward's mayoralty in October 1678, designed by Thomas Jordan, celebrated the reduction of barbarous peoples through commerce in every part of the world and included many depictions of blacks and Indians, while Sir John Peake's pageant in 1686 included representations of Europe, Africa, Asia, and America.[7] Some contemporary printed materials relating to these annual events have survived.[8] Whether or not the costumes and properties worn and used at these pageants were based on any real acquaintance with the New World objects discussed by Christian Feest elsewhere in this volume, or even included any of these, is an interesting speculation and might be worth further inquiry. Some of them could be seen, of course, in various cabinets of curiosities in London.[9] Later seventeenth- and eighteenth-century plays[10] also need specialized attention; my investigations of these have been limited.

Problems of inclusion and exclusion certainly made it necessary to look at many hundreds of works in order to discover the exact nature of their (North) American relevance. Probably somewhat arbitrarily, a decision was taken not to list general collections of voyages, editions of treaties, most works relating to tobacco after it reached Britain, and works relating to the Royal African Company that had only very marginal North American references. Also, unless they contained material about America, works by temporary residents who were not born in the colonies and which were published after their residence there had finished were not included. For example, Nathaniel Ward returned to England from New England at the start of the Civil Wars and published many tracts. These are not listed since they contain no American references, but his writings published in London while he lived in Massachusetts are. Further, are the works of those born in North America who settled permanently in Britain, unless they contained North American references, "Americana"? These are not significant exclusions, but were they correct ones? The major eighteenth-century American-born writers who produced most of their works in England were the Pennsylvanian James Ralph and the New York–born Charlotte Lennox, daughter of Lieutenant-Governor James Ramsay of that colony.[11]

However, I have included one important category of imprint which *European Americana* omits: the European publications, whether reprints or originals, of items by American authors without material relating to the Americas. The first printing or reprinting in the Old World of works by, for example, John Cotton, Cotton Mather, Benjamin Franklin, and Jonathan Edwards should surely be considered by the bibliographer as much as the cultural historian as an intrinsic component of "European Americana."

The publication of *European Americana* has made more straightforward the wholesale identification of items printed in more than one European country in a way that has not been easy before and therefore places discussions of the validity of the idea of "European Americana" or of a "European" consciousness of America based on printed works on a firm footing. However, was there a European consciousness or was there a series of national consciousnesses? One could certainly argue that after the sixteenth century, divergences between, for example, Spanish and British views of America were more significant than similarities. Also, generally, and in the context of printed Americana, southern and northern Europe probably formed two distinct regions, Catholic and Protestant, with some shared publications in cities like Venice and Paris.

Another question of definition is raised by the approach of *European Americana.* Should a bibliography of "Americana" after, say, 1660 include works with a few very conventional or incidental short references to the Americas? Such imprints tend to outnumber, surround, and even obscure the most important and significant works. Criteria for the inclusion of sixteenth-century imprints, when American references were sparse, may not be as helpful for the eighteenth century, when casual references to the New World were commonplace and much Americana was merely part of other general categories of material: commercial legislation, the fiscal concerns of governments, the administration of colonies, slavery, and so on. I listed too only some of the more important botanical works rather than following *European Americana* in including every such work, even those published after 1700, which includes, for example, perhaps only a mention of cochineal or Peruvian bark among hundreds of non-American entries.

Indeed, what is clear about these botanical and horticultural imprints is that by the eighteenth century, classification of the once-exotic natural products of the New World[12] was becoming less important than their commercialization and domestication. This occurred quickly in the area of drugs and medicines. By the middle of the eighteenth century, such works as Thomas Short's *Medicina Britannica or, A treatise on such physical plants, as are generally to be found in . . . Great-Britain . . .* (London, 1746) included with little comment many transplanted New World items. Similarly, Christopher Gray, whose *Catalogue of American trees and shrubs that will endure the climate of England* appeared in 1737, was one of several horticulturists who specialized in American trees and plants. Propertied families could purchase these New World garden flora almost as easily as they could buy furniture made from American woods.

On the other hand, if numerous herbals and plant books are to be included, why not Matthew Prior's *Carmen Seculare* (London, 1699). This mentions the "Indies" only once but is still significant for an understanding of the development of European (or British) attitudes to the extra-European world, including the Americas, with its celebration of Britain's "active commerce" and powerful fleets that will go "In World's unknown to plant BRITANNIA's power; / Nations yet wild by Precept to reclaim, / And teach 'em Arms, and Arts, in WILLIAM's Name." Similarly, Alexander Pope's *Essay on Man* has only a few lines on the "poor Indian" and his "untutor'd mind," but these are certainly as important for the study of European consciousness of the Americas as any number of references to sarsaparilla or syphilis.

A checklist of British North Americana obviously takes a national approach. This, I think, appropriately fits the context (the growing nation states of Europe) within which most printed works relating to America were generated and within which they relate to each other. A cursory inspection of the four printed volumes of *European Americana* does reveal that the majority of imprints listed in it were indeed published only in one country. And, after about 1600, many works published in more than two countries were often surveys of botany, medicine, geography, and other subjects which contained only incidental or very general references to the Americas.

One great difference between British Americana before about 1620 and after was, of course, its quantity. Indeed, in the sixteenth century much British Americana was adapted or translated from works first published in continental Europe. Only from the 1570s did the voyages of Frobisher and Gilbert begin the process that led to the flowering of English works with American themes, and even in the last three decades of the sixteenth century indigenous British Americana was still outnumbered by translations or borrowings from continental European sources. This was both an indication of the relative contemporary balance of national strengths in the New World and a reflection of the general cultural dependence of the British Isles on Italy, Spain, and France. Such continental books, beginning with Sebastian Brant's *Shyppe of Fooles* in 1509 and including texts by Thevet, Oviedo, Las Casas, Acosta, Du Bartas, Gómara, and Aléman, constituted a high percentage of all British Americana before 1601. From about 1630 they comprised a diminishing percentage of works published in the British Isles relating to America. *European Americana* lists few British editions of continental books in the years 1701 to 1750, and these few were a tiny fraction of the total works relating to America published in the British Isles in the same years.[13]

Britain, indeed, became a net exporter of works with American themes (probably in the second half of the seventeenth century). Yet some of the British works listed in the currently published volumes of *European Americana* with the widest republication outside of the British Isles actually contained little American material. The medical works of John Allen, Walter Harris, and Charles Sydenham are such cases. Allen's *Synopsis universae medicinae practicae* was first published in London in 1719. By 1750 it had been reprinted a total of fourteen times, four issues appearing in Paris, three in Amsterdam, two in Venice, one in Leipzig, four more in London, and one in Bautzen. It therefore has fifteen entries in *European Americana*, but its American references seem to be limited to the (by then) hackneyed question of syphilis and the probability that the disease was transmitted by Spaniards to Europe. At the other extreme, Daniel Defoe's works were obviously fully

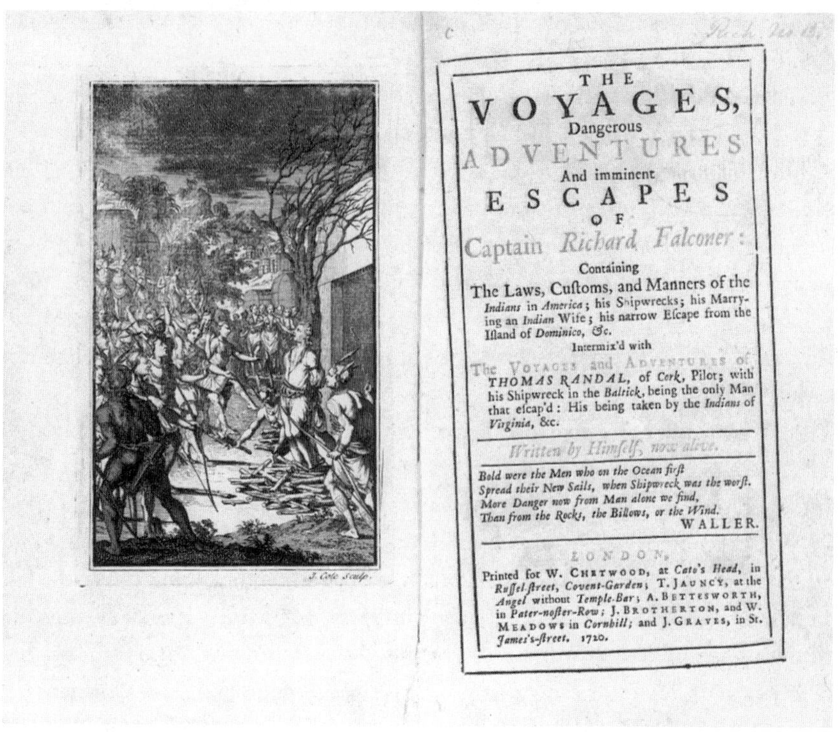

THE
VOYAGES,
Dangerous
ADVENTURES
And imminent
ESCAPES
OF
Captain *Richard Falconer*:
Containing
The Laws, Customs, and Manners of the *Indians* in *America*; his Shipwrecks; his Marrying an *Indian* Wife; his narrow Escape from the Island of *Dominico*, &c.
Intermix'd with
The Voyages and Adventures of *THOMAS RANDAL*, of *Cork*, Pilot; with his Shipwreck in the *Baltick*, being the only Man that escap'd: His being taken by the *Indians* of *Virginia*, &c.

Written by Himself, now alive.

Bold were the Men who on the Ocean first
Spread their New Sails, when Shipwreck was the worst.
More Danger now from Man alone we find,
Than from the Rocks, the Billows, or the Wind.
WALLER.

LONDON,
Printed for W. CHETWOOD, at *Cato's Head*, in *Russel-street*, *Covent-Garden*; T. JAUNCY, at the *Angel* without *Temple-Bar*; A. BETTESWORTH, in *Pater-noster-Row*; J. BROTHERTON, and W. MEADOWS in *Cornhill*; and J. GRAVES, in St. *James's-street*. 1720.

Frontispiece and title page of William Rufus Chetwood, *The voyages, dangerous adventures and imminent escapes of Captain Richard Falconer* (London, 1720). John Carter Brown Library.

conscious of the New World and were reprinted throughout Europe. William R. Chetwood's fictional Americana was also popular outside Britain.[14]

The publication of *European Americana* has made it possible to make some quantitative comparisons of British imprints relating to the Americas with those of other European countries. The following table reveals the large number of items containing "Americana" printed in Great Britain compared with other European countries. This was a function of the rising wealth and growing population of Britain and of British America. Certain periods also produced relatively higher numbers of imprints than others for specific reasons. For example, the 1640s witnessed the interchange of arguments and ideas between English, Scottish, and New England participants in the church controversies of the period, the 1740s saw great transatlantic activity resulting from the Great Awakening, and the 1750s witnessed the impact on the printing presses and the booksellers of the struggle with France for trade and colonies.[15]

Another quantitative assessment relates to the places of printing of British Americana. If the diffusion of knowledge about or the practice of activities con-

TABLE 1.

Entries by Region in European Americana, *1621–1650, 1701–1725, 1726–1750: A Trial Tabulation*

	1621–1650		1701–1725		1726–1750	
	Total	Yearly Average[a]	Total	Yearly Average[a]	Total	Yearly Average[a]
Austria	8	–	12	–	31	–
British Isles	1,296	43	2,431	97	3,214	128
England	1,271	42	2,295	–	2,827	113
Ireland	7	–	61	–	240	10
Scotland	18	–	75	–	147	6
France	736	24	439	17	512	20
Germany	499	16	685	27	750	30
Italy	329	11	183	7	294	12
Low Countries and Luxembourg	86	–	71	–	42	–
Poland	2	–	2	–	4	–
Portugal	76	–	75	–	160	6
Prague, Brno, and Tranava					9	–
Russia	–	–	6	–	8	–
Scandinavia	15	–	37	–	70	–
Spain	701	23	787	31	1,483	59
Switzerland	85	–	36	–	96	–
United Provinces	1,227	41	735	29	680	27

[a]If more than four.

cerning America are among the factors to be related to the place of publication, the predominance of London is always significant. Yet the steady rise of provincial publishing is also noticeable. *ESTC* lists about 108,000 British entries for 1701–60, of which about 25,800 were printed outside of London.[16] The provincial printings that appear in my checklist are slightly more than 10 percent of total printings, still not a negligible figure.[17] By the 1740s at least, this provincial output reflected the intensifying impact of the New World on provincial middle- and even lower-class consciousness, especially consciousness of the Americas as an aspect, even as an engine, of the beneficial growth of commerce.

This increasing volume of provincial printing certainly reflected the wide interest in the events leading to the Seven Years' War and in the war itself. An extensive circulation throughout the British Isles of works relating to the war, from simple broadside verses or cheap garlands[18] to expensive atlases and other descriptive

TABLE 2.

Trial List of British North Americana, 1641–1760, by Place of Publication

	Decade												
	1641	1651	1661	1671	1681	1691	1701	1711	1721	1731	1741	1751	To
Aberdeen								1			1	2	
Bath												1	
Belfast								1		2	2	1	
Berwick										1			
Birmingham										2			
Bristol									1	1	11	5	
Bury												2	
Cambridge	3											1	
Canterbury												1	
Chester					1							1	
Coventry												1	
Dublin					2		4	4	18	34	32	34	1
Edinburgh	3	2			10	6	7	8	5	20	43	40	1
Exeter											4	3	
Glasgow						1			2	2	20	20	
Gloucester	1											1	
Hull										1			
Ipswich											1	2	
Leeds										1		1	
Leominster												1	
Liverpool												1	
London	246	187	102	135	174	208	322	300	307	516	567	605	3,6
Manchester											1		
Newcastle								3		1	6	2	
Norwich							2					1	
Oxford	4	1		3	1				1				
Portsmouth												1	
Reading											1		
Sherborne											1		
Shrewsbury												1	
Tewkesbury							1						
Tunbridge							1						
Wells												1	
Whitby											1		
Wolverhampton											1		
Yeovil											1		
York												4	
Total	257	190	102	138	188	215	337	317	334	581	693	732	4,0

works, illustrates the extent to which it both familiarized large numbers of Britons with matters of trade, colonies, and empire and produced an outpouring of patriotism, which also identified British successes with the providentially directed victory of Protestantism. For example, Bristol's eight first imprints were dated 1739 and after, and many British provincial cities and towns first produced a first edition of a work relating to America in or after 1754, including Aberdeen, Belfast, Canterbury, Coventry, Leominster, Liverpool, Portsmouth, Shrewsbury, Tewkesbury, and Wells. Of the total items of British Americana in the period 1641 to 1760, about 730 imprints, or nearly 20 percent, were printed from 1751 through 1760. There is certainly room for a bibliographical survey and for reprints of works relating to the origins of the war and to the war itself, similar to those produced by Thomas R. Adams and Colin Bonwick for British books in the years of the American Revolution.[19]

The continuing importance of the historic capitals of Ireland and Scotland also merits comment. Outside of London, Edinburgh with 144 and Dublin with 128 imprints had the largest number of printings, demonstrating the continuing and increasing importance of old national capitals as centers both of printing and of American contacts. Moreover, the third largest number of first printings outside of London occurred in Glasgow, certainly a result of that port city's burgeoning commercial and personal links to North America. In these cities not only were certain popular London books reprinted, but indigenous works made their first appearances, so that by the 1760s it becomes necessary to consider not only Americana in British books but Americana in English, Scottish, and Irish books. Welsh imprints still need study.[20]

In the case of Scotland, in the seventeenth century such indigenous productions were mainly tracts aimed at promoting emigration to the Americas; in the eighteenth century, works that reflected the activities of the Scottish churches and the considerable repercussions of the Great Awakening in Scotland were seen in Glasgow and Edinburgh imprints. There were also such works as *Britain, a poem; in three books . . .* (Edinburgh, 1757), a poetical survey of the Seven Years' War ("Behold the ghost of Braddoc [*sic*], brave in fight, / With generous Halket, stalking round / Ohio's red streams, unburied, unavenged"), which show well how the disloyal Scots of the 'forty-five became transformed into the loyal Highlanders of a decade later! Nor should Scottish popular literature be overlooked; for example, *The jovial gamester's Garland, composed of several excellent new songs . . .* (Edinburgh, 1750?) tells of the "betray'd Maid" who was taken to Virginia and "served seven years to Captain Gulshaw laird." In Ireland there was a concentrated interest in emigration. *A Letter from a gentleman in the North of Ireland, to a person in an eminent post under his majesty; concerning the transportation of great numbers from that part of the kingdom to America* (Dublin, 1729) seems to have slipped out of

European Americana. There is a single copy of it in Trinity College, Dublin, one of many Irish imprints dealing with the same topic. In both Scotland and Ireland, works also appeared on the problem of developing specific beneficial, mainly commercial, links with the Americas while avoiding English constraints.

Out of numerous books, pamphlets, broadsides, chapbooks, garlands, parliamentary bills, court briefs, and so on, it is only possible to mention a few other publications, some because they represent important categories among British imprints, others because they are more obscure but interesting. Drama, poetry, and fiction, for example, are relatively strongly represented. As well as works that are still widely read, such as Daniel Defoe's novels, there are many now largely forgotten, like the Abbé Prévost's *The life of Mr Cleveland, natural son of Oliver Cromwell, written by himself. Giving a particular account of . . . his great sufferings in Europe and America . . .* (London, 1731) or William Moraley's *The infortunate: or, the voyages and adventures of William Moraley . . . Containing, whatever is curious and remarkable in . . . Pennsylvania and New Jersey . . . several adventures through divers parts of America . . .* (Newcastle-upon-Tyne, 1743). The first novel written by a North American woman, Charlotte Lennox's *The life of Harriot Stuart, written by herself* (London, 1751), is partly set in New York, where Lennox was born. Anthony Aston's *The Fool's Opera; or, the taste of the age. Written by Mat. Medley . . . To which is prefixed, a sketch of the author's life, written by himself* (London, 1730) describes his experiences as an actor in the West Indies and North America. The sketch is appended, not prefixed, in the British Library copy. Several eighteenth-century poems and collections of poems, such as William Donaldson's *North America, a descriptive poem. Representing the voyage to America; a sketch of that beautiful country; with remarks upon the political humour and singular conduct of its inhabitants . . .* (London, 1757) or John Dyer's *The fleece, a poem. In four books* (London, 1757), which contains substantial American references, are less well known than similar kinds of seventeenth-century works. This whole category of material has not been looked at in much depth by historians.[21]

Popular and of very great importance in forming a view of America were numerous works on kidnapping and transportation. The operations of confidence tricksters, of "spirits" and "crimps" who either with kindly cunning or with great brutality kidnapped boys and girls, young men and women to servitude as laborers in the colonies, had entered the literature of British America at an early period. During the seventeenth century, references to it remained generally in the broadside and chapbook section of the market, as, for example, in the *Kid-napper trapan'd . . . being a pleasant relation of a man that would have sold his wife to Virginia . . .* (London, 1675?), a tale of a kidnapper who found himself taken up, or in the story of an innocent in the big city, *The Trappan'd Welsh man, sold to Virginia* (London, 1685?), who on his first marveling visit to London was entrapped by a pretty woman. Other references were to real cases, for example, William Lauder's process against four fellow Scots for trepanning his son to Boston in 1716.[22]

In the eighteenth century, fact, fiction, and fantasy contributed to and mingled in more substantial works. The kidnapping theme was often found in sometimes lurid fictions. In Penelope Aubin's account of *The life of Charlotta du Pont* (London, 1723), a lovely thirteen-year-old virgin was kidnapped and sent to Virginia on the instructions of her wicked stepmother's lover, Captain Farley. In Edward Kimber's *History of the life and adventures of Mr. Anderson. Containing his strange varieties of fortune in Europe and America . . .* (London, 1754), a young boy of respectable family is seized by a seafaring man on the pavements of genteel London and then exposed to the lust of a homosexual sea captain before his sale to a Maryland planter. Other publications referred to true or purportedly true kidnappings. The most famous was certainly that of James Annesley, who claimed to be the legitimate heir to the earldom of Annesley, which had passed (illegally, he said) to his uncle, Richard, in 1727. Annesley stated that he had been kidnapped as a young boy and sent as a "common slave" to North America before finding his way back to Ireland via Jamaica in Admiral Vernon's fleet. Accounts of his life and a subsequent trial of his claims certainly entered the best-seller lists, with regional and provincial reprintings (and European translations), and inspired a number of supplemental and auxiliary accounts and satires.[23] All these publications still repay study, and the question of the derivation of the American background and other material in them has not been fully explored.

Equally popular were accounts, also both fictional and "true," of rogues and unfortunates sent forcibly but legally to the New World. Several of the printed Newgate "confessions" involved persons who at one point had been transported, including those of James Dalton, who, from a humble background, claimed to have been sentenced five times to transportation to Virginia, to have arrived there on four of these—on the other occasion, as the result of various adventures, he ended up in Spain—and once to have journeyed voluntarily to the Chesapeake. At least two of the criminals whose confessions were published claimed to be old Etonians: one, William Parsons,[24] was a confidence trickster who had been taken up by Governor Fairfax of Virginia; the other, Henry Simms, was the son of a favored upper servant, spoiled by his employer's patronage. *The life of Henry Simms, alias Young gentleman Harry* (London, 1747) took his story to his death at Tyburn on 17 June 1747 and recounted his "extraordinary adventures . . . at home and abroad." A recent study, drawing in part on contemporary printed accounts, suggests that many of those hanged in eighteenth-century London had had experience of one kind or another in the Americas and comments on the cosmopolitan nature of the London proletariat, which included many American blacks.[25]

Such generally masculine accounts were widely read, but probably the most famous eighteenth-century real-life transportee and certainly the most famous fictional one were both women. Elizabeth Canning (1734–73) was sentenced to transportation in 1754 after a sensational trial, which divided London society, involving her claimed perjury in a previous court case about her alleged kidnapping.[26] Her later virtuous behavior was reported in *Virtue triumphant; or, Elizabeth Canning in America; being a circumstantial narrative of her adventures, from her setting sail for transportation, to the present time . . .* (London, 1757) and was said to have included her running away from a New York family in order to escape the advances of the head of the household (after which she was captured by Indians) and her eventual marriage, after which she became an accomplished charitable worker. Another publication, a remarkable broadside, includes a colored depiction, the *Sceene of sceenes* (London, 1755), of Canning's "dream for the good of her native country," which was said to have occurred shortly after she arrived in Boston (not New York). Here the spin-off of a factual event into fictitious reconstructions demonstrates a typical eighteenth-century genre presenting several difficulties to the compilers of historical bibliographies.

The actual fictional character was, of course, the heroine of Daniel Defoe's *Moll Flanders* (London, 1722), who journeyed twice to Virginia, once as a voluntary emigrant and once as a transportee, and who found there the wealth and gentility which she could not obtain in England. Her adventures were quickly used by the chapbook makers. A useful study might be made of the way in which they handled the American content and altered Defoe's story.

The largest group of involuntary migrants to the New World were African slaves. Most works appearing before 1760 accepted the naturalness of slavery, though some called for the catechizing, baptism, and humane treatment of slaves. In the eighteenth century, Edmund Gibson, bishop of London, took seriously his responsibility for the ecclesiastical oversight of the American plantations; his letters to the master and mistresses of slaves were published in 1727. Some of the writings of American clergy, such as Thomas Bacon of Maryland and Samuel Davies of Virginia, who stressed the slaveowners' duty to propagate Christianity, were reprinted in London. However, a few works—Richard Baxter's *A Christian directory: or, A summ of practical theology* of 1673, for example, which contains a typical chapter on the duties of masters toward their servants, of which the second section is "Directions to Masters in Forain Plantations who have Negro's and other Slaves; being a solution of several cases about them"—discuss whether blacks are "reasonable creatures" and refer to the "natural liberty" of all humans.

Unless there is material in the numerous accounts of the travels of members of the Society of Friends in North America and the West Indies or in the official letters sent between Friends' meetings in America and Britain, such discussions of

A Sceene of sceenes (London, 1755). John Carter Brown Library.

slavery as a moral or ethical question were rare, nor was the justification of the African trade questioned. Malachy Postlethwayt's tract of 1745, *The African trade, the great pillar and support of the British plantations in America*, argued in part for its continuation in terms of control over the American plantations, which dependence on the supply of slaves by British merchants made certain. Readers who sought novel challenges to slavery were forced to look to Montesquieu, whose *Esprit Des Lois* first appeared in an English publication in 1750, or to the Scottish philosophers George Wallace and Francis Hutcheson. The latter's *System of Moral Philosophy* was published in Glasgow and London in 1755. Five years later J. Phillmore published his attack on the slave trade and on slavery in the plantations, *Two Dialogues on the Man Trade.* These writings are part of the prehistory of the great flowering of antislavery arguments and sentiments that appeared after about 1770. Perhaps the most remarkable related book of the period was Thomas Bluett's *Some memoirs of the life of Job, the son of Solomon the high priest of Boonda in Africa; who was a slave about two years in Maryland; and afterwards being brought to England was set free, and sent to his native land in 1734 . . .* (London, 1734), the biography of an enslaved African who finally benefited from his noble pedigree.

Stories of adventure, whether true or invented, were important in the corpus of British Americana. Besides the themes of transportation and kidnapping, other exotica arose naturally from the double hazards of maritime travel—exposing individuals to the threats of both shipwreck and piracy—and, if the crossing was safely completed, those arising from the New World environment itself. The sea voyage also figured in pietistic contexts because of its analogy with the passage of the soul. On land, encounters, friendly or otherwise, with native Americans were also commonplace occurrences in such works. In John Dennis's play published in 1704, *Liberty Asserted,* Indians occupied the stage for the first thirty-two pages of dialogue, while many fictional or individual accounts of America included pages of description of various Indian communities and the writer's personal experiences with native Americans. This was the continuation, or imitation, of a tradition that can be dated back at least to the adventures of Captain John Smith and of Pocohontas. Other narratives, such as Peter Williamson's widely circulated *French and Indian cruelty exemplified in the life . . . of P. W. . . . written by himself . . . ,* published in York in 1757, in Glasgow in 1758, and in London in 1759, reflected the author's experience or alleged experience in warfare with the Indians, dwelling on the tortures which they inflicted and their savagery. I have treated some aspects of the theme of the "savage" in British Americana elsewhere—incidentally, the index of *European Americana* contains no headings under "savage" or "savagery"—but another look at eighteenth-century sermons, drama, and poetry rather than at works directly treating the Amerindian suggests itself as highly desirable from my readings in a large number of these sources.[27]

Williamson's work also dealt with his captivity among the Indians, and "captivity narratives" have, of course, been seen as an important American genre. However, they were not widely republished in the British Isles. Although Mary Rowlandson's 1682 work, *A true history of the captivity and restoration of Mrs Mary Rowlandson, a minister's wife in New England . . . ,* was reprinted in London in the seventeenth century, it was not reprinted in the eighteenth.[28] The first American female captivity narrative to be reprinted after 1700 seems to have been that by Elizabeth Hanson, in 1760, *An account of the captivity of Elizabeth Hanson, now or late of Kachecky; in New England: who, with four of her children and servant-maid, was taken captive by the Indians, and carried into Canada . . . ,* a work first published in 1728 in Philadelphia. Only a handful of others appeared before 1800, and these do indicate the growing impact of the wars in North America from the late 1750s. But certainly before 1760, works dealing with Europeans captured by the Moors were more frequent, and these reflect the point that contemporary Britons were more interested in the slavery and captivity of Europeans among the Moors than European captivity in North America. The release of English captives from Morocco in 1721 was celebrated by a service in St. Paul's Cathedral.[29] Many plays and novels, of course, treated this theme.

The numerical importance of works on religion, theology, and church government, associated especially with puritanism and with the Society of Friends in the seventeenth century, continued during the eighteenth, reinvigorated by the effects of the transatlantic wave of revivalism of the late 1730s and the 1740s. Jonathan Edwards's account of conversions at Northampton, *A faithful narrative of the conversion of many hundred souls in Northampton . . . New England. In a letter to Dr. B. Colman . . . and published with a preface by Dr. Watts and Dr. Guyse . . .* was published in Edinburgh and London in 1736, and his famous *Sinners in the hands of an angry God* was reprinted in Edinburgh in 1745. Numerous works by or about George Whitefield appeared almost simultaneously in England and America. Whitefield continued, perhaps expanded, the habit of leading clerics who sought publication and republication for the sake of reputation as well as for the advancement of religion. Evident throughout the period is the large number of printed sermons. The Church of England was most strongly represented by the annual sermon before the Society for the Propagation of the Gospel, to which was usually appended an account of the work of the society overseas, with a strong North American section. Many of the sermons before the Georgia Trustees also contained North American material, as did some of those before the Scottish Society for Propagating Christian Knowledge, the less well-known Scottish missionary body, founded in 1709 in Edinburgh. It badly needs a modern study. Nor have I seen any assessment of *The females advocate: or, an essay to prove that the sisters in every church of Christ, have a right to church-government as well as the brethren* (London, 1718), a work which cites Cotton Mather on the New England churches but is not listed in *European Americana*.

All these series of sermons merit reassessment in the light of new historical approaches to non-Europeans, especially to the Amerindian and the African, and to the poor. Nor have questions of commerce and liberty been looked at in the sermon literature, which is where many contemporaries would have become acquainted with them. Excellent examples are the sermons delivered throughout Britain on 29 November 1759 on the capture of Quebec, a unique window into contemporary views of providence, empire, commerce, and liberty at the peak of British eighteenth-century imperial success. Thirty-one have been located, many in single copies in libraries as far apart as the Huntington in California and the Rylands in Manchester. A short study of these sermons is now being finished.[30]

More esoteric and more vulgar fare was provided by works relating to the prophecies, to horrible acts allegedly committed under the delusions of religion, and by tales of supernatural horror, including Richard Chamberlayne's *Lithobolia: or, The stone-throwing devil . . . account . . . of infernal spirits . . . and the great disturbance . . . they gave to George Waltons family, at . . . Great island in . . . New-Hantshire in New-England . . .* (London, 1698). New England witchcraft naturally also featured not only in the Mathers' eagerly promoted specific accounts, but in general works on witchcraft and magic.[31]

LITHOBOLIA:

OR, THE

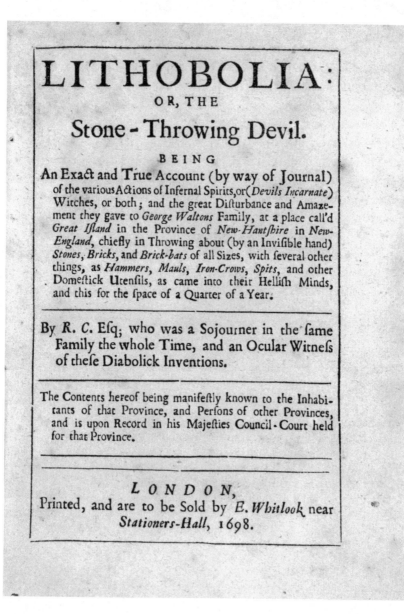

Stone-Throwing Devil.

BEING

An Exact and True Account (by way of Journal) of the various Actions of Infernal Spirits, or (*Devils Incarnate*) Witches, or both; and the great Diſturbance and Amazement they gave to *George Waltons* Family, at a place call'd *Great Iſland* in the Province of *New-Hantſhire* in *New-England*, chiefly in Throwing about (by an Inviſible hand) *Stones*, *Bricks*, and *Brick-bats* of all Sizes, with ſeveral other things, as *Hammers*, *Mauls*, *Iron-Crows*, *Spits*, and other Domeſtick Utenſils, as came into their Helliſh Minds, and this for the ſpace of a Quarter of a Year.

By *R. C.* Eſq; who was a Sojourner in the ſame Family the whole Time, and an Ocular Witneſs of theſe Diabolick Inventions.

The Contents hereof being manifeſtly known to the Inhabitants of that Province, and Perſons of other Provinces, and is upon Record in his Majeſties Council-Court held for that Province.

LONDON,
Printed, and are to be Sold by *E. Whitlook* near *Stationers-Hall*, 1698.

Title page of Richard Chamberlayne, *Lithobolia* (London, 1698). John Carter Brown Library.

Some of the most frequently reprinted works were those first published in the seventeenth century. Thomas Shepard's *Sincere Convert* was first printed in London in 1640 and republished about nineteen times by 1692; it seems to have received its last printing in Edinburgh in 1714. Shepard's *Sound Beleever*, another work dealing with the conditions of religious conversion, first published in London in 1645, was also popular until the third quarter of the seventeenth century. George Herbert's *The Temple*, with its famous lines on religion and the "American strand," was also frequently reprinted in the seventeenth century. The "Bay Psalm Book" had appeared in many British editions by 1760.

The closest rivals to these works of devotion seem to have been works of geography. Peter Heylyn's *Microcosmus; or a little description of the great world . . .* had reached eight editions by 1639; his *Cosmographie in four books . . .*, first published in 1652, was reprinted many times to 1703. In both books the text relating to North America hardly changed over the years.[32] The same was true of Patrick Gordon's book, discussed below. Nathaniel Crouch's *English empire in America* (London, 1685) also had about eleven editions through 1760. Some explanation of the extraordinary popularity of Bernard Le Bovyer de Fontenelle's *A discourse of the plurality of worlds . . .*, the text of which appeared under numerous slightly changed titles from 1687 for the next one hundred years, is also needed.

Other works went into many editions over a shorter period. Accounts of military successes were always popular; Thomas Prince's *Extraordinary events the doings of God and marvellous in pious eyes . . . seen on . . . taking the city of Louisbourg, on the Isle of Cape Breton . . .* (1747), first printed in Boston in 1746, appeared in at least five London editions and one Belfast and one Edinburgh edition in the same year. John Brown's attack on luxury and corruption, which he linked to British failures in the war against the French, *An estimate of the manners and principles of the times . . .*, first printed in 1757, had reached eight or nine editions by the end of 1758.

Calculations based on British North Americana printed between 1621 and 1760 suggest that about half of the works listed were printed in one edition and about another quarter in two or three. The remainder ranged up to about thirty editions. But the number of editions is, of course, no guide to the number of copies printed; the number of copies per edition could number from about 250 upward. Without direct information about the publishing history of individual imprints, sometimes found in printers' or publishers' records or other sources, there is no way of discovering the size of editions or assessing the readership for different works. What does seem clear is that some frequently issued works were little changed over time and must have presented an inaccurate and antique view of America to their readers, perhaps with an effect on their attitudes and beliefs. Patrick Gordon's *Geography anatomized: or, a compleat geographical grammer . . .* was first published in London in 1693 and seems to have been issued in more than twenty issues/editions with slight title alterations to 1754 with the text hardly altered.[33]

About 143 works in this checklist of British North Americana seem to have been first printed in North America. The first British North American imprint to have been reissued in the mother country was *The Capitall Lawes of New-England* of

1643, printed in London during the intense debate (involving the "New England way") over forms of church and civil government in the early years of the English Revolution. The second—although all or part of its preface had in fact been reprinted in 1644 in London in Nathaniel Holmes's *Gospel Musick*—was the Bay Psalm Book, *The Whole book of psalmes, faithfully translated into English metre; whereunto is prefixed a discourse* . . . (London?, 1647). Although there has been discussion of whether some subsequent editions of this work from 1648 onward were printed in Cambridge, Massachusetts, or Cambridge, England, it has recently been convincingly argued that these were produced in Amsterdam, probably for the American market.[34] However, it is fairly clear that at least from the last quarter of the seventeenth century, the publication of the New England form of psalms was frequent in England and in Scotland. Twenty-three or so editions had appeared in England and Scotland by 1759. Whether these were for export to America or for use in nonconformist churches in the British Isles is not known, although, of course, books were a substantial export to the New World.[35]

Although numerous works by (mainly) divines living in New England were first published in London in the 1640s and 1650s, no other direct republication of a work first printed in North America seems to have happened until 1652, when a version of the Massachusetts Platform of Church Discipline attributed to Richard Mather, first printed in Cambridge, Massachusetts, in 1649, was printed in London by W. Bentley for J. Ridley. According to Holmes,[36] this was technically flawed and was suppressed. Only one copy is now extant. A second, more successful version, printed by Peter Cole, appeared in the following year with a foreword by Edward Winslow. Seven years later, in 1660, Quakers—voracious customers of the printing shops—had a declaration of the Massachusetts General Court justifying the trials and executions of Quakers in Boston reprinted in London, in *A True relation of the proceedings against certain Quakers, at the generall court of the Massachusetts . . . October 18, 1659* . . . . In the same year, John Norton's apologia for the prosecutions of Quakers in New England, *The heart of New-England rent at the blasphemies of the present generation,* was also reprinted in London. These two works are examples of the very much larger quantity of Americana published in Britain in order to present a case to the authorities, influence the opinion of the political nation, or gain public sympathy. The printing press, of course, was the only cheap machine for making multiple copies of items available to give to influential figures as well as to sell.

The frequency of London reprints of New England works hardly increased after the Restoration of Charles II. In 1666 Michael Wigglesworth's *The day of doom: or, A description of the great and last judgement* was printed in London. This would be reprinted again in 1673 and 1687 in London and in 1711 in Newcastle-upon-Tyne.

The Newcastle imprint may well have been the first reprint outside of London of a book first published in North America. Despite the book's presumed allure for nonconformists, Wigglesworth's verses were not to be reprinted again in Great Britain until 1774, when an edition appeared in Norwich. In 1675–76 several accounts of the serious Indian war in New England, King Philip's War, appeared in London, either closely adapted or directly reprinted from Boston originals. Rowlandson's captivity narrative was also printed in London in 1682.[37]

By the 1680s another category of works from America was becoming more common—those by individuals whose wish for literary or other forms of recognition led them to seek as many British printings as possible for both their previously unpublished or their previously American-published writings. Increase Mather's first London reprint was in 1684, when G. Calvert issued his essay on "illustrious providences" published earlier in the same year in Boston. This had a degree of success and was republished in London in 1687. Thereafter his British reprints were frequent. Cotton Mather followed his father's example. His works on the New England witchcraft cases were reprinted in London and Edinburgh, while he either had certain Boston publications reprinted in London or arranged for other writings to be first printed there. I have not calculated how many of his works had been printed or reprinted in the British Isles by the time of his death in 1728. One of the Mathers' London contacts and agents was John Dunton, who had visited New England and published an account of his travels. The Mathers' example was to be followed by other clergy in the following years.

Probably the first work from an American press outside of Massachusetts to be reprinted in London resulted from Leisler's rebellion in New York. Although *A modest and impartial narrative of several grievances . . . that the peaceable and most considerable inhabitants . . . of New-York . . . lye under, by the extravagant and arbitrary proceedings of Jacob Leyster and his accomplices . . .* (London, 1690) claimed that this tract had been first "printed at New York," its actual place of first publication was Philadelphia. An earlier justification of the Protestant Revolution of 1689 in Maryland, *The Declaration of the reasons and motives for the present appearing in arms of their majesties protestant subjects in Maryland*, was also "reprinted" in London in 1689, but despite this claim on the title page no evidence has been found of a first printing in Maryland. A popular and entirely different work, the Reverend J. Dickinson's *God's Protecting Providence, man's surest help and defence . . .*, a story of shipwreck and cannibals, was first printed in Philadelphia in 1699 and reprinted in London in 1700, 1701, 1720, and 1759.

After 1700 there were frequent reprintings of New York and Philadelphia publications, later to be joined by those of the presses located in the colonial South. These included many works relating to political controversies in the colonies,

A TRUE

HISTORY

OF THE

Captivity & Reſtoration

OF

Mrs. *MARY ROWLANDSON*,

A Miniſter's Wife in *New-England*.

Wherein is ſet forth, The Cruel and Inhumane Uſage ſhe underwent amongſt the *Heathens*, for Eleven Weeks time: And her Deliverance from them.

Written by her own Hand, for her Private Uſe: And now made Publick at the earneſt Deſire of ſome Friends, for the Benefit of the Afflicted.

Whereunto is annexed,

A Sermon of *the Poſſibility of God's Forſaking a People that have been near and dear to him*:

Preached by Mr. *Joſeph Rowlandſon*, Husband to the ſaid Mrs. *Rowlandſon*: It being his Laſt Sermon.

Printed firſt at *New-England*: And Re-printed at *London*, and ſold by *Joſeph Poole*, at the *Blue Bowl* in the *Long-Walk*, by *Chriſts-Church* Hoſpital. 1682.

Title page of Mary Rowlandson, *A true history of the capitivity and restoration of Mrs. Mary Rowlandson* (London, 1682). John Carter Brown Library.

which, for various reasons, it was felt might advantageously be reprinted in London. Among other topics were Indians and Indian converts and the dispute relating to the treatment of smallpox. But, as we have seen, works relating to religion and the churches predominated during much of the eighteenth century, as they had in the seventeenth. There were also increasing republications of American pieces concerned with military relations between France and Britain in the New World, such as the patriotic sermons of the Reverend Samuel Davies of Virginia. Of these militaria, *The Journal of Major George Washington . . .*, first printed in Williamsburg in 1754 and reprinted by Thomas Jefferys in London in the same year, is the most celebrated. By the 1750s quite substantial historical works were also being reprinted in London, including William Stith's *The history of the first discovery and settlement of Virginia . . .* (Williamsburg, 1747; London, 1753) and William Douglass's two-volume *A summary, historical and political of the first planting, progressive improvements, and present state of the British settlements in North America* (Boston, 1749, 1753; London, 1755).

A short essay can only deal with aspects of British Americana, some representative, some of individual interest. The huge corpus of printed British Americana for the latter seventeenth and the eighteenth centuries has still not properly been appreciated or explored by cultural historians or historians of ideas, who have tended to concentrate on well-known "key" texts. My own view of British consciousness of America is that from about the 1690s to the 1770s it existed within a general idea of "maritime Augustanism"—of a God-approved seaborne empire that would extend commerce, liberty, and Protestantism throughout the world and which also would bring wealth and material improvements to individuals and to the nation. This belief, productive of a profound and resonant patriotism that crossed social boundaries, is to be found in the literature of the streets[38] as well as that of the salons. It penetrated very deep into English and later into Scottish society, underlying the Scottish enlightenment.[39] It is to be found in the works of poets, historians, philosophers, and clergymen.[40] Adam Smith's *The Theory of Moral Sentiments* (London and Edinburgh, 1759) compared the characteristics of those living in an age of civility and politeness and wealth—a wealth to some extent based on Europe's contact with the Americas—with those of the poor savages of the New World. The Reverend Richard Price, celebrating Britain's victory at Quebec and expansion into the New World, praised the virtues and charities of the British as well as British liberty. The title that he gave his sermon was *Britain's happiness, and the proper improvement of it . . .* and, while regretting the fact that "the greatest part of the rest of mankind are slaves," he congratulated his audience on living in "a more improved and enlightened age." He looked forward to the realization of the "everlasting gospel," when universal peace, prosperity, and liberty would prevail and all the nations of the earth would have become "kingdoms of the Lord."[41] Edward Gibbon, a rationalist without millennial dreams, nevertheless also believed that "War, commerce, and religious zeal" had diffused civilization around the world and that "every age of the world has increased, and still increases, the real wealth, the happiness, the knowledge, and perhaps the virtue of the human race."[42] By the 1780s, however, the loss of America and the events in France had shattered this complacency. Moreover, the American New World had lost most of its mystery and had become a largely conventional prospect in an English mental landscape whose new and more exotic horizons were to be found in the Pacific and Australasian worlds.

APPENDIX

Shown below are some authors listed in *European Americana* published in Britain and then in continental Europe (number of items printed/number of continental cities in which published), grouped by period.

1601–1650

Bacon, Francis 51/10
Camden, William 4/3
Hall, Joseph 7/3
Hariot, Thomas 2/1
Owen, John 17/8
Sandys, Edwin 4/4
Selden, John 3/1

1701–1725

Allen, John 1/1
Behn, Aphra 1/1
Beverley, Robert 5/2
Boyle, Robert 1/1
Burchett, Josiah 1/1
Burnet, Gilbert, Bishop 5/2
Chamberlayne 2/2
Clarendon, Edward 2/1
Chevrau, Urbain 7/3
Colman, Benjamin 1/1
Dale, Samuel 1/1
Dampier, William 20/6
Defoe, Daniel 29/13
Dickinson, Jonathan 1/1
Hare, Francis 2/1
Harris, Walter 2/2
Kimber, Isaac 1/1
Law, John 3/3
Lawson, John 3/2
Maitland, Charles 2/2
Oldmixon, John 3/2
Ray, John 7/4
Rogers, Woodes 4/1
Sewel, William 2/1
Sidney, Algernon 1/1
Smith, John 5/1
Southerne, Thomas 3/1
Stillingfleet, Edward 1/1
Stubbs, Philip 1/1
Swift, Jonathan 13/5
Sydenham, Thomas 5/2
Temple, William 2/1
Wafer, Lionel 5/4
Wagstaffe, William 1/1
Whiston, William 1/1
Woodward, Josiah 1/1

1726–1750

Allen, John 11/5
Bacon, Francis 2/1
Baker, J. 1/1
Behn, Aphra 2/2
Berkeley, George 4/2
Blackwell, Elizabeth 1/1
Bollan, William 3/2
Bradley, Richard 1/1
Browne, Thomas 8/4
Burnet, Gilbert, Vicar 1/1
Campbell, John 3/1
Chetwood, William 7/4
Churchill, Awnsham 1/1
Cockburn, John 1/1
Crouch, Nathaniel 2/1
Dale, Samuel 1/1
Defoe, Daniel 22/7
Derham, William 10/5
Dryden, John 1/1
Edwards, Jonathan 4/3
Ellis, Henry 7/3
Gee, Joshua 3/2
Gibson, Edmund 3/1
Gordon, Patrick 1/1
Harrington, James 1/1
Harris, Walter 4/3
Hoadly, Benjamin 6/1
Hutchinson, Francis 1/1
Ker, John 2/2
Kimber, Isaac 1/1
Kolb, Peter 5/2
Logan, James 1/1
Macky, John 1/1
Miller, Philip 2/2
Mun, Thomas 1/1
Oglethorpe, William 1/1
Oldmixon, John 2/2
Rapin-Thoyras, Paul de 9/4
Ray, John 3/3
Salmon, Thomas 4/2
Sewel, William 4/3
Snelgrave, William 1/1
Sydenham, Thomas 6/3
Walter, Richard 7/4
Wilson, Thomas 1/1

NOTES

1. See, for example, J. H. Elliott, *The Old World and the New: 1492–1650* (Cambridge, 1970; rev. ed., 1992), and Antonello Gerbi, *The Dispute of the New World: The History of a Polemic, 1750–1900* (Pittsburgh, 1973).

2. *European Americana: A Chronological Guide to Works Printed in Europe Relating to the Americas, 1493–1750*, vol. 1, *1493–1600*, vol. 2, *1601–1650*, ed. John Alden with the assistance of Dennis C. Landis (New York, 1980, 1982); vol. 5, *1701–1725*, vol. 6, *1726–1750*, ed. Dennis C. Landis (New York, 1987, 1988). These volumes contain full lists of other catalogs and guides to relevant materials.

3. *The Eighteenth-Century Short Title Catalogue: 1990* (London, 1990). The CD-ROM version became available in 1992. It is also available and is being added to on-line.

4. Alfred W. Pollard and Gilbert R. Redgrave, *A Short-Title Catalogue of Books Printed in England, Scotland, and Ireland and of English Books Printed Abroad, 1475–1640* (London, 1926), and 2d ed., rev. and enl., by William A. Jackson, F. S. Ferguson, and Katharine F. Pantzer (London, 1976–92); Donald F. Wing, comp., *Short-Title Catalogue of Books Printed in England, Scotland, Ireland, Wales, and British America, and of English Books Printed in Other Countries, 1641–1700* (New York, 1972–88).

5. A useful study for British imprints relating to America before 1621 is John Parker, *Books*

to Build an Empire: A Bibliographical History of British Overseas Interests to 1620 (Amsterdam, 1965).

6. Gertrude M. Sibley, *The Lost Plays and Masques* (Ithaca, 1933), 30, 123, 183.

7. *The triumph of London: performed on Tuesday, October XXIX, 1678* (London, 1678); *London's yearly jubilee perform'd on Friday, October XXIX, 1686 . . .* (London, 1686).

8. August W. Staub and Robert W. Pinson, "Fabulous Wild Men: American Indians in European Pageants, 1493–1700," *Theatre Survey* 25 (May 1984): 43–53. For Lord Mayor's pageants in London and civic pageantry in London and elsewhere, see David M. Bergeron, *English Civic Pageantry, 1558–1642* (London, 1971). John Nichols, *London Pageants* (London, 1831) lists Lord Mayor's pageants to 1708. See also F. C. Brown, *Elkanah Settle, His life and Works* (Chicago, 1910), and R. T. D. Sayles, *Lord Mayor's Pageants of the Merchant Taylor's Company in the 15th, 16th, and 17th centuries* (London, 1931).

9. See Christian F. Feest's essay in this volume.

10. See, for example, Pierre Danchin, *The Prologues and Epilogues of the Restoration, 1660–1700: A Complete Edition*, 6 vols. (Nancy, 1981–88).

11. See Robert W. Kenny, "James Ralph: An Eighteenth-Century Philadelphian in Grub Street," *Pennsylvania Magazine of History and Biography* 64 (1940): 218–42. Charlotte Lennox has entries in both the *Dictionary of National Biography* and the *Dictionary of American Biography*.

12. See the essay in this volume by Henry Lowood for the theme of "managing new information" about natural history. British horticulturists and botanists are dealt with by Blanche Henrey, *British Botanical and Horticultural Literature before 1800: Comprising a History and a Bibliography of Botanical and Horticultural Books Printed in England, Scotland, and Ireland from the Earliest Times to 1800*, 3 vols. (London, 1975).

13. A quick check revealed the following (dates of first British publication given): 1701, Moréri; 1703, Lahontan; 1707, Vallemont, Pierre de; 1707, Jesuit Relations; 1710, Bayle; 1713, Huet; 1720, Hennepin; 1720, Boerhaave, Herman; 1724, Solís; 1727, Voltaire; 1731?, Bernard, Jean Frédéric; 1731, Prévost; 1731, Rivadeneira; 1735, Palafox; 1739, Pluche; 1749, Savary des Bruslons.

14. William Rufus Chetwood, *The voyages, dangerous adventures and imminent escapes of Captain Richard Falconer: containing the laws, customs, and manners of the Indians in America . . . Intermix'd with the voyages and adventures of Thomas Randal . . . His being taken by the Indians of Virginia, etc.* (London, 1720); *The voyages and adventures of Captain Robert Boyle . . .* (London, 1726); *The voyage, shipwrack, and miraculous escape of Richard Castleman . . . With a description of Pensylvania . . . and . . . Philadelphia . . .* (London, 1726).

15. See John Feather, "British Publishing in the Eighteenth Century: A Preliminary Subject Analysis," *The Library*, 6th ser., 8 (1986): 32–46, for an attempt at a general survey of types of publication.

16. I have not included as provincial imprints books printed in London for provincial booksellers. Therefore there are fewer tabulations of non-London entries than in *European Americana*.

17. The numerical information in this essay reflects my research in spring 1991 and is provisional. These numbers are currently being revised upward.

18. The following are some examples of cheap "popular" works: *A New song* (Edinburgh, 1755), a broadside, concerns recruiting of Scots troops for French and Indian war; *Great Britain's glory. Being a loyal song on the taking of Cape Breton from the French 26 of July by Admiral Boscawen* . . . ([London?], [1758?]); *The Northumberland garland. Containing four excellent new songs* (London, 1759), with verses on "Britain's conquest" mentioning Cape Breton, Crown Point, Senegal, etc., and "Quedec's [*sic*] mighty fall"; *The Soldier's delight. Being a choice collection of songs* (London, [1760?]), a garland, contains "Britannia's glory" with verses on Boscawen, Amherst, and Cape Breton; *Chapter of Admirals. To which are added . . . Patrick O'Neal's return from drubbing the French. An Anacreonic song* (London, [1760?]), a chapbook, a mockery of Irish boasting; *The Highlander's march a garland. Composed of several new songs viz. 1. The Highlander's march to America* . . . (Edinburgh, [1760?]), damaged part of an 8p. chapbook, "O the French like Foxes do lie in the Wood," etc.; *A Hint to the fair sex. A garland, containing six new songs* (Leominster, Worcester, Gloucester, 1760), a chapbook, with patriotic verses referring to Amherst, Wolfe, etc.

19. See Thomas R. Adams, *The American Controversy: A Bibliographical Study of the British Pamphlets about the American Disputes, 1764–1783*, 2 vols. (Providence and New York, 1980). Thomas R. Adams and Colin Bonwick, *British Pamphlets Relating to the American Revolution . . . 1764–1783* (East Ardsley, n.d.), forty-nine reels of microfilm.

20. Wales had no printing presses until the early eighteenth century, and their output was mainly in Welsh. I am not aware that any study was made of this Welsh language literature for *European Americana*, and I have not investigated it myself. Future studies will be considerably facilitated by the publication of Eiluned Rees, *Libri Walliae: A Catalogue of Welsh Books and Books Printed in Wales, 1546–1820*, 2 vols. (Aberystwyth, 1987).

21. David S. Shields, *Oracles of Empire: Poetry, Politics, and Commerce in British America, 1690–1760* (Chicago, 1990), is a pioneering work, surveying some of the major British poetry.

22. William Lauder, *Memorial or state of the process at the instance of William Lauder of Wine-Park* . . . (N.p., [1718?]). A seemingly unique copy of this pamphlet is in the John Carter Brown Library.

23. For a popular, if under-researched, treatment, see Andrew Lang, *The Annesley Case* (Edinburgh and London, 1912).

24. *A genuine, impartial, and authentick account of the life of William Parsons, esq; executed at Tyburn, Monday Feb. 11, 1751, for returning from transportation* . . . (London, 1751).

25. Peter Linebaugh, *The London Hanged: Crime and Civil Society in the Eighteenth Century* (London, 1991). See also Lincoln B. Faller, *Turned to Account: The Forms and Functions of Criminal Biography in Late Seventeenth- and Eighteenth-Century England* (Cambridge, 1987). There has been no detailed study of English seventeenth- and eighteenth-century criminal biographies that seeks to elucidate all the New World material in them.

26. For a recent reexamination, see John Treherne, *The Canning Enigma* (London, 1989).

27. See Richard C. Simmons, *Savagery, Enlightenment, Opulence* (Birmingham, 1989).

28. For a discussion of its publishing history, see K. Z. Derounian, "The Publication, Promotion, and Distribution of Mary Rowlandson's Indian Captivity Narrative in the Seventeenth Century," *Early American Literature* 23, no. 5 (1988): 239–61.

29. See, for example, William Berriman, *The great blessings of redemption from captivity. A sermon preached at the cathedral church at St. Paul, December 4, 1721. Before the captives redeem'd by the late treaty with the Emperor of Morocco* (London, 1722).

30. Richard C. Simmons, "God and Victory: The Quebec Thanksgiving Sermons of 29 November 1759" (in progress).

31. Richard Baxter, *The certainty of the world of spirits, fully evinced by the unquestionable histories of apparations and witchcrafts . . .* (London, 1691); William Turner, *A compleat history of the most remarkable providences, both of judgement and mercy, which have hapned [sic] in this present age . . .* (London, 1697); John Beaumont, *An historical, physiological and theological treatise of spirits, apparitions, witchcrafts . . .* (London, 1705); Richard Boulton, *A compleat history of magick, sorcery, and witchcraft . . .* (London, 1715); Francis Hutchinson, *An historical essay concerning witchcraft . . . And also two sermons . . .* (London, 1718); and Richard Boulton, *The possibility and reality of magick, sorcery and witchcraft . . . In answer to Dr. Hutchinson's Historical essay . . .* (London, 1722) all contain more or less substantial sections on New England witchcraft.

32. John Huber Walker, "A Descriptive Bibliography of the Early Printed Works of Peter Heylyn" (Ph.D. diss., The University of Birmingham, 1978).

33. Patrick Gordon, *Geography anatomized: or, a compleat geographical grammer . . .* (London, 1693), appeared in a second enlarged edition in 1699 and then from 1701–60 in more than twenty issues/editions with slight title alterations. *European Americana* lists editions in 1702, 1704, 1708, 1711, 1716, 1719, 1722, 1725, 1730, 1733, 1735, 1737, 1740, 1741, and 1744. *ESTC* has also London, 1728 (11th ed., corrected and enlarged), 1749 (19th ed.), and 1754 (20th ed.), and Dublin, 1739 (15th ed., corrected) and 1747 (16th ed.). For a discussion of the size of editions and related points on eighteenth-century books, see Marjorie Plant, *The English Book Trade: An Economic History of the Making and Sale of Books*, 3d ed. (London, 1975), and John Feather, *The Provincial Book Trade in Eighteenth-Century England* (Cambridge, 1985). An accessible source, with frequent and representative references to sizes of editions, is James E. Tierney, ed., *The Correspondence of Robert Dodsley, 1733–1764* (Cambridge, 1988).

34. Thomas J. Holmes, *The Minor Mathers: A List of Their Works* (Cambridge, Mass., 1940), no. 51B. I am very grateful to Hugh Amory of the Houghton Library for providing me with information on this point.

35. Giles Barber, "Books from the Old World and for the New: The British International Trade in Books in the Eighteenth Century," *Studies on Voltaire and the Eighteenth Century* 151 (1976): 185–224.

36. Holmes, *Minor Mathers*, no. 51B.

37. See above, note 28.

38. A very great number of English songs and chapbooks have oceanic themes, deal with the "Indies" as a source of wealth for individuals, and celebrate the valor of British sailors in the struggle against France and Spain. Very few have any measure of critical social comment. Linda Colley, *Britons: Forging the Nation, 1707–1837* (New Haven, 1992), deals with British patriotism.

39. James Thomson, author of "Rule Britannia" and other quasi-imperial songs and

poems as well as of *The Seasons*, was, of course, a Scot. He was also appointed to the sinecure office of surveyor-general of the Leeward Islands in 1744.

40. J. G. A. Pocock, *Virtue, Commerce, and History: Essays on Political Thought and History, Chiefly in the Eighteenth Century* (Cambridge, 1985), touches on many of the contrasting views of these ideas held by the learned. See esp. chap. 11. However, merchants, politicians, and the vulgar were more robust in their acceptance of the value of commercial progress than the intellectuals.

41. Richard Price, *Britain's happiness, and the proper improvement of it*... (London, 1759), 4, 8, 10–11, 19, 22–23.

42. Edward Gibbon, *History of the Decline and Fall of the Roman Empire*, ed. J. B. Bury (London, 1925), 4:167n.

Part v

Conclusion

J. H. ELLIOTT

Final Reflections

THE OLD WORLD AND THE NEW REVISITED

Twenty-three years and two international conferences have now passed since the publication in 1970 of *The Old World and the New, 1492–1650*,[1] my study of the consequences for early modern Europe of Columbus's landfall and the European occupation of the Americas that followed it. The first of these conferences, which was directly prompted by my book, was organized in 1975 by Fredi Chiappelli, then director of the Center for Medieval and Renaissance Studies at the University of California, Los Angeles. The conference brought together a large number of specialists, who addressed almost every conceivable aspect of the impact of the New World on the Old in some fifty-five papers, subsequently published in two impressive volumes.[2] The second conference, organized by the John Carter Brown Library at Providence in 1991, confined itself specifically to the theme of the impact of the New World on the European consciousness and again generated a substantial number of papers, a selection of which appears in this book.

It is clear from the convening of these conferences and from the willingness of so many scholars to take part in them that I must have stumbled on some historical questions of more than passing interest. The word "stumbled," it should be said, is used advisedly. At the time of embarking on this particular voyage of discovery I was not, like Columbus, inspired by some grand vision. A lengthy trip to Latin America in 1964 had opened my eyes to the sheer size and scale of the Spanish colonial achievement and made me vividly aware, as I think I had not previously been, that no serious historian of Spain could afford to exclude from the reckoning the transatlantic dimension of the Spanish past. This was appreciated in his time by one of the most eminent foreign historians of Spain, Roger B. Merriman, who chose *The Rise of the Spanish Empire in the Old World and in the New*[3] as the title of his four-volume work—a title which, resonating in my mind, would later provide the inspiration for my own.

Because of the attention paid by Earl J. Hamilton[4] and subsequent historians to the consequences for the sixteenth-century Spanish economy of silver remittances from the Indies, I was already turning over in my mind some of the problems connected with the impact of overseas empire on metropolitan society. Subsequently, the need to prepare a course of lectures on the conquest of Mexico led me to immerse myself in contemporary accounts of the Indies. The pleasure to be found in reading such writers as Fernández de Oviedo and Bartolomé de Las Casas naturally widened my interest in the interaction between early modern Spain and America to embrace intellectual and cultural history, and the whole problem of European perceptions of the New World. It was at this point that I received an invitation to give the Wiles Lectures for 1969 at the Queen's University, Belfast, on a "broad issue relating to the general history of civilization," and realized that I had the makings of a series of lectures to hand.

I was conscious that, given a brief that specified the "general history of civilization," I could not confine myself to Spain and should properly extend my concerns to early modern Europe as a whole, although Spain, as the pioneer imperial power in the Americas and as the first to be seriously confronted by the challenge of lands and peoples unknown to earlier Europeans, was likely to provide me with much of my evidence. But I soon came to see that a vast amount of reading would be needed, both in primary sources and in the secondary literature, if I were to cast a European-wide net—reading for which the deadline of the lectures allowed me insufficient time. In the circumstances, I was able to do no more than take a small number of soundings, as was all too obvious when the lectures appeared in print.

But those soundings in themselves proved revealing, less perhaps for what they trawled up than for what they did not. The secondary literature was neither as overwhelming nor as impressive as I had originally expected when I first turned to it for guidance about European responses to the newfound world. I naturally read what I could in the historiography of discovery and picked up some valuable ideas and information from standard works like Geoffroy Atkinson's *Les Nouveaux Horizons de la Renaissance Française*,[5] and those of Gilbert Chinard on exoticism in French literature.[6] In general, the Spanish contribution was disappointing, as also was the Anglo-American contribution, in spite of the abundance of good writing on the early voyages and settlements. Somehow, the wider theme of the impact of America on the consciousness of sixteenth- and seventeenth-century English men and women seemed largely to have eluded British and American historians, although it had attracted the attention of literary scholars, notably Robert Rawston Cawley, whose *Unpathed Waters*[7] explores the influence of the overseas voyages on the Elizabethan imagination. The interest shown by literary scholars has remained a constant in the subsequent development of the subject, and the interaction of historians and literary specialists proved to be one of the most encouraging features of the John Carter Brown Library conference.

But there were two major contributions by Italian scholars which did much to help me formulate my approach. The first of these was Rosario Romeo's investigation into the sixteenth-century Italian response to reports of the newly discovered lands—an investigation which moved beyond the realms of literature, explored by Chinard, to consider more generally the impact of those reports on the ways in which sixteenth-century Italians thought about the world.[8] The other outstanding Italian contribution, which appeared in 1955, the year following the publication of Romeo's work, was Antonello Gerbi's *The Dispute of the New World*,[9] a book which I found enormously suggestive in its indications of how America helped to shape a European debate, even if that debate fell chronologically outside the limits of the period to which I had confined myself.

Although I had already visited the John Carter Brown Library at Brown University, it was only now that I became fully aware of its central importance to my current interests, and I managed to return to it, for what proved all too brief a visit, shortly before delivering my Wiles lectures in 1969. It was during this visit that I was introduced to Durand Echevarria's *Mirage in the West*, first published in 1957, another study which, although concerned, like Gerbi's, with a subject relating to a later period than my own—in this instance the image of America in the France of the Enlightenment and the Revolution—helped to influence my approach. In particular, it confirmed what was by this stage becoming a dominant theme in my own formulation: the importance of *images* of America, and the remoteness of many of those images from the American reality. Echevarria identifies in 1783 three distinct interpretations of "the westward expansion of European civilization into the new frontier environment of America." "The oversimplification of all these interpretations," he argues, "produced a gross distortion of the image. In spite of the greatly increased flow of information on America into France, the supply of facts was by far inadequate to give a balanced picture or to support the top-heavy superstructures of hypothesis. Moreover, the reporting of the facts was inaccurate because of the carelessness, inexperience and ignorance of the reporters." But, he concludes, and his conclusion seemed to me fundamental, "the main cause of distortion . . . was that the image was a reflection not of reality but of domestic preoccupations."[10]

The image as a reflection of metropolitan preoccupations rather than of colonial realities was something that had haunted me since I first read the *Decades* of Peter Martyr, with its vision of a golden age society now transposed to the farther shores of the Atlantic; and the evidence adduced by Echevarria to show that Europe's domestic preoccupations were still shaping the image of America three centuries after its discovery probably did more than anything else to confirm me in my decision to make this a leading motif of my book. Without it I doubt if I would have risked the concluding words of my book: ". . . perhaps dreams were always more important than realities in the relationship of the Old World and the New."

Those words have not met with universal acclaim, but twenty-three years later I remain unrepentant. In a book that deals not only with the reception and diffusion of ideas, but also with such apparently matter-of-fact questions as bullion transfers, transatlantic migration, and the European balance of power, they will inevitably strike some readers as far-fetched. But the discussions that took place at the John Carter Brown Library conference amply confirmed that even the most mundane concerns are attended by a fair share of illusions—that bullion remittances cannot be divorced from images of wealth, nor the movement of peoples from images of an alternative society developing in the new American environment.

Even allowing for an element of exaggeration, my assertion of the importance of dreams at the expense of realities does have the merit of highlighting what has emerged as a central problem of method in any approach to the theme of "America in European consciousness." Time after time we find on inspection that the America we are seeking in the European consciousness turns out to be a fantasy America—an America as Europeans either believed it or wanted it to be. There is no doubt that reports from America, whether of Indians living as innocent beings in a state of nature or as members of ordered polities like Inca Peru with its network of paved highways and its impressive stone buildings, excited the European imagination, nor that this excitement was reflected in an important utopian literature. But to go on from here to assert that ideas of liberty or authority in Europe would have been very different without the presence of a "real" America which offered alternative models of social organization strikes me now, as it struck me when originally writing my book, as a much riskier proposition, although even my minimalist approach seemed to some critics to take me several steps too far.

The papers presented to the John Carter Brown conference have served to remind us that for sixteenth-century Europeans preoccupied by the current condition of their own society, an impressive range of alternative models already existed in the biblical tradition and the literature of classical antiquity. The primitive Christian church, the world of the Golden Age, the Scythians, the Spartans, the Romans—all these provided models and points of reference. America, precisely because of the fantasy elements that attended its conceptualization, had no trouble in taking its place in this assortment of models, offering as it did a convenient range of possibilities that could provide confirmation or refutation for preexisting views. Accordingly, America looks at first sight more like an optional extra than a necessity for that amorphous, and very notional, entity, the early modern European consciousness.

As we seek to determine whether this is in fact a fair impression, it seems to me that we have constantly come up against three interrelated, but different, questions, to none of which we have yet discovered ways of formulating satisfactory answers. The first question, and the one most likely in the long run to prove amenable to some kind of answer, since part of it at least can be reached by statistical analysis, is the degree of *interest* generated by news from the newfound world. The second question is that of the *assimilation* of this world into the European consciousness; and the third, and most complex of all, relates to the *transforming effect* of America on that consciousness.

As I listened to the papers and discussions at the John Carter Brown conference, it seemed to me that opinion remains pretty sharply divided on all three questions. As far as the first is concerned, those who have started from a bibliographical standpoint, like Jan Lechner in his study of the private libraries of Dutch humanists, or Richard Simmons in his examination of British publications relating to America,[11] have argued persuasively that there was more "interest" in America than is often asserted, assuming that "interest" can be measured by publishing decisions and the library catalogs of scholars. In the light of their findings, and of those which are likely to arise from the kind of systematic work now made possible by that great bibliographical tool, *European Americana*,[12] I suspect that, in common with many others, I overemphasized the degree of indifference shown by early modern Europeans to the new discoveries. As Lechner pointed out, the head start enjoyed by the authors of classical antiquity is liable to give rise to misleading impressions, at least when they are derived from a statistical comparison between the printings of classical texts and works devoted to America.

Yet sufficient evidence was presented at the conference to suggest that the interest was tempered by a fair degree of indifference, even in circles where interest might have been expected, like those of Henry Lowood's sixteenth-century naturalists, who "hardly cited the literature of exploration and passed over the voyages of discovery in silence."[13] But here Lowood comes up with an interesting suggestion, which may help to explain what can appear to modern scholars a surprising indifference, when he remarks that, at least where its plant life was concerned, the New World had in some respects become "too familiar" by the later sixteenth century to provoke much discussion about the original American habitat of plants that had long since lost their novelty.[14] The idea is attractive, but, in the nature of things, the evidence provided by silence is disturbingly ambiguous.

Ultimately this would appear to be a problem without a solution, since no historian can say what represents a reasonable degree of "interest." Given the intractable nature of the problem, it is not surprising that the John Carter Brown conference, like the Los Angeles conference that preceded it, was divided between maximalists and minimalists—the former impressed, and the latter unimpressed, by the degree of space occupied by America in the mental world of sixteenth-century Europeans. But before a verdict of stalemate is delivered, it would be desirable to explore further the similarities and the differences in European and non-European reactions to alien civilizations. Already, in *The Old World and the New*, I had used Edward Schafer's *The Vermilion Bird* to point up the contrasts between the responses of medieval Chinese to the tropical southern lands of Nam-

Viet and those of sixteenth-century Europeans to the New World of America.[15] The Chinese of the T'ang period were not only dismissive of other societies but lacked those governing metaphysical principles of "order," "harmony," or even "nature" which helped Europeans to conceptualize the American world.[16] More recently, Bernard Lewis has examined the profound indifference of the Islamic world over many centuries to the changing civilization of Europe.[17] In the light of a comparative approach, therefore, we should perhaps be seeking to explain the degree of European interest, rather than lack of interest, in America. An approach along these lines would undoubtedly bring us back to the internal tensions, and the competing traditions, within an early modern European civilization that was far from monolithic.

Accepting a relatively substantial degree of interest, our standard instrument of measurement, the counting of titles or even of references to America, has obvious limitations. Curiosity is only crudely quantifiable, but the kind of work being done by scholars like Lechner and Simmons does at least enable us to get a more precise picture than we once had of the particular aspects of the American world that generated curiosity at any given moment. More work could be done to establish the distinctive kinds of readership for Americana, by means of the systematic study of library catalogs and inventories, while details of the holdings of booksellers can inform us about the anticipated demand for particular books. Much remains to be discovered, too, about the dissemination of information about America—a process that was far from being solely dependent on the printing press. Letters from America, like those that have been preserved of sixteenth-century Spanish settlers in the Indies,[18] can provide fascinating clues to the networks of communication linking the Americas to different parts of Europe.

Publishing decisions also provide an important indicator of the aspects of America most interesting to a European readership, since publishers, if they are to survive, need to know and gauge their markets. It is clear, for instance, that Theodore de Bry, in embarking in 1590 on his great series of illustrated volumes on America,[19] judged his potential market well. On the basis of publishing history it should be possible to determine with some degree of precision what particular topics, or what aspects of the American scene, excited particular interest at any given moment. This in turn can provide valuable insights into shifts and changes in European preoccupations; and it is European preoccupations that set the agenda and largely determined the degree of interest inspired by one aspect of America rather than another.

The past, present, and future of America were all shaped to make it conform as closely as possible to European hopes, aspirations, and requirements. In this sense, America was from the beginning more directly the "invention" of Europe, to use the phraseology of Edmundo O'Gorman,[20] than were either Africa or Asia, even if these also allowed considerable latitude to the European imagination. America, after all, was both destroyed and created by Europe, and the parallel process of destruction and creation at the hands of Europeans makes it unique among the continents of the early modern world. It was precisely this question of the European invention and perception of America that most fascinated me as I looked at differing European accounts of the New World and its peoples and became aware of the degree to which those accounts were shaped and constrained by the European mental and cultural inheritance. I believe that my concern with this aspect of the question possessed the merit of directing attention away from the traditional preoccupation of historians with relatively static images of America and its peoples and shifting it to the observers themselves, and to the wider question of the education of the eye. But it also exposed me to the danger, which I suspect from the responses to my book that I did not entirely avoid, of creating the impression that there was some linear advance in understanding as observers disencumbered themselves by degrees of their traditional constraints and belatedly got to grips with an American "reality."

It was to dispel this impression that I argued in the paper that I wrote for the Los Angeles conference of 1975[21] that we should abandon the Ruskinian doctrine of the innocent eye and think rather in terms of eyes that were selective, but selective in different ways at different times, so that over the centuries we are faced not so much with the progressive unfoldment of a real America as with an America seen from constantly changing angles of vision, each with its distinctive areas of focus and distortion. But this line of approach still does not dispose of the problem of method, which, I suggested, confronts all of us who work on the theme of America in the European consciousness.

Even to talk about "areas of focus and distortion" is to suggest the possibility, in certain ideal circumstances, of capturing an objective reality out there. But the pursuit of any such objective reality was not the purpose of early modern European observers of America, whose intentions were different. Their principal concern, as Anthony Pagden reminds us in *The Fall of Natural Man*, was "to bring within their intellectual grasp phenomena which they recognized as new and which they could only make familiar, and hence intelligible, in the terms of an anthropology made authoritative precisely by the fact that its sources ran back to the Greeks."[22]

The pursuit of an objective reality would become the principal goal only of a later Europe—the Europe of the self-proclaimed scientific observers and the topographical artists, and subsequently of the ethnographers, the anthropologists, and the photographers. It was that Europe—the Europe roughly of the mid-eighteenth to the mid-twentieth centuries—which provided the criteria that many of us still instinctively employ for judging those early interpreters of alien civilizations. It is a Europe whose voice we can hear in the *Cosmos* of Humboldt, when he writes:

> If . . . a taste for accurate observation was in a manifold way developed in Columbus, simply through contact with the grand phenomena of Nature . . . yet we may by no means conclude that a similar development of taste took place among the rude and warlike multitudes of the Conquistadores. Europe has gradually and incontestably obtained, by the discovery of America, an increase in her natural history and in her physical knowledge. . . . For this she has to thank another, more peaceable class of travellers, a small number of distinguished men among the civil officers in the towns, the ecclesiastics and the physicians. They were enabled, during their long sojourn in the old Indian towns . . . to observe with their own eyes, and to confirm and arrange what others had seen, to collect natural specimens, to describe them, to send them to their friends in Europe.[23]

But we no longer share the profound faith of our nineteenth- and early-twentieth-century forebears in the possibilities of accurately recording an objective reality. The reality itself has become too complex and is starting to disintegrate. Our generation has become deeply suspicious of the alleged objectivity of the observer and asks skeptical questions about the nature of his or her relationship to the observed. Photographs, like all other evidence, can be faked or contrived. Instead of an objective reality, now thought to be unattainable or unworthy of attainment, we seek instead to achieve a sympathetic understanding of "the other." This in turn becomes the criterion by which the early observers of America are judged and found wanting.

While this desire to grasp in all its complexity the "otherness" of the "other" has given a valuable stimulus in recent years to the ethnohistorical study of non-European peoples, it has also, in my view, led to expectations of sixteenth- and seventeenth-century European observers and chroniclers which are as unreasonable in their way as the expectations entertained of them by nineteenth-century positivists. Where once they were rated by their degree of success in achieving truth to nature, they are now rated according to their ability to understand the "other." But this latter form of judgment seems to me as ahistorical as the former, since it demands of an Oviedo or even of a Las Casas a set of mental processes entirely alien to them. Their concern, like that of the civilization from which they sprang, was directed to the finding not of otherness but of commonality, for it was only by establishing commonality that they could secure the full incorporation of the peoples of America into the human community and so look forward to the possibility of hailing them, either at once or in due course, not as others but as brothers.

What has happened, in other words, is that our contemporary discovery of the presumed "otherness" of others has embraced the non-European world to the exclusion of the conquerors, colonists, and chroniclers of the sixteenth century; the observed have been accorded a privileged status that has been denied their observers, whose individual voices, reduced to an unattractive unison, are dismissed as "the hegemonic voices of the West."[24] But in reality there are many voices, among the conquerors and the conquered alike. We may not like what some of those voices are saying, but, as historians, we have an obligation to give a hearing to each and every one. There is no more crying need at this moment than to observe the observers with that same sensibility to historical context and environment which we pride ourselves on possessing when we come to reconstruct the world of the observed. To what extent, for instance, are their reactions affected by differences of nationality, generation, or religious affiliation? Does America call forth a different kind of observation from that to which other parts of the world are subjected? Here the Jesuits, with their missions to Canada and Paraguay, India and China, provide a control group which affords valuable opportunities for close analysis.

Those recorders of an alien world were doing their best to find a meaningful vocabulary with which to describe and make sense of landscapes and peoples that were new and strange to them. *Our* problem, as I see it, is to find an adequate vocabulary for explaining the enterprise on which they were embarked. The papers given at the John Carter Brown conference suggest to me that neither historians nor literary scholars have yet succeeded in this. Take, for instance, the phrase "the process of assimilation," which I used as the title of the second chapter of *The Old World and the New*. I do not think that I knew then, and I certainly do not know now, what that phrase really means. What criteria do we possess for judging whether some thing, or some idea, has been truly assimilated? Has assimilation been finally achieved when new impressions and new information have become so routine that they have ceased even to be discussed—when, for instance, the Spanish expression for extreme wealth, *vale un Potosí*, has become so commonplace that its original American connotations are effectively forgotten?

In a highly suggestive article called "Assimilating New Worlds in the Sixteenth and Seventeenth Centuries," published in 1981, Michael Ryan points to a further difficulty arising from the concept of assimilation. "One wonders," he writes, "whether the capacity for these more empathetic encounters was merely idiosyncratic, whether Sahagún, Zorita, Acosta and Las Casas were isolated moments, or part of a larger process."[25] This seems to me a fair question, and one which casts real doubt on an approach which, like mine, was cast in terms of "process." I would see these as individuals whose particular combination of concerns and talents, when filtered through their cultural traditions, gave them unusually sharp insights

"III. Indi, qua arte aurum ex montibus eruant," from Johann Theodor de Bry, *Grands Voyages*, pt. IX (Latin) (Frankfurt, 1602)

into certain aspects of the new lands and peoples. But whether those insights were widely communicated, and subsequently helped to promote further understanding, depended on a variety of circumstances largely outside the author's control.

Authors, as Lowood reminds us,[26] tended to be the hostages of their printers—that is, if they ever got as far as the printer. Acosta, on the whole, did well. The seventeen editions, in a variety of languages, of his *Historia natural y moral de las Indias*, listed in *European Americana* for the period between 1590 and 1650, testify vividly to his enormous popularity and influence. Further confirmation was provided at the conference by Jan Lechner's paper on the Dutch humanists' knowledge of America, which showed Acosta at the top of popularity tables based on 114 printed auction catalogs. To obtain this kind of success, a book needs to respond to contemporary concerns, and the success of Acosta requires further examination from this point of view. Yet the part played by sheer chance in determining the fortunes of an author should never be discounted. It is instructive, for instance, to compare the contrasting fate of two Spanish eyewitness accounts of the sixteenth century New World. Agustín de Zárate alleges in the dedication to his *Historia del descubrimiento y conquista del Perú*[27] that he would never have dared subject his work to public scrutiny if Prince Philip had not read his manuscript during his 1554 voyage from Corunna to England and ordered him to publish it. On the other hand, it was not until 1891 that the *Breve y sumaria relación de los señores de la Nueva España*, by another Spanish royal official of the same period, Alonso de Zorita, finally appeared in print, although the number of manuscript copies in circulation indicates that Zorita, too, was not without his readers.[28]

A further problem posed by the concept of assimilation is to be found in the element of disjunction which can so easily divide an individual's world into separate compartments. The John Pym who fought so hard for representative government in England displayed no wish to see it established in that overseas extension of England, the Providence Island colony.[29] It is hardly surprising, therefore, to find symbolic and naturalistic representations of Cuzco existing side by side.[30] One of the inherent problems of the history of *mentalités* is that it tends to take for granted the existence of an intellectual or cultural coherence which is rarely to be found. The absence of coherence means that there is bound to be something quixotic about any attempt, like my own, to establish when and how "America" became assimilated into the European "consciousness."

Having for long blunted my energies against the intractable question of "A blunted impact?," I am now inclined to agree with Ryan that "it will be necessary to alter somewhat the idea of assimilation," by shifting attention away from the use of the idea to cover the working out of a tension between reality and projected fantasies, and concentrating instead on the "conceptual strategies through which contemporaries interpreted their world."[31] He is certainly right to emphasize early modern Europe's deep distrust of novelty, and its consequent desire to domesticate the new worlds by incorporating them with as little disruption as possible into the framework of the familiar and the traditional. The impact, in effect, was deliberately blunted, as part of Europe's defensive strategy against an outside world that in some ways it was afraid to understand. In resorting to this defensive strategy Europeans could neutralize the disturbing religious beliefs and practices of the indigenous peoples of America by relating them to such familiar concepts as idolatry, paganism, and the machinations of the devil. This was the treatment meted out to the most celebrated of the Aztec deities, Huitzilopochtli, who was safely domesticated into the European tradition through a series of engravings which sought either to classicize him or else to transform him into the familiar figure of a devil, but a devil whose exotic accoutrements effectively served to deprive him of his diabolical malignity.[32]

One of the problems, however, about the search for similarities between different peoples or beliefs is that sooner or later it establishes the fact of diversity, and diversity, once established within a conceptual framework based on the idea of a fundamental unity, cries out for explanation. Early modern Europe was accustomed to the concept of diversity and during the sixteenth century, as its own internal dissensions multiplied, was to become increasingly aware of its dangers. But even if its growing intolerance encouraged a seventeenth-century search for a new uniformity and universalism to hold in check what it saw as the forces of disorder, the extreme varieties to be found among its own peoples and languages made some acceptance of diversity a necessary fact of life. This in turn must have made it easier for Europeans, when confronted with the phenomena of American peoples and nature, to sharpen and refine the conceptual strategies that could be used to explain diversity.

A convenient explanation of diversity was to be found in the theory which related character to climate—a theory which had been reformulated and popularized by Bodin in the sixteenth century.[33] European overseas discoveries helped sustain the acceptability of this theory, which was to enjoy an eighteenth-century apotheosis in the work of Montesquieu.[34] At the same time, the establishment of Europe's overseas colonies was providing powerful ammunition with which to subvert it. "The same set of manners," wrote David Hume, "will follow a nation, and adhere to them over the whole globe, as well as the same laws and language. The Spanish, English, French, and Dutch colonies, are all distinguishable even between the tropics."[35] In the controversy between nature and nurture, the contribution made by America would cut both ways.

An alternative conceptual strategy, which engaged the attention of the John Carter Brown conference as climatic theory did not, was the recourse to history in order to fashion a developmental theory of a civilizing process from barbarous to civil society. Diversity could thus be explained, or explained away, by placing disparate societies into one or another of a few broad bands on the evolutionary scale. The effect of this strategy, as pursued by Las Casas and then by Acosta, was to breathe new life into the "civilization myth" inherited from Seneca, Lucretius, Vitruvius, and Cicero.[36] Only recently, in *The Architecture of Conquest*, Valerie Fraser has drawn attention to another aspect of this myth—the hierarchy of building materials and techniques. This provided a further yardstick for measuring the relative civility of indigenous peoples of the Americas.[37] Their skilled use of stone placed the Incas on a higher plane of civilization than peoples who constructed their buildings of straw and mud and appeared to justify their inclusion in the same category as the Romans. Yet the underlying European assumption that a society would maintain the same levels of civility right across the spectrum made for some disturbing anomalies. It was difficult to understand, for instance, why the Peruvians, who had progressed so far in their building techniques, had failed to develop the art of writing—another yardstick for measuring stages on the ascent from barbarism.

Sixteenth-century writers failed to get to grips with these anomalies, and I suspect that the seventeenth century was less interested in pursuing historical or other reasons for diversity than in searching for origins and for new uniformities. This at least is suggested by John Headley's discussion of Campanella and world evangelization.[38] Here we see an attempt by Lord Herbert of Cherbury and others, after the religious upheavals of the sixteenth century, to reduce religion to a few natural principles accessible to all. This aspiration toward a new universalism had its intellectual roots in the Platonic and Stoic revivals. But it was also a response, as Headley shows, to the need to reshape Christianity to meet the demands of a global missionary endeavor.

The new attempt to establish the existence of a universal religious instinct among the peoples of the world seems to me comparable in its effects to the sixteenth-century attempt to establish the existence among them of a universal rationality. The apostle of the search for a universal rationality was Las Casas; the apostle of the search for a universal religiosity was Lafitau, whose Jesuit order still preserved its evangelizing zeal in a new, more skeptical, and disillusioned age.[39] Both men were driven by the attack on their most profoundly held convictions to develop a comparative approach designed to mitigate the implications of cultural diversity. "On the surface of things," Sabine MacCormack tells us, "Lafitau's was a deeply conservative book."[40] The same could be said of the writings of Las Casas. Yet each man in his way, while starting from the most conservative of standpoints, made a revolutionary contribution to European understanding of the diverse peoples of the world.

This points to the third and most complex of the issues raised by the theme of America in European consciousness—the degree to which it had a genuinely transforming effect. There is a natural desire in a conference devoted to "America in European Consciousness" to establish the revolutionary implications of America for that consciousness, and yet the effort remains bafflingly inconclusive. Over and over again we return to the dilemma posed by Peter Burke when he discusses the new interest in the primitive in late-seventeenth-century Europe: do we explain this interest by reference to the "impact" of America, or does the new concern with America derive from a revival of interest in the primitive?[41] Here my own conviction remains that between 1493 and around 1650 the effect of America is not so much to generate new departures in European consciousness as to reinforce existing proclivities and predispositions, including often contradictory ones. America, for instance, encouraged Fernández de Oviedo to laud the superiority of personal experience over classical authority.[42] Yet growing acquaintance with the New World also worked to reinforce the hold of authority when the civilization of the Greco-Roman world was made a standard point of reference for the history and development of Amerindian societies.[43]

Here I regret that my own book stopped rather arbitrarily at the year 1650. If I had continued it to 1750, the closing date chosen for the John Carter Brown Library conference, my perspective would undoubtedly have been rather different. The cumulative effect of the papers presented to the conference on the whole range of the period 1493–1750 was to leave me feeling that on balance they confirmed John Headley's assertion that "Columbus creates for Campanella—and for succeeding European generations—a more ample and comprehensive vision of the physical, moral, and religious world."[44] This assertion, indeed, can reasonably be applied also to the generations before Campanella. The sense of one interconnected world was establishing itself as a commonplace in the sixteenth century, assisted by the new conceptualization of space made possible by the Renaissance device of the globe.[45] "All men," observed Bodin, "surprisingly work together in a world state, as if in one and the same city-state."[46] For Giovanni Botero,[47] as for Francisco de Vitoria before him, it was maritime communication that linked the different parts of this world state together, facilitating mutual commerce and Christianizing missions.

This more ample vision of the world was in part a more ample vision of Europe and its past, for, as more than one of the conference papers argued, an important by-product of the discovery of America was the stimulus it gave to the rediscovery of Europe. An insular version of this process is described in David Armitage's "The New World and British Historical Thought," when he shows how English antiquarians and early historians were inspired by the conceit of Britain as another world to explore their own country with fresh eyes and to set it for the first time in a comparative context.[48] It is impressive to find John Selden referring specifically to Acosta in his musing as to how foxes had found their way to Britain.[49] This is the kind of hard evidence of direct influence which has until now been in short supply, but of which more should come to light as the literature of early modern Europe is systematically explored.

From the beginning, however, the vision looked to the future as well as to the past. The Franciscan millenarians, for instance, were looking not to history but to the end of history as they contemplated America as a theater for the realization of long-cherished hopes and expectations.[50] But if America revived or generated among Franciscans, Jesuits, or Sephardic Jews expectations that tended to express themselves in utopian experiments, it also encouraged a less apocalyptic, but still progressive, current of thinking which seems to me to have been considerably more significant as a transforming influence in European consciousness.

This progressive strain of thought is visible in the sixteenth century, but it is only in the eighteenth that it comes fully into its own. Perhaps it is most neatly described as the "doctrine of improvement." One aspect of it is exemplified in those words taken from *An American Garland* (1612): ". . . And so Virginia may in time / be made like England now."[51] But it is already present in Spanish writings about America in the sixteenth century, as in López de Gómara's expression of pride in 1552 at the way in which his compatriots had "improved" Hispaniola and New Spain, or in Bishop Landa's list of the benefits conferred by the Spaniards on the Indians, including animals, plants, and tools, which, in his words, enabled them to live "incomparably more like men."[52]

Improvement, as this quotation suggests, had cultural as well as technological connotations and offered a means by which Europeans could speed up the civilizing process of the indigenous peoples of America and give it an "accelerating push."[53] Both the peoples and the land were, thanks to European efforts, being steadily "improved." By the later seventeenth century, at a time when colonial societies, and especially those of the English-speaking world, were showing themselves to be viable communities with obvious potential for the mother country, the language of improvement was beginning to be widely spoken and was helping to pave the way for the full-blown philosophy of eighteenth-century economic imperialism.

With the advent of this philosophy, America was integrated, as it had not previously been, into the economic thinking of Europe. This process of integration was to have important repercussions in the field of historical writing. For the historians and social theorists of the Enlightenment, the past and present of America offered unique insights into the development of civil society, and in particular into the decisive contribution made by the progress of commerce to the civilizing process. This was to be the theme of William Robertson's great *History of America* of 1777, which, as David Armitage points out, resolved in a grand synthesis the "twin challenges to antiquity and modernity which America had presented to European consciousness."[54]

The triumph of the new Enlightenment historiography involved the rejection of an alternative, and less well known, historiographical tradition which had also sought to find a place for America in the great historical design. This alternative tradition, which has recently been magisterially surveyed by David Brading,[55] was that of Jesuit baroque historiography, with the seventeenth-century Austrian Jesuit Athanasius Kircher as a principal founding father. Eagerly embraced by the creoles of seventeenth- and eighteenth-century New Spain, who saw in it a historical legitimation for their newfound sense of a distinctive Mexican identity, this tradition exalted the Aztec past in order to establish Mexico's claim to imperial origins and an imperial destiny.

Although such historical preoccupations were largely confined to creole patriots, they also had European repercussions in the work of the Milanese noble Lorenzo Boturini, who managed the improbable intellectual feat of simultaneously looking back to Kircher's arguments for the Egyptian origins of all religion and wisdom and applying Vico's theories about the stages of cultural development to the indigenous peoples of America.[56] But Kircher, and baroque historiography in general, had little to offer a Western world increasingly confident that civilization and commerce marched side by side, and that it alone could endow America with the priceless benefits of modernity.

"The age of sophisters, economists and calculators" was dawning, and once again the domestic preoccupations of Europe were helping to determine its perception of America. It is no doubt true that the rise of economic imperialism was accompanied by the rise of a countercurrent of economic anticolonialism, which questioned the privileged importance of foreign trade. But the critics of the dominant economic philosophy criticized it only in order to put forward their own version of the doctrine of improvement—an improvement to be secured by a more intensive development of domestic resources. In both instances the underlying assumption was that humanity—and specifically European humanity—held the future of the universe in its hands.

While it can be argued that this assumption was implicit in the scientific and technological achievements of early modern Europe, I believe that the conquest, colonization, and (from a European standpoint) the civilization of America played a critical, and perhaps even a decisive, part in making it explicit. America had given Europe space, in the widest sense of that word—space to dominate, space in which to experiment, and space to transform according to its wishes. This transformation of American space left Europe with a lasting sense of guilt which it periodically sought—and still seeks—to purge in a round of collective breast-beating as it looks nostalgically back to the noble savage and laments the fate of the innocent peoples whom it exploited and destroyed. But it also left Europeans with a lasting sense of their own providential position in the historical design. Of all the continents which European artists of the seventeenth and eighteenth centuries delighted in portraying in allegorical form, Europe alone had created, or re-created, another in its own likeness. This signal achievement left it in no doubt of its superior skills. By transforming America as a prelude to its transformation of the world, Europe transformed its image of itself.

NOTES

1. J. H. Elliott, *The Old World and the New, 1492–1650* (Cambridge, 1970; rev. ed., 1992).

2. Fredi Chiappelli, ed., *First Images of America: The Impact of the New World on the Old*, 2 vols. (Berkeley, 1976).

3. Roger B. Merriman, *The Rise of the Spanish Empire in the Old World and in the New* (New York, 1918–34).

4. Earl J. Hamilton, *American Treasure and the Price Revolution in Spain, 1501–1650* (Cambridge, Mass., 1934).

5. Geoffroy Atkinson, *Les Nouveaux Horizons de la Renaissance Française* (Paris, 1935).

6. Gilbert Chinard, *L'Exotisme Américain dans la Littérature Française au XVIe Siècle* (Paris, 1911), and *L'Amérique et le Rêve Exotique dans la Littérature Française au XVIIe et au XVIIIe Siècle* (Paris, 1913).

7. Robert Rawston Cawley, *Unpathed Waters* (Princeton, 1940).

8. Rosario Romeo, *Le Scoperte Americane nella Coscienza Italiana del Cinquecento* (Milan-Naples, 1954).

9. Antonello Gerbi, *La Disputa del Nuovo Mondo* (Milan, 1955), trans. Jeremy Moyle as *The Dispute of the New World: The History of a Polemic, 1750–1900* (Pittsburgh, 1985).

10. Durand Echevarria, *Mirage in the West: A History of the French Image of American Society to 1815* (Princeton, 1957; reprint with corrections, 1968), 77–78.

11. Jan Lechner, "Dutch Humanists' Knowledge of America," subsequently published in *Itinerario* 16 (1992): 101–13. See Richard Simmons's essay in this volume.

12. John Alden and Dennis C. Landis, eds., *European Americana: A Chronological Guide to Works Printed in Europe Relating to the Americas, 1493–1776* (New York, 1980–).

13. See Henry Lowood's essay above, 297.

14. Ibid., 299.

15. Elliott, *The Old World and the New*, 16–17.

16. Edward H. Schafer, *The Vermilion Bird* (Berkeley, 1967), 115.

17. Bernard Lewis, *The Muslim Discovery of Europe* (New York and London, 1982).

18. Collected in Enrique Otte, *Cartas privadas de emigrantes a Indias, 1540–1616* (Seville, 1992).

19. See Teodor de Bry, *America de Bry, 1590–1634* (Berlin and New York, 1990; Spanish ed., with preface by J. H. Elliott, Madrid, 1992) for a one-volume abridgment, reproducing the original plates.

20. Edmundo O'Gorman, *The Invention of America: An Inquiry into the Historical Nature of the New World and the Meaning of Its History* (Bloomington, 1961).

21. J. H. Elliott, "Renaissance Europe and America: A Blunted Impact?," in Chiappelli, *First Images of America*, 1:11–23.

22. Anthony Pagden, *The Fall of Natural Man: The American Indian and the Origins of Comparative Ethnology* (Cambridge, 1982; reprint with corrections and additions, 1986), 6.

23. Alexander Von Humboldt, *Cosmos*, 2 vols. (London, 1845–48), 2:311–12.

24. Beatriz Pastor, "Silence and Writing: The History of the Conquest," in *1492–1992: Rediscovering Colonial Writing*, ed. René Jara and Nicholas Spadaccini (Minneapolis, 1989), 158.

25. Michael Ryan, "Assimilating New Worlds in the Sixteenth and Seventeenth Centuries," *Comparative Studies in Society and History* 23 (1981): 522.

26. See Lowood above.

27. Agustín de Zárate, *Historia del descubrimiento y conquista del Perú* (Antwerp, 1555).

28. See the prologue by Joaquín Ramírez Cabañas to Alonso de Zorita, *Breve y sumaria relación de los señores de la Nueva España*, 2d ed. (Mexico City, 1963), xx.

29. See Karen Kupperman's essay above.

30. See Sabine MacCormack's essay above.

31. Ryan, "Assimilating New Worlds," 523.

32. See Elizabeth H. Boone, "Incarnations of the Aztec Supernatural: The Image of

Huitzilopochtli in Mexico and Europe," *Transactions of the American Philosophical Society* 79, pt. 2 (1989), esp. chap. 6.

33. Elliott, *The Old World and the New*, 49.

34. See Gerbi, *The Dispute of the New World*, 39–42.

35. David Hume, "Of National Characters," in *Essays: Moral, Political and Literary* (Oxford, 1963), 210.

36. Cf. Arthur B. Ferguson, *Clio Unbound: Perception of the Social and Cultural Past in Renaissance England* (Durham, N.C., 1979), 347.

37. Valerie Fraser, *The Architecture of Conquest* (Cambridge, 1990), 25–33.

38. See John Headley's essay above.

39. See Luca Codignola's essay above for the Propaganda's waning interest after the 1650s.

40. See MacCormack above, 108.

41. See Peter Burke's essay above.

42. See Elliott, *The Old World and the New*, 40.

43. For the continuing use of the classical canon, its persistent richness, and its often self-contradictory character, see Anthony Grafton, *New Worlds, Ancient Texts: The Power of Tradition and the Shock of Discovery* (Cambridge, Mass., 1992).

44. See Headley above, 254.

45. One of the weaknesses of my book was its neglect of cartographical developments in the sixteenth century, which ought to be incorporated into any assessment of the influence of America on European consciousness. Unfortunately, they were equally neglected in the John Carter Brown Library conference.

46. Cited in Elliott, *The Old World and the New*, 53.

47. For a convenient compilation of those pages from Botero's works relating to America, see Aldo Albònico, *Il Mondo Americano di Giovanni Botero* (Rome, 1990).

48. See David Armitage's essay above.

49. Ibid., 60.

50. See Georges Baudot, *Utopie et Histoire au Mexique* (Toulouse, 1977).

51. *An American Garland* (1612), ed. C. H. Firth (Oxford, 1915), 24. I owe this reference to David Armitage.

52. *The Maya: Diego de Landa's Account of the Affairs of the Yucatán*, trans. and ed. A. R. Pagden (Chicago, 1975), 162–63. For Gómara and other references, see my article on "The Seizure of Overseas Territories by the European Powers," in *The European Discovery of the World and Its Economic Effects on Pre-Industrial Society, 1500–1800*, ed. Hans Pohl (Papers of the Tenth International Economic History Congress, Stuttgart, 1990), 53.

53. David Armitage's phrase, from his paper "The New World and English Historical Thought," presented at the conference on America in European Consciousness.

54. See Armitage above, 69. See also, most recently, on Robertson and the Enlightenment's encounter with America, Anthony Pagden, *European Encounters with the New World* (New Haven, 1993).

55. David A. Brading, *The First America: The Spanish Monarchy, Creole Patriots, and the Liberal State, 1492–1867* (Cambridge, 1991).

56. See ibid., 381–86.

Conference Program

America in European Consciousness, 1493–1750: An International Conference on the Intellectual Consequences of the Discovery of the New World, June 5 to 9, 1991, Organized by the John Carter Brown Library

SESSION 1. *European Americana: The Bibliographical Basis in European Books for the Study of the Colonial Americas.* Chair: Michael Ryan, Stanford University. Jackson C. Boswell, University of the District of Columbia, "Americana in the STC." Richard C. Simmons, University of Birmingham, "Americana in British Books, 1641 to 1760." Discussant: Dennis C. Landis, Editor, *European Americana*, John Carter Brown Library.

SESSION 2. *America in European Consciousness.* Chair: Vartan Gregorian, President, Brown University. An address by Emmanuel Le Roy Ladurie.

SESSION 3(A). *The New World as Alternative Space: Political and Social Thought.* Chair: Nancy Roelker, Brown University. Frank Lestringant, University of Lille III–Charles de Gaulle, "Geneva and America in the Renaissance: The Dream of a Huguenot Refuge, 1555–1600." Stelio Cro, McMaster University, "Utopian Foundations of the Jesuit Mission in Paraguay." Discussant: Harvey Mansfield, Harvard University.

SESSION 3(B). *The Building of European Collections of American Artifacts.* Chair: Shephard Krech III, Brown University. Marie-Noëlle Bourguet, University of Paris VII-Jussieu, "The French Museum in America." Christian Feest, Museum für Völkerkunde, Vienna, "The Collection of American Indian Artifacts in Europe." Henry Lowood, Stanford University Libraries, "New World Observations and European Books on Natural History." Discussant: George Kubler, Yale University.

SESSION 4. *The New World in Popular Imagination; the New World in Literary Imagination.* Chair: José Amor y Vazquez, Brown University. David Cressy, California State University at Long Beach, "The Limits of English Enthusiasm for America." Jan Lechner, University of Leiden, "Dutch Humanists' Knowledge of Spanish America." Discussants: Jacques LaFaye, Harvard University, and Richard Simmons, University of Birmingham.

SESSION 5. *The Concept of Man and the Origins of Racism.* Chair: Sheldon Watts, American University, Cairo. Henry Kamen, University of Warwick, "America and Its Impact on Racial Attitudes and 'Blood Purity' in Early Modern Spain." Geoffrey Scammel, Pembroke College, Cambridge, "The Other Side of the Coin: The Discovery of the Americas and the Spread of Intolerance, Absolutism, and Racism in Early Modern Europe." (Professor Scammel was unable to attend the conference and his paper was read by Professor Sheldon Watts.) Discussant: Perez Zagorin, University of Rochester.

SESSION 6. *Art and Iconography: Beyond the Textual Documentation of America.* Chair: Frank Robinson, Museum of the Rhode Island School of Design. Samuel Edgerton, Clark Art Institute, Williams College, "Images of Human Blood in the Visual Arts of Renaissance Europe and Pre-Columbian Meso-America: Toward an Understanding of a Five-Century-Old Problem of Cultural Misconception."

SESSION 7. *The Concept of Man and the Origins of Racism* (cont'd). Chair: Perez Zagorin, University of Rochester. Karen Ordahl Kupperman, University of Connecticut, "The Challenge of America to English Social Thought." David Quint, Princeton University, "Montaigne's Cannibals in the Larger *Essais*." Discussant: Kirkpatrick Sale, New York City.

SESSION 8. *America in European Consciousness.* Chair: William H. McNeill, University of Chicago. Anthony Pagden, King's College, Cambridge, "Old Worlds and New: America and the Ancients in the European Imagination."

SESSION 9(A). *American History and Universal History in Early Modern European Historiography.* Chair: Philip Benedict, Brown University. Sabine MacCormack, University of Michigan, "America and the Rebirth of the Historical Study of Religion in Early Modern Europe." David Armitage, Emmanuel College, Cambridge, "The New World and English Historical Thought." Peter Burke, Emmanuel College, Cambridge, "America and the Rewriting of World History." Discussant: John Pocock, Johns Hopkins University.

SESSION 9(B). *New World Empires, Specie, and National Wealth: The Stimulus of the "Discovery" to Economic Thought.* Chair: Robert Litchfield, Brown University. Jonathan Israel, University of London, "The New World in the Social and Economic Thought of the 18th-Century Dutch Sephardic Jewish *Philosophe*, Isaac de Pinto." John E. Crowley, Dalhousie University, "Empire versus Wealth: Economic Anti-Colonialism in the Enlightenment." Discussant: Terence W. Hutchison, University of Birmingham.

SESSION 10(A). *The New World as Alternative Space* (cont'd). Chair: Anthony Pagden, King's College, Cambridge. Georges Baudot, University of Toulouse, "The Renewal of Utopian Societies and the Indians in Sixteenth-Century Mexico." Francisco Sánchez-Blanco, Ruhr University, "America: Hope of Those Persecuted for Religion." Discussant: Anthony Pagden.

SESSION 10(B). *The Roman Catholic Church in Response to America.* Chair: Sabine MacCormack, University of Michigan. John Headley, University of North Carolina, "Campanella, America, and World Evangelization." Luca Codignola, University of Genoa, "The Holy See and the Conversion of the Indians." Thomas Cohen, Catholic University, "The Jesuits in Brazil and Their Impact in Europe." Discussant: Sabine MacCormack.

SESSION 11. *The New World in the Literary Imagination* (cont'd). Chair: Stephen Foley, Brown University. Hans Galinsky, Gutenberg University of Mainz, "German Baroque Authors and the Rediscovery of Europe as a By-Product of the Discovery of America." Roland Greene, Harvard University, "Petrarchan Experience and the Colonial Americas: The Rape of Florida." Discussant: Gustav Siebenmann, Hochschule St. Gallen, Switzerland.

SESSION 12. *America in European Consciousness.* Chair: Norman Fiering, John Carter Brown Library. John H. Elliott, Oxford University, "The Old World and the New Revisited."

Contributors

David Armitage is Assistant Professor of History at Columbia University and the author of recent essays in the *Journal of the Warburg and Courtland Institutes* and the *Historical Journal.* He is also coeditor (with Armand Himy and Quentin Skinner) of *Milton and Republicanism* (forthcoming).

Peter Burke is Reader in Cultural History, University of Cambridge, and Fellow of Emmanuel College. His books include *The Italian Renaissance, Popular Culture in Early Modern Europe,* and *The Fabrication of Louis XIV.*

Luca Codignola is Associate Professor of Early European Expansion at the University of Genoa and the author of *The Coldest Harbour of the Land, 1621–1649* and *Guide to French and British North America in the Archives of the Propaganda Fide, 1622–1799.*

Sir John Elliott, Regius Professor of Modern History in the University of Oxford, is the author of, among other titles, *The Old World and the New, 1492–1650, The Count-Duke of Olivares,* and *Spain and Its World, 1500–1700.*

Christian F. Feest is Professor of Anthropology at the Johann Wolfgang Goethe University, Frankfurt am Main, and the author of *Native Arts of North America* and the editor of *Indians and Europe: An Interdisciplinary Collection of Essays.*

Roland Greene, Professor of Comparative Literature and English at the University of Oregon, is the author of *Post-Petrarchism: Origins and Innovations of the Western Lyric Sequence* and the forthcoming *Unrequited Conquests: Love and Empire in the Colonial Americas.*

John M. Headley is Distinguished University Professor of History at the University of North Carolina, Chapel Hill, and the author of *The Emperor and His Chancellor: The Imperial Chancellery under Gattinara.*

Karen Ordahl Kupperman, Professor of History at the University of Connecticut, is the author of *Settling with the Indians* and *Providence Island, 1630–1641: The Other Puritan Colony.*

Henry Lowood is Curator for Germanic Collections and Bibliographer for History and Science and Technology Collections in the Stanford University Libraries and the author of *Patriotism, Profit, and the Promotion of Science in the German Enlightenment: The Economic and Scientific Societies, 1760–1815.*

Sabine MacCormack, Professor of History at the University of Michigan, is the author of *Art and Ceremony in Late Antiquity* and *Religion in the Andes: Vision and Imagination in Early Colonial Peru.*

David Quint is Professor of English and Comparative Literature at Yale University. He is the author of the recent *Epic and Empire* and coeditor of *Creative Imitation: New Essays in Honor of Thomas M. Greene.*

Richard C. Simmons is Professor of American History at the University of Birmingham and the author of *The American Colonies from Settlement to Independence* and *British Imprints Relating to North America, 1621–1760* (forthcoming).

Index